# Electronic Government Strategies and Implementation

Wayne Huang
Ohio University, USA

Keng Siau
University of Nebraska at Lincoln, USA

Kwok Kee Wei
City University of Hong Kong, Hong Kong

IDEA GROUP PUBLISHING
Hershey • London • Melbourne • Singapore

| Acquisitions Editor: | Mehdi Khosrow-Pour |
| Senior Managing Editor: | Jan Travers |
| Managing Editor: | Amanda Appicello |
| Development Editor: | Michele Rossi |
| Copy Editor: | Ingrid Widitz |
| Typesetter: | Sara Reed |
| Cover Design: | Lisa Tosheff |
| Printed at: | Yurchak Printing Inc. |

Published in the United States of America by
    Idea Group Publishing (an imprint of Idea Group Inc.)
    701 E. Chocolate Avenue
    Hershey PA 17033
    Tel: 717-533-8845
    Fax: 717-533-8661
    E-mail: cust@idea-group.com
    Web site: http://www.idea-group.com

and in the United Kingdom by
    Idea Group Publishing (an imprint of Idea Group Inc.)
    3 Henrietta Street
    Covent Garden
    London WC2E 8LU
    Tel: 44 20 7240 0856
    Fax: 44 20 7379 3313
    Web site: http://www.eurospan.co.uk

Library of Congress Cataloging-in-Publication Data

Electronic government strategies and implementation / Wayne Huang, Keng Siau and Kwok Kee Wei, editors.
     p. cm.
   Includes bibliographical references and index.
   ISBN 1-59140-348-0 (h/c) -- ISBN 1-59140-349-9 (s/c) -- ISBN 1-59140-350-2
  1. Public administration--Information resources management. 2. Administrative agencies--Technological innovations--Management. 3. Internet in public administration. 4. Electronic government information. I. Huang, Wayne, 1964- II. Siau, Keng, 1964- III. Wei, Kwok Kee.
    JF1525.A8E43 2004
    352.3'8'02854678--dc22
                              2004016286

British Cataloguing in Publication Data
A Cataloguing in Publication record for this book is available from the British Library.

# Electronic Government Strategies and Implementation

# Table of Contents

### Section II: E-Government Implementations and Practices

# Preface

The Internet has not only transformed the way of doing business, but it has also enabled the transformation of government and democratic processes. E-government uses information and telecommunication technologies to facilitate the daily administration of government and provide better services to citizens, businesses, and other government agents. For citizens, e-government empowers them to actively participate in the democratic institutions and political processes.

This book is on *E-Government Strategies and Implementation.* The book consists of 18 chapters. All the chapters have undergone a thorough review process and extensive revisions. These chapters are grouped into two sections. The first section is on "E-Government Strategies, Concepts, and Issues". The second section is on "E-Government Implementations and Practices". Together, these 18 chapters provide an excellent overview on the topic of e-government and the practices of e-government in various countries.

Section One consists of seven chapters that focus on "E-Government Strategies, Concepts and Issues". Chapter 1, "The Paradigm of E-Commerce in E-Government and E-Democracy," compares and contrasts e-government to e-democracy, and discusses the application of e-commerce in the governments and administration system. Chapter 2, "Implementing and Assessing Transparency in Digital Government: Some Issues in Project Management," looks into ways of assessing greater transparency in e-government and presents the benefits of a private-sector-based assessment of fiscal and monetary transparency. Chapter 3, "The Dimensions of Business Process Change in Electronic Government," describes the four developmental stages of electronic government and the impacts of change in government business processes. Chapter 4, "A Strategic Framework for a G2G E-Government Excellence Center," proposes the creation of an e-government Excellence Center that increases visibility and enhances consulting services to the clients. Chapter 5, "Access Control Model for Webservices E-Government Infrastructure," presents a powerful and flexible mechanism in supporting interoperability among heterogeneous legacy government systems and specifying the access rules to government resources. Chapter 6, "Online One-Stop Government: A Single Point of Access to Public Services," describes the concept of online one-stop government, its applications and impacts. Chapter 7, "Privacy and Trust in E-Government," explores the challenges, requirements, issues, and solutions associated with satisfying requirements for privacy and trust in e-government.

Section Two consists of 11 chapters and the section focuses on "E-Government Implementations and Practices". Chapter 8, "A Comparative Study of Strategic Issues of Digital Government Implementations Between Developed and Developing Countries," compares and contrasts the different strategic issues of digital government implementation between developed and developing countries. Chapter 9, "Effectiveness of E-government: Online Services in Australia," proposes a research model and identifies the underlying factors influencing the effectiveness of e-government and gives insights into the future trends of e-government. Chapter 10, "Implementing Digital Government in the Finnish Parliament," describes the concepts, implications and outcomes of the standardization process in the Finnish parliament and discusses the plans for extension of standardization of metadata. Chapter 11, "Participants' Expectations and the Success of Knowledge Networking in the Public Sector," highlights the importance of the behind-the-scenes interorganizational collaboration for public sector agencies and examines the benefits and problems of its application. Chapter 12, "Shanghai's E-Government: Implementation Strategies and a Case Study," introduces the Social Security Card System implemented in Shanghai and highlights the differences in e-government implementation strategies between China and USA. Chapter 13, "E-Government: Implementation Policies and Best Practices from Singapore," highlights Singapore's best practices and policies in incorporating e-government in the public administration infrastructure. Chapter 14, "Towards an E-Government Solution: A South African Perspective," discusses the challenges of establishing an e-government environment in the multicultural and multilingual society of South Africa. Chapter 15, "Building the Network State," describes how the Uniform Resource Name is used as the administration portal for Switzerland in creating a network state. Chapter 16, "Semiotic Analysis of E-Policing Strategies in the United Kingdom," presents a semiotic approach to the business and information technology systems and discusses the applicability of the framework in the e-government in UK. Chapter 17, "Digital Government Development Strategies: Lessons for Policy Makers from a Comparative Perspective," provides policy makers a comprehensive framework for developing national digital government strategies by describing the framework used in Poland and Taiwan. Chapter 18, "E-Government Applications and User Acceptance in Taiwan," explores the e-government developments and applications in Taiwan.

These 18 chapters provide a comprehensive coverage of the current issues and practices in e-government. The book is recommended for both researchers and practitioners in the e-government area. For researchers, this book provides the necessary conceptual foundation and knowledge in the area. For practitioners, this book discusses issues and concerns related to e-government implementation that are invaluable to practice.

*Wayne Huang, Keng Siau, Kwok Kee Wei*
*February, 2004*

# Section I:

# E-Government Strategies, Concepts, and Issues

**Chapter I**

# The Paradigm of E-Commerce in E-Government and E-Democracy

Bernd Carsten Stahl, De Montfort University, United Kingdom

## Abstract

*During its relatively short history, e-commerce, the use of information and communication technology (ICT) in business, has been more successful and glamorous than e-government or e-democracy, the comparable use of ICT in governments and administration. This may be the reason why many government initiatives try to emulate the success of e-commerce by using concepts, processes, technologies, and approaches pioneered by businesses. This chapter analyses the relevance and limits of this use of e-commerce as a paradigm in government. For this purpose it starts out by distinguishing between e-government and e-democracy. In the following step the chapter discusses which factors have led to the success of e-commerce and might therefore be applicable as parts of the paradigm. It then discusses the strengths and the weaknesses of e-commerce as applied to government. The conclusion will be that there are good reasons to use the commercial paradigm in e-government and e-democracy. However, this may lead to an unintended shift towards e-government. E-democracy may even be weakened by the paradigm, which might turn out to be detrimental to the democratic legitimacy of e-government and e-democracy.*

# Introduction

Many governmental initiatives aimed at promoting the use of information and communication technology (ICT) for the purposes of government and administration try to transfer ideas from the area of e-commerce to the area of e-government. Most notably, one can find any number of initiatives worldwide that emphasise the idea of citizen-centeredness, which is based on the example of customer-centeredness in e-commerce. Furthermore, governments try to take advantage of the strengths of e-commerce in order to improve their e-government initiatives. Such attempts to import successful examples from e-commerce into e-government refer to all sorts and aspects of information systems. On the one hand governments buy hardware and software that was originally developed for the private sector and apply it to their tasks. On the other hand, governments take over arguments and whole discourses from the commercial sector. Customer or citizen-centeredness is only one example of this. Others would be the ideas of efficiency, optimisation, or cost-benefit analysis. While these ideas are not confined to the commercial world, they have a strong association with it and during the last decades have mostly been developed in the context of private enterprises.

The attempts by governments to improve and optimise their services are usually met with approval. One of the central and frequently voiced criticisms of governments is that they are slow, do not react to the demands of their citizens, and that they are generally bureaucratic and wasteful. The business world, on the other hand, does not seem to be bothered by these problems. Businesses are deemed to be efficient, quick, and responsive. Commercial entities that do not take their customers seriously are quickly replaced in the marketplace by those that do. A large portion of the criticism levelled at governments and the way they do their business can therefore apparently be taken care of by doing things the way they are done in business.

However, things may not be quite as simple as they seem. While citizens are the customers of governments to a certain extent, there are also limits to this analogy. The question that this chapter will analyse is therefore where the limits of the application of commercial ideas to government are. In order to be able to discuss this question on a meaningful basis the chapter will start out by discussing the concepts of e-government and e-democracy. In the following section the strengths of e-commerce are analysed insofar as they are relevant or translatable to e-government. After that the strengths and weaknesses of using the paradigm of e-commerce in e-government are discussed. The result of the chapter will be that the commercial paradigm is useful for most service delivery tasks that we find in e-government but that it is quite less useful for most applications in e-democracy. At the same time the strength of electronic service delivery along the lines of e-commerce is such that it threatens to blend out e-democratic applications. If this is so, then the commercial paradigm may turn out to become a threat to the legitimacy of democratic e-government.

# E-Government and E-Democracy

In order to understand the impact of the commercial paradigm on e-government and e-commerce we will first of all have to clarify the concepts. This section will therefore start out with a brief introduction of the concept of a paradigm and will then continue to discuss e-government as well as e-democracy. The importance of the distinction between the two will be the reintroduction of the separation of powers, which in discussions about e-government is often neglected.

## Paradigms and Information and Communication Technology

The term *paradigm* will in this chapter be used in accordance with Kuhnian epistemology and the current use in information systems literature. While paradigm originally means something like "example," the term has taken on a more specific meaning following the publication of Kuhn's (1996) classic of the philosophy of science: *The Structure of Scientific Revolutions*. For Kuhn, a paradigm is a framework for understanding the world that is on the one hand "sufficiently unprecedented to attract an enduring group of adherents away from competing modes of scientific activity" (Kuhn, 1996, p. 10). On the other hand it must be "sufficiently open-ended to leave all sorts of problems for the redefined group of practitioners to resolve" (ibid.). Examples are Aristotle's *Physica* or Newton's *Principia and Opticks*. These are works that shape the perception of researchers and provide them with a theoretical framework to carry out their work. Kuhn's writings seem to suggest that only great scientific developments constitute frameworks but the term has since evolved to be used for specific ways of approaching research.

In the area of information systems, the term has been used to denote "the most fundamental set of assumptions adopted by a professional community that allow them to share similar perceptions and engage in commonly shared practices" (Hirschheim & Klein, 1994, p. 108). Paradigms in information systems are thus the lenses that are used to perceive and understand reality. They are contained in the narratives that are used to make sense of technology and its impact on social relationships (cf. Pentland, 2003). There is a multitude of paradigms in most academic disciplines, and information systems are no exception. Where the term "paradigm" is used explicitly it usually refers to questions of methodology and epistemology. However, it can also be used to analyse the use of ICT within organisations and here it may be used to explain why certain technologies are successful or fail. It can also be used to give explanations for problems of change management and changing perceptions. Finally, it has also been applied to the area of e-government and the understanding of developments in there (Wastell, 2003).

In this chapter we will regard e-commerce as a paradigm in e-government and e-democracy. This is not to say that e-commerce is nothing but just that, a paradigm. E-commerce can be seen as an important part of the economy, as a particular channel of doing business, as an academic discipline, and many other things. For us the main point of interest here is whether and in what way e-commerce can influence or determine the perception of another, albeit related, field, namely e-government. This means that we will necessarily have to abstract from the totality of phenomena in e-commerce and try to distil those aspects that render it useable as a paradigm, as a lens for perception or a framework for understanding. Before we return to the question of why e-commerce is a paradigm and what the specifics of the e-commerce paradigm are, we should first clarify what the area is that is supposedly affected by the paradigm, namely e-government and e-democracy.

# E-Government

In order to understand where and how the paradigm of e-commerce can be useful and also where its limits are when applied to public administration and political processes it is useful to distinguish between e-government and e-democracy. It will later become clear that e-commerce may be rather useful as a paradigm in e-government but it may be less so or even dangerous in e-democracy. To make this argument transparent we need to define the terms more clearly.

E-government will in this chapter be understood as those aspects of public administration that have to do with the tasks of the executive. When these tasks are discharged with the help of ICT we speak of e-government. Typically these are administrative tasks, service delivery, but they may also include other executive duties such as the interpretation or enforcement of laws. E-government in this sense can aim at internal processes, meaning the use of ICT for the optimisation of internal processes. It can also aim at international processes, where computers and networks can be used for all sorts of international political matters from the exchange of statistics over cultural collaboration to combining efforts in crime prevention and detection. Finally, and this is the aspect that tends to be most clearly emphasised, e-government can have to do with the interaction of the administration with its citizens. Here, most of the examples revolve around service delivery where certain governmental or administrative functions are discharged with the use of computers.

It should be noted that this chapter concentrates exclusively on the use of ICT in democratic governments. This is a non-trivial limitation of the scope of the topic because it implies several aspects. Democratic governments are supposed to represent their citizens and to act in their best interests. Democratic governments have to adhere to legal processes, they are subject to checks and balances and they have to adhere to the underlying ethical expectation that they do "the right thing," whatever that may mean in any specific situation. This limitation of the concept of e-government is also important because e-government is just as well imaginable in non-democratic environments. In fact, Orwell's *1984* is a good example for potential use of ICT in an administration without a democratic background.

Another interesting aspect that will be largely ignored for the rest of this chapter is the interaction between technology and administration. The central question of this chapter is whether e-commerce is a useful paradigm for e-government and where the limits of this approach are. The role of technology in this area is not discussed in any depth. However, it should be conceded that there can be a close connection and mutual influence of technology and e-government. On the one hand, governments can be large or even the largest users of ICT and thus shape the market for this technology. On the other hand, governments and administrations usually set the technical and legal framework within which technology is developed. Decisions about technology development can play a central role in governments (Weiser & Molnar, 1996). Finally, existing technology from other realms can influence which types of policies or service deliveries are deemed possible. "[…] policy is often tightly coupled with, or biased by, the technology it applies to, and vice versa" (Reagle, 1996, p. 18).

To come back to e-government, one can conclude that it mainly occupied with administrative and bureaucratic tasks. When we hear of e-government initiatives then these tend to concentrate on innovative and better ways to provide citizens with services. At the same time e-government also has a deep influence on the internal processes in administrations. External service delivery and internal process optimisation go hand in hand. The bureaucratic nature of e-governmental service delivery may be one of the reasons why computerisation appeals to administrative decision makers. Following Wiener, Postman (1992) argues that computers are the technology of command and control and that they need something to control. Given that bureaucracies are there to control and supervise, they may have a natural affinity to ICT that other aspects of democratic governments lack.

# E-Democracy

Many authors define the notion of e-government much wider than we do here and include other political elements as long as they are related to ICT. On a local level, Wastell (2003), for example, sees three functions of government, namely to provide the mechanisms of local democracy, to be the focus for public policy making and to provide a range of public services, mostly in the social domain. If one defines the scope of government this wide, then e-government, consequentially, is the use of ICT in these three domains. Given the classical division of powers in executive, legislative, and judiciary, however, it seems useful to distinguish between the different aspects by introducing different terms. In this chapter we will therefore distinguish between e-government, which stands for the use of ICT for the purposes of the executive branch of government and e-democracy, which represents the use of ICT in all other aspects of political processes in democracy. This choice of terms is not perfect because it may be misunderstood to imply that e-government is not democratic. Also, it may be too limiting because it subsumes all non-executive functions of government under one term and the different applications of ICT in the legislative branch as well as all other sorts of democratic processes may require a further distinction. For the purposes of this chapter, however, the dichotomy between e-government and e-democracy will suffice because it highlights the two most important branches of the use of ICT in government and public administration.

There is another reason why the distinction between e-government and e-democracy is of importance. Looking back at the idea of the division of power since Montesquieu, there has always been the belief that different parts of government should be responsible for making the rules, for enforcing them, and for judging breaches. The division of power was supposed to put checks and balances to the powers and thereby avoid misuses of power. In this sense, e-democracy can be seen as a possible check on the powers of e-government.

Most factual uses of ICT in government are examples of what we have named e-government instead of e-democracy. However, one should note that e-democracy has at least a strong theoretical influence. Ideas of computer use for the purposes of democratic discourse and decision making have long accompanied the rhetoric surrounding computers and particularly the Internet. Johnson (2001, p. 211) summarises the argument as follows: "(1) Democracy means power in the hands of individuals (the many); (2) information is power; (3) the Internet makes vast quantities of information available to individuals; (4) therefore, the Internet is democratic." The Internet can thus be called a "democratic technology, suggesting that it is inherently democratic" (Johnson, 2000, p.181). And, indeed, the idea of democratic participation was one of the inspiring factors that led Al Gore to his political efforts that promoted the development of the Internet and the World Wide Web as we know it today (cf. Gore, 1995).

There is a number of possible ways in which ICT and particularly the Internet might be beneficial to democracy. On the one hand, technology might allow the formation of democratic interest groups and the development of open democratic discourses. Electronic deliberation could allow the incorporation of a multitude of voices and stakeholders into the process of decision making (cf. Lévy, 1997). The new technology might "free us to build a better world, promote democratic equality, improve the quality of education, and create new economic opportunities for underdeveloped nations" (Stichler & Hauptman, 1998, p. 1). Optimists envisage a world where the increase in bandwidth will eliminate the difference between haves and have-nots in terms of information access and telecommunication will form the backbone of society (Meeks, 2000). On the other hand, ICT can have a positive effect on the individual and thereby improve the functioning of democratic societies. ICT has frequently been described as a means of emancipation and empowerment (cf. Hirschheim & Klein, 1994). If it helps people live up to their psychological and intellectual potential and helps them optimise their organisations then this would again strengthen the basis of democracy.

## Problems of E-Democracy

While e-democracy is a central aspect of the use of ICT in democratic societies, it is not without drawbacks. There are a number of areas where e-democracy either fails to live up to its expectations or where it may even have negative effects. One of the fundamental critiques of e-democracy is that instead of expanding dialogues and discourses it may do the opposite and result in a restriction of information flows. It may allow ICT-literate elites to separate themselves from other parts of society (Breen 1999). The question of power distribution does not have an unambiguous answer with regard to ICT. While the ideal developed in the last section is one of emancipation, decentralisation, and empowerment, ICT can be used for the exact opposite as well. Stallman (1995) argues that the computer system and the societal system can be designed in such a way as to keep the elite in power (cf. Weizenbaum, 1976). Similar power issues can appear in other social settings such as commercial organisations. Ischy and Simoni (2002) emphasise that many of the problems of ICT development are linked to power struggles that link them to politics, be it organisational politics or politics on a wider scale. Another argument against e-democracy is that despite the promising rhetoric that accompanies it, the examples we see of it so far do not seem to deliver on the promises. For example, computerisation does not seem to empirically promote decentralisation of power and public communication, which can be seen as conditions of functioning democracy (cf. Yoon, 1996).

A fundamental problem of e-democracy that might materialise in case e-democracy is introduced successfully is populism. The fundamental idea of e-democracy seems to be some kind of direct democracy, of electronic plebiscites based on the idea of direct democracy as we know it from the Greek Polis. It is debatable, however, whether and in what form this would be applicable and useful in complex modern societies. One could argue that e-democracy might lead to a shallow exchange of phrases. Instead of developing a political will it could lead to a simplification of issues and to non-optimal solutions. Instead of a democratic utopia we might end up with anti-democratic plebiscites (cf. Ess, 1996). Instead of including larger groups or even all of society, e-democracy can lead to the creation or petrification of special interest groups (cf. Paletz, 2000), to lobbying, and to a skewed idea of public interest.

A final problem of e-democracy that needs to be mentioned here because it can have an influence on which effects the commercial paradigm may have is that of the change of society. This is a highly complex problem with many different aspects that cannot be analysed comprehensively in this chapter. It is based on the fact that the ubiquitous use of ICT changes not only the way we can use democratic institutions but affects most parts of society. Furthermore it seems to do so without being subject to the intentional steering of any one actor and it seems to take away power from the nation state. In the literature this development is often called *globalisation*. Globalisation is at least partly based on the use of ICT and many of its aspects are not possible without this. The networking of international financial and information markets, for example, is dependent on a functioning ICT infrastructure. Globalisation can be seen as a chance for e-democracy because it may enable international networks and international consultations on political issues. An interesting aspect here is that the opponents of globalisation are using the very technologies that it is based on to organise their resistance to it as could be seen in the anti-globalisation protests in Seattle, Milan, and other places in the last few years.

However, globalisation also seems to threaten the classical political basis of democracy, namely the nation-state. ICT allows the creation of international networks from global trading networks over internationally working NGOs to international crime syndicates. Most individual nation-states are powerless to control or oversee these institutions. Worse, the power of globalised developments forces individual states to adhere to certain rules without their having an equitable voice in the development of these rules (cf. Johnson, 2001).

Finally, e-democracy and globalisation may just be aspects of a fundamental change in the fabric of our states and societies. The nation-state may evolve into networks and parts of wider networks, as Castells (2001) predicts. In this network of networks e-democracy may take on new forms and meanings. We may be witnessing the evolution of a truly new form of society, the network society, or even a new age, the information age (Castells, 2000). All of this forms the background to our understanding of e-government and e-democracy and it is important for seeing how the paradigm of e-commerce can affect the development of these notions. In the following section we will now analyse what exactly the paradigm of e-commerce stands for and which of its aspects can be of relevance to e-government and e-democracy.

# The Paradigm of E-Commerce

This section will attempt to give an overview over e-commerce with regards to its use as a paradigm. It does not claim to be conclusive and exhaustive of the topic. Rather, it will attempt to isolate those factors that might affect our perception of the use of ICT in government. For this purpose it will try to capture the positive aspects frequently used to explain the success of e-commerce but also the characteristics that might become problematic when applied to democratic processes.

## Characteristics of E-Commerce

In this chapter we will take the term "e-commerce" to denote the buying and selling of products, services, or other commodities through the use of information and communication technology. Furthermore, we will include internal processes of companies that are geared toward the support and facilitation of such commercial exchanges. That means that we will ignore the difference between e-commerce and e-business as external and internal aspects of commerce using ICT. This is justified by the fact that we are looking for the possibility of transfer from the economic sphere to the administrative sphere and the boundaries between internal and external may not be comparable between the two. On the basis of this wide and inclusive definition of e-commerce one can note that it is not a radically new phenomenon. Companies have exchanged business data over a variety of communication networks for a number of years (Currie, 2000). However, the rapid expansion of the Internet and its use for commercial purposes has increased the volume of e-commerce immensely. In some areas this has led to completely new business models, while in many cases old business models have been adapted to be able to make use of the technology. It is debatable how deep the changes introduced by e-commerce really are, whether we are looking at a revolution of the business world or just a gradual change of some aspects. Independent of the answer to this question, there are some aspects of e-commerce that could be observed during the last few years which are important enough to speak of a new paradigm when applied to e-government.

The use of the Internet to buy and sell goods has introduced a new form of competition to many markets. While competition is at the heart of capitalist economic models and generally recognised as a positive part of market economies, competition in traditional markets is often limited. Individual consumers may have a choice of shopping in supermarket A or B but they rarely have the necessary information and resources to get an overview over markets and make economically rational decisions. Markets in economic theory tend to have a number of characteristics such as an infinite number of participants, complete transparency, and infinite reaction speed, which are not even approximated by most real markets. E-commerce has in many cases led to an evolution of markets in the direction of perfect markets of economics. The use of the Internet as a market platform facilitates access to information and reduces barriers to access (Spinello, 2000). The individual market participant can get an overview over markets more easily and technology allows access to vendors and customers far beyond the regional area of traditional markets. A customer who wants to buy a book, for example, can now choose between hundreds of booksellers located all over the world. She can easily compare prices and conditions and make a better-informed decision. E-commerce thus realises the promises of market economies by providing better service to customers.

E-commerce does not only optimise existing markets but it also creates new ones. There are a number of goods and services for sale online that are only possible through the use of ICT in commerce (Schiller, 1999). Examples might be online information databases, outsourcing of company tasks to Web-based companies, and a whole host of services related to information as a commodity. Again, this may not be radically new (Stichler, 1998), but it has taken on new meaning through the Internet and related technologies.

The ease of obtaining information on the Internet has brought with it the disadvantage of information overload. The amount of information available to each and every Internet use is greater than the capacity for processing it. This has produced the side effect that attention has become more important than clear information. Even the best information is useless if it does not reach potential users. Information suppliers on the Internet are therefore concentrating more on grabbing potential customers' attention than on providing them with useful information. The Internet and e-commerce have thereby created a sort of attention economy where attention is the scarce good instead of goods, services, or information (Liebl, 1999; Zerdick et al., 2001).

The most important positive aspect of e-commerce, the aspect that may have facilitated the success of the Internet economy and the one that renders it desirable to politicians and administrators is that it is supposed to save costs. Shin (2003, p. 127) quotes three reasons why e-commerce can be less costly than traditional exchanges: the use of ICT decreases information processing costs, it decreases the costs of product selection, and it allows decreasing inventories, thereby saving capital costs. Another view of the cost-saving capacities of e-commerce concentrates on transaction costs. These costs that appear when transactions are prepared and realised consist of different costs, including search costs, information costs, bargaining costs, decision costs, policing costs, and enforcement costs (Welty & Becerra-Fernandez, 2001, p. 68). The use of computers and networks does not necessarily affect all of these components but it does bring down the overall transaction costs, which can form a considerable part of transactions. At the same time, the use of ICT within businesses can also produce cost savings by optimising structures and processes, by allowing reaction to customer preferences and so forth. These aspects carry different weight in different industries but they are probably the most important reason why e-commerce was and is successful.

## Advantages of E-Commerce

The above characteristics are a collection of reasons why e-commerce may make sense as a business institution. In order to understand why it might be tempting to use the ideas in e-government it is helpful to translate them into manifest advantages for the customer.

This section will therefore describe why e-commerce is good for customers (mainly working with the model of business-to-consumer (B2C) e-commerce) because this explains best why politicians and bureaucrats believe it to be good for citizens. The point of this section is therefore to translate the economic advantages named above into more general advantages for the customer.

The central theme of the last section was that e-commerce makes good business sense by improving efficiency and decreasing costs. For companies this translates into higher earnings which, given the supposed purpose of companies, namely to create profits, does not need further justification. But why should the consumer care? The answer comes from fundamental assumptions about the nature and functioning of markets. In functioning markets (and we have seen that e-commerce is supposed to create these) producers and service providers will not be able to retain the gains they make through efficiency and productivity gains but they will eventually have to pass them on to customers. Customers can therefore save money, which then translates into a greater freedom of choice. Cost savings thus take on an ethical meaning, which can easily be translated into something a democratic government can identify with. Following this line of reasoning one can see other ethical benefits in e-commerce, which stem from its realisation of functioning capitalist markets. Cost savings not only increase freedom of choice but they also allow production of more with the same amount of resources and they are therefore a necessary condition of redistribution and thus of justice (Kreikebaum, 1996). The ethical advantages of e-commerce are thus of a fundamental nature and they touch deep-seated ethical concerns such as freedom and distribution. While most of these are of course double-edged swords, it is nevertheless easy to make a case for e-commerce in these terms. Another example might be tele-working, which can also be understood to be one aspect of e-commerce. This, too, can be seen as an increase of freedom of the employees. It can also have negative consequences (McCalman, 2003), but for the moment we are more interested in positive sides, as these may be used as arguments for the use of the commercial paradigm in e-government.

One big advantage for customers that e-commerce promises is that it facilitates a more personalised service. The use of ICT allows vendors and service providers to accumulate great amounts of information on the customers and this information allows them to cater to individual preferences and needs. An integral part of many e-commerce applications is the so-called customer relationship management (CRM). CRM systems can be bought as complete packages or they can form a part of other e-commerce applications. Their use varies between industries and sellers but the overall defining feature is that the customers' views are taken seriously. Again, this is a very important point for governments, and it is the reason why the use of the term "customer-centred," which is closely linked to e-commerce and CRM, is transformed to "citizen-centred" in e-government.

# The Paradigm of E-Commerce in E-Government and E-Democracy

Having discussed the concepts of e-government and e-democracy as well as the positive sides of e-commerce we are now in a position to discuss the advantages and disadvantages of the transfer of the concept of e-commerce to democracy and administration. In the first part of this section we will look at the reason why governments may want to use the commercial paradigm. The second part will be dedicated to the limits of the commercial paradigm.

## Reasons for the Adoption of the Commercial Paradigm in E-Government and E-Democracy

The reasons why governments and administrations might want to use ideas and concepts from e-commerce for their own activities should have become quite clear from the enumeration of the advantages of e-commerce. Fundamentally, one can summarise the advantages of e-commerce as those of a functioning capitalist market economy and those advantages should be transferable to the activities of government. Among these positive points we have found efficiency, which should allow governments to deliver the same or better services at lower costs. This idea of efficiency also mirrors a hope that government bureaucracies, which are traditionally seen as inefficient and reluctant to change, could be accelerated and streamlined. Here, the commercial paradigm tends to aim at motivational structures, at the fact that e-commerce companies have found it possible to become much more flexible than traditional companies. The hope is that bureaucracies may find it possible to become as flexible by using processes and motivational measures copied from the commercial sector.

But efficiency in service delivery is no end in itself. In e-commerce efficiency gains are supposed to maximise profits, whereas in government they have different justifications. These can best be understood when the state is seen as a representative of its citizens, which requires the state to act in the sense of the citizens and to do what they believe to be right. Saving costs may be something citizens desire but that only counts in the context of the other wishes citizens have. The ethical advantages of e-commerce therefore play a central role for the adoption of the paradigm in government. Efficiency and cost savings can then be seen as measures that increase the citizens' freedom. E-government can thus be seen as an aspect of liberty, which is something that democratic states are supposed to provide their citizens with. This liberty includes the freedom of choice, and again, the use of ICT can improve this by providing information. In the extreme, e-government could be seen as an introduction of competition between governments because the increased information flow might allow citizens to make an informed decision in which jurisdiction they want to live.

The adoption of the concept of customer-centeredness in the form of citizen-centeredness should also be understood in this context. Since, fundamentally, the state is there for the citizens it should be focused on the citizen anyway. If governments try to become more citizen-centred, then this is an expression of the reflection of the government on their original purpose. As such, it is clearly positive if e-government following e-commerce focuses the awareness of administrations on their *raison d'être.*

## Limits of the Commercial Paradigm in E-Commerce and E-Democracy

As we have just seen, there are numerous good reasons for trying to extend the ideas of e-commerce to e-government and e-democracy. However, there are also limits to how far this transfer of ideas can go. These will be discussed in this section, starting with the differences between customers and citizens, proceeding with the limitations of economic analogies in government and administration and ending with genuine political problems caused by the adoption of e-commerce as a paradigm.

The starting point of this discussion of the limits of the commercial paradigm is the difference between customers and citizens. As we have seen above, the idea of customer-centeredness, which is closely linked to e-commerce, is quite attractive to administrators in public bodies. Just like companies have to satisfy their customers to receive orders and survive, governments should satisfy their citizens. Accepting the commercial paradigm should lead to desirable developments such as speedier service and more efficient processes. However, there are limits to this analogy. The role of citizens in state and government is fundamentally different from the role of customers in a company. Companies exist for purposes that are defined by their owners. These may include profit generation, power exertion, reputation enhancement, and many others. Customers are important for companies as means to achieve these ends but they carry no intrinsic value. This is different for governments, which exist for the citizens. The citizens are at the same time the owners and decision makers of governments. Governments have to realise the collective will of citizens. Without citizens governments would cease to exist. To return to the commercial paradigm, citizens are not only customers, they are also the shareholders. This means that while some aspects of the analogy of the customer apply to citizens, these have a richer meaning in governments. Citizens are the ultimate sovereign and they should have a voice in decision making. Some companies try to give their customers a voice in decision making or product design, but again, the motivation for doing so is different. Governments are there for their citizens in a fundamental ontological sense, whereas companies are only there for their customers as long as it suits their needs.

Another group of limits of the commercial paradigm results from the dissimilarity of states and markets. Markets are self-organising entities whereas states are directed and led. Furthermore, markets are not natural occurrences but they require a framework of rules, regulations, and enforcement that can only be supplied by political entities (cf. De George, 1999; Hayek, 1994). Markets are thus fundamentally different entities from states and governments and, consequentially, some of the characteristics and advantages of e-commerce may not be transferable from one to the other.

One example of this is the idea of competition, which is so central to success of e-commerce. There are several reasons why competition may not be equally desirable in government and administration. First, competition, by definition, produces winners and losers. Not everybody can survive in competition and the threat of losing is one of the main motivators in markets. This very idea is not suitable to the way governments treat their citizens. Citizens retain their status as citizens independent of their personal abilities and the state cannot accept a system that necessarily leads to some people losing out. Second, competition is only relevant for those players who have market power, meaning who have financial resources. E-commerce may be highly customer-centred but this applies only to those customers who can afford the products. Again, governments cannot copy this aspect, as their citizens have rights to services, independent of their financial means. In fact, those citizens who have little financial means are the same ones that need the services of the state most. Finally, competition does not apply to states and governments. Citizens do not generally have a choice between who they want to be governed by and ICT does little to change this. In order for the e-commerce paradigm to develop all of its potential, there would have to be competition between different e-government agencies or initiatives and this is impossible because of the nature of governments as natural monopolies.

Another problem is the concept of efficiency. Our description of the advantages of the commercial paradigm has emphasised efficiency by using a common sense understanding of efficiency. However, looking closer at the term shows that it is quite difficult to define efficiency in such a way that it reflects the common sense understanding. Because of this difficulty economics defines efficiency as Pareto-optimality (Hausman & McPherson, 1996; Sen, 1987). This definition means that an economic state is efficient if there are no more possible exchanges between two agents that are mutually advantageous. This is fundamentally problematic because it means that an economic state is efficient when one agent owns everything and nobody else owns anything at all. By definition this would be efficient but it would not be something that people and governments strive for.

A further problem of the commercial paradigm is that it may not be applicable to the goods that states are responsible for. Arguably one of the more important tasks we need states and governments for is the allocation of public goods. Public goods are those that belong to the community and can be used by all or some members thereof. They are highly problematic because the benefits of using them can be reaped by individual users whereas the costs tend to be socialised. They therefore create incentives for anti-social behaviour where individuals optimise their benefits and minimise their costs. Since these incentives are similar for all users, public goods can be overused and destroyed, to the detriment of all users. Pure market tools are incapable of dealing with this sort of situation. The situation requires state intervention and thus goes against the commercial paradigm. Interestingly, the information age seems to create new cases of public goods. The entire network structure of the Internet, for example, is a public good. It is questionable whether this can be managed by principles of capitalist business (Chapman & Rotenberg, 1995), even though it is the basis for most of today's e-commerce activities. Furthermore, the idea of information itself also seems to be a public good. Democracies need some sort of information to be workable. Applying the principles of private ownership to this may be harmful to the very idea of democracy (Blanke, 1998).

Finally, there is the character or e-commerce as an attention economy. In terms of e-government and e-democracy this might be taken to mean that only those topics are taken serious that are at the top of current attention. While this is the case to some degree in any democracy, and maybe even stronger in modern media democracy, it is not necessarily a desirable development. If the increased use of ICT leads to an overflow of information and to citizens who are disoriented because of too much rather than too little information then e-commerce may be better used as a bad example than as a paradigm that one should follow.

Apart from these points where there is a lack of fit between the paradigm of e-commerce and the reality and requirements of government and democracy, there are some issues of genuine political importance that stand against the use of e-commerce ideas. Generally, these issues can be summarised by saying that the introduction of ICT into government, administration, and democracy can have political results that are not desirable.

The first point here is that ICT can lead to a redistribution of power. By their very nature, government and democracy have to do with power. However, the idea of democracy is to render the distribution and use of power transparent and understandable. ICT may lead to more or less subtle power shifts which are not transparent and which are not coupled to institutions of accountability. Much of the literature on how ICT changes power structures starts with the works of Foucault and analyses the power relationships within organisations and companies (cf. Healy & Iles, 2002; Introna, 2001). The same processes of power shifts might take place within governments and between different stakeholders of governments. One aspect of this is that of access, where e-government and e-democracy will favour those who have access to technology. A similar argument can be made in international relationships as well. The increasing use of ICT in commerce can be seen as a facilitator of international trade but it can also easily become an expression of cultural imperialism (Weckert, 2000). The rich western countries force the developing world to subscribe to their values and rules because it allows them to increase profits.

The most serious political problem produced by the use of e-commerce as a paradigm is that it may promote a particular ideology under the guise of addressing technical problems. When we look back at the advantages of the commercial paradigm then these could be summarised as saying that ICT can improve processes, mostly without changing the substance of activities. One could hold against this that e-commerce is not value-neutral but rather that it is deeply entrenched in the ideology of liberalism. The use of the paradigm in e-government would consequentially lead to a shift toward liberalism. This is in itself not a negative thing but the problem is that this might happen masked as a technical change. In fact, it has been noticed that digital technology, including personal computers, networks, and the Internet, and the mindset of those who developed this technology are quite closely related to liberalism or even libertarianism (Fagin, 2000). Many of the aspects of e-commerce that allow it to produce its positive effects are based on the ideas of free markets and can be related to neo-liberalism and the Chicago School of economics (Winner, 2000). These ideas, which originally aim mostly at the economic sphere, also have consequences in the political system. Many of the aspects and advantages of what is sometimes called "information democracy" are close to or originate from liberal thoughts. The free flow of data assumes independent and equal individuals with a sufficient amount of knowledge and freedom to act according to the information. This is, of course, the very starting point which liberalism takes (cf. Kester, 1998). It should thus be noted that e-government and e-democracy, as long as they work on the basis of this view of humanity, are using presuppositions, which move them closely to liberalism.

The use of the term "ideology" here should not be misunderstood to be something entirely negative. An ideology can be seen "as a set of assumptions of which we are barely conscious but which nonetheless directs our efforts to give shape and coherence to the world" (Postman, 1992, 123). As Postman himself points out in the next sentence, according to this view, language itself is pure ideology. It is impossible to exist without ideologies as these are the building blocks of our world. In this they are very close to the concept of a paradigm, which is so central to this chapter. This part of the argument should thus not be misconstrued to be overly critical of liberalism. Rather, it is meant to show that the adoption of one paradigm, e-commerce, may lead to or be influenced by another set of fundamental assumptions, namely liberalism. This is nothing bad in and of itself. But it can become politically problematic if is not admitted openly and made subject of discussion and political decisions.

# Conclusion

The question of this chapter was whether the success of e-commerce could somehow be emulated or imported into state, government, and democracy. The chapter discussed why e-commerce might be used as a paradigm as well as the strengths and weaknesses of this approach. The result was somewhat ambivalent. Some of the aspects of e-commerce can be used and applied in administration and democratic decision making whereas others seem to run counter to the idea of democracy. So where does this leave us; what should the decision maker try to achieve?

The answer to this question becomes a bit clearer when one looks at the areas where e-commerce as a paradigm displays strengths and weaknesses. As a general rule, one can say that the success of the paradigm is the greater the closer the government application is to e-commerce. That means that in those areas where governments provide goods and services for the citizens, where citizens can thus justly be seen as customers, e-commerce may provide a useful role model. The further government applications move away from this service provision model into the genuine tasks of democratic politics, the less useful e-commerce will be. Democratic decision making including elections, representation, parliamentarianism, and so forth have few or no equivalents in the business world. E-commerce can therefore not provide governments with suggestions for how ICT can be used in these areas.

Returning to our distinction between e-government and e-democracy, one could now say that e-commerce is a useful paradigm for the former but less so for the latter. At the same time one can observe a tendency of many of the organisations and institutions charged with using ICT in government to adopt the language of e-commerce and thus presumably the paradigm (cf. Remenyi & Bannister, 2003). This can be seen as a good sign because it means that the advantages of e-commerce may be realised in government. At the same time it can also mean that the emphasis of governments will move toward service provision and e-government and away from the politically more important e-democracy. This may lead to a growth of the power of the executive to the detriment of the legislature. If this is so then it might be deeply damaging to democracy as we know it.

This chapter was meant to draw attention to this hidden danger. It was not intended to say that we should not make good use of positive experiences in the business world and use them to improve the workings of our states and administration. However, we should realise that there are fundamental differences between democratic government and business. Neglecting to take these differences seriously may in effect do more harm than good by weakening the participative basis of democracy.

# References

Blanke, H.T. (1998). Librarianship and public culture in the age of information capitalism. In R.N. Stichler & R. Hauptman (Eds.), *Ethics, information and technology: Readings* (pp. 184-199). Jefferson, NC: MacFarland & Company.

Breen, M. (1999). Counterrevolution in the infrastructure - A cultural study of techno-scientific impoverishment. In L.J. Pourciau (Ed.), *Ethics and electronic information in the 21ˢᵗ century* (pp. 29-45). West Lafayette, IN: Purdue University Press.

Castells, M. (2000). *The information age: Economy, society, and culture. Volume I: The rise of the network society* (2nd ed.). Oxford: Blackwell.

Castells, M. (2001). Epilogue: Informationalism and the network society. In P. Himanen(Ed.), *The hacker ethic and the spirit of the information age* (pp. 155-178). London: Secker & Warburg.

Chapman, G., & Rotenberg, M. (1995). The national information infrastructure: A public interest opportunity. In D.G. Johnson & H. Nissenbaum (Eds.), *Computers, ethics & social values* (628-644). Upper Saddle River, NJ: Prentice Hall.

Currie, W. (2000). *The global information society.* Chichester: John Wiley & Sons.

De George, R.T. (1999). *Business ethics* (5th ed.). Upper Saddle River, NJ: Prentice Hall.

Ess, C. (1996). The political computer: Democracy, CMC, and Habermas. In C. Ess (Ed.), *Philosophical perspectives on computer-mediated communication* (pp. 197-230). Albany: State University of New York Press.

Fagin, B. (2000). Liberty and community online. In R.M. Baird, R. Ramsower & S.E. Rosenbaum (Eds.), *Cyberethics - Social and moral issues in the computer age* (pp. 332-352). New York: Prometheus Books.

Gore, A. (1995). Global information infrastructure. In D.G. Johnson & H. Nissenbaum (Eds.), *Computers, ethics & social values* (pp. 620-628). Upper Saddle River, NJ: Prentice Hall.

Hausman, D.M., & McPherson, M.S. (1996). *Economic analysis and moral philosophy.* Cambridge University Press.

Hayek, F.A. von (1994). *The road to serfdom* (50th anniversary ed.). Chicago: The University of Chicago Press.

Healy, M. & Iles, J. (2002). The impact of information and communications technology on managerial practices: The use of codes of conduct. In I. Alvarez et al. (Eds.), *The transformation of organisations in the information age: Social and ethical implications.* Proceedings of the sixth ETHICOMP Conference, November 13-15, 2002, Lisbon, Portugal. Lisbon: Universidade Lusiada.

Hirschheim, R., & Klein, H. K. (1994, March. Realizing emancipatory principles in information systems development: The case for ETHICS. *MIS Quarterly, 18*(1), 83–109.

Introna, L. (2001). Workplace surveillance, privacy, and distributive justice. In R.A. Spinello & H.T. Tavani (Eds.), *Readings in cyberethics* (pp. 418-429). Sudbury, MA: Jones and Bartlett.

Ischy, F., & Simoni, O. (2002). Representations as factor of organizational change. In I. Alvarez et al. (Eds.), *The transformation of organisations in the information age: Social and ethical implications* (pp. 355-367). Proceedings of the sixth ETHICOMP Conference, November 13-15, 2002, Lisbon, Portugal. Lisbon: Universidade Lusiada.

Johnson, D.G. (2000). Democratic values and the Internet. In D. Langford (Ed.), *Internet ethics* (pp. 181-196). London: McMillan.

Johnson, D.G. (2001). *Computer ethics* (3rd ed.). Upper Saddle River, NJ: Prentice Hall.

Kester, G.H. (1998). Access denied: Information policy and the limits of liberalism. In R.N. Stichler & R. Hauptman (Eds.), *Ethics, information and technology: Readings* (pp. 207-230). Jefferson, NC: MacFarland & Company.

Kreikebaum, H. (1996). *Grundlagen der unternehmensethik.* Stuttgart: Schaeffer-Poeschel.

Kuhn, T.S. (1996). *The structure of scientific revolutions* (3rd ed.). Chicago: The University of Chicago Press.

Lévy, P. (1997). *Cyberculture.* Paris: Editions Odile Jacob.

Liebl, F. (1999). What system have you announced? Impressionen aus einer Ökonomie der Ankündigung. In F. Liebl (Ed.), *E-conomy - Management und Ökonomie in digitalen Kontexten* (pp. 7-10). Marburg: Metropolis Verlag.

McCalman, J. (2003). What can we do for corporate nomads? IT and facilities aanagement. In L.A. Joia (Ed.), *IT-based management: Challenges and solutions* (pp. 130-142). Hershey, PA.: Idea Group Publishing. Meeks, B.N. (2000). Better democracy through technology. In R.M. Baird, R. Ramsower & S.E. Rosenbaum (Eds.), *Cyberethics - Social and moral issues in the computer age* (pp. 288-294). New York: Prometheus Books.

Pentland. (2003). Panel contribution to: Ackerman, M., Pentland, B.T., Qureshi, S., & Yakura, E.K. Visual elements in the discourse on information technology. In E. Wynn, E. Whitley, M.D. Myers & J. DeGross (Eds.), *Global and organizational discourse about information technology* (pp. 527-531). Ifip Tc8/Wg8.2 Working Conference on Global and Organizational Discourse About Information Technology, December 12-14, 2002, Barcelona, Spain. Dordrecht: Kluwer Academic Publishers.

Paletz, D.L. (2000). Advanced information technology and political communication. In R.M. Baird, R. Ramsower & S.E. Rosenbaum (Eds.), *Cyberethics - Social and moral issues in the computer age* (pp. 285-287). New York: Prometheus Books.

Postman, N. (1992). *Technopoly - The surrender of culture to technology.* New York: Vintage Books.

Reagle, J.M., Jr. (1996). Trust in electronic markets. *First Monday, 1*(2). *www.firstmonday.dk.*

Remenyi, D., & Bannister, F. (Eds.). (2003). *Proceedings of the European Conference on e-Government,* Trinity College Dublin, June 3-4, 2003, Dublin.

Schiller, D. (1999). *Digital capitalism: Networking the global market system.* Cambridge, MA: MIT Press.

Sen, A. (1987). *On ethics and economics.* Oxford, NY: Basil Blackwell.

Shin, N. (2003). Productivity gains from IT's reduction of coordination costs. In N. Shin (Ed.), *Creating business value with information technology: Challenges and solutions* (pp. 125-145). Hershey, PA: Idea Group Publishing.

Spinello, R. (2000). *Cyberethics: Morality and law in cyberspace.* London: Jones and Bartlett.

Stallman, R. (1995). Are computer property rights absolute? In D.G. Johnson & H. Nissenbaum (Eds.), *Computers, ethics & social values* (pp. 115-119). Upper Saddle River, NJ: Prentice Hall.

Stichler, R.N. (1998). Ethics in the information market. In R.N. Stichler & R. Hauptman (Eds.), *Ethics, information and technology: Readings* (pp. 169). Jefferson, NC: MacFarland & Company.

Stichler, R.N., & Hauptman, R. (Eds.), (1998). *Ethics, information and technology: readings.* Jefferson, NC: MacFarland & Company.

Wastell, D.G. (2003). Organizational discourse as a social defense: Taming the tiger of electronic government. In E. Wynn, E. Whitley, M.D. Myers & J. DeGross (Eds.) *Global and organizational discourse about information technology* (pp. 179-195). Ifip Tc8/Wg8.2 Working Conference on Global and Organizational Discourse About Information Technology, December 12-14, 2002, Barcelona, Spain. Dordrecht: Kluwer Academic Publishers.

Weckert, J. (2000). What is new or unique about Internet activities? In D. Langford (Ed.), *Internet ethics* (pp. 47-63). London: McMillan.

Weiser, M., & Molnar, K.K. (1996). Advanced telecommunications infrastructure policies - A comparative analysis. *Proceedings of the Americas Conference on Information Systems 1996.*

Weizenbaum, J. (1976). *Computer power and human reason.* San Francisco: W. H. Freeman and Company.

Welty, B., & Becerra-Fernandez, I. (2001). Managing trust and commitment in collaborative supply chain relationships. *Communications of the ACM, 44*(6), 67–73.

Winner, L. (2000). Cyberlibertarian myths and the prospects for community. In R.M. Baird, R. Ramsower & S.E. Rosenbaum (Eds.), *Cyberethics - Social and moral issues in the computer age* (pp. 319-331). New York: Prometheus Books.

Yoon, S.-H. (1996). Power online: A post-structuralist perspective on computer-mediated communication. In C. Ess (Ed.), *Philosophical perspectives on computer-mediated communication* (pp. 171-196). Albany: State University of New York Press.

Zerdick, A. et al. (2001). *European Communication Councel report: Die Internet-Ökonomie: Strategien für die digitale wirtschaft* (3rd ed.). Berlin: Springer.

## Chapter II

# Implementing and Assessing Transparency in Digital Government:
## Some Issues in Project Management*

Bryane Michael, Oxford University, United Kingdom

Michael Bates, Oxford Analytica, United Kingdom[1]

## Abstract

*The IMF has been leading efforts to develop and implement codes of monetary and fiscal transparency. Such codes aim to increase disclosure of public sector information on the Internet-representing a type of "e-transparency". Do such codes and increased Internet-based public sector information achieve their objectives? Much e-government theory sees electronic presence and e-transparency as a first step toward transformationary e-government. Yet, e-transparency itself represents a transformation in e-government. This chapter will first describe the results of a private-sector based assessment of fiscal and monetary transparency and report cross-country ratings. Second, it will describe a new method of assessment that emphasizes the role of knowledge management and the critical role played by assessment project design. Lastly, this chapter will discuss the extent to which such e-government efforts aimed at greater transparency achieve broader objectives - such as increased trust, predictability, credibility, oversight, and political accountability in the public sector. The lessons in this chapter are applicable to governments engaged in promoting and assessing transparency as well as corporations.*

# Introduction

Since the mid-1990s, governments around the world have been making efforts to put documents on the Internet, report fiscal data electronically and provide more transparent descriptions of public sector activities. At the international level, such an effort has been led by the International Monetary Fund (IMF) - in collaboration with the World Bank, the Bank for International Settlements, and other international organisations - in their development and implementation of codes of monetary and fiscal transparency.[2] According to the Fund, "the adoption of internationally recognized standards and codes of good practice can help to improve economic policymaking and strengthen the international financial system" (IMF, 2001). Implicit in both the improvement of policymaking and the strengthening of the international financial system is the use of information and communications technologies (ICTs) in government for the creation of an "e-government" capable of transmitting information required by the codes. Universal access to public sector information, then, reduces information asymmetries - thereby lessening principal-agent problems related to monitoring public sector performance (Bertelsmann Foundation, 2002). The availability of public sector information also reduces the panic selling of portfolio investments (Lane, 1999).

At the national level, the disclosure of public sector information through e-government initiatives (and the purported transparency such disclosure entails) has been seen as a way to promote democracy (Cullen & Houghton, 2000), increase trust in government (Heichelbech, 2002), increase predictability in public service performance (United Nations, 2001), promote credibility through better incorporation of citizen needs and access to information (Martin & Feldman, 1998; Roberts, 1999), and encourage oversight in the fight against corruption (Fenner & Wehrle, 2001; Radics, 2001). Heeks (2001), however, found mixed results for the impact of e-government on government effectiveness.

*Figure 1: A teleology of e-government*

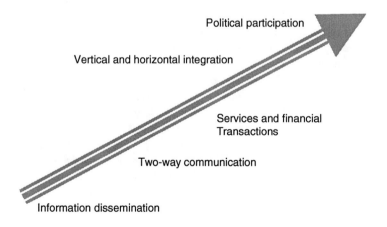

*Source: Hiller and Belanger (2001)*

Most of these points are illustrated in a diagram which has become commonplace in the e-government literature. Figure 1 depicts the purported evolution of e-government along a linear teleological continuum of presence, interaction, transaction and transformation (Backus, 2001; Herman, 2002; Hiller & Belanger, 2001; Moon, 2002). In the first stages, e-government is supposed to promote the dissemination of information. As e-government "evolves," governments are said to have the increasing capacity to interact (or achieve two-way communication in Hiller and Belanger's terminology). The third stage represents "transactions" between government and citizens such as in tax and registration payments. The final stage of e-government represents a "transformation" or a new way of engaging in political participation. While the details about each of these steps differ slightly between authors (for example Hiller and Belanger also include a stage dedicated to vertical and horizontal integration), the basic premise that e-government "evolves" along a continuum remains canonical. The e-government teleology has become so fundamental in the e-government literature that these stages are used by the United Nations' (2001) "e-government" international index as evaluation criteria.

If such a "life cycle theory" of e-government holds at the international level, then the IMF's Codes of Monetary and Fiscal Transparency represent the early phases (the "presence" and "interaction" phases) of a broader trend toward the "transformation" of government into a public service provider and a representative of collective interests. Assuming the e-government teleology is correct, codes establishing orderly rules of "presence" and assessments ascertaining the degree of presence would both promote such an evolution and lay the basis for broad-based involvement by local actors, government, the international community, and business in each stage of this "growth". Lessons from early "phases" - such as the establishment of e-transparency phase - of e-government implementation and the consequences of e-government projects would be valuable for practitioners working in later stages.

However, as we will argue, work on public sector transparency is more than simple stage 1 information dissemination. Instead, it provides a service and represents a change in political participation that represents the late stages of the e-government "revolution". The drive to implement "e-transparency," just like the drive to promote e-government, depends not on technology but the methods of project design, implementation, and assessment (Herman, 2002). The first section of the chapter will describe the project design of one specific assessment - Oxford Analytica's Assessment of Monetary and Fiscal Transparency.[3] The second section will present some comparative data from this international assessment of monetary and fiscal transparency - showing that most governments have some level of "e-transparency," albeit with large differences between groups of countries. The third section will present the lessons learned in the assessment exercise for both other assessors and for implementing governments. The fourth section will present some issues that must be confronted in future stages of e-transparency work involving the use of codes and standards. We will argue for a demand-driven approach focusing on the role of third parties. We also argue that e-transparency is not a final objective, but only a target for other objectives such as increased public sector predictability, trust, credibility, oversight, and political accountability.

# Assessing Monetary and Fiscal Transparency

In 2001, Oxford Analytica undertook, on behalf of the California Public Employees Retirement System (CalPERS), an assessment of monetary and fiscal transparency in 25 countries. [4] These assessments were based on evaluation modalities used in the IMF's Reports on the Observance of Standards and Codes (ROSC). [5] Assessment reports evaluated the degree of compliance with two IMF codes: Code of Monetary Transparency and Code of Fiscal Transparency.[6] Both codes are divided into four main sections evaluating the clarity of roles and responsibilities, public availability of information, open processes for formulating and reporting policy decisions and assurances of integrity.[7] Each of these main sections is further divided into sub-sections (35 sub-sections for monetary transparency and 37 for fiscal transparency) addressing specific organisations or reporting requirements.

The assessments extended on work already being done by Oxford Analytica's eStandards project aimed at assessing transparency against a number of pre-established standards in over 100 countries.[8] According to the eStandards Web site, the goal of this evaluation exercise is to "present assessments of key economies in a user-friendly format that will for the first time allow our subscribers to get a quick snap shot of a country's standing in thirteen key standard categories" (Oxford Analytica, 2002). [9] The "quick snap shot" refers to the 5- point assessment ratings given for each standard. The standards covered by eStandards relate to national-level data dissemination, monetary transparency, fiscal transparency, insolvency framework, accounting, corporate governance, auditing, money laundering, payment system of the Central Bank, payment systems principles, banking supervision, securities regulation and insurance regulation.

*Figure 2: Simplified representation of the evaluation procedure used to assess monetary and fiscal transparency*

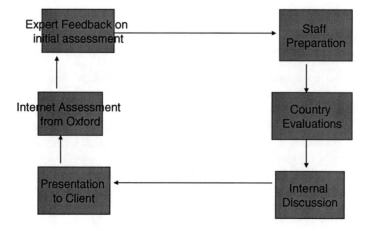

As shown in Figure 2, the evaluation process for monetary and fiscal transparency followed roughly six steps. The first step concerns project preparation. Besides having strong academic backgrounds and work experience in areas of relevance to the project, staff spent up to two weeks reading the IMF's Codes, supplementary readings, looking at examples of ROSCs and discussing the methodology internally. Most staff working on the assessment already had developed assessment competencies and in-country contacts while working on the eStandards Forum. Country embassies in London were also contacted to inform them of the evaluations and to seek their assistance. The second step involved an Internet assessment. Using data collected over the Internet from Oxford, five researchers looked for data for each sub-point addressed by the Codes - following a well-defined search procedure and augmenting the procedure as information was discovered. Emphasis was placed on the Internet search component given that information available by Internet would have the lowest "transactions costs" for all stakeholders interested in the information.[10]

The third step involved the commissioning of expert opinions based on the preliminary data. These experts are normally contracted for Oxford Analytica Briefs and thus have significant in-country experience and are recognised experts in their fields. The fourth step consisted of country evaluations. These evaluations were conducted by a pair of assessors - one Oxford Analytica staff member and one country expert. In-country partners consisted of government officials, businesspersons and NGO representatives. Initial evaluations were shared with in-country partners beforehand for line-by-line feedback and assessors did receive extensive feedback in several instances. A large number of non-government actors were consulted as a way of "triangulating" scores - given biases that may result due to individual responses, inconvenient meeting times or other factors.[11] The fifth step consisted of internal discussion with country experts and project staff using a type of Delphi method (Sackman, 1975). These discussions served to generate a global overview to facilitate inter-country comparisons and to eliminate individual judgement biases. Finally, the results were presented to the client.

# International Comparative Data on "Compliance" with Transparency Standards

The results of the assessment yield insights into general trends about the adoption of international transparency standards. Figure 3 shows three different country examples along with monetary and fiscal transparency scores for each component of the IMF Codes. These countries - Hungary, Indonesia, and Venezuela - have been chosen because they represent a cross-section of different geographical locations and transparency scores. For the reported scores, 1 represents "no compliance," 2 represents "intent declared," 3 represents "enacted," 4 represents "compliance in progress" and 5 represents "full compliance". Even for only these three countries, two points are observable. First, there is a degree of variability within each type of Code. Fiscal transparency scores for Hungary range between 3-4 while for both Indonesia and Venezuela, they range

*Figure 3: Three examples of transparency scores*

|  | Hungary | Indonesia | Venezuela |
|---|---|---|---|
| **Fiscal Transparency** |  |  |  |
| 1. Clarity Of Roles, Responsibilities and Objectives | 4 | 2 | 3 |
| 2. Public Availability of Information | 3 | 3 | 2 |
| 3. Open Budget Preparation, Execution and Reporting | 3 | 2 | 2 |
| 4. Accountability and Assurance of Integrity | 4 | 3 | 2 |
| **Monetary Transparency** |  |  |  |
| 1. Clarity of Roles, Responsibilities and Objectives of Central Banks | 5 | 4 | 3 |
| 2. Open Process for Formulating and Reporting Monetary Policy Decisions | 4 | 4 | 2 |
| 3. Public Availability of Information on Monetary Policy | 5 | 3 | 2 |
| 4. Accountability and Assurance of Integrity by the Central Bank | 5 | 4 | 3 |

*Source: CalPERS (2002)*

between 2-3. Second, there is no consistently strict country ranking for individual sections of the Codes.[12] For clarity of fiscal roles, Venezuela ranks higher than Indonesia even if Indonesia ranks higher than Venezuela for the other fiscal code sections. These points are generalisable to all the countries in the survey.

Despite the ostensible ease that numerical country rankings give for cross-country comparison, the interpretation of these scores is not straightforward. First, they do not represent "compliance" with the standard. "Compliance" implies a cause and effect relationship where countries simply "react" to standards. Instead, these scores represent countries' actions - often undertaken on their own initiative - which have been grouped together into categories. Second, there are bands of errors around these estimates. A country score of 2 for Indonesia is not a precise and immutable parameter estimate. Instead, numbers represent some degree of absolute compliance and some degree of relative compliance compared with other countries. External factors involving language, events in the country, and personalities in government all affect these scores. Third, these scores - like the Codes upon which they are based - to a large extent reflect the creation and evaluation of legislation and regulation. Countries that have enacted legislation aimed at transparency but have public sector processes that make obtaining information very difficult will rank higher than countries that have the opposite situation. In other words, the Codes put a greater weight on formal compliance than on substantive compliance.

*Figure 4: Monetary and fiscal transparency worldwide*

|       | Monetary | | | |
|-------|---|---|---|---|
|       | 1 | 2 | 3 | 4 |
| **4** |   |   |   | Argentina   Czech Rep<br>Brazil       Hungary<br>Chile |
| **3** |   |   | India<br>Malaysia<br>Morocco<br>Taiwan | Colombia   Peru<br>Israel     Poland<br>Mexico     S. Korea<br>Phillipines |
| **2** |   | Venezuela<br>Sri Lanka | Jordan<br>Russia<br>Thailand | Indonesia |
| **1** |   | Pakistan<br>China |   | Turkey |

(Row labels: F i s c a l)

*Note: Higher scores imply greater transparency. These data are illustrative only and do not represent direct inter-country comparisons.*

Individual sections of the IMF Codes have been "aggregated" to arrive at an overall country transparency score for each Code. Aggregation was based on qualitative factors rather than on a mathematical formula between sub-components. Figure 4 presents aggregate ratings for monetary transparency compared with aggregate ratings for fiscal transparency for each country assessed by Oxford Analytica. There appears to be a correlation between fiscal and monetary transparency. However, the correlation is not very strong.[13] Argentina and Indonesia receive relatively high marks for monetary transparency (both countries scoring 4). Yet, Indonesia rates 2 and Argentina rates 4 on fiscal transparency. Given the variability and country specificity of these data, it is not possible to define a "transparent country". Any reference to the transparency of a country must define clearly the institution and standard being discussed.

A second, and closely related point refers to the "lower rectangular matrix" form of Figure 3. All the countries appear on or below the diagonal. Fiscal transparency appears to be the constraining variable in the transparency problem. Given that fiscal transparency always received a score at least as high as monetary transparency or lower, this suggests that improving fiscal transparency should be a priority of e-transparency activity. However, part of the reason for these data may involve the diffuseness of the fiscal measure. Central Bank transparency focuses mainly on one institution and to a great extent is influenced by legislative and Central Bank regulation. Fiscal transparency, however, covers a wide range of organisations and their relations. Thus, just as it is difficult to draw inter-country comparisons, one must be circumspect in directly comparing fiscal and monetary transparency.

Third, despite the difficulty involved in making inter-country comparisons, the data suggest there are "clusters" of countries with high and low transparency.[14] Argentina, Brazil, Chile, Colombia, Czech Republic, Hungary, India, Indonesia, Israel, Malaysia,

*Figure 5: Fiscal transparency and e-governance*

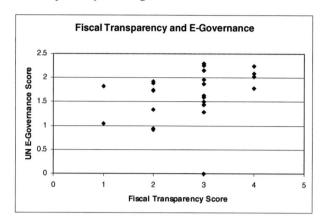

Mexico, Morocco, Peru, Philippines, Poland, S. Korea, and Taiwan roughly form a higher transparency set of countries. To some degree, there is a correlation between this country group and the set of upper-middle and high-income countries - except for Turkey, which is outside the "high transparency group" and Colombia, India, Indonesia, Morocco, and Peru, which are in the group. However, comparing countries, one sees that OECD countries and a set of middle-income countries tend to be more transparent, while lower-middle income and low-income countries such as China, Egypt, Jordan, Pakistan, Russia, Sri Lanka, Thailand, Turkey, and Venezuela rate low on both fiscal and monetary transparency.

Ostensibly, the degree of "e-government" (namely the degree to which government uses the Internet as part of its operations and information dissemination) should be a determining factor in a partially Internet-based transparency assessment. The hypothesis underlying much work on transparency is that information and communications technologies (ICTs) are key in promoting transparency (Heeks, 2001; Reilly, 2002). Yet, the data show a weak correlation between transparency assessments and the level of e-government.

Figure 5 shows the correlation between Oxford Analytica's fiscal transparency scores and the United Nations' (2001) "e-Government index". Scores range from 3.25-2.0 ("high e-govt capacity"), 2.0-1.6 ("medium e-govt capacity"), 1.6-1.0 ("minimal e-govt capacity") and below 1 indicate "deficient e-govt capacity". Scores are partly constructed by subjective measures of the country's progress along the e-government teleology mentioned previously rather than objective assessments of technological connectivity. The quantitative correlation between e-government and fiscal transparency appears weak (correlation co-efficient of 0.57).[15] The qualitative evidence from the assessment exercise also suggested a weak correlation. In several cases, such as Turkey and Russia, e-government was well developed and yet public sector organisations had not undertaken efforts to increase the transparency of their operations. Second, each transparency score corresponds to a different variability (or range) of e-government scores. "Compliance in progress" has the largest range of e-government variability, with most countries clustered mostly in the high e-govt capacity group. Such variability might reflect "binning effects" in the fiscal transparency assessments (fiscal transparency scores are broad enough to include a wide range of differing countries into one score). However, for countries that have "enacted" fiscal transparency measures, e-govt capacity ranges from minimal to high. Given these data, transparency appears to depend less on e-government capacity than on specific country and organisational policies – which also affect e-government policy decisions.

# Lessons Learned in Assessing E-Government Information

During the course of the evaluation, there were a number of lessons learned about evaluation strategy that may be of interest to organisations working on similar assessment exercises. While these lessons may only seem relevant for transparency assessments, given the close links between transparency and e-government, these lessons are generalisable to e-government assessments. Figure 6 shows the "emergent strategy" that developed as a result of project needs.[16] The first step involved deciding on optimal evaluation targets - which meant combining quantitative and qualitative indicators. The second step involved the optimal allocation of information and knowledge use to make assessments on these indicators. The third step focused on process design necessary for adhocratic flexibility to make best use of information and knowledge resources. The fourth step involved participatory evaluation that capitalised on external information and knowledge assets most important for the assessment.

## Selecting Indicators to Maximise Quantitative And Qualitative Data

For most evaluation exercises, decisions must be made about the optimal mix of quantitative versus qualitative indicators (Bulmer & Warwick, 1993; King et al., 1994). Prior assessments of transparency have used measurements that rely on perceptions surveys such as those employed by the World Bank (2002) and Transparency International (2001). However, these indicators may be unreliable due to biases in respondent selection, cognitive biases, or other problems. Such "soft data," which may rely on qualitative judgements, may be contrasted with "hard data" indicators, which use relatively objective and impartially recordable measures - such as the enactment of laws or the availability of certain types of documents. The IMF codes are not completely objective (allowing for a completely dispassionate evaluation of transparency) but their reliance on the availability of strictly and narrowly defined documents is objective and measurable. The Oxford Analytica assessment consisted of a "combined" approach that used both quantitative indicators with qualitative evaluations conducted by experts or groups of experts. Mostly hard indicators were used such as recording the number of non-budgetary entities in a country or recording article numbers in legal documents that addressed a particular type of transparency issue. However, soft data such as newspaper

*Figure 6: Process lessons: Knowledge management for e-governance*

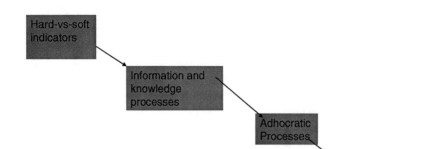

articles, key informant interviews, and focus group discussions were rigorously incorporated into the evaluation exercise. The formal search procedure for these soft data included Internet searches on key words in each Code section for each country and routinised searches for business associations and NGO representatives to discuss draft assessments with - thereby addressing both formal and substantive measurement targets. For example, if there was formal compliance with a particular provision – such as institutional clarity in Peru - then interviews and newspaper articles could "fill in" the assessment, verifying if the assessment was correct.

There were a number of problems with the indicators used. First, the Codes are overly broad in some areas and too narrow in others. For example, Section 1.1 of the Code of Fiscal Transparency refers to institutional clarity covering a wide range of activities. Section 1.2.3 though addresses the existence of a very particular and specialised code of civil servant ethics. Obtaining a roughly uniform assessment instrument will be a challenge for both the IMF and other assessment bodies. Second, these Codes rely too little on "hard-soft" indicators - namely indicators of subjective perceptions collected from standard bodies using a standard format. For example, point 1.2 about clarity of institutional rules might bring in advice from civil society and specific searches about conflicts in budgetary allocation. In many ROSCs, IMF expert evaluations are used in much the same way that Oxford Analytica expert evaluations were used - drawing upon the investigators' tacit knowledge of qualitative factors affecting transparency along a particular dimension.[17] Having an increasingly standardised interview questionnaire and method of engaging non-government organisations (measuring for example the use of a transparency law by NGOs rather than simply its existence) would be an important step in developing such "hard-soft" indicators.

# Managing the Information versus Knowledge Trade-Off

Beneath the apparent need to simply collect information and perform an assessment lies a deep trade-off between the need to collect information and produce knowledge in a cost-effective way. Information generally refers to simple facts and figures that are organised in some way, while knowledge refers to the giving of meaning to information by human actors (Davenport & Prusak, 2000). In a transparency assessment context, information can be obtained in a relatively cost effective way via the Internet; but the creation of knowledge requires in-country experience and "being there" (Watson, 1999). The Oxford Analytica assessment sought to combine the advantages of Internet information management with interview and experience-based knowledge management.[18]

In general, there are several advantages to using Internet-based assessments.[19] The first advantage refers to the low cost of Internet assessment. Many international organisations send teams on mission to a country for extended periods to assess certain standards. However, this work shows that Internet evaluation has an important role to play in the overall evaluation exercise in terms of saving time and money. eStandards has a team of approximately six staff who are able to monitor over 100 countries with the help of proprietary work designs and technologies. The monetary and fiscal transparency evaluations were conducted by a staff of five and covered 25 countries in about 9 months.

The second advantage refers to the large amount of information that can be collected per unit time - as these statistics show. A rough draft assessment for a country can be done in about 3-6 days. Part of this speed is attributable to low processing times. An Internet assessment can use keyword searches and links in ways that personal contacts cannot. Many commentators have noted public sector organisational forms have changed - reflecting delayering and restructuring – reducing the number of steps involved in obtaining information. Yet, few have commented on changes in the organisation of public sector information structures. Given both the conversion to e-government and third-party hosting of government information, public sector information increasingly represents a rhizomatic structure - where every point is connected to every other point.[20] Such structure affects e-government as well as the transparency assessment exercise. Such a structure implies a degree of "natural transparency" given the reduction in the number of steps needed to acquire information. In the Latin American case, rather than consulting thick budget documents, budget figures for several countries could be electronically queried and standardised tables produced. Less reliance on local "infrastructure" also reduced the number of steps needed to obtain information. Telephone assessments would involve patchy lines. Even in-person interviews involve scheduling difficulties, whereas Internet is almost always available even if only on a mirror site.

There are also several advantages to "being there," especially for subjective information. First, perhaps one of the biggest advantages of face-to-face interviews is the ability to assess organisational culture and non-verbal dispositions toward transparency. In Thailand, the assessment team had difficulty in contacting Thai officials using both

Internet and telephone methods. Yet, when the assessment team arrived in the country, Thai officials were generally supportive and helpful. In many cases, the assessment team was given books and documents that were not on the Internet. A second advantage refers to the nature of information itself. The provision of information services - like the provision of other government services - often requires guidance from the service provider.[21] Even for simple services like ticket reservations, service users often prefer direct contact with a service provider representative rather than contact over the telephone or Internet. The reception of public services - just like the assessment of public services - often requires the same physical interaction with the service provider. Third, face-to-face interviews allow for an understanding of the "deep institutional logics" behind the Codes. Often these logics are responsible for conflict that can affect the political will to be transparent. Especially important were conflicts created by institutional arrangements which pitted Central Bank independence (with its prioritisation of price stability) against government objectives of promoting economic growth (through coercing Central Bank expansionary monetary policy). Such conflicts are not described on the Internet. Finally, personal interviews are important due to outdated and inaccurate information. In the case of Morocco, interviews were the only method of evaluation available, as the Central Bank had not yet established an Internet site. In many countries, projects that were "in progress" were reported on or assessment teams were informed that information collected via the Internet was inaccurate.

## Managing "Adhocracy"

Once indicators are chosen and the best methods of obtaining information and knowledge are obtained, evaluation processes must be in place. As presented previously in Figure 2, the assessments appear to follow a particularly mechanistic process of project

*Figure 7: Adhocracy in e-transparency assessment*

|  | April | May | June | July | August | Sept | Oct. | Nov. | Dec. |
|---|---|---|---|---|---|---|---|---|---|
| Staff Prep | X | X |  |  |  | X | X |  |  |
| Internet Assessment |  | X | X |  |  |  | X | X |  |
| Expert Feedback |  |  |  | X |  |  |  | X |  |
| Country Evaluations |  |  |  |  | X | X | X |  |  |
| Internal Discussion |  |  | X |  |  |  |  | X |  |
| Presentation to Client |  |  |  |  | X |  |  |  | X |

design. However, this representation misses two important points about the assessment methodology that are reflected in much of the business literature. First, much of the design was not sequential but parallel (Iansiti & MacCormack, 1997). As shown in Figure 7, each phase of the project was not carried out in a discrete and sequential manner, but often steps were done and redone based on new information. In-country interviews were chances both to obtain any information not found over the Internet as well as obtain focus group and individual-based feedback on our findings. If new information was found, this would prompt verification by Internet to the extent possible and collective assessment to determine if similar information sources could be used for other countries. In other cases, one team might lag behind - working on translating Internet material - while another team conducts country assessments. In November, for example, most of the project steps were running in parallel as codified and tacit knowledge was combined to deliver the greatest client value in terms of quality, responsiveness to client needs, process innovation, and process cost-reductions. Rather than simply "sharing information" through e-mail updates, the building of codified and tacit knowledge emerged from the project design. This observation reflects other studies such as "time-geography" studies (Nandhakumar & Avison, 1999) in other service industries - showing that optimal process cannot be "routinised". Instead, e-government implementers and assessors need the ability to draw knowledge and form competencies as necessary.

Given the parallel project design, organisational structure was based around flexible adhocracy (Mitzberg, 1983). Rather than following strictly defined divisionalised structure with roles strictly defined, project teams assembled and disassembled based on the immediate needs of the assessment in question - crossing functional and hierarchical lines. Adhocracy served three purposes. First, adhocracy in this context reflected the need to combine the knowledge of an assessment expert with a country expert. In many cases, Oxford Analytica staff did not know country-specific detail- being experts in the IMF codes and assessment methods generally.[22] The country expert did not possess specific competencies related to assessment or knowledge about institutional arrangements impacting upon monetary and fiscal transparency. These binary teams required "co-management". Oxford Analytica staff had to manage the country experts' assessment practices and country experts had to manage the way Analytica staff managed their relationships, interview procedures, and references to country-specific institutional arrangements.

Second, flexible project-based teams allowed for the generation of synergies. Contacts from the Daily Brief editorial staff as well as learning from eStandards generated much codified knowledge needed for the assessment and especially for quality control. Strong informal norms of co-operation and trust ensured continuous communication between these groups.[23] Third, attendant with adhocracy was project modularity (Langlois, 1992). Every stage of the assessment process was broken down and substitutable so any individual could perform the task of any other. Given such modularity, staff could be used based on needed competencies at any point in time. Because of the need for these competencies, modularisation did not imply standardisation.[24]

## Using "Assessment" as a Participatory Process

The traditional model of assessment involves a two party interaction of assessor and assessee. In our experience, not only were our interlocutors more qualified to make these assessments, but in most cases seemed genuinely interested in transparency. The assessors established a tone of mutual evaluation rather than a confrontation tone by inviting country embassies in London into the process at the beginning and keeping in regular contact with in-country interlocutors. Such a tone led to collaborative learning. Learning occurred for both the evaluator and in-country partners. Assessor learning occurred in two ways. First, Oxford Analytica was able to collect large amounts of information about transparency practices around the world and develop a pool of tacit knowledge that could be applied to a wide range of projects. Second, Oxford Analytica was able to "learn about learning" - developing processes and assessment methodologies applicable to a wide range of assessment problems.[25] Many of the process lessons presented here are the result of this type of learning. Both of these forms of learning are participatory in the sense that they are reiterative and rely on continuous interaction with in-country practitioners. Both of these forms of learning may also be leveraged for other work  - such as participation at the Caux Roundtable.[26]

Oxford Analytica's in-country partners' learning occurred in two ways. First, in many cases, the Internet assessment revealed information that government officials did not directly know about – especially about information in different ministries or institutions. Thus, the evaluation exercise resulted in dissemination effects in the ministries undertaking the transparency exercise. Given these dissemination effects, there is qualified support for the theory that transparency reduces information asymmetries within the public sector. E-transparency projects alone do not necessarily lead to long-run reductions in information asymmetries. Periodic assessment is crucial for sustainability. Second, for the country visits, much of our assessment was based on the interviewees' own assessments. In some cases such as in India and Philippines, the government employees themselves were realistically critical of their own performance. Many of the in-country interlocutors demonstrated pride in discussing particularly innovative measures they had undertaken to comply with certain information dissemination requirements or in discussing the extent to which they exceeded minimum requirements. In the case of India, many officials showed curiosity about how practices are in other countries. Both of these forms of learning also create a pool of competencies that may be used nationally and internationally.[27]

# Does E-Government Promote E-Transparency?

During the course of the evaluation exercise, we had the opportunity to observe how e-government - focused on increasing public sector transparency - was evolving both across space and time. Indeed, the methods of project organisation discussed in the previous section were strategic reactions to these trends. First, assessment priorities are shifting from supply-driven to demand-driven evaluation. Second, e-transparency is not just a step on the way toward more "advanced" forms in e-government. E-transparency encompasses all the phases of e-government and is a vital end in itself for standards based assessment. Third, e-transparency is not an unambiguous "end-state" but serves public sector objectives - be they increased trust, predictability, oversight, credibility, and political accountability. Given these trends, project organisation issues discussed in the previous section become vital.

# From Supply-Driven to Demand-Driven Evaluation

Preliminary work on the IMF Codes and their evaluation might arguably be considered to be driven by the supplier of this work - the IMF. Many e-government assessments are driven by the needs of the evaluators, whether addressing returns from the client (Oxford Analytica's project), academic returns (Ho, 2002) or business returns (Accenture, 2002). Supply driven evaluation is based on expert assessments and external actor involvement is limited to "consultation". Supply-driven evaluation is useful - especially during the preliminary phases of a project where leadership is required given a lack of initial demand.[28] Yet, there is demand for the existence of monetary and fiscal codes even if preferences about their exact form have not been determined: "the international community has called on the IMF and other forums and standard setting agencies to develop standards and codes covering a number of economic and financial areas" (IMF, 2001). Even at this early stage, some future "market" preferences are already discernible. The Codes are a useful guide for interviewing public sector, businesses and civil society organisations. They seek to provide a mutually exclusive and collectively exhaustive list of assessment criteria. They also carry a degree of gravitas given their association with the Fund. However, it was unclear how much these codes represent the long run needs and concerns of non-public sector actors.[29] Our client had indicated that the IMF codes matched their interests. Other stakeholder groups we interviewed though in the public sector and NGO sector expressed concern about the lack of IMF consultation in the elaboration of these Codes.

Demand-driven assessment entails asking the ultimate users of transparency "services" which items are most important to them. Many of the obvious demanders of public sector information are national and international business, NGOs, and media - in order to programme project decisions. However, as these assessments demonstrated to us, there is also demand within the public sectors concerned. Many public sector officials appeared to take the Codes very seriously. Almost all the countries responded quickly to requests for meetings and during meetings talked about the standards, not as a burdensome obligation, but as a necessity. In many ways, the IMF is responding to changing preferences given more complete knowledge in civil society about the Codes. As preferences are formed and experience acquired about implementing and assessing e-transparency, these standards can better respond to these multi-stakeholder preferences.

# From Actor-Based to Standards-Based Assessment

The Codes of Fiscal and Monetary Transparency are founded upon a type of multi-lateral negotiation between the IMF and its member states. To differing extents, these country representatives, who are middle-level non-elected civil servants, offered feedback on the Codes and the evaluation process used by the Fund. However, these Codes were principally a document discussed by the Fund and member countries. Any attempts at incorporating the views of outside actors - such as business or NGOs -[ constituted "outreach"[30].

Yet, work on the Codes is becoming a multi-actor forum. The Codes, along with the extensive documentation that accompanies them, involve an important type of "public good" which entails significant knowledge "spill-over effects". Standards, as public information goods, benefit from network externalities that promote compliance to one common standard (Sharpiro & Varian, 1998) at relatively low cost to external actors. Standards also entail the "reuse knowledge" (Langlois, 1999) given the knowledge transfer implicit in "spill-over effects" which allow public sector evaluation to be conducted outside of the public sector. Yet, such knowledge reuse is adapted to different actors' needs. The Codes themselves - much like an open architecture of the software industry - can be modified, used, reused, or discarded by external actors. As a public good, they can be (and have been) appropriated and used by different parties. Given this open and public nature of the Codes, much of the demand-driven nature of the Codes will not be determined by IMF sympathy for the "third sector" (business and NGOs) or even by political lobbying of the IMF by third sector groups. A new evaluation criterion for the Codes is not the degree to which country representatives in Washington endorse them. The ultimately success of the IMF's Codes of Monetary and Fiscal Transparency will rest on the degree to which they are "demanded" and used by third parties. Oxford Analytica's use of the Codes represents in one aspect a market test of these Codes.

There are three broader implications for the public nature of this work and the effects of standards on e-government more generally. First, this initiative represents a new type of public-private partnership where codified standards serve as a public good. As the business literature shows, the first-mover does not have to actively co-operate with fringe movers for there to be tacit co-operation.[31] Given the size of the Fund and the large amount of resources it had deployed on the Codes, it was rational for Oxford Analytica to use these Codes rather than formulate its own. Both organisations' interests in the Codes represent a type of co-operation or implicit partnership based around standards instead of an explicit bilateral relationship. Second, the "monopoly" on the governance agenda held by the Bretton Woods institutions - purportedly following Post-Washington Consensus doctrines - is not as strong as some advocates of this position suggest (Phillips & Higgott, 1999). There is a radical literature in development that argues that the Bretton Woods institutions are using the governance agenda as a way of strengthening their hegemony over developing countries. Our work shows this argument is an exaggeration. Work on governance can be reshaped and reused by external actors. Third, given that these public goods represent a service as a vital as the transaction or interaction aspects of e-government, the e-government teleology is false because transparency *is* a service.

# From E-Transparency Targets to E-Transparency Objectives

The appropriability of Codes and Standards by a variety of actors suggests that codes of transparency are not ends in themselves – but serve political and administrative objectives. Broadly conforming with the results in Figure 4, technological issues or e-government "capacity" was rarely, if ever, mentioned as a specific incentive or obstacle to e-transparency. In the quantitative and qualitative data collected, a number of reasons for e-transparency emerged which roughly follow the typology developed in Posen (2002). According to this typology, transparency may be sought by the public sector in order to promote trust, predictability, credibility, oversight, or political accountability in the public sector. [32] The informal and mostly qualitative results from the assessment suggest that each of these objectives was concern for e-transparency to differing degrees.[33]

Figure 8 shows each of these e-transparency objectives compared with their overall specific importance for monetary and fiscal institutions, examples of stakeholders who would find a particular objective important, and the impact of transparency codes and their assessment on promoting each objective.

Increasing trust and predictability were low-level concerns. Increased trust appeared to be a relatively minor reason for promoting e-transparency, as no Web site particularly made mention of trust. In interviews, one NGO representative from an Asian country mentioned that there is a very low level of trust in public servants. Given the contractual and formal nature of public sector services, the only group of people who would need to trust government are the poor and marginalised members of society (whom were not consulted by the Oxford Analytica assessment). There was no indication that the creation and assessment of Codes would have an effect on trust. Predictability also appears to be a relatively minor reason for e-transparency. Much transparency work does not directly impact on predictability given that laws and data concerning transparency reflect prior rather than expected events. Moreover, while laws may establish the nominal independence of certain bodies, they may be less predictable in practice. The Thai Central Bank Law establishes the Bank Governor's independence. Yet, Bank of Thailand Governor Chatumongkol Sonakul was fired by Prime Minister Thaksin Shinavatra. Web

*Figure 8: An assessment of objectives*

| | Degree of importance | Area of importance | For whom? | Assessment Important |
|---|---|---|---|---|
| **Trust** | Low | Neither | Poor | Not important |
| **Predictability** | Low | Monetary | Investors, business | Not important |
| **Oversight** | Medium | Fiscal | Civil servants, media | Very Important |
| **Credibility** | Medium | Fiscal | Citizens, investors, civil servants | Important |
| **Politicisation** | High | Both | All | Important |

*Source: Adapted from Posen (2002)*

sites made some mention of predictability, especially Central Bank sites. If predictability was an issue, it was businesses and investors concerned about Central Bank policy, who are understandably concerned about predictability given the important role of rational expectations about interest rates and inflation in broader investment behaviour. The creation of Codes appeared to slightly increase confidence in Central Bank predictability while Code assessment appears to have little impact on beliefs about public sector predictability.

Increasing oversight and credibility of public sector policies appeared to be a moderately important concern for e-transparency. Oversight, which the IMF holds as a key reason for e-transparency work, was only moderately important. Few public sector Web sites stated that information was being provided to promote oversight of the public sector. There was also little indication that the data being posted to the Internet were actively used or discussed. If Web sites did mention the role of oversight, or if data were used by third parties to exercise oversight, it was mostly fiscal data used. Yet, the anecdotal evidence suggests that fiscal data and procedures posted to the Internet served to facilitate the collection of information (such as tax procedures) rather than promote the use of information to "check" government behaviour. While the creation of codes appears only moderately important for oversight, their assessment appears vital. There was general support both within governments and outside of governments for assessments. Given the link between the assessment results and international portfolio investment decisions - where portfolio managers will often exit a country based on an evaluation - there appears to be a substantive impact from evaluation.

Web sites did not mention credibility directly. Instead they showed concern for it by cross-links with other institutions and in assurances of integrity such as in auditor reports. Code-based credibility appeared to be an issue mainly in fiscal transparency. Reference was often made of the need for credibility both for civil servants to believe in government and external actors such as citizens, media and NGOs to believe in policy pronouncements and the integrity of data. Credibility appears to be an important reason in the creation of the Codes - which often discuss the degree to which there is outside or independent evaluation of data. Yet, assessment appeared not to necessarily increase perceptions of credibility - perhaps due to questions about the credibility of the assessment exercise?

As a high-level concern, concerns about political accountability appeared to affect both monetary and fiscal transparency. The official Web sites never discuss the political aspects of transparency - given that transparency might harm short-term interests attached to opacity in certain types of arrangements. Yet, the interviews picked up the political aspects affecting all actors. At the international level, one Asian country noted that they did not have a certain requirement because they did not have to follow everything the IMF told them to do. At the national level, constant mention was made of the conflicts arising between government and the Central Bank. During the assessments, we rarely heard stories about technology or work processes - but about people. Even for laws and administrative acts, the stress was always on the bureaucratic or party politics underlying various measures. Both the creation of codes and their assessment appeared to be seen as a highly political process for both monetary and fiscal transparency. Indeed, the results of Oxford Analytica assessments are likely to have political as well as informational impacts. Much work will need to be done to ascertain the effects and interests behind such politicisation that impact on evaluation.

# Conclusion

International work on codes and standards related to fiscal and monetary transparency is moving into a new stage. Yet, reflection about the methods of assessing transparency and about the objectives in promoting transparency can be fruitful for others working on e-government. In general three main lessons emerge from this chapter. First, nothing ensures the teleological evolution of e-government. The existence of laggard countries, the importance of e-transparency in all phases of e-government, and the trend toward standards-based governance highlight the important role of institutions and policy. Second, if governments aim to promote e-transparency and third parties seek to assess e-transparency, adhocratic methods of project organisation and knowledge management have many advantages. Assessment is a vital part of the e-government agenda. Yet, given the need for flexibility and increasing reliance on generalised standards, adhocratic structures become vital for performing these assessments. Third, e-transparency - much like e-government - relies on the objectives of the programme rather than simply on technological capacity. As transparency standards become more "demand-driven," they should take into account these multiple objectives such as increasing trust, credibility, predictability, oversight, and political accountability in government.

# References

Accenture. (2002). *eGovernment leadership-Realizing the vision. http://www. accenture.com/xdoc/en/industries/government/eGov_April2002_3.pdf.*

Argyris, C., & Schön, D. (1978). *Organizational learning: A theory of action perspective.* Reading, MA: Addison Wesley.

Backus, M. (2001, April). E-governance in developing countries. *Research Report* 3. *http://www.ftpiicd.org/files/research/reports/report3.pdf.*

Bertelsmann Foundation. (2002). *Balanced e-government - Connecting efficient administration and responsive democracy. http://www.begix.de/en/studie/studie.pdf.*

Bulmer, M., & Warwick, D. (1993). *Social research in developing countries: Surveys and censuses in the third world.* London: UCL Press.

CalPERS. (2002). *Oxford Analytica research. http://www.calpers.ca.gov/invest/ emergingmkt/oxford.htm.*

Coalition for Healthcare eStandards. (2002). *Consortium and standards list. www.consortiuminfo.com/ssl/links.php?go=15.*

Cohen, D. (2001). *In good company: How social capital makes organizations work.* Cambridge, MA: Harvard Business School Press.

Columbia International Affairs Online. (2002, February 27). *In perspective: The Oxford Analytica weekly column. http://www.ciaonet.org/pbei/oxan/oxa02272002.html.*

Cullen, R., & Houghton, C. (2000). Democracy online: An assessment of New Zealand government Web sites. *Government Information Quarterly, 17*(3), 243-267.

Davenport & Prusak. (2000). *Working knowledge.* Cambridge, MA: Harvard Business School Press.

Department of Environmental Protection. (2002). *eStandards workgroup home page.* *http://www.dep.state.pa.us/dep/deputate/oit/estandards/.*

Economist Intelligence Unit. (2002). *Business environment ratings.*

Evans, P., & Wurster, T. (1999). *Blows to bits.* Cambridge, MA: Harvard Business School Press.

Fenner, G., & Wehrle, F. (2001). The Internet culture in the fight against corruption. *Progress in the fight against corruption in Asia and the Pacific: Conference papers and proceedings.* Manila: Asian Development Bank.

Fetterman, D. (1998). Empowerment evaluation and the Internet: A synergistic relationship. *Current Issues in Education, 4*(1). College of Education at Arizona State University.

Geraats, P., & Eijffinger, S. (2002, February). How transparent are central banks? *CEPR Discussion Paper* 3188.

Handy, C. (1991). *Gods of management: The changing world of organisation.* Century Business.

Heeks, R. (2001). A framework for national and donor action. *I-Government Working Paper Series* 12.

Heichelbech, J. (2002). *E-government and public trust: What we should be doing. http://64.91.236.79/ethicscommunity/documents/E-GOV%20and%20Trust.pdf.*

Herman, L. (2001, June 11-12). *The hype and the myth: The future isn't what it used to be.* Presentation at the World Bank/Development Gateway Conference, E-government in developing countries: Achievements & prospects, Washington, D.C.

Hiller, J. & Belanger, F. (2001). Privacy strategies for electronic government. *E-Government Series.* Arlington, VA: PricewaterhouseCoopers Endowment for the Business of Government.

Ho, A. (2002, July/August). Reinventing local governments and the e-government initiative. *Public Administration Review.*

Iansiti, M., & MacCormack, A. (1997, September/October). Developing products on Internet time. *Harvard Business Review, 75,* 108-117.

IMF. (2001, April 2). International standards and codes. *IMF Survey.*

IMF. (2002a). *Standards & codes. http://www.imf.org/external/standards/index.htm.*

IMF. (2002b). *Quarterly report on the assessments of standards and codes-June 2002.*

King, G., Keohane, R.& Verba, S. (1994). *Designing social inquiry: Scientific inference in qualitative research.* Princeton University Press.

Lane, T. (1999, September). The Asian financial crisis: What have we learned? *Finance and Development, 36*(3).

Langlois, R. (1999). Scale, scope, and the reuse of knowledge. In S. Dow & P. Earl (Eds.), *Economic organisation and economic knowledge: Essays in honour of Brian Loasby.* Cheltenham: Edward Elgar.

Langlois, R. & Robertson, P. (1992). Networks and innovation in a modular system: Lessons from the microcomputer and stereo component industries. *Research Policy, 21*(4), 297-313.

Martin, R. & Feldman, E. (1998). Access to information in developing countries. *Transparency international working papers. http://www.transparency.org/working_papers/martin-feldman/index.html.*

Michael, B. & Langseth, P. (2002, July 4-6). *Anti-corruption project design, new political economic interests, and knowledge management in a globalising world.* Paper presented at the conference Toward a New Political Economy of Development: Globalisation and Governance, Sheffield.

Mintzberg, H. (1983). *Structure in fives: Designing effective organisation.* Englewood Cliffs: Prentice-Hall.

Moon, M. (2002, July/August). The evolution of e-government among municipalities: Rhetoric or reality? *Public Administration Review, 62*(4).

Nandhakumar, J., & Avison, D. (1999). The fiction of methodological development: A field study of information systems development. *Information Technology and People, 12*(2), 176-191.

Oxford Analytica. (2002). *eStandards forum. http://www.estandardsforum.com/.*

Petrotechnical Open Software Corporation. (2002). *Energy eStandards News.* www.posc.org/news/een20020401

Phillips, N., & Higgott, R. (1999). Global governance and the public domain: Collective goods in a 'post Washington consensus' era. *CSGR Working Paper 47-99.* University of Warwick.

Posen, A. (2002). *Six practical views of central bank transparency.* International Institute of Economics.

Potter, B, & Humphreys, R. (1999, February 23). *The IMF transparency code.* Presentation. Cape Town. *http://www.internationalbudget.org/conference/2nd/imf.htm.*

Premchand, A. (2001, November). *Fiscal transparency and accountability: Idea and reality.* Paper prepared for the workshop on Financial Management and Accountability, Rome. *unpan1.un.org/intradoc/groups/public/documents/un/unpan 001892.pdf.*

PriceWaterhouseCoopers. (2002). *Opacity index. http://www.opacityindex.com/ind_fullindex.html.*

Quinn, J., Mintzberg, H.,& James, R. (1991). *The strategy process: Concepts, contexts, and cases.* Englewood Cliffs, NJ: Prentice-Hall.

Radics, G. (2001). *Cristal: A tool for transparent government in Argentina. http://www1.worldbank.org/publicsector/egov/cristal_cs.htm.*

Reilly, K. (2002). *Government, ICTs and civil society in Central America: Is national government ICT use contributing to more democratic states? http://www.katherine.reilly.net/e-governance/reports.html.*

Roberts, A. (1999, May). Access to government information: An overview of issues. *Transparency International Working Papers. http://www.transparency.org/documents/work-papers/robertsFOI.html.*

Sackman, H. (1975). *Delphi critique.* The Rand Corporation, Lexington Books.

Sharpiro, C., & Varian, H. (1998). *Information rules: A strategic guide to the network economy.* Cambridge, MA: Harvard Business School Press.

Transparency International. (2002). Corruption perceptions index. *http://www.transparency.org/cpi/index.html.*

UNDP. (2001). *Human development report 2001: Making new technologies world for human development.* United Nations.

United Nations. (2001). *Benchmarking e-government: A global perspective - Assessing the progress of the UN member states. http://www.unpan.org/egovernment2.asp.*

Vaillancourt, R. (2000). *Public-private partnerships.* MIT Press.

Walker, D. (2001, July 11). *E-government in the information age: The long view.* E-Gov 2001 Conference. *http://www.gao.gov/cghome/ia/egov.htm.*

Watson, C. (1999). *Being there: Fieldwork in anthropology.* London: Pluto Press.

World Bank. (2002). *Governance dataset. http://www.worldbank.org/wbi/governance/gov_data.htm.*

# Endnotes

\*     This chapter is based on an earlier version published in the *International Public Management Journal 6*(2).

1     The authors would like to thank the eStandards Forum and transparency assessment teams for their feedback. The opinions expressed here represent those of the authors and do not represent the opinions of their institutions or Oxford Analytica's clients. Mr. Michael consulted on Oxford Analytica's monetary and fiscal transparency project during the summer of 2001. An earlier draft of this chapter was discussed at the Second Annual European Conference on E-government.

2     As of April 30, 2002, 59 fiscal and monetary assessments have been published by the IMF.

3     There are many references to Oxford Analytica throughout this chapter. As a "best practice," such references are largely unavoidable and we have tried to put critiques and lessons learned where appropriate.

4     These countries were Brazil, Chile, China, Colombia, Egypt, Hungary, India, Indonesia, Israel, Jordan, Korea (South), Mexico, Malaysia, Morocco, Pakistan, Peru, Philippines, Poland, Russia, South Africa, Sri Lanka, Taiwan, Thailand, Turkey, and Venezuela. For some countries, only one assessment - either monetary or fiscal - was conducted.

5     For a critical background on the project, see Columbia International Affairs Online (2002).

6     See IMF (2002a) for specific copies of these codes.

7       See Potter and Humphreys (1999) for an informal introduction to the Code of Fiscal Transparency.

8       While Oxford Analytica's eStandards focuses on standards used by investment managers, other types of "E-Standards" also exist in the public sector (Department of Environmental Protection, 2002) as well as in the private sector in areas such as chemicals (Chemical Industry Data Exchange, 2002), energy (Petrotechnical Open Software Corporation, 2002), and health care (Coalition for Healthcare eStandards, 2002). Thus, assessment issues raised in this chapter may apply to a more general class of projects.

9       For a discussion of the eStandards methodology, see Oxford Analytica (2002). Similar types of evaluation techniques are offered by a number of organisations such as Economist Intelligence Unit (2002) and PricewaterhouseCoopers (2002). The Transparency International (2002) Corruption Perceptions Index is perhaps the best-known indirect subjective measure of transparency.

10      For other examples of e-government Internet assessments using similar methodologies, see Ho (2002), Accenture (2002), or Bertelsmann Foundation (2002).

11      Given the subjective nature of social science data, "triangulation" procedures should generally be used in the assessment or evaluation exercise (see Bulmer & Warwick, 1993 for more).

12      A country *strictly* ranks higher than another if and only if not only the aggregate score for a country ranks higher than another, but also all the sub-points of a code rank higher.

13      The non-parametric Spearman rho correlation coefficient between fiscal and monetary transparency is 0.64. Given a Wilcoxon matched pairs test Z-statistic of 3.4 (p value = 0.0007), it is unlikely that there is a country specific transparency process driving both fiscal and monetary transparency.

14      To remove subjectivity from the clustering process, Statistica's formal statistical 2-means clustering technique was used to differentiate these groups.

15      Similar trends emerge looking at measures of "technological achievement" UNDP (2001). Given the subjectivity of both data sets, these correlations are only suggestive - thus we do not plot regression lines.

16      Where Figure 1 represents project operational logistics, Figure 5 represents an "emergent strategy" (Quinn et al., 1991) more than a preconceived project design. Its utility lies in its empirically inductive rather than theoretically deductive origins.

17      Tacit knowledge refers to the distinction often made in the knowledge management literature between codified and tacit knowledge (Davenport & Prusak, 2000). Codified knowledge can be written down and applied by anyone. Tacit knowledge exists in the heads of individuals in the form of "know-how".

18      Many projects in development, and especially in the field of transparency, downplay the important role of tacit and local knowledge (Michael & Langseth, 2002).

19      Internet helps with the implementation of evaluation in a variety of contexts (Fetterman, 1998).

20    During the assessments, a number of laws were found through public and private Internet sites based in the US and elsewhere.

21    In the terminology of Evans and Wurster (1999), such individuals comprise "information navigators".

22    Given eStandards broad range of assessments, Oxford Analytica staff possessed a wide range of contacts and codified knowledge about a range of institutions - such as Central Bank payment systems and data dissemination - which could impact indirectly on transparency.

23    Such norms - social capital - have been found in a number of contexts to improve project performance (Cohen, 2001). In Oxford Analytica's case, these norms largely stem from company size, prior process decisions, recruitment from a particularly focused section of the labour market, and a mix of "power" and "people" cultures (Handy, 1991).

24    Oxford Analytica has a particular organisational form based on modularity that gives it a sustainable competitive advantage in its small market niche.

25    Such "learning to learn" reflects Argyris and Schön's (1978) "double-loop learning".

26    One disadvantage of the capacity-development model is the relatively high staff turnover occasioned by staff's increased labour market value. The modularisation approach discussed previously serves Oxford Analytica as a way of both providing staff with competencies needed to pursue their long-term career objectives while at the same time maximising the use of knowledge for short-term project requirements.

27    In the long run, Oxford Analytica's most important rivals for this work will be public sector officials who consult independently or with international organisations.

28    There is an analogy to the marketing context (in new technologies for example) where the innovative producer must estimate future market demand for a product with which the market has no experience.

29    The international and national public sector ideally is simply a democratic representative of civil society actors. Thus, these final preferences should be of ultimate concern to the Fund and the governments it negotiates with.

30    IMF (2002b) describes such outreach efforts that consist of speeches given by senior IMF officials at private sector meetings.

31    Much of the public-private partnership literature focuses on the consensual and active participation of all actors in the partnership (Vaillancourt, 2000). Our work indicates that such partnerships can emerge as the result of tacit co-operation caused by asymmetries between the actors.

32    While Posen focused only on Central Banks, we would extend his taxonomy to both Fiscal and Monetary Transparency.

33    These results are tentative and are only presented to suggest future rigorous research.

**Chapter III**

# The Dimensions of Business Process Change in Electronic Government

Hans J. (Jochen) Scholl, University of Washington, USA

## Abstract

*Governments at all levels and across all branches have been urged to become leaner and smarter, providing better and faster service at lower cost. Such fundamental change, however, inevitably impacts the business processes governments work by. So far, though, business process change has mostly been studied in the private sector. Electronic government (e-government, e-gov) appears as a potent enabler when reinventing the way government is doing business. According to Layne and Lee (2001), four stages of development can be distinguished in electronic government. This chapter maps the dimensions of business process change into the developmental stages of electronic government, providing a roadmap for business process change through electronic government.*

# Introduction

When government began using telegraphs and telephones in the 19th century, the old messenger-based processes and organizational formats did not immediately disappear. They were gradually and then increasingly rapidly and radically replaced by new formats and processes that greatly enhanced the immediacy of government action and reaction. Similar patterns it appears underlie the changes in the context of electronic government.

If so, it follows that for the inevitable change to occur with minimal friction the implications of emerging computer-mediated networks for existing business processes in government need to be well understood. Surprisingly, literature dedicated to this particular subject is in short supply. The various literature on information technology-enabled business process change in the private sector (cf., for example, (Champy, 1995; Grover, Teng, Segars & Fiedler, 1998; Gunasekaran & Nath, 1997; Hammer, 1996; Hammer & Champy, 1993; Kettinger & Grover, 1995; Kettinger, Teng & Guha, 1997)) has only recently been studied for its applicability and relevance to electronic government (Scholl, 2003). Despite certain obvious differences (Huang, d'Ambra & Bhalla, 2002; Mohan & Holstein, 1990), there are many similarities in technology-induced organizational and business-process change between public and private sector (cf., for example, (Rubin, 1986)). This literature has developed four key ideas: (1) any business can be re-thought and redesigned from the bottom rather than only incrementally improved (Hammer & Champy, 1993; Kettinger & Grover, 1995), (2) information and communication technology (ICT) might play a major enabling role in such fundamental change processes (Gunasekaran & Nath, 1997; Hammer & Champy, 1993), (3) the development, deployment, and use of information systems and business process change (BPC) have to be treated as two sides of the same coin ( Kettinger et al., 1997), and (4) the organizational-culture context and the human interests involved in the change process greatly matter (cf., (Orlikowski, 1992; Orlikowski & Gash, 1994; Pardo & Scholl, 2002)).

As Layne and Lee propose, electronic government can analytically be grouped into four stages of development: In the (early) cataloguing stage, government establishes an online presence of presentation including downloadable forms (Layne & Lee, 2001). This stage has empirically been documented by a number of studies (cf., (Chen & Gant, 2001a, 2001b; Gant & Gant, 2002; Gefen, Warkentin, Pavlou & Rose, 2002)). In the transaction stage, services are made available for online use and databases are readied for the support of such transactions (cf., also, (Gant & Gant, 2002; Huang & Chao, 2001)). In the vertical integration stage local, state, and federal systems in all three branches of government (legislative, executive, and judicial) serving similar functions are linked together. Finally, in the horizontal integration phase, systems of all levels and branches, and across functions are linked in a one-stop fashion (Layne & Lee, 2001). The Layne and Lee model bears a certain resemblance with the original IT-growth model presented by Gibson and Nolan, and also with its revised and more frequently cited version by Nolan (Gibson & Nolan, 1974; Nolan, 1979), which will be further detailed in the next section.

While the first Layne and Lee stage does not yet require any business process change, more fundamental and substantial changes become the norm in subsequent stages. Adaptations and redesigns of existing information systems, along with the incorporation of completely new systems become a necessity. This in turn requires significant and

*Figure 1: Business process change project dimensions mapped into the Layne and Lee framework of e-government*

| Dimensions of Business Process Change in E-Government | | | | |
|---|---|---|---|---|
| | The Layne & Lee Framework of Electronic Government (2001) | | | |
| **Business Process Change Project Dimensions** | Stage I - Cataloguing | Stage II - Transaction | Stage III - Vertical Integration | Stage IV - Horizontal Integration |
| | | | | |

increasing changes to the underlying business processes. These latter three stages, then, are where BPC literatures and practices are relevant for understanding the implications, likely effects, and necessities of changes to either information systems, or business processes, or both. Electronic government projects, hence, present a special case of business process change or reengineering along the following dimensions.

In this chapter, Layne and Lee's four-stage framework is used to discuss the implications of electronic government with regard to business process change (BPC). The main ideas of the BPC literature are mapped to each stage of the framework (see Figure 1). Special attention is directed towards the management and participation of constituents or "stakeholders" in these e-government-related business process change initiatives.

# Layne and Lee's Analytical Framework

In the 1970s, the phenomenon of IT proliferation and its profound impact on the organization was studied for the first time on a wider scale. For many organizations, this was when computer-based systems were implemented for the first time. In that decade, the then ubiquitous mainframe computing was complemented by smaller and cheaper departmental systems. Instead of processing batches of sequential jobs, online trans-action processing became more widely available. Also, software applications became more diverse and numerous. Towards the end of the decade, the first standalone personal computers appeared. Network-based client/server computing and communications had not yet arrived, though. Two studies from that era directed towards explaining the phenomenon of rapid IT growth may, however, still have certain utility for the study of the equally rapid unfolding of electronic government and directly relate to the aforementioned Layne and Lee framework (Layne & Lee, 2001) presented in this section. Gibson and Nolan propose a four-stage model of IT growth comprising (1) initiation, (2) expansion, (3) formalization, and (4) maturity, with each stage exhibiting growth patterns in three dimensions: (a) computer applications, (b) IT expert specialization, and (c) formal management and organization (Gibson & Nolan, 1974). The two authors foresee an S-shaped growth pattern in the proliferation of IT. In his revised model, Nolan distinguishes six stages: (1) initiation, (2) contagion, (3) control, (4) integration, (5) data administration, and (6) maturity (Nolan, 1979); however, without mapping the revised stages to the previous model. Yet, to some extent the stages of contagion and control may correspond to the expansion stage of the early model, while the integration and data administration stages seem to overlap with the formalization stage of the 1974 version of the model. Looking from an end-of-decade perspective in 1979, Nolan particularly revises the pure S-shaped growth assumption in favor of nested and overlapping schemes of S-shaped growth sub-patterns throughout the stages. Between the third (control) and fourth stage (integration), Nolan also introduces what he calls a transition point where the emphasis in IT growth shifts from technology management towards one of data resource management (p. 119, p. 124), which in essence foreshadows the contemporary concepts of information management (Earl, 1996) and knowledge integration (Boer, Bosch & Volberda, 1999). Although Layne and Lee do not refer to those two models at any point in their discussion, some obvious similarities and synergies between the three models should not go unattended.

Layne and Lee describe the four stages of their model by (1) defining the stage, (2) detailing the types of functionality, which is typically provided at this stage, and (3) discussing the challenges of the particular stage (Layne & Lee, 2001).

## The Cataloguing Stage

In the first stage of *cataloguing,* government agencies make information available via the Web. As a consequence, citizens begin looking for government information on the Web in the same fashion they would look for information from private businesses. Governments at this stage may build portals through which the information of various agencies of a particular government branch or government level is bundled together. For both citizens and government employees the immediate availability of government information increases the ease of access and, hence, convenience. Since fewer requests for information occur via the traditional channels, Layne and Lee conclude that the workload for front-office workers might be reduced. The functionality at this stage in the two authors' view is confined to providing the government agency with a basic Web presence. However, this already includes the availability of official forms, which can be downloaded, printed out, and used in the same way the government-provided hardcopy forms would be used. Among the challenges that the two authors identify for this first stage of e-government are (1) competition for Web-related resources among departments and agencies, (2) maintaining the currency of information on the Web site, (3) flagging (and consequently managing) the temporal nature of some information, (4) privacy issues regarding the log file analysis of Web traffic, and (5) managing the responses to incoming e-mails (Layne & Lee, 2001, pp. 126-128). The first stage in Layne and Lee's framework bears some resemblance with the initiation stages of the two IT-growth models (Gibson & Nolan, 1974; Nolan, 1979), in which "low-level operational systems in a functional area...are automated" (Nolan, 1979, p. 119).

## The Transaction Stage

When they reach the second stage of *transaction,* governments and citizens alike want to take advantage of the potential of computer-mediated networking as provided by the Internet/Intranet in terms of two-way communication and transactional fulfillment. All parties involved begin to play an active role of requesting and providing information online. Rather than downloading forms, those can be completed online. Also, payments can be made online. Government portals become more integrated and multifunctional, both in an informational and transactional sense. As opposed to the *cataloguing* stage, in the *transaction* stage the moderate modification and extension of existing processes appears at the agenda for the first time. Among the challenges of this stage, issues of authentication, confidentiality, security, and the integration of transactional online services with legacy databases and applications move to center stage. Government agencies are confronted with the challenge of maintaining the traditional service delivery formats, while developing and offering new online formats at the same time (Layne & Lee, 2001, pp. 128-129). As electronic government progresses through the transaction stage, it rapidly builds up towards a critical mass where new needs and opportunities for integration and process change become visible and feasible. This translates directly to Nolan's observation of a transition point between the earlier stages of IT proliferation and the later integrative stages. In his words, the "transition involves not only restructuring the DP organization but also installing new management techniques" (Nolan, 1979, p. 117)

## The Vertical Integration Stage

At the third stage of *vertical integration,* the change of business processes becomes a major focus in the unfolding of e-government and begins to transform government operations. The interoperability and integration of formerly dispersed applications and databases will also gradually lead to redefining and redesigning the underlying business processes in a vertical dimension. Transactions at any level of government, hence, will have visibility and impact on the other vertical levels of governments, once business processes and the enabling technologies are integrated. Layne and Lee give the example of applying for a business license, which, integration provided, can be obtained in a single step for all involved vertical levels of government. The authors also foresee that this stage may greatly benefit government-to-government (g2g) integration aiming, for example, at law enforcement and governmental oversight. Challenges at this stage include the legal and constitutional aspects of blurring the division of powers and once intentionally implemented federalist boundaries. Vertical integration also requires more standardization at the information system and database level, the authors hold (Layne & Lee, 2001, pp. 129-132).

## The Horizontal Integration Stage

At the fourth and final stage of *horizontal integration* services and functions will be integrated not only vertically within one functional area between levels of government, but also across functions, departments, and agencies at the same level. From a citizen perspective, this integration provides for "one-stop service" (p. 132). Business processes and information systems/databases need to be thoroughly integrated for this to happen. The authors do not give an example for stage-IV functionality; however, they anticipate gains in effectiveness and efficiency deriving from this type of integration. The challenges for this tight type of integration are posed by the heterogeneity of the existing IT landscape making it difficult to accomplish any interoperability between those existing systems and databases. Again, the similarity of Layne and Lee's framework to Nolan's older growth model becomes obvious; that is, process redesign and the integration of services and sources of information "are opening up new opportunities for doing business at the operational level" (Nolan, 1979, pp. 124-125). Major changes and redesigns of business processes and their enabling information technology might become necessary for achieving the goal of horizontal integration. The traditional breakdown of functions in government may need reassessment and redesign at this stage (Layne & Lee, 2001, pp. 132-135).

## Summary

Layne and Lee's framework helps distinguish the degree of development of electronic government. Except for perhaps the first two stages, the framework does not represent a temporal continuum, where one stage follows the other. For example, horizontal integration may coincide with and even antecede vertical integration. While at the first stage of *cataloguing* no business process change is required, certain extensions and even minor changes to existing business processes can be observed already during the stage of *transaction*. The two stages of *horizontal* and *vertical integration*, however, are those, in which a Nolanian transition point is passed and true transformation with change of business processes and of underlying IT structures is inevitable. Currently, most governments have mastered the first stage. Quite many governments at all levels provide transactional services and functions, while some governments have already entered the early phases of integration.

# E-Government Projects are Business Process Change Projects

As mentioned above, unlike in the private sector, business process change has not been widely studied in the public sector. Government has been criticized for its slow adoption of new technologies and innovative practices (Mohan & Holstein, 1990). In systems of democratic governance of checks and balances, however, the element of change has been deliberately constrained in extent and in speed. Criticizing government for relatively slow rates of change may, therefore, be regarded as pointless (cf., (Halachmi & Bovaird, 1997)). With respect to the high number of reengineering disasters in the private sector during the 1990s, governments may have even acted quite wisely by sticking to the slow adoption scheme (Champy, 1995; Hammer, 1996; Hammer & Champy, 1993).

In the next sections, the private-sector-oriented reengineering literature is presented as a proxy for the main motives, the strategies and objectives, and the focal areas potentially underlying such business process change projects in electronic government. The implications and insights of this literature are then discussed in the context of the Layne and Lee framework for each section.

## Motives and Needs Underlying Business Process Change Projects

A challenge in major change projects has reportedly been the organization's inertia and the stakeholders' active and passive resistance to change. Some authors have argued that (real or artificial) crises may be instrumental in increasing the willingness to embrace the proposed change (cf., (Hurst, 1995; Peters & Waterman, 1984)). However, as the literature unveils, in particular, business process change appears as highly problematic under circumstances of organizational crisis (Mallalieu, Harvey & Hardy, 1999), which is characterized by loss of control over important variables. A change project may unduly and untimely add to the number of variables out of control, potentially setting the organization up for disaster. Consequently, the best times for business process changes may be those when business is normal or thriving. Decision-makers, on the other hand, may question the necessity of burdensome, proactive change, if the business is humming. In addressing those concerns, mainly effectiveness- and efficiency-oriented arguments of (1) expected or desired cost savings, (2) speedups of the processes, and (3) customer service improvements have been used for making the case for business process change (Ranganathan & Dhaliwal, 2001). Although projected cost savings remain an attractive and appealing line of argument presented to decision-makers when justifying change projects including technology-based projects, due to unanticipated or hidden costs those projections have rarely materialized. As quite a few authors document, among technology project failure causes, significant cost overruns rank among the most prominent (cf., for example, (Lyytinen & Hirschheim, 1987)). More recent textbook literature (cf., for example, (Laudon & Laudon, 2002)) explicitly denounces the cost arguments in the context of technology investments as a weak and insufficient line of argument and constrains it to opportunity costs (of doing business). Tam also points out that ICT investments, although they may indirectly add to shareholder returns, do not necessarily produce above-normal profits (Tam, 1998). Hitt finds evidence for the reduction of external coordination costs through ICT (Hitt, 1999). By and large, the cost savings argument for justifying BPC and related ICT investments increasingly appears as a supplemental argument. Cost savings, however, may eventually result from speeding up processes through streamlining and via improving customer service, although such savings cannot be projected in advance with any credible accuracy nor can they reliably be measured from hindsight. Decisions in favor of major change projects therefore are of relatively high risk, made on the basis of incomplete information and under high outcome uncertainty, which is why other arguments such as seizing a perceived (market) opportunity, reacting to or preempting competitive pressure, or addressing customer demands are regularly invoked for support.

While rationally grounded motives play an important role in electronic government-related business process change projects, other (locally rational) motivations such as personal, departmental, economical, and political interests of various constituents may also be of major influence for launching electronic government projects. For example, in recent years, governors, commissioners, mayors, and other elected officials have made better online service for citizens as well as leaner and smarter government operations through electronic government center pillars of their campaign promises. Besides those globally and locally rational motives human decision-making is always tempered with emotion and bias (Simon, 1979, 1991). In fact, in the literature on information systems-related change projects (with their anteceding or ensuing change in business processes) there is ample evidence that those systems are developed and deployed for multiple motives, including personal and non-rational ones (Markus, 1983). As Markus points out in a rather early paper on the subject in the context of information systems, non-rational or locally rational purposes play a role in the decision-making in any socio-technical context (ibid.). Vested self-interest of project planners rather than the shareholders' best interest or the pursuit of the public good is also found by others in the context of ICT-related decisions (Tillquist, 2002). Once major constituents in the project are given the opportunity to influence the project trajectory, such self-interest may be contained, he argues (ibid.). In sum, it must be assumed that multiple (including personal and non-rational) interests affect electronic-government projects.

## Motives Underlying E-Government in the Context of the Layne and Lee Framework

According to the President, the "{i}mplementation of E-Government is important in making Government more responsive and cost-effective" (Bush, 2002). Also, the break-down of e-government functions into government-to-government (g2g), government-to-business (g2b), government-to-citizen (g2c), internal efficiency and effectiveness (IEE), and e-authentication in the presidential e-government initiatives evinces the underlying motives of improved citizen-orientation and expected efficiency/effectiveness gains in government operations through e-government (ibid).

Improving services and speeding up business processes can be observed in all four stages, however, to different degrees. In a fully transformed, both vertically and horizontally integrated government, that is, in fully developed electronic government, internal and external services may, indeed, be greatly improved and sped up. Due to unavoidable system and networking overhead, the process speed of highly integrated processes and systems may not always appear as dramatically superior. Also, while the process redesign undoubtedly will tap vast potentials of efficiency and effectiveness gains in government operations, the desired extent of integration may hit certain limits of complexity and technology besides the federalist and constitutional concerns (Jaeger, 2002). As we will discuss below, the more constituents involved the more the process change aspect of electronic government requires a thorough identification, involvement, and management of salient stakeholders (constituents). Since those stakeholders' needs and motives will rarely converge towards the same means and ends without intervention and moderation, aligning motives, needs, and expectation will be more challenging with more people involved and more integration targeted. Among the motives in the first two stages of e-government the reaping for lower-hanging fruits appears as a tactical move agencies may opt in favor of. Web-based screen-scraper applications, for example, for requesting a driver's license renewal online requires no legacy application and no process change, while it truly provides a transactional online service. Though there is little transformational impact, citizens and front-office workers benefit alike. Agency and political leadership use this to point at those easy wins for demonstrating their commitment towards e-government. Also, by providing some quick solutions of this kind, agencies gain time and experience for approaching the more challenging tasks in the integration stages.

## Aligning Business Process Change Projects with Strategy and Objectives

In this section, the holistic understanding of the organization is portrayed as a prerequisite to successful change projects. Strategic, long-term view and flexible planning emanate from this understanding. This view also allows for defining modest objectives and project scopes, however, within a long-term context. Another critical success factor for BPC is its intertwining with ICT strategies.

Changing the business processes of an organization needs to be performed in alignment with its strategic objectives. In the private sector, the desire to quickly meet newly formulated objectives has sometimes led to change rush. Even academics explicitly recommended such ambush-like approaches (Stoddard & Jarvenpaa, 1995). Once private firms executed change projects at those scholars' and consultants' behest, however, they met an extremely high, 70%, rate of failure of those projects (Hammer, 1996). The brute-force fashion of change has not only bred resistance on behalf of parties negatively affected by the imposition, but also ignored the overwhelming number of variables, which need to be, but hardly can be controlled in case of such an approach. Consequently, a more considerate, carefully phased, and inclusive approach to change appears mandatory rather than ambush and rush.

Various authors advocate establishing and maintaining a holistic and shared view of the organization throughout a BPC project (Gunasekaran & Nath, 1997; Pardo & Scholl, 2002). If electronic government in fact is a major initiative of transforming government, then of course it clearly needs a holistic view of the (governmental) organization, its culture, systems, processes, and constituencies. Governments in the West, however, inherently meet certain difficulties in maintaining a holistic and shared perspective over longer periods of time.

Change processes cannot completely be controlled. Change is dynamic, unpredictable, and full of surprise. Organizational systems have a tendency to return to their original state, such that relatively long periods of time are necessary for the change to take a hold. The organization's leaders have to master the challenge of developing and maintaining a shared vision of the process from the outset to its completion (Gunasekaran & Nath, 1997). If business processes change fundamentally, then those changes cannot be planned in the traditional and incremental fashion, because fundamental change entails more than just business process and workflow mapping. Social networks and informal organizations will be affected too. Change, hence, needs to be more loosely coupled and supposedly relies on coordination by feedback rather than formal planning ( Mitchell & Zmud, 1999). This directly applies to the context of electronic government, which requires both long-term view and flexible planning due to the iterative and disruptive nature of the change process.

Some authors have shown that more radical and far-reaching BPC projects expose a higher failure rate than those less ambitious projects (Kallio, Saarinen, Salo, Tinnila & Vepsalainen, 1999). Since the number of variables involved is greater, the complexity of the change project may rise to overwhelming levels in the more radical projects, particularly with respect to soft variables such as, for example, cultural readiness (Gunasekaran & Nath, 1997). However, even modest changes in business processes can affect any combination and depth of organizational tasks, structure, information systems, and culture (Stoddard & Jarvenpaa, 1995) with an inherent complexity that defies straightforward planning and execution.

Another, related tenet of the early reengineering movement has not lived up to its promise in practice, either. Contrary to the recommendations of the original reengineering advocates (Hammer & Champy, 1993), projects that incorporated the so called clean-slate approach ran a higher risk of failure. O'Neill and Sohal argue that in the clean-slate approach at least three problems arise: (1) for the lack of analyzing and understanding the current situation and system, another equally inefficient system can be the result, (2) important and valuable knowledge embedded in the current system and processes may be ignored, and (3) the scope of the problem may be underestimated (O'Neill & Sohal, 1999).

While, in principle, business processes could be streamlined without the use of ICT, the enabling role of ICT in BPC is emphasized within and beyond the BPR literature. A number of authors have argued that the perspective of technological change driving organizational change is mistaken. Those authors rather observe that both aspects of change co-evolve with co-occurring changes in business and technology strategies (cf., (El Sawy, Malhotra, Gosain & Young, 1999; Kambil, Kamis, Koufaris & Lucas, 2000)). It follows that the designs of both business rules and information systems are and should be carefully integrated (Giaglis, 1999), especially considering the rare match of  life cycles of information systems and those of business-relevant information (van Wingen, Hathorn & Sprehe, 1999). Mismatches between business strategy and ICT strategy typically result in organizational frictions (for example, through multiple system standards at the expense of organizational efficiency (cf., (Beaumaster, 2002)). Quite many organizations, therefore, added the role and function of the Chief Information Officer (CIO) to their organizational practice, whose main and ongoing task is to ensure the alignment of both business and ICT strategies leading to greatly improved success rates in redesign projects  (Mitchell & Zmud, 1999; Teng, Fiedler & Grover, 1998). Integrating both strategies allows for a pre-project assessment of the organization's (a) overall innovative capacity along with (b) its ICT maturity (Teng, Jeong & Grover, 1998). Consequently, the evaluation of the final outcome in terms of business process redesign and supporting information systems has to be integrated as well (Giaglis, 1999). Finally, in the context of private-sector firms, Hitt argues that ICT may have the capacity to both vertically and horizontally impact the boundary definition of the organization (Hitt, 1999). This may not be any different for the public sector, once more mandating business and ICT strategy integration.

In summary, when using the general BPC literature within an e-government context the following insights emerge: For aligning business process change projects with organizational strategies and objectives, a holistic view of the organization, its culture, systems, processes, and stakeholder seems to be required, which in turn facilitates a long-term perspective paired with flexible planning. Modest objectives and project scope when defined within the long-term perspective seem to yield better prospects for success than aggressive objectives and wide scope. Finally, it appears that e-government and general ICT strategies need to be tightly coupled for electronic government to succeed.

## Aligning BPC Projects with Strategy and Objectives in the Context of Layne and Lee's Framework

At the *cataloguing* stage, the holistic view of the organization may be dispensable, by and large, though a misrepresentation of the organization even at this stage may be detrimental. Further, unlike private organizations, government agencies cannot simply dispose of the content of government Web sites without further consideration and obligation. Content provided by government is of authoritative and legally binding nature. Previous states of content must be preserved for future scrutiny. Statutory and other legally binding archiving rules apply. In other words, even in the early section of the learning curve, government agencies have to meet more demanding challenges than their private-sector counterparts. Presenting content over the Web not only draws an unintended self-portrait of the agencies including their elected and appointed officials, but also sets the level of expectation in the public eye. A Web site whose content is easy to navigate and understand will more frequently be used than a convoluted and ill-designed page. While maintaining sufficient flexibility for incorporating future functionality, some stability of appearance and functioning of, for example, a government portal based on a long-term, evolutionary view through the various stages is necessary to provide consistency and ease of orientation for portal users. It may deter users and usage, when with the change in political leadership the appearance and navigation of government Web sites dramatically changes. No new administration, for example, would dare to alter the uniforms of the military personnel just for making visible a change in leadership. In this regard, the *cataloguing* stage has already posed many more challenges than most officials had originally anticipated.

At the *transaction* stage, although business process change is still minor and e-government-related transactions appear more like an extension or a partial automation of existing processes, the necessity of applying a longer view towards more integration of services and functions becomes increasingly clear. With a higher number of transactions performed online, the demand for more and smoother online processing increases. Satisfying the initial demand creates even more demand. The transactional stage also brings together traditional IT departments and new Web services, in case they have been separated in the first place. At this stage at the latest, the intertwining of Web-based and traditional IT-functionality becomes a reality. Separate databases become linked together or even integrated. New developments at one end no longer happen with ignorance of the other end. Transactional projects are performed with an increasingly improved understanding of the risks involved. Security measures and authentication procedures are tested and incorporated. Modesty in scope of transactional projects creates demonstrable benefits at limited exposure. Middleware interfacing legacy and Web-front-end systems is first tested and implemented at this stage.

At the two integration stages when passing a Nolanian type of transition point, assuming a holistic perspective becomes a necessity. While the assessment of the technical and organizational aspects, once two or more agencies begin to integrate their business processes and information systems, appears to be straightforward, the understanding of nuances and outright differences between agency cultures may be more challenging. Agencies with deeply divergent cultures may find it harder to integrate their processes and systems than agencies with less divergent cultures. For example, a transaction-intensive, external input-oriented agency environment may find it difficult to understand and appreciate an environment with an individual case orientation and service mission. As pointed out before, projects with modest objectives and scope are less risky and can serve long-term goals, provided they are aligned to the long-term perspective. Also, due to the increasing complexity of the integration task, the scope of e-government projects at these two stages typically extends over more than one budgetary cycle. However, due to the prevailing annual funding schemes those projects may be broken down into smaller projects. At the two integration stages, the distinction between ICT functions and e-government functions loses its meaning. Backend and backbone systems, both legacy and non-legacy, will be tightly integrated with front-end systems such that for any requested information the physical location of its various pieces becomes completely transparent to the user.

# Focal Areas of Business Process Change Projects

Due to their high potential for improvements in performance (Earl, Sampler & Short, 1995), the organization's core processes and those processes crossing functional and organizational borders have been proposed as good candidates (Harkness, Kettinger & Segars, 1996) for business process change. Earl also argues that BPC must be seen "as a means of building core capabilities" (Earl et al., 1995, p. 50) where focusing on core processes presents a high-leverage opportunity for organizational learning (Kettinger & Grover, 1995). Such BPC projects may at first have only a functional scope, but then shortly advance into a cross-functional reach encompassing core processes and later cross-organizational core processes (Harkness et al., 1996).

## Focal Areas of Business Process Change Projects in the Layne and Lee Framework

Although at the *cataloguing* stage, primary or core processes remain unchanged, core business process-related information appears on government Web sites. At the *transaction* stage, portions of core business processes become automated without changing them. At this stage, agency projects encompass elements of exploration and discovery (Harkness et al., 1996) regarding the extent and direction of e-government-induced business process change. At the *vertical* and *horizontal integration* stages, core-process, cross-functional, and core-cross-organizational changes become the major foci of e-government projects. Transactional and informational integration in all three areas of inter- and intra-government (g2g), government-to-business (g2b), and government-to-citizen (g2c) will be targeted at this stage.

Integrated transactional services to both citizens (for example, applying for, receiving, and paying for a license online) and businesses (for example, bidding, contracting, and billing for a service) deliver measurable benefits to all parties involved. However, since the g2g domain is said to have the highest volume of transactional processing (Balutis, 2001), it may be become a primary target for e-government integration efforts as the area with a high potential for internal efficiency and effectiveness (IEE) gains (Bush, 2002). The other huge potential for integrated e-government applications, though it may be tapped fully only as a result of a longer integration effort, resides in the informational domain. Linking government information sources horizontally and vertically will provide for an unprecedented wealth of information.

# Identifying Salient Constituents in E-Government Projects

In recent years, the two terms *constituents* and *stakeholders* have increasingly been utilized interchangeably (Tennert & Schroeder, 1999). Whereas the former term has been used for a long time in both political practice and science, the term *stakeholder* has been coined in the more recent past, particularly in the private sector. Stakeholders, for example, in a private enterprise have been distinguished from *stockholders*. While the latter own the enterprise in the legal sense, the former may have vested interests ("stakes") in it as well. Private-firm oriented *stakeholder theory* has studied the particular relationships between the organization, its stockholders, and its other stakeholders.

Despite those roots of the theory in the private domain, the theory has attracted wide attention and interest in applying at least parts of its findings to public sector organizations. While some proponents of stakeholder theory are extremely skeptical in this regard, governmental decision processes, which typically involve numerous parties with divergent interests, are intriguingly similar to stakeholder scenarios in the private sector. E-government, in particular, with its tremendous change and integration agenda appears as a natural candidate for stakeholder analysis and stakeholder management. In this section, a short overview of stakeholder theory is presented along with a discussion of how it may apply to the Layne and Lee framework.

# Stakes and Stakeholders

Before outlining the tenets of stakeholder theory, the two terms "stake" and "stakeholder" need to be defined. A "stake" in an organization in terms of stakeholder theory rests on "legal, moral, or presumed" claims, or on the capacity to affect an organization's "behavior, direction, process, or outcomes" ( Mitchell, Agle & Wood, 1997, p. 858). According to Reed, stakes represent interests, "for which a valid normative claim can be advanced" (Reed, 1999, p. 467). The classical definition of stakeholder is Freeman's: "A stakeholder in an organization is (by its definition) any group or individual who can affect or is affected by the achievement of the organization's objective" (Freeman, 1984, p. 25). Freeman first gave this widely accepted definition in a 1983 article, in which the broader term "organization's mission" was still used instead of "organization's objective" (Freeman, 1983, p. 38). Some scholars criticized the broadness of Freeman's definition, which would make it possible to include even such groups as terrorists and competitors (Phillips, 1997). However, using Clarkson's argument (Clarkson, 1994), Mitchell et al. outline that the use of risk as a second defining property for the stake in an organization helps "narrow the stakeholder field to those with legitimate claims, regardless of their power to influence the firm or the legitimacy of their relationship to the firm" (Mitchell et al., 1997, p. 857). Alkhafaji also suggested that stakeholders must have a vested interest in the survival of the organization (Alkhafaji, 1989). Frooman offers three questions for characterizing the scope of stakeholder theory: "(1) Who are they? (2) What do they want? (3) How are they going to try to get it?" (Frooman, 1999, p. 193). From the theory's perspective, managers regard stakeholders for the "intrinsic justice" of stakeholder claims, and because information on stakeholder interests makes the organization more manageable (Jones & Wicks, 1999, p. 208).

As opposed to Freeman's static and equidistant view on stakeholders, Mitchell et al. have developed a dynamic perspective, which distinguishes between stakeholder attributes of power, legitimacy, and urgency. Based on these attributes seven classes of stakeholders are identified who need different managerial attention at different times (Mitchell et al., 1997).

Some proponents of stakeholder theory do not welcome its use beyond the private-sector firm. For example, Donaldson and Preston doubt the appropriateness of applying stakeholder theory to public-sector organizations, since in their view the theory appears as governed by private sector-oriented principles and implications (Donaldson & Preston, 1995). Such concerns notwithstanding, stakeholder theory has found its way into both public-sector practice and research (Tennert & Schroeder, 1999). Although most public-sector managers perform their tasks for different ends (e.g., public interest rather than profit seeking), public-sector managers' decisions have the same capacity of affecting individuals or groups when pursuing their organization's objective. Similar to private-sector managers and firms, stakeholders can affect public managers and governmental organizations, so that Freeman's stakeholder definition applies to managerial decision-making within a governmental context as well.

Also, instrumental and normative considerations apply to public-sector stakeholder scenarios very much like in the private sector. However, as Tennert and Schroeder (Tennert & Schroeder, 1999) remark, public sector managers seem to lack a proper toolkit for stakeholder identification and management. Since the public-sector managers' mindset undergoes a shift from administration towards facilitation, the authors see an even greater necessity for stakeholder management in the public sector. "Working in the public sector has become a multi-jurisdictional and multi-sector endeavor" (p. 5). Moreover, shifting from more hierarchical to more network-type organizations further demands inclusion and management of constituencies.

Tennert and Schroeder propose the combination of Mitchell et al.'s concept of stakeholder identification along the lines of power, legitimacy, and urgency (cf. (Mitchell et al., 1997)) with Blair and Whitehead's (Blair & Whitehead, 1988) diagnostic topology of stakeholders' potential for collaboration versus their potential for threatening the organization. The authors propose a survey instrument by which those five capacities can be assessed (Tennert & Schroeder, 1999, p. 33).

# Identifying Salient Constituents in the Context of the Layne and Lee Framework

At any stage of the Layne and Lee framework constituents are affected by and can affect an e-government project. Hence, the identification, the management, and the involvement of salient constituents become important elements of the project's management on a continued basis. As Aldrich et al. ask, "{i}s E-Government *really* providing citizens with what they want?" (Aldrich, Bertot & McClure, 2002, p. 351), and also "is E-Government what government agencies want?" (ibid). Further, the discussion regarding the *digital divide* illustrates to what extent e-government may or may not have an impact on all citizens. Constituents are affected in the way they are able to participate in e-government in terms of physical access (technology), connectivity (telecommunications), economic infrastructure, information access, and information literacy (Bertot, 2003). Since government is chartered with providing equitable service to all citizens, e-government projects need to take into account how the requirement of universal access can be met. As in previous times of technology-induced change, old and new ways of doing business need to coexist for a considerable amount of time in e-government.

Already at the *cataloguing* stage the posting of government information on the Web may affect citizens in terms of privacy and confidentiality, as Layne and Lee have pointed out (Layne & Lee, 2001). The needs for protecting the rights of individual constituents and groups of constituents to privacy and confidentiality, hence, must be addressed and met even at the early stage. While the information government provides over the Internet may be subject to change, at least a portion of the obliterated information has to be archived for future scrutiny. The requirement for archiving and documenting previous states of government Web sites may become more evident over time. The archiving task in this regard has the potential to become burdensome, but might prove necessary for protecting constituents' rights regarding the proper maintenance and completeness of government records. As outlined above, using the integrated salient stakeholder/constituent identification framework of Mitchell et al. and Blair and Whitehead (Blair & Whitehead, 1988; Mitchell et al., 1997) helps to pinpoint constituents who are important along the dimensions of power, urgency, and legitimacy, as well as potential for collaboration and potential for threatening. Salient stakeholders who are most influential along those five dimensions would represent the primary stakeholders/constituents. At this stage, for example, government agencies and departments, which are affected by or can affect the Web presence, and also the elected administration (the President's, Governor's, Commissioner's, or Mayor's office), House committees, lobbyists, private businesses (vendors), and organized groups of the citizens may rank among those most salient stakeholders who must be identified, their needs analyzed, and who may be actively involved in the evolution of the project.

At the *transaction* stage, constituents involved at either end of the transaction processing, but also intermediaries in the process, move into the focus of e-government project teams. While the transaction initiating and receiving agencies can be counted among the primary constituents, other intermediary agencies or process-involved departments such as, for example, Finance/Comptroller, Budget, or IRS have high salience as constituents in the process. The same holds true for businesses and vendors, and initially to a lesser degree, citizens, who represent the other end of the transaction chain. The identification of salient constituents' needs at this stage includes the nature, scope, formats, and cost of transactional services offered and requested. At either end of the transaction processing chain the integration with existing systems may be desired. Also at this stage, the coordination of various salient constituents and their specific needs and wants determines the perceived success of the service. For example, enabling credit card payments requires certain statutory, or even legislative, prerequisites, but also the sheer technological infrastructure as well as the budgetary provisions for such a service feature. Again, the integrated stakeholder/constituent identification framework helps in identifying and involving all salient constituents. However, at this stage the tasks of identifying, managing, and involving salient constituents reaches a higher level of complexity, because (a) the number of salient constituents increases, (b) their salience may change over time, and (c) the interests of salient constituents become harder to align.

In the stages of *vertical* and *horizontal integration* salient constituents' identification and involvement become both even more important for the success of e-government projects and more complex. The number of primary constituents who score high along all five dimensions of salience increases as a consequence of the integration effort within and between government departments, agencies, levels, and branches. With respect to the high potential of both collaboration and threatening at the same time, at the integration stages quite a few salient constituents might qualify as what Blair and Whitehead have called the "Mixed Blessing Stakeholders" (Blair & Whitehead, 1988, p. 162). The two authors strongly recommend the collaboration with those constituents and the proactive management of their involvement, since the risk of this group converting towards non-supportive behavior would significantly increase otherwise (ibid).

# Discussion and Conclusion

In the past two decades, the notion of reinventing government has been discussed (cf., for example, (Milward, 1994; Osborne & Gaebler, 1992; Savas, 1982)) from various perspectives. Government, as it has been called for, would require a leaner and more efficient way of doing the business while at the same time it would emphasize its focus on citizens' and businesses' needs. For changing old-style, bureaucratic government toward this new model, Osborne and Gaebler discuss 10 avenues, many of which relate to electronic government (Osborne & Gaebler, 1992). With information and information technology as enablers, principles such as catalytic, community-owned, competitive, mission-driven, and results-oriented government may carry a practical meaning and translate into an organizational reality. Electronic government may also help converting government toward the orientations of "customer" needs, enterprise, prevention, decentralization, and markets as Osborne and Gaebler foresee them (ibid).

As Layne and Lee implicitly suggest through their framework (Layne & Lee, 2001), in electronic government business processes in government need to change and are changed. History and observation tells us that such changes first occur slowly, but then after a transition point (Nolan, 1979) increasingly rapidly and radically. The change of business processes has to encompass more than the technical dimension. As Hollings notes, this change is "more than 'quick fix' solutions to complex problems, it is an examination of what government does, why it does it, where government does it, and when government does it" (Hollings, 1995). Through electronic government the philosophy underlying Osborne and Gaebler's proposal of a reinvented government finds a timely and powerful enabler. Although business process change has not been widely

*Table 1: The dimensions of business process change in electronic government - a detailed view*

| Dimensions of Business Process Change in E-Government | | | | |
|---|---|---|---|---|
| **Business Process Change Project Dimensions** | **The Layne & Lee Framework of Electronic Government (2001)** | | | |
| | Stage I - Cataloguing | Stage II - Transaction | Stage III - Vertical Integration | Stage IV - Horizontal Integration |
| Motives/Needs | Provide basic information services over the Web; Provide information quickly and conveniently | Extend services to online transaction; Reduce costs; Simplify service | Provide true one-stop service; Speed up and greatly improve government processes and services; Provide wide-scope integration | |
| Strategic Objectives | Create a public image on the Web; Set up the evolutionary path for later stages | Make online transactions attractive; Link e-Gov systems and legacy systems; Establish standards for security and authentication | Integrate appropriate vertical and horizontal functions within meaningful constraints; Integrate and align business cultures; Merge e-Government and ICT systems; | |
| Focal Areas | Webified print content; Forms downloading; Fringe areas; Identification of potential future e-Gov areas | Legacy transaction systems in select areas; Other transactional services in fringe areas | Redesign busines core processes (in an evolutionary approach); Link sources of information; Newly design or redesign intra- & inter-agency, intra- & inter-level, and intra- & inter-branch functions as appropriate | |
| Stakes and Stakeholders | Identifying salient stakeholders and their needs | Identifying and managing salient stakeholders and their needs | Identifying, managing, and involving salient stakeholders and their needs | |

studied in the public sector, the private sector-based literature provides a wealth of lessons learned for performing those changes in a government setting, thus helping reap the benefits while avoiding the potential pitfalls.

As Table 1 illustrates, the stages of e-government correspond to various levels and challenges in governmental business process change. At the first stage, business process change does not yet occur; however, this phase of e-government provides an important stepping-stone for the changes in the later stages. At this stage, among the major motives and needs for electronic government projects one finds the desire to provide basic information services via the Internet, which is seen as a speedier and more convenient way for information delivery. The strategic objective at the *cataloguing* stage is to create a Web-based public image of the government agency. Another objective may be to set up the evolutionary path for the later stages. At this stage, the main focus rests on bringing print content to the agency's Web site, to provide forms for downloading, and to potentially identify opportunities for future change. Typically, electronic government projects remain at the fringes of the core business process at this stage. Although stakeholders/constituents can affect and may be affected by placing information on government Web sites, those constituents and their needs are identified and noticed, but typically not actively managed yet.

At the *transaction* stage, major motives and needs for electronic government projects encompass desire (a) to extend online services by a transactional component leading to improvement and speed-up, (b) to reduce costs, and (c) to simplify service delivery for the user. Strategic objectives include making online transaction processing attractive to users, linking e-government systems and legacy systems, and establishing security and authentication standards for online transaction processing. Electronic government projects at this stage focus on the Web-enablement of select legacy applications, which are in "customer" demand but do not pose extreme security risks and performance penalties on existing legacy systems. Projects providing online interactivity and transaction processing are also conducted for fringe; that is, non-core, areas of the agency's business. Stakeholders/constituents and their needs are identified and the relationships with them begin to be actively managed at this stage.

Beyond the transition point, at the transformational stages of *vertical* and *horizontal integration* e-government projects are motivated by the desire and need for truly one-stop services based on greatly improved and speeded-up processes with wide-scope integration. Strategic objectives include the meaningful integration of appropriate vertical and horizontal functions, the alignment of organizational cultures to make that integration feasible and maintainable, and, at the ICT side, the complete merger of e-government with other ICT systems. At this stage, finally, the core business processes move into the focus of e-government projects. In an evolutionary approach, those processes will be newly designed or redesigned capturing intra-agency, inter-agency, intra-level, inter-level, intra-branch, and inter-branch opportunities for meaningful integration. Linking and integrating information sources represents another explicit strategic thrust at this stage. For reaching the desired high level of integration, stakeholders/constituents and their needs are not merely identified and managed as in the previous stages, but at this stage the stakeholders are and remain actively involved in those projects. Since stakeholder salience can change over time, collaborative e-government projects, which are typical at this stage, become more complex than in first two stages, and the stakeholder environment in the transformational stages needs close attention from e-government project managers on an ongoing basis.

Although it has not been empirically studied in detail for its process change impact yet, electronic government seems to be a special case of business process change, which can be mapped with some confidence and specificity to each of its predicted developmental stages. An illustrative case in this regard is the overhaul of New York State's (NYS) Central Accounting System (CAS) (cf., ( Pardo & Scholl, 2002; Pardo, Scholl, Cook, Connelly & Dawes, 2000; Scholl, 2001)). The currently used, almost quarter-of-a-century-old mainframe system, although it has proven a robust transaction-oriented workhorse, falls short of providing the 90-plus agencies in the state with modern financial management (FM) and planning capabilities. As a result NYS agencies began developing their local systems for that particular purpose, leading to a massive reduplication of effort and unacceptable increase in cost to the taxpayer. NYS, hence, had to decide whether the existing system could serve for another 10 to 15 years, or needed to be replaced rather quickly. While the Web enablement of existing transactional CAS functionality (stage 2) along with some additions of FM capabilities would have tactically served the immediate needs to some extent, NYS officials felt that that course of action might create an even larger roadblock into the future, in which more sophisticated FM capabilities along with other, not yet identified applications might be required. The core motives for considering the fundamental overhaul of CAS were to provide statewide users with one-stop, seamless service at higher speed and with extended and improved functionality. The state, therefore, decided to conduct a reassessment of business processes and user requirements from the ground up before embarking on any particular course of action. In other words, the state officials had a clear sense of both the change and integration opportunities as well as of the enormity of the undertaking. In a multi-year project, the overhaul of the old CAS and its subsystems has been pursued carrying NYS, once the project is completed, well beyond the transition point into the two integration stages of electronic government. In this project, the complexity of the integration task at hand quickly became visible. For example, beyond the lack of certain FM functionality, the old CAS would even not smoothly support certain transactional functions such as state revenues, which had no great importance a quarter of a century earlier when CAS was built. NYS also found most business processes and underlying workflows supported by CAS duplicative and unnecessarily fragmented. Business process streamlining, hence, became both a necessity and enabler of integration. With over 90 state agencies and numerous non-governmental users the new CAS has to satisfy the needs of a huge and diverse constituency. The project, hence, had to involve salient constituents at all stages. Whether or not the NYS CAS overhaul effort will be successful is not certain as of this writing. However, cases of this order of magnitude will provide ample empirical evidence for the intricacies of the integration stages, which will lead to further enhancement and refinement of the framework proposed in this chapter.

It might be interesting to study whether or not the unfolding of e-government as proposed in this framework will as well be observable in developing countries, which typically do not have as mature administrative and third-generation IT legacies to cope with as have the developed countries. In this regard, governments in developing countries may rather enjoy a higher degree of freedom when pursuing truly integrated e-government applications. This may prove instrumental for the more rapid creation of both administratively effective and efficient structures of government in developing countries. However, superior technological and organizational structures always need to be supported by a co-evolving societal and social context of governance. Technology has a dual character (Orlikowski, 1992), which not only shapes its environment, but is rather equally shaped by it. In an analysis of readiness factors for (commercial) electronic business in China, for example, Huang et al. define "internal requirement, external environment, and organization competence and IT application and acceptance as the keys for success (Huang, Huang, Huang & Zhao, 2003, p. 1111) and develop a readiness indicator system along those key factors. If applied to a governmental context, those factors, although defined for the private-sector assessment, may provide valuable information regarding the degree of readiness for electronic government in developing countries.

With regard to the framework proposed in this chapter, the depth and the extent of business process change increases, as the degree of integration throughout the four stages increases, also marking an ever-increasing degree of readiness. Electronic government, hence, may one day become the synonym for the most dramatic changes in government practice in decades.

# References

Aldrich, D., Bertot, J.C., & McClure, C.R. (2002). E-government: Initiatives, developments, and issues. *Government Information Quarterly, 19*(4), 349-355.

Alkhafaji, A.F. (1989). *A stakeholder approach to corporate governance: Managing in a dynamic environment.* New York: Quorum Books.

Balutis, A.P. (2001, Spring). E-government 2001, Part I: Understanding the challenge and evolving strategies. *The Public Manager, 33-37.*

Beaumaster, S. (2002). *Local government IT implementation issues: A challenge for public administration.* Paper presented at the Proceedings on the 35th Hawaii International Conference on System Sciences, Hawaii.

Bertot, J.C. (2003). The multiple dimensions of the digital divide: More than the technology 'haves' and 'have nots'. *Government Information Quarterly, 20*(2), 185-191.

Blair, D.L., & Whitehead, C.J. (1988). Too many on the seesaw. Stakeholder diagnosis and management for hospitals. *Hospital and Health Administration, 33*(2), 153-166.

Boer, M.D., Bosch, F.A.J.V.d., & Volberda, H.W. (1999). Managing organizational knowledge integration in the emerging multimedia complex. *Journal of Management Studies, 36*(3), 379-398.

Bush, G.W. (2002). *e-Gov: The official Web site of the President's e-Government initiatives.* Retrieved October 23, 2003, from: *http://www.whitehouse.gov/omb/egov/.*

Champy, J. (1995). *Reengineering management: The mandate for new leadership* (1st ed.). New York: HarperBusiness.

Chen, Y.-C., & Gant, J. (2001a). *Transforming e-government services: The use of application service providers in U.S. local governments.* Paper presented at the AMCIS, Boston.

Chen, Y.-C., & Gant, J. (2001b). Transforming local e-government services: The use of application service providers. *Government Information Quarterly, 18*(4), 343-355.

Clarkson, M. (1994). *A risk based model of stakeholder theory.* Paper presented at the Proceedings of the 2nd Toronto Conference on Stakeholder Theory, Toronto.

Donaldson, T., & Preston, L.E. (1995). The stakeholder theory of the corporation: Concepts, evidence, and implications. *Academy of Management Review, 20*(1), 63-91.

Earl, M.J., Oxford Institute of Information Management, & PA Consulting Group. (1996). *Information management: The organizational dimension.* Oxford, UK: Oxford University Press.

Earl, M.J., Sampler, J.L., & Short, J.E. (1995). Strategies for business process reengineering: Evidence from field studies. *Journal of Management Information Systems, 12*(1), 31-56.

El Sawy, O.A., Malhotra, A., Gosain, S., & Young, K.M. (1999). IT-intensive value innovation in the electronic economy: Insights from Marshall Industries. *MIS Quarterly, 23*(3), 305-335.

Freeman, R.E. (1983). Strategic management: A stakeholder approach. In R. Lamb (Ed.), *Advances in strategic management* (Vol. 1, pp. 31-60). Greenwich, CT: JAI.

Freeman, R.E. (1984). *Strategic management: A stakeholder approach.* Boston: Pitman.

Frooman, J. (1999). Stakeholder influence strategies. *Academy of Management Review, 24*(2), p. 115, 191.

Gant, J.P., & Gant, D.B. (2002). *Web portal functionality and state government e-service.* Paper presented at the Proceedings on the 35th Hawaii International Conference on System Sciences, Hawaii.

Gefen, D., Warkentin, M., Pavlou, P.A., & Rose, G.M. (2002, August 9-11). *E-government adoption.* Paper presented at the AMCIS, Dallas, TX.

Giaglis, G.M. (1999). Integrated design and evaluation of business processes and information systems. *Communications of AIS, 2*(1), 1-33.

Gibson, C.F., & Nolan, R.L. (1974, January/February). Managing the four stages of EDP growth. *Harvard Business Review, 52*(1), 76-88.

Grover, V., Teng, J., Segars, A.H., & Fiedler, K. (1998). The influence of information technology diffusion and business process change on perceived productivity: The IS executive's perspective. *Information & Management, 34*, 141-159.

Gunasekaran, A., & Nath, B. (1997). The role of information technology in business process reengineering. *International Journal of Production Economics, 50*(1997), 91-104.

Halachmi, A., & Bovaird, T. (1997). Process reengineering in the public sector: Learning some private sector lessons. *Technovation, 17*(5), 227-235.

Hammer, M. (1996). *Beyond reengineering: How the process-centered organization is changing our work and our lives* (1st ed.). New York: HarperBusiness.

Hammer, M., & Champy, J. (1993). *Reengineering the corporation: A manifesto for business revolution* (1st ed.). New York: HarperBusiness.

Harkness, W.L., Kettinger, W.J., & Segars, A H. (1996). Sustaining process improvement and innovation in the information service function: Lessons learned from Bose Corporation. *MIS Quarterly, 20*(3), 349-367.

Hitt, O.M. (1999). Information technology and firm boundaries: Evidence from panel data. *Information Systems Research, 10*(2), 134-149.

Hollings, R.L. (1995). *Reinventing government: An analysis and annotated bibliography.* Commack, NY: Nova Science Publishers.

Huang, C.J., & Chao, M.-H. (2001). Managing WWW in public administration: Uses and misuses. *Government Information Quarterly, 18*(4), 357-373.

Huang, J., Huang, H., Huang, W., & Zhao, C. (2003, August 4-6). *An indicator system for assessing enterprises e-readiness and its application in Chinese retailing.* Paper presented at the AMCIS, Tampa, FL.

Huang, W., d'Ambra, J., & Bhalla, V. (2002, August 9-11). *Key factors influencing the adoption of e-government in Australian public sectors.* Paper presented at the AMCIS, Dallas, TX.

Hurst, D.K. (1995). *Crisis & renewal: Meeting the challenge of organizational change.* Boston: Harvard Business School Press.

Jaeger, P.T. (2002). Constitutional principles and e-government: An opinion about possible effects of federalism and the separation of powers on e-government policies. *Government Information Quarterly, 19*(4), 357-368.

Jones, T.M., & Wicks, A.C. (1999). Convergent stakeholder theory. *Academy of Management Review, 24*(2), 206-221.

Kallio, J., Saarinen, T., Salo, S., Tinnila, M., & Vepsalainen, A.P.J. (1999). Drivers and tracers of business process changes. *Journal of Strategic Information Systems, 8,* 125-142.

Kambil, A., Kamis, A., Koufaris, M., & Lucas, H.C. (2000). Influences on the corporate adoption of Web technology. *Communications of the ACM, 43*(11), 264-271.

Kettinger, W.J., & Grover, V. (1995). Toward a theory of business process change management. *Journal of Management Information Systems, 12*(1), 9-30.

Kettinger, W. J., Teng, J.T.C., & Guha, S. (1997). Business process change: A study of methodologies, techniques, and tools. *MIS Quarterly, 21*(1), 55-80.

Laudon, K.C., & Laudon, J.P. (2002). *Management information systems: Managing the digital firm* (7th ed.). Upper Saddle River, NJ: Prentice Hall.

Layne, K., & Lee, J. (2001). Developing fully functional e-government: A four-stage model. *Government Information Quarterly, 18*(2), 122-136.

Lyytinen, K., & Hirschheim, R. (1987). Information systems failures–a survey and classification of the empirical literature. *Oxford Surveys in Information Technology, 4,* 257-309.

Mallalieu, G., Harvey, C., & Hardy, C. (1999). The wicked relationship between organizations and information technology (industry trend and event). *Journal of End User Computing, 11*(4), 40-50.

Markus, M.L. (1983). Power, politics, and MIS implementation. *Communications of the ACM, 26*(6), 430-444.

Milward, H.B. (1994). Nonprofit contracting and the hollow state. *Public Administration Review, 54*(1), 73-77.

Mitchell, R.K., Agle, B.R., & Wood, D.J. (1997). Toward a theory of stakeholder identification and salience. Defining the principle of who and what really counts. *Academy of Management Review, 22*(4), 853-866.

Mitchell, V.L., & Zmud, R.W. (1999). The effects of coupling IT and work process strategies in redesign projects. *Organization Science, 10*(4), 424-438.

Mohan, L., & Holstein, W.K. (1990). EIS: It can work in the public sector. *MIS Quarterly, 14*(4), 434-448.

Nolan, R.L. (1979, March/April). Managing the crises in data processing. *Harvard Business Review, 57*(2), 115-126.

O'Neill, P., & Sohal, A.S. (1999). Business process reengineering: A review of recent literature. *Technovation, 19,* 571-581.

Orlikowski, W.J. (1992). The duality of technology: Rethinking the concept of technology in organizations. *Organization Science, 3*(3), 398-427.

Orlikowski, W.J., & Gash, D.C. (1994). Technological frames: Making sense of information technology in organizations. *ACM Transactions on Information Systems, 12*(2), 174-207.

Osborne, D., & Gaebler, T. (1992). *Reinventing government: How the entrepreneurial spirit is transforming the public sector.* Reading, MA: Addison-Wesley Pub. Co.

Pardo, T.A., & Scholl, H.J.J. (2002, January 7-10). *Walking atop the cliffs: Avoiding failure and reducing risk in large-scale e-government projects.* Paper presented at the 35th Hawaiian International Conference on System Sciences, Maui, HI.

Pardo, T.A., Scholl, H.J., Cook, M.E., Connelly, D.R., & Dawes, S.S. (2000). *New York State central accounting system stakeholder needs analysis.* Albany, NY: Center for Technology in Government.

Peters, T.J., & Waterman, R.H. (1984). *In search of excellence: Lessons from America's best-run companies* (Warner Books ed.). New York: Warner Books.

Phillips, R.A. (1997). Stakeholder theory and a principle of fairness. *Business Ethics Quarterly, 7*(1), 51-46.

Ranganathan, C., & Dhaliwal, J.S. (2001). A survey of business process reengineering practice in Singapore. *Information and Management, 39,* 125-134.

Reed, D. (1999). Stakeholder management theory: A critical theory perspective. *Business Ethics Quarterly, 9*(3), 453-483.

Rubin, B.M. (1986). Information systems for public management: Design and implementation. *Public Administration Review, 46*(Special Issue), 540-552.

Savas, E.S. (1982). *Privatizing the public sector: How to shrink government.* Chatham, NJ: Chatham House Publishers.

Scholl, H.J.J. (2001, October 3-5). *Applying stakeholder theory to e-government: Benefits and limits.* Paper presented at the 1st IFIP Conference on E-Commerce, E-Business, and E-Government (I3E 2001), Zurich, Switzerland.

Scholl, H.J.J. (2003, January 6-9). *E-government: A special case of ICT-enabled business process change.* Paper presented at the 36th Hawaiian International Conference on System Sciences, Waikoloa, Big Island, HI.

Simon, H.A. (1979). Rational decision making in business organizations. *The American Economic Review, 69*(4), 493-513.

Simon, H.A. (1991). Bounded rationality and organizational learning. *Organization Science, 2*(1), 125-134.

Stoddard, D.B., & Jarvenpaa, S.L. (1995). Business process redesign: Tactics for managing radical change. *Journal of Management Information Systems, 12*(1), 81-107.

Tam, K.Y. (1998). The impact of information technology investments on firm performance and evaluation: Evidence from newly industrialized economies. *Information Systems Research, 9*(1), 85-98.

Teng, J.T.C., Fiedler, K.D., & Grover, V. (1998). An exploratory study of the influence of IS function and organizational context on business process reengineering project initiatives. *Omega, Int. J. Mgmt Sci., 26*(6), 679-698.

Teng, J.T.C., Jeong, S.R., & Grover, V. (1998). Profiling successful reengineering projects. *Communications of the ACM, 41*(6), 96-102.

Tennert, J.R., & Schroeder, A.D. (1999, April 10-14). *Stakeholder analysis.* Paper presented at the 60th Annual Meeting of the American Society for Public Administration, Orlando, FL.

Tillquist, J. (2002). Rules of the game: Constructing norms of influence, subordination and constraint in IT planning. *Information & Organization, 12,* 39-70.

van Wingen, R.S., Hathorn, F., & Sprehe, J.T. (1999). Principles for information technology investment in US Federal Electronic Records Management. *Journal of Government Information, 26*(1), 33-42.

**Chapter IV**

# A Strategic Framework for a G2G E-Government Excellence Center*

Roberto Evaristo, The University of Illinois at Chicago, USA

Beomsoo Kim, The University of Illinois at Chicago, USA and
Yonsei University, Seoul, Korea**

## Abstract

*The business of government can be streamlined by offering interactive services for the public and placing procurement mechanisms and relationships with contractors online. However, traditional government has not maximized its ability to benefit from these initiatives. We propose that the creation of an e-government Excellence Center can help with this transition of traditional to digitalized government. Such an e-government Excellence Center would be beneficial to different stakeholders: traditional governments, by making them aware of the alternatives or potential options available to them; experienced government structures, by increasing their visibility and by offering consulting services to a host of potential clients; and even to IT solution providers, by making their products and services more visible.*

# Introduction

For centuries, government has endeavored to serve its various constituents. Bureaucracy and lengthy delays in communication have been some of the unfortunate consequences of many of the services provided by the government to the public and to other organizations, be they private or governmental at different levels (Becker, George, Goolsby & Grissom, 1998). Now this situation is changing, partly due to the use of advanced applications of information technology. Much of this can be seen with the newest e-government solutions available for federal, state and municipal governments and their agencies (Pardo, 2000). The significance of collaboration and coordination among government agencies and the use of new innovative technologies as enablers or means of achieving effective and efficient governments are important issues constantly being addressed by academics, governments, and the public. After the first wave of electronic government initiatives, many researchers in the field of public administration and government have started emphasizing the need to take advantage of new technological advances in promoting efficient and effective collaboration among government organizations (Ho, 2002).

The plethora of alternatives in electronic government creates an immediate problem for decision makers who need to decide how to invest tax dollars in the solutions that offer the highest return in satisfaction and usefulness to the original customers, or to those who have paid for it with their taxes. Which solutions are more efficient? What are the most appropriate solutions to a particular situation? The only thing that seems to be clear – other than the traditional statement, "we need a Web presence" – is a general state of confusion about what resources are available and what may be a good starting point. To make things even more complicated, there is a proliferation of information sources about different e-government alternatives, providers, services, and even lists of e-government sites worldwide (e.g., eGov Links, 2003; FirstGov.com, 2003) that to a limited extent were created to answer subsets of these questions.

*Table 1: Five stage frameworks for e-government development*

| Stages of E-government | Moon (2002) | United Nations (2002) |
|---|---|---|
| Stage 1 | Simple information dissemination | Emerging |
| Stage 2 | Two-way communication | Enhanced |
| Stage 3 | Service and financial transactions | Interactive |
| Stage 4 | Integration | Transactional |
| Stage 5 | Political participation | Seamless |

However, still missing is an unbiased source providing not only evaluations and critical analysis of different e-government services but also extended discussions of what is available, what is appropriate for different constituencies, and the reasons for such.

This chapter proposes to develop a blueprint for a Center of Excellence on e-government – from government to government (G2G). By its very nature, the Center may also become an interesting site for businesses to observe and publish what they are offering in e-government solutions, but this is anticipated to be a smaller part of the total traffic. The Center would be a visionary project where all the above questions and many more can be answered, providing a forum from which stakeholders in e-government can learn and to which they can contribute. This would add value not only for governmental areas not yet digitalized in developed countries but also for the much larger audience of developing countries.

In particular, as Moon's (2002) and United Nations' (2002) frameworks for e-government development in Table 1 suggest, we find that approaches to e-government initiatives evolve from relatively simple Web pages offering plain data and information, to two-way communication, to financial transactions, to vertical and horizontal integration, and finally to political participation. Stages 1 and 2 are relatively simple and easy to implement and require very little exchange of information on how other agencies or governments have acted in the past. The need for collaboration and information exchange among government agencies and governments increases radically from stages 3 to 5. The proposed Center for Excellence in e-government would add the most value in these later stages of e-government development.

In the next section, we will analyze the needs of different stakeholders for different e-government efforts: the public, private organizations, and governmental agencies. The complexity of these needs may require coordination across two or more of these stakeholders. Finally, we will use conclusions gleaned from the earlier sections in this chapter to elaborate on a framework for a Center of Excellence on e-government as well as to provide recommendations for future research in the area.

# Stakeholder Needs

In this section we will examine the diverse needs of G2G e-government initiative stakeholders. However, one should keep in mind that the reason we are looking at the public as one of the stakeholders is because the public constitutes the ultimate customers of goods and services offered by a government. Other stakeholders rally around the issue of e-government in order to improve the quality of services rendered to the public. So, although learning about e-government alternatives is something that would not be interesting to the average citizen, knowledge of e-government approaches is very important for officials trying to decide which e-government services to offer to that citizen.

# Stakeholder # 1: The Public

On a daily basis, people need information to go about their lives. Some of this comes from newspapers, some from interactions with other people in different venues, and some from using basic services provided by different levels of government. For example, in Brazil, people can both prepare and pay their taxes on the Web (Brazilian Government, 2003). In Canada, citizens can access their favorite hospital or the post office (Canada Post, 2003). In the UK, passport applications are available on the Web (UK online, 2003). In Atlanta, one can look at bus and train schedules on the web (MARTA, 2002). In Chicago, people can not only pay their parking tickets or renew their license plates, but also find out more about reported crimes from the Chicago police department's database (City of Chicago, 2003; Fulla & Welch, 2002). In Korea, a centralized e-government portal site offers over 4,000 services including paying taxes, accessing government records, applying for government-issued documents, paying for vehicle registration, applying for and tracing social security, and filing citizen complaints or suggestions (Korea Ministry of Government Administration and Home Affairs, 2002). People judge the quality of these services on a daily basis. Erin Research Inc. (1998) and others address that customer satisfaction with the government is derived from interacting with these online services. In summary, the key points seem to be:

1.  Ratings for e-government services in general are lower than ratings for specific offerings, potentially showing a gloomy view of government by citizens. Specific services, typically ones that have been used recently, are evaluated based on one's own experience. This suggests that if people actually used e-government services, their satisfaction would likely increase.

2.  Forty-two percent of respondents believe that government should provide better quality service than the private sector.

3.  The main problem seems to be to know where to find the service. Without that knowledge one cannot use it.

4.  Timely delivery is the most important characteristic that contributes to higher satisfaction ratings. The other drivers are courtesy, competence, fairness and outcome.

The root of customer satisfaction seems to be a perception of value from the public - partly due to time and cost savings, but mainly from convenience. And the most interesting part is that most people, once they try e-government services, are likely to keep coming back, therefore increasingly lowering the costs of offering such services (Kaylor, Deshazo & Van Eck, 2001). Moreover, their approval of the government tends to increase.

This seems to be a powerful argument for carefully planned marketing campaigns to increase the reach and knowledge of such e-services to clients who have access to the Web or who can be given such access as part of further e-government efforts.

## Stakeholder # 2: Private Organizations

There are different categories of private organizations that interact with government. They can be customers or providers, sometimes concurrently. For instance, a garbage hauler may take the role of a provider and want to offer its services to the government and may need to access the e-procurement area of the government to whom they are marketing their services. The same provider eventually needs to be paid for services rendered. Alternatively, some organizations will be buying services from the government and may be paying taxes, import duties, or other information services (Jorgensen & Cable, 2002).

Their interaction needs will be very similar to the ones discussed above for public-centered services. However, since the amounts involved are much higher and the government can actually force providers to go through an e-procurement solution, stakeholder awareness will be much higher from the onset.

## Stakeholder # 3: Government Agencies

There are government agencies at several levels: municipality (county), state and federal. Some of these agencies are self-contained, whereas others may benefit from exchanging information with other agencies at their level or at a different one.

Similarly to private organizations, government agencies can be seen as providers or suppliers of products/services from other stakeholders. That can be quite involved: for instance, a particular government agency at the county level may develop a solution that could be marketed partially or in full to other counties countrywide. This is in addition to traditional G2C services, and can be thought of as G2G. This is the crux of this chapter. In our experience, most governments that try to start or improve their own e-government efforts face a daunting task. First, it is difficult to identify which tools exist or how much they cost, or even which agency is using what so that it could be asked for its opinion. Second, there may be several tools or services addressing a typical problem being marketed and it is hard to know which one may be more appropriate to a particular agency's needs. Worse yet, it may be that the best-fit application is not even on the market because its developers are the only users and have not thought that it may be marketable. Third, a slew of consultants are available, each touting a different solution. Good as they may be, an unbiased opinion is hard to come by to people whose private network does not include people in those agencies most experienced with e-government solutions.

Alternatively, the exchanged commodity could be information about citizens. For instance, let us discuss the example mentioned by Becker et al. (1998). They describe the reorganization of the Illinois Department of Social Services into one body from several erstwhile dispersed services: Department of Mental Health and Development Disabilities, Department of Alcoholism and Substance Abuse, Department of Rehabilitation Services, Department of Public Aid, Department of Public Health, Department of Children Services, and the Department of Aging. They describe a fictitious customer, "Jane Doe," who would benefit from such reorganization. Under the previous system, this social services user would have had to offer her information several times to agencies with different and sometimes contradictory requirements. She might have had as many as three or four agents, each addressing only the concerns of a specific agency, and may not have been informed about other agencies more appropriate to her needs. The single shop window situation (only one agency) is able to be much more efficient in recognizing the complex issues surrounding a case, providing more complete help to the individual, while also lowering costs for the government.

Furthermore, other authors position e-government not only as the best service offered digitally, but also as a change in philosophy and cross-agency interaction to enable one-stop shopping (akin to reengineering the way government offers services as in Moon, 2002).

At the heart of efforts to create enhanced e-government services, however, there is an inherent concern for privacy. The more the state knows about a particular citizen and all his/her needs, the more likely it is that a solution addressing those problems in an all-encompassing and consistent manner will be possible. But this of course creates the shadow of "Big Brother". The solution may be a compromise not palatable to any of the strong political forces rallying around the problem.

In the next section, we will address how a G2G Center of Excellence on e-government can address most of these problems and create real added value.

# A G2G Solution: Creating Added Value through a Center of Excellence

Value-addition is the holy grail of any information technology effort, and any e-government initiative is not an exception. Problems observed in the literature, coupled with a careful analysis of e-government sites all over the United States (2002), suggested some of the issues raised in the previous section. In this section, we discuss how some of these problems can be addressed through a set of features proposed for a Center of Excellence on e-government.

First, it is interesting to observe a key difference between e-commerce and e-government and what opportunities and problems this brings. E-commerce or e-business has a potentially unlimited number of stakeholders in each of its categories, buyers and suppliers. On the other hand, G2G e-government has a limited number of buyers of e-government solutions (even though the number of buyers of products and services themselves offered by e-government solutions may be quite large). Likewise, the number of suppliers is limited, particularly if we think of suppliers as government agencies. On the one hand, this makes all buyers relatively easily identifiable and therefore reachable. However, it also means that the high costs of building an infrastructure to support this group need to be shared among a relatively small number of paying "customers," increasing the difficulty in delivering services to this group. Again, customers are here defined as government agencies that are purchasing e-government solutions.

Such an excellence center would have to be focused on the customers. As seen before, the critical problem for these customers is that they do not know what online products or services are available, prices, the quality of the product/service, who has been using what with which results, and which consultant is good. Therefore, the initial step would be to identify government agencies exemplary in their use of e-government solutions, and to invite them to participate in the G2G Center for Excellence. Their motivation to accept participation is that their visibility would increase among their peers, and even more importantly that they would gain possibilities for marketing their know-how or products. Their role would be to provide content and credibility for the Center. The content provided by these "senior members" of particular interest to potential would-be adopters is several fold: who is using what (own development or purchased solutions), at what cost, with what results. Moreover, not only is ad hoc consultancy possible via simplified discussion lists, but also the "advertisement" of solutions that might otherwise never be used by anybody else would create a low-cost secondary market for the initial developer.

There are several assumptions in the above proposal. First, some of the services provided by such a center would be centralized, such as content structure and requests for participation. However, each senior member would also have some level of latitude in the way he/she presents content. This would simplify the task of managing the Center and also increase the accuracy and currency of the information, since information ownership would tend to be closer to actual stakeholders. Therefore, this Center would not be a venture based on the efforts of one owner or single agency. This multiplicity increases the chances of success.

Another key issue is to maintain motivation for both senior members as well as onlookers or less experienced stakeholders to keep coming back. This is where customer relation-

*Figure 1: G2G E-Government Excellence Center framework and stakeholders*

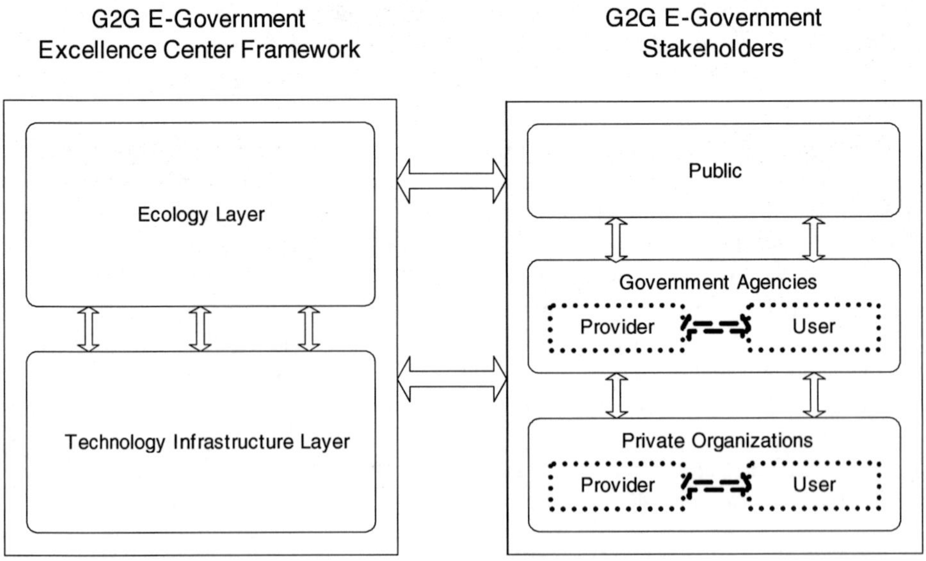

ship management can play an important role. Critical mass of visitation can be initially attained with careful print marketing about the existence of the Center. At that point, interest from less experienced stakeholders will originate from their need to solve their informational needs, and the fact that they find value in the information will prompt them for return visits. Each return visit may mean accessing more information from a senior member, and potentially either purchasing from that member or requesting their (possibly paid) unbiased help.

An interesting consequence of this enhanced visibility of success cases is that customers may start seeing the potential for citizen information exchange across agencies as well as the reasons why past efforts have or have not worked. For instance, it may be possible that when one person changes his or her address in one agency the same change of address could be propagated to separate databases. Integrated databases are a dream not achievable even in government agencies working very closely, but there are intermediate solutions that with 20% of the effort may reach as much as 80% of the possible results. The trick is to identify the candidates for such efforts, and the Center of Excellence on e-government can facilitate or assist such information exchange and learning. As in Figure 1, we propose a framework for a G2G e-government Excellence Center that corresponds to the concerns and needs of e-government stakeholders addressed in the above.

# The Framework for a G2G Excellence Center

By adopting approaches and applying lessons learned from e-business and e-commerce, we establish a framework for a Center of Excellence on e-government. In this framework, we propose a two-layer approach: a technology infrastructure layer and an ecology layer as in Figure 2.

## Technology Infrastructure Layer

The technology infrastructure layer is the required infrastructure that involves hardware, software, and networks as well as the topology for the G2G excellence center.

The development principles for this technology infrastructure layer for the G2G center are the following: (1) simplify application development and deployment, (2) support heterogeneous client and server platforms, (3) leverage existing skills and assets, (4) deliver a secure, scalable, reliable, and manageable environment, and (5) provide the freedom to implement using many vendors' products.

From a review of the adoption and implementation of electronic commerce and electronic business projects in various businesses in recent years, we can expedite the development of G2G center while minimizing possible inefficiencies. As IBM (2002) defines, an e-business is an organization that connects critical business systems directly to key constituencies (customers, employees, suppliers and distributors) via the World Wide

Web on the Internet, intranet and extranet. As customers, employees, suppliers and distributors are all connected to the business systems and information they need, this simple concept actually transforms key business processes. The framework developed for e-business also helped its development and adoption in the IT and other industries. As we find from IBM's approach in e-business, this framework for e-business often followed guidelines like the following: (1) maximize ease and speed of development and deployment; (2) accommodate any client device; (3) ensure portability across a diverse server environment; (4) leverage and extend existing assets. These principles help us define the goals for technology infrastructure layer of the G2G excellence center.

This infrastructure layer consists of the following six components, which are interconnected to each other:

- **Internet clients** - Through various Internet clients, users communicate with Internet and Web application servers (using traditional Internet standards such as TCP/IP, HTTP, XML, HTML and WML) to access knowledge and data. The primary role of the client is to accept and validate user input, and present results received from the Web application server to the user. Clients supported by the framework span a diverse range of products from information appliances, such as digital mobile telephones and personal data assistants (PDA) to personal computers (PC). While the individual capabilities of each of these clients vary significantly, they are unified by their reliance upon a set of Web based technologies. This set includes Java, TCP/IP, HTTP, HTTPS, HTML, DHTML, XML, MIME, SMTP, IIOP, SOAP, WAP, and X.509, among others.

- **Networks and network services** - Network and network services include wireless and wired Internet, extranet, and intranet. Different network connections can be utilized according to the format and usage of information and data. The extranet and intranet can be used for development and deployment purposes. In addition, the

*Figure 2: G2G E-Government Excellence Center framework*

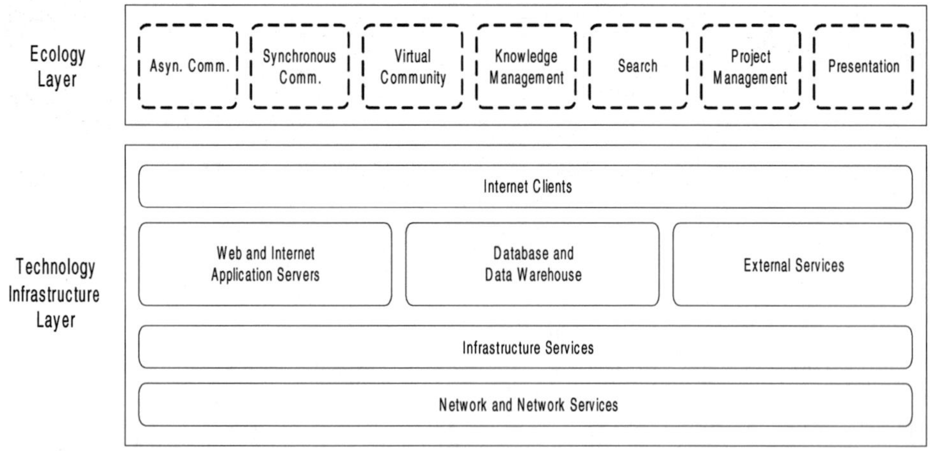

extranet can enable distributed administration and utilization of the Center by multiple government organizations at a time.

- **Infrastructure services -** Infrastructure services provide Web application servers and their system logic and components with directory and security services. Included in these services are firewalls, which shield an organization's network from exposure when connecting to the Internet, and which prevent hackers and unauthorized others from gaining access to internal data, and computing resources. Security systems that block or filter malicious applications are also part of the services provided.

- **Internet and Web application servers -** Internet and Web application servers serve as the hubs of the Web application topology by processing requests from clients. These servers orchestrate access to systems logic and data on the server and, in turn, return Web pages composed of static and dynamic content back to the client. The Web application server provides a wide range of programming, data access, and application integration services for writing the systems logic part of a Web application. This server also supports templates that translate data in different formats for supporting various client devices and network connections.

- **Databases and data warehouses** - Databases and database management systems (DBMS) store, update, and retrieve data in distributed and centralized database systems. For the safe storage of data, mirroring and creating backup data in these databases are important measures. Data warehouse takes advantage of parallel and multi-node database configuration. This warehouse also provides classification of users and users' input, and analysis of transactions.

- **External services** - External services consist of existing mission critical applications and data within the center as well as external information services. Authentication and certification services are also examples that can be used to prevent network infrastructure from security threats such as spoofing or repudiation on the computer networks.

It is also important to note that the Web application server, data warehouse and external services are logical tiers capable of running on the same physical machine. In addition, functionality on the Web application server, data warehouse and external services can be spread across multiple physical machines.

## Ecology Layer

As more and more governments of various levels seek new services and processes on the network and as Internet growth skyrockets, it is becoming apparent that there is a demand for mechanisms to find and share knowledge and expertise on the Internet. An important source of information published in the Center and on the Internet is the users themselves. A natural effect of this center will be to have people and organizations with similar interests and responsibilities interact with one another conveniently. Moreover, increasing user awareness of new e-government methods and approaches will benefit digital-government-savvy organizations or IT vendors providing products and services. This in turn benefits users, as IT vendors or other contractors produce better products and services targeted more accurately to real governments' needs. This ecology layer turns the technology infrastructure layer into a meaningful and effective venue for information searching and sharing among various digital governments.

The ecology layer defines how this G2G Center collects data, information and knowledge; how the Center facilitates its users or its constituents in participating in discussions, disseminating and acquiring information and knowledge useful and relevant to their government and organizations. The topology of this layer includes the following seven services: (1) asynchronous communications, (2) synchronous communications, (3) search, (4) knowledge management, (5) system management, (6) virtual communities, (7) project management and tracking, and (8) presentation services. In order to make this community effort on the Internet successful, high traffic and quality information become the management goals. The effective development, integration and presentation of these components in this layer determine the fate of the Center in achieving this goal of a highly efficient information center on digital government.

- **Asynchronous Communications Services** - This is the most prevalent way of supporting the information needs of stakeholders. After several years of Internet development, most Web sites and clearinghouses on the Internet still provide data and information via this channel. That is, site managers provide information to users and visitors to the site, who can read and acquire information. Users participate by downloading intangible assets from the center. This relatively low cost way of providing and utilizing information and the high demand for austere knowledge sharing is still the dominant way of communication. It is also worth noting that frequent access and high volume transactions are not always directly related to significant improvement due to communications. The efficacy and quality of communications is also an important aspect to consider. To improve quality of communications, customized information along with un-customized information is provided in this framework. The customization of the content (e.g., Copeland, 2001; Ketchell, 2000; Schwartz, 2000) according to user characteristics is supported from the Web applications server and data warehousing in the technology infrastructure layer and the knowledge management service in the ecology layer.

- **Synchronous Communications Services** - Another venue for information sharing in this framework is the synchronous communications channel, which includes message boards, forums, chatting rooms, and video-conferencing. In addition to these traditional approaches, we propose that in the Center some services should be administered by stakeholders rather than by the Center itself. That is, even if the e-government Center is a centralized information clearinghouse, this Center up-dates itself by having some of its services run by the stakeholders themselves. This is an ultimate form of active participation in sharing information, knowledge, and applications by those people involved in the daily transactions of such information. This distributed administration simultaneously benefits the Center and all participants. Moreover, this distributed management and administration could also allow governments of different sizes to build positive relationships with each other, to discover new needs and to identify solutions for themselves. Considering the fact that these stakeholders are the primary producers and consumers of data and information on digital government (while the Center itself is a secondary producer/consumer), having them at the center of information sharing is key to this Center's success.

- **Search Services** - Search is incredibly cost-effective in bringing a wealth of underutilized information and knowledge to the surface (Copeland, 2001; Kim, Chaudhury & Rao, 2002). The scope of the domain that a search engine covers is not limited by the physical boundary of the e-government center but encompasses all electronically available data, information, and expertise related to digital government. This will result in much better informed stakeholders and the manual and automatic search outputs will also be used to update data and the information set through the asynchronous communication channel.

- **Knowledge Management Services** - Most information repository applications (Heintz, 2003) require business intelligence tools integrated into the infrastructure. Knowledge management includes the aggregation of information from multiple heterogeneous data sources; content management including versioning, auditing, and lifecycle management; content analysis supported by visualization tools to identify patterns and relationships in data and interactions; records management (Hunter & Jupp, 2002; Zahir, Dobing & Hunter, 2002); and click-stream analysis.

- **System Management Services** - A variety of system management services includes: user registration from which the center collects and manages participant information; notification service of newly available applications and knowledge; user activity logging and tracking; setting cookies for easier user access; Web applications server and data warehouse server log-file analysis; providing a set of tools administration, and system workspace management.

- **Virtual Communities** - Participants in this project can work not only as individuals, but they can also build and participate in a community. Stakeholders and users of this e-government center can classify themselves as members of involved communities. Once a community is formed and the members of each community identified, information exchange and communication in the community become more efficient and focused. Concentrated and in-depth information exchange and sharing will be preeminent in this community. Large projects or joint-project follow-ups can be supported easily in this Center. In addition, it becomes easy to deploy multiple, focused communities, because the technology infrastructure proposed has already taken this into account.

The quality of information and services voluntarily posted by participants is very difficult to evaluate. This information asymmetry - in which the quality of information is not fully available to the consumers - often leads to undesirable results, that of an inefficient community outcome. There is often no critical mass for an information clearinghouse to deliver synergetic outcome through this new intermediation channel. To maintain or enhance the quality of information and applications shared in the excellence center, especially in its early stage of deployment, we propose to create peer evaluation programs that provide additional sets of information quality assessment instruments, and to provide affiliate programs to make this active participation as an incentive compatible mechanism.

- **Project Management and Tracking Services** - Clearinghouses or portals in businesses often provide services to communicate appropriate information to each type of user throughout its supply chain. In e-government systems, we expect that the same feature will be required. This leads to the challenge of connecting the Center to legacy or back-end information systems. Within our framework, connectivity will be provided by an *external service* in the technology infrastructure layer. From various supply chain management functionalities, we can incorporate project management features including a customized calendar and RFP (request for proposal) deadlines posting services. The data collected from this project tracking system will be used as a measure for effectiveness, efficacy, and improvement.

- **Presentation Services** - This framework includes the presentation services that manage the look and feel of the user interface and enhance user experience. Customization of data provided by the center occurs at various levels. The information provided to the users by the center may require tailoring to support various client devices and needs as well as their usage based on the taxonomy of applications and the task at hand.

In order to avoid having this Center become simply a collection of pockets of standalone information and knowledge, administration strategies are another important element. The development and launching of other information portals offer us ready lessons in how to prevent a portal from becoming an information island. An excellence center needs to keep as its goal and strategy its integration into existing business processes and organizational culture.

# Future Research

There are two separate sets of suggestions for future research. One addresses how such a Center for Excellence in e-government can work in intra-country situations, and the second addresses how cross-cultural issues may affect a more international use of the Center. First, the Center would allow for the study of patterns of communications among different stakeholders. Such analysis would allow for development of more efficient communication and knowledge exchange patterns. Moreover, it would be possible to understand the diffusion of innovations with direct implications for public policy and investment.

One of the most interesting observations related to the second set of suggestions regards the differences in e-government implementations across the world (Hunter & Jupp, 2002). Countries like Canada (Allen, Juillet, Paquet & Roy, 2001) have maintained their lead almost from the very beginning of the e-government trend, while others have not yet been able to make large strides toward digitalization of government. Clearly, some of this is due to the digital divide (Compaine, 2001), but other issues are also relevant. An analysis of other countries shows the relevance of cultural and political reasons (e.g., Li, 2003; Wong, 2003).

This raises an interesting set of future research questions: first, how one can take advantage of the cultural make-up of certain countries to create synergies toward e-government implementation; second, how an e-government excellence center can help bridge such differences.

# Conclusion

In this chapter we have proposed a Center of Excellence on G2G e-government as an approach to helping the transition from a traditional government to a digital government. The customers for such a Center are government agencies, both as suppliers and as consumers, thus defining a G2G environment. We believe that such a Center will enhance the value of e-government, creating a level of awareness of solutions already existing or able to be developed. At the same time, the creation of such Center is likely to improve the service level even of agencies very experienced in e-government solutions, since they will be challenged or benchmarked by newcomers. As an added bonus, we expect that such an understanding may bring the very tangible benefit of lowered risk in large expensive e-government projects (Pardo & Scholl, 2002).

Our framework for an e-government Center presents a concrete vision for its development and implementation, including (1) the basic technology infrastructure layer and (2) the ecology layer describing the e-government environment. The drafting of this framework follows the needs analysis for G2G e-government at different levels and the lessons learned from deploying e-commerce and e-business clearinghouses.

The primary objective of our Center is a value-added e-government, but what we describe in this chapter is only the beginning of an open-ended opportunity. We expect not only that this Center will deliver direct value to its immediate customers (first to government agencies and then on to citizens), but also indirect value through its ability to provide research tools which will lead to yet further benefits to scholars and to citizens.

# References

Allen, B.A., Juillet, L., Paquet, G., & Roy, J. (2001). E-governance & government on-line in Canada: Partnerships, people and prospects. *Government Information Quarterly, 18,* 93-104.

Becker, D., George, M., Goolsby, A., & Grissom, D. (1998). Government: The ultimate service turnaround. *The McKinsey Quarterly, 1.*

Brazilian Government. (2003). *Brasil: Um pais de todos.* Retrieved on October 15, 2003, from *http://www.brazil.gov.br.*

Canada Post. (2003). *Canada Post.* Retrieved October 15, 2003, from *http://www.canadapost.ca.*

City of Chicago. (2003). *City of Chicago.* Retrieved October 15, 2003, from *http://egov.cityofchicago.org/city/webportal/home.do.*

Compaine, B. (2001). Re-examining the digital divide. In *The digital divide: Facing a crisis or creating a myth.* Boston: MIT Press.

Copeland, R. (2001, May 21). More than a pretty interface. *InformationWeek.*

eGov Links. (2003). *E-government starting point. http://www.egovlinks.com/.*

Erin Research Inc. (1998). *Citizen centered service network and the Canadian Centre for Management Development.* Canada.

FirstGov.com. (2003). *Official U.S. gateway to all government information. http://firstgov.gov/.*

Fulla, S., & Welch, E. (2002). *Framing virtual interactivity between government and citizens: A study of feedback systems in the Chicago Police Department.* Paper presented at the 35th Hawaii International Conference on System Sciences, Hawaii.

Heintz, J.P. (2003). Migration of government information products to the Internet. *Portal: Libraries and the Academy, 3*(3), 481.

Ho, A.T.-K. (2002). Reinventing local governments and the e-government initiative. *Public Administration Review, 62*(4), 434-444.

Hunter, D.R., & Jupp, V. (2002). *eGovernment leadership - Realizing the vision.* Accenture.

IBM. (2002). *IBM framework for e-business. http://www-3.ibm.com/e-business/index.html.*

Jorgensen, D., & Cable, S. (2002). Facing the challenges of e-government: A case study of the city of Corpus Christi, Texas. *SAM Advanced Management Journal,* 15-30.

Kaylor, C., Deshazo, R., & Van Eck, D. (2001). Gauging e-government: A report on implementing services among American cities. *Government Information Quarterly, 18,* 293-307.

Ketchell, D.S. (2000). Too many channels: Making sense out of portals and personalization. *Information Technology and Libraries, 19*(4), 175.

Kim, Y.J., Chaudhury, A., & Rao, H.R. (2002). A knowledge management perspective to evaluation of enterprise information portals. *Knowledge and Process Management, 9*(2), 57.

Korea Ministry of Government Administration and Home Affairs. (2002). *Korea eGovernment egov.go.kr.* Retrieved April 5, 2003, from: *http://www.egov.go.kr/.*

Li, F. (2003). Implementing e-government strategy in Scotland: Current situation and emerging issues. *Journal of Electronic Commerce in Organizations, 1*(2), 44-65.

MARTA. (2002). *The Metropolitan Atlanta Rapid Transit Authority. http://www.itsmarta.com.*

Moon, M.J. (2002). The evolution of e-government among municipalities: Rhetoric or reality? *Public Administration Review, 62*(4), 424-433.

Pardo, T. (2000). *Realizing the promise of digital government: It's more than building a Web site.* Unpublished manuscript, Albany, NY.

Pardo, T., & Scholl, H.J. (2002). *Walking atop the cliffs: Avoiding failure and reducing risk in large scale e-government projects.* Paper presented at the 35th Hawaii International Conference on Systems Sciences, Hawaii.

Schwartz, K. (2000). Companies spin personalized portals to their advantage. *InformationWeek, 3.*

UK online. (2003). *UK online. http://www.ukonline.gov.uk/.*

United Nations. (2002). *Benchmarking e-government: A global perspective.* New York: United Nations.

Wong, P.-K. (2003). Global and national factors affecting e-commerce diffusion in Singapore. *The Information Society, 19,* 19-32.

Zahir, S., Dobing, B., & Hunter, M.G. (2002). Cross-cultural dimensions of Internet portals. *Internet Research, 12*(3), 210.

# Endnotes

[*]   An earlier version of this chapter was published in the Proceedings of the European Conference in e-Government, Dublin, September, 2001.

[*]   This research is sponsored in part by a grant from the Center for Research in Information Management, University of Illinois at Chicago.

[**]   The names of the authors are in alphabetical order.

## Chapter V

# Access Control Model for Webservices E-Government Infrastructure

Kam Fai Wong, The Chinese University of Hong Kong, China

Matthew Ka Wing Tam, The Chinese University of Hong Kong, China

## Abstract

*E-government is an exciting area for applying information and communication technologies (ICT). ICT can improve the efficiency and effectiveness in the provision and delivery of citizen services. A critical issue for the e-government implementation is the interoperation problem among heterogeneous legacy government systems. In this aspect, the universal system interoperability supported by the XML-based Web service technologies can be a useful component in a holistic e-government infrastructure. A key requirement of the e-government systems is the establishment and the implementation of the right access policy to the government resources. This in turn requires an appropriate mechanism to specify the access rules. Due to the nature of Web service and the specific requirements in the e-government context, we propose that a more powerful and flexible mechanism is required to express the access policy more effectively in a Web services e-government infrastructure.*

# Introduction

The recent rapid development of e-commerce has demonstrated how the advancement in data communication technology (in particular the explosion of Internet connections) can enable business transactions to be conducted electronically and in a more efficient way than the traditional business process. Given the successful e-commerce implementation in the private sector, we naturally develop the same expectations for applying data communication technology in government systems. E-government projects may be viewed as the answers to meet these expectations.

As pointed out in Arcieri's article (Arcieri, Cappadizzi, Nardelli & Talamo 2001), a critical issue for the e-government projects is the interoperability problem among heterogeneous legacy government systems. A general solution to the problem requires effective tools and methodologies to provide easy and seamless connections between systems that were developed by different people, running in different environments and under different software/hardware platforms. Although there have been a whole family of distributed computing solutions developed by different software vendors and standard bodies, none has received sufficient acceptance to ensure that e-government systems building upon which can achieve universal interoperability.

In this aspect, the Web service technology is probably a breakthrough in the area of system integration. Building upon XML, which is a truly platform-neutral technology, the Web services interoperability standards are quickly accepted by the major software industry vendors. For the first time in the software history, we now have the core technologies that promise to achieve universal software interoperability on the Internet. As a tool to solve the interoperability problem, it is not difficult to see that the Web services technologies can serve as a useful component in e-government.

Due to the dependency of citizens on government services, e-government must be highly trustworthy. According to an e-government survey conducted by Taylor Nelson Sofres (Taylor Nelson Sofres, 2001), security is a major concern of most potential users of the e-government services. We believe that the enforcement of the appropriate access policy is an essential prerequisite of any e-government solution, including the Web service based one. We have examined the detailed requirements on access control for a Web service based e-government. Based on our analysis, we conclude that the traditional access control mechanisms are inadequate for the Web service based e-government environment. To address this predicament, we propose a flexible framework that is composed of two key components: the Web service specific access control and the subject based control.

# Webservice as an Interoperability Solution

Most organisations are faced with the problem of integrating a large number of legacy systems, and solutions for enterprise application integration (EAI) have always been in strong demand. Driven by the market, a whole family of distributed computing solutions have been invented over the years. These include RPC from Sun, COM/DCOM from Microsoft and COBRA from the Object Management Group (OMG). Unfortunately, none of these products have enjoyed widespread acceptance and this has greatly limited the usefulness of these solutions for universal interoperability. As a result, integration solution providers are often forced to build new adapters when a new connection is required, effectively reinventing the wheel every time.

The lesson learnt is that to achieve universal interoperability, we need standards that are both vendor neutral and supported by all vendors. With the recent emergence of XML, the industry has been quick to recognize its potential as the building block for truly language and platform-neutral standards. To this end, a suite of eXtensible Markup Language (XML)-based Web service technologies (Chappell & Jewell, 2002; Graham et al., 2001) has been evolved as the most promising solution to *enable* global system interoperation:

- Simple Object Access Protocol (SOAP) is an XML-based protocol for exchanging structured information in a decentralized, distributed environment. SOAP provides an "http-friendly" protocol for systems to talk over the Internet, to request and to serve for Web services (W3C, 2000);

- Web Service Description Language (WSDL) is an XML format for describing network services. WSDL allows the client to understand how to invoke a Web service (W3C, 2001);

- Universal Description, Discovery, and Integration (UDDI) is a Web service based standard for registration and search of network services. UDDI provides a Web services discovery platform on the Internet (Boubez, Hondo, Kurt, Rodriguez & Rogers, 2002).

As we can see from the definitions of Web services given by the major players (IBM [Feller, n.d.], Microsoft ["XML Web Services," n.d.] and Sun [Sun, 2002]), Web services are about providing services over the network via standard XML wire format. Thus, each vendor can have a different Web service architecture that is most appropriate to its proprietary platform (Myerson, 2002), and at the same time adhering to the same XML standards, which facilitates successful interoperation with any service consumers sticking to the same standards. The wide acceptance of these standards by the major software industry players, and the fact that the standards are platform and language neutral, makes Web services technologies a promising solution to solve the universal interoperation problems presented by many of today's software systems, including e-government.

# Webservices for E-Government – A Marriage for Interoperability

There are a number of structural differences between the public sector and the private one (Traunmuller & Wimmer, 2000):

- The legal framework plays a vital part in the government systems.
- There is a high level of non-instrumental rationality in the public sector.
- Usually there are many stakeholders involved in a government process, which requires high level of collaboration.

In addition, there are also different expectations to the government bodies as compared to the private sector. In particular, government is dealing with the well-being of a society as a whole and there should be equal access of its services to all citizens (Traunmuller & Wimmer, 2000). This provides a strong justification for the implementations of e-government-on-the-Web projects.

We will examine the application of Web service technologies to meet the following expectations:

- efficient operation;
- citizen-centric government;
- security;
- support of e-business.

## Efficient Operation

E-government or digital government can enhance the efficiency of the public sector by automating labour intensive government processes. However, a more significant efficiency and productivity gain is usually achievable when a fundamental redesign of the processes is done together with a new system, effectively a reengineering of the government using information technology (Mechling, 1994). This may also involve back office integration within the government body to eliminate the manual transmittal of data between system components.

Both the process reengineering and back office integration stops at the boundary of the individual government departments. However, there are large numbers of government processes that require collaboration among different departments, which offer ample opportunities for another level of streamlining and process reengineering beyond a single government body.

The recent SARS disease outbreak in Hong Kong does offer a good example to demonstrate the importance of information sharing across the government departments.

The task to fight against the disease involved different activities including the hospital treatment for the infected, the trace of infection source, the quarantine of the potential infected, public education and the release of latest statistics of the disease to the public. Each of these activities may be responsible by a single or jointly by several government departments. The effort of each department must however be well coordinated to achieve the desired result. For example, the trace of infection source was based on the information of patients obtained from the hospital treatment and any new reported SARS case should initiate a trace. In this case, it would be very useful if the systems of the responsible departments could exchange the information automatically to fit in a workflow. As another example, during the critical period, the government of Hong Kong was expected to release the latest statistics of the disease to the public every day. This required the collection of the data from the individual hospitals receiving SARS patients. The ability to extract the data from the systems of the hospital directly would make it possible to automate the entire task and certainly improve the efficiency of the reporting significantly.

In addition, as observed by Virili (Virili, 2001), a large source of government inefficiency exists simply because the database systems of government branches are implemented independently. As a result, citizen data are distributed and often duplicated among these databases and there is no easy way to get a consistent view of the citizen's data across the departments.

Without the technology to achieve interoperation between the systems, inter-department or G2G (government-to-government) streamlining is difficult to achieve. We can thus see that Web services as an integration tool will have great value in facilitating the streamlining of G2G processes. To a less extent, the technology is also valuable in the intradepartment process reengineering exercise as a tool for back office integration.

# Citizen-Centric Government

Unlike a private organisation, one of the government's missions is to make the services available to *all* citizens. To meet this goal, e-government systems are required to provide equal accessibility to all the citizens in an easy-to-use way. Putting all the government services on the Web is a major step toward this end, which provides around-the-clock access to the government services in any location via the Internet. This can be achieved in different stages ("No Gain Without Pain," 2000), with each subsequent stage requiring integration of more legacy functions to the Web server in a more sophisticated way, and it is obvious that application of webservice technologies should be able to simplify the work. For example, the last stage calls for a portal that integrates the complete range of government services, and provides a path to them that is based on need and function, not on department or agency. Usually the portal provides grouping of government services by "life events": few people visit the government sites for information surfing and citizens usually use e-government for a purpose; the "life events" grouping provides a means for a citizen to locate the required service quickly. Building such a portal should be much easier if all the required legacy functions have been exposed as Web services.

The access of e-government using a Web browser is a major improvement to government service delivery. The expectation will however be for more means to access the e-government. Sooner or later, following a similar access pattern in e-commerce services, the requirement to access the e-government over other electronic devices like smart mobile phones and PDAs will be taken for granted. In particular, service delivery to non-computing devices like the touch-tone telephone handset is viewed as a way to narrow the digital divide, so that access to electronic government service is not limited to those PC-literates. Without the Web service technologies to achieve universal interoperability, the connection of the legacy government systems to all these different types of devices can be a daunting task requiring tedious case-by-case integration efforts.

The term "joined-up government" is sometimes used to describe a holistic government structure, in which the citizens requiring government services does not need to care about which department does what. One example of such vision can be found in the Italian e-government action plan (Virili, 2001):

- Any authorised "front office" administration should supply any service to any entitled citizen;
- After being identified, the citizen should not be requested to furnish any personal information already in procession by another administration;
- Citizens should communicate any changes of their personal information only once.

For a truly citizen-centric e-government, the joined-up government should be an important goal to achieve. It is easy to see that the achievement of joined-up government would require a high level and seamless integration among the government systems.

## Security

Due to the dependency of citizen on government services, e-government is expected to be highly trustworthy. This demands strong security built in the e-government systems. To achieve true security to access government systems, we need to protect against unintended interruption of the e-government services, whether caused by accident or as a result of malicious attacks. This is very important especially for those government services related to the public security. Indeed, the importance of the government systems availability has received increasing attention recently when people start to think about the possible fatal consequences of breakdown in a life maintaining service (e.g., the fire-fighting service) during a critical moment.

Much of the means to enhance e-government availability will have to do with the overall system infrastructure, for example a more resilient data network or more redundancy incorporated in the processing equipment. However, in terms of e-government access the expectation will be a wider range of supported channels to provide mutual backup of access. In particular, wireless access to e-government systems will become more important to ensure the availability of essential services during crisis situations. This will require the connection of government systems not only to the Web browser, but also to different types of electronic devices that are capable to utilise the service, for example smart mobile phone, PDA device, and so forth.

# Support of E-Business

Today few governments would allow the economy to run entirely on its own. In fact, all the modern governments have economic policies to safeguard the economic well-being of society. As one of these economic goals, promotion of IT adoption is pursued by most governments as an opportunity to improve the living standard of the citizens and enhance the competitiveness of the society's economic power. For example, the Hong Kong SAR government has put "promoting the wider use of IT in the community and improving public access to online services" as part of the "Digital 21" Strategy (HKSAR ITSD, 2001).

To this end, the government has at least two roles to play. Firstly, as the e-business facilitator the government is expected to ensure that the necessary infrastructure and environment is in place for electronic transactions to take place efficiently and securely. In particular, as the government is the provider of a large number of services essential to the operation of every business, the efficient delivery of the e-government services is an important driver to the adoption of e-commerce. One way this can be done is to provide an easy means to achieve G2B system integration to allow straight through consumption of e-government services.

Secondly, as a major player in the economy, the government can play the role as a leader in adoption of new technologies. Being both an effective tool for enterprise application integration and an inexpensive alternative to the EDI solutions to support exchange of information between businesses (B2B integration), the Web service technologies have a lot of applications in the private sector. In this aspect, successful applications of Web service technologies in e-government projects can set good examples on how the technologies can be used beneficially.

# Related Researches

As we have seen, interconnectivity among government systems is a prerequisite to address many of the existing problems in the public sector (efficiency and citizen usability problems due to fragmented government processes, insufficient means of e-government access to ensure accessibility to key government resources during disaster situations, etc.). The interoperability problem among the heterogeneous legacy government systems is thus a critical issue of e-government (Arcieri, Cappadizzi, Nardelli & Talamo, 2001). There have been much research efforts to address the issue and the solutions suggested can be broadly classified into two categories:

- use of metadata and information integration technique to provide a single integrated user interface for access to diversified but interrelated databases from different government departments, for example the Energy Data Collection (EDC) (Ambite et al., 2001) and COPLINK (Chen, Zeng, Atabakhsh, Wyzga & Schroeder, 2003) projects;

- development and migration of existing applications to a cooperative information system (CIS) architecture (Mylopoulos & Papazoglou, 1997) based on middleware and distributed computing technologies, for example the Unitary Network (Mecella & Batini, 2001) of the Italian Public Administration.

The two approaches are not mutually exclusive and can be applied in combination to supplement each other. An interesting example can be found in the work of Bouguettaya et al. (Bouguettaya, Ouzzami, Medjahed & Cameron, 2001) on the databases of the Indiana Family and Social Services Administration (FSSA) and the US Department of Health and Human Services (HHS).

The metadata approach attempts to solve the e-government problems at the user interface level. Its main purpose is to hide the diversity of government databases from the users to alleviate the usability problem. The approach per se does not address the interconnectivity issue directly. It seems that further research is required to demonstrate its usefulness beyond data query applications.

As a more general approach, the CIS architecture is targeted to enable seamless and painless interconnections among e-government processes at the method level. It is thus able to provide a more complete built-in solution to the interoperability problem. To meet its goal, the architecture must however be built on the right distributed computing technologies. While this is an area used to be fitted in by the traditional tools like COBRA and Java RMI, the universal interoperability promised by the webservice technologies make them an attractive option for the CIS approach [Medjahed, Rezgui, Rouguettaya & Ouzzani 2003]. The Web service based e-government architecture can thus be viewed as an implementation of the CIS architecture based on the XML Web service technologies.

# E-Government Webservices Access Control

To safeguard the government resources in a Web service environment, we need to control the accesses to the government Web services. With the control in place, whenever there is a request (from outside or within the government domain) to use a government Web service, the access will be accepted or rejected according to whether the requesting party is authorised to use the service.

A key issue in the Web service based e-government system is that we need an infrastructure to support the access control requirement. The Web service technologies are to achieve interoperability between the government systems. The implementation of the access control at the individual department or Web service level will, however, be likely to introduce new interoperability problems, which could defeat the whole purpose of using the technologies.

To better understand the requirements of such a global access control mechanism, we will have a closer look of the following components:

- e-government Web service
- access to e-government Web service
- e-government access policy

# E-Government Web Service

In a Web service based e-government system, government services are provided to the users in the form of service components deployed as Web services. These include internal services provided within a government body to facilitate system integration, inter-department services provided across government departments to support inter-department process streamlining, or delivery of citizen services requiring cross-department processing, and public services provided to allow government services to be embedded in private business systems.

Different access control requirements apply to each type (internal, inter-department, public) of government Web services. For example, a public government service that involves citizen data access would require citizen level access right, to ensure that each citizen can only access his/her own data via the Web service. The access control mechanism should thus support authentication of the Web service user identity. On the other hand, a G2G Web service not involving citizen data may be accessible by all or selected government departments, and thus the access right would solely be determined by the identity of the Web service consumer.

The diversity of access control requirements must be adequately addressed by the e-government access control mechanism. In particular, the mechanism must provide adequate flexibility to express the different types of Web service access rules precisely and efficiently. More important, the mechanism should be able to provide a level of infrastructure support such that the Web service developers do not have to worry about the access control. In other words, this should allow each Web service to be developed without any knowledge of who will and should access it. The Web service developer should focus on the business logic of the service; the mechanism to grant or reject an access request to the Web service should be the sole responsibility of the access control mechanism and must not be "hardwired" in the Web service. This is to isolate and thus protect the Web service from any changes in access policy. Any changes in the access policy related to a Web service (e.g., a change of access right due to a reorganization) should only affect the access control setting for the Web service and should require nothing more than the modification of its access control parameters. In what follows we will refer to the requirement to allow a Web service to be developed independent of the access policy as the "policy neutral" requirement.

# Request of Access

The access control mechanism is responsible to determine whether each access request to a Web service should be accepted or rejected. In terms of the network environment, a Web service request can be made from a system connected to the same LAN as the Web service provider, a system connected to the government intranet, or just from the Internet. As one of the requirements, the access control mechanism should support access rules based on the means of access.

To illustrate the requirement, let us look at an internal Web service that provides electronic filing service to other electronic processes of the same government department. It is likely that this Web service should be provided only to systems of the department that owns the electronic filing. This would translate into an access policy that only access requests from the department LAN should be accepted.

Another example would be an e-procurement Web service offered by the central government procurement department. While this service should be offered to a much wider user base than the electronic filing Web service in the previous example, the access should still be limited to within the government. The access policy for this service will have some parts tied up with a requirement that all access requests not from the government intranet should be rejected.

Association of access rights based on the means of access is a useful way to capture the e-government Web service access policy. However, a more general access policy should have rights associated with the identities of parties requesting for the service. This is in close analog with the access control commonly employed on a time-sharing system, which provides access rights based on the user identity. To access a resource on the system, for example a database file, a user should first request the necessary "privilege" of the file and subsequently all processes associated with that user will be granted access to the file.

Unlike the access to an object in a time-sharing system, an access to a Web service can be associated with more than one party (the equivalence of the "system user" in a time-sharing system). This can be illustrated with a Web service example. As a legal requirement in Hong Kong, the owner of a private car must submit his/her car for an inspection for roadworthiness every year starting from the seventh year after the manufacture date. The inspection service is outsourced to a few testing centres, who will issue a Certificate of Roadworthiness to the vehicle owner if the car passes the tests. The certificate must be presented for the subsequent vehicle licence renewal. Suppose that the process is streamlined to eliminate the physical Certificate of Roadworthiness. To achieve this, a Web service can be provided to the test centers to update the examination record of the vehicle directly to reflect the test result. Renewal of the vehicle can then be based on the updated record and the certificate will no longer be required. Such Web service will be accessed by the system of the test center as a consumer, acting on behalf of the vehicle owner as the end user.

Since the Web service would update the vehicle record, access to the Web service should be granted only if the request is made on behalf of the vehicle owner. In addition, the service should only be accessible from the test centers, not from anyone on the Internet. As such, the access should be granted based on the identity of both the end user and the consumer.

There are other possibilities. For instance, access right may be determined based on the identity of the consumer only, as in our previous example of the electronic filing Web service, which should serve all the systems on the same LAN. On the other hand, for most public citizen information enquiry Web services, for example a tax assessment enquiry service, it is sufficient to have end user based access right, as the identity of the consumer is not important for the access decision.

A more complicated (and interesting) situation arises when a service is requested as a result of a chain of Web service execution. The chained Web service model is useful to support processes that require collaboration from different government departments. In this situation, when an end user initiates the process, a request will be made to access the first Web service on the chain. As all the subsequent Web services except the last one in the chain need an additional service from another department to fulfill its function, each will request for another Web service along the chain, until the end of the chain is reached, which will be a Web service that can complete on its own. In terms of the access right, we should view each access request as made jointly by the owner system(s) of the Web service(s) on the chain preceding that Web service. If the Web service is accessible by any one or more of these systems, the access should be accepted. In other words, we should combine the access rights of all the consumer systems when there is more than one consumer involved in an access request.

# E-Government Access Policy

The data access policy for the systems of any modern governments is inherently a complicated subject. Firstly, the size of the problem is huge in terms of the number of potential users (including all citizens, civil servants and government departments) and the number of government systems. Also, government systems and databases are largely developed independently of one another, usually with little consideration for security interoperability. As a result, it is likely that significant effort needs to be taken to tackle the problems of semantic heterogeneity and conflicting security policies in the different government domains (Joshi, Ghafoor, Aref & Spafford, 2002) to work out a government access policy on a global basis.

Perhaps not as a surprise, the adoption of a Web service e-government infrastructure, the primary objective of which is to solve the general interoperability issues of e-government projects, also helps to resolve the security interoperability problem. This is because by extracting into Web service components, only those existing business functions provided by the legacy system, a Web service based e-government system can be viewed as a group of business objects accessible by potential users and systems and the access to information resources are through the well-defined Web service interfaces.

## Administration Based Policy

It is useful to distinguish between two types of Web service access policies. The first type covers those access rules that are based on administrative arrangements at a department level. Most of the access rules for the internal Web services fall in this category, as the access to these Web services should be formulated based on the organization structure of the Web service owner department. Also, administration based access rules may be derived from explicit arrangements (e.g., in the form of a legal contract or inter-department agreement) between the Web service provider and another party to provide the business service to that party. For example, if the transport department may have an outsourcing agreement to subcontract the vehicle inspection service to a private operated testing center, the testing center should be granted with the access right to the appropriate vehicle record update Web service as a consumer, on behalf of the vehicle owner. Lastly, this type of policy also applies to the infrastructure or administration related Web services, as the right to access the services is covered by the service level agreement (also known as performance pledge in Hong Kong) committed by the service department.

The above examples reveal a few properties of the administration based access policy. Firstly, it is to deal with the Web service specific access, as the access right is based on the service to be provided to the potential consumers/users. Therefore, we will have specific access rules for each Web service. Secondly, security interoperability is not an issue here, as all the access decisions can be made within the department, either based on the organisation or explicit agreements with outsiders. Lastly, there is no mandatory need to disclose the access policy in force to parties outside the department. In some cases, the disclosure is actually undesirable, as it will reveal some sensitive organisational information of or confidential arrangements made by the service department. Therefore, it is more appropriate to handle the administration based access policy within the service department.

## Legislation Based Policy

Administration based access policy is not adequate when the provider of the Web service does not have the authority to decide all the access rights. In this case, we need a source of access policy that can be applied in the global government level. This is when the legislation based access policy comes into play. It is a norm in modern governments that a comprehensive legal framework should be in place to provide the legal basis for all government activities, and in particular the interaction between government bodies and the citizen or among different government bodies. The formulation of access policy beyond the provider's domain can and should thus be based on the legislation relevant to the government service provided.

In the Web service environment, the legislation based access policy dictates access right to a Web service if the access by the user to the business service offered or the information resources encapsulated by the Web service is explicitly approved by the law. The law does not however specify the access right in the form of Web services. Instead, the security subjects (the business service/information resources) are described by legal terms in the relevant pieces of legislation. As such, legislation based access policy is based on the legal subjects and specifies who can access these subjects. The full set of legislation based access policy can thus be viewed as a set of the legal subjects and the authorised parties to access each of them. It is thus important for any access control mechanism to support an easy translation of the access rule from the policy extracted from government rulebooks or statutory documents.

To apply the policy by a Web service access control mechanism, a mapping between the security subjects and the legal subjects is necessary. This mapping can be a many-to-many one, which means that multiply legal rules can apply to a single Web service, and one rule can apply to more than one Web service.

The task of working out the mapping for all security subjects is a complicated task requiring significant efforts from both technical and legal experts. For e-government Web services that are based on existing business services, however, it is likely that the provider of the Web service is familiar with the relevant legislatures and thus the legal subjects that should apply to the underlying business service. As such, it is unnecessary to work out the mapping from scratch. This is certainly an advantage of the Web service based e-government structure.

The task is less straightforward when a Web service is introduced for a new business service. In this case, the most difficult part of the task is to locate the relevant statutory applicable to the service. In reality, however, most government departments are established based on a well-defined piece of legislation. For example, the Inland Revenue Department and Company Registrar of Hong Kong are based on the Inland Revenue Ordinance (Chapter 112 of Laws of Hong Kong) and the Companies Ordinance (Chapter 32 of Laws of Hong Kong), respectively. It is highly probable that the relevant legal subjects of the services provided by a department are covered in the corresponding legislation; for example the submission of tax return to the Inland Revenue Department is covered in Part IX of the Inland Revenue Ordinance. Accordingly, if a Web service is to be set up for tax return submission, each citizen should have the access right to submit his/her own return.

The legal framework does not only provide an authoritative source for access policy. It also provides a common vocabulary to describe the security subjects and thus serves to resolve the problem of semantic heterogeneity in different e-government domains. In addition, provided that the legal framework is reasonably well integrated and self-consistent, the chance of conflicting security policies derived is minimal. (Nevertheless, there is still a need to resolve the possible inconsistency within the legal framework, as we will return to this point later.)

The legal subject referred to in a legislation based access rule may either be specific or general. The power to obtain the tax return is an example of a rule with a specific subject. Another example can be found in the Land Registration Regulations of Hong Kong (Chapter 128A of Law of Hong Kong), which stipulates in section 4 that the "Land Registry" should be open to the public.

An example for the general legal subject can be found in Hong Kong's Personal Data (Privacy) Ordinance (Chapter 486 of Law of Hong Kong), which spells out the access right for all "personal data" as any data that are "relating directly or indirectly to a living individual and from which it is practicable for the identity of the individual to be directly or indirectly ascertained and in a form in which access to or processing of the data is practicable" (HKSAR, 1996). The rule is that the "data subject" of each piece of personal data should be allowed to access the data. As such, any Web service encapsulating personal data should be granted with access to the subject of the data. This clearly applies to a large range of government services.

A similar example can be found in the Official Secrets Ordinance of Hong Kong (Chapter 521 of Law of Hong Kong), which covers sensitive information relating to security, intelligence and criminal investigation. In effect, no access to these data from anybody should be allowed other than those working directly with the data as part of their duty.

Normally, the law provides right to access to the general public (the "Land Registry" example), the data subject of the service (the "Personal Data" example), or a specific government body. The right of a tax assessor of the Inland Revenue Department in Hong Kong to obtain all tax related information of a citizen as stipulated in section 51 of the Inland Revenue Ordinance (Chapter 112 of Law of Hong Kong) is an example of the right provided to a specific government body. Unlike the administration based policy, the legislation based policy never spells out rights to individual service users. This is an important observation, which we will rely on later in our proposed access control mechanism.

Another interesting point is that there can be more than one source of access policies applying to the same legal subject. This may result in conflicting access rules applied to the same Web service. This is actually the result of inconsistent legislation and there is no easy way to resolve this other than the request for a court decision. Nevertheless, for legal systems that provide a hierarchical legislation structure (for example, the US Constitution takes precedence over all other forms of law in the state), some priority system can be adopted and this should be catered in the access control mechanism.

It is worthwhile to point out that legislation based access policy is not something new that is invented for the Web service based e-government structure. The legal framework is a key part of any modern government infrastructure and there must be an element of the legislation based access policy in any e-government structures. However, as illustrated above, the e-government Web services component model, which views each Web service as a well-defined interface to the security subjects, makes it easy to utilize this type of access policy.

Due to the different natures, it is more appropriate to handle the administration and legislation based access policies differently. When both types of policies apply to the same Web service, we can refer to the Web service specific (administration based) rules first, which are set up by the service provider. If the rules cannot determine whether an access request should be accepted or not, the subject (legislation based) rules can then be consulted.

# Existing Access Control Models

The traditional access control or access matrix mechanism (Lampson, 1971) can be modeled by an object system with a set of objects $X$ and a set of domains $D$. Objects are the things to protect, which can include program and data files. The domains related to the process execution environments with distinct access rights and the domain concept can cover ideas like user profile and other protection contexts. An authorization is specified by a triple $<d, x, p>$ to state that the domain $d$ is authorized to exercise privilege $p$ on object $x$. All the authorization triples are stored in an access matrix.

The access matrix is a fairly low-level mechanism that maps directly to the concepts in distributed operating systems and can thus be easily and efficiently accommodated in an operating system. However, it suffers from the problem that business access policy may not be translated naturally into triples in the access matrix. The Role-Based Access Control (RBAC) (Ferraiolo & Kuhn, 1992), on the other hand, is a more business oriented access control model. RBAC is based on the fact that access decisions in an organisation are often based on the roles individual users take on within the organisation. To apply this concept RBAC mechanism defines access rights by well-defined roles.

The basic RBAC scheme consists of three components: a set of well defined roles *R,* a set of subjects *S* and a set of transactions *T.* The subject set *S* corresponds to the users of the protected system. Each transaction *t* represents a transformation procedure on specific information resources. In the RBAC model, access decision is based on transactions; that is,  access right is expressed as whether a subject can execute a transaction. Authorisation is based on the roles and the access right set-up involves two steps: specification of transactions for each role, and the assignment of subject members to the role.

More recently, a family of Task Based Authorisation Control (TBAC) (Thomas & Sandhu, 1997) models were proposed to address the access control requirement in workflow-based processing. In the TBAC models, authorisation is granted and controlled via authorisation-steps. To obtain access to a protected resource, a process need to invoke the appropriate authorisation step, which can be granted from a number of pre-defined trustees of the authorization step. A key feature of the models is that there is a lifetime associated with each invoked authorisation step, based on either usage or time parameter. TBAC also allows interrelationships to be defined between authorization steps in the form of dependencies. There is however still a lot of work required before TBAC can be applied to a real-world problem like the e-government environment. For examples, a formal means is needed to specify the access policy according to the models.

All these models are based on the simple user concept in the traditional time-sharing system, and the access control decision can be made based on the identity of a single user party associated with the access request. An access to a Web service, on the other hand, can be associated with more than one party and a Web service access control infrastructure must therefore be able to accommodate access policies based on combination of user and consumer identity. For example, if a Web service to update the vehicle record of the transport department was provided to the police department to report vehicle theft, an access to the Web service should be accepted when the consumer is from the police department and the user is the owner of the vehicle. As a result, all these models failed to accommodate the access control requirement for a Web service environment.

In addition, these models are non-domain specific ones. As general solutions to the access control problems, these models do not cater well to some of the e-government specific situations:

- There are a lot of e-government services to provide access to citizen data. For these services, each citizen should be authorized to access his/own data only.  However, citizen level access right cannot be conveniently supported in these models and must be implemented within the Web service, which implies that the Web service cannot be developed in an "access policy neutral" manner.

- As we have seen, infrastructure or administration G2G Web services should be accessible by all consumer systems connected to the government intranet. Similarly, internal services provided to support integration of systems in the same government department should allow access from consumer systems via the department LAN. These access means based access right is not supported directly in the existing models and thus must be done indirectly on a consumer-by-consumer basis. This requires a separate access rule for each government or internal consumer, which is a tedious and inefficient way to specify the right.

- There is no provision for legal subject based authorization. Legislation based access policy cannot be expressed directly in the model and must be translated into object (Web service) access rights.

To provide a mechanism that work for Web services, and to provide a solution that better addresses the need for e-government access control, we propose a flexible access control framework that is composed of two key components: the Web service specific access control and the subject based access control.

# A Two-Level Access Control Model

In order to meet the requirements for a secured Web service based e-government system, we propose that a two-level access control mechanism can be used. We propose a scheme based on the access model developed by Bertino et al. (Bertino, Perego, Farrari, Adam & Atluri, 2002). The original model is to address digital libraries' access rights and we have made enhancements to apply to the Web service and provide the two-level access control.

The proposed two-level access control mechanism consists of two key components, namely: the Web service specific access control and subject based access control. We will first examine each of the two access right control components. We will then explain how these access rights can be applied to the Web service based e-government environment.

## Web Service Specific Access Control

The first level of access rights in the mechanism is those rights associated with individual e-government Web services. These access rights correspond to the administration based access policies, which, as we have demonstrated, are all Web service specific. This is the level of access control that should be implemented within the domain of the Web service provider.

## Web Service Access Rules

The Web service specific access rights are expressed by Web service access rules. Specifically, each rule consists of the following elements:

- a *user specification USER,* which specifies to the end user that the access rule applies. This may be the digital identification of a specific citizen or a government staff member, *ANONYMOUS (anonymous access), *CITIZEN (any citizen with a valid identification). Note that there is a difference between the anonymous and "any citizen" right when only access to the individual data subject is granted (see below). In this case, the former specifies unrestricted rights to use the Web service, while the latter implicitly specifies that the right granted is limited to use of the Web service to access the citizen data related to the end user. As such, *CITIZEN should only be applied to Web services that involved access to personal data.

- a *consumer specification CONSUMER,* which specifies the Web service consumer that the rule applies. This may be the digital identification of a specific government department or a private organization, *ANONYMOUS (anonymous access), *GOVERNMENT (access from the government intranet), or *LOCAL (access from the provider's LAN). The last two special values are to provide for specification of access right based on the physical means of access.

- a *Web service specification WS,* which specifies the government Web service governed by the rule. It is assumed that there is a naming system in place in each e-government domain to provide a unique identification for each individual government Web service within the domain.

- the *sign* of the access right; that is, whether the right to access the Web service is granted "+A" (right to access any data subject via the Web service), "+I" (right to access the user's data only via the Web service); or not "-".

We can denote a Web service access rule in the form of *<USER, CONSUMER, WS, "+/ -" >*. The following examples illustrate the working of the Web service access rule:

- <*citizen, *anonymous, ws-1, +I>: a request to access the Web service *ws-1* from any consumers will be accepted. If *ws-1* requires access to personal data, the access right is limited to the data of the requesting citizen. This is an example of a public government Web service that requires citizen level access right.

- <*anonymous, *government, ws-2, +A>: a request to access the Web service *ws-2* from any consumers connected to the provider of *ws-2* via the government intranet will be accepted. This is an example of a G2G infrastructure Web service not involving citizen data.

- <*anonymous, *local, ws-3, +A>: a request from any user to access the Web service *ws-3* via any consumers connected to the provider of *ws-3* via the local LAN will be accepted. This is an example of an internal service provided within a government department

- *<staff-1, *local, ws-4, +A>*: a request from *staff-1* to access the Web service *ws-4* via any consumers connected to the provider of *ws-4* via the local LAN will be accepted. If *ws-4* requires access to personal data, *staff-1* will be able to access the data of all data subject via the Web service. In this case, *staff-1* should be a staff whose day-to-day responsibility requires access to the corresponding citizen data. This is an example of a Web service specific right granted based on the status of the user.

- *<*citizen, consumer-1, ws-5, +I>*: a request to access the Web service *ws-5* from consumer *consumer-1* will be accepted. If *ws-5* requires access to personal data, the right granted by this rule is limited to data of the requesting citizen. This is an example of a government service that is to be embedded in the system of selected party.

- *<*anonymous, consumer-2, ws-6, ->*: any request to access the Web service *ws-6* from consumer *consumer-2* will be rejected. This illustrates the use of the "-" sign to explicitly revoke access from a particular consumer.

## Authorisation Conflict Resolution

Resolution of authorisation conflict is required when both positive ("+*A*" or "+*I*") and negative ("-") rights have been defined for the same access. Certainly we can require that all the rules specified are consistent with one another to avoid the conflict. However, allowing different access rights to be specified at different levels of user/consumer specificity is useful when we want to provide access to a general group of user/consumer, with a few individuals excluded. To utilise this feature, we provide an authorisation resolution rule, which specifies that a specific access right always take precedence over a more general right.

*Table 1: Priority of access rules based on the specificity of the user/consumer*

| Priority | User | Consumer |
|---|---|---|
| 1 (most specific) | A specific user | A specific consumer |
| 2 | *CITIZEN | A specific consumer |
| 3 | *ANONYMOUS | A specific consumer |
| 4 | A specific user | *GOVERNMENT/*LOCAL |
| 5 | *CITIZEN | *GOVERNMENT/*LOCAL |
| 6 | *ANONYMOUS | *GOVERNMENT/*LOCAL |
| 7 | A specific user | *ANONYMOUS |
| 8 | *CITIZEN | *ANONYMOUS |
| 9 (least specific) | *ANONYMOUS | *ANONYMOUS |

The rule of precedence is expressed in Table 1. To illustrate, suppose there are two rules: *<user-1, consumer-1, ws-1, ->* and *<*citizen, consumer-1, ws-1, +A>* both apply to an access request to *ws-1* made by *user-1* via *consumer-1*. Here, the first rule is of priority 1 (specific user and consumer) while the second rule is of priority 2 (*CITIZEN and specific consumer). As such, the first rule takes precedence and thus access will be rejected on the request. In effect, this combination of rules provides access of the Web service to all citizens via *consumer-1* except *user-1*. Without the authorisation conflict resolution rule, this situation would require a large number of access rules to explicitly grant the right to all citizen users individually except *user-1*.

# Subject Based Access Control

The second level of access rights in the mechanism is those rights associated with Web service subjects. These access rights correspond to the legislation based access policy, which is based on the legal subjects and specifies who can access these subjects. Subject based access control is to be operated over the individual government departments and this is the level of access control that should be implemented at a global level.

## Subject Category

The subject category is a repository of all the legal subjects that are the objects of access rights. The category should contain an entry for each legal subject with both the proper legal term and its source, which specifies the piece of legislature that is the source of the legal term. The source is included as reference information to the legal subject and usually it should be a pointer to the relevant interpretation section in the corresponding legislature. Inclusion of this reference provides a means to retrieve the legal interpretation of the subject when there are questions to the details of the underlying access policy later.

The subject category should provide a unique identification for each subject. The subject ID will be used in the subject access rules to associate the access rights to the subject.

## Subject Access Rules

The subject based access rights are expressed by subject access rules. Specifically, each rule consists of the following elements:

- a *user specification USER,* which specifies the end user to whom the access rule applies. The use and interpretation of this element is the same as in the Web service access rule except that only two values are allowed: *ANONYMOUS (anonymous access) or *CITIZEN (any citizen with a valid identification).

- a *consumer specification CONSUMER,* which specifies the Web service consumer to whom the rule applies. Same as in the Web service access rule.

- a *subject specification SUBJECT,* which specifies the legal subject Web service governed by the rule. This should contain the unique ID of legal subject that can link up with the subject category.

- a *privilege specification PRIVILEGE,* which specifies privilege granted or revoked by this rule. This may be *READ (read privilege) or *UPDATE (update privilege, which implies the *READ privilege).

- a *source specification SOURCE,* which specifies the legal source of the rule. This should contain a reference to the relevant piece of legislature which is the basis of the access right.

- a *priority specification PRORITY,* which optionally provides a priority number of the rules that can be used to resolve conflicting rules. This applies only to legal system that provides a hierarchical legislation structure (for example, the US Constitution takes precedence over all other forms of law in the state).

- the *sign* of the access right; that is, whether the right to access the Web service is granted "+*A*" (right to access any data subject via the Web service), "+*I*" (right to access the user's data only via the Web service); or not "-".

We can denote a subject access rule in the form of *<USER, CONSUMER, SUBJECT, PRIVILEGE, SOURCE, PRIORITY, "+/-">*. The following examples (which are based on the law of Hong Kong) illustrate the working of the subject access rule:

- *<*anonymous, *anonymous, "Land Registry," *read, "Land Registration Regulations s4," 1, +A>*: specifies that any user can request via any consumer system to Web services requiring read-only access to the Land Registry information;

- *<*citizen, *anonymous, "personal data," *update, "Personal Data (Privacy) Ordinance s22," 1, +I>* specifies that any user can request via any consumer system to Web services that will update his/her own personal data;

- *<*anonymous, "Inland Revenue Department," "tax related information data," ,*read, "Inland Revenue Ordinance s51," 1, +A>* specifies that request will be accepted via the Inland Revenue Department's system to Web services requiring read-only access to the "tax related information data".

## Web Service Registration

To apply the subject based access right to a Web service, we need to associate the Web service with the subject(s) representing the security subjects (the business service/ information resources) it encapsulates. This can be done by registering the Web service in the subject category, effectively mapping the Web service to the applicable subject(s). Note that the registration can be done locally within the provider's domain and a global registration database is not required.

A registration entry for a Web service should contain the following:

- the Web service to register;
- the subject id of the subject that the Web service should be associated with;
- the privilege of the subject that is required to access the Webservice; this can be *READ (read privilege) or *UPDATE (update privilege).

Once the registration is done, the subject based access control mechanism operates by referring to the access rules of all the subject(s) associated with the Web service. A request to access the Web service should be accepted if the necessary privilege on the associated subject has been granted by one of the rules in effect.

It is possible that a Web service is registered under more than one subject. This would happen when the security subjects are governed by more than one piece of legislation, or when the Web service encapsulates more than one security subject. In this case, the access test must be performed for all the associated subjects and a request should be accepted if the necessary privileges required for all the subjects are granted.

### Authorisation Conflict Resolution

Similar to the Web service access rules, it is possible that both positive ("+A" or "+I") and negative ("-") rights are defined for the same access in the subject based access control. This may reflect the need to define a general access rule supplemented by a few exceptions, as we have seen in the Web service access control example. However, this may also be the result from more than one source of access policy in force for the same legal subject. In each case, we need a similar schema to resolve the conflicts in authorisation.

When there is a conflict between two rules applying to the same subject, we will first resolve the conflict by the priority of the rule. The rule with the higher priority will take precedence. If both rules are of the same priority (or no priority is specified), the "specific over general" rule can be applied, although some modification on the rule of precedence is required to take into account the different values supported by the subject based access rules.

If all the above fail to resolve the conflict, the mechanism should reject the access and report the case as an exception (this is only possible when there is a conflict between different legislation provisions). This is the safe approach as the user can always request the business service with an alternative means.

## Combining Two-Level Access Control

In general the two levels of access control work independently. The Web service access rules work in a local context within the Web service provider's domain. The subject access rules work across the government and are controlled centrally. The Web service provider's role is restricted to the registration of the Web service.

It is possible that both types of access rights apply to the same Web service. Our rule is that the Web service access rules should always be consulted first. If the rules cannot determine whether an access request should be accepted or not, the subject rules can then be consulted. This is based on the assumption that the Web service provider should take into account all the relevant facts when the administration based (Web service specific) access policy is worked out and thus the rule should take precedence over the more general legislation based rights.

An exception will occur if both levels of access control cannot determine whether a request should be accepted. In this case, the request should be rejected. This is actually an arbitrary decision based on the fact that the user can always request the business service with an alternative means.

## Application to Chained Web Service Request

Both the Web service and subject access rules only accommodate one consumer party. As a result, the rules cannot be applied directly in the more complicated situation when a service is requested as a result of a chain of Web service executions. We have argued that we should view such access requests as made jointly by the owner systems of the Web services on the chain preceding the Web service. For the purpose of access control, we can view these requests as made with multiple consumers and we should combine the access rights of all the consumer systems. Along these lines, it is possible to extend the proposed mechanism to cover the chained Web service requests.

For the Web service access rights, we can first determine whether the request of a chained request should be accepted based on the identity of each consumer. To combine the access rights, the request should be accepted if any consumer has got the right to access the service.

Similar arrangement can be applied to the subject based rights. Here the schema should, however, work on the subject level. We should determine whether the required privilege on a subject is granted based on the identity of each consumer. If the privilege has been granted to any of the consumers in the request, it should be treated as granted. As such, when a Web service requires privileges to several security subjects, it is possible to access the Web service with a request made jointly by a group of consumers if their access rights add up to the required privileges, even though individually neither of them can access the Web service.

## Comparison with the Existing Access Control Models

As we have mentioned, the existing access control models cannot address the requirement of e-government Web service as they fail to support access rules based on combination of user and consumer identity.

In the proposed system, both a user specification and a consumer specification are in place in the access rules. This allows specification of rules based on combination of user and consumer identity and makes the system adequate to address the Web service requirements.

In contrast to the existing models, the proposed system also caters better to the e-government access control infrastructure with support for the following domain-specific requirements:

- citizen level access right can be specified directly with the sign of "+*I*";
- special consumer specification values *LOCAL and *GOVERNMENT are provided to express access rules based on physical means of access;
- the subject based access control component is in place to support legislation based access policy.

# An Implementation Reference Model

## System Architecture

To implement the two level access control model, a typical system architecture consists of the following:

- e-government Web services gateway
- authentication engine

*Figure 1: Proposed system architecture*

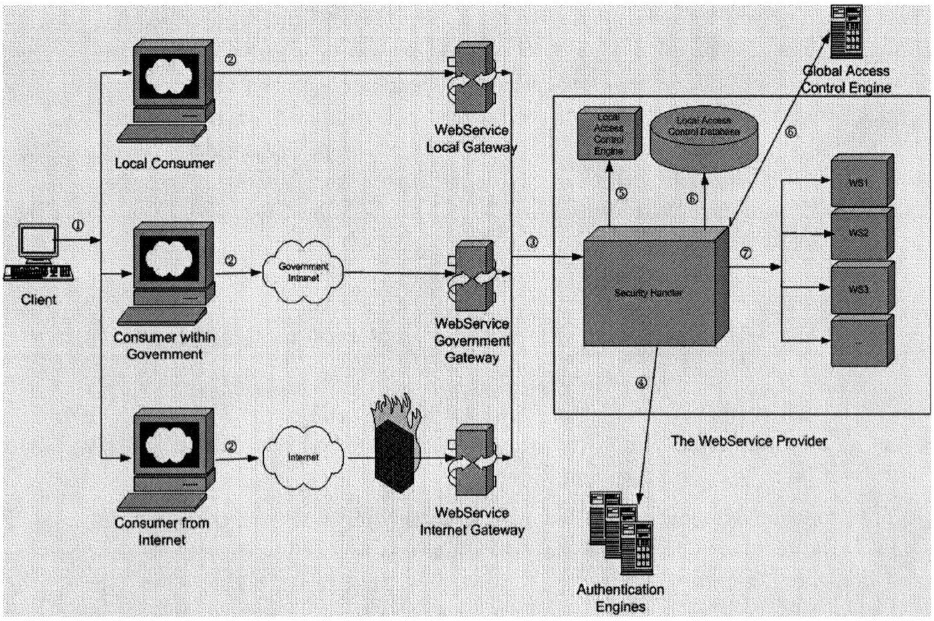

- access control database
- access control decision engine.

## E-Government Web Services Gateway

To protect the e-government Web service resources, access to the Web services should be restricted to well-defined access points. This can be achieved by e-government Web services gateways, which provide connection to the Web service from different network environments. A different gateway can be set up for access via the local LAN, the government intranet and the Internet.

For public service, consumer systems will able to submit the Web service request to the appropriate Internet Web service gateway via the Internet. Similarly, government consumer systems can access the e-government Web services via the government intranet gateway. For internal service, consumer systems connected to the Web service provider on the same LAN will request the Web service via the LAN gateway.

In each gateway, additional protection hardware and software (e.g., firewall) appropriate to the corresponding network environment can be added.

## Authentication Engine

The request for a Web service may contain the digital identification of the user and/or consumer. The access control decision will be made based on the identity of the user/ consumer corresponding to the digital identification.

It is the responsibility of the authentication engines to provide and prove the identity of the user/consumer based on the digital identification provided. To provide adequate protection to the citizens' privacy, there is a need to support multiple identity domains, both global and local ones managed by different departments. We have assumed that an authorization engine will be available for each identity domain. The security infrastructure of the provider should be able to locate and access the proper authorization engine corresponding to the digital identifications.

## Access Control Database

To implement the access control models, a number of databases should be maintained. In the local level, specific to the service provider, a database storing the Web service access rules for all the local Web services is required. This will be consulted to determine locally whether a request should be accepted based on the Web service access rights. In addition, the local database will also include the registration information of the local Web services. To invoke the subject based access control decision, this database provides information of the subjects associated with the Web service in question, which will be required to retrieve the appropriate subject access rules.

At the global level, a database storing the subject access rules will be maintained.

## Access Control Decision Engine

To handle the two levels of access control independently, two access control decision engines will be required. The local access control engine will make decision based on the Web service access rules. A subject access control engine that runs outside the provider's domain will be responsible to make decisions based on the subject rules.

In both cases, the engine should decide not only whether a Web service request should be accepted. It also has to determine whether the access right granted is based on a data subject specific access rule (e.g., a rule with the "+$I$" sign). If this is the case, the Web service request should be examined to check that the data subject accessed is that of the requesting citizen.

An important feature of the global engine is that the query should be based on generic citizen identity (*CITIZEN or *ANONYMOUS) and the legal subject. The use of generic citizen identity ensures that access request information of a citizen will not be disclosed outside of the service provider's domain. This is possible because the subject access rules only refer to generic user identifies. Also, use of legal subjects in the access control query instead of the Web service provides another privacy protection, as the global engine will not have any knowledge of the specific service the citizen is requesting.

## A Working Scenario

To illustrate how the different architecture components would work together, the UML sequence diagram of a working scenario to make the access control decision for a Web service request is provided in Figure 2. The step numbers referred in the example correspond to the same numbers in Figure 1.

1.  The user invokes a Web-based application on the consumer's system. The application requires the service of an e-government Web service.

2.  The consumer system prepares the necessary Web service request, with the digital identities as required by the Web service. The request is submitted to the appropriate gateway, depending on the type of consumer.

3.  The gateway routes the Web service requests to the appropriate provider, which is intercepted by the security handler of the provider's Web service engine.

4.  The security handler locates and invokes the appropriate authentication engine to use based on the digital identity. The request will be rejected if authentication fails. This step may be skipped if the request is an anonymous one.

5.  The local access control decision engine will be consulted to see whether the request should be accepted. The engine will make use of the local access control database to retrieve the rules applicable to the requested Web service. If the access is based on an access rule with specific data subject (ie a "+$I$" rule), the Web service request will be examined to check that the data subject accessed is that of the requesting citizen. If a decision can be made, the request will either be routed to the appropriate Web service (step 7) or rejected right away.

*Figure 2: Sequence diagram for a working scenario*

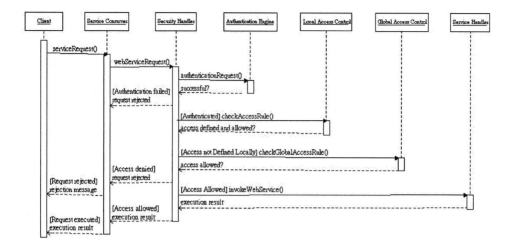

6.    If a decision cannot be made within the provider's domain, the subject(s) associated with the requested Web service will be retrieved from the local access control database and the global access control decision engine will be consulted to make a decision. If the access is based on an access rule with specific data subject (ie a "+*I*" rule), the Web service request will be examined to check that the data subject accessed is that of the requesting citizen. The request will be rejected according to the result of the decision.

7.    The request will be passed to the corresponding Web service.

## Implementation

We have implemented a prototype system on top of Apache Axis using the Java platform. The developed system is largely according to the architecture described previously with some minor simplifications.

Figure 3 shows a screenshot of the system when a request is prepared for a Web service invocation.

Once all the information has been input into the system, a SOAP request message will be generated and sent to the Web service provider. The access control information (user, consumer and medium type) is incorporated in a header element compatible with the WS-Security (Atkinson et al., 2002) standard. The following is an example of a header generated:

```
<soapenv:Header>
    <wsse:Security soapenv:actor="" soapenv:mustUnderstand="0"
        xmlns:wsse="http://schemas.xmlsoap.org/ws/2002/0
        4/secext">
        <wsse:UsernameToken>
            <wsse:Username>global:user1</wsse:Username>
        </wsse:UsernameToken>
        <ns1:ConsumerName
            xmlns:ns1="http://www.se.cuhk.edu.hk/~kwtam/
            eGov/">global:consumer1</ns1:ConsumerName>
        <ns2:AccessMeans
            xmlns:ns2="http://www.se.cuhk.edu.hk/~kwtam/
            eGov/">*GOVERNMENT</ns2:AccessMeans>
    </wsse:Security>
</soapenv:Header>
```

*Figure 3: A WebService request*

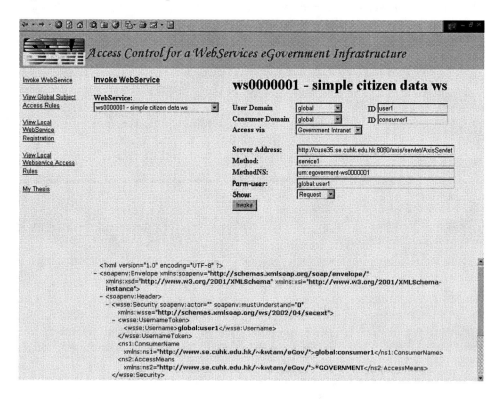

On the server side, the security handler (Figure 1) is implemented via a SOAP Message Handler, which is defined by the JAX-RPC standard. With Apache Axis, the access control can be "plugged-in" to the e-government Web service by incorporating the handler information in the Web Service Deployment Descriptor (WSDD) for the published Web service.

The implemented security handler performs the following functions:

- intercept the SOAP request message before the request is processed by the provider
- extract the access control information from the WS-Security header
- check the local Web service based access control database for access right
- consult the Global Access Control Engine (Figure 1) for subject based access right, if necessary
- check that the data subject accessed is that of the user, in case the access right is "+*I*" (this is done by inspecting the appropriate element of the SOAP body for the request parameter that is representing the data subject based to the provider)
- reject the request if the access right is not granted, or a data subject other than the requesting user is tried to be accessed without a "+*A*" right
- pass the request to the provider if the request is authorized

The Global Access Control Engine is implemented as a separate Java function, which can either be invoked locally as a Java method, or consumed as a published Apache Axis Web service.

Both the local and global access control databases are maintained as xml files, which are loaded by the local security handler and Global Engine respectively during each invocation.

# Conclusion

We have examined the key requirements of the e-government, which reveals that most of the issues faced by e-government are about integration and inter-connectivity. Web service technology, which is a tool for universal interoperability, is therefore a logical solution to most e-government problems. In additional, we have argued that a security infrastructure implemented at the global level is essential to protect a Web service based e-government environment. The detailed requirements of such a mechanism are examined and an access control mechanism that is suitable for the Web service based e-government is proposed. The proposed system enables the e-government Web services to be developed in an access policy neutral manner and can accommodate access right rules based on the physical means of the Web service access, as well as combination of the end-user and consumer identity. More importantly, the system supports both the administration and legislation based access policy that are applicable to e-government Web services.

Throughout this chapter, we have argued that interoperability is a key e-government issue that can be addressed with a Web service based structure. However, a number of recent events indicate a trend of much more and closer cooperation among governments of different countries. These include, for example, the formation of the European Union and the joint effort to fight against terrorism and more recently, the SARS disease. As a closing remark, we speculate that this may in time call for more integration of the systems among governments from different nations to achieve the necessary coordination of the efforts. It is thus a challenging but interesting question to see whether and how the e-government Web service framework can be extended to accommodate the level interoperability beyond a single government.

# References

Ambite, J.L., Arens, Y., Hovy, E., Philpot, A., Gravano, L., Hatzivassiloglou, V., & Klavans, J. (2001). Simplifying data access: The Energy Data Collection project. *IEEE Computer, 34*(2), 47-54.

Arcieri, F., Cappadizzi, E., Nardelli, E., & Talamo, M. (2001). SIM: A working example of an e-government service infrastructure for mountain communities (extended abstract). *Proceedings of 12th International Workshop on Database and Expert System Applications,* 407-411, Munich, Germany.

Atkinson, B., Libera, G.D., Hada, S., Hondo, M., Baker, P.H., Klein, J., LaMacchia, B., Leach, P., Manferdelli, J., Maruyama, H., Nadalin, A., Nagaratnam, N., Prafullchandra, H., Shewchuk, J., & Simon, D. (2002). Web Services Security (WS-Security). *IBM developerWorks: WS-Security Specification Version 1.0.* Retrieved April 7, 2003, from: *http://www.ibm.com/developerworks/library/ws-secure/.*

Bertino, E., Perego, A., Farrari, E., Adam, N.R., & Atluri, V. (2002). DLAM: An access control model for digital libraries. *Proceedings of the Second International Conference on Information Security,* 149-155, Shanghai, China.

Boubez, T., Hondo, M., Kurt, C., Rodriguez, J., & Rogers, D. (2002). UDDI Data Structure Reference V1.0. *UDDI Published Specification,* 28 June 2002. Retrieved August 1, 2002, from: *http://www.uddi.org/pubs/DataStructure-V1.00-Published-20020628.pdf.*

Bouguettaya, A., Ouzzami, M., Medjahed, B., & Cameron, J. (2001). Managing government databases. *IEEE Computer, 34*(2), 56-64.

Chappell, D., & Jewell, T. (2002). *Java Web Services.* Sebastopol, CA: O'Reilly.

Chen, H., Zeng, D., Atabakhsh, H., Wyzga, W., & Schroeder, J. (2003). COPLINK: Managing law enforcement data and knowledge. *Communication of the ACM, 46*(1), 28-34.

Feller, J. (n.d.). IBM Web Services Toolkit – A showcase for emerging Web services technologies. *Web services by IBM.* Retrieved August 1, 2002, from: *http://www-3.ibm.com/software/solutions/webservices/wstk-info.html.*

Ferraiolo, D.F., & Kuhn, D.R. (1992). Role based access control. *15th National Computer Security Conference,* 554-563, Baltimore, MD.

Graham, S., Simeonov, S., Boubez, T., Davis, D., Daniels, G., Nakamura, Y., & Neyama, R. (2001). *Building Web services with Java: Making sense of XML, SOAP, WSDL and UDDI.* Indianapolis, IN: SAMS.

HKSAR. (1996). PERSONAL DATA (PRIVACY) ORDINANCE. *Laws of Hong Kong* (ch. 486), s 2 (Interpretation).

HKSAR ITSD Hong Kong Special Administrative Region Government Information Technology Services Department. (2001). General policy. *Building a digitally inclusive society* (ch. 3, p 22).

Joshi, J., Ghafoor, A., Aref, W.G., & Spafford, E.H. (2001). Security and privacy challenges of a digital government. In W.J. McIver & A.K. Elmagarmid (Eds.), *Advances in digital government: Technology, human factors, and policy* (ch. 7, pp. 121-136). Norwell, MA: Kluwer Academic Publishers.

Lampson, B. (1971). Protection. *Proceedings of 5th Princeton Conference on Information Sciences and Systems*, 437, Princeton. Reprinted in *ACM Operating Systems Rev. 8,* 1 (Jan. 1974), 18-24.

Mecella, M., & Batini, C. (2001). Enabling Italian e-government through a cooperative architecture. *IEEE Computer, 34* (2), 40-45.

Mechling, J. (1994). Reengineering government: Is there a 'there' there? *Public Productivity & Management Review, Thousand Oaks, 18*(2), 189-197.

Medjahed, B., Rezgui, A., Bouguettaya, A., & Ouzzani, M. (2003). Infrastructure for e-government Web services. *IEEE Internet Computing, 7*(1), 58-65.

Myerson, J.M. (2002). *Web service architectures - How they stack up.* Chicago, IL: Tect. Retrieved August 1, 2002, from: *http://www.webservicesarchitect.com/content/articles/webservicesarchitectures.pdf.*

Mylopoulos, J., & Papazoglou, M. (1997). Cooperative information systems. *IEEE Expert Intelligent Systems & Their Applications, 12*(5), 28-31.

No Gain Without Pain. (2000, June 24). *The Economist.* Also available from: *http://www.economist.com/displayStory.cfm?Story_ID=80764.*

Sun Microsystems. (2002). Delivering services on demand. *Sun ONE Architecture Guide* (ch. 1). Retrieved March 20, 2002, from: *http://wwws.sun.com/software/sunone/docs/arch/chapter1.pdf.*

Taylor Nelson Sofres. (2001). Government online – an international perspective. *2001 Benchmarking Research Study.*

Thomas, R., & Sandhu, R. (1997). Task-based authorization controls (TBAC): A family of models for aActive and enterprise-oriented authorization management. *Proceedings of the 11ᵗʰ IFIP WG 11.3 Workshop on Database Security*, 166-181, Lake Tahoe, CA.

Traunmuller, R., & Wimmer, M. (2000). Processes-collaboration-norms-knowledge: Signposts for administrative application development. *Proceedings of 11th International Workshop on Database and Expert System Applications,* 1141-1145, Greenwich, London.

Virili, F. (2001). The Italian e-government action plan: From gaining efficiency to rethinking government. *Proceedings of 12th International Workshop on Database and Expert System Applications*, 329-333, Munich, Germany.

W3C. (2000). Simple Object Access Protocol (SOAP) 1.1. *W3C Note*, 08 May 2000. Available at: *http://www.w3.org/TR/SOAP/*.

W3C. (2001). Web Services Description Language (WSDL) 1.1. *W3C Note*, 15 March 2001. Available at: *http://www.w3.org/TR/wsdl/*.

XML Web Services. (n.d.). *MSDN Library*. Retrieved August 1, 2002, from: *http://msdn.microsoft.com/library/default.asp?url=/library/en-us/bts02kit/htm/bts_netsdk_gettingstarted_hgsr.asp*.

**Chapter VI**

# Online One-Stop Government:
## A Single Point of Access to Public Services

Efthimios Tambouris , Archetypon SA, Greece

Maria Wimmer, University of Linz, Austria

## Abstract

*One-stop government refers to the integration of public services from a customer's (citizen, business) point of view. One-stop government suggests that customers may request any public service through a single point of access using the communication channel of their choice (e.g., citizen center, call center, Internet, etc.). The one-stop concept further attempts to reduce the number of contacts with the authorities per service consumption to a minimum— one single interaction at best. The information and public services offered are organized and integrated in a customer-focused manner to address the personal needs and to cover the exact requirements of the citizens and business customers. To exploit the potential of one-stop government, the public sector should be accommodated with a set of information and communication technology tools that allow the back-office processes to interoperate. The public servants may thereafter use these tools in order to create and manage information and integrated public services that match the needs of their customers. In this chapter, the concept of online one-stop government is examined and a framework for realizing one-stop government is proposed. The proposed framework consists of process models and an open interoperable software architecture. A demonstrator that has been developed to implement the architectural design is also presented. Furthermore, the results of the trial use of the demonstrator in three European countries are outlined. Finally, experiences gained are provided and impact is assessed.*

# Introduction

In the last few years, an increasing number of countries worldwide allocate significant resources in e-government initiatives in order to modernize the public sector. Among the objectives of these initiatives is the improvement of service provision to citizens and businesses, by employing information and communication technologies (ICT). Improved service provision stands for increased quality, faster provision, accessibility of services anywhere and anytime independently of the government agencies offering them, and provision in terms of the needs of the respective customer at a low cost rate. One-stop government is a concept of e-government that strives for implementing these demands.

One-stop government refers to the integration of public services from a customer's (citizen, business) point of view. One-stop government is becoming a powerful driving vision for e-government initiatives worldwide. It suggests that customers may request any public service through a single point of access using the communication channel of their choice (e.g., citizen center, call center, Internet, etc.). Consequently, customers no longer need to be aware of the fragmentation of the public sector. The one-stop concept further attempts to reduce the number of contacts with the authorities per service consumption to a minimum - one single interaction at best. The information and public services offered are organized and integrated in a customer-focused manner to address the personal needs and to cover the exact requirements of the citizens and business customers.

To exploit the potential of one-stop government, the public sector should be accommodated with a set of ICT tools that allow the back-office processes to interoperate. The public servants may thereafter use these tools in order to create and manage information and integrated public services that match the needs of their customers.

In this chapter, the concept of online one-stop government is examined and a framework for realizing one-stop government is proposed. The proposed framework consists of process models and an open interoperable software architecture. A demonstrator that has been developed to implement the architectural design is also presented. Furthermore, the results of the trial use of the demonstrator in three European countries are outlined. Finally, experiences gained are provided and impact is assessed.

It should be acknowledged that most of the work presented in this chapter has been conducted within the IST project eGOV[1], which was a two-year research and technology development project co-funded by the European Commission within the 5th framework program (2001). For a detailed description of the project see Tambouris (2001).

# Background

## Overall Scope of One-Stop Government

### *Expectations of E-Government*

Expectations of e-government focus on advanced instruments to improve service provision to all types of customers: individual citizens, communities, commercial and non-profit organizations as well as public authorities themselves. Its overall vision implies (cf. Traunmüller & Wimmer, 2003):

- Modernization of the whole machinery of governments including reorganizing and restructuring of public organizations,
- Re-engineering of administrative processes to provide public services via modern access means,
- Citizen- and customer-centred service provision including a more active participation in government and democracy, and
- Integrating tools and connecting organizations and people over time and distances to implement seamless government.

Massive usage of modern information and communication technology is seen as the enabler to access governmental services and knowledge resources. ICT provides the basic means for collaboration over time and distance between the different actors across borders of various kinds. Advanced ICT has also become the driving force to modernize authorities and other institutions of public governance and service provision. The expectations imply efficient and transparent possibilities for more active participation, a higher level for the control of public affairs and of those to whom people invest their trust.

Recently, a number of collective volumes on e-government have appeared. Among them are the conference proceedings of the annual international EGOV conferences (cf. Traunmüller, 2003; Traunmüller & Lenk, 2002) and the KMGov (knowledge management in e-government) conferences (cf. Wimmer, 2003), the collective volume on e-government of Grönlund (2002) or the brand new report of the European Commission on the state of affairs in e-government (see Leitner, 2003). The latter reflects the reality and visions of e-government and it awards good practices in European e-government developments in 2003 in the following three categories:

- The role of e-government in European competitiveness
- A better life for European citizens
- European, central and local government e-cooperation.

In the second category, the Austrian one-stop government online guide to authorities, offices and institutions, "Amtshelfer online"[2], has been awarded.

## E-Government Policies Towards Better Service Provision for Citizens

One has to note that the concept of one-stop government is not a newly invented one. Several governments provided their services through a physical one-stop center in the past. However, in the era of new information and communication technology, this concept was not implemented for a long time. Hindrances were the bureaucratic structures of public administration grown in the last centuries, the strong argument of personal data protection hampering the electronic inter-connection of government agencies and the potential loss of power of rather autonomous local authorities through a centrally organized single face (portal and front-office) to the customer.

Only in the last few years, the importance of citizen-centered, online one-stop public service provision has been recognized again. E-government is one of the first priorities of the eEurope2005 policy of the European Commission (eEurope, 2002; ERA, 2002). A study in the United States of America (Governmental Advisory Board, 1999) states that "governments have traditionally focused on processes but are beginning to shift their perspective to providing citizen-centered services". Furthermore, one of the aims of the office for intergovernmental solutions in USA is "the delivery of integrated services"[3]. Another study in Europe (Wauters & Kerschot, 2002) points out that "the online development of public services can be enhanced by coordinated e-government solutions, which allow local service providers to take advantage of centralized online initiatives offering a single point of contact in the form of e-portals or ASP-related

*Figure 1: Traditional access to public services versus one-stop government*

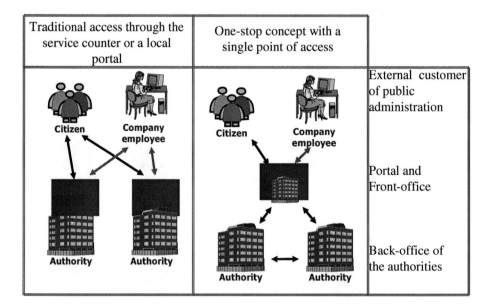

solutions (Application Service Providers), with a citizen/customer-oriented approach rather than a procedural approach".

Through the current vision and national policies for implementing e-government at all levels of the public sector (local, regional, national, supranational), the one-stop government concept has received much attention for many countries to be amongst the first to offer customer-focused services and information through a single window.

The concept of one-stop government is demonstrated in Figure 1 as opposed to the traditional access at public service counters or local portals. As can be recognized, the one-stop concept requires integrating public service offers of various local authorities at the front-office side. In this way, the customer of public administration is provided the requested service without him/her needing to know which authorities are involved in the actual service provision.

## Portals as Key Access Means

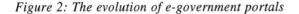

The use of online portals for providing electronic public services has recently received considerable attention. Figure 2 demonstrates the evolution of e-government portals.

As the figure demonstrates, recent developments were rather restricted to providing mainly information and download of forms to the citizens. Current investigations focus on the implementation of advanced transaction portals, where a wide range of online services is provided. Among the conceptual ideas are one-stop government portals, which provide online access to public services from a single point of access to a wide range of offers from different public authorities. Such one-stop portals should be accessible through the Internet, through mobile access channels or through one-stop citizen counters, where the counter servant uses the one-stop portal and acts as an

*Figure 2: The evolution of e-government portals*

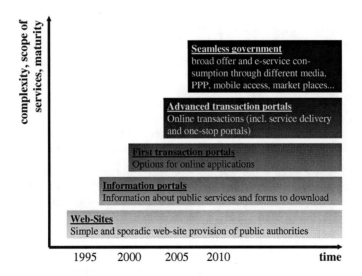

intermediary for the citizen that does not want to use the online portal platform himself/herself.

In order to provide the online service offers through a self-service portal in a customer-focused way, an adequate structure reflecting the needs and ease of comprehension from the customer's point of view is crucial. The concept of *life events* has been invented (see Winter, 2000) and has been recognized as an effective way to present the wide range of public service offers in an easy to navigate and understandable way to citizens. This concept is now used in many national one-stop government portals to structure public service offers and information. An evaluative study on the maturity of various life event portals is provided in Leben and Bohanec (2003).

# Current One-Stop Portals, Research Projects and Technologies

## National One-Stop Government Portals and Current EC Research Projects

Some current good practices of national one-stop government portals in the field include *www.firstgov.gov* (USA), *www.direct.gov.uk* (UK), *www.fonction-publique.gouv.fr* (France), *www.help.gv.at* (Austria), and *www.ecitizen.gov.sg* (Singapure). These portals offer information and public services; however, they rarely offer integrated public services. In some cases, national initiatives address the challenge of information and public service integration by implementing relevant infrastructures. Examples are the UK Government Gateway[4], the Irish Broker (Basis, 2002), and standards such as the Online Services Computer Interface (OSCI)[5] in Germany. At the European level, the European Commission (EC) initiative "Interchange of Data between Administrations" (IDA)[6] has launched a relevant project named e-Link, which aims at providing a common communication platform for various public authorities to exchange information.

Since the electronic form of one-stop government is a concept investigated only recently, the EC has supported a series of research and development projects in its 5th framework program. The projects are targeted at investigating the concept of one-stop government and on proposing relevant frameworks and architectures. Examples include:

- the INFO-CITIZEN project (cf. Tarabanis & Peristeras, 2002) aiming at assisting citizens to conduct electronic transactions in multi-agent settings (e.g., multi-country involvement) in a manner as transparent as possible.

- the CB-Business project (see Legal et al., 2002) that intended to develop, test and validate an intermediate scheme that integrates the services offered by government, national and regional administration agencies as well as commerce and industry chambers of European Union Member States and Enlargement countries in the context of cross-border processes.

- the CITATION project (cf. Anagnostakis et al., 2002) that aimed at developing an innovative software platform to facilitate access to administrative information sources by providing effective information structure, indexing and retrieval.

- the VISUAL ADMIN project (see Drion & Benamou, 2002) aiming at providing citizens and businesses with a global online view for information relevant to them. It also intended to organize the flow of information between administration services for handling customers' cases and to act as a portal for getting access to relevant online information services.

- the eGOV project that intended to investigate and implement an integrated platform for online one-stop government including a central access portal platform and the respective middleware. Its conceptual framework and implementation are presented in this contribution.

## State-of-the-Art in Technical Matters Concerning Online One-Stop Government

The realization of online one-stop government presupposes advances in a number of areas including interoperability, metadata, and emerging Web technologies. State-of-the-art in these areas is introduced in the following and includes results from research projects as well as experiences from good practices worldwide.

- **Interoperability Frameworks:** Existing interoperability frameworks for e-government include the UK e-Government Interoperability Framework (e-GIF)[7], the German Standards and Architectures for e-Government Applications (SAGA, (KBSt, 2002)), the Swedish Spridnings och HämtningSystem (SHS)[8], or the Greek e-Government Interoperability Framework[9]. Furthermore, the European Commission IDA initiative had a plan to propose a European interoperability framework within 2003 following the recommendations of eEurope2005 policy (eEurope, 2005).

- **Metadata:** Examples of national e-government metadata standards include the e-Government Metadata Standard (e-GMS) in UK[10], the Australian Governmental Locater Service (AGLS)[11], the New Zealand Government Locator Service (NGLS)[12], the Governmental Information Locator Service (GILS) in USA[13]. Also Finland[14], Canada[15] and Ireland[16] have defined national standards. Most of these are based on Dublin Core (DC)[17]. The IDA "Managing Information Resources for e-Government" (MIReG) project also aims to present a European metadata standard[18]. Likewise since September 2002, the European Committee for Standardization (CEN)[19] runs yearly projects with the same objective (see CEN Working Agreements CWA 14860 "Dublin Core eGovernment Application Profiles" and CWA 14859 "Guidance on the use of metadata in eGovernment").

- **Web technologies:** Relevant technologies include the eXtendible Markup Language (XML), the Resource Description Framework (RDF) and Web Services by W3C[20]. The concept of Web services integration is the main objective of the recently established "Web Services Choreography Working Group"[21].

- **Commercial tools:** A large number of IT companies have proposed their portal solutions to explicitly target the needs of the public sector (see Deloitte Research, 2000; IBM Global Industries, 2000; Microsoft, 2000). Portal servers are provided by companies such as IBM and BEA. Metadata management tools include those by

Profium but also tools based on open source. Modeling tools for processes are here for quite some time (e.g., ADONIS by BOC or ARIS by IDS Scheer). More recently, advanced products have emerged, such as XMLBus by IONA, which allow Web Services management and orchestration.

# Requirements for Designing One-Stop Access to Public Services

The implementation of online one-stop government should take into consideration a series of requirements from stakeholders. First of all and based on the motivation of providing better services to the citizens, the portal users have to be interviewed on their real needs and ability to serve themselves through an online portal.

Implementing online public services through a one-stop portal also requires a careful investigation of the business processes at stake: not all public services are suitable for online provision. Sometimes only steps within the chain of activities to complete a service can be provided online; in other cases the service delivery cannot be performed through the online portal due to the nature of the service.

Apart from these basic principles, the following general requirements have to be investigated properly for an integrated online one-stop government platform (see also Wimmer, 2002):

- Smoothly adapting traditional processes to modern technology;
- Providing access to public services via a single entry point even when these services are actually provided by different departments or authorities (single window);
- Enabling access via different media channels and devices (Internet, Personal Digital Assistants - PDAs, WAP-enabled devices, call centers, citizen offices, etc.);
- Guaranteeing the necessary level of security, authenticity and privacy in communication and transactions via the Internet, especially for personal data and information that is highly sensitive;
- Adapting both the internal (workflow, databases, Intranets, etc.) and external (information and communication services to the citizens and customers, transactions of goods and services via the Internet) change requests for public activity;
- Smoothly coordinating internal and external public activity to facilitate cross-border operations (i.e., seamless government);
- Enabling customers to access public services in terms of life events or business situations and without knowledge of the functional fragmentation of the respective public authorities;

- Allowing customers to approach and monitor different stages of service provision and delivery, for example, simple information gathering; interacting with an authority; contracting (online application); service delivery and payment; complaints and other aftercare needs such as feeding statistics or feedback;

- Providing customers with pre-information at various stages and in various depths;

- Providing help in filling in online forms and so forth;

- Clarifying and updating underlying legal issues, laws and prescriptions;

- "Translating" the demand for a service (a license, etc.) from the citizens'/businesses' world to legal-administrative jargon and vice versa;

- Matching online public services with the jurisdictional structure (competencies in the legal sense) and routing the citizen demand to the relevant back office;

- Keeping track of the process, handling "freedom of information" requests and other "due process" requirements.

One of the first requirements to be investigated is the re-engineering of the official proceedings that should be implemented for the online one-stop government platform. One-stop government calls for the integration of public services to a single point of access from a customer of public administration's point of view. The following section provides insight into process modeling and re-organization of public services for the one-stop government concept.

# Re-Organizing Public Services for the One-Stop Concept

Realizing the single window concept brings an important organizational shift: from public services structured around the fragmentation of public administration towards a customer oriented structure of public services. This shift implies that, on the one hand at the one-stop portal, the services are provided according to the customers' context and situations (e.g., life events, business situations and specific topics). The customers must be able to access these services in a well-structured and clear manner meeting their perspective and needs. This view needs to be uncoupled from the different public authorities or private service providers that actually deliver the public service. So on the other hand, the specific responsibilities and fragmentation of public administration in respect to service production and service delivery must not be hampered. Hence, a smooth integration of two distinct views is required: an external, customer oriented view; and an internal, public administration oriented view.

The framework for integrated process modeling presented in Figure 3 provides a guideline of process re-engineering based on the life event metaphor. It is based on the holistic reference concept as presented in Wimmer (2002).

The left side of the figure reflects the taxonomy of the life event concept. Based on this taxonomy, process models can be developed for various public services reflecting the

*Figure 3: Framework for integrated process modeling*

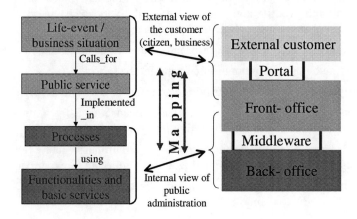

business structure and life event approach. The models provide the description for implementing the public services through an online one-stop government technical platform. In general, the following modeling structure and process information on public services should be provided through integrated process models:

- *Abstraction level 1:* life events for citizens and business situations for businesses
- *Abstraction level 2:* public services in the context of a life event/business situation including conditional relations between different public services
- *Abstraction level 3:* specific process and (nested) sub-process descriptions by means of: activities (sequential and parallel), roles (e.g., citizen, public servant, expert, business, etc.) performing the activities; resources (documents, IT systems, etc.) feeding into an activity and resulting from an activity; input/output data during service performance; service workflow (business logic); pre-/post-conditions (e.g., validity proof, time constraints, etc.) per activity; legal grounding; locations (e.g., portal, public authority, etc.) where the performance of the activities takes place; conditional references to other public services - semantic interdependencies (service bundling, that is, the involvement of other public services) depending on the specific contextual situation of the applicant; involvement of basic services (such as payment or signature); further comments where required.

To allow appropriate and consistent process modeling, a clear methodology for process modeling is essential. For example within the eGOV project, a modeling methodology has been adopted that is based on the holistic reference framework developed by Wimmer (2002) as well as on standard process modeling and systems engineering concepts (see e.g., Carroll, 1995; Diaper, 1989). Such a methodology guides the engineers in the elicitation of user requirements for the process models, in the re-engineering of the traditional processes towards online public services and in a comprehensive description of the target process models. The proposed steps are:

1.   Analysis of the current model for a public service

2.   Documenting the analysis results in models and scenarios

3.   Evaluation of the analysis results

Analysis iteration (steps 1 and 2)

4.   Design of target process models

5.   Evaluation of target process models

An iteration between steps 4 and 5 is performed.

It is strongly recommended that the process modeling be supported by an off-the-shelf modeling tool (e.g., ADONIS®, ARIS®, UML modeling, etc.).

Providing well-structured and understandable information and structures of online services to the customer of public administrations is of utmost importance for a successful take-up of such online one-stop portals. Negligence of a careful investigation of user needs and targeted designs of the user interface may be grounded in the fact that the wide user group of online services is very heterogeneous. So it is a big challenge to design a portal structure and interface for one-stop government that meets the requirements and expectations of the distinct groups in one single access point.

In the next section, a platform to provide online services through a one-stop portal is introduced. This platform follows the concept of providing services to citizens and businesses through a single point of access structured around the life events approach and linking distinct back-offices through the middleware.

# An Integrated Platform for Realizing Online One-Stop Government

Within the eGOV project, an integrated platform for realizing online one-stop government has been specified and developed (Tambouris & Spanos, 2002). This one-stop government platform allows the public sector to provide citizens, business partners and administrative staff with information and public services based on life events and business situations, hence increasing the effectiveness, efficiency and quality of public services.

More specifically, the eGOV online one-stop government platform:

*   Implements the concept of online one-stop government.

*   Allows public authorities to provide integrated services. The proposed approach enables the administrations to offer customer (citizens, businesses) focused

functionality based on life events, target groups, and so forth. Service integration is based on advanced, open technologies such as Web Services, Universal Description, Discovery and Integration (UDDI), Web Services Description Language (WSDL) and Simple Object Access Protocol (SOAP).

- Achieves interoperability with legacy systems of different public authorities by means of open standards such as XML.

## The eGOV Service Provision Model for Online One-Stop Government

A simple service provision model for online one-stop government is depicted in Figure 4.

The assumptions and basic method of service provision depicted in this model are:

- We assume that there are many different communication channels
- We assume that a large number of public authorities wish to provide their public services through these channels
- We assume that a large number of public authorities wish to provide information about their public services (termed *service descriptions*) through these channels

The main idea is that between the communication channels and the back-office, a new layer is introduced, termed *mid-office*. The mid-office acts as a broker between the communication channels and the back-office processes.

*Figure 4: A simple online one-stop government service provision model*

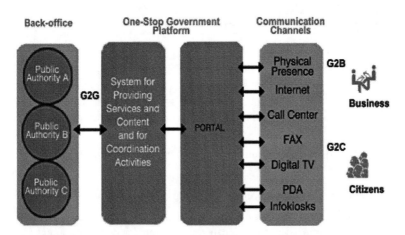

This service provision model suggests that:

- There is one public authority where the central one-stop government portal is located.

- The communication channels register all their customers' (citizens, businesses) requests in the portal. Clearly, when the channel is the Internet then actually the customers register their requests by themselves.

- All participating public authorities establish relevant processes to support the mid-office. In the figure this is denoted as the "System for Proving Services and Content and for Coordination Activities".

- The "System for Proving Services and Content and for Coordination Activities" is responsible for two main activities. Firstly, it provides all necessary technological tools for public servants to integrate and manage public services. Secondly, it is responsible for handling the communication between the portal and the back-offices.

## The eGOV Technical System Architecture

From a technical point of view, the eGOV project identified and addressed three key development and implementation modules:

- The eGOV one-stop government portal and network architecture.

- The eGOV middleware containing the content and service repository, the service creation environment and the service runtime environment.

- A common format for the data flow between the portal and the service repositories in different public authorities, which is termed *Governmental Markup Language* (GovML). GovML is based on open standards such as XML, RDF and Dublin Core. It contains data vocabularies for describing content of life events and public services, and it provides a standard set of metadata for life events and public service resources.

The overall technical architecture of the eGOV platform is depicted in Figure 5.

The eGOV system architecture recognizes and supports four user stereotypes:

- Customers: these are citizens (businesses) who are in a life (business) episode and require public services or relevant information. More specifically, through the eGOV platform, customers can register and authenticate themselves; retrieve information on a life event/business situation or information on a specific public service; request (invoke) a public service; view a specific document, and so forth.

- Public servants: staff of public authorities or the central authority hosting the eGOV portal and central eGOV middleware. These public servants are responsible

*Figure 5: The eGOV overall system architecture*

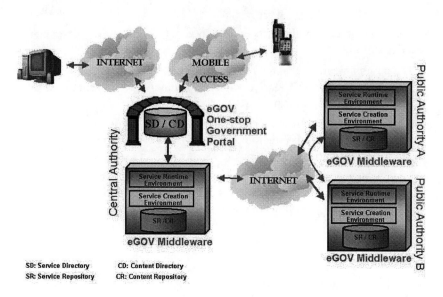

SD: Service Directory   CD: Content Directory
SR: Service Repository   CR: Content Repository

for publishing information on public services and life events/business situations as well as executable public services on the eGOV platform. They are using the service creation environment, the process modeling toolset, and the metadata management tool to create and publish eGOV services, modify relevant service descriptions and track the execution of public services invoked by customers.

• Portal Administrators: these are technical administrators who are responsible for managing the central portal.

• Middleware Administrators: these are technical administrators who are responsible for managing the "System for Proving Services and Content and for Coordination Activities". More specifically, they are implementing Web services and Applets to run executable services that are published at the eGOV platform by the public servants.

The components of the eGOV architecture as well as relevant technologies are depicted in Figure 6.

As already mentioned, the use of standard technologies is crucial when providing an online one-stop government platform. Standard technologies can guarantee interoperability among various legacy systems of back offices that provide their public services through the one-stop platform. This was an important criterion for the eGOV team to select technologies for specific purposes as follows:

• The extensible Markup Language (XML). The most important XML application utilized is the Resource Description Framework (RDF) for creating appropriate graphs for life events and handling metadata for service descriptions. Furthermore,

*Figure 6: The eGOV technical architecture in terms of technologies and components*

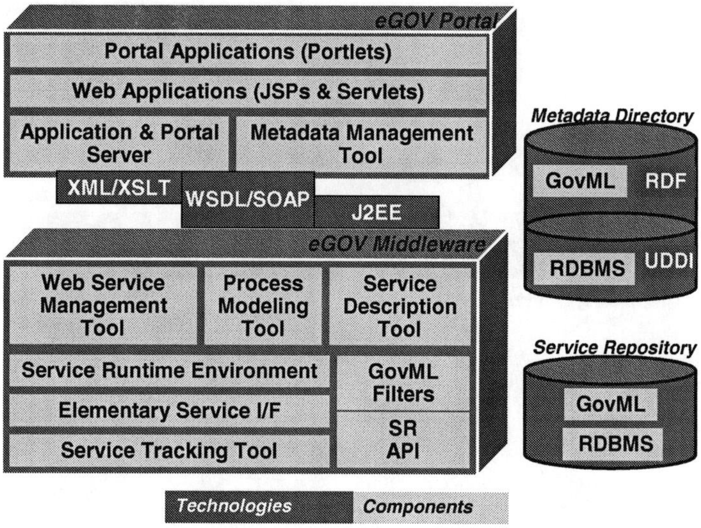

specific XML vocabularies are needed for describing life events and public services in standard format while a metadata element set is also essential for management and retrieval of governmental resources. In Figure 6 these are referred to as Governmental Markup Language (GovML).

- The Web Service Framework based on SOAP/UDDI/WSDL is utilized for the invocation of online services.

- Figure 6 demonstrates that for the eGOV portal and eGOV middleware, a series of components and tools have been integrated.

In the next sections the two main modules of the eGOV architecture are presented in more detail. Furthermore, the Governmental Markup Language is described as a sufficient structure for metadata handling and for describing life events and public services.

## The Portal Platform Module

The Portal module combines content (i.e., information) and services to a Web site in a loosely coupled way. For this purpose, metadata directories are utilized, which contain descriptions of both content and services.

With the Portal Module the user can view life events, retrieve content related to them and activate services.

The Portal consists of a group of services that provide aggregation and integration of content and services from public authorities. These services are based on the concept of life events.

*Figure 7: The eGOV portal platform*

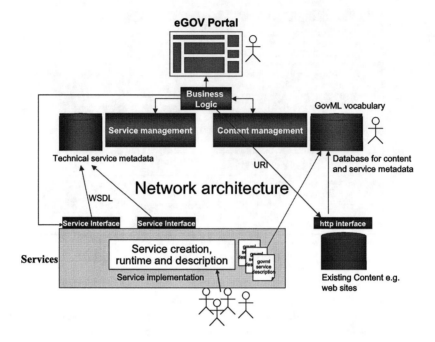

Portal functionality can be provided by using the Web services concept, where the services are described in WSDL. References to WSDL descriptions are stored in a UDDI directory. An RDF metadata directory can be used for storing additional metadata descriptions of services. Web services are based on loosely coupled functionality using common Internet communications protocols and standard message vocabularies.

The portal supports multi-channel functionality. Therefore, the portal user can connect to the portal using various devices such as a workstation, mobile phone, or other PDAs.

The Portal Platform (Figure 7) is divided into two parts: the portal and the network architecture. The portal consists of service metadata management, content metadata management, the functionality for combining these two, and the data stores for service and content metadata. The network architecture comprises the application level protocols for the communication between service interfaces and data stores and the components needed for this.

The service information is retrieved from a UDDI register and has been described with a WSDL description. An HTML form is created from the description by eXtensible Stylesheet Language (XSL) transformation. The actual service is a Web service located in an access point.

The user can personalize his/her view of the portal. The look and feel of the portal can be changed and the preferred language can also be selected.

## The Middleware

The **Service Repository** (SR) stores all service related information required for describing services and tracking service execution. Public services are described by means of standard templates (termed GovML and explained in the next section) that are stored inside the repositories. During service execution, information necessary for tracking the execution status of services is stored in the service repositories. Moreover, authentication information for application operators is stored in the SRs. The implementation of SRs can be based on an RDBMS.

The **Service Runtime Environment** (SRE) processes incoming service requests, dispatches those requests to the appropriate service implementations and/or back-office systems, and returns the results of the service execution to the requestor, which in our case is the portal.

In order to map the service framework to the Internet infrastructure the Web service framework based on SOAP/UDDI/WSDL is utilized. For the creation, management and execution of Web services the Web Service Management Tool is utilized. This could be a development and execution framework and a collection of technologies based on XML and Java for building, exposing and executing Web services. This should enable business-to-business (B2B) transactions and application integration across the Internet, using the existing Internet/Intranet infrastructure available in enterprises or public authorities.

The **Service Creation Environment** (SCE) provides a collection of tools that allow a public authority to create and manage public services. This covers the creation and management of public services in terms of GovML as well as in terms of Web services. The creation and management of Web services is covered by the Web Service Management Tool, which provides a full set of tools to accomplish the required tasks (Web Service Creation Environment). Furthermore, the SCE provides a set of tools to monitor and keep track of the service execution.

# Governmental Markup Language (GovML)

The Governmental Markup Language (GovML) is a recommendation of the eGOV project for standardizing document templates that can be used from public authorities in order to describe public services and life events. Public organizations as well as consumers of public services benefit from such a common information structure. Public authorities are able to manage (create, modify, store, etc.) information in a unified way, exchange and reuse it. On the other hand, citizens and businesses enjoy better quality when searching for information regarding public services and life events.

From a more technical perspective, GovML data vocabularies are proposed XML patterns for the public sector, validated against the XML Schema mechanism.

Interoperability among public authorities is ensured, as the rules, which dominate the document syntax, are common for all public authorities. Moreover, GovML compliant information exploits XML potential and can be displayed in multiple formats and devices, for example Web browsers, mobile phones and so forth.

GovML vocabularies are separated into two categories:

- Three data vocabularies, which standardize the format of the governmental information about life events/public services.

- A metadata vocabulary (or application profile) for governmental resources, which includes the most appropriate and necessary elements from existing metadata standards like the Dublin Core, e-GMS and PRISM (Publishing Requirements for Industry Standard Metadata)[22].

## Generic Description Data Vocabulary for Public Services

This vocabulary defines a common standard for the content of all public authorities at a national level. Such governmental content is created only once, at a national level. This type of content could be normally based upon a governmental law, so it can be adopted by all public agencies of a country. Examples of data elements are: title, procedure, required documents, and so forth.

## Specific Description Data Vocabulary for Public Services

This vocabulary caters for the creation of content related to a public service provided by a specific public authority. It can be considered as a specialization of the generic description vocabulary because the values of some elements of this vocabulary depend on the public authority that provides the service. Some of its elements are: name and address of the public authority, public servant contact details, delivery channel of the service, and so forth.

It should be noted that the generic and specific data vocabularies for public services have many common elements.

## Data Vocabulary for Life Events and Business Situations

This vocabulary defines a set of elements necessary to describe any everyday life event or business situation. Elements of this vocabulary are a subset of the generic description data vocabulary for public services. The three GovML data vocabularies are listed in Table 1.

*Table 1: GovML data vocabularies*

| | Public Services | | Life Events |
|---|---|---|---|
| | **Generic description** | **Specific description** | **Description** |
| 1 | identifier | identifier | identifier |
| 2 | language | language | language |
| 3 | title | title | title |
| 4 | description | description | description |
| 5 | attention | attention | attention |
| 6 | faq-list | faq-list | faq-list |
| 7 | eligibility | eligibility | |
| 8 | required-documents | required-documents | |
| 9 | procedure | procedure | |
| 10 | periodicity | periodicity | |
| 11 | time-to deliver | time-to deliver | |
| 12 | cost-info | cost-info | |
| 13 | service-hours | service-hours | |
| 14 | employee-hints | employee-hints | |
| 15 | citizen-hints | citizen-hints | |
| 16 | related-services | | related-services |
| 17 | | public-authority-name | |
| 18 | audience | | |
| 19 | | Public authority department | |
| 20 | public-authority-type | | |
| 21 | | e-documents | |
| 22 | law | | law |
| 23 | | delivery-channel | |
| 24 | result | | |
| 25 | | cost | |
| 26 | | contact-details | |
| 27 | | service-code | |
| 28 | | automation-level | |
| 29 | | public-authority-address | |
| 30 | | state | |
| 31 | | service-name | |

## Implementation of GovML

From a technical point of view, the Governmental Markup Language (GovML) vocabularies are implemented using XML technologies. More specifically, in order to serialize GovML documents in XML format, an XML schema was implemented for the validation of their structure. The XML schema validation mechanism[23] was preferred from Document Type Definition (DTD) because it provides a richer set of data-types (including byte, date, integer, etc.) and allows users to derive their own data types and take advantage of inheritance of elements, attributes and definitions of data-types.

New XML documents describing public services or life events can emerge from the XML schema of GovML. Consequently, the appropriate XSL Transformations (XSLT) should be applied for transforming GovML documents to the required format (HTML, WML, etc).

XML schema can be easily extended, modified and maintained in the future according to consumers' needs.

## eGOV Metadata Element Set (Application Profile)

The aim of the eGOV metadata element set is to enhance and facilitate search and retrieval of governmental resources across the Internet. The core of the eGOV metadata element set is the Dublin Core (DC) Element set. Furthermore, the UK e-GMS framework and PRISM have been utilized.

Technically, mixing and matching of elements from different sets (such as DC, e-GMS and PRISM) is achieved using mechanisms available in RDF and XML.

Table 2 presents the eGOV metadata element set.

*Table 2: GovML metadata application profile*

|    | Element         | Brief Description                                                            |
|----|-----------------|------------------------------------------------------------------------------|
| 1  | Title           | A short name given to the resource                                           |
| 2  | Creator         | Creator of the content of the resource                                      |
| 3  | Subject         | Topic of the resource                                                       |
| 4  | Publisher       | Entity making the resource available                                       |
| 5  | Date            | Date of the creation / availability of the resource                        |
| 6  | Type            | Nature of the content of the resource                                      |
| 7  | Format          | Format of the digital content of the resource                              |
| 8  | Language        | Language of the content of the resource                                    |
| 9  | Relation        | A reference to a related resource                                          |
| 10 | Coverage        | The extent in terms of spatial location of the content of the resource     |
| 11 | Audience        | Group of people, businesses or public authorities the resource focuses on  |
| 12 | Has Translation | Reference to a resource in a translated version                           |

# eGOV Demonstrator

The technical architecture proposed in the previous section has been implemented within the eGOV project. The resulting demonstrator was derived by integrating off-the-shelf products with components that were developed within the project. The implementation language for the eGOV components is Java, leaned on existing J2EE standards. Furthermore, within the eGOV project this demonstrator was deployed in Austria and Greece and subsequently evaluated by three public authorities.

## The eGOV Platform

The eGOV Demonstrator is an implementation of the proposed architecture for one-stop government presented in Figure 4. In Figure 8 the demonstrator is depicted by explicitly differentiating between off-the-shelf products and components developed within the eGOV project.

The eGOV demonstrator operates on Microsoft Windows 2000 Server[24]. It uses the Tomcat 4.0 Web Application Server[25] while the application environment is Java (J2EE and JDK 1.3.1[26]). Furthermore, the eGOV demonstrator includes the following off-the-shelf tools:

*Figure 8: The eGOV demonstrator for one-stop government*

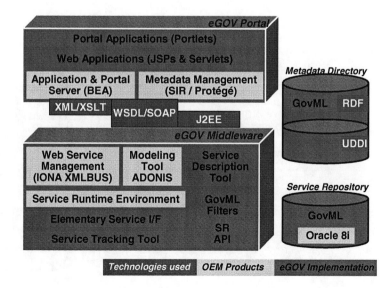

- Portal Server: BEA WebLogic Portal 4.0[27] and Wokup! Server 2.0[28]
- Metadata Management tool: Profium SIR 3.0.4[29] and Protégé by Stanford University[30].
- Web Services Management tool: XMLBus by IONA[31].
- Relational DataBase Management System: Oracle 8.1.7[32].
- Modeling tool: ADONIS by BOC[33].

## Sketching Two Scenarios of Using the eGOV Platform

As stated earlier, eGOV demonstrator supports four groups of users. In the following two pictures, scenarios for the main user groups are presented. For these users, the life event metaphor is the basic underlying concept applied at the presentation layer. The consumers of public services can access information regarding a life event/business situation they are looking for. They can also invoke online public services they are in need of. Figure 9 demonstrates the invocation of a public service by a customer via the eGOV platform. The customer accesses the eGOV portal and retrieves the respective service either by navigating through the live event structure or through direct search of the service s/he is interested in. The portlet sends a request to the application, which itself retrieves the reference of the invoked service from the service directory through the metadata management system. With this reference, the portal server calls the service runtime environment at the respective public authority (which can be at the central installation or at an installation of a local authority where the service is provided) and places the application request of the customer. The application server sends itself a

*Figure 9: Demonstration of the invocation of a public service through the eGOV platform*

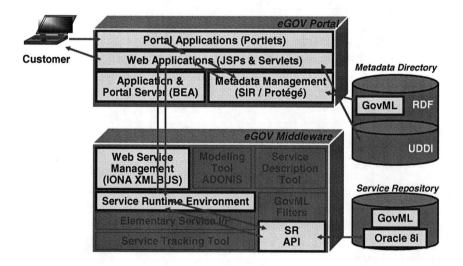

*Figure 10: Demonstrator of publishing public services at the oeGOV platform*

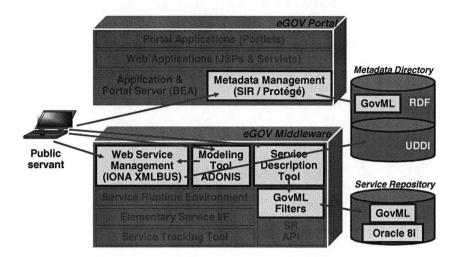

confirmation of successful receipt of application at the authority in charge of the service provision to the portal server, which is shown to the customer as feedback.

The eGOV middleware contains as well a toolset (Service Description Tool, Metadata Management Tool, ADONIS Modeling Tool, Web Service Management Tool) for public servants to publish and manage online public services and information regarding public services or life events. Figure 10 demonstrates the use of tools for a scenario of publishing a new online public service. A public servant of a local authority develops a model for a public service via the ADONIS modeling tool. The front-office service flow is then implemented in Web services via IONA XMLbus (normally, the Web service development is done through a software programmer) and published in the Service Repository. With the use of the Service Description Tool, the public servant publishes information regarding the public service in the Content Repository and inserts the references of the information and Web services regarding the public service at the portal's Service and Content Directories via the Metadata Management Tool.

# Trials and Evaluation

Within the eGOV project, the eGOV demonstrator was deployed at three public authorities: the Hellenic Ministry of Interior, Public Administration and Decentralization, the Austrian Federal Computer Center and the Greek Municipality of Amaroussion. The platform was subsequently evaluated by citizens and public servants in Greece, Austria and Switzerland (for the latter the platform installed in Austria was utilized).

The basic validation criterion was that the developed architecture has to meet the requirements of the users. In other words, the eGOV system had to satisfy end-users and had to fall in line with organizational needs of the public authorities.

On the basis of the "observed user tests" methodology, a number of scenarios that simulated real-life cases and assigned tasks to test-participants (citizens and public servants) were created in terms of electronic services and/or GovML descriptions:

- Marriage at the civil office
- Work permits for foreigners (for citizens)
- Applying for a work permit of a foreigner (for businesses)
- Applying for a building permit
- Application for a trade license/new business registration
- Elections (voting relocation)
- Passport application

Questionnaires were utilized in order to collect the views of the test participants as well as demographic data. The user tests focused on the components developed within the eGOV project as opposed to off-the-shelf tools that were incorporated in the eGOV platform.

The most important conclusion that can be drawn from the user trials of the eGOV demonstrator is that, in general, both types of users have a positive attitude towards the introduction of public services that are provided through an online one-stop government platform. Citizens recognize the benefits to be gained from the use of the eGOV system (one-stop shop capability, saving time from queuing or waiting on the phone, having services available where and when the user wants, etc.) and have strong expectations for the future. Also public employees, although at points they appear to be more skeptical, recognize the benefits of the eGOV system from the content and service creator's point of view. They agree that the system in principle supports the goals of e-government and state that it could be the base for full-scale applications in the future.

# Lessons Learned and Impacts

The concept of one-stop government is a driving vision for e-government worldwide. It suggests that the public sector is transparent to its customers (citizens or businesses). More importantly, it suggests that the public sector is able to provide integrated services that match the needs of its customers. We anticipate that pursuing this vision will continue with more density in the years to come from an increasing number of governments worldwide.

However, realizing one-stop government faces multiple challenges. Organizational changes including the re-assignment of local competencies and re-organization of processes might be needed; technology based on open standards must mature; the legal and statutory framework might have to change and a change of culture of public servants is probably necessary. The following sub-sections dig deeper into these arguments.

# Organizational Impacts

Implementing an online one-stop government platform as realized in the eGOV project has strong impacts on the organizational structures of public administrations. One has to bear in mind the overall objectives and vision of one-stop government. As Wimmer and Tambouris (2002) state, *"One-stop government refers to the integration of public services from a citizen's - or customer of public services - point of view. This implies that public services are accessible through a single window even if they are provided by different public authorities or private service providers. ... Online one-stop government allows citizens to have 24 hours access to electronic public services from their homes, libraries, schools, shopping malls or even on the move."*

As expressed in this definition, the customers must be able to access public services in a well-structured and well understandable manner meeting their perspectives and needs. One-stop government reflects a new structure of public administration as demonstrated in Figure 1, which has significant impact on how public services are offered and delivered to the customer.

With the concept of one-stop government, the organizational structure of public administrations is going to change. Public authorities will have to provide their offerings in a harmonized way for the parts that are handled at the portal side. Some of the tasks that were traditionally performed at the local service counter move to the one-stop portal. This has as well an impact to the public servants' work.

As a consequence, a smooth change management has to be performed by all public authorities providing their online services through the one-stop portal. This task is not only an organizational issue of one authority, but as well a political matter and an issue of the overall e-government strategies in each country.

# Technological Impacts

One of the most important prerequisites of one-stop government is that public services must be integrated. As already discussed above, the concept of life events and public services for external customers needs to be properly mapped to the functional responsibilities and core competencies of the public administration landscape. This requirement has high technological impact in several dimensions (see discussion in the subsections above):

- appropriate process modeling integrating the external and internal point of view of service performance as well as harmonization of the understanding of life events and public services at the portal layer (external view) are needed;

- an appropriate technical infrastructure with seamless interfaces between the portal and the local legacy systems and overall interoperability are required;

- a standardized data and service vocabulary to describe the content and services of public administration according to the life event approach are needed.

If a public authority wants to offer its services through the one-stop government platform, this may require the adaptation of local legacy systems and introduction of interfaces.

Another significant characteristic of one-stop government is accessibility through multiple delivery means (or communication channels), including physical presence at designated offices, call centers, Internet, mobile devices, digital TV and so forth. So, apart from the Web-based applications, mobile access and other channels have to be enabled and integrated. Therefore, a technological challenge (i.e., addressing integration and interoperability requirements) emerges with the implementation of online one-stop government.

## Society Impacts

The concept of online one-stop government presents a way of providing and consuming public services through a single point of access. Partially, the implementation of offers through the Web shifts tasks to the customer (citizens and businesses that perform the entry of data and completion of forms based on online help and online proof). A kind of self-service culture is established throughout the landscape of public service offers. Expectations of customers in compensation for these tasks are faster treatment and service delivery as well as application from home at any time.

However, we have to be aware that not all customers of public administration may be able to serve themselves through the Internet. Public administration has to secure that also non-Internet users have access to, and get the same quality of service as Internet users do.

With the concept of one-stop government, all public authorities need to be interconnected. Hence, data exchange among authorities and collaboration between them is a must. Yet, data protection and the phenomenon of "big brother is watching you" may still hinder the effective take-up and usage of the one-stop offers. Without a careful investigation and accordance with the legal grounding for cross-organizational collaboration and integration of sensitive data, society will not accept this innovative concept.

## Conclusions

One-stop government suggests that public services are integrated according to customers' (citizens, businesses) needs. The concept of one-stop government provides a clear and powerful vision for e-government initiatives. However, the realization of the full potential of one-stop government is a challenging task that requires integration effort on different levels[34]. For example:

- At the organizational level, different public administrations have to collaborate and to become networked to provide services according to the customers' needs and expectations.

- At the process level, process chains that are performed in different authorities need to be integrated. Apart from that, a common electronic act is needed to fully enable online provision of services. On this level, a strong effort for standardization and interchangeability of process content is of utmost importance.

- At the technical level, integration of the platform with the local legacy systems is to be addressed. Hence, the interoperability of front-office and various back-office systems has to be guaranteed.

In this chapter, the integration on the process level and on the technical level are partially addressed.

As stressed in this chapter, advances in one-stop government are related to advances in many areas. The concepts of joined-up government and interoperability are highly relevant and actually comprise prerequisites to achieve true one-stop government. Investigations and pilot solutions are now under way. However, further effort is needed on a global scale to implement integration on all three levels above in order to succeed with effective implementation and take-up of the one-stop government concept. It is a fascinating trip that has just started!

# Acknowledgments

The work presented in this chapter has been conducted within the IST project "An Integrated Platform for Realising Online One-Stop Government" (eGOV), a two-year RTD project co-funded by the European Commission under contract IST-2000-28471. The consortium partners are: Siemens Austria (A); Archetypon S.A. (EL); TietoEnator Corporation (FIN); IKV ++ GmbH (D); University of Linz (A); National Centre for Scientific Research "Demokritos" (EL); Hellenic Ministry of Interior, Public Administration and Decentralization (EL); Municipal Technology Company of Amaroussion (EL); University of Lausanne (CH); Austrian Federal Computing Center (A).

# References

Anagnostakis, A., Sakellaris, G.C., Tzima, M., Fotiadis, D.I., & Likas, A. (2002). CITATION: Citizen information tool in smart administration. In R. Traunmüller & K. Lenk (Eds.), *Electronic government. First International Conference* (pp. 307-312). Heidelberg: Springer.

Basis. (2002). *Public services broker study.* Basis Project report. Retrieved July 17, 2003, from: *http://www.basis.ie/topics/abstract.jsp?parentKey=WCList;id-36424&topicsType=Topics&language=english.*

Carroll, J.M. (1995). *Scenario-based design: Envisioning work and technology in system development.* Wiley.

Deloitte Research. (2000). *Through the portal: Enterprise transformation for e-government.* Retrieved July 17, 2003, from: *http://www.deloitte.com.*

Diaper, D. (1989). *Task analysis for human-computer-interaction.* Ellis Horwood Ltd.

Drion, B., & Benamou, N. (2002). VISUAL ADMIN – Opening administration information systems to citizens. In R. Traunmüller & K. Lenk (Eds.), *Electronic government. First International Conference* (pp. 319-325). Heidelberg et al.: Springer.

eEurope. (2002). *eEurope 2005 - an information society for all.* European Commission. Retrieved July 22, 2003, from: *http://europa.eu.int/information_society/eeurope/news_library/documents/eeurope2005/eeurope2005_en.pdf.*

ERA. (2002). ERA objectives of the European Commission: Towards a European research area. Retrieved July 24, 2003, from: *http://www.cordis.lu/rtd2002/era-debate/era.htm.*

European Commission. (2001). *5th Framework Program, user-friendly information society (IST), Key Action I: Systems and services for the citizen.* Retrieved July 23, 2003, from: *http://www.cordis.lu/ist/ka1/home.html.*

Governmental Advisory Board. (1999). *Integrated service delivery: Governments using technology to serve the citizen.* Retrieved July 17, 2003, from: *http://policyworks.gov/integov.*

Grönlund, A. (Ed.). (2002). *Electronic government - Design, applications and management.* Hershey, PA: Idea Group Publishing.

IBM Global Industries. (2000). *Creating and implementing an e-government portal solution.* Technical report. Retrieved July 17, 2003, from: *http://ibm.com/solutions/government.*

KBSt (2002). *SAGA – Standards and Architectures for e-Government Applications.* Document version 1.1. of the Federal Ministry of the Interior, Unit IT2 (KBSt). Retrieved July 24, 2003, from: *http://www.kbst.bund.de/Anlage302807/SAGA+Version+1.1+-+English+(445+kB).pdf.*

Leben, A., & Bohanec, M. (2003). Evaluation of life event portals: Multi-attribute model and case study. In M. Wimmer (Ed.), *Knowledge management in electronic government. 4th IFIP International Working Conference, KMGov 2003* (pp. 25-36). Heidelberg: Springer.

Legal, M., Mentzas, G., Gouscos, D., & Georgiadis, P. (2002). CB-BUSINESS: Cross-border business intermediation through electronic seamless services. In R. Traunmüller & K. Lenk (Eds.), *Electronic government. First International Conference* (pp. 338-343). Heidelberg: Springer.

Leitner, C. (Ed.). (2003). *eGovernment in Europe: The state of affairs.* Report of the European Institute of Public Administration, Maastricht.

Microsoft. (2000). *Microsoft in government.* Company report. Retrieved July 17, 2003, from: *http://www.microsoft.com/europe/industry/government.*

Reinermann, H., & von Lucke, J. (2002). *Speyerer definition von electronic governance.* Forschungsinstitut für Öffentliche Verwaltung Speyer. Retrieved July 22, 2003, from: *http://foev.dhv-speyer.de/ruvii/SP-EGvce.pdf.*

Tambouris, E. (2001). An integrated platform for realising one-stop government: The eGOV project. *Proceedings of the DEXA International Workshops 2001* (pp. 359-363). Los Alamitos, CA: IEEE Computer Society Press.

Tambouris, E., & Spanos, E. (2002). An architecture for integrated public service delivery based on life events. *Electronic Markets, 12*(4), 281-288.

Tarabanis, K., & Peristeras, V. (2002). Requirements for transparent public services Provision amongst public administrations. In R. Traunmüller & K. Lenk (Eds.), *Electronic government. First International Conference* (pp. 330-337). Heidelberg: Springer. Traunmüller, R. (Ed.). *Electronic government. Second International Conference EGOV 2003.* Heidelberg: Springer.

Traunmüller, R., & Lenk, K. (Eds.). *Electronic government. First International Conference.* Heidelberg: Springer.

Traunmüller, R., & Wimmer, M. (2003). e-Government at a decisive moment: Sketching a roadmap to excellence. In R. Traunmüller (Ed.), *Electronic government. Second International Conference EGOV 2003* (pp. 1-14). Heidelberg: Springer.

Wauters, P., & Kerschot, H. (2002). *Web-based survey on electronic public services.* Summary report and annex. Brussels: European Commission, Directorate General Information Society. Retrieved July 23, 2003, from: *http://europa.eu.int/ information_society/eeurope/benchmarking/list/2002/index_en.htm.*

Wimmer, M. (2002). Integrated service modelling for online one-stop government. *EM – Electronic Markets, 12*(3), 1-8.

Wimmer, M. (Ed.). (2003). *Knowledge management in electronic government. 4ᵗʰ IFIP International Working Conference, KMGov 2003.* Heidelberg: Springer.

Wimmer, M., & Tambouris, E. (2002). Online one-stop government: A working framework and requirements. In R. (Ed.), *Information systems: The e-business challenge. Proceedings of the 17th World Computer Congress of IFIP in Montreal* (pp. 117 – 130). Boston: Kluwer Academic Publishers.

Winter, A. (2000). www.help.gv.at – Die österreichische Verwaltung im Internet. In H. Reinermann (Ed.), *Regieren und verwalten im informationszeitalter, unterwegs zur virtuellen verwaltung* (pp. 170–85). Heidelberg: R.v. Decker.

# Endnotes

[1]   IST eGOV project, *http://www.egov-project.org*

[2]   *http://www.help.gv.at/*

[3]   *http://estrategy.gov/*

[4]   *http://www.gateway.gov.uk/*

5    *http://www.osci.de/*

6    Interchange of Data between Administrations, *http://europa.eu.int/ISPO/ida/ jsps/index.jsp*

7    *http://www.govtalk.gov.uk/schemasstandards/egif_document.asp?docnum=731*

8    *http://www.statskontoret.se/gel/shortdesc.pdf*

9    *http://www.infosociety.gr/content/downloads/Greek-eGIF-TechSpecs_v_1_3 .pdf (in Greek)*

10   *http://www.govtalk.gov.uk/interoperability/metadata_document.asp? docnum=473*

11   *http://www.naa.gov.au/recordkeeping/gov_online/agls/summary.html*

12   *http://www.e-government.govt.nz/nzgls/index.asp*

13   *http://www.dtic.mil/gils/documents/naradoc*

14   *http://www.intermin.fi/juhta/suositukset/jhs143.htm*

15   *http://www.cio-dpi.gc.ca/im-gi/meta/clf-nsi-meta/clf-nsi-meta_e.asp*

16   *http://www.gov.ie/webstandards/metastandards/index.html*

17   *http://www.dublincore.org/*

18   *http://dublincore.org/groups/government/mireg-metadata-20010828.shtml*

19   *The European Committee for Standardization, http://www.cenorm.be*

20   *http://www.w3c.org/*

21   *http://www.w3c.org/2002/ws/chor/*

22   *http://www.prismstandard.org/*

23   *http://www.w3.org/XML/Schema*

24   *http://www.microsoft.com/windows2000/server/default.asp.*

25   *http://jakarta.apache.org/tomcat/tomcat-4.0-doc/index.html.*

26   *http://java.sun.com/products/archive/j2se/1.3.1/index.html*

27   *http://e-docs.bea.com/wlp/docs40/index.htm.*

28   *http://www.wokup.com/*

29   *http://www.profium.com/gb/products/sir.shtml*

30   *http://protege.stanford.edu/*

31   *http://www.xmlbus.com/*

32   *http://otn.oracle.com/software/htdocs/devlic.html?/software/products/oracle8i/ htdocs/winsoft.html*

33   *http://www.boc-eu.com/english/adonis.shtml*

34   A recent working document of the European Commission speaks of interoperability required on technical, semantic and organizational level, see (accessed 03/11/2003) *http://europa.eu.int/information_society/eeurope/egovconf/doc/ interoperability.pdf.*

## Chapter VII

# Privacy and Trust in E-Government[1]

George Yee, National Research Council Canada, Canada

Khalil El-Khatib, National Research Council Canada, Canada

Larry Korba, National Research Council Canada, Canada

Andrew S. Patrick, National Research Council Canada, Canada

Ronggong Song, National Research Council Canada, Canada

Yuefei Xu, National Research Council Canada, Canada

## Abstract

*This chapter explores the challenges, issues, and solutions associated with satisfying requirements for privacy and trust in e-government. Accordingly, the first section presents the background, context, and challenges. The second section delves into the requirements for privacy and trust as seen in legislation and policy. The third section examines available technologies for satisfying these requirements. In particular, as examples, we describe and analyze two solutions being implemented in Canada: the Secure Channel and the Privacy Impact Assessment. We describe some new technologies for privacy policy negotiation and ensuring privacy policy compliance. The fourth section presents two case studies, e-census and e-voting, and shows how these e-government activities can be equipped to protect privacy and engender trust. Finally, the chapter ends with conclusions and suggestions for future research.*

# Introduction

## Background and Context

The Internet has brought about profound changes in society, enabling users to access almost any information they desire. One effect is that Internet users are becoming better informed than those who do not use the Internet. At the same time, merchants have taken advantage of the Internet to sell their wares to Internet-connected buyers with the proliferation of e-commerce. This combination of receiving knowledge online together with the experience of receiving goods online is leading to user expectations of receiving government services online. This is a good result, because on the supply side, governments want to take advantage of the economies to be gained by supplying services online. To the user or consumer, receiving services online means convenience and timeliness. Governments supplying their services online receive savings in the cost of staffing requirements and information distribution. These benefits will multiply as more and more citizens use online government services. For example, once a government online service is established, the government's savings will increase as more people use the online service, instead of using the traditional more labor-intensive form of the service. However, a major factor in whether or not an online service is used is the user's level of trust in the ability of the service to protect personal information supplied by the user to the service. In the case of Canada, research has shown that Canadians expect more from their government than they do from the private sector in terms of privacy and security. This is due in large part to the fact that the government holds so much sensitive personal information about them, spanning their health, educational attainment, job history, utilization of social benefits, and marital and financial status. Their perceptions about how seriously the government views its stewardship responsibilities for safeguarding their personal data and respecting their privacy will have a tremendous impact on their adoption of online services. This is probably true of other countries as well.

The focus of this chapter is on privacy and trust issues of e-government: the requirements for privacy, the issues faced in providing for privacy, the standards and technologies available (e.g., security safeguards) for ensuring that privacy preferences are followed, and the technologies available (e.g., human factors design techniques) that promote trust.

## *Definition of E-Government*

We define e-government as the application of information and Internet technology to provide electronic access to government information and services. It is similar to using the Internet to access various Web sites for information or services such as buying and selling goods (e.g., eBay). Here are some typical e-government scenarios:

- Job seekers can go online to a government employment center and search for opportunities or submit a skills profile that automatically matches them with interested employers.

- Travelers could renew their passports online with instant turnaround, and businesses could use Internet-based customs clearance.

- Seniors could apply for all applicable benefits online – such as old age security and pension benefits – or make a direct deposit request, or find all information relevant to their needs in a variety of subject areas.

- Citizens could vote online during regularly scheduled political elections, or during referenda on important national issues (e-voting), providing almost instant turnaround.

- People could receive their questionnaire and submit their data online during a census (e-census) with significant savings in costs for forms printing, distribution, and processing.

## Benefits of E-Government

The benefits of e-government are many, and include:

- Users can have one-stop access to all the services they need in daily life.

- Compared to non-electronic means, this one-stop access is more convenient (24-7) and more efficient through automation.

- E-government improves the choice that people have to access government services by adding Internet access to conventional means such as postal mail and telephone.

- E-government gives people access to expanded services made possible through computerization, for example access to new tools for job search.

- E-government can provide better and much more responsive government by increasing opportunities for citizen engagement – citizens can provide instant feedback on government policy or the services they use and identify areas needing improvement.

- E-government can act as a powerful stimulant for e-commerce by familiarizing the population with online transactions and services.

## Challenges of E-Government

### Overall Challenges

In order for the above benefits to accrue, e-government must first be implemented or deployed. Here we find some obstacles and challenges to full implementation. We list some of these as follows:

- Many people are still computer illiterate.

- Not everyone has adequate access to the Internet. This may be due to lack of appropriate equipment, or the speed/bandwidth of the access may be inadequate.

- To be widely used, e-government services requiring private information must be reliable, secure, and protect the privacy of the information. In short, people must trust the service. This is the challenge we address in this chapter.

- There are legal, administrative, regulatory, social, and political hurdles that lead to a delicate mix of stakeholders of e-government. Managing these stakeholders is a daunting task (Accenture, 2002).

**The Challenge of Trust**

Building any online system or service that people will trust is a significant challenge. For example, consumers sometimes avoid e-commerce services over fears about their security and privacy. As a result, much research has been done to determine factors that affect users' trust of e-commerce services (e.g., Egger, 2001; Riegelsberger & Sasse, 2001). Building trustable e-government services, however, represents a significantly greater challenge than e-commerce services for a number of reasons. First, government services are often covered by privacy protection legislation that may not apply to commercial services, so they will be subject to a higher level of scrutiny. Second, that nature of the information involved in an e-government transaction may be more sensitive than the information involved in a commercial transaction (Adams, 1999), such as the case of an e-census service discussed below. Third, the nature of the information receiver is different in an e-government context (Adams, 1999). Some personal information, such as supermarket spending habits, might be relatively benign in an e-commerce situation, such as a loyalty program, but other information such as medical records would be considered very sensitive if shared amongst all government agencies. Fourth, the consequences of a breach of privacy may be much larger in an e-government context, where, for example, premature release of economic data might have a profound effect on stock markets, affecting millions of investors (National Research Council, 2002).

E-government services also involve significant privacy and security challenges because the traditional trade-offs of risks and costs cannot be applied. In business contexts it is usually impossible to reduce the risks to zero and managers often have to trade off acceptable risks against increasing costs. In the e-government context, because of the nature of the information and the high publicity, no violations of security or privacy can be considered acceptable (National Research Council, 2002). Although zero risk may be impossible to achieve, it is vital to target this ideal in an e-government service.

In addition, government departments are often the major source of materials used to identify and authenticate individuals. Identification documents such as driver's licenses and passports are issued by government agencies, so any breach in the security of these agencies can lead to significant problems. Identity theft is a growing problem worldwide, and e-government services that issue identification documents must be especially vigilant to protect against identity theft (National Research Council, 2002).

Another significant challenge for e-government systems is protecting the privacy of individuals who traditionally have maintained multiple identities when interacting with the government (National Research Council, 2002). Today, a driver's license is used when operating an automobile, a tax account number is used during financial transactions, while a government health card is used when seeking health services. With the rollout of e-government services it becomes possible to match these separate identities in a manner that was not being done before, and this could lead to new privacy concerns.

## *Privacy, Trust, and Security in E-Government*

We explain here what we mean by "privacy," "trust," and "security" in the context of e-government. An e-government service user's "privacy" represents the conditions under which she is willing to share personal information with others. Privacy is violated when the underlying conditions for sharing are violated. A user's "trust" is her level of confidence in the ability of the e-government system to a) comply with the conditions she has stated (her privacy preferences) for sharing information, b) comply with the government's policies and regulations for handling personal information, c) function as expected, and d) act in her best interest when she makes herself vulnerable. "Security" refers to all of the electronic and physical means (e.g., encrypted traffic, secure servers, firewalls) used by an e-government system to a) comply with the user's privacy preferences, and b) function correctly without being compromised by an attack.

# State of Privacy and Trust Research for E-Government

In the literature, there are relatively few papers on security and privacy for e-government. A search through the ACM Digital Library and IEEE Explore on August 13, 2003 using the search term "e-government" turned up a total of 101 documents of which 13 were security/privacy related. This gives a rough indication that only about 13% of research on e-government is focused on security and privacy issues. Thus we can conclude that researchers are only beginning to examine the issues of security and privacy for e-government. Papers on e-government that are not concerned with security and privacy are concerned with the implementation of e-government: the design of portals, services integration, human factors, social impacts, service flow management, specific examples of implementations, and others.

We mention here some of the papers on e-government that are concerned with security and privacy. Rezgui et al. (2002) present their WebDG Web-based infrastructure for efficient privacy-preserving access to government Web services. Their approach is based on digital privacy credentials, data filters, and mobile privacy enforcement agents. Wimmer and von Bredow (2002) describe security layers in a holistic approach that views the e-government system as a whole. Their layers range from security management at the upper layers to specific security mechanisms at the lower layers. Benabdallah et al. (2002) describe an e-government model defining steps that need to be taken to develop e-government. They then describe a security model containing tasks that need to be carried out to develop a corresponding security infrastructure. They state that their approach is especially applicable to emerging countries. Boudriga (2002) discusses security requirements for e-government and what security measures can be applied. Boudriga considers essential security requirements such as authentication, access authorization, transaction protection, and intrusion protection. Caloyannides et al. (2003) talk about the efforts by the U.S. government to expand e-government services through the implementation of centralized trust-transfer mechanisms based on PKI.

This chapter differs from the existing literature in at least three ways: 1) we identify and analyze the measures for security and privacy being implemented by Canada, the world's leading e-government services provider according to the Accenture (2002) study (see below), 2) we present some of the new research we are doing in the areas of privacy and trust using privacy policies, and 3) we give descriptions and proposals for two new and important e-government services, e-voting and e-census.

# Canada's E-Government Initiative and Implementation

Canada's e-government initiative is called Government On-Line (GOL) and began in 2000. In an annual report prepared in 2002 (Government of Canada, 2002), the purpose of the initiative is described as "to use information and communication technologies (ICTs) to enhance Canadians' access to improved citizen-centred, clustered services, anytime, anywhere and in the official language of their choice". Progress in GOL to September 2002 has been described in terms of higher levels of satisfaction among Canadians, with "surprisingly resilient positive perceptions of government service". The report claims that the Canadian public's overall rating of the quality of service received from the federal government has been rising steadily every year, from 59% saying "good" in 1999 to 67% in 2002.

GOL was initially conceived as a separate initiative focusing solely on the delivery of e-services using the Internet. It has now evolved to reflect a broader multi-channel service vision covering not only delivery by the Internet but also delivery by the telephone or in person. This broader vision necessitated a new interdepartmental governance structure to better coordinate the multi-channel strategies. In this chapter we are only concerned with delivering services using the Internet.

## GOL Key Areas

The Government of Canada has been working in the following key-areas [1] to provide for multi-channel service improvement, including the delivery of key e-services:

**Service transformation and multi-channel integration** – applying a user-centric approach to multi-channel service delivery, as driven by client priorities and expectations;

**Common, secure infrastructure** – building the enterprise-wide electronic service platform that enables integrated services and supports secure access;

**Common Look and Feel Standards** – ensure that all visitors to government Web sites have a consistent experience, no matter which Web site they visit, by providing standards and guidelines dealing with issues such as accessibility of Web sites, an easily understood visible identity, and a consistent set of navigation aids. Further, it provides a standard for important information addressing issues such as copyright and privacy.

**Federated Architecture Program** – supports systems interoperability across departments and agencies by basing systems on three architectures: a technical architecture, an information architecture, and a business architecture [1];

**Policy and standards frameworks** – addressing information management privacy and security to build trust in e-services;

**Communications and marketing** – encouraging the adoption of high quality electronic service options in sync with the government's capacity to deliver, through public reporting and marketing, while assuring citizens of the government's commitment to respect their channel preferences; and

**Human resources** – developing the necessary skills in the government's workforce to adapt to change and operate effectively as a provider of client-centered services in a technology enabled, integrated, multi-channel environment.

## Example GOL Online Services

Some examples of GOL online services are: a) income tax filing for both individuals and companies, b) address changes, c) one stop submission of consumer complaints, d) job search (post resume and receive e-mail notification of matching jobs), and e) calculation of federal pension benefits. Descriptions of other services can be found in Government of Canada (2003).

## Provision for Privacy, Trust, and Security

The security infrastructure for GOL is called Secure Channel and has the following objectives (Government of Canada, 2002) from the public's point of view:

- Provide assurance of secure transactions.
- Provide assurance of the authenticity and integrity of government sites and databases.
- Protect against network intrusion.
- Provide directory services and secure messaging.
- Provide identification and authentication of individuals and businesses.
- Provide brokerage services and connectors to departmental enterprise-wide and administrative systems.

Further on in the chapter a more detailed account of Secure Channel is given. In addition to Secure Channel, policy frameworks have been developed for privacy, security, and information management. These frameworks contribute to ensuring that the public can use e-government services with trust and confidence. To ensure that privacy is protected whenever e-services are developed or re-designed, mandatory privacy impact assessments (PIAs) are applied prior to the development or re-design. The PIA procedure identifies areas in the proposed development or re-design which fail to comply with required privacy, or comply in a weak or risky manner, and thereby allow for informed design choices. PIAs are described in detail at a later point.

E-government is sometimes described as having three phases: *publish, interact,* and *transact* (Dempsey, 2003). These phases are all facilitated by information and telecommunication technology. The publish phase refers to making government information available to the population. The interact phase concerns government interacting with the population through such means as providing contact e-mail addresses or feedback forms on government proposals. The transact phase refers to the provision of e-government services. We wish to note here that the publish and interact phases can be largely carried out with little concern for security and privacy (assuming the interact phase is not requesting private information). Canada has been and continues to be a leader in the publish phase.

## World Progress in E-Government

We summarize here some results of an e-government study made by Accenture (Accenture, 2002), a world leading management and technology services organization. Accenture has carried out this study each year for the past several years, in which it assesses the maturity level of e-government initiatives around the world. Accenture researchers in the 23 selected countries sampled the Web sites of national government agencies to determine the quality and maturity of services, and the level at which business can be conducted electronically with government. This research was carried out between January 7 and January 18, 2002.

The countries/regions selected for the study were: Australia, Belgium, Brazil, Canada, Denmark, Finland, France, Germany, Hong Kong, Ireland, Italy, Japan, Malaysia, Mexico, the Netherlands, New Zealand, Norway, Portugal, Singapore, South Africa, Spain, the United Kingdom and the United States. A total of 169 national government services across nine major service sectors were investigated. The nine service sectors researched were Human Services, Justice & Public Safety, Revenue, Defense, Education, Transport & Motor Vehicles, Regulation & Democracy, and Procurement and Postal.

The ranking of countries on progress in e-government was based on "overall maturity," which is made up of 70% "service maturity" plus 30% of a customer relationship management component (CRM), which measures the sophistication level of service delivery (helping the user to get the best value from interacting online with government). Service maturity measures the degree to which a government has developed an online presence, and depends on both the number of online services and the completeness of each service. Overall maturity is broken down into four levels, from high to low, as follows:

- Innovative Leaders- overall maturity score greater than 50%, characteristics: high number of mature services, stand apart from the rest;
- Visionary Challengers - overall maturity score between 40% and 50%, characteristics: solid base of online services, some development in CRM;
- Emerging Performers - overall maturity score between 30% and 40%, characteristics: large breadth of services at lower levels of maturity, has significant opportunities to improve online services;

*Figure 1: Overall maturity by country in 2002 (relative country levels are accurate, individual country levels are approximate, data from Accenture, 2002)*

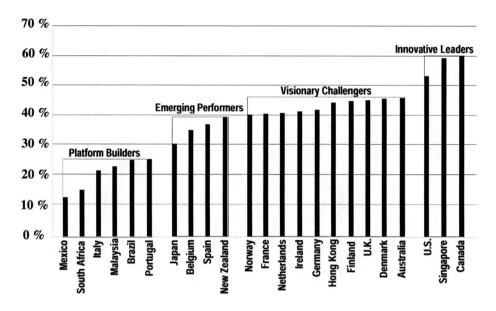

- Platform Builders - overall maturity score less than 30%, characteristics: low levels of online services that are concentrated on information publishing, significant infrastructure issues, late start in e-government.

Using this breakdown of overall maturity, Accenture published the country ranking in Figure 1. As shown in this Figure, Canada is in first place (as it was in 2001) with Singapore coming close, and followed by the United States. In 2001, the same three countries were in this category, and all had overall maturity scores of greater than 38%, with Canada having the highest score of 50%.

The Accenture report (Accenture, 2002) has much additional detail, including e-government topics, comparisons of 2002 study results with 2001 results, and individual country reports. The interested reader is invited to consult it.

Readers who are interested in a discussion of e-government issues for Eastern Europe may access the publication *Local Government Brief* (2003).

As we go to press, the latest edition of the Accenture report (Accenture, 2004) just became available. The maturity levels have of course changed over 2002-2004. Figure 1a adds the increases in the maturity levels to Figure 1 using data from Accenture (2004). We note from Figure 1a that Canada remains in first place in terms of overall maturity level. Singapore and the United States are tied in second place. Accenture (2004) contains many

*Figure 1a: Increases in overall maturity, 2002-2004, relative country levels are accurate, individual country levels are approximate, data from Accenture (2002) and Accenture (2004).*

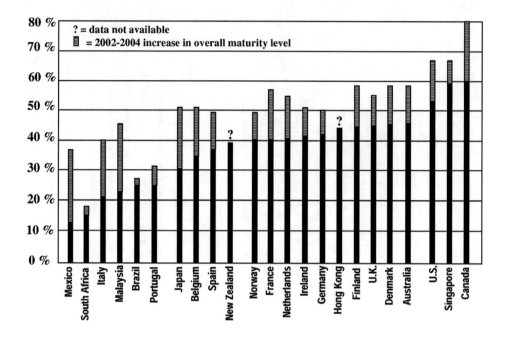

other insights into the 2004 international scene for e-government and the reader is encouraged to consult it.

# Privacy Legislation and Established Policy – The Canadian Perspective

## Privacy and Trust Requirements from Privacy Legislation

Governments in North America and Europe have realized the need for legislation to protect consumer privacy. The privacy legislation enacted by these governments requires individual control for the use of personal information, including the collection, use, disclosure, retention, and disposal of personal data by organizations that may handle that information. Privacy principles have been developed to expose the implications of either privacy laws or privacy policy adopted by online organizations. Governments are counted as belonging to the set of such organizations. In Canada, 10 Privacy Principles (CSA, 1996) (see Table 1), incorporated in the *Personal Information Protec-*

*tion and Electronic Documents Act* of Canada (Department of Justice), spell out the requirements for use of personal information. As a set of privacy requirements, the Privacy Principles serve as a reference to determine how well an online system that handles private information meets these requirements.

These principles may be implemented in computer systems to varying degrees due to the nature of each principle. For example, Principle 1 is largely handled by policy but portions of it can still be implemented to facilitate its compliance. The following suggests ways in which each principle may be "implemented" in government online systems:

*Table 1: The ten privacy principles used in Canada.*

| Principle | Description |
|---|---|
| 1. Accountability | An organization is responsible for personal information under its control and shall designate an individual or individuals accountable for the organization's compliance with the privacy principles. |
| 2. Identifying Purposes | The purposes for which personal information is collected shall be identified by the organization at or before the time the information is collected. |
| 3. Consent | The knowledge and consent of the individual are required for the collection, use or disclosure of personal information, except when inappropriate. |
| 4. Limiting Collection | The collection of personal information shall be limited to that which is necessary for the purposes identified by the organization. Information shall be collected by fair and lawful means. |
| 5. Limiting Use, Disclosure, and Retention | Personal information shall not be used or disclosed for purposes other than those for which it was collected, except with the consent of the individual or as required by the law. In addition, personal information shall be retained only as long as necessary for fulfillment of those purposes. |
| 6. Accuracy | Personal information shall be as accurate, complete, and up-to-date as is necessary for the purposes for which it is to be used. |
| 7. Safeguards | Security safeguards appropriate to the sensitivity of the information shall be used to protect personal information. |
| 8. Openness | An organization shall make readily available to individuals specific information about its policies and practices relating to the management of personal information. |
| 9. Individual Access | Upon request, an individual shall be informed of the existence, use and disclosure of his or her personal information and shall be given access to that information. An individual shall be able to challenge the accuracy and completeness of the information and have it amended as appropriate. |
| 10. Challenging Compliance | An individual shall be able to address a challenge concerning compliance with the above principles to the designated individual or individuals accountable for the organization's compliance. |

1.  Accountability: The name and contact information of the person who is account-able can be clearly advertised in the online system.

2.  Identifying Purpose: The purpose is clearly identified by the online system and can be retrieved at will.

3.  Consent: The person's consent is obtained by the online system in the form of a signed certificate to guarantee authentication and non-repudiation.

4.  Limiting Collection: The online system limits the collection of information to that which is necessary for the purposes identified and ensures that the collection will be done by fair and lawful means. In addition, the online system keeps secure logs of its data collection so that it can prove that it has complied with this principle if challenged.

5.  Limiting Use, Disclosure, and Retention: The online system keeps secure logs of its uses, disclosures, or retention of the data so that it can prove that it has complied with this principle if challenged.

6.  Accuracy: The system can a) ask the individual providing the data to verify the data and sign-off on its accuracy and completeness, b) periodically request the individual to update his or her personal information, and c) run rule-based checks on the data to identify inconsistencies.

7.  Safeguards: Security safeguards such as authentication and encryption can be implemented.

8.  Openness: The online system can advertise its policies and practices relating to the management of personal information as well as provide easily accessible links to this information.

9.  Individual Access: The online system can provide facilities for the individual to perform all access functions required by this principle.

10. Challenging Compliance: The online system can provide a facility for the individual to address a compliance challenge to the person who has been identified as accountable by Principle 1.

## Privacy and Trust Requirements from Policy

To facilitate the transition to e-government, the Government of Canada has developed policy frameworks that address the critical areas of security, privacy, and trust. One framework gives requirements for a privacy impact assessment to ensure that privacy is safeguarded before the development of a new e-government service or the modification of an existing service. Another framework requires the government to follow certain baseline IT security standards in order to provide a safe, secure environment for its data.

We give an overview of what these frameworks require.

Privacy Impact Assessments (PIAs) became mandatory in May 2002 for the design or redesign of programs and services where there are potential privacy issues that may violate the Privacy Principles. For example, a design or redesign could call for increased collection, use or disclosure of personal information, potentially violating principle 4, or may represent a shift from direct to indirect collection of personal information, possibly violating principle 3. PIAs identify the degree to which service design or redesign proposals comply with legislative and policy requirements. They promote fully informed service design choices, and assist in avoiding or mitigating privacy risks. A further requirement is that summaries of the assessments be made publicly available.

In terms of security, the baseline IT security standards are a critical part of the Government of Canada's revised Government Security Policy that became effective on February 1, 2002 (Treasury Board of Canada Secretariat, 2002). This policy calls on government departments and agencies to meet baseline security requirements, to perform continuous security risk management, and to assure continuous service delivery. The departments and agencies are challenged to treat information security as an ongoing dynamic process, not only implementing layers of protective mechanisms, but also being prepared to detect, respond, and recover from attacks on those mechanisms.

## Putting it All Together in the Context of E-Government Services

For e-government services, the above privacy legislation and policy frameworks imply the following:

- An e-government service must not violate any of the Privacy Principles.

- Before an e-government service is designed or modified, a Privacy Impact Assessment must be done to ensure that there are no privacy issues with the design or modification.

- The private information gathered by the service is stored in a secure environment that is protected from attack.

- The service itself is secured from attack, allowing for continuous service delivery.

Thus, privacy legislation and policy frameworks work together to promote trust among those in the population who are users of the services.

# Privacy Enhancing Technologies for E-Government

## Existing Solutions

### Secure Channel

E-government is the use of information technology to support government operations, engage citizens, and provide government services. In order to provide highly secured,

*Figure 2: The Secure Channel*

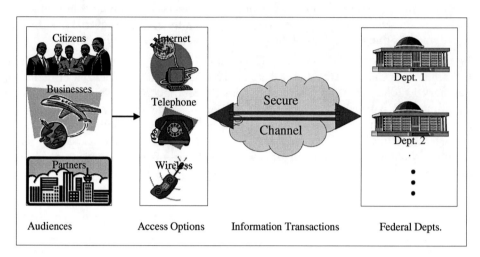

responsive and economical access to government services for citizens, businesses, and trusted partners, the Government of Canada proposed the Secure Channel project. The primary goal of the Secure Channel is to build a secure infrastructure foundation for Canadian government electronic service delivery. Accordingly, the Secure Channel will serve as a fundamental component of the electronic platform, providing a single electronic window for Canadians and companies to conduct business with the federal government. It will enhance the privacy, timing, and ease of accessibility and interaction for applications. It will also provide network connectivity and underlying support services including access, authentication, authorization, confidentiality, inter-communication, data integrity, non-repudiation and brokering. Figure 2 depicts the Secure Channel, which could make a secure connection between the citizens and the government departments, and provide a variety of secure services such as security access control, authentication, authorization, confidentiality, data integrity, non-repudiation, privacy protection, inter-communication, public key infrastructure (PKI) (CCITT, 2001), certificate registration and issue, intelligent brokering, and so on.

## Secure Channel Components

The Secure Channel consists of several services according to its conceptual design. They are application services, security services, information services, network infrastructure services, and platform infrastructure services. Figure 3 depicts the Secure Channel conceptual architecture.

- Secure Services: The secure services are the fundamental services for the Secure Channel. Current secure services include authentication, authorization, encryption, data integrity, non-repudiation, time stamping, PKI, certificate authority (CA), registration authorities, facilities management, operations, Secure Sockets Layer (SSL) (SSL, 1996), and so forth. They will provide other secure services in the future,

*Figure 3: The Secure Channel conceptual architecture*

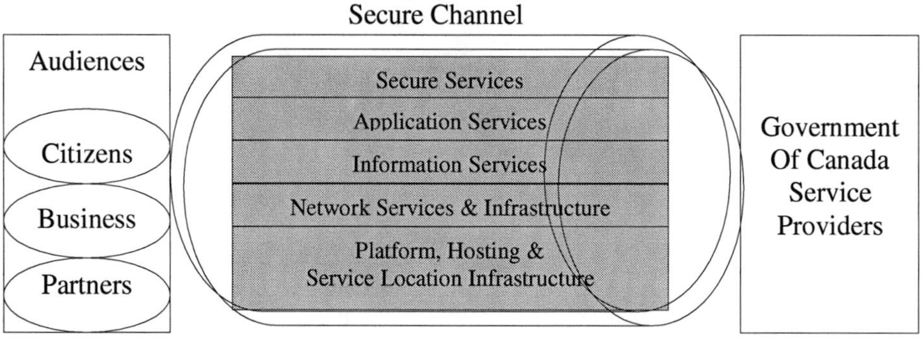

for example, IPSec (Kent & Atkinson, 1998), virtual private network (VPN), secure systems, secure remote access (SRA), managed firewall, intrusion detection system, anti-virus, content filtering services, and so on.

- Application Services: Current application services include service broker, logging, operations, secure store, and facilities management in the Secure Channel. The Secure Channel also will provide other application services in the future, such as service integration engine, service registration, access administration, search engine, session management, transaction management, profile management, and so forth. In addition, the application services also include the interface services, which provide the interfaces to contact with the government departments like Canada Customs and Revenue Agency (CCRA), Human Resources Development Canada (HRDC), and so on.

- Information Services: The Secure Channel will provide the following information services in the future, such as data security (i.e., safeguarding the data), data management, search services, directory services, and so on.

- Network Services and Infrastructure: The current network services include call services, interactive voice response (IVR), call center, telephony, connectivity, Web hosting, VPN Remote Access (RA), network operation center (NOC), facilities management, and operations, and so forth. The Secure Channel will provide other network services such as MPLS VPN, QoS, remote access, and Internet access, and so on.

- Platform, Hosting and Service Location Infrastructure: The Secure Channel currently could provide core IT services, PKI directory services, facilities management, operations, and so forth, It will provide other services in the future, for example, user registry, data security, data management, and so on.

In the Secure Channel, the service broker takes an important role. It provides the fundamental security services such as PKI, CA management, Authentication management, profile management, secure store, and so forth. Figure 4 depicts the Secure Channel service broker model.

*Figure 4: The Secure Channel service broker model*

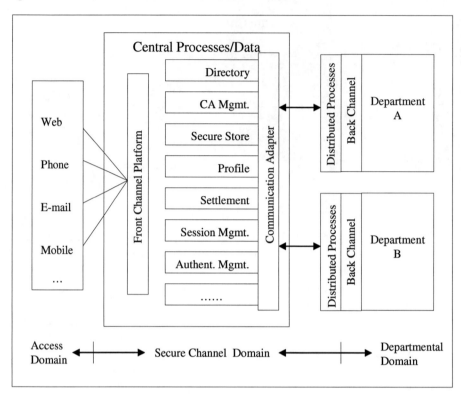

In addition, the current Secure Channel provides epass for common security services registration. Epass has the following features:

- Single Sign On (SSO): It is a session/user authentication process that permits a user to enter one name and password in order to access multiple government department applications, and also offers increased security. Note however that a citizen may have as many epasses as departments she associates with online. This was done to allay any concern over information aggregation associated with SSO.
- Online Registration
- Online or In-Person ID Proving
- Authentication, Confidentiality, Signature Verify, Non-repudiation and Time Stamp
- Secure Sockets Layer (SSL)

**Strengths and Weaknesses**

The Secure Channel will be a robust, reliable infrastructure for Canadian government electronic service delivery. It will provide many advanced services as follows.

- A common set of processes and services for authentication and registration for departments and their individual programs, for example, epass service
- Simple and strong authentications according to the security levels of the applications
- Centralized administration of PKI certificates
- Issue a digital certificate to the user to provide strong authentication along with protection of privacy, and allow for single or multiple certifications according to user preference
- Auditable transaction trail and non-repudiation
- Provide robust IP network perimeter defense capabilities such as intrusion detection, firewall, anti-virus, content filtering and security consulting services
- Provide secure remote access (SRA)
- Fast and reliable communication for inter and intra-departmental communications
- Multiple performance levels tied to traffic priority
- Serve as the backbone for timely citizen-centric service delivery
- Provide an online interface for credit card payments and integrated with Receiver General systems (the Receiver General is the official recipient for payments made to the Government of Canada)
- Much better services such as improved accounting and reconciliation functionality, a variety of back-end technologies and applications seamlessly, and so on.

Since the Secure Channel is employing the existing secure technologies such as SSL, IPSec, SRA, and so forth, especially the fundamental cryptographic algorithms such as RSA (Rivest, Shamir & Adleman, 1978), DSS (FIPS 186, Digital Signature Standard, 1994), AES (FIPS 197, Advanced Encryption Standard, 2002), IDEA, MD5, SHA-1, and so forth, the weaknesses that these technologies have still exist in the Secure Channel.

In addition, some important e-government applications such as e-voting have not yet been described in the Secure Channel. Since these applications may need to be supported by special privacy enhancing technologies such as anonymous communication networks (e.g., MIX network) (Chaum, 1981, 1985; Chaum & Evertse, 1986) pseudonym systems, and so forth, the Secure Channel still needs to be improved in the future to support these technologies for the requirements of democracy.

## Privacy Impact Assessment

Privacy concerns are requiring more positive and proactive approaches to addressing privacy issues (CIO, 2000). The Privacy Impact Assessment (PIA) is emerging as an efficient means to resolve and evaluate privacy impacts on e-services.

A PIA is a process that helps an organization determine the impacts of a program on an individual's privacy and then provide ways to mitigate or avoid any adverse effects (Canada, 2002). The program may include new initiatives, policies, services, information systems, or applied technologies. When designing a new program, making changes on an existing program, or converting existing service modes, and where such a program has potential involvements of collecting, processing, retaining, or disclosing personal information, a PIA process should be carried out to check the privacy impacts and ensure compliance with privacy related legislations and principles.

The PIA has been accepted as an important assistant to assure compliance with applicable laws and regulations governing privacy (E-government Unit, 2003), or even as a compulsory process (Greenleaf, 2002). It is also taken as a strategic consideration for government agencies (Clarke, 2000). Canada's program of "Government Online" specified the PIA process based upon the Canadian federal privacy legislation and policies, as well as the universal privacy principles identified in the Canadian Standards Association's Model Code for the Protection of Personal Information (Canada, 2002).

The PIA may benefit e-government by:

- Anticipating the privacy implications of e-government applications on the public's privacy
- Understanding the privacy risks and the options available for mitigating those risks
- Providing decision-makers with the information necessary to make informed policy, system design or procurement decisions
- Ensuring that the cost of compliance is kept as low as practicable, by avoiding expensive re-work
- Integrating privacy protections into the lifecycle of e-government systems
- Enhancing the integrity, efficiency and fairness of the system, which then enhances public trust and confidence in e-government services

**PIA Process**

Different counties and departments are developing respective PIA processes and steps. The process defined by CIO (2000) consists of four steps: privacy training, data gathering, privacy risks identifying and resolving, and approval by the Privacy Advocate. Other organizations, such as New Zealand (2002), Office of Justice Programs (2000), or Ontario (2001) have suggested detailed steps.

While there is no standard process for a PIA, the basic ideas are the same: analysis and assessment. As an example, Figure 5 shows a PIA process suggested by the Treasury Board of Canada (Canada, 2002):

- The *Project Initiation* determines the scope of the PIA, designates the project team and adapts appropriate tools for PIA analysis. A preliminary PIA or a full PIA may be conducted depending on the progress of the program initiative, such as if detailed information and processes have already been defined or known.
- The *Data Analysis* involves the analysis of business processes, data flow and system architecture, which involves the collection, use, retention, and disclosure of personal information and private behaviors.

*Figure 5: PIA process suggested by the Treasury Board of Canada*

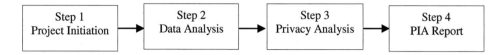

- The *Privacy Analysis* examines the data flows in the context of applicable privacy policies and legislations. Questionnaires are used as a checklist that facilitates the identification of major privacy risks or vulnerabilities associated with the program.

- With outcomes from the previous steps, the *PIA Report* documents the privacy risks and the associated implications along with discussions of possible remedy strategies. This report is to be used by the program strategist, analyst, designer, and developer for the development of the program. It may also be presented to a variety of stakeholders, including program manger and privacy commissioner.

### Suggestions and Potential Improvements

The PIA process should be considered from the earliest stages of a system proposal and design (CIO, 2000). This way the privacy impacts and protection methods can be incorporated into the whole development life cycle, from initiation to implementation. Also, it is worthwhile to mention that the PIA is a dynamic and ongoing process. A PIA may need to be reviewed and refined with the program's development and evolution.

For e-government applications, the PIA results are normally reviewed by specified privacy officials, such as the Privacy Commissioner's office. Besides these, public comment and/or external privacy reviews are also important and should be considered, especially for broad applied systems or policies, like Taxpayer Privacy Rights (CIO, 2000) or e-voting systems.

Also, it will be a limited privacy assessment process if only personal data privacy issues are addressed in a PIA. The scope should extend to "the full gamut of privacy concerns" (Clarke, 2000), including privacy of person, privacy of behavior, and privacy of communications (Clarke, 1999).

PIAs require the involvement of those who are familiar with both the privacy requirements (legal and as stated in the government's privacy policy) and the details of the workings of the databases and Web sites associated with the e-government service under review. Techniques that would automate the PIA and provide assistance in the assessment of privacy needs and the discovery of implementation details would be of great benefit. For instance, research, underway now for some time, attempts to translate laws into knowledge and rules (ontologies). Once a knowledge base of privacy policies and laws is in place, this information can be interpreted automatically to determine how private information should be dealt with for any service.

The PIA alone cannot guarantee privacy. Experience over time has demonstrated that the most effective way to protect privacy is to combine PIA with legislation, strategies, policies, methodologies, and enforcement tools. These include privacy legislation, privacy and data protection policies, privacy-enhancing technologies, as well as engaging in public education.

# Technologies Based on Privacy Policies

## *Privacy Policies*

Policy-based management approaches have been used effectively to manage and control large distributed systems. In such a system, policies are usually expressed in terms of authorization, obligation, delegation, or refrain imperatives over subject, object, conditions, and actions. Privacy policies can be used to manage or control the collection and use of private information in order to comply with the Privacy Principles. An example of such an application is the Platform for Privacy Preferences Project (P3P) (P3P: The Platform for Privacy Preferences Project, 2001), developed by the World Wide Web Consortium (W3C). P3P enables Web sites to express their privacy policies in a standard format that can be automatically retrieved and interpreted by a software agent acting on behalf of or under the control of a user (i.e., a user agent). P3P defines a machine-readable format (XML) for data collection practices, such as:

- What information does the Web site gather and for what purpose?
- How can the user gain access to the information related to her privacy?
- How long is this information kept?
- Is this information revealed to other companies and if so, for what purpose?

A user usually applies the P3P exchange language (APPEL) to express her preferences (rules) over the P3P policies. Based on these preferences, a software agent can make automated or semi-automated decisions regarding the acceptability of machine-readable privacy policies from P3P enabled Web sites. This allows P3P-enabled client software or user agents to retrieve Web site privacy policies and to compare them against the user's privacy preferences. If the user's privacy preferences are satisfied by the privacy policy of the Web site, then the user may proceed with the service; otherwise, the user might be warned that the Web site does not conform to her privacy preferences.

For e-government services, the P3P approach can be taken, but we can go beyond it to allow the user to negotiate her privacy policy with the government service provider to try to get a match between her privacy policy and the service provider's privacy policy. The service can only proceed if a match is negotiated. In this way, more users will be able to use the service, where otherwise, they may not want to give up some of their private information. We describe privacy policy negotiation in a later section.

Interestingly, while a policy-based approach makes it possible to specify and manage privacy aspects of system operation, there is a challenge in implementing the actual controls within or around the objects themselves. Consider the principle of Limiting Collection. This principle may be readily expressed as obligation policies. Unfortunately, in implementation, limiting the extent of collection of personal information is difficult, if not impossible. For instance, a government department may specify that it will only collect names of people strictly for the purpose of managing record keeping during the execution of a government program (e.g., giving a community free access to the Internet). Yet it is difficult to imagine a system that would automatically prevent collection of other information regarding the participants in the program, or the data mining of other information sources for further information about the user for any purpose the department chooses. Indeed, especially for the principles of Limiting Collection and Limiting Use, rather than automated means of compliance, trust and audit approaches are the most obvious recourse. We describe some of these approaches for privacy policy compliance in a later section.

## Negotiation of Privacy Policies

In policy-based privacy and trust management, policies must reflect the wishes of the service consumer as well as the service provider. Yee and Korba (2003) describe an agent-based approach for the negotiation of privacy policies between a distance learning consumer and a distance learning provider. They examined negotiation under certainty and uncertainty (where the offers and counter-offers are known or unknown, respectively) and proposed a scheme for resolving the uncertainty using the experience of others who have undergone similar negotiation. The choice of whom to call upon for negotiation experience is resolved through the identification of common interest and reputation.

In this work, stationary non-autonomous user agents act on behalf of the learner (see Figure 6). Similar provider agents act on behalf of the provider. The learner and the provider each must provide negotiation input to their respective agents. These agents facilitate the negotiation process through a) timely presentation and edit of the separate privacy policies, b) providing access to reputations and negotiation experience, and c) carrying out communications with the other party's agent. The decision to employ non-autonomous agents is justified by the fact that privacy is a very inexact concept that depends on many factors, including culture and education level, so that it would be extremely difficult to build an autonomous agent that learners would trust to carry out privacy negotiations.

The scheme proposed for a negotiator to resolve negotiation uncertainty using the experience of others is summarized as follows:

- Given: Stored negotiation experience of others (a data structure for this experience was given in the chapter), stored reputation for the owners of the negotiation experience (a method to calculate the reputation from past transactions is given in Yee and Korba (2003)).

Perform the following steps in order:

1. Identify which parties are reputable by asking a reputation agent for parties whose reputations exceed a pre-determined threshold. Call the resulting set A.

*Figure 6: Negotiation of privacy policies (PP) between consumer agent (CA) and provider agent (PA)*

2.   Among the parties in A, identify parties that have the same interest as the negotiator. Call the resulting set B.

3.   Among the parties in B, identify parties that have negotiated the same item as the negotiator is currently negotiating. Call the resulting set C.

4.   Retrieve the negotiation experience of parties in C, corresponding to the item under negotiation. The negotiator can then use this experience (negotiation alternatives and offers) to resolve his/her uncertainty.

The authors have also implemented a working prototype of privacy policy negotiation that incorporates the above scheme for negotiating in uncertainty.

## Ensuring Privacy Policy Compliance

As online users demand more online privacy protection, legislators and courts around the world responded with a number of laws and rulings (e.g., EU Privacy Directive, U.S. Safe Harbor Agreement, COPPA (the Children's Online Privacy Protection Act), HIPAA (the Health Insurance Portability and Accountability Act), and the Canadian PIPEDA (Personal Information Protection and Electronic Documents Act) (Department of Justice)). Most of these laws hold online organizations accountable for personal information under their control. Importantly, these laws require online organizations to designate an individual, commonly referred to as the Chief Privacy Officer (CPO), who is accountable for the organization's compliance with the applicable laws and rulings.

Generally speaking, a Chief Privacy Officer (CPO) is the person in charge of the organization's privacy compliance with the applicable privacy laws. His/her duties include the definition of the organization's privacy policy and compliance verification with the policy. His or her duties would also include raising the people's awareness of privacy within the organization. A major part of his or her duty is to create an easy and simple process for receiving complaints and resolving disputes.

Ensuring online organization compliance with the applicable laws and the posted policy is a daunting task, especially for complex Web sites. Killingsworth (1999) recommended a process for the CPO to follow in order to ensure that all online users' privacy concerns are properly addressed. The recommended process identifies the following fours steps:

1.   Auditing of the current practice of the organization: during the audit step, the CPO is required to know exactly how the personal information is handled. This step requires the CPO to analyze how each piece of information is collected, stored, used, disseminated within the organization as well as with third parties that share the information. During the process, the CPO would be able to answer questions such as how the data are analyzed, what references are made from the analysis, how long the data will be stored, with whom the data will be shared, and so on. These questions should also be answered for any third party that receives the information from the organization.

2.   Setting the goals or purpose for collecting personal information: this second step can be skipped in case the organization has some futuristic plans to perform on the collected data. This does not mean that the organization should focus on what data it can collect but on how services could be improved using additional data with less impact on privacy concerns.

3.   Formulating and drafting the policy and site design: the third step, policy development, drafting, and site design, focuses mainly on expressing the organization's data handling process in a privacy policy that is easily accessible.

4.   Implementing and maintaining the policy and data practice: this final step revolves around using the right technologies to implement the policy and data practices. This step also requires that any changes to the organization site or data handling be reflected in the policy.

Part of the design and implementation of the policy and equally important to setting security parameters, closing security holes and selecting the right data storage facility, is raising the awareness of all employees handling the data in regard to the privacy policy. Because employees are always considered the weakest link in the security chain, educating them helps reduce the risk of unauthorized use or disclosure of the personal information.

An essential responsibility of the CPO is to have a procedure in place for receiving and responding to complaints or inquiries about the privacy policy and the practice of handling personal information. This procedure should be easily accessible and simple to use. The procedure should also refer to the dispute resolution process that the organization has adopted. An online organization might also join some "privacy seal" programs such as BBBOnLine or TRUSTe, and agree to their compliance reviews. While most seal programs do not actively check for an organization's compliance with its privacy policy and laws, they usually have some conflict resolution procedures that member organizations adhere to in case online users feel that the organization has violated its privacy policy.

Most of the time, CPOs usually set up some secure logs to help them check the compliance of their organization. Such secure logs would record all of the transactions that the organization performs on the collected data during and after the collection. Cryptographic techniques (Schneier & Kelsey, 1999) can help provide assurance that any modification, deletion or insertion into the secure log would be detectable. These secure logs can also be audited for proofs of compliance or non-compliance with a particular law or regulation. Available technologies such as Oracle9i allows also for tagging the data with its privacy policy and to evaluate the policy every time the data are accessed. Actions can be associated with the result of the policy evaluation process, such as logging the access or warning the CPO in case of privacy violation. A similar concept is used in Jiang, Hong and Landay (2002) to preserve the privacy of the data even when they cross the boundaries of the organization that collected the data.

# Trustable and Compliant Interfaces

## Interfaces and Users

As mentioned in the Introduction earlier, developing trust in e-government services is especially difficult. The interface that the end user interacts with plays a central role in building or breaking that trust. It is the interface, whether it is a computer screen, a WWW site, a stand-alone kiosk, or a telephone system, that must convey all the features and limitations of the underlying service to the user. Decades of interface research and design have demonstrated that a useful and usable interface is crucial for the success of a product or service, and this is true for e-government systems. When it comes to privacy, this means that the privacy protection measures must be reflected in the interface. Since the e-government services will have to be accepted by the users, the perception of privacy will be as important as the actual privacy protection itself. A completely secure system with strong data handling policies and procedures will still be rejected if the users perceive the system or service to be untrustable (Adams, 1999).

Understanding users' perceptions falls in the discipline of psychology, and the psychology of human-computer interaction (HCI) has an important role to play in the development of e-government systems (e.g., Kossak, Essmayr & Winiwarter, 2001). HCI research has begun to examine how people perceive and cope with security and privacy concerns. Security, for example, is often perceived to be a secondary or enabling task (Sasse, 2003) that is less important than the primary task to be accomplished (e.g., providing a login and password as an enabler to reading my e-mail). Thus, security measures are often seen as barriers that users may wish to avoid, or delegate the responsibility to others (Adams & Sasse, 1999; Dourish, Delgado de la Flor & Joseph, 2003). This perception, along with the poor usability of many security systems (e.g., requiring users to memorize multiple meaningless usernames and passwords), accounts for many of the problems seen in today's security systems.

Users' perceptions of privacy concerns are also complex. For example, users' perceptions of what constitutes personal, private information is not so much determined by the content of the information but by how it is perceived by the user (Adams, 1999). Each user makes personal decisions about what he or she considers personal and private that are dynamic depending on the context of use. As mentioned previously, the receiver of the information plays a large role in determining the users' level of concern. Other contextual factors include the users' risk perception bias, prior history, level of technical knowledge of the systems involved, and so forth (see Patrick, 2002). Users may also behave in a way that is inconsistent with their stated privacy preferences and be willing to make privacy trade-offs depending on the context (e.g., allowing Web tracking when shopping for a book, but not when researching health information; Cranor, 2003).

Users may also have limited understanding of the privacy domain and the possible areas of concerns. Cranor (Cranor, 2003; Cranor, Argula & Guduru, 2002) has developed a user interface to the P3P system, the AT&T Privacy Bird, and conducted a series of studies examining people's understanding and use of the interface. She has found that users often have limited understanding of basic privacy concepts let alone the jargon that is found in the P3P vocabulary (e.g., "pseudonymous analysis"). Moreover, Cranor's studies show that most Internet users have little understanding of how privacy violations may come about, such as not understanding how cookies can be used and abused.

## Building Trustable Interfaces

Research on human decision making has shown that people assess both the trustability and the risk of a particular situation, and then weigh the two against each other to decide on an action (e.g., Grandison & Soloman, 2000; Lee, Kim & Moon, 2000; Patrick, 2002; Rotter, 1980). Trustability can be low, for example, if the perceived risk is also relatively low. On the other hand, a system might need to be very trustable if the perceived risk is very high.

The issue of building trust and reducing perceived risk has most often been studied for e-commerce transactions (e.g., Rielgelsberger & Sasse, 2001), but the lessons are also applicable to e-government. One of the most important factors for building trust in e-commerce is the visual design of the interface, and users often make rapid trust decisions based on a shallow analysis of the appearance of a WWW site (Fogg et al., 2002). A visual appearance that is clean, uses pleasing colors and graphics, is symmetrical, and is professional looking is usually rated as more trustable. Other design factors that can build trust are the amount of information provided to the user, such as the information on how a system operates and the status of any processing. This transparency of operations can be particularly important for e-government systems because users may not understand the internal procedures and policies that are involved in a government service. Predictable performance can also be an important factor, with systems that respond rapidly and consistently instilling higher levels of trust.

The most important factors for determining the level of perceived risk in e-government transactions are the sensitivity of the information involved and the receiver of the information. As previously discussed, users will perceive situations to be more or less risky depending on the nature of the personal information that is involved and the eventual destination.

Halabi (2003) has recently summarized some simple design principles for e-government interfaces. The most important is usability, which is the ability to perform the necessary tasks with ease. If users cannot accomplish the tasks they set out to perform, the service will not be accepted. There are a number of usability test methods that can be used to assess problems in this area, and HCI has developed a number of user-centered design techniques that can improve usability (e.g., Nielsen, 1993). Kossak et al. (2001) have illustrated how these techniques can be applied to e-government services.

The second factor is providing comprehensive information. For example, if an e-government service for paying parking tickets does not provide detailed information about how quickly the payments are processed, users may not trust it in fear that they will incur further penalties. A related factor is feedback and reassurance. The interface should ensure that users receive acknowledgement when information is received, and a capability to track the processing of requests or transactions will often reduce apprehension.

Finally, accessibility and flexibility are especially important design features for e-government services. Not only must the services support different languages, but they must also support users with widely different reading abilities. Flexibility in access methods, such as supporting the Internet, automated telephone services, and direct human contact, will also be important for building a service users will trust.

Another useful resource for building trustable e-government interfaces is the research results on Web site credibility. Fogg (2002) has summarized this research into a set of design guidelines that are very relevant to e-government services. Perhaps the most important is to make the site useful. This means providing the information and services that the users really want, rather than what the government wants to provide. A related principle is to make it usable, as was discussed above.

Second, the service should clearly identify itself as a legitimate organization, which means using the appropriate government logos and appearance. Third, the interface should show the real people behind the site, rather than providing a faceless corporate look. Although showing the names and faces of individuals may not be possible in a large government bureaucracy, putting some kind of human face on the interface will be important for building trust. A related design guideline is to make it easy to contact the service organization (e.g., by telephone or e-mail), and this is related to the flexible access design goal discussed above. Fogg's research also supports the importance of a professional look and feel, which includes layout, typography, colors, images, and consistency. The most colorful design is not always the most appropriate and it is important to match the visual design to the site's purpose. It is also important to avoid errors, including typographical errors and missing links. Even the smallest errors can decrease the credibility of a site. Finally, providing up-to-date and dynamic information that is clearly time-stamped is important for building trust and return visitors.

## Implementing Privacy Principles in Interfaces

In addition to building trustable interfaces, e-government developers must also create compliant interfaces. That is, the systems must comply with the privacy legislation and principles that are applicable. These might be national or local laws and regulations, government policies or procedures, or informal best practices. Building usable, privacy compliant systems involves supporting specific activities or experiences of the potential users.

Patrick and Kenny (2003) have recently described a technique called "Privacy Interface Analysis," which can be used to examine privacy requirements coming from legislation or principles and determine interface design solutions to meet the requirements. The foundation for the analysis is a review of the applicable privacy requirements and a derivation of the HCI requirements that are stated or implied. This has been done for the European Privacy Directive (95/46/EC; European Commission, 1995), and the result is a set of specific activities or experiences of the potential users that must be supported. These user needs have been summarized into four categories: comprehension, consciousness, control, and consent.

*Comprehension* refers to the users understanding the nature of private information, the risks inherent in sharing such information, and how their private information is handled by the government agencies. Design factors that can support comprehension include training, documentation, help messages, and tutorial materials. Designers can also use familiar metaphors or mental models so that users can draw on related knowledge to aid understanding. The layout of the interface can also support comprehension, such as when a left-to-right arrangement is used to convey the correct order of sequential operations.

*Consciousness* refers to the user being aware of, and paying attention to, some aspect or feature at the desired time. Design techniques that support consciousness include alarms, alert messages, and pop-up windows. Interface assistants, such as the animated help character in Microsoft Office, are also an attempt to make users aware of important information at the time it is needed. Users can also be reminded of some feature or function by the strategic placement of a control element on an interface screen, as is seen when similar functions are arranged together. Other methods to draw users' attention to something can include changing the appearance, either by using a new color or font, or by introducing animation or movement. Sounds are also a powerful technique to make the user pay attention to a particular activity or event. Privacy-aware designers should use these techniques to ensure that the users are aware of the privacy features of a system, and that they are paying attention to all the relevant information when they perform a privacy-sensitive operation.

*Control* means the ability to perform a behavior necessary to use the interface. Supporting control means building interfaces that are obvious and easy to use. Door handles that reflect the behavior that is required, such as push plates for doors that open outwards and metal loops for doors that open inwards, are good examples of obvious controls. Another useful technique is mapping, where the display or arrangement of the controls is somehow related to the real-world objects they manipulate. This might be seen, for example, when light switches are arranged on a wall in a pattern than reflects how the light fixtures are installed on the ceiling. In the privacy domain, the concept of control is important for ensuring that users actually have the ability to manipulate their private information and their privacy preferences. Thus a good interface design for an e-government system might include easy-to-use controls for limiting who can receive personal information.

*Consent* refers to users agreeing to some service or action. It is most common that there is a requirement for *informed consent,* which means that the user fully understands all the information relevant to making the agreement. Supporting informed consent implies supporting the comprehension and conscious factors listed above, since the users must both understand and be aware of the relevant information when the agreement is made. In the privacy domain, consent to the processing of personal information is often obtained when a user enrolls for a service. At that time, users are often presented with a large, legally worded user agreement that specifies how their personal information will be handled. It is well known that users often ignore these agreement documents and proceed to using the service without considering or understanding the privacy implications. This is not what is meant by informed consent, and in our laboratory we are experimenting with interface designs that allow users to make informed decisions in the appropriate context.

These HCI requirements, being derived from the European Privacy Directive, are fairly general and universal, but they will need some modification and extension depending on the national and local legislation and policies. The end result, however, will be a set of detailed interface requirements that must be met (see Table 2 in Patrick & Kenny, 2003, for an example).

Once these HCI requirements have been specified, a new application or service can be analyzed. This involves five steps:

1.   Developing a detailed description of the application or service from a use case and internal operation point of view (UML is a valuable tool here);

2.   Examining each HCI requirement to see if it applies to this application;

3.   For each requirement that must be met, scrutinizing the generic privacy solutions available to determine an appropriate specific solution;

4.   Organizing the solutions according to use cases and capturing the solutions in an interface requirements document;

5.   Implementing the interface according to the requirements document.

The result of a well-conducted privacy interface analysis is a set of design solutions that will ensure an effective and usable application that will satisfy the privacy requirements.

In summary, interface design techniques, properly used, can increase users' feelings of trust and reduce their perceptions of risk. In addition, paying attention to the users' privacy needs in the areas of comprehension, consciousness, control, and consent and ensuring these needs are satisfied by the e-government service will be an important step for building a system that is usable and trusted.

# Case Studies

We examine here how security and privacy may be provided for two obvious and important applications of e-government: e-census and e-voting. To our knowledge, these applications have not been implemented as part of the Government of Canada's offering of e-government services, although e-census is being rolled out for Canada's

2006 census. We were not able to find any references in the literature for e-census, although we found many references for e-voting.

# E-Census

In Canada, the census has been traditionally carried out by asking people to fill out a form which asks for various kinds of personal data such as address, birth date, occupation, salary range, number of people in household, and so on. The form usually contains a statement by the government agency that is conducting the census (in Canada, Statistics Canada) to the effect that all information provided will be kept confidential. Generally it is the "head of the household" (husband, or wife if the husband is not available) who is asked to provide the information. The form is delivered by Post Office mail and returned by Post Office mail when completed.

The concerns for privacy are of course centered on the fact that personal individual and household information is to be provided. All such information is private and must be governed by the Privacy Principles. In particular, the Limiting Collection Principle seems very relevant to a census, to ensure that the collecting agency does not collect more information than it needs by assuming the "while we're at it" attitude. Other principles that are highly relevant to a census are Limiting Use, Disclosure and Retention, Individual Access, and Challenging Compliance. Since the population is required by law to participate in a census, personal privacy policies really do not apply. The government is required by law to comply with the Privacy Principles and has to be trusted to do so. It would be impractical for the government to maintain secure logs as evidence of its compliance due to the sheer size of the population. Nevertheless, if news of non-compliance is leaked, the government is subject to probes by the Auditor General or the opposition parties.

An e-census simply replaces the paper census form with an electronic form hosted by an e-government Web site, with the appropriate safeguards for security and privacy (Safeguards Privacy Principle only - as mentioned previously, the government is trusted to comply with the other Privacy Principles). Figure 7 illustrates the system components for e-census.

*Figure 7: System components for e-census*

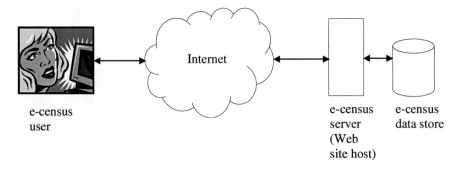

e-census
user

Internet

e-census
server
(Web
site host)

e-census
data store

The requirements for security and privacy (Safeguards Privacy Principle) for e-census are the requirements for any e-government service in which private information is collected from the user. These requirements are:

- Authentication – The government needs to be assured that the census data are coming from the genuine party and not someone who is masquerading as the party. Likewise, the user has to be assured that the e-census Web site is genuine. Since there does not seem to be any strong incentive for someone to pretend to be someone else in order to give misleading information in a census, this requirement may not be as important as in other applications such as banking.

- Authorization – The user of the e-census service must be authorized to use it. If the user completes the census over several sessions, authorization would ensure that the user is the legitimate person who should be allowed to complete it. In addition, authorization could be used to ensure that an electronic census form is completed only once.

- Non-repudiation – The user of the e-census service should not be allowed to repudiate or deny the fact that she has knowingly submitted private data requested by the e-census. Without this requirement, the user could bring a lawsuit against the government claiming that the private information was somehow obtained from her without her consent.

- Data Transmission Integrity and Confidentiality – The private data received by the government must be the same as the data submitted by the user. In addition, the data must not be intercepted in a readable form by an eavesdropper while en route from the user to the government.

- Secure Data Storage – The Census data must be stored in a secure environment. This requirement is needed for both traditional census and e-census.

In Canada, the federal government provides a means for people to register for an "epass" (Just, 2003), which then provides the person with an electronic credential that will permit her to access e-government services and programs. In fact, epass is based on SSL technology and can be used for authentication (both user and Web site), non-repudiation, and data transmission integrity, and confidentiality.

To fulfill these requirements we propose the use of epass in combination with security measures such as firewalls and intrusion detection systems for protecting the data in storage. Table 2 maps the above requirements to the proposed security technologies.

Authorization is done by the e-census software running on the Web site, which can simply access a secure table to see if the user is allowed to proceed. We do not say too much about technologies for providing secure data storage since this is a common topic and already well-treated elsewhere. We only mention some common sense safeguards such as the use of firewalls, an intrusion detection system, and restricting access to authorized personnel only.

*Table 2: Security technologies for e-census*

| Requirement | Security Technology | Comments |
|---|---|---|
| Authentication | epass | User identifies herself by supplying an electronic credential obtained by registering for epass; authenticates both Web site and user |
| Authorization | Application | E-census system checks if user is authorized |
| Non-repudiation | epass | By means of user-supplied electronic credential containing electronic signature |
| Data Transmission Integrity, Confidentiality | epass | Data are encrypted before transmission |
| Secure Data Storage | Firewall, intrusion detection system, authorized access | These measures are also needed in a regular census; authorized access means access only by authorized personnel |

# E-Voting

In this section we provide an overview of e-voting. We include a definition and the driving forces behind e-voting, a description of the requirements for e-voting systems, and the controversies and challenges for e-voting systems.

## E-Voting Definition and the Driving Forces

### Definition

We define e-voting as: "A voting system in which the election data is recorded, stored and processed primarily as digital information" (Network Voting System Standards). Note that this definition includes systems that are network-based, closed-box systems (specially developed hardware and software: e.g., Direct Recording Electronic Voting Systems), as well as Web-based solutions. Traditional electronic voting is over 134 years old. For instance, Thomas Edison introduced the Electrographic Vote Recorder with a US Patent in 1869.

### Driving Forces

There has been a great deal of research, development and use of e-voting systems. The driving forces for this level of activity include the following:

- The prospect of greater voter turnout offering greater support for the democratic process
- An electronic approach leads to the possibility of:
  - Longer ballots, especially useful in situations where there may be many candidates, or many additional questions an organization or government

wishes to poll their population on. For instance, some US State elections have had over 100 candidates (Califorinia, 2003). A paper ballot simply listing the candidates would look more like a pamphlet.

- Multiple languages on the ballot. This is an important issue in a bilingual country such as Canada, or large multilingual countries such as Russia, or the European Community. Rather than having multiple copies of ballots and instructions written in different languages, the voting terminal may present appropriate languages according to users' preferences or selections.

- Once the required infrastructure is in place (e.g., networks, voting servers and other equipment) there is a potential for reducing costs of putting on a vote.

- Electronic voting could lead to a different relationship between governments and citizens wherein governments would rely upon referenda or polling to make all major and (perhaps minor) decisions. All this would hopefully result in more responsive and representative governance.

Figure 8 illustrates a hierarchy of different types of voting processes that could be fulfilled through electronic voting means.

Another driving force in the path toward the development and deployment of electronic voting systems includes advances in telecommunications:

- Telephone systems: both wireless and wired systems offer a pervasive network (in western countries) of communication devices that may be used as voting terminal devices. The networks over which western telephone systems operate are also well managed, have high availability, and are not easily compromised.

- Short Messaging Service: Text messaging services are now commonly available in many countries. In fact, the growth in subscribers for such services has been explosive (e.g., NTT DoCoMo).

- Interactive Digital Television (IDTV): IDTV is available in large urban centers. Municipal referenda or votes could be supported through this private network.

*Figure 8: Hierarchy of voting processes*

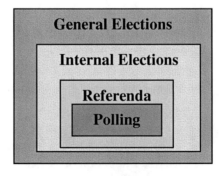

- Internet: Web-based and peer-to-peer applications offer yet another means of communication that has been widely used for electronic voting.

## E-Voting Requirements

E-voting systems should have five key attributes: anonymity, scalability, speed, audit and accuracy (Dill, Schneier & Simons, 2003). Shamos created six commandments of electronic voting which put in practical voting terms, represent the basic needs within an e-voting system (Shamos, 1993). These attributes and commandments may be expanded into the key requirements these systems should meet for effective deployment, as follows:

- Authentication - All those involved in the vote (voters and those in charge) must be checked for their validity. For electronic voting systems, several approaches have been attempted. One of them has been a public key infrastructure to offer identification of voters. Another approach is the assignment of an identity by way of usernames and passwords via a registration system.

- Uniqueness - Each voter must be unique, so that voters may vote only once. The one-person-one-vote is core to democratic principles and as such must be maintained within an e-voting system.

- Accuracy - A vote that is not accurate is useless. Worse than that rendering a vote useless, inaccurate voting would undermine the democratic process. E-voting systems must then contain safeguards for the accuracy of the process.

- Integrity - The systems supporting e-voting must have an integrity that may not be compromised. The often quoted example of the Florida 2000 election and the inadequacies of the punch-card voting approach have led to high expectations for integrity and reliability for any alternative.

- Verifiability - For the voter, there must be provisions for verifying the choice made has been accepted correctly by the system.

- Auditability - The e-voting system must offer a means of auditing the election process. To meet the auditability requirement, the e-voting system must log activities within its subsystems and provide a way to analyze the logs so as to accurately reconstruct and analyze events that occurred during the voting process. In addition, the logs must be tamperproof and secure from examination by unauthorized individuals.

- Reliability - If an e-voting system were to fail during an election, voter confidence in the system would be lowered or lost completely. The design of the e-voting system should not include any single point of failure and should include a "watchdog" operation to ensure all subsystems are operating and communicating correctly.

- Secrecy - A fundamental operational requirement of paper ballot systems is the secrecy of the vote.

- Privacy - The e-voting system should protect the privacy of the voters. Ideally the system should offer total anonymity of the voter throughout the voting process.

- Non-Coercible- It should not be possible for one to be coerced to vote against one's wishes.

- Flexibility and Convenience - Flexibility is expected from electronic voting systems. They must be able to accommodate different types of votes including write-in votes, offer quick changes in ballots, and function flexibly for different types of votes. Also, e-voting systems are expected to offer a heightened level of convenience for voters (e.g., Web or phone voting) and those in charge of the voting process. With heightened convenience, there is an expectation of higher vote participation rates.

- Certifiable - All voting systems must be certified for elections in all levels of governments. This often involves a rigorous testing process. Other organizations will have their own policies regarding the system requirements and testing required before deployment.

- Availability - The system must have a certain level of responsiveness irrespective of level of voting participation. Availability is affected by network issues (for network-based e-voting systems) and machine failures.

- Transparency - Voters should be able to understand easily how an e-voting system works.

- Cost-Effectiveness – E-voting systems are expected to offer efficiencies over paper alternatives that are measurable.

These requirements are rather broad. Standards have been set for election systems, most notably by the Federal Election Commission (FEC). In the USA, individual states have their own standards for election systems, based on the FEC standard. These include requirements for durability, maintainability, mean time between failures, mean time to repair, expected environmental operating conditions (temperature, humidity, drop tests), and so on.

## E-Voting Systems: General Organization

E-voting systems are much more than the protocols and individual processes that might be put in place to create the system. To gain some understanding of what an e-voting system might look like, it is important to consider the actors involved in holding a vote For the sake of this discussion we consider a federal election.

The *election organizers* manage and orchestrate the voting process and ensure it is properly conducted. The *election personnel* carry out the orders of the election organizers. The *party representatives* are generally members from all parties involved in the election, appointed to monitor the election process. *Judicial officers* oversee the correct legal operation of the election. *Independent third parties* are people who have no vested interest in the outcome of the vote, and may be appointed to assure the integrity of the process. The *voters* are all those eligible to participate in the vote.

An e-voting system will have the following set of services (see Figure 9):

- Voter Registration – Registration involves checking the eligibility of the individual for the vote and managing the identity of the voter for the purposes of the vote. In order to respect the privacy of the voter and the importance of vote confidentiality and non-traceability, a variety of different voting protocols have been developed (Cranor). These are very challenging requirements, and there are still many improvements that could be made to the registration service (Rivest, 2001).

- Vote Casting – This service handles all aspects associated with a voter casting a vote.

- Security – Separate from the other services is the security service. It handles many of the functions required during the election. These include: authentication, authorization, data privacy, data integrity and non-repudiation. Authentication and authorization assure that the voter and others who have access to the system are indeed who they say they are and that they are eligible to perform the function they are attempting to perform. For instance, in vote casting, the authentication service will assure that the voter is correctly identified, while the authorization service will determine whether the person is registered to vote and has not yet voted.

- Vote Tallying – This service involves tallying eligible votes.

- Election Result Verification – Under the guidance of the election organizer, the judicial officer and independent third party would use this service to verify the election results.

- Election Audit – The audit service would be used to examine details of the operations of any of the e-voting services. The audit service would comprise various means for searching and examining the many logs associated with the other services. Clearly the logs must be protected by cryptographic and other means to ensure they are tamper proof.

*Figure 9 : E-Voting system from the services point of view.*

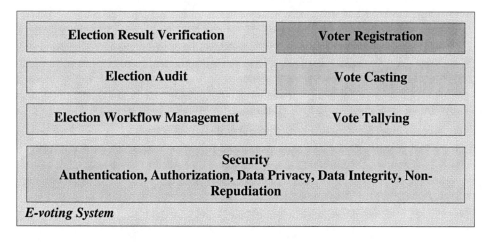

- Election Workflow Management – Launching and administering an election is a complicated process involving many different steps. The workflow management service would help the election officials manage the process more effectively.

There have been many types of e-voting systems developed. Some are in the public domain (FREE e-democracy project, 2003). Several implement reasonably effective mechanisms to assure the operating requirements for e-voting systems.

## E-Voting Security Issues

Due to the many potential benefits of electronic voting, there has been a flurry of activity in the development and deployment of e-voting systems within the USA. This is especially true for Direct Recording Electronic (DRE) systems. These systems completely eliminate paper in the voting process, using an electronic terminal to capture vote casting. A growing number of states within the USA have adopted systems from various manufacturers. While they may have passed testing certification requirements based upon FEC and state requirements, concerns remain over their deployment. The technical challenges associated with e-voting have led to investigations by numerous researchers of protocols and other technologies to promote private and secure electronic voting. At the same time there has been a rush to market by many companies to deliver new systems to meet the demand from various governments. Most companies have developed their own hardware and software rapidly in order to meet the perceived market need. Similarly, standards for e-voting equipment were also developed to provide a certifying process for e-voting equipment and software. Systems have been approved and used for voting processes in many jurisdictions. Many votes have been cast using this new technology. Why then are there any security issues left with "proven technology"? A review of recent public discussions of the security systems put in place by a well-known e-voting technology developer and manufacturer follows:

### Diebold Systems

An interesting case study in this area is Diebold, Incorporated (Diebold, Incorporated Web site). Diebold has a lengthy history in the manufacturing of security systems, commencing with safes and vaults in 1859. Today the company is the market leader for self-service transaction systems in North America, Latin America and the Middle East, with projected revenue (2003) of about 2 billion US dollars. They manufacture automated teller machines (ATMs), self-service systems, provide security consulting services and engineering, currency processing systems, card-based systems and election systems. They consider themselves to be a market leader in election systems.

Their Accuvote-TS™ is a direct record entry device (DRE). This is a special purpose computer device designed as a voter terminal. It has features to support voting by the visually impaired. The company also claims election results stored securely "utilizing world-class encryption techniques," among other features. Diebold has also developed application software called Global Election Management System (GEMS) to provide the back-end for the Accuvote terminal.

In January of 2002, what appears to be code for the Diebold Voting System appeared on Diebold's public access FTP server. The code has since been redistributed through other Internet sites (Jones, 2003). It was announced by Bev Harris and discussed in her book, *Black Box Voting* (Harris, 2003) and other articles (Harris, 2003). The code appears to be from an earlier version of Diebold's Accuvote-TS and GEMS. Harris has illustrated how the multiple sets of books for the vote ledgers are open to tampering – leading to incorrect election results (Harris, 2003). GEMS appears to use Microsoft Access for its database. Another vulnerability described involves the ease with which one can work around password access to the Access database. The author also questions the audit trail process, showing how the audit trail may be modified.

A group of researchers at Johns Hopkins University has studied the source code for what appears to be Diebold's Accuvote-TS voting terminal from security and software engineering points of view. Their report (Kohno et al., 2003) describes a wide range of security problems in the code and outlines questionable software engineering practices. While many security issues are described, those that are core and have not been refuted through the public responses from Diebold (Diebold systems follow-up, 2003) and the authors (Kohno, Stubblefield, Rubin & Wallach, 2003) include:

- Key management:
  - Cryptographic keys stored as static entries in the source code. If a single voting machine is compromised, any/all parts running the same software are compromised.
  - No description of Diebold's new approach for handling smartcard keys. It appears that Diebold still uses techniques that would make the keys available in physical storage.
- Votes and audit logs are encrypted using the Data Encryption Standard (DES).
  - The source code uses DES in Cypher Block Coding CBC mode, yet the source code fails to provide the necessary initialization vectors.
  - DES is an old symmetrical key encryption technology. It is widely known to be subject to efficient brute force attacks.
- Data Integrity: Diebold uses the Cyclic Redundancy Check (CRC) method in an attempt to provide data integrity. This technique is known to be unsafe. Message Authentication Codes (MACs) can detect tampering with data.
- Smart Cards: It appears that it would be possible for an attacker to use a counterfeit smart card to tamper with the results or the process of an election. This may be done with or without knowledge of the software of the election terminal.

While the previous comments pertain more to the technical analysis of e-voting, Jones (2003) offers yet another perspective on the issues raised by the Johns Hopkins analysis as well as other issues related to the FEC standards.

## E-Voting: Further Work Required

The above discussion concerning a particular voting system underscores several issues related to e-voting. Indeed, as has already been discussed by several researchers (Cranor; Jones, 2003; Kohno, Stubblefield, Rubin & Wallach, 2003; Mercuri, 2003), e-voting requires some work before it is ready for prime time (Campaign to demand verifiable election results, 2003). Here we outline some of the work still needed related to this field.

### Scalable Private E-Voting

Research to date describes security protocols for possible implementation in e-voting systems. These offer privacy and integrity advantages, often against a wide range of attack models. Unfortunately, technologies that make a system secure and private can make implementations complex, leading to computational and network costs. More work is needed in the development of approaches for testing protocols and systems for scalability early in the design phase. New ideas must be implemented and tested for scalability and resilience to attack in order to meet the reliability requirements for e-voting systems. Within the research community there are a few efforts towards practical open implementations (Cranor, 1996) (EVOX voting system) (FREE e-democracy project, 2003) (SOLON – The free election program, 2003). Some describe scalability issues (Cranor, 1996).

### Secure Distributed Logs

As described above, logging activities during a voting process is important to enable auditing. An audit service makes extensive use of logs maintained by the e-voting system. Logs are typically distributed over many computing platforms (e.g., voting terminals, servers). They must contain detailed information that links with other sub-systems and their activities. The records must be secure from unauthorized access, and resistant to alteration. The records must also maintain the privacy of individual voters (i.e., voters must not be identified, and they are not linkable to their votes). Developments to standardize format for secure logs would be an improvement for e-voting and many other Internet applications.

### Citizen Engagement

Critical to democratic elections is the involvement of as many citizens as possible. While a driving force for e-voting is the opportunity to engage more citizens in the voting process, there are more fundamental approaches to engage citizens in democracy. Citizen engagement is larger than offering electronic voting. Services ancillary to e-voting, if put in place, would play an important role in citizen engagement. For instance, Web-based access to voter's lists, and e-government services that make it easier to correct voter information.

### Trustworthy Computing Platforms

In an environment where the attack model may include computing platforms (hardware and software) that may be compromised, meeting the security and privacy requirements for e-voting is very challenging. Special protocols and procedures have been developed in an attempt to deal with a computing platform attack. While no trustworthy computing platform currently exists, several companies and research organizations are attempting to build the technology. Improvements in the trustworthiness of computing platforms will make many applications (including e-voting) viable.

### Open Software Review

The Diebold case underscores the importance of open review of software for e-voting systems. Voting is core to democracy. Systems must meet the expectations for security and privacy. Scrutiny of the inner workings of e-voting systems by leading experts is essential. To effectively open the review process, systems, protocols and source code would be described in detail at the manufacturers' Web sites. Developers would attempt to publish details of new approaches at recognized security conferences.

# Conclusions and Future Research

We have introduced the reader to the benefits and challenges of e-government. We defined what we mean by privacy, trust, and security as applied to e-government and surveyed the state of the current research in this area. We next summarized Canada's e-government initiative and implementation and gave a comparison of progress in e-government from the Accenture report. This report puts Canada in first place in 2002 (as it was in 2001) with Singapore coming close, followed by the United States. We updated this picture of e-government progress with data from the latest 2004 Accenture report, which again put Canada in first place, with Singapore and the United States sharing second place. We next presented an overview of privacy legislation and policy from the Canadian perspective. In particular, the Privacy Principles play a key role in identifying privacy requirements. We next discussed existing privacy enhancing technologies for e-government as seen in the Canadian initiative, and examined the Secure Channel and Privacy Impact Assessment. We looked at other privacy enhancing technologies driven by privacy policies, and discussed privacy policy negotiation and how to ensure policy compliance. We then examined the important role of trustable interfaces in promoting trust among users of e-government services. Finally, we presented two case studies of potential e-government services: e-census and e-voting.

There is still much to be done in terms of privacy and security research for e-government, as demonstrated by the relative lack of literature in this area. New e-government services may require more stringent privacy protection mechanisms such as anonymous communication networks and pseudonym systems. The whole area of policy-driven privacy management needs to be further explored in terms of privacy policy negotiation and assurance of policy compliance. More research is also needed for building usable and trusted interfaces, in terms of service customization and user acceptance. In the application domain, further work is needed for e-voting in terms of scalability, auditing, citizen engagement, trustworthy computing platforms, and open software review. Another area requiring attention is the development of techniques that would lower the cost but keep up the security of authentication maintenance for access to government services. Twenty-four hour helpdesk support is expensive to maintain and any approach that can automate username/password recovery while maintaining secure access would be beneficial.

Governments must maintain equal service access to all citizens. Not all citizens will have equal access to computers and the Internet due to physical handicap, economic restrictions or personal preferences. Governments must then have alternate means for providing their services. In the future, with e-government fully deployed, we will still see government offices, but there may well be considerably fewer people staffing those offices.

# References

Accenture. (2002). E-government leadership – Realizing the vision. The Government Executive Series, 2002-04. Retrieved July 2003, from: *http://www.gol-ged.gc.ca/ pub/pub_e.asp* (labeled as Accenture - Third Annual E-Government Study – Realizing the Vision (2002-04)).

Accenture (2004). E-government leadership: High performance, maximum value. The Government Executive Series, 2004-05. Retrieved June 9, 2004 from: *http:// www.accenture.com/xdoc/en/industries/government/gove_egov_value.pdf.*

Adams, A. (1999). *The implications of users' privacy perception on communication and information privacy policies.* Proceedings of Telecommunications Policy Research Conference, Washington DC.

Adams, A., & Sasse, M.A. (1999). Users are not the enemy: Why users compromise security mechanisms and how to take remedial measures. *Communications of the ACM, 42*(12), 40-46.

BBBOnLine. Retrieved July 12, 2003, from: *http://www.bbbonline.org.*

Benabdallah, S. et al. (2002, October 6-9). *Security issues in e-government models: What governments should do.* Proc. of IEEE International Conference on Systems, Man and Cybernetics SMC'2002, Hammamet, Tunisia.

Boudriga, N. (2002, October 6-9). *Technical issues in securing e-government.* Proc. of IEEE International Conference on Systems, Man and Cybernetics SMC'2002, Hammamet, Tunisia.

Caloyannides, M. et al. (2003, May/June). US e-government authentication framework and programs. *IT Pro,* 16-21. IEEE Computer Society.

Campaign to demand verifiable election results. (2003). Retrieved August 18, 2003, from: *http://www.verifiedvoting.org/resolution.asp.*

Canada. (2002, April). Privacy impact assessment policy. Treasury Board Secretariat, Government of Canada. Retrieved August 22, 2003, from: *http://www.tbs-sct.gc.ca/ pubs_pol/ciopubs/pia-pefr/siglist_e.asp.*

CCITT. (2001). Rec. X.509 (03/00) I ISO/IEC 9594-8: 2001, *Information technology – Open systems Interconnecion – The Directory: Public-key and attribute certificate frameworks.*

Chaum, D. (1981). Untraceable electronic mail, return address, and digital pseudonyms. *Communications of the ACM, 24*(2), 84-88.

Chaum, D. (1985). Security without identification: Transaction systems to make big brother obsolete. *Communication of the ACM, 28*(10), 1030-1044.

Chaum, D., & Evertse, J. (1986). A secure and privacy-protecting protocol for transmitting personal information between organizations. *Advances in cryptology—CRYPTO'86* (pp. 118-167). Springer-Verlag.

Chou, W. (2002, July/August). Inside SSL: The secure sockets layer protocol. *IT Pro, 47-52.* IEEE Computer Society.

CIO. (2000, February). Best practices: Privacy, internal revenue service model information technology. CIO Council Sub-Committee on Privacy. Retrieved August 22, 2003, from: *http://www.cio.gov/Documents/pia_for_it_irs_model.pdfb.*

Clarke, R. (1999). Introduction to dataveillance and information privacy, and definitions of terms, 1997-1999. Retrieved August 23, 2003, from: *http://www.anu.edu.au/people/Roger.Clarke/DV/Intro.html.*

Clarke, R. (2000). Privacy impact assessments, 1997-2000. Retrieved August 22, 2003, from: *http://www.anu.edu.au/people/Roger.Clarke/DV/PIA.html.*

COPPA (the Children's Online Privacy Protection Act). Retrieved July 12, 2003, from: *http://www.cdt.org/legislation/105th/privacy/coppa.html.*

Cranor, L. Electronic voting hot list. Retrieved August 15, 2003, from: *http://lorrie.cranor.org/voting/hotlist.html.*

Cranor, L. (1996). Sensus prototype. Retrieved August 16, 2003, from: *http://lorrie.cranor.org/voting/sensus/.*

Cranor, L.F. (2003, April 6). *Designing a privacy preference specification interface: A case study.* CHI 2003 Workshop on Human-Computer Interaction and Security Systems, Ft. Lauderdale, FL.

Cranor, L.F., Arjula, M., & Guduru, P. (2002, November 21). Use of a P3P user agent by early adopters. Proceedings of Workshop on Privacy in the Electronic Society, Washington, D.C.

CSA. (1996). Privacy code, Canadian Standards Association ten privacy principles. Retrieved July 10, 2002, from: *http://www.csa.ca/standards/privacy/code/Default.asp?language=English.*

Dempsey, J.X. (2003). What e-government means for those of us who cannot type. Local Government Brief, Winter 2003, p. 22. Retrieved Sept. 3, 2003, from: *http://lgi.osi.hu/publications/2003/217/english.pdf.*

Department of Justice. Privacy provisions highlights. Retrieved April 4, 2002, from: *http://canada.justice.gc.ca/en/news/nr/1998/attback2.html.*

Diebold, Incorporated Web site. Retrieved August 17, 2003, from: *http://www.diebold.com/.*

Diebold systems follow-up (2003). Retrieved August 20, 2003, from: *http:// www.diebold.com/followupstatement.pdf; http://www.diebold.com/technical response.pdf; http://www.diebold.com/checksandbalances.pdf.*

Dill, D., Schneier, B., & Simons, B. (2003). Voting and technology: Who gets to count your vote? *Communications of the ACM, 46*(8), 29-31.

Dourish, P., Delgado de la Flor, J., & Joseph, M. (2003, April 5). *Security as a practical problem: Some preliminary observations of everyday mental models.* CHI 2003 Workshop on Human-Computer Interaction and Security Systems, Ft. Lauderdale, FL.

Egger, F.N. (2001, June 27-29). Affective design of e-commerce user interfaces: How to maximise perceived trustworthiness. In M. Helander, H.M. Khalid & Tham (Eds.), *Proceedings of CAHD2001: Conference on Affective Human Factors Design,* Singapore (pp. 317-324). ASEAN Press.

E-government Unit. (2003, March). Preliminary privacy impact assessment of models being considered for inclusion in a proposal for online authentication for e-government. E-government Unit, State Services Commission. Retrieved August 23, 2003, from: *http://www.e-government.govt.nz/docs/authent-pia-prelim/.*

EU Privacy Directive. Retrieved July 12, 2003, from: *http://www2.echo.lu/legal/en/ dataprot/directiv/directiv.html.*

European Commission. (1995). Directive 95/46/EC of the European Parliament and of the Council of 24 October 1995 on the Protection of Individuals with Regard to the Processing of Personal Data and on the Free Movement of such Data. *Official Journal of the European Communities, 31.*

EVOX voting system. Retrieved August 16, 2003, from: *http://theory.lcs.mit.edu/~cis/ voting/voting.html.*

Federal Election Commission. Voting systems standards. Retrieved August 16, 2003, from: *http://www.fec.gov/pages/vss/vss.html.*

FIPS 186, Digital Signature Standard. (1994). Retrieved August 15, 2003, from: *http:// www.itl.nist.gov/fipspubs/fip186.htm.*

FIPS 197, Advanced Encryption Standard. (2002). Retrieved August 15, 2003, from: *http:/ /csrc.nist.gov/CryptoToolkit/aes/.*

Fogg, B.J. (2002). Stanford guidelines for Web credibility. A research summary from the Stanford Persuasive Technology Lab. Stanford University. Retrieved August 25, 2003, from: *www.webcredibility.org/guidelines.*

Fogg, B.J., Marable, L., Stanford, J., & Tauber, E.R. (2002). How do people evaluate a web site's credibility? Results from a large study. Consumer Webwatch News. *http:/ /www.consumerwebwatch.org/news/report3_credibilityresearch/stanfordPTL_ TOC.htm.*

FREE e-democracy project. (2003). Retrieved August 17, 2003, from: *http://sourceforge. net/projects/free/.*

Government of Canada. (2002). *Sustainable, secure electronic services – Building the base for government-wide, multi-channel service transformation.* Annual report on Canada's progress on GOL prepared for the 36th Conference (2002) of the

International Council for Information Technology in Government Administration (ICA), 2002-09. Retrieved July 2003, from: *http://www.gol-ged.gc.ca/pub/pub_e.asp.*

Government of Canada. (2003). 2nd Annual Report on GOL: Government On-line 2003, 2003-06. Retrieved July 2003, from: *http://www.gol-ged.gc.ca/pub/pub_e.asp.*

Grandison, T., & Sloman, M. (2000). A survey of trust in Internet applications. IEEE Communications Surveys, Fourth Quarter 2000. *http://www.comsoc.org/livepubs/surveys/public/2000/dec/grandison.html.*

Greenleaf, G. (2002). Canada makes privacy impact assessments compulsory. *Privacy Law & Policy Reporter, 8*(10), 189-190.

Halabi, L. (2002, January). Implementing e-government, the key to success is good 'usability'. *The Source Public Management Journal.*

Harris, B. (2003, July 8). Inside a U.S. Election Vote Counting program. *SCOOP.* Retrieved August 20, 2003, from: *http://www.scoop.co.nz/mason/stories/HL0307/S00065.htm.*

Harris, B.-1 (2003, July). *Black box voting: Vote tampering in the 21st century.* Elon House/Plan Nine.

HIPPA (the Health Insurance Portability and Accountability Act). Retrieved July 12, 2003, from: *http://cms.hhs.gov/hipaa/.*

Jiang, X., Hong, J., & Landay, L. (2002, September 29-October 1). *Approximate information flows: Socially-based modeling of privacy in ubiquitous computing.* Proceedings of the 4th International Conference on Ubiquitous Computing (Ubicomp'2002), GÖTEBORG, Sweden.

Jones, D.W. (2003, July). The case of the Diebold FTP site. Retrieved August 18, 2003, from: *http://www.cs.uiowa.edu/~jones/voting/dieboldftp.html.*

Just, M. (2003). An overview of public key certificate support for Canada's Government On-Line (GOL) initiative. Retrieved August 22, 2003, from: *http://www.cio-dpi.gc.ca/pki-icp/gocpki/opkcs-veuccpf/opkcs-veuccpf01_e.asp.*

Kent, S., & Atkinson, R. (1998, November). *IP authentication header.* IETF RFC 2402.

Kent, S., & Atkinson, R. (1998, November). *IP Encapsulating Security Payload (ESP).* IETF RFC 2406.

Kent, S., & Atkinson, R. (1998, November). *Security architecture for the Internet protocol.* IETF RFC 2401.

Killingsworth, S. (1999, fall). Minding your own business: Privacy policies in principle and in practice. *Journal of Intellectual Property Law.*

Kohno, T. et al (2003). *Analysis of an electronic voting system.* Johns Hopkins Information Security Institute Technical Report TR-2003-19. Retrieved August 18, 2003, from: *http://avirubin.com/vote.pdf.*

Kohno, T., Stubblefield, A., Rubin, A., & Wallach, D. (2003). Response to Diebold's technical analysis. Retrieved August 20, 2003, from: *http://avirubin.com/vote/response.html.*

Kossak, F., Essmayr, W., & Winiwarter, W. (2001, June). *Applicability of HCI research to e-government applications.* Proceedings of the 9th European Conference on Information Systems, Bled, Slovenia.

Lee, J., Kim, J., & Moon, J.Y. (2000). What makes Internet users visit cyber stores again? Key design factors for customer loyalty. *Proceedings of CHI '2000,* The Hague, Amsterdam, 305-312.

Local Government Brief. (2003, Winter). *Of modems and men: Installing e-government in the e-east.* Local Government Brief, Open Society Institute. Retrieved September 3, 2003, from: *http://lgi.osi.hu/publications/2003/217/english.pdf.*

Mercuri, R. (2003, January). On auditing audit trails. *Communications of the ACM, 46*(1).

Mercuri, R. Web page on electronic voting. Retrieved August 28, 2003, from: *http://www.notablesoftware.com/evote.html.*

National Research Council, Committee on Computing and Communications Research to Enable Better Use of Information Technology in Government. (2002). *Information technology research, innovation, and e-government.* Washington, DC: National Academy of Sciences. Retrieved August 25, 2003, from: *http://search.nap.edu/html/itr_e_gov/.*

Network Voting System Standards. Retrieved August 15, 2003, from: *http://www.votehere.net/ada_compliant/nvss/NetworkVotingSystemStandards.pdf.*

New Zealand. (2002, March). Privacy impact assessment handbook. Office of the New Zealand Privacy Commissioner. Retrieved August 23, 2003, from: *http://www.privacy.org.nz/comply/pia.html.*

Nielsen, J. (1993). *Usability engineering.* Boston, MA: Academic Press.

NTT DoCoMo. Retrieved August 16, from: *http://www.nttdocomo.com/home.html.*

Office of Justice Programs. (2000, August). Privacy impact assessment for justice information systems. Office of Justice Programs. Retrieved August 24, 2003, from: *http://www.ojp.usdoj.gov/archive/topics/integratedjustice/piajis.htm.*

Ontario. (2001). Privacy impact assessment guidelines 1999, re., 2001. Management Board Secretariat, Government of Ontario. Retrieved August 24, 2003, from: *http://www.gov.on.ca/mbs/english/fip/pia/pia1.html.*

P3P: The Platform for Privacy Preferences Project. (2001). In S. Garfinkel & G. Spafford (Eds.), Web security, privacy & commerce (2nd ed., pp. 699-707). Sebastopol, CA: O'Reilly & Associates, Inc.

Patrick, A.S. (2002) Building trustworthy software agents. IEEE *Internet Computing, 6*(6), 46-53.

Patrick, A.S., & Kenny, S. (2003, March 26-28). *From privacy legislation to interface design: Implementing information privacy in human-computer interfaces.* In R. Dingledine (Ed.), Proceedings of Privacy Enhancing Technologies Workshop (PET2003), Dresden, Germany. LNCS 2760, pp. 107-124 (NRC 45787).

Rezgui, A. et al (2002, November 8). *Preserving privacy in Web services.* Proceedings, WIDM'02, McLean, VA.

Riegelsberger, R., & Sasse, M.A. (2001, October 3-5). *Trustbuilders and trustbusters: The role of trust cues in interfaces to e-commerce applications.* Presented at the 1st IFIP Conference on e-commerce, e-business, e-government (i3e), Zurich. *http://www.cs.ucl.ac.uk/staff/jriegels/trustbuilders_and_trustbusters.htm.*

Rivest, R. (2001, May 24). Security in voting technology. Testimony before the committee on house administration.Retrieved August 17, 2003, from: *http://theory.lcs.mit.edu/~rivest/rivest-may-24-01-testimony.doc.*

Rivest, R.L., Shamir, A., & Adleman, L. (1978, February). A method for obtaining digital signatures and public-key cryptosystems. *Communications of ACM, 21*(2), 120-126.

Rotter, J.B. (1980). Interpersonal trust, trustworthiness, and gullibility. *American Psychologist, 35*(1), 1-7.

Sasse, M.A. (2003, April 5). *Computer security: Anatomy of a usability disaster, and a plan for recovery.* CHI 2003 Workshop on Human-Computer Interaction and Security Systems, Ft. Lauderdale.

Schneier, B. & Kelsey, J. (1999, May). Secure audit logs to support computer forensics. *ACM Transactions on Information and System Security, 2*(2), 159-176. ACM.

Shamos, M. (1993, March 9-12). *Electronic voting – Evaluating the threat.* 3rd conf. on Computers Freedom and Privacy, Burlingame, CA. Retrieved August 15, 2003, from: *http://www.cpsr.org/conferences/cfp93/shamos.html.*

SOLON – The free election program. (2003). Retrieved August 17, 2003, from: *http://sourceforge.net/projects/solon/.*

SSL. (1996). 3.0 Specification. Retrieved August 15, 2003, from: *http://wp.netscape.com/eng/ssl3/.*

Treasury Board of Canada Secretariat. (2002). Government Sscurity policy. Retrieved on August 20, 2003 from: *http://www.tbs-sct.gc.ca/pubs_pol/gospubs/tbm_12a/gsp-psg_e.asp.*

TRUSTe. Retrieved July 12, 2003, from: *http:www.truste.org.*

U.S. Safe Harbor Agreement. Retrieved July 12, 2003, from: *http://www.export.gov/safeharbor/.*

Wimmer, M., & von Bredow, B. (2002, January 7-11). *A holistic approach for providing security solutions in e-government.* Proceedings of the 35th Hawaii International Conference on System Sciences (HICSS), Hawaii.

Yee, G., & Korba, L. (2003, May 18-21). *The negotiation of privacy policies in distance education.* Proceedings, 14th IRMA International Conference, Philadelphia, PA. NRC Paper Number: NRC 44985.

# Endnote

[1]  NRC Document No. NRC-46528.

# Section II:

# E-Government Implementations and Practices

Chapter VIII

# A Comparative Study of Strategic Issues of Digital Government Implementations Between Developed and Developing Countries

Yining Chen, Ohio University, USA

Wayne Huang, Shanghai Jiaotong University, China and Ohio University, USA

D. Li, Peking University, China

H.Z. Shen, Shanghai Jiaotong University, China

P.Z. Zhang, Shanghai Jiaotong University, China

Lori Klamo, Ohio University, USA

## Abstract

*Over the last decade, the Internet has become one of the most important means of communication in all social areas. The success of Web technology adoption in the private sector has put pressures on the public sector to adopt the Internet to present information and service resources. The concept of creating more efficient and convenient interaction between government and the interacting parties using Internet technology is referred to as digital government (or e-government). Recent studies have shown an increase in the adoption of digital government by various countries. Nevertheless, the level of implementation diverges from country to country. This study compares strategic issues of digital government implementation between developed and developing countries. Critical success factors for digital government implementation are discussed. In addition, recommendations are made to developed and developing countries for their implementation of digital government.*

# Introduction

With the Internet surging, governments at all levels are utilizing it to reinvent their structure and efficiency, coining the term "digital government" to describe this initiative. Bill Gates of Microsoft claims that digital government is one of the most exciting fields in electronic commerce in the near future. The *Economist* magazine estimates that the potential savings of implementing digital government could be as much as $110 billion and 144 billion English pounds in the US and Europe respectively (Symonds, 2000). Though a new subject, digital government has attracted more and more research interest and focus from industries, national governments, and universities, such as IBM's Institute for Electronic Government and various "E-government Task Forces" in different countries.

Digital government is a permanent commitment by government to improve the relationship between the private citizen and the public sector through enhanced, cost-effective, and efficient delivery of services, information, and knowledge. Broadly defined, digital government includes the use of all information and communication technologies, from fax machines to wireless palm pilots, to facilitate the daily administration of government, exclusively as an Internet driven activity that improves citizens' access to government information, services and expertise to ensure citizens' participation in, and satisfaction with government process (UN and ASPA, 2001). Narrowly defined, digital government is the production and delivery of government services through IT applications; used to simplify and improve transactions between governments and constituents, businesses, and other government agencies (Sprecher, 2000).

## From Traditional Government to Digital Government

The development and implementation of digital government will have big effects on and bring about some changes to the structure and functioning of the public administration (Snellen, 2000). Unlike the traditional bureaucratic model where information flows only vertically and rarely between departments, digital government links new technology with legacy systems internally and in turn links government information infrastructures

*Table 1: Main differences between traditional and digital government*

| Traditional Government | Digital Government |
|---|---|
| Bureaucratic controls, clear authority hierarchy | Client service and community empowerment, leveled/blurred hierarchy |
| Process centricity | Customer centricity |
| Isolated administrative functions and data collection | Integrated resource service and knowledge focus |
| Functional specialization of units or geographic bias | Breakdown of unit barrier, government integration |
| Decision based on uniform rules and awkward reporting approvals | Decision based on negotiation and implicit controls and approvals |
| Isolated administrative functions | Integrated resource services |
| Disjointed information technologies | Integrated network solutions |
| Time-consuming process | Rapid streamlined responses |

externally with everything digital (Tapscott, 1995). Traditional government process focused on internally driven service delivery, whereas in digital government, priority will be placed on establishing mutually beneficial relationships between customers and governments. Furthermore, decision making based on uniform rules will shift to negotiation based. Information capture and data collection will shift from isolated administrative functions to integrated resource service and knowledge focus. The table below summarizes the characteristic differences between the traditional government and digital government organizations.

# Digital Government Implementation Benefits

Governments are capitalizing on information technology to improve people's lives. Generally governments are aiming to make information technology the servant of society in order to improve living standards, to make economies stronger, and to bring people closer together. The benefits of digital government are enormous. Some of these are listed below:

- Break down the barriers: Digital government will help breaking down agency and jurisdictional barriers to allow more integrated whole-of-government services across the three tiers of government (Federal, State, and Local). With digital government, the provision of seamless access will be taken much further and will make government much more approachable.

- More accessible government: Government in the offline environment can be difficult to access. While some business can be conducted by phone, it often requires a visit to a government office. This can be problematic for people in regional and remote locations. Digital government offers a potential to dramatically increase access to information and services.

- Improved service quality: The underlying goal of digital government is to improve service quality for all citizens. Digital government represents convenient and reliable services, with lower compliance costs as well as higher quality and value.

- Integration of agencies: Cross-agency initiatives can lead to high value services that provide efficiency benefits for both citizens and government. Scope for cross-agency initiatives exists where several services are closely related – that is, where information needs to be acquired from more than one agency (e.g., business services).

- Improved reputation: Digital government helps build up an image of a country as a modern nation, an attractive location for people to visit and business to invest in.

- Greater participation by people in government: Digital government makes it easier for those who wish to contribute to governmental issues.

## Digital Government Implementation Stages

According to the government and the Internet survey (2000), the implementation of digital government includes four major internal and external aspects:

- the establishment of a secure government intranet and central database for more efficient and cooperative interaction among governmental agencies
- Web-based service delivery
- the application of e-commerce for more efficient government transaction activities, such as procurement and contract
- digital democracy for more transparent accountability of government

Various stages of digital government reflect the degree of technical sophistication and interaction with users (Hiller & Belanger, 2001). The five stages listed below are just a conceptual model to examine the recent evolution of digital government. Not all levels of government follow this linear progression. Many studies of technological innovation also indicate that the diffusion and adoption of technology may even follow a curvilinear path (Moon, 2002).

- Stage 1: the most basic form of digital government; uses IT for disseminating information by posting data on the Web sites that are viewable
- Stage 2: two-way communication between government and constituents; e-mail systems are incorporated as well as data-transfer technologies

- Stage 3: Web-based self services where online service and financial transactions are available
- Stage 4: various government services are connected internally and externally for enhanced efficiency, user-friendliness, and effectiveness
- Stage 5: the promotion of Web-based political participation, including online voting; highlights Web-based political activities by citizens

# Developed versus Developing Countries

Every year, the United Nations releases a report on the least developed countries (LDC) and compares their economic conditions in several different categories. For 2002, 49 countries were designated as the least developed. These countries were decided based on their low GDP per capita, their weak human assets, and their high degree of economic vulnerability (UNCTAD, 2002). Digital government implementation and development is a high-priority issue on various countries' agenda. Some countries have surpassed others in online services that they offer to their citizens. Indicators on education and literacy show that in Mozambique, only 7% of the total population was enrolled in secondary school. Indicators on communications and media show that in Bangladesh, only 3.4% of the population has a telephone, while 9.3% are in the circulation of daily newspapers (UNCTAD, 2002).

Although digital government technologies have a potential to improve lives of the 80% of the world's population that lives in the developing countries, so far the developed countries such as USA, Canada, UK, and Australia are leaders in digital government (Annual Global Accenture Study, 2002), reaping the vast majority of initial gains of digital government implementation. Actually, the gap between developed and developing countries in Internet technological infrastructures, practices, and usage has been wider rather than narrower over recent years. Besides the lack of sufficient capital to build up expensive national information infrastructure (NII) on which digital government is based, developing countries also lack sufficient knowledge and skills to develop suitable and effective strategies for establishing and promoting digital government.

An estimated 500 digital government programs were launched in the year 2001 by governments worldwide (Palmer, 2002). Digital government strategies have had a tremendous impact on the way governments interact with their citizens. More than 75% of Australians file income taxes online, while the mayor of Minnesota receives about 13,000 e-mails from the public each week (Palmer, 2002). According to the 2002 Annual Global Accenture (former Anderson Consulting: AC) Study, Canada is the leader in digital government implementation. The remaining top 10 countries are (in order): Singapore, the United States, Australia, Denmark, the United Kingdom, Finland, Hong Kong, Germany, and Ireland. A recent survey by the United Nations found that of its 190 member states, only 36 out of the 169 available Web sites had one-stop portals and less than 20 offered online transactions (Jackson, 2002). This clearly shows a big gap in current digital government implementation status in different countries.

*Table 2: Main differences between developed and developing countries*

| | Developed Countries | Developing Countries |
|---|---|---|
| **History and Culture** | • Government and economy developed early, immediately after independence<br><br>• Economy growing at a constant rate, productivity increasing, high standard of living | • Government usually not specifically defined; economy not increasing in productivity<br><br>• Economy not growing or increasing productivity; low standard of living |
| **Technical Staff** | • Has a current staff, needs to increase technical abilities and hire younger professionals<br><br>• Has outsourcing abilities and financial resources to outsource; current staff would be able to define requirements for development | • Does not have a staff, or has very limited in-house staff<br><br>• Does not have local outsourcing abilities and rarely has the financial ability to outsource; current staff may be unable to define specific requirements |
| **Infra-structure** | • Good current infrastructure<br><br>• High Internet access for employees and citizens | • Bad current infrastructure<br><br>• Low Internet access for employees and citizens |
| **Citizens** | • High Internet access and computer literacy; still has digital divide and privacy issues | • Low Internet access and citizens are reluctant to trust online services; very few citizens know how to operate computers |
| **Government Officers** | • Decent computer literacy and dedication of resources; many do not place digital government at a high priority | • Low computer literacy and dedication of resources; many do not place digital government a high priority due to lack of knowledge on the issue |

In comparison with other countries around the world, the United States along with Australia, Singapore, and Canada are the early leaders in the march toward digital government. Governments in the United Kingdom, France, Germany, Spain, Norway, Hong Kong, and New Zealand have vowed to change their policies towards the implementation of digital government in order to take the full advantage of the digital information age. Other cautious implementers include Italy, Japan, Netherlands, and South Africa. Though there has been significant progress made in developed countries, many developing countries have been left behind with a long way to catch up toward digital government. To this day, one third of the world's population has never made a phone call and 63 countries have less than 1% access to the Internet (ICeGD, 2002).

Table 2 summarizes differences between developed and developing countries in various aspects of government.

# History and Culture

The history and culture between developed and developing countries are different in many aspects. Developed countries are known more for their early economic and governmental growth, with many governments forming in the 1500s. Several of the developing countries have just recently gained their independence, and still do not have a specific government structure. Culture is also a major difference between developed and developing countries. Religious and other backgrounds among citizens of developing countries defer them from doing certain activities that are commonplace among developed countries. War is also notorious among developing countries, which depletes their economy and their government structure.

## Technology Staff

The in-house staff for most developed countries has been in existence and well established. Although many of them are old, with half of the existing United States government information technology (IT) workers eligible to retire within the next three years (Ledford, 2002), the existing department is up and working. In contrast, many developing countries do not have an IT department in place or have an IT department that is low skilled and insufficiently equipped. Education in these countries is a major problem, as well as lack of financial resources to pay skilled workers. This brings up major issues with the development and maintenance of systems.

Governments in many developed countries choose to outsource digital government projects. Developed countries often house companies specialized in digital government development within their border, which makes outsourcing an affordable and convenient alternative. Though companies specialized in digital government development may be available in developing countries, the competitive systems development rates they charge may not be affordable for many developing countries. Even if affordable, without appropriate understanding of IT, many government officials of developing countries will find it difficult to specify requirements and resources to devote for the projects to be outsourced.

## Infrastructure

The size and abilities of infrastructures between developed and developing countries differ dramatically. For example, India's capacity for international telecom traffic reached just 780 Mbps by the end of 2000, which is a mere 1.4% of the capacity available in the neighboring country, China (Dooley, 2002). Developed countries have the infrastructure size and abilities to make Internet and telephone access available to almost all of their residents, with some populations over 300 million. The insufficient infrastructure of developing countries is due to economic conditions, war or destruction that may have recently occurred and governmental regulations of the telecommunications industry. A dilemma of government regulations also exists in India, where the sector has been a monopoly since its independence from Great Britain in 1947 (Dooley, 2002). All of these factors unfortunately hinder the progress of digital government in developing countries.

## Citizens

The difference of Internet accessibility between developed and developing countries is a reflection of the countries' infrastructure and telecommunication abilities. As mentioned previously, developing countries lack financial resources and government stability and structure to contain a sizable infrastructure. This results in low access to the Internet and telephone. One third of the world's population has never made a phone call and 63 countries have less than 1% percent access to the Internet (ICeGD, 2002). In developed countries, almost every citizen has access to the Internet and the rate of computer literacy surpasses that in developing countries.

## Government Officers

It is imperative that government officials understand and value digital government. The level of resources they are willing to allocate is dependent on their understanding of technology and the benefits that will ensue. In developed countries, most government officials use the Internet or computers on a daily basis. Therefore, government officials in developed countries are familiar with technology and realize how efficient it is, increasing their dedication to allocating additional resources for further implementation. In developing countries, IT is a vague concept and government officials are somewhat unwilling to allocate already scarce resources towards something they are not familiar with.

# Digital Government Implementation

Most, if not all, digital government strategies and implementation plans in developing countries have been based on theories and experiences of developed countries (Huang, D'Ambra & Bhalla, 2002). Feeling the pressure and demand from citizens to provide digital government services online, many developing countries have no choice but hastily jump into the digital government implementation wagon by following digital government development strategies proposed and carried out by developed countries. However, due to substantial differences in many key aspects of digital government related technological and social conditions between developed and developing countries, digital government development strategies and experiences from developed countries may not be directly applicable to developing countries. Even in developed countries, about 20-25% of digital government projects are either never implemented or abandoned immediately after implementation, and a further 33% fail partially in terms of falling short of major goals, causing significant undesirable outcomes or both (Heeks, 2000). Therefore, it would be important to conduct a comparative study on digital government strategies and implementations between developed and developing countries. Only through the study from the perspective of developing countries, digital government strategies and implementation for developing countries may be practical and eventually successful.

The Center for International Development at Harvard University, USA, supported by IBM, identified what we would term as National e-Commerce Infrastructure (NeI) factors describing differences between developing and developed countries in terms of implementing e-Commerce (Kirkman, Osorio & Sachs, 2002).

1)  Network Access - What are the availability, cost and quality of information & communication technology (ICTs) networks, services and equipment? More specifically, it includes the following key issues:

- **Infrastructure Development** - Infrastructure development is a necessity before countries can consider any large projects dedicated to digital government. Citizens must have access to services before any of the cost saving benefits will apply. Also, with a lack of back-end infrastructure, governments and their employees will be unable to move into transactional process and further stages of digital government implementation.

- **Resources and IT Support** - Outsourcing can be an option for countries to implement digital government. The private sector has an obligation to support governments throughout the world in their dedication to digital government. Developing countries need financial discounts and support from the private sector to successfully develop applications due to their lack of resources and staff.

- **Utilization** - The citizen utilization of the Internet is based on the access to the Internet and the Web site. Technical support must provide 24/7 access, in addition to providing a better infrastructure so that more citizens can utilize the Internet. Much like in developed countries, citizen utilization is an important part of the cost savings for countries.

2)  **Networked Learning** - Does an educational system integrate ICTs into its processes to improve learning? Are there technical training programs in the community that can train and prepare an ICT workforce?

- Technical staffing and training is a major issue in digital government implementation in developed and developing countries. In developing countries, the problems lie in the lack of financial resources to hire full time in-house support and in the inability to find such support, due to the lack of education in these countries. Outsourcing is usually a better option; however, issues lie in the inability to find companies in the area, and again, finances are limited. Even if a country can find the finances to support an outsourcing project, stability and maintenance of the application are often difficult.

3)  **Networked Economy** - How are businesses and governments using information and communication technologies to interact with the public and with each other? Some key issues involved include collaboration, partnership, public-private sector partnership, e-community creation, and so forth.

- Boundary removal between different agencies in a government is a major issue in digital government. In many developing countries, government structure is undefined and destabilized by corruption and communism. Consequently, boundary removal and department collaboration is a difficult and slow process. In many countries, war and terrorism is a constant issue that disrupts government operations on a daily basis. Government departments must collaborate with each other, with private sectors and related communities in order for digital government to be implemented in an efficient way. Due to the low computer literacy and high cost of online access, long and unnecessary transactions need to be cut down in processes to allow users to quickly access documents and print them or fill them out online.

4)   **Network Policy** - To what extent does the policy environment promote or hinder the growth of ICT adoption and use? Some related key issues include legislations, laws, strategies (visions and missions), accountability and so forth.

- Government agencies and departments must be accountable for their information and processes they support. It is essential for processes and duties to be segregated and responsibilities to be assigned to appropriate agencies and departments. These agencies and departments then need to work together to design their Web pages and IT flows. After implementation, they must have the abilities and be held accountable to support the Web pages and troubleshoot them. Governments must also be accountable for their financial and accounting systems. Many developing countries have issues and economic problems due to their lack of responsibility accounting systems.

E-commerce largely deals with business transactions in private sector whereas digital government deals with services in public sector. Due to key differences between private and public sectors (e.g., Bozeman & Bretschneider, 1986; Caudle, Gorr & Newcomer, 1991; Rainey, Backoff & Levine, 1976), factors other than the ones identified by the above-mentioned Harvard University e-commerce research project may also be important to digital government strategies and implementations. Prior relevant research suggested some key factors for digital government strategies and implementations, which can be used to identify differences in digital government between developed and developing countries. Those suggested factors include society factors like *history, citizens* (Huang, D'Ambra & Bhalla, 2002), *government staff and governance* (Wimmer, Traunmuller & Lenk, 2001), *organizational structure* (Baligh, 1994); and cultural factors like *national culture* (Hoftstede, 1980, 1991), *organizational culture* (Hoftstede, 1980; Schein, 1993), and *social norms* (Ajzen, 1988).

Based upon the above literature review and discussion, a research framework identifying critical success factors (CSFs) that influence digital government strategies and implementations is proposed and shown in Figure 1. This proposed research framework identifies key factors influencing digital government strategies and implementations in both developed and developing countries. Some factors could be more important to developed countries than to developing countries, or vice versa. Future studies can examine the relative importance of these factors to developed countries versus developing countries. For developing countries, the importance of those key factors to digital

*Figure 1: A conceptual research framework*

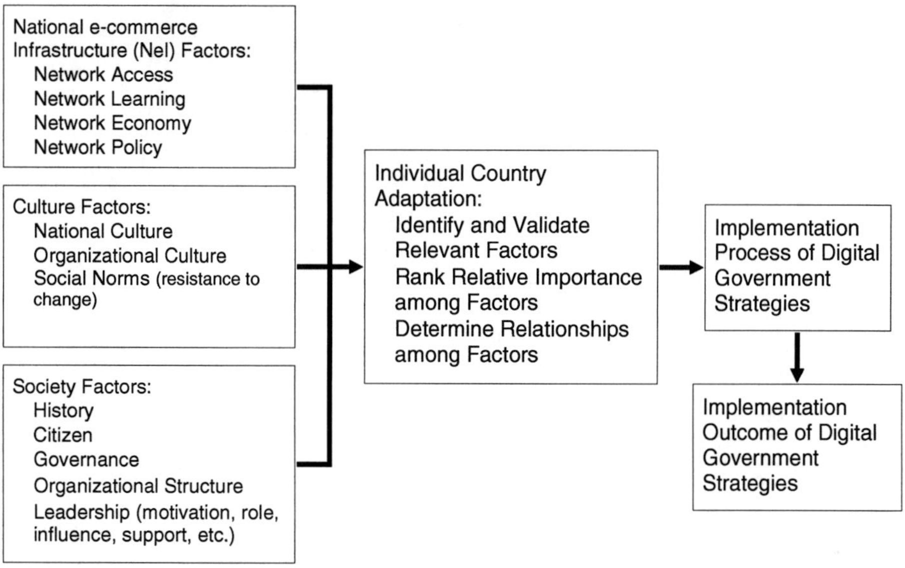

*Table 3: Stages of National e-Commerce Infrastructure (NeI) factors*

| Panel A. Network Access | | | | |
|---|---|---|---|---|
| | **Speed & Availability** | **Business** | **Government** | **Home** |
| **Initial Stage** | • 56k dial-up available to 100% of homes and businesses <br> • Only analog mobile wireless services offered. | • Employees dial-up for Internet access <br> • 25% of employees have e-mail accounts. | • 50% of government buildings have always-on connection <br> • 25% of employees have e-mail. | • 25% of homes have a computer access device <br> • 15% of homes use the Internet. |
| **Developing Stage** | • High-speed (DSL/Cable or fixed wireless equivalent) access available to 20%-80% of home and businesses. <br> • Mobile digital wireless data service covers 30%-50% of the community at 12kbps. | • 30%-60% of employees have access to an always-on connection to the Internet. <br> • 50%-75% of employees have e-mail accounts. <br> • 50%-100% of mobile employees use wireless devices. | • 100% of government buildings have always-on connection to the Internet. <br> • 100% of employees have e-mail. <br> • 50%-100% of mobile employees use wireless devices. <br> • Public terminals are available in 50% of buildings that are accessible to the public. | • 50%-80% of homes have a computer/access device. <br> • 30%-80% of homes use the Internet. |
| **Mature Stage** | • Every business has access to high-speed connections and employees can access the Network wirelessly from anywhere in the community. | • All businesses of all sizes and in all sectors are always connected to the Network and every employee is able to access the Network when it is needed to perform their job, even when mobile. | • Governments make the Network always available to employees and become a point of Network access for the public when they are in a public building. | • All homes are connected to the Network and enable people and devices to access the Network from multiple sites in the home. |

*Table 3: Stages of National e-Commerce Infrastructure (NeI) factors (continued)*

| Panel B. Network Learning | | |
|---|---|---|
| | K-12 | Higher Education | Home |
| **Initial Stage** | • 100% of schools have an informational Web site.<br>• 25% of teachers trained to use digital content and Web-based learning for instruction.<br>• 25% of classes use digital content and/or Web-based learning. | • 25% of campuses offer online registration.<br>• 25% of faculty trained to use digital content and Web-based learning for instruction.<br>• 25% of classes use digital content and/or Web-based learning. | • 25% of community-based organizations have an informational Web site. |
| **Developing Stage** | • 25-75% of schools have interactive Web site including access to homework assignments and e-mail contact with teachers and administrators.<br>• 50%-100% of teachers trained to use digital content and Web-based learning for instruction.<br>• 50%-100% of classes use digital content and/or Web-based learning. | • 50%-75% of campuses offer online registration.<br>• 50%-75% of faculty trained to use digital content and web-based learning for instruction.<br>• 50%-100% of classes use digital content and/or Web-based learning. | • 50%-75% of community-based organizations have an informational Web site.<br>• A unified community portal provides access to a broad range of community information and services. |
| **Mature Stage** | • Schools use the Network to connect students, teachers, and parents; improve learning using digital content; and manage administrative responsibilities more efficiently. | • All aspects of higher education are available through the Network including instruction, content and administration. | • Community-based organizations are able to use the Network to engage people in the community and make their services available to everyone. |

| Panel C. Network Economy | | |
|---|---|---|
| | Innovation | Workforce | Consumer |
| **Initial Stage** | • Business permits and licenses take up to 3 months to secure.<br>• 25% of existing businesses have transformed their internal and external practices due to the Internet. | • 10% of the workforce participates in training/education programs either online or in person every 5 years.<br>• 10% of employers post job opening on online job listing services. | • 10% of households purchase goods or use services online. |
| **Developing Stage** | • Business permits and licenses take up to 1 month to secure.<br>• 50%-75% of existing businesses have transformed their internal and external practices due to the Internet. | • 25%-50% of the workforce participates in training/education programs either online or in person every 5 years.<br>• 25%-75% of employers post job opening on online job listing services.<br>• 5%-15% of the workforce telecommutes at least once a week. | • 33%-75% of households purchasegoods or use services online. |
| **Mature Stage** | • Starting a new business has minimal bureaucratic and economic barriers and support mechanisms are in place to assist and encourage new business development. Existing businesses are embracing new technologies and best practices. | • People are continually upgrading their skills to adjust to new technologies and best practices. Online job banks are able to dynamically match employees with openings and connect to training/education programs to identify changing workforce skill requirements. Telework becomes a standard operating procedure in most work environments. | • Consumers can find information about, compare, and buy any good or service located anywhere in the world online. |

*Table 3: Stages of National e-Commerce Infrastructure (NeI) factors (continued)*

| Panel D. Network Policy | | |
|---|---|---|
| | **Privacy** | **Policy** |
| **Initial Stage** | • 75% of public and private sector Web sites post privacy policy.<br>• 10% of people feel they understand how to protect their privacy when online. | • Policy makers and business leaders are familiar with key connectedness policy, telecommunications competition, taxation, authentication, intellectual property, security, and online criminal activity. |
| **Developing Stage** | • 25%-50% of public and private sector Web sites meet the privacy guidelines of BBBOnline or TRYSTe.<br>• 25%-75% of people feel they understand how to protect their privacy when online. | • Policy makers and business leaders are working to ensure that new policies are in place to encourage and support the emergence of connectedness.<br>• Policy makers and business leaders are working to eliminate barriers to connectedness, such as requirements for physical signatures.<br>• Regular assessments of connectedness are made as well as the effect policies are having on connectedness. |
| **Mature Stage** | • Users are enabled to easily protect their privacy through a combination of technology tools and best practices.<br>• Public and private sector organizations make it easy for users to understand how information is collected and used. | • Policies related to privacy, telecommunications competition, taxation, authentication, intellectual property, and criminal conduct for disrupting networks are clearly established and are favorable to promoting connectedness and use of the Network. |

government strategies and implementation can be ranked through using survey research methodology. Further, the relationships between key factors can be determined using Structure Equation Modeling technique. In this way, key critical successful factors (CSFs) for implementing digital government strategies in developing countries can be specifically identified and validated, rather than directly using those key CSFs identified by the experiences of developed countries. Consequently, digital government strategies and implementations in developing countries could be more effective and efficient than they would be.

Table 3 proposes and discusses stages of NeI factors that can be used for readiness assessment or strategy planning purposes for digital government implementation, which is based on prior studies of The Computer Systems Policy Project (CSPP), sponsored by leading US information technology corporations such as IBM, Intel, Sun and HP (www.cspp.org, accessed in 2002).

# Case Study

The following case studies present snapshots of current digital government implementation in the USA (a developed country), China, and India (two major developing countries).

# United States

The potential number of users of digital government in the United States is estimated to be 250 million people (Ledford, 2002). According to another report, more than 68 million Americans say that they have visited government Web sites, compared to only 40 million two years ago (Perlman, 2002). Due to this, the United States dedication to digital government and Internet initiatives has become a major issue in the Senate and Congress. FirstGov (*www.firstgov.gov*), the federal portal for the US government that was launched in September 2001, reports that they receive three million hits per month (Keston, 2002). Besides, the recently passed e-Government Act of 2001 holds the federal government responsible for policy guidance and resource development.

The United States Web portal, FirstGov, is currently in Stage 4 of implementation, which integrates various government services internally and externally for the enhancement of efficiency, usability, and effectiveness. The policy environment in the United States is an important consideration in understanding the strategy for digital government implementation. A related complete set of laws relating to the development of digital government has been in the place already, including Privacy Act, Computer Matching and Privacy Protection Act, Electronic Freedom of Information Amendments, Computer Security Act, Critical Infrastructure Protection, Government Paperwork Elimination Act, and Electronic Government Act (Relyea, 2002).

The Electronic Government Act budgets $345 million to be spent over four years to promote and improve the federal government's use of the Internet and other technology (Garretson, 2002). It also proposes the creation of an office of electronic government. Now, more than 90% of Americans surveyed said that they were likely or very likely to utilize the Internet and e-government to do business with the public sector (Ledford, 2002). By 2003, it is projected that $1.3 trillion of transactions related to the Gross Domestic Product (GDP) will be conducted online through digital government (Ledford, 2002).

# China

The digital government implementation in China began in 1999. According to the 11th Report of the Statistic of China National Network Development (RSCNND) by China National Network Information Centre (CNNIC), up to the end of 2002, the Internet users had achieved 59.1 million. It added up to 9% of the Internet users in the world (655 million). There were 371,600 WWW Web sites, among which 291,323 were in com.cn, 6,148 in gov.cn, 54,156 in net.cn and 1,783 in org.cn. And the number of computers linked to Internet was more than 20.83 million.

Though China has maintained its position as the fastest developing economy in the world in recent years, there still exists a big gap in terms of National e-commerce Infrastructure (NeI) between China and other developed countries.

1)    **Network Access** - Subscribing to Internet service is much more costly in China than in developed countries such as the United States. In China, the charge of ISP is bi-directional; users pay for not only sending but also receiving information. Table 4 shows the expense (in US dollars) difference between China and the United States. As for a business organization using ISP (Internet Service Provider) service, the cost of paying for leasing communication line to total costs of the company is more than 50% in general. Such a situation slows down the development of e-government/e-commerce in China.

CNNIC forecasts that the Internet users in China will exceed 85 million by the end of the 2003. As a country with a 1.3 billion population, China, exceeding Japan, has the second largest number of Internet users. Yet, the percentage of Internet users compared to the total population is rather low. Table 5 shows differences between China and US in terms of NeI infrastructure, Internet usage, e-commerce turnover, and so forth.

2)    **Network Learning** - According to the *Human Development Report in 2001* by the United Nations Development Program (UNDP), which first publishes Technical Achievements Index (TAI) in the world, China is listed as the 45th among the 72 countries. The report identifies that the average value of TAI is 0.374 and the TAI of developing countries is 0.2~0.34. Part of the UNDP's statistics of TAI is shown in Table 6.

3)    **Network Economy** - As shown in Tables 4, 5, and 6, due to the big differences between China and developed countries like USA in terms of NeI's technical infrastructure, China's e-commerce turnover is relatively small in size, accounting for only 0.23% of US' annual e-commerce turnover (see Table 5).

*Table 4: The ISP expense difference between China and United States*

| Country | 2M Special communication line | 64Kbps communication line | Proportion of paying line to total costs of the Co. |
|---------|-------------------------------|---------------------------|-----------------------------------------------------|
| China   | $40000/month                  | $5000/month               | more than 50%                                       |
| US      | $2000/month                   | $260/month                | 5.26%                                               |

*Source: Guangming Daily in China 07/21/1999*

*Table 5: The proportion of the data in China to that in United States in eight measures*

| SCI | Patents | High tech exports | Phones line | Personal computer | Internet user | E-Commerce turnover | Enrolment rate of education |
|-----|---------|-------------------|-------------|-------------------|---------------|---------------------|------------------------------|
| 45% | 8%      | 3.5%              | 61.8%       | 3.8%              | 4.6%          | 0.23%               | 70%                          |

*Source: China Quality News 01/03/2001*

*Table 6: UNDP's statistics of TAI*

| Country | Finland | US | Korea | Italy | Malaysia | China | India | Mozambique |
|---------|---------|-----|-------|-------|----------|-------|-------|------------|
| Order | 1 | 2 | 5 | 20 | 30 | 45 | 63 | 72 |
| TAI | 0.744 | 0.733 | 0.666 | 0.471 | 0.396 | 0.299 | 0.201 | 0.066 |

*Source: Human Development Report in 2001*

4)   **Network Policy** - Network policy might be the weakest part of the four NeI factors for China. China has been transiting its economic system from the old Soviet Union's "planned economy" model to the capitalist's "market economy". The transition period, though seems to be on a right track, is painful and far from the completion. The legal systems, laws, and regulations have been gradually established. Yet, there is a long way to go to complete its legal system and structure in managing the big developing economy, not to mention the completeness of its network economy policy and related laws.

Because of the substantial differences in all four key aspects/factors of NeI between China and developed countries like US, China should adopt a different strategy to implement digital government, not to exactly follow up the strategies adopted by developed countries like the US. For example, US used a "market-driven" strategy for digital government implementation (www.firstgov.gov); however, China adopted a different strategy that could be characterized as "government-push and partnership with private sector". In this strategy, governmental departments consolidate all forces and resources available to promote and lead the implementation of digital government in some focused areas while establishing the partnership with the private sector. So far, China's digital government implementation is still in its early stage but it has achieved some initial results. Figures 2 and 3 show the system architecture of e-government systems in China.

*Figure 2: eGovernment system architecture*

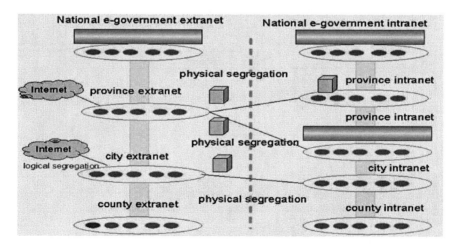

*Figure 3: e-Government application systems*

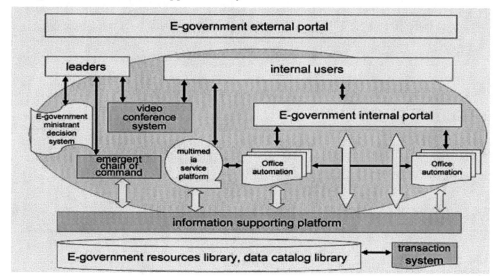

# India

As a developing country, India has a population of more than one billion, and is the largest country in South Asia and the second most populous country in the world. However, the country has only 4.3 million PCs, and its phone network is one of the least accessible even in the third world countries. Besides, it lacks a complete set of relevant laws guiding the development of digital government in India.

Despite India's size, it has only the 14th largest telecom market in the world. According to Dooley (2000), India has one of the lowest ratios of telephone accessibility among developing countries, at 0.03, and there is still no telephone connection in nearly 40% of small villages in India. The capacity for international telecom traffic reached just 780 Mbps by the end of 2000. The cost of implementing telephone lines and Internet access is outrageous, at $775 to install a new fixed line. In addition to underdeveloped infrastructure, India has a high level of poverty and unequal income distribution. Limited Web access is only available to the privileged few who are able to afford it.

India's residents may have to wait years before getting a phone line installed. The current going price for Internet service is $200 for 500 hours of use (Dooley, 2002). With this limitation, it is hard to encourage businesses and citizens to utilize IT and digital government for cost cutting and efficient enhancing. Although the Internet Service Providers (ISPs) offer a broad range of services, the network access is so slow that many only use the Internet for e-mail. Until the infrastructure is built and capacity is increased, data services, especially multimedia data services, will remain unattainable. As a result, India government has been careful to develop its own suitable e-government implementation strategy, which cannot directly be based on those e-government implementation models adopted in US and other developed countries. India government's portal (*http://www.nic.in/*) is operational and is continuing to be improved.

# Recommendation for Developed Countries

Following up the case study, some specific suggestions for enhancing digital government implementation are summarized next.

## Technical Staff

The current staff of the government IT departments are generally inexperienced in highly technical fields, which is true for the United States and many other developed countries. To correct this problem, the federal governments must offer highly competitive benefits packages and salary compensation. Governments must compete with the IT departments of the private sector. College and entry level recruiting is also necessary to bring in young staff. In addition, training programs need to be improved to allow for inexperienced staff to be technically able to support the existing applications and to deliver enhancements.

## Stabilization and Support

About half of the existing US Federal IT workers will be eligible to retire within the next three years, with less than 1% of the workforce under 25 and only 10% under 32 (Ledford, 2002). This would limit the in-house IT abilities of the government. In-house ability and stability is critical, especially for digital government applications. Without 24/7 availability, it is unlikely that citizens will continue to visit the site frequently in the future. The Web site must be stable and up at least 99% of the time. Specific goals must be set for each IT department and if there is downtime on any application, logs and documentation must be provided on why the outage occurred and what steps are being taken to prevent this from a repeat occurrence. Whether the support is outsourced or completed in house, IT management and project leaders must offer support to internal applications through support phones and assigned IT employees.

## Collaboration

In the shift to a Weberian bureaucracy, government departments will stay individualized and make decisions on their own. However, it is important that there is an effective communication between departments and agencies. To do this, internal applications need to be developed and utilized by employees to share information and improve communication. E-mail is the most obvious success story for improved communications, but other applications can be enhanced to improve communications as well.

## Resource Allocation

A government Web site takes time, money, and professional talent to achieve its maximum quality. All of these resources are hard to come by, depending on budget criteria and government officials' dedication to the project. Governments must budget and plan ahead for digital government resources and allocate them. A specific analysis of the benefits of digital government must be estimated to determine the anticipated savings and the length of delay time in those savings. By examining that, governments can appropriately budget for the return on investment.

# Recommendation for Developing Countries

Given the key differences between developed and developing countries, such as limited financial, technical, and human resources in developing countries, the digital government implementation strategies adopted by developed countries, such as the "market-driven" strategy adopted in the US (www.firstgov.gov), may not be directly applicable to developing countries. Developing countries may need to use governments' administrative and legislative power to consolidate and better make use of limited available resources to implement digital government.

## Internal Support

Financial problems are the most prevalent among developing countries. The finances needed for implementing digital government can be drawn from a stricter tax structure and a concentrated effort on formal business transactions. Developing countries need to build upon their retail market for their citizens' necessities, like grocery and clothing outlets. This will generate additional taxes to bring the country out of its economic demise.

## External Financial Support

In an effort to assist developing countries in coming out of the economic demise, external financial support from non-profit groups and other government agencies can help implement digital government. Not only can the developing countries designate money into IT budget, they can also use external financial assistance to do so. For example, Italy and the United Nations have already started this initiative with their Palmero Conference of digital government by assisting several developing countries financially.

## Infrastructure Development

Infrastructure development is a necessity before countries can consider any large projects dedicated to digital government. Throughout the world, 63 countries have less than 1% of their population with the access to the Internet (ICeGD, 2002). To improve infrastructure, developing countries must have financial resources to build up their IT infrastructure and to pay for technical support. Outsourcing is an option that needs to be carefully considered due to the lack of internal technical staff.

## Technical Staffing

Technical staffing is a major issue in digital government implementation in developing countries. In developing countries, the problems lie in the lack of financial resources to hire full time in-house support, and in the inability to find such support, due to the lack of education in these countries. Outsourcing would be recommended for many countries that do not have the proper education and training to hire in-house staff. However, it is detrimental for outsourcing to be successful if a minimum of in-house staff is not available to understand maintenance issues and support.

## Collaboration

Boundary removal between different agencies in the government is a major issue in digital government. In several developing countries, their government structure is undefined and unstable due to corruption and communism. However, government departments in developing countries must strive to obtain a specific structure and boundary between themselves before the departments can align with each other. With the disorganization that most developing countries have in their government system, it is important that tasks are accounted for and distributed among the departments before digital government implementation can be successful.

## Accountability

Departments and governmental divisions must be accountable for their information and the processes they support. They must be able to separate processes and information so that an appropriate department is responsible for certain parts of the Web site. They must also work together to make their pages and IT flow together. After the implementation, they must have the abilities to support the site and troubleshoot it. By being accountable for the appropriate segments of the site, it will make troubleshooting easier if problems occur.

## Simplification of Transactions

Long and unnecessary transactions need to be cut down in processes to allow users to quickly access documents and print them or fill them out online. To do this, government departments must first define their structure and accountability as mentioned above. After the departments are determined and structure is in place, the transactions need to be simplified and a decision making process must be determined. By simplifying transactions, citizens will be more likely to access the site.

# Conclusion

Although there are prior studies published on digital government strategies and implementation (e.g., Glassey, 2001; Greunz, Schopp & Haes, 2001; Huang, D'Ambra & Bhalla, 2002; Wimmer, Traunmuller & Lenk, 2001), to our knowledge, there has been little research published on digital government strategies and implementation specifically from the perspectives of developing countries. Therefore, the current study intends to do some initial work to bridge the gap.

This study compares strategic issues and implementations of digital government between developed and developing countries. More specifically, the following issues are addressed:

- Implementation benefits and stages of digital government
- Comparison of digital government implementation aspects between developed and developing countries
- Critical success factors influencing digital government strategies and implementations for developed and developing countries
- Recommendations for developed and developing countries in their implementation of digital government

# References

Ajzen, I. (1988). *Attitudes, personality and behavior.* Milton Keynes: Open University Press.

Annual Global Accenture (former Anderson Consulting: AC) Study Report. (2002).

Baligh, H.H. (1994). Components of culture: Nature, interconnections, and relevance to the decisions on the organization structure, *Management Science*, 40(1), 14-28.

Bozeman, B., & Bretschneider, S. (1986). Public management information systems: Theory and prescription. *Public Administration Review* (Special Issue), 47-487.

Caudle, S.L., Gorr, W.L., & Newcomer, K.E. (1991, June). Key information systems management issues for the public sector. *MIS Quarterly, 15*(2), 171-188.

Dooley, B.L. (2002, February). Telecommunications in India: State of the marketplace, *faulkner information services*. Docid 00016872.

Garretson, C. (2002). Senate passes e-Government bill. *InfoWorld Daily News*, June 28.

Glassey, O. (2001, June 27-29). Model and architecture for a virtual one-stop public administration. *The 9th European Conferences on Information Systems,* 969-976.

Government and the Internet Survey. (2000). *The Economist, 355* (8176), 33-34.

Greunz, M., Schopp, B., & Haes, J. (2001). *Integrating e-government infrastructures through secure XML document containers.* Proceedings of the 34th Hawaii International Conference on System Sciences.

Heeks, R. (2000). *Reinventing government in the information age.* London: Roultedge Press.

Hiller, J., & Belanger, F. (2001). Privacy strategies for electronic government. *E-government series.* Arlington, VA: PricewaterhouseCoopers Endowment for the Business of Government.

Hofstede, G. (1980). *Culture's consequences: International differences in work-related values.* Newbury Park, CA: Sage Press.

Hofstede, G. (1991). *Cultures and organizations: Software of the mind.* London: McGraw Hill.

Huang, W., D'Ambra, J., & Bhalla, V. (2002). An empirical investigation of the adoption of eGovernment in Australian citizens: Some unexpected research findings. *Journal of Computer Information Systems, 43*(1), 15-22.

International Conference on e-Government for Development (IceGD). Retrieved September 25, 2002, from: *http://www.palermoconference2002.org/en/home_a.htm.*

Jackson, N. (2002, February). State of the marketplace: E-Government gateways. *Faulkner Information Services*. Docid 00018296.

Keston, G. (2002, February). US self-service government initiatives. *Faulkner Information Services*. Docid 00018287.

Kirkman, G.S., Osorio, C.A., & Sachs, J.D. (2002). The networked readiness index: Measuring the preparedness of nations for the networked world. The global information technology report: Readiness for the networked world (pp. 10-30). Oxford University Press.

Ledford, J.L. (2002, February). Establishing best practices for e-government within the U.S. *Faulkner Information Services.* DocId: 00018275.

Moon, J.M. (2002, July/August).. The evolution of e-government among municipalities: Rhetoric or reality? *Public Administration Review, 62*(4), 424-433.

Palmer, I. (2002, January). State of the world: E-government implementation. *Faulkner Information Services.* Docid 00018297.

Perlman, E. (2002, September). E-government special report: The people connection. *Congressional Quarterly DBA Governing Magazine, 32.*

Rainey, H.G., Backoff, R.W., & Levine, C.H. (1976, March/April). Comparing public and private organizations. *Public Administration Review,* 233-243.

Relyea, H.C. (2002). E-gov: Introduction and overview. *Government Information Quarterly, 19,* 9-35.

UN (United Nations) and ASPA (American Society for Public Administration). (2001). *Global survey of e-government.*

UNCTAD. (2002). *Least developed countries at a glance.* United Nation Information Communication Technology Task Force.

Sachs, Schwab & Cornelius, (2002).

Schein, E.H. (1993, Autumn). On dialogue, culture, and organizational learning. *Organizational Dynamics,* 40-51.

Snellen, I. (2000). Electronic commerce and bureaucracies. *Proceedings of the 11th International Workshops on Database and Expert System Application,* 285-288.

Sprecher, M. (2000). Racing to e-government: Using the Internet for citizen service delivery. *Government Finance Review, 16,* 21-22.

Symonds, M. (2000, June 24) The next revolution: After e-commerce, get ready for eGovernment. *The Economist. http://www.economist.com/l.cgi?f=20000624/index_survey.*

Tapscott, D. (1995). *Digital economy: Promise and peril in the age of networked intelligence.* New York: McGraw-Hill.

Wimmer, M., Traunmuller, R., & Lenk, K. (2001). *Electronic business invading the public sector: Considerations on change and design.* Proceedings of the 34th Hawaii International Conference on System Sciences.

## Chapter IX

# Effectiveness of E-Government Online Services in Australia

Xuetao Guo, University of Technology Sydney, Australia

Jie Lu, University of Technology Sydney, Australia

## Abstract

*Electronic government (e-government) breaks down the barrier of distance and time, and offers the potential for government to better deliver its contents and services, and interact with citizens and businesses. Australia has been recognized as one of e-government leaders internationally. All the three levels (federal, state and local) of Australian government organizations have increasingly embraced e-government. With few years of e-government practices in Australia, it is critical to evaluate the current applications and explore more effective strategies for the next phase of e-government. This study aims to identify what factors affect the effectiveness of Australian e-government online services. In the study, a research model is proposed and data collections are completed based on two questionnaire-based surveys from internal and external users of Australian e-government Web sites respectively. Furthermore, data analyses are conducted to test proposed hypotheses. The findings show that Web presence quality and information quality influence effectiveness of e-government online services more than system quality from user perspectives. Several recommendations and future trends are also presented in the chapter.*

# Introduction

The Internet offers a tremendous opportunity for government to better deliver its contents and services and interact with citizens, businesses, and other government partners (Chen, 2002). Electronic government (e-government) breaks down the barrier of distance and time, and therefore offers the potential to enhance government service quality. E-government online services may not only provide benefits to citizens and businesses, but also offer the potential to reshape the public sector and remake the relationships between the citizens, businesses, and government (West, 2000).

A number of definitions of e-government have been offered in the existing literature (Devadoss, Pan & Huang, 2003); however, no single definition has been widely accepted (Scholl, 2003). The applications of information technology to government services are commonly referred to as e-government (Gordon, 2002; Holmes, 2001; Marchionini, Samet & Brandt, 2003; Scholl, 2003). Tapscott (1996) defined e-government as an Internet worked government, while Sprecher (2000) considered e-government as any way technology is used to help simplify and automate transactions between governments and constituents, businesses, or other governments. Wimmer and Traunmuller (2000) considered e-government as a guiding vision towards modern administration and democracy. According to them, e-government is concerned with the transformation that government and public administration have to undergo in the next decades. World Bank Group (worldBank, 2002) defined e-government as the use by government agencies of information technology (such as wide area networks, the Internet, and mobile computing) that have the ability to transform relations with citizens, businesses, and other arms of government, while New Zealand government (Anonymous, 2002) defined e-government as government agencies working together to use technology so that they can better provide individuals and businesses with government services and information. Taking a more comprehensive view, Aicholzer and Schmutzer (2000) saw e-government covering changes of governance in a twofold manner: (1) transformation of the business of governance, that is, improving service quality delivery, reducing costs and renewing administrative processes; (2) transformation of governance itself, that is, re-examining the functioning of democratic practices and processes. These definitions may be slightly different for each organization based on the community's values, goals and culture. However, a complete definition of e-government has to identify with consideration of all its users. In this study, we consider e-government users in two categories, internal and external users. The external users are citizen and business, while the internal users mainly imply the administration staff of a government agency or other government agencies.

E-government is much more than getting information and services online. It is transforming government administration, information provision and service delivery by the application of new technologies. It is delivering government services in ways that are most convenient to the client and citizen, while at the same time realizing efficiency gains, and streamlining government processes (Rimmer, 2002). E-government applications are very comprehensive. The challenges to e-government are not only technological but also economic, legislative and political; for example, electronic business, electronic management, electronic democracy and electronic politics (Pilipovic et al., 2002). Based on the involved parties, the most important classes of e-government applications are: government- to-citizen (G2C), citizen-to-government (C2G), government-to-business (G2B), business-to-government (B2G) and government-to-government (G2G). G2C applications focus on online services where government is working for citizens. G2B applications refer to supplying, information gathering and services for business. C2G and B2G applications are meant by communication between citizens, business and government agencies. And G2G concerns with communication amongst e-government users. Three components are required to support the e-government operational models that deliver a government-wide response. The three components are effective governance, business system, and physical infrastructure, which are explained below. Effective governance - the mandate or authority to act in a given situation, a framework for reporting and accountability, a recognised budget process and reward system. Business system - the operating business and decision-making processes that support cross-government activities. These include models for how response teams operate internally and processes to secure cooperation from different areas of government. Physical infrastructure – the information communication technology (ICT) and other systems needed to combine agency services for presentation to the community in an integrated way (Victoria, 2002).

So much of technology and information policy debate and discussion fall broadly under the header of e-government (Aldrich, Bertot & McClure, 2002). With the nearly all-inclusive domain of e-government, it is hard to conduct evaluation of e-government success. Thus, our study addresses online services delivery of e-government, which is termed as e-government online services. The concept of e-government online service implies those not-for-profit services delivered in the Internet environment by government agencies. Not-for-profit services address how to attract and keep customers returning, and to improve the service quality. The main contents of e-government online services are the delivery of all appropriate government services electronically, including complement (not replacement) of exiting written, telephone, fax and counter services; government information accessing; electronic payment and government-wide intranet for secure online communication (OGO, 2001).

Australia is a pioneer in the practices of e-government. Since the early 1990s Australia already had a clear e-government vision and began to develop its own e-government strategies. In February 2002, the Prime Minister announced that the 1997 commitment for all appropriate Commonwealth Government services to be online by 2001 had been achieved (NOIE, 2002b). Recently, Rimmer (2002), CEO of National Office for the Information Economy (NOIE) Australia, announced that the phase of government information and service online has been successfully completed, with over 1,600 Commonwealth government services online.

Internationally, Australia has been recognized as one of leaders in e-government. In 2001, on the basis of the assessment criteria developed by World Markets Research Centre (http://www.wmrc.com) to evaluate the "functionality" of national government Web sites around the world, Australia was ranked 3rd with 50.7% of federal government Web sites assessed conforming to all the assessment criteria. The US was ranked 1st with 57.2% of federal government Web sites conforming to all criteria (NOIE, 2002a). Australia was ranked second only to the United States according to a report from the United Nations released in June 2002, which had several key criteria such as sophistication of online services, Internet penetration rates, and Web presence of government (NOIE, 2002b). The Australian government has an important leadership role in enhancing the extent to which businesses and the community takes full advantage of the opportunities provided by the new technologies.

With few years of practices on e-government, it is clear that evaluating the current applications and exploring more effective ways for the next phase of e-government are critical. However, what factors influence the effectiveness of e-government online services? This study aims to identify and empirically establish the dimensions that underlie e-government online service effectiveness. We believe that our outcome will contribute to management scholars' and practitioners' understanding and developing efforts of effective e-government with accomplishment of the following tasks:

- identifying the development model and current practices of Australian e-government online services;
- identifying the underlying dimensions of the construct;
- developing a measure to evaluate user satisfaction from both internal and external user perspectives;
- empirically validating the construct; and
- exploring the theoretical and managerial implications of the findings.

The remainder of this chapter is structured as follows. Following a development model of Australian e-government online services and literature review in background section, the main thrust of the chapter is described, including a proposed research model, research methodology, data analyses and results, summary of findings, and several recommendations. Next, future trends in the area are presented. Finally, the conclusions are drawn.

# Background

## Development Model of Australian E-Government Online Services

The government is committed to maximize the opportunities provided by the Internet. The potential for government using Internet to enhance services are now more evident than ever before. The challenge for government is to continually embrace the opportunities that the Internet provides and ensure that citizens, business and community needs and expectations are met. In addition to providing information, communication and transformation services, exciting and innovative transformation could occur with the new technologies and practices (Chen, 2002). E-government is an evolutionary phenomenon (Layne & Lee, 2001). The use of new technology and the demand of new service features will be required for the transformation of e-government. Therefore, we believe that the development model of e-government initiatives should be accordingly derived and implemented. Based on the observation on Australian e-government applications and

*Figure 1: Development model of e-government online services*

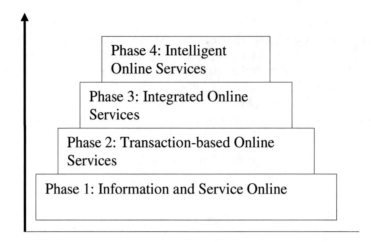

our previous research (Guo & Lu, 2003), a development model of Australian e-government online services (shown in Figure 1) is proposed on the basis of Layne and Lee's
(Layne & Lee, 2001) fourth-stage growth model of e-government. Our model is developed
according to different levels of interaction ordered by complexity (Chen, 2002; Elmagarmid
& McIver Jr., 2001; Gordon, 2002) and it is in four phases: phase 1 - information and service
online; phase 2 – transaction-based online services; phase 3 – integrated online services;
and phase 4 – intelligent online services. The detailed explanations of each phase are
presented next. It is expected that this model reflects the growth phases of Australian
e-government online services and offers a strategic direction from technological perspective.

- **Phase 1** - information and service online. One of the most common e-government
  applications is providing citizens with access to information and services. Governments produce vast volumes of information and an increasing amount of it is now
  available through the Internet and other electronic venues (Marchionini, Samet &
  Brandt, 2003). At this level, government information and services are delivered to
  its citizens and business through the Internet. Furthermore, by adding simple
  groupware functionalities such as Web forms, e-mail, bulletin and chat room, two-
  way communication is supported. Most early G2C and G2B services fall into this
  category (Chen, 2002). Most Australian governments' efforts on Web development belong to the first phase. Examples of functionalities at this phase are mostly
  limited to online presentations of government information. Our previous study
  (Guo, Lu & Raban, 2002) showed that the e-government Web sites deliver the static
  information in this phase. The Web site on this level provides catalogues of
  information, e-mail inquires and downloadable forms. "Provision of policy or
  service information (of 96.7% agencies offer the function)," "publication of
  organization information (of 90% agencies offer the function)," and "e-mail inquires (of 90% agencies offer the function)" are the three main functions that the
  majority of sample agencies provide on their Web sites.

- **Phase 2** - Transaction-based online services. People also use government Web sites to complete transactions. Linked to direct deposit and other commercial transaction systems, increasing numbers of citizens are avoiding long lines, complicated phone menu systems, and postal delays by using government transaction processing systems. Around one quarter of Australian commonwealth e-government online services are in the second phase (Rimmer, 2002). The second phase of e-government focuses on service-oriented e-government activities, including linking database to online interfaces and paying bills online. For instance, citizens in New South Wales may renew their licenses via the Roads and Traffic Authority Web site (http://www.rta.nsw.gov.au/) with online payment. In Australian e-government context, many e-government applications fall into this phase. According to our previous research (Guo, Lu & Raban, 2002), the three functions fall into this level with reasonable complexity of functions, which are "site search engine," "directory" and "access to database," with percentage of 60%, 53.3% and 46.7% respectively. Four functions can provide two-way data interchange between clients and an agency, which are "online payment/online transaction (26.7%)," "registration (16.7%)," "sale of information, service or products (13.3%)," and "lodgement of return (6.7%)". In addition, in this phase agencies also move towards electronic procurement, by putting requests for proposal and bidding regulations online.

- **Phase 3** - Integrated online services. Increasingly there are some whole-of-government requirements that cut across all agencies, some that bind a number of agencies together, and some that agencies can decide on an individual basis. The integrated online service delivery channels will be needed and it will link with existing delivery channels such as shop fronts and call centres. This phase would be able to provide clients with "one-stop shop," and make it unnecessary for clients to know the structure of government (Rimmer, 2002). This integration may happen in two ways: vertical and horizontal. Vertical integration refers to the different levels (local, state and federal) of government connected for different functions or services. Some Australian agencies' e-government activities are currently in this phase. As an example of vertical integration, a Tax File Number (TFN) registration system (http://www.ato.gov.au) at a state might be linked to a national database for cross checking. Another example is Australian Business Number (ABN). ABN was introduced through *A New Tax System (Australian Business Number) Act 1999,* which also called for a system to share ABN information with all levels of government via the Australian Business Register (ABR). ABR allows clients to access or change their own details on the register. It allows businesses and their endorsed representatives to access and maintain their business information online. In contrast, horizontal integration deals with different functions and services in the same level of government. Customers are getting better services that are streamlined and integrated with other services offered by other governments or the private sector, and that make it easier to use the services and transact with government. Centrelink's Overseas Direct Deposit and the Department of Immigration, Multicultural and Indigenous Affairs' Citizenship e-lodgement services are prime examples of these services. With system integration of Australian Taxation

Office, Medicare offices and Centrelink, Australian Family Assistance Office (http://www.familyassist.gov.au/) can process the claim of family assistance payments.

- **Phase 4** - Intelligent online services. Providing high quality information and integrated communication services are no less challenging and may evolve into knowledge management services and become adaptive, personalized, proactive and accessible from a broader variety of devices (Gordon, 2002). In the previous three phases of E-government, although there have been a huge number of emails sent to government officials and agencies each year, there is not evidence to show their impact on government decision-making. This phase emphasizes on intelligent presentation of Web content, intelligent decision support, and direct citizen participation in government decision-making. In this phase, governments use information technology to provide more effective access to appropriate services by making more pathways available so that there is "no wrong door" to services. Governments can anticipate which service or information a citizen or business is likely to want in a given set of circumstances and then use information technology to fast track client access to these services or information. By using information technology in these ways governments have the opportunity to streamline business processes so that services are structured around clients rather than around government service providers.

# Literature

Briggs et al. (2003) pointed out that the Internet is perhaps the most successful information system. As information systems ushered in flatter organizational structures, so the Internet ushers in globally distributed organizations and electronic commerce (e-commerce). Based on Briggs et al.'s (2003) point of view, e-government may be a new paradigm of information systems. In this study, like many research efforts (Gordon, 2002; Holmes, 2001; Marchionini, Samet & Brandt, 2003), e-government is considered as an application type of information technology, especially Internet. Although e-government can be seen as a sub-area of information systems, the evaluation of e-government can simply not adopt the measures of information system success. It should draw lessons from the measures of e-commerce success as well. Thus, literature from both areas may be appropriate for the research context.

## *Information System Success*

There are many different definitions of information system success in the existing literature. Briggs et al. (2003) summarized them according to four perspectives. (1) From the end user's perspective, successful systems may be those that improve the user's job performance without inflicting undue annoyance. (2) From a management's perspective, successful systems are those that reduce uncertainty of outcomes and have lower risks, and leverage scarce resources. (3) From a developer's perspective, successful information systems are those that are completed on time and under budget, with a completed set of features that are consistent with specifications and that function correctly. (4) From an innovator's perspective, successful information systems may be those that attract a large, loyal, and growing community of users.

A large number of research efforts on information system success evaluation can be found in the literature. Broadly, Garrity and Sanders (1998) viewed information system from two perspectives, an organizational viewpoint and a socio-technical viewpoint. The organizational perspective focuses on the quality of the interface and the information provided by an information system. The socio-technical viewpoint focuses on individual needs. According to Kim (1989), the surrogates developed for measuring information system success fall into three categories: user satisfaction (US) (Bailey & Pearson, 1983), level of system usage (Srinivasan, 1985), and information value regarding user decision performance (Gallagher, 1974). Seddon et al. (1999) reviewed 186 empirical papers in three major information system journals and proposed a two-dimensional matrix for classifying information system success measures. One dimension is the type of system studied, and another one is the stakeholder in whose interests the system is being evaluated. Communication theory is also used to understand the impact of information system at the individual level. For instance, Mason (1978) used the model of Shannon and Weaver (1949) to conduct a model. The basic elements of the Mason (Mason, 1978) model are receipt of the information, the evaluation of the information, and the application of the information leading to a change in recipient behavior and a change in the system performance.

More importantly, building on the work of Mason (1978) and comprehensive review of different information system success measures, DeLone and McLean (1992) proposed a model of information system success (shown in Figure 1) which depicted information system success measures in terms of six dimensions – system quality, information quality, use, US, individual impact and organization impact. The six interdependent and interrelated categories or components form DeLone and McLean (1992)'s information system success model. DeLone and McLean (1992) suggested that the effects of user participation on the subsequent success of different information systems may use satisfaction as their primary measure. System quality and information quality singularly and jointly affect both use and US. Use and user satisfaction are direct antecedents of individual impact. Additionally, the amount of use can affect the degree of US. The impact on individual performance should eventually have some organizational impact.

*Figure 1: DeLone and McLean's (1992) model of information system success*

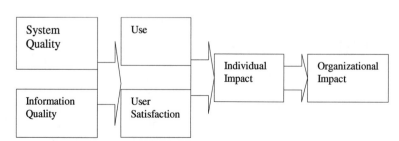

Since DeLone and McLean's (1992) model was proposed, a number of studies have undertaken empirical investigation of the multidimensional relationships amongst the measures of information system success (Rai, Lang & Welker, 2002; Seddon, 1997; Seddon & Kiew, 1996; Seddon et al., 1999; Wilkin & Castleman, 2003). However, it is difficult to measure information system success, because the general aim of information system development is to contribute to organizational effectiveness, to lead to higher productivity, better customer service, and better quality of working life. This has led to various measures of information systems to serve as surrogate for information system success (Iivari & Ervasi, 1994). US probably has been the most studied construct in information system research (Woodroof & Burg, 2003). Many researchers have investigated various dimensions of US (Bailey & Pearson, 1983; Davis, Bagozzi & Warshaw, 1989; Igbaria & Nachman, 1990), such as system accuracy, system timeliness, usefulness, ease-of-use, task importance, and quality of output. Other ways include content (such as accuracy and relevance), presentation (such as format and mode), and service quality (Woodroof & Burg, 2003). Much literature indicates that DeLone and McLean's (1992) model has been used as a basis of information system success measurement.

## E-commerce Success

The quality of e-commerce Web sites may vary from high quality sites developed by professionals, to low quality sites constructed by inexperienced site developers. Many problems can arise when using Web sites, including page loading time which is often lengthy, out-of-date site content, privacy concerns, access to site contents, and lack of acceptance (Gehrke & Turban, 1999). Therefore, evaluation of e-commerce applications has been studied in many aspects and by different approaches, such as factors affecting customer relationship, consumer requirements, customer support, customer satisfaction, cost/benefits, and operational-qualitative and strategic-qualitative approaches. Based on the success stories from companies, Seybold (1998) provided eight success factors for e-commerce: targeting the right customers; owning the customer's total experience; providing a 360 view of the customer relationship; letting customers help themselves; helping customers do own jobs; delivering personalized service; and fostering community. Farquhar, Langmann and Balfour (1998) identified some generic consumer requirements, including ease of use, consistency in user interface, privacy, security, cost transparency, reliability, error tolerance, design for different type customers, order confirmation and system status information. Turban et al. (2002) proposed some Web-related metrics that a company can use to determine the appropriate level of customer support: response time; site availability; download time; up-to-date; security and privacy; fulfilment; return policy; and navigability.

Liu and Arnett (2000) identified four factors that were critical to e-commerce Web site success, including information and service quality, system use, playfulness, and system design quality. Elliot, Morup-peterson and Bjorn-andersen (2000) proposed a framework for evaluation of commercial Web sites to identify the key features and facilities of business-to-customer Web sites. The framework consists of six categories: company information and function; product/service information and promotion; transaction processing; customer services; ease of use; and innovation in services and technology.

More research efforts can be found in the existing literature for e-commerce success measures (D'Ambra & Rice, 2001; Molla & Licker, 2001; Palmer, 2002; Teo & Choo, 2001).

## E-Government Success

Some research efforts pay attention to the design of e-government. Heeks (2001) developed an ITPOSMO model and discussed the gap between current realities and design conceptions of e-government projects. ITPOSMO means Information, Technology, Processes, Objectives and values, Staffing and skills, Management systems and structures, and other resources (time and money). The research also suggested that mismatch of e-government initiatives can be assessed along those seven dimensions, and concluded that success or failure of an e-government initiative depends on the degree of mismatch between the design of that initiative and the realities.

Others focus on the measurement of e-government success. From a user's perspective, Lisle-Williams (2002) defined the successful e-government in three criteria: service quality, choice, and user experience. Service quality focuses on objective measures. Choice addresses not only personalization, but also privacy and anonymity. User experience refers to subjective and often influenced by small factors. Steyaert (in press) adopted e-commerce performance indicators – consumer awareness, popularity, contact efficiency, conversion, and retention, proposed by Watson et al. (2000) to analyze federal and state e-government service cases in USA. Consumer awareness deals with the number of visitors to a site. Popularity refers to the rank of the site. Contact efficiency indicates site usability and content. Conversion refers to customer satisfaction, transactions and time on the site. Retention deals with customer loyalty.

Two main categories of research results are government Web site evaluation and e-government success or failure criteria. Concerning the government Web site evaluation, DeConti (1998) proposed a methodology to evaluate and analyse the government Web sites in six areas: audience; purpose statement; objectives; Web specification; domain information; and Web presentation. Smith (2001) applied the evaluation criteria of Eschenfelder et al. (1997) to a sample of five Web sites of New Zealand government. The Eschenfelder et al. (1997) evaluation criteria are divided into two groups, information content criteria and ease-of-use criteria. Information content criteria are used to evaluate the nature of the information and services provided by the Web site, including orientation to the Web site, the content of site, currency, metadata, availability of services, accuracy and privacy. Ease-of-use criteria are used to evaluate the ease of use of the Web site, which includes links, feedback, accessibility, design and navigability. Huang, D'Ambra and Bhalla (2002) examined the adoption of e-government in Australian public citizens based on the technology acceptance model (TAM) (Davis, 1989). Huang, D'Ambra and Bhalla (2002)'s research effort focused on an actual system usage with two constructs, perceived usefulness and perceived ease of use. Their research indicated that the prediction of TAM theory was not supported by the findings. In addition, Burgess and Cooper (1999) proposed a Web site evaluation model called Model of Internet Commerce Adoption (MICA). The MICA model classified Web sites into three stages: inception, consideration and maturity. Sites in the inception stage provide basic information or have a basic Web presence. Sites classified in the consideration stage demonstrate an extension of basic information including e-mail, online inquiry and contact, information on extended services and general value-added information. Maturity stage sites include high-level value-added services, such as secure online transaction processing. Boon, Hewett and Parker (2000) tested the MICA model in the context of Australian local government Web sites and modified the model to make a clear distinction between the more progressive, sophisticated sites and those relatively simplistic sites.

# Main Thrust of the Chapter

## Research Model

This study focuses on the issue: what factors affect the effectiveness of e-government online services in Australia? DeLone and McLean's (1992) model explains the impact of information system at the individual and organizational level. A number of prior studies have used the DeLone and McLean (1992) model as basis of information system success (Rai, Lang & Welker, 2002; Seddon, 1997; Seddon & Kiew, 1996; Seddon et al., 1999; Wilkin & Castleman, 2003). In this study, our research model (shown in Figure 2) is partly adopted and extended from the DeLone and McLean (1992) model. Furthermore, another new construct, namely Web presence quality, is added to the DeLone and McLean (1992) model. We believe that Web presence quality is crucial in the online environment. The research model conceptualized information system success as effectiveness of e-government online services, which is measured by US. The research model shown in Figure 2 focuses on the investigation of the first two phases related to the development model of e-government online services (see Figure 1). This model presents the impact of three independent constructs (system quality, information quality and Web presence

*Figure 2: Research model in this study*

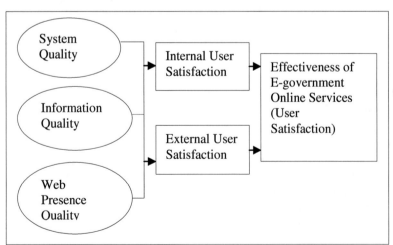

quality) on the dependent construct US, including both internal US and external US. The external US focuses on the public users, while the internal US emphasizes the inter-organizational users.

The effectiveness of e-government online services deals with both measures of information system success and that of e-commerce success. In the information systems arena, a search involved information system success measures and US. In the e-commerce arena, commercial Web site success measures were investigated. The measures in the research model are mostly derived from the measurement of information system success and e-commerce success. The relevant literature indicates that these measures are important for the three constructs, system quality, information quality and Web presence quality. However, there are no criteria to justify the weights of each measure (Liu & Arnett, 2000). Thus, the average scores of the variable, adopted in the prior study (Liu & Arnett, 2000), are used as a criterion for selection of the measures in this study.

## User Satisfaction

Since the success of information systems is difficult to measure directly, many researches have turned to indirect measures such as US (Iivari & Ervasi, 1994). Cyert and March (1963) proposed the concept of US as a surrogate of information system success. Since then, many prior research efforts employed US to measure information success. US has been considered one of the most important determinants (Downing, 1999) and the most widely used measure of information system success (DeLone & McLean, 1992).

Moreover, in this study, US has been employed as a surrogate measure for e-government effectiveness. It is supposed that US can be affected by the three independent instructs - system quality, information quality and Web presence quality. Each independent construct includes a few measures. The constructs and the corresponding measures and labels are shown in Table 1.

*Table 1: List of constructs, measures and labels*

| Construct | Measure | Label |
|---|---|---|
| System Quality (SQ) | Accessibility | V1 |
| | Feedback speed | V2 |
| | Security | V3 |
| Information Quality (IQ) | Information currency | V4 |
| | Functionality | V5 |
| | Content importance | V6 |
| Web Presence Quality (WPQ) | User-friendly | V7 |
| | Display format | V8 |
| | Navigation efficiency | V9 |
| User Satisfaction (US) | Internal user satisfaction | Internal US |
| | External user satisfaction | External US |

## System Quality

System quality refers to the technical details of the information system interface (DeLone & McLean, 1992). Many different measures of system quality have been adopted in the previous literatures, such as accuracy (Hamilton & Chervany, 1981), convenience of access, and reliability (Bailey & Pearson, 1983), rapid access, security, quick error recovery, precise operation and computation (Bhimani, 1996), and responsiveness and follow-up services.

In this study, the following three measures are adopted for system quality construct: accessibility, feedback speed, and security. In the Web-based e-government context, accessibility refers to access convenience of the system. Customers should be able to reach the company Web site at any time. This means that downtime should be as close to zero as possible. Feedback speed refers to availability and speed of responsiveness and contact management. Security concerns reliability of information systems. Security of online transaction is necessary to transmit financial information over the Web, because of increasing involvement of online transaction in e-government services.

Better system quality has been expected to lead in better effectiveness of e-government online services. Therefore, the following hypothesis is caused.

$H_1$: system quality is positively associated with effectiveness of e-government online services.

Three measures, V1, V2 and V3, affect system quality. Therefore, this leads to sub-hypotheses $H_{1-1}$, $H_{1-2}$, $H_{1-3}$.

$H_{1-1}$: accessibility (V1) is importantly associated with system quality.

$H_{1-2}$: feedback speed (V2) is importantly associated with system quality.

$H_{1-3}$: security (V3) is importantly associated with system quality.

## Information Quality

Information quality concerns the characteristics of information (DeLone & McLean, 1992). Many different information characteristics have been used as the measures of information quality, such as currency (Bailey & Pearson, 1983), accuracy, timeline, completeness, relevance (Ahituv, 1980; Bailey & Pearson, 1983), flexible and customized information presentation, service comparability, and service differentiation (Baty & Lee, 1995).

Based on the previous information quality construct, information quality is viewed as having three aspects, information currency, functionality, and content importance in this study. Information currency - it is relevant to timeline of information. Functionality – it concerns with website functions and information completeness to meet user needs. Content importance - this refers to relevance, completeness, and accuracy of information.

It is expected that increases of information quality will lead to the increase of effectiveness of e-government online services. This causes hypothesis 2.

**H₂:** information quality is positively associated with effectiveness of e-government online services.

We have proposed that three measures, V4, V5 and V6, affect information quality. Thus, the following three sub-hypotheses are resulted in.

**H$_{2.1}$:** information currency (V4) is importantly associated with information quality.

**H$_{2.2}$:** functionality (V5) is importantly associated with information quality.

**H$_{2.3}$:** content importance (V6) is importantly associated with information quality.

## *Web Presence Quality*

Web presence quality refers to the quality of e-government Web sites. There are a considerable number and variety of factors associated with Web site quality: for instance, high quality, text, graphics, image and animation (Ho & Wu, 1999), consistency in user interface, design for different customers, system status information (Farquhar, Langmann & Balfour, 1998), well defined hyperlink, help function, ease to use (Hamilton & Chervany, 1981), information availability and friendliness (Wan, 2000), present style, format and processing efficiency (Swanson, 1986). In this study, three measures are employed for Web presence quality, which are user-friendly, display format, and navigation efficiency. User-friendly concerns the availability of attracting users. Display format refers to presentation style of Web sites. Navigability efficiency means that a Web site must be easy to navigate in order to please customers.

In e-government online services, a Web site acts as an interface interacting with users. Thus, it is hypothesized that better Web presence quality will positively influence the effectiveness of e-government online services. This leads to hypothesis 3.

**H₃:** Web presence quality is positively associated with effectiveness of e-government online services.

It is assumed that the measures V7, V8 and V9 affect Web presence quality. Therefore, the following three sub-hypotheses are led to.

**H$_{3.1}$:** user-friendly (V7) is importantly associated with Web presence quality.

**H$_{3.2}$:** format (V8) is importantly associated with Web presence quality.

**H$_{3.3}$:** navigation (V9) is importantly associated with Web presence quality.

# Research Methodology

## Sampling Method

In this study, non-probability sampling method (Dickman, 1998) was used to select sample Web sites from the federal or state entry point and their links. Non-probability sampling is usually based on someone's expertise about the population and can be used successfully even though the sample validity is unable to measure (Dickman, 1998). The samples were selected from those Web sites which the public can frequently use to find relevant information or do online transaction, other than those Web sites which offer only organizational information.

## Questionnaire Design

Based on the Likert (1982) scale technique, a satisfaction score can range between one and five, where one represents the highest satisfaction and five is the highest dissatisfaction. For example, score 1 - extremely satisfied, score 2 - satisfied, score 3 - adequate, score 4 - dissatisfied, and score 5 - extremely dissatisfied. Our questionnaire was based on the four questions shown in Table 2. The content of each construct has been explained in Table 1. Target audiences need to highlight one number of the five scores. V1 – V3 are related to Question1, V4 – V6 refer to Question 2, V7 – V9 concern with Question 3, and "user satisfaction" offers the responses for Question 4.

Table 2: Questions in the questionnaire form of this study

| Q.1. How do you assess the satisfaction of the following factors in system quality? | | | | | |
|---|---|---|---|---|---|
| V1: Accessibility | 1 | 2 | 3 | 4 | 5 |
| V2: Feedback speed | 1 | 2 | 3 | 4 | 5 |
| V3: Security | 1 | 2 | 3 | 4 | 5 |
| Q.2. How do you assess the satisfaction of the following factors in information quality? | | | | | |
| V4: Information currency | 1 | 2 | 3 | 4 | 5 |
| V5: Functionality | 1 | 2 | 3 | 4 | 5 |
| V6: Content importance | 1 | 2 | 3 | 4 | 5 |
| Q.3. How do you assess the satisfaction of the following factors in web presence quality? | | | | | |
| V7: User-friendly | 1 | 2 | 3 | 4 | 5 |
| V8: Display format | 1 | 2 | 3 | 4 | 5 |
| V9: Navigation efficiency | 1 | 2 | 3 | 4 | 5 |
| Q.4. Based on all the variables (V1 – V9), how do you assess the satisfaction of this E-government website? | | | | | |
| User satisfaction | 1 | 2 | 3 | 4 | 5 |

## Data Collection from Internal Users

In the study, the internal users imply the related government agency's staffs and they are familiar with the government online service activities. An e-mail-based survey was employed for data collection. The survey was operated through measures based on the previous literatures. Three pilot studies were conducted from selected agencies. Based on the responses from them, the format and readability of survey questions were modified. To test the organization level satisfaction, an Australian-wide government Web site search was completed to select the relevant government agencies. A hundred government agencies were selected from the Australian government entry point http://www.australia.gov.au and its links. Because some of these Web sites indicate to share one port with others and a few delivery failures occurred, only 80 valid questionnaires were sent out successfully. The data collection was undertaken during May and June 2002. In total 30 valid responses were received and a 37.5% response rate was obtained. Among the responses, it indicated that five (17%) were obtained from federal government, 19 (63%) were from state government, and six (20%) were received from local government. In addition, according to Dickman (1998), a small sample is one of less than 25 observations, while a sample of 25 or more will be deemed as large. The sample size is sufficiently large for valid data analysis.

## Data Collection from External Users

The external users are those customers who regularly use the e-government Web sites. To test the external user satisfaction, eight questionnaires were e-mailed to research students and academic staff in Faculty of Information Technology at University of Technology Sydney, who were our colleagues and we were sure that they were regular users of e-government Web sites. Also it was assumed the participants should have certain knowledge of Web site design. Although the amount of questionnaires was not very large, the targeted audiences were, to a certain degree, experts on Web site design and Web site quality, so that more useful response than random audiences had been achieved. These expert audiences were required to visit all the 30 assigned Web sites and complete the survey questions. Six responses were received and a 75% valid response rate was obtained, which was considered a very high response rate.

# Data Analysis and Results

## Comparison of Internal and External User Satisfaction

The investigation results of US are shown in Table 3. From an internal user's viewpoint, the statistical data show that about 1/3 of agencies classify their feelings about the government Web sites as "satisfied," including 26.7% "satisfied" (ranking in 2) and 6.7% "extremely satisfied" (ranking in 4). Forty percent of agencies feel their site is "adequate" (ranking in 1). However, there are 23.3% that appeared "dissatisfied" (ranking in 3) and

*Table 3: Comparison of internal and external user satisfaction (US)*

| Scale of US | Internal US | | | External US | | |
|---|---|---|---|---|---|---|
| | *No* | *%* | *Ranking* | *No* | *%* | *Ranking* |
| 1 - extremely satisfied | 2 | 6.7 | 4 | 10 | 5.6 | 4 |
| 2 - satisfied | 8 | 26.7 | 2 | 91 | 50.5 | 1 |
| 3 - adequate | 12 | 40 | 1 | 63 | 35 | 2 |
| 4 - dissatisfied | 7 | 23.3 | 3 | 14 | 7.8 | 3 |
| 5 - extremely dissatisfied | 1 | 3.3 | 5 | 2 | 1.1 | 5 |
| Total | 30 | 100 | Nil | 180 | 100 | Nil |

3.3% "extremely dissatisfied" (ranking in 5). From an external user viewpoint, half of users consider their feeling about the government Web sites as "satisfied" (ranking in1) and 35% feel "adequate" (ranking in 2).

More importantly, we have found that the average US from internal and external users are basically consistent, with 2.9 of the average US for internal users and 2.5 for external users. The responses show the score 1, score 4 and score 5 are in the same ranking, respectively ranking in 4, 3, and 5. The only difference is the ranking of score 2 and 3. Internal users ranked score 3 (adequate) on first, while external users ranked score 2 (satisfied) on first. The consistencey of two survey results have confirmed the validation of this survey. The little difference might be caused by the small population of external users. Furthermore, the total score of US may be obtained by averaging the whole responses, which is 2.7, beween satisfied (score 2) and adequate (score 3), and it is closer to score 3 (adequate). Thus, we conclude that the US of Australian Ee-government online services lies on an "adequate" level.

## Reliability Analysis

The construct reliability is assessed in terms of Cronbach's $\alpha$ coefficient (Cronbach, 1951). Cronbach's $\alpha$ coefficient is regarded as a measure of internal consistency at the time of administration of the questionnaire. Cronbach's $\alpha$ coefficient of greater than 0.70 is an acceptable reliability (Nunnaly, 1978), but a lower threshold (e.g., 0.60 or above) has also been used in research literature (Huang, D'Ambra & Bhalla, 2002). In this study, model reliability of EUS are examined, which confirmed all Cronbach's $\alpha$ coefficients are above 0.7. Then total Cronbach's $\alpha$ coefficient of each construct is obtained by simply averaging the coefficients contained in each construct. Cronbach's $\alpha$ coefficient of both internal US and external US are listed in the Table 4. The results show that the constructs are reliable.

*Table 4: Reliability analysis with Cronbach's α coefficient*

| Construct | No. of Indicator | Cronbach's α (Internal US) | Cronbach's α (External US) |
|---|---|---|---|
| System Quality | 3 | 0.76 | 0.73 |
| Information Quality | 3 | 0.71 | 0.72 |
| Web Presence Quality | 3 | 0.80 | 0.73 |

## Hypotheses Testing

The three factors are examined in relation to their impacts on US. A one-way analysis of variables (ANOVA) is conducted with each factor as the independent variable, and internal US and external US as the dependent variables, separately. The ANOVA results with $p$-values of internal US are shown in Table 5. The ANOVA results with $p$-values of external US are shown in Table 6-1, Table 6-2, and Table 6-3, which show respectively the relationship between SQ, IQ, WPQ and external users.

It may be found from Table 5 that all nine measures have $p$-value<0.05. According to $p$-value, the measures fall into two groups: group 1 – two (V2 and V6) of the nine measures, which have $p$-value greater than 0.01 and less than 0.05. This means that V2 and V6 have important effects at 5% level; group 2 – the other seven measures (V1, V3, V4, V5, V7, V8, V9), which have $p$-value less than 0.01. This implies that the seven measures V1, V3, V4, V5, V7, V8, and V9 have significant effects at 1% level. Furthermore, the average $p$-values are 0.009 for SQ, 0.007 for IQ, and 0.001 for WPQ. Thus, the results from viewpoint of internal users support all three hypotheses, $H_1$, $H_2$ and $H_3$. Meanwhile, all nine sub-hypotheses are also supported because of each $p$-value is less than 0.05.

*Table 5: ANOVA results to test relationship between constructs and internal US*

| Construct | Measure | Sum of Squares | df | Mean Square | F | p-value | Mean p-value |
|---|---|---|---|---|---|---|---|
| System Quality | V1 | 9.810 | 4 | 2.452 | 4.961 | .004** | 0.009** |
| | V2 | 5.980 | 4 | 1.495 | 3.486 | .021* | |
| | V3 | 10.843 | 4 | 2.711 | 5.203 | .003** | |
| Information Quality | V4 | 3.760 | 4 | .940 | 6.514 | .001** | 0.007** |
| | V5 | 7.742 | 4 | 1.935 | 4.779 | .005** | |
| | V6 | 8.621 | 4 | 2.155 | 3.756 | .016* | |
| Web Presence Quality | V7 | 5.411 | 4 | 1.353 | 7.110 | .001** | 0.001** |
| | V8 | 7.986 | 4 | 1.996 | 6.918 | .001** | |
| | V9 | 9.821 | 4 | 2.455 | 7.356 | .000** | |

*$p<0.05$, **$p<0.01$

232   Guo and Lu

*Table 6-1: ANOVA results to test relationship between SQ (V1, V2, V3) and external US*

| Measure | User no. | Sum of squares | df | ms | f | p-value | Mean p-value | |
|---|---|---|---|---|---|---|---|---|
| V1 | 1 | 1.750 | 2 | .875 | 3.399 | .048* | 0.045* | |
| | 2 | 2.567 | 2 | 1.283 | 3.726 | .037* | | |
| | 3 | 3.819 | 3 | 1.273 | 1.753 | .181 | | |
| | 4 | 22.578 | 4 | 5.644 | 8.162 | .000** | | |
| | 5 | 5.800 | 3 | 1.933 | 5.484 | .005** | | |
| | 6 | 2.904 | 1 | 2.904 | 27.440 | .000** | | |
| V2 | 1 | 1.642 | 2 | .821 | 3.026 | .065 | 0.033* | 0.042* |
| | 2 | 2.042 | 2 | 1.021 | 2.434 | .107 | | |
| | 3 | 4.065 | 3 | 1.355 | 3.857 | .021* | | |
| | 4 | 11.978 | 4 | 2.994 | 5.051 | .004** | | |
| | 5 | 5.188 | 3 | 1.729 | 6.011 | .003** | | |
| | 6 | 2.904 | 1 | 2.904 | 27.440 | .000** | | |
| V3 | 1 | 1.617 | 2 | .808 | 8.559 | .001** | 0.047* | |
| | 2 | 3.600 | 2 | 1.800 | 6.750 | .004** | | |
| | 3 | 3.708 | 3 | 1.236 | 3.386 | .033* | | |
| | 4 | 10.411 | 4 | 2.603 | 4.210 | .010* | | |
| | 5 | 2.133 | 3 | .711 | 3.467 | .031* | | |
| | 6 | .181 | 1 | .181 | 2.018 | .167 | | |

*p<0.05, **p<0.01

*Table 6-2: ANOVA results to test relationship between IQ (V4, V5, V6) and external US*

| Measure | User no. | Sum of squares | df | ms | f | p-value | Mean p-value | |
|---|---|---|---|---|---|---|---|---|
| V4 | 1 | 5.267 | 2 | 2.633 | 6.971 | .004** | 0.014* | |
| | 2 | 2.417 | 2 | 1.208 | 6.591 | .005** | | |
| | 3 | 3.919 | 3 | 1.306 | 3.122 | .043* | | |
| | 4 | 11.711 | 4 | 2.928 | 3.724 | .016* | | |
| | 5 | 19.008 | 3 | 6.336 | 6.514 | .002** | | |
| | 6 | 1.337 | 1 | 1.337 | 6.650 | .015* | | |
| V5 | 1 | 7.750 | 2 | 3.875 | 15.973 | .000** | 0.031* | 0.019* |
| | 2 | 3.300 | 2 | 1.650 | 2.621 | .091 | | |
| | 3 | 1.708 | 3 | .569 | 2.403 | .090 | | |
| | 4 | 18.411 | 4 | 4.603 | 5.363 | .003** | | |
| | 5 | 14.721 | 3 | 4.907 | 15.046 | .000** | | |
| | 6 | 2.504 | 1 | 2.504 | 72.800 | .000** | | |
| V6 | 1 | 8.800 | 2 | 4.400 | 8.486 | .001** | 0.011* | |
| | 2 | 4.950 | 2 | 2.475 | 8.100 | .002** | | |
| | 3 | 2.832 | 3 | .944 | 5.295 | .006** | | |
| | 4 | 18.478 | 4 | 4.619 | 2.970 | .039* | | |
| | 5 | 4.000 | 3 | 1.333 | 4.000 | .018* | | |
| | 6 | .300 | 1 | .300 | 12.600 | .001** | | |

*p<0.05, **p<0.01

*Table 6-3. ANOVA results to test relationship between WPQ (V7, V8, V9) and external US*

| Measure | User no. | Sum of squares | df | ms | f | p-value | Mean p-value | |
|---|---|---|---|---|---|---|---|---|
| V7 | 1 | 4.692 | 2 | 2.346 | 12.239 | .000** | 0.074 | |
| | 2 | 3.442 | 2 | 1.721 | 2.918 | .071 | | |
| | 3 | 10.994 | 3 | 3.665 | 11.379 | .000** | | |
| | 4 | 30.567 | 4 | 7.642 | 7.320 | .000** | | |
| | 5 | 4.762 | 3 | 1.587 | 2.733 | .064 | | |
| | 6 | .185 | 1 | .185 | 1.089 | .306 | | |
| V8 | 1 | 7.467 | 2 | 3.733 | 31.500 | .000** | 0.033* | 0.024* |
| | 2 | 4.950 | 2 | 2.475 | 4.243 | .025* | | |
| | 3 | 5.094 | 3 | 1.698 | 11.398 | .000** | | |
| | 4 | 19.678 | 4 | 4.919 | 5.777 | .002** | | |
| | 5 | 5.221 | 3 | 1.740 | 3.942 | .019* | | |
| | 6 | .448 | 1 | .448 | 2.144 | .154 | | |
| V9 | 1 | 2.250 | 2 | 1.125 | 7.500 | .003** | 0.014* | |
| | 2 | 4.492 | 2 | 2.246 | 3.593 | .041* | | |
| | 3 | 12.375 | 3 | 4.125 | 14.315 | .000** | | |
| | 4 | 23.578 | 4 | 5.894 | 7.447 | .000** | | |
| | 5 | 3.008 | 3 | 1.003 | 3.576 | .027* | | |
| | 6 | 2.700 | 1 | 2.700 | 7.088 | .013* | | |

$*p<0.05, **p<0.01$

In contrast, the Table 6-1, Table 6-2 and Table 6-3 indicate the viewpoint of external users. All measures (V1 – V6 and V8 – V9) have mean $p$-value less than 0.05, except V7 (user-friendly) with means $p$-value 0.074 (greater than 0.05). This result indicates that user-friendliness is not importantly associated with Web presence quality, and user-friendliness does not have significant effects on internal US. The hypothesis $H_{3-1}$ should be rejected from the construct WPQ. The average $p$-values are 0.042 for SQ, 0.019 for IQ, and 0.024 for WPQ. The sub-hypotheses $H_{1-1}$, $H_{1-2}$, $H_{1-3}$, $H_{2-1}$, $H_{2-2}$, $H_{2-3}$, $H_{3-2}$, and $H_{3-3}$ are supported as well as $p$-values of V1 (0.045), V2 (0.033), V3 (0.047), V4 (0.014), V5 (0.031), V6 (0.011), V8 (0.033) and V9 (0.014) are less than 0.05. Therefore, we conclude that the results from the viewpoint of external users support all the three hypotheses. All sub-hypotheses are also supported by the results.

## Summary of Findings

Apparently, the research outcomes indicate that the user satisfaction on Australian e-government online services lies only on an "adequate" level. Customers' expectations are only satisfied to a limited extent. The two surveys from both internal and external users have caused consistent results. All three main hypotheses, $H_1$, $H_2$ and $H_3$, have been validated by the results of data analyses. According to the previous data analyses and results, we summarized the findings as follows.

System quality is positively associated with effectiveness of e-government online services ($H_1$); thus an increase in the quality of system leads to an increase in effectiveness of e-government online services. System quality includes accessibility, feedback speed, and security. A net positive effect from these factors will result in a positive effect on effectiveness of e-government online services. These factors should remain important considerations for the e-government developers and managers.

Information quality is positively associated with effectiveness of e-government online services ($H_2$); thus an increase in the quality of information leads to an increase in effectiveness of e-government online services. Information currency, functionality and content importance constitute the construct of information quality. Thus, a net positive effect from these factors has resulted in a positive effect on effectiveness of e-government online services. Information currency, functionality and content importance should be considered as important factors when presenting information.

Web presence quality is positively associated with effectiveness of e-government online services ($H_3$); thus an increase in the quality of Web presence leads to an increase in effectiveness of e-government online services. User-friendly, display format, and navigation efficiency are used to measure Web presence quality. Thus, a net positive effect from these factors will result in a positive effect on effectiveness of e-government online services. User-friendliness, display format, and navigation efficiency should be considered as important factors for Web designers. On the other hand, public users do not care about the user-friendliness factor. Easy to navigate and easy to find the relevant information are most important for them.

The results indicate that the viewpoints of evaluating the effectiveness of e-government online services are slightly different between the internal users and external users. Internal users address all nine factors to evaluate the satisfaction, which are accessibility, feedback speed, security, information currency, functionality, content usefulness, user-friendliness, display format and navigation efficiency. However, external users emphasize only the other eight factors except user- friendliness. We believe this is due to external users paying more attention to the service quality of e-government, and a small size of population from external users can also be another reason to cause the difference.

According to the internal users, all sub-hypotheses in the research model are fully supported. All the measures (accessibility, feedback speed, security; information currency, functionality, content importance; user-friendliness, display format, navigation efficiency) are positively associated to constructs separately. In contrast, from external users, the statistical conclusions partially support the sub-hypotheses in the research model. That is, user-friendliness is not positively associated with the Web presence quality. Others are positively associated with the constructs separately.

In addition, the results also demonstrate that the three constructs have different weight on affecting effectiveness of e-government online services. According to the internal users, the quality of Web presence has a highest weight among them, while system quality and information quality have almost equal weight on influencing effectiveness of e-government online services. Web presence quality is most important for promotion of effectiveness of e-government online services. That is, the quality of Web presence influences effectiveness of e-government online services most. On the other hand, from the external users, information quality and Web presence quality influence have approximately higher weight than system quality on influencing effectiveness of e-government online services. That is, information quality and Web presence quality influence effectiveness of e-government online services more than system quality.

## Recommendations

In general, effectiveness of e-government online services may be achieved through making high user satisfaction. Based on the results, several recommendations are advanced to develop better e-government online services.

Firstly, government agencies and organizations should actively seek ways to promote quality of information and Web presence. This requires assisting users to find the information and services from the Web sites. It can be achieved by: improving navigation by adopting standard navigational devices and using them consistently throughout the site; facilitating browse through the provision of better site maps and/or indexes and the provision of navigational information on every page; providing more links to high demand content and ensuring that descriptive information is clear; providing search engines and stating clearly what and how they search.

Secondly, government agencies and organizations should focus on the way in which customers use the Web sites, so that Web developers can maintain user-oriented Web site design and content development. This includes: determining the purpose of the site and making this clear to the users and orienting them to the site; developing and organizing the site content around user groups. This requires identification and knowledge of the relevant user groups, their information and service needs and any access issues; improving the quality of instructions generally and providing for different level of skills and expertise from the novice to the sophisticated user where necessary.

Last but not the least, government agencies and organizations should also focus on assisting users to find the information that is not on the Web sites. This can be achieved by what follows. (1) Offering a comprehensive list of agency contacts and users should be able to send an e-mail enquiry directly to the relevant section/person. Users should expect appropriately detailed and relevant answers within a set period of time. (2) Facilitating links across government Web sites and other relevant Web sites.

# Future Trends

E-government is a dynamic concept of varying meaning and significance. Because e-government continues to evolve, the full measure of its success awaits assessment (Relyea, 2002). With the transformation of e-government and the changes of client needs, the applicable evaluation model would be developed to match the future practices of e-government. The limitation of this study should be addressed in further studies. First, a much larger sample should be required for greater precision. Second, more factors should be added to match more comprehensive applications. In order to attribute to maturity of e-government, we will need to continue to develop empirical-based theories of e-government evaluation.

A particular priority for Australian e-government is the integration or linking of related services that might be provided by the same agency, different agencies, agencies in other jurisdictions, and private sector partners, so that customers can carry out multiple transactions during a single instance of service (Rimmer, 2002). After completion of integrated e-government online service phase, higher level of e-government would implement intelligent services (Guo & Lu, 2003); for example, personalized relationship between citizen and government. All citizens can have an electronically maintained, personal profile of their financial interactions with the government to improve their personal efficiency. Thus, we identify personalization as one of our main direction in the future study. Personalization is a technique used to generate customized content for each client. Through personalization an organization can focus on customer intimacy and enhance its overall value. Although the full potential of personalization techniques have not broadly been realized, a few government agencies have launched to offer simple personalization function through provision of online personal profile.

# Conclusions

This study has developed a research model to evaluate the effectiveness of Australian e-government online services. The specification of the research model is based on the theoretical and empirical sources. We have identified the underlying factors, system quality, information quality and Web presence quality, which influence significantly the effectiveness of e-government online services. The research results empirically demonstrate the relationships between the three conducts - system quality, information quality, Web presence quality, and user satisfaction. These relationships are useful in determining the development strategies of e-government online services. Government agencies need to understand these relationships in order to achieve better services.

E-government online services are still in an early stage. Demands of customers have not been understood completely and agencies are not so clear on how to present their information and services based on the needs of customers. Furthermore, the results obtained in this study have some important implications for development of e-government online services. Our results suggest that Web presence quality and information quality influence effectiveness of e-government online services more than system quality from user perspectives. This will help the relevant participants of e-government addressing management concerns of success strategy.

Although the study has been conducted in the context of Australian e-government online services, the research outcomes may assist practitioners and researchers, in the developed countries especially, who recognize the critical importance of e-government online services but remain unsure of how to implement the strategies effectively. On the other hand, the practitioners and researchers in the developing countries can draw lessons from the practices and experiences of e-government online services in Australia, and develop an effective strategy in combination with their own status.

# References

Ahituv, N. (1980). A systematic approach toward assessing the value of an information system. *MIS Quarterly, 4*(4), 61-75.

Aicholzer, G., & Schmutzer, R. (2000, September). *Organizational challenges to the development of electronic government.* Paper presented at the 11th International Workshop on Database and Expert Systems Applications, Greenwich, London.

Aldrich, D., Bertot, J.C., & McClure, C.R. (2002). E-government: initiatives, development and issues. *Government Information Quarterly, 19,* 349-355.

Anonymous. (2002). *What is e-government?* Retrieved March 18, 2003, from: *http://www.e-government.govt.nz/programme/faqs.asp#a1.*

Bailey, J.E., & Pearson, S.W. (1983). Development of a tool for measuring and analyzing computer user satisfaction. *Management Science, 29*(5), 530-545.

Baty, J.B., & Lee, R.M. (1995). Intershop: Enhancing the vendor/customer dialectic in electronic shopping. *Journal of Management Information Systems, 11*(4), 9-31.

Bhimani, A. (1996). Securing the commercial Internet. *Communications of ACM, 39*(6), 29-35.

Boon, O., Hewett, W.G., & Parker, C.M. (2000, June). *Evaluating the adoption of the Internet: A study of an Australian experience in local government.* Paper presented at the 13th International Bled Electronic Commerce Conference, Bled, Slovenia.

Briggs, R.O., Vreede, G.D., Nunamaker Jr, J.F., & Sprague Jr., R. H. (2003). Special issue: Information systems success. *Journal of Management Information Systems, 19*(4), 5-8.

Burgess, L., & Cooper, J. (1999, June). *A model for classification of business adoption of Internet commerce solutions.* Paper presented at the 12th International Bled Electronic Commerce Conference, Bled, Slovenia.

Chen, H. (2002). Digital government: Technologies and practices. *Decision Support Systems, 34*(3), 223 - 227.

Cronbach, L.J. (1951). Coefficient alpha and internal structure of tests. *Psychometric, 16,* 297-334.

Cyert, R., & March, J. (1963). *A behavioral theory of the firm.* Englewood Cliffs: Prentice-Hall.

D'Ambra, J., & Rice, R.E. (2001). Emerging factors in user evaluation of the World Wide Web. *Information and Management, 38*(6), 373-384.

Davis, F.D. (1989). Perceived usefulness, perceived ease of use, and user acceptance of information technology. *MIS Quarterly, 13*(3), 319-340.

Davis, F.D., Bagozzi, R.P., & Warshaw, P.R. (1989). User acceptance of computer technology: A comparison of two theoretical models. *Management Science, 35*(8), 982-1003.

DeConti, L. (1998). *Planning and creating a government website: Learning for the experience of US states.* Retrieved, June 16th, 2002, from: *http://www.amn.ac.uk/ idpm.*

DeLone, W.H., & McLean, E.R. (1992). Information systems success: The quest for the dependent variable. *Information Systems Research, 3*(1), 60-95.

Devadoss, P.R., Pan, S.L., & Huang, J.C. (2003). Structural analysis of e-government initiatives: A case study of SCO. *Decision Support Systems, 34*(3), 253-269.

Dickman, G. (1998). *Business statistics.* Melbourne: Nelson.

Downing, C.E. (1999). System usage behavior as a proxy for user satisfaction: an empirical investigation. *Information and Management, 35*(4), 203-216.

Elliot, S.R., Morup-Peterson, A.S., & Bjorn-Andersen, N. (2000, June). *Towards a framework for evaluation of commercial websites.* Paper presented at the 13th International Bled Electronic Commerce Conference, Bled, Slovenia.

Elmagarmid, A.K., & McIver Jr., W.J. (2001). The ongoing march toward digital government. *IEEE Computer, 34*(2), 32-38.

Eschenfelder, K.R., Beachboard, J.C., McClure, C.R., & Wyman, S.K. (1997). Assessing US federal government Web sites. *Government Information Quarterly, 14*(2), 173-189.

Farquhar, B., Langmann, G., & Balfour, A. (1998). Consumer needs in global electronic commerce. *Electronic Markets, 8*(2), 9-12.

Gallagher, C.A. (1974). Perceptions of the value of a management information system. *Academy of Management Journal, 1*(1), 46-55.

Garrity, E.J., & Sanders, G.L. (1998). Dimensions of information systems success. In E.J. Garrity & G.L. Sanders (Eds.), *Information systems success measurement.* Hershey, PA: Idea Group Publishing.

Gehrke, D., & Turban, E. (1999, January). *Determinants of successful Web design: Relative importance and recommendation for effectiveness.* Paper presented at the 32nd Hawaii International Conference on System Science (HICSS'99), Hawaii, USA.

Gordon, T.F. (2002). Introduction to e-government. *European Research Consortium for Information and Mathematics, 48,* 12-13.

Guo, X.T., & Lu, J. (2003, September). *Building intelligent e-government: A strategic development model in context of Australia.* Paper presented at the CollECTeR (LatAm) Conference on Electronic Commerce, Santiago, Chile.

Guo, X.T., Lu, J., & Raban, R. (2002, October). *An assessment of the characteristics of Australian government e-services.* Paper presented at the 7th annual CollECTeR Conference on Electronic Commerce, Melbourne, Australia.

Hamilton, S., & Chervany, N.L. (1981). Evaluating information system effectiveness: comparing evaluation approaches. *MIS Quarterly, 5*(3), 55-69.

Heeks, R. (2001, September). *Explaining success and failure of e-government.* Paper presented at the European conference on E-government, Dublin.

Ho, C.F., & Wu, W.H. (1999, January). *Antecedents of customer satisfaction on the Internet: An empirical study of on-line shopping.* Paper presented at the 32nd Hawaii International Conference on System Science (HICSS'99), Hawaii, USA.

Holmes, D. (2001). *eGov: eBusiness strategies for government.* London: Nicholas Brealey Publishing.

Huang, W., D'Ambra, J., & Bhalla, V. (2002). An empirical investigation of the adoption of eGovernment in Australian citizens: Some unexpected research findings. *Journal of Computer Information Systems, 43*(1), 15-22.

Igbaria, M., & Nachman, S.A. (1990). Correlates of user satisfaction with end user computing. *Information and Management, 19,* 73-82.

Iivari, J., & Ervasi, I. (1994). User information satisfaction: IS implementability and effectiveness. *Information and Management, 27*(4), 205-220.

Kim, K.K. (1989). User satisfaction: A synthesis of three different perspectives. *Journal of Information Systems, 4*(1), 1-12.

Layne, K., & Lee, J. (2001). Developing fully functional e-government: A four stage model. *Government Information Quarterly, 18,* 122-136.

Likert, R.A. (1982). A technique for the measurement of attitudes. *Archives of Psychology, 142,* 44-53.

Lisle-Williams, M. (2002). Successful eGovernment. Retrieved November 6, 2002, from: *http://www.egov.vic.au/Documents/webchannelsinfutureegov.pps.*

Liu, C., & Arnett, K.P. (2000). Exploring the factors associated with Website success in the context of electronic commerce. *Information and Management, 38,* 23-33.

Marchionini, G., Samet, H., & Brandt, L. (2003). Digital government. *Communications of the ACM, 46*(1), 25-27.

Mason, R.O. (1978). Measuring information output: A communication systems approach. *Information and Management, 1*(5), 219-234.

Molla, A., & Licker, P.S. (2001). E-commerce systems success: An attempt to extend and respecify the DeLone and McLean model of IS success. *Journal of Electronic Commerce Success, 2*(4), 1-11.

NOIE. (2002a). The current state of play. Retrieved June 16th, 2003, from: *http://www.noie.gov.au.*

NOIE. (2002b). Advancing Australia: The information economy progress report 2002. Retrieved December 16, 2002, from: *http://www.noie.gov.au/publications/NOIE/progress_report/NOIE_AA_S.pdf.*

Nunnaly, J. (1978). *Psychometric theory.* New York: McGraw-Hill.

OGO. (2001). Government online: The commonwealth government's strategy. Retrieved June 16, 2002, from: *http://www.govonline.gov.au/projects/strategy/GovOnlineStrategy.htm.*

Palmer, J.W. (2002). Web site usability, design, and performance metrics. *Information Systems Research, 13*(2), 151-167.

Pilipovic, J., Ivkovic, M., Domazet, D., & Milutinovic, V. (2002). E-government. In V. Milutinovic & F. Patricelli (Eds.), *E-business and e-challenges*. Amsterdam: IOS Press.

Rai, A., Lang, S.S., & Welker, R.B. (2002). Assessing the validity of IS success models: An empirical test and theoretical analysis. *Information Systems Research, 13*(1), 50-69.

Relyea, H.C. (2002). E-gov: Introduction and overview. *Government Information Quarterly, 19,* 9-35.

Rimmer, J. (2002). E-government - better government. Retrieved March 26, 2003, from: *http://www.noie.gov.au/publications/speeches/Rimmer/Breakfast/egov_sep18. htm.*

Scholl, H.J. (2003, January). *E-government: A special case of ICT-enabled business process change.* Paper presented at the 36th Hawaii International Conference on System Science (HICSS'03), Hawaii, USA.

Seddon, P. (1997). A respecification and extension of the DeLone and McLean model of IS success. *Information Systems Research, 8*(3), 240-253.

Seddon, P.B., & Kiew, M.Y. (1996). A partial test and development of the DeLone and McLean model of IS success. *Australian Journal of Information Systems, 2,* 1-61.

Seddon, P.B., Staples, S., Patnayakuni, R., & Bowtell, M. (1999). Dimensions of information systems success. *Communications of the AIS, 1*(20), 1-39.

Seybold, P.B. (1998). *Customer.com: How to create a profitable business strategy for the Internet and beyond.* London: Random House.

Shannon, C.E., & Weaver, W. (1949). *The mathematical theory of communication.* Urbana, IL: University of Illinois Press.

Smith, A.G. (2001). Applying evaluation criteria to New Zealand government Website. *International Journal of Information Management, 21,* 137-149.

Sprecher, M.H. (2000). Racing to e-government: Using the Internet for citizen service delivery. *Government Finance Review, 16*(5), 21-22.

Srinivasan, A. (1985). Alternative measures of system effectiveness: Associations and implications. *MIS Quarterly, 9*(3), 243-253.

Steyaert, J.C. (in press). Measuring the performance of electronic government services. *Information and Management.*

Swanson, E.B. (1986). A note of informatics. *Journal of Management Information Systems, 2*(3), 86-91.

Tapscott, D. (1996). *Digital economy.* New York: McGraw-Hill.

Teo, T.S.H., & Choo, W.Y. (2001). Assessing the impact of using the Internet for competitive intelligence. *Information and Management, 39*(1), 67-83.

Turban, E., King, D., Lee, J., Warkentin, M., & Chung, H.M. (2002). *Electronic commerce 2002: A managerial perspective.* New Jersey: Pearson Education.

Victoria, M. (2002). *Putting people at the centre: Government innovation working for Victorians.* Retrieved March 18, 2003, from: *http://www.mmv.vic.gov.au/egov.*

Wan, H.A. (2000). Opportunities to enhance a commercial Website. *Information and Management, 38*(1), 15-21.

Watson, R.T., Berthon, P., Pitt, L., & Zinkhan, G. (2000). *Electronic commerce - the strategic perspective.* Texas: Dryden Press.

West, D.M. (2000). Assessing e-government: The Internet, democracy, and service delivery by state and federal government. Retrieved June 16, 2002, from: *http://www.insidepolitics.org/egovtreport00.html.*

Wilkin, C., & Castleman, T. (2003, January). *Development of an instrument to evaluate the quality of delivered information systems.* Paper presented at the 36th Hawaii International Conference on System Science (HICSS'03), Hawaii, USA.

Wimmer, M., & Traunmuller, R. (2000, September). *Trends in electronic government: managing distributed knowledge.* Paper presented at the 11th International Workshop on Database and Expert Systems Applications, Greenwich, London.

Woodroof, J., & Burg, W. (2003). Satisfaction/dissatisfaction: Are users predisposed? *Information and Management, 40*(4), 317-324.

WorldBank. (2002). A definition of e-government. Retrieved March 16, 2003, from: *http://www1.worldbank.org/publicsector/egov/definition.htm.*

Chapter X

# Implementing Digital Government in the Finnish Parliament*

Airi Salminen, University of Jyväskylä, Finland

Virpi Lyytikäinen, University of Jyväskylä, Finland

Pasi Tiitinen , University of Jyväskylä, Finland

Olli Mustajärvi, The Parliament of Finland, Finland

## Abstract

*The Finnish Parliament has been active in utilizing information and communication technologies in the parliamentary work as well as in communicating with citizens and other organizations. As common in public sectors, work, knowledge management, and communication in the environment is document-centric. A strategic issue in implementing digital government has been SGML/XML standardization. The Finnish Parliament has been a pioneer in the adoption of SGML/XML technologies. The chapter reports experiences from the standardization efforts. The implications of the standardization will be examined from the viewpoints of documents, information technology, work with documents, the Finnish Parliament, and the whole society. From the point of view of a citizen, the major effect of the standardized document production is the improved accessibility to legislative information through the Internet. Plans for new knowledge management solutions and semantic Web services will be discussed at the end of the chapter.*

# Introduction

In democratic societies, the rules of the societies, as well as the history of the development of the rules, are documented by government agencies. The work in the agencies is document-centric. Therefore, a critical factor in the implementation of digital government is effective implementation of electronic document management. Digital governments of the future will be complicated inter-organizational networks where parties involved share, send, receive, and distribute documents. Data and system integration in the networks requires major efforts in document standardization.

The importance of document standardization was realized in the Finnish Parliament already in the middle of 1990s. Incompatibilities of systems, inconsistencies in representations, heterogeneity in retrieval techniques, and uncertainty of the future usability of archived digital documents activated major standardization efforts. After a careful analysis, the Standard Generalized Markup Language (SGML) (Goldfarb, 1990) was chosen for the standard format of documents in the Parliament. The implementation of SGML has been a demanding task. The effects of the standardization have concerned documents, document production, archiving practices, information distribution, and inter-organizational collaboration. From the point of view of a citizen, the major effect of the new solutions is the improved accessibility to legislative information through the Internet. Currently work is going on to implement a transfer from SGML to its subset XML (Extensible Markup Language) (Bray, Paoli & Sperberg-McQueen, 1998).

In the chapter we will describe the standardization process in the Finnish Parliament. We will also describe the outcomes of the standardization project, which has been a major redesigning and rethinking effort. In standardizing documents, the rules for representing information in them were defined. The standardization affected not only the documents themselves. Also the roles of the people working with the documents, the workflows of the document production, and the tools used in the domain changed in implementing the standards (Salminen, 2000; Salminen, Lyytikäinen, Tiitinen & Mustajärvi, 2001). The standardization was quite a complicated process and required a lot of motivation and resources. In the background section of the chapter we will first discuss the document standardization process in general. Then we will describe the environment of the Finnish Parliament and the pre-standardization situation of the document management there. After that a chronological narrative of the standardization efforts follows. The implications of the standardization will be examined from the viewpoints of documents, information technology, work with documents, the Finnish Parliament, and the whole society. Finally, the plans for the extension of the standardization to concern metadata will be discussed.

# Background

## SGML Standardization Process

The use of SGML (or its subset XML) on a specific domain requires document standardization. The standardization means agreement upon rules that define the way information is represented in the documents of the domain. SGML standardization does not concern documents only. Successful implementation of the standards of a domain may require major changes in work processes as well as in the tools used in the work. Especially interorganizational document standardization covering many document types has proven to be an extremely complicated task. It may take several years before the first operational solutions are implemented and cause tremendous costs.

Figure 1 shows a model for SGML-based standardization in an organization or a group of organizations. The circles in the figure depict activity phases, and the arrows show the control flow specifying the order for starting the activities. The small black circle indicates that all of the following three activities can be started either in parallel or in any order. The analysis phase in the beginning of the process produces preliminary standards for a specified domain. Design of new solutions requires evaluation and redesign of the preliminary DTDs parallel with the development of new document production practices and selection of new systems. The new electronic document management solution will then be implemented. The solution may require a lot of changes in document processing, as has been noticed in reported cases (e.g., Braa & Sandahl, 1998; Fahrenholz-

*Figure 1: SGML standardization process*

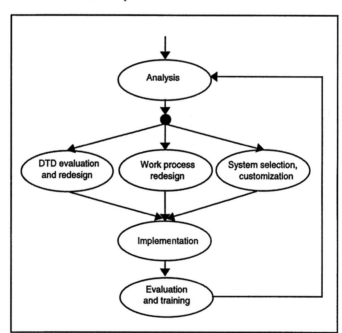

Mann, 1999). After the implementation phase, a phase including both a careful evaluation of the new solutions and training of the people involved is important. After the evaluation, the implementation may need corrections, further redesigning may be called for, or a new domain is selected for analysis.

SGML standardization activities in public administration have taken place in many organizations, for example in the Norwegian Parliament and ministries (Johanson, 1997; Sundholm, 1997), the Supreme Court of Canada (Poulin, Lavoie & Huard, 1997), and the Tasmanian government (Arnold-Moore, Clemes & Tadd, 2000). SGML has also been utilized in the preparation of the Budget of the European Union (Catteau, 1997). XML in turn have been considered as a basis for document production, for example in Estonia (Heero, Puus & Willemson, 2002) and United States Congress (Carmel, 2002). This chapter describes SGML standardization of the Finnish legislative documents.

# The Case Environment

The legislative process in Finland usually begins when officials and a minister in one of the ministries start preparing a Government Bill. The impulse for initiating the preparation may come, for example, from the European Union, which Finland joined in the beginning of 1995. The Council of State (also called government), which includes all the ministries, submits the finalized Bill to the Parliament as a proposal for a law. Each year approximately 250 Government Bills are submitted to the Parliament. Not only the government, but also a Member of the Parliament (MP) may present a proposal concerning law. In this case the proposal document is called a Law Initiative. Annually MPs produce around 150 Law Initiatives.

The Finnish Parliament has 200 MPs and employs 600 civil servants. The unicameral Parliament was established in 1906. Its main tasks are to enact legislation, decide on taxes and state expenditures, oversee the ministries and their subordinates, and approve international treaties. The Parliament also participates in the national preparation of EU affairs. The handling of a bill in the Parliament begins with a preliminary debate in the plenary session. In the session no decisions are made concerning the content of the proposals, but the purpose is to provide a basis for the committee work.

The Parliament has 14 permanent Special Committees. The main task of the committees is to handle bills. In addition to Special Committees there is also a Grand Committee mainly for dealing with EU matters. For each bill, the plenary session appoints one of the Special Committees to work with it and prepare a statement in a form of a Special Committee Report. The other committees may express their opinion on the matter by preparing a Special Committee Statement, and send the statement to the responsible committee. When the report is finalized, it is sent back to the plenary session for two readings.

In the first reading a general debate precedes a more detailed discussion where the content of the bill is decided. In the second reading the bill can either be approved or rejected. In rare cases (besides EU matters) the Grand Committee has to state its position over the bill by preparing a report. The total time for handling one bill in the Parliament is usually 2-4 months. After the Parliament has approved the law, it is sent to the President of the Republic to be ratified. The President and the responsible minister sign the law, and it will be published in the statute book.

Since Finland has two official languages, Finnish and Swedish, all legislative documents have to be available in both of the languages. The translations from Finnish to Swedish, or in some cases from Swedish to Finnish, are done either in the Swedish Office of the Parliament or in the Translation Unit of the Council of State.

## The Baseline

In the Finnish Parliament automatic text processing started in 1980, in the ministries in 1985. In the following we describe the situation around 1994, at the time standardization was activated.

In the Parliament, the first versions of documents were created using Word Perfect (WP) v. 5.1 with help of templates and styles. The final composing was done in a publishing house owned by the state. The WP documents were transferred online from the Parliament to the publishing house. The layout was designed only for printed documents and planned in the publishing house. Many proofreading iterations were needed between the Parliament and the publishing house. A complex manual system was used for managing different document versions. Documents with quite a poor layout (first versions) were distributed during document handling processes, for instance, for the readings in the plenary session. The reference data concerning the legislative documents were stored in a tracking system; the WP documents themselves were archived in a text archive. The user interfaces were character based.

In the 13 ministries, the systems for managing digital documents differed in each ministry. For the creation of legislative documents the ministries used mostly either WP or MS Word. The word processor versions varied. The official copies of legislative documents were printed in the publishing house from the WP documents. The ministries used 13 different diary systems for document management: each ministry had its own system. The systems included reference data concerning documents, not the documents themselves. There was no electronic archival system in the government at the time.

The functional center of document management was the publishing house. Only printed documents were available to citizens and other users outside the legislative organizations. The publishing house had a key position to dominate the document handling processes. The inter-organizational document traffic was organized via the publishing house. On one hand it was a pleasant situation for people working in the Parliament and ministries: they did not need to take care of the distribution or of the form of the distributed documents. On the other hand, from the information management and service point of view, the situation was not satisfactory. From time to time publishing costs also inspired vivid discussions.

## Standardization Activities

The standardization was activated in 1994. At the time, several work groups had discussed document management in the Parliament and ministries. Constant changes in word processing applications and incompatibilities of document formats caused problems in information transfer and extra work. In the following, the main phases of the standardization effort are discussed.

# Analysis

In spring 1994 a project called RASKE was commenced by the Parliament and a software company in cooperation with researchers at the University of Jyväskylä. The goal of the project was to evaluate alternatives for standard document formats, to design preliminary standards for parliamentary documents, and to develop methods for standardization. During later phases also the Ministry of Foreign Affairs, Ministry of Finance, Prime Minister's Office, and a publishing house participated in the RASKE project. The coordination and management of the project however was all the time on the responsibility of the Parliament. In the beginning of the project the objectives for the practical efforts were defined:

- uniform parliamentary documents,
- standard document formats and instructions for document authoring,
- better and richer Internet services in both official languages (Finnish and Swedish),
- speeding up the document production,
- savings in printing costs, and
- guaranteeing the long-term accessibility of information.

It was recognized early in the RASKE project that to achieve long lasting new solutions in the management of parliamentary documents, careful analysis of the documents and cooperation between different stakeholders in developing the standards was needed. The following were identified as the major characteristics causing difficulties in the standardization:

- The collection of different document types was large.
- The interrelationships of different document types were complicated.
- The documents were created in inter-organizational processes.
- Traditions to handle documents as paper documents were long.
- The instructions developed for document authoring were designed for paper documents.
- The number of people involved was large.
- The users and user needs concerning documents were diverse.
- It was unclear who were the persons having authority to make decisions about document standards.
- Document standards could not be implemented without changes in work processes and IT tools used in the work.

•   Changes in document management were recognized as a possible cause for changes in power relationships.

During 1995-1998, a method for document analysis was developed in the project and four domains were analyzed: the enquiry process, national legislative work, Finnish participation in the EU legislative work, and national budgetary work. The analysis method has been described by Salminen (2000, 2003), Salminen, Kauppinen and Lehtovaara (1997), and Salminen, Lyytikäinen and Tiitinen (2000). The analysis covered documents, their use and users, current systems, work processes and user needs. As part of the analysis, preliminary DTDs were designed for 21 document types including, for example, Government Bill, Special Committee Report, Private Bill, Communication of Parliament, and Budget Proposal. The publishing house implemented a prototype document archive. The archive included three types of documents in SGML format: Government Bills, Special Committee Reports, and Parliament Replies. The prototype implementation was systematically evaluated by researchers. The results of the evaluation are described by Salminen, Tiitinen, and Lyytikäinen (1999).

# Redesign and Implementation

The work of the RASKE project has been followed by projects where selected companies have developed and implemented SGML solutions (DTDs and tools) for a specific subset of documents, and the Parliament and ministries have redesigned their work processes. The first implemented document repository in SGML form was the archive of laws and statutes, which was published by the Ministry of Justice in 1997. The archive was built by the publishing house printing the statute book. In the archive there are automatically formed links to the document archives of the Parliament. The SGML format was produced by a conversion from word processing files. Conversion of text files was also used in the early version of new SGML based budgeting system implemented by the Ministry of Finance in 1998. In the Parliament, the goal was to initiate document production where documents would be originally authored in structured form. Changing the document production processes and authoring tools has been a major reengineering effort.

The document types selected in the Parliament as pilot cases in producing structured documents were the Committee Report and Committee Statement. Those document types were chosen because there are a limited number of people involved in their authoring; namely the committee councilors and their secretaries, about 30 people altogether. Another reason that favored the chosen document types was that during the document analysis and preliminary DTD design phase some of the committee councilors had shown strong interest and commitment in improving document management.

The actual redesign of the Committee Report and Committee Statement started while planning a new workflow system for special committees. It was decided to realize ideas developed in the RASKE project when the committee work processes were under reconstruction anyway. The redesign proceeded by two separate projects. One of the projects considered the layout of documents; the other designed their logical structure. Along with these, a third project concentrated on building a new information system for storing data concerning the status of affairs in discussion in the Parliament. Together with the DTD design, a considerable amount of work was carried out in customizing the software needed for document authoring. The software chosen for the purpose was FrameMaker+SGML. At the time it was considered the most mature editor in market. WordPerfect 6+SGML was also tested in the Parliament but legislative documents were too complicated for the software. In order to make the authoring work easier and thus to lessen the possible resistance towards the new authoring system, additional features were tailored to the editor. Examples of such features are automatic numeration of lists and connections to the databases of the Parliament. The connections enable, for example, automatic inclusion of information concerning MPs.

The DTDs of the pilot document types were designed by document management consultants in cooperation with people having responsibility for authoring documents of the types and also having a long experience in their work. The design work proved to be an iterative one, mainly due to communication difficulties and lack of coordination between the two ongoing projects. Even though the consultants were familiar with the document production in the Parliament, it took a while to establish a common vocabulary between all of the participants in the project. Since the project was a pilot one, there was only little knowledge related to SGML in the Parliament, and it was hard for the document authors to imagine and express all their needs and wishes towards the new system. In addition, the results of the layout project reflected as needs to alter the definition of the logical structure of the documents, and consequently caused changes in the customized editor.

After the pilot SGML implementation, the production of structured documents was extended to concern also budgetary petitions, minutes of the plenary session, law initiatives, and written questions. The number of people involved in the production of structured documents has increased to 50. By the end of 2000 the SGML implementation was extended to concern all parliamentary legislative documents.

## Training

The SGML implementation has been associated with training offered to people whose work has changed, particularly office secretaries of the committees, counselors, and officials in the Document Office and Swedish Office. Training has also been a way to disseminate information about the standardization and as such, it has been successful in promoting interest in the use of SGML. At the moment there is still need to improve the support services for document authoring. Authors have pointed out the importance of getting assistance from people who know the legislative work besides the technical issues.

## Impacts

The SGML implementation has had various effects. It has been characterized as the most important document management project in the Finnish public administration ever

(Kuronen, 1998a, 1998b). The effects can be recognized both in the legislative organizations and outside them. In the legislative organizations the major changes have taken place in the document management of the Parliament. In the following the impacts of the SGML implementation on the document management of the Parliament are discussed. In the discussion the three components of document management are considered: documents, information technology, and work with documents. At the end of the section impacts from the organization's and whole society's point of view will be discussed.

## Documents

As described above, the SGML implementation in the Parliament started from the Committee Reports and Committee Statements. Earlier many committees used their own special document structures. Currently all committees follow the same standardized structure and layout for reports and statements. The standardization has also concerned document identifiers. The standardization of the document structures and identifiers has facilitated automated generation of links to different parts of documents. This is an essential benefit for users.

*Figure 2: Committee statement in HTML form*

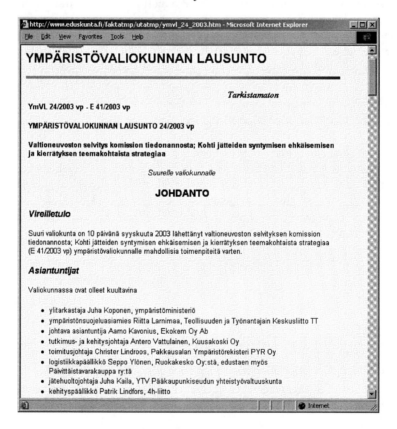

Finnish legislative documents were accessible on the Web already before the SGML implementation. The quality of the documents available on the Web has however improved as a consequence of the SGML implementation. Some document types are now available in three forms: HTML, PDF, and SGML. The layout of the documents in HTML form has been improved, for example by using different fonts in titles, subtitles and other specific parts of the document (Figure 2). The PDF form is especially useful for printing and reading paper documents (Figure 3). The printed PDF copies look practically the same as the corresponding paper documents printed by the publishing house. By the changes made to the layout of printed documents their structure has become more explicit. This is important especially to people who do not read parliamentary documents regularly. People working in the Parliament are able to print documents with slightly different layouts for different purposes, for example for different phases of legislative drafting. The possibility for on demand printing with high quality layout has significantly decreased the need for personal archives in the Parliament. To companies the SGML form available on the Web offers an opportunity to create new kinds of products and services by enriching the freely available information (Figure 4). The goal in the Parliament is to offer all parliamentary documents in the three forms introduced above. The texts of documents have been publicly available also earlier. The SGML form should however improve the capabilities for automatic processing of the texts, which in turn, when properly used, may support effectiveness and reliability.

The SGML format for legal texts opens new chances for semiautomatic consolidation of legal documents. Consolidation based on SGML has been realized earlier in a project of the Tasmanian government (Arnold-Moore et al., 2000). In February 2000 the Finnish Parliament decided about new goals for information distribution, including a goal for the

*Figure 3: Committee statement in PDF form*

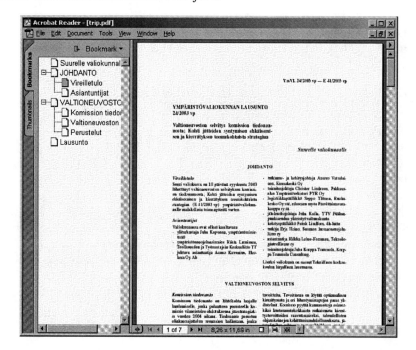

*Figure 4: Committee statement in SGML form*

distribution of consolidated legal texts. After the decision the Ministry of Justice commenced a project for implementing an SGML-based consolidation. A pilot system implemented in the Parliament demonstrated that using the SGML form as a basis, the consolidated legal database is possible to be realized and updated with reasonable costs. The consolidated Finnish legal database was opened for public use in February 2002. It is a free service for all the Web users at *www.finlex.fi*.

## Technologies and their Functionalities

In the SGML document production environment it is possible to combine information from many sources, originally authored by different tools and in different formats. WP is the tool favored by MPs and some officers. The content authoring is supported by suitable templates and styles. A document created using WP is afterwards edited using FrameMaker+SGML. Documents coming from interest groups outside the Parliament, for example, Government Bills coming from ministries, are converted to SGML with Balise software before the final editing in FrameMaker+SGML. Information can also be retrieved to the FrameMaker+SGML environment from the databases of the Parliament like from Trip text databases containing information about MPs, or from relational Ingres databases containing work flow information.

Documents created in the SGML environment are saved to a Trip database especially designed for the purpose. Documents are stored in four different formats and in two languages:

- The SGML format is for archival purposes and for creating HTML pages.
- The PDF format is for distributing printed-like documents.
- The Trip text fields are for text retrieval purposes for structured queries (a search can be directed only to some parts of the documents).
- The ASCII text is for full text retrieval.

The text databases of the Parliament are connected to the Web servers of the Parliament. There are two Web servers: one is for public use on the Internet (*http://www. parliament.fi, http://www.riksdagen.fi, http://www.eduskunta.fi*) and the other, called Facta, is for internal use. Between the two servers there is the firewall and mirroring technique is used for the data transfer from the internal server to the public server. Because the Trip databases form the basis of the Parliament's text processing system, all Internet users can get up-to-date information about the Parliament's work, documents, speeches and voting in sessions, and so forth. The Web services offer powerful retrieval capabilities utilizing document structures. Compared to the pre-standardization situation, capabilities for defining queries have significantly improved. The latest version of the Trip system, including support for XML, will cause some further changes. According to some preliminary testing, the SGML form of the documents in the Parliament does not cause essential problems in the new Trip/XML database.

## Work with Documents

The new way of producing documents in structured form changed work tasks of different groups of people. The most remarkable changes can be seen in the tasks of office secretaries of the committees, officials in the Document Office, and officials in the Swedish Office.

The office secretaries of the committees were the first people in the Parliament who actually used the customized FrameMaker+SGML editor in their work. From the committee counselors only some obtained the new tools for content authoring from the beginning of the structured document production. Therefore, the secretaries were required to have detailed understanding of the creation of Committee Reports and Statements. Since then, there have been several training sessions for the counselors, and as a result the counselors and office secretaries of the committees can now work in pairs as they earlier used to do.

Previously, people in the Document Office were responsible for the final revision and proofreading of documents, and for the communication with people in the publishing house. The new software enables the content authors themselves to take care of the layout of documents. Thus their responsibilities have increased while the work tasks in the Document Office and publishing house have decreased. The Swedish Office uses in the translation the same structure editor as other organizational units of the Parliament. The software has been customized in such a way that the constant parts of documents of a specific type are translated automatically. In the case of a large document, the translator can have access to the text already during its drafting. The translators have found this feature as a clear improvement, speeding up their work.

As a consequence of the SGML implementation, people working on document production in the Parliament need more versatile professional skills than earlier. Not only expertise for using new authoring software, but also some other technical skills not needed earlier, knowledge concerning parliamentary work, and ability to produce correct texts are essential.

## Impacts for the Organization

The availability of the parliamentary documents on the Web has significantly decreased the dissemination of paper documents both in the Parliament and from the Parliament. Although the costs of the standardization project have been rather high, they are still very acceptable compared to annual printing costs or annual expenditure to information technology in general. A major change at the organizational level can be recognized in the relationship of the Parliament and the publishing house. Compared to the situation earlier, the deployment of SGML has made the Parliament less dependent on the publishing house. The Parliament is able to place a call for bids for printing parliamentary documents. This is expected to lead to savings in the printing costs in the future. The current savings in printing costs have already been remarkable, 10-15%, and future savings are estimated to be as high as 40-50%.

In relationship to the society, the feedback received has indicated a clear improvement in the public image of the Parliament. The Parliament has been referred to as a pioneer in its work for improving openness, Web services, and usability. The activities in the Parliament have been seen as a model for other organizations, offering them a chance at least to evaluate, and possibly apply the new solutions for their own purposes. The Parliament's Web service has often received recognition for its advanced and wide content of information (Ronaghan, 2002).

## Impacts for the Society

The implementation of SGML standards in the Finnish legislative work has radically improved the accessibility of information and thus supports democracy and transparency of governance. All documents are available to all citizens free of charge. The Finnish public libraries have traditionally had an important role in the distribution of legislative documents to citizens. The tasks of the libraries are changing towards services by which citizens are helped to reach legislative archives via the Internet. In fact, many libraries do not order any more printed parliamentary legislative documents because the same information is available on the Internet in better format.

As a consequence of the implementation of the SGML-based consolidation the Finnish society got access to consolidated law on the Web. Now, both legal experts and laymen alike have improved capabilities for legal information retrieval. They no longer need to search for all the amendments to the original law texts, but instead they find the up-to-date version of the law on the Finlex service on the Internet.

As a whole, the document management development activities in the Parliament can encourage other organizations in public sector, both in Finland and in other countries, to work for delivering their documents more quickly and with improved quality to everyone who needs them.

# Lessons Learned

SGML implementation in inter-organizational processes clearly is a tedious task. In the case, the work in the first implementation projects proceeded very slowly; there was lack of SGML knowledge in the legislative organizations and lack of knowledge about legislative work among SGML consultants. The situation changed, however, during the work: in the later projects the resources needed were considerably more minor than in the beginning.

Experiences in the case emphasize the need for inter-organizational co-operation from the early phases of standardization. The involvement of many organizations in legislative work increases the complexity of the planning and implementation of new solutions. In the case environment, some problems were caused, for example, by the limited co-operation between simultaneous standardization activities in the Parliament and Ministry of Finance. After one budget round, however, it was relatively easy to harmonize the document structures of the Parliament and the Ministry of Finance. Currently problems are caused by the fact that the Government Bill is not produced in SGML format in ministries, although the text of the Bill is used in the documents produced in the Parliament.

Changes in document production cause changes in the work of several groups of people in the organization. In the beginning, a group of people may seem to get benefits of the new practices while people in other groups may find their workload to be increasing. Motivating the needs for changes and demonstrating future benefits is extremely important. A way for motivating authors in the Parliament to new working practices has been the customized editor making the authoring work easier.

One of the lessons learned concerns the role of the external representation of documents on specific media. DTD design is often introduced as a phase where the logical structure of documents is considered and the external representation for different media is then separately planned. The experiences show, however, that it is important to plan the external representation at least to some extent together with the DTDs.

The need for profound analysis of documents and work processes in the beginning of the standardization has become clear. It is important to elicit information about the requirements and needs from all parties involved. A large test material in SGML format helps in figuring out also the exceptional constructs in documents. It is also important to model the present and future processes carefully for understanding the requirements towards the DTDs and new work processes. This will lessen the need for potentially expensive later changes.

# Future Trends

The document standardization process is essential to increase the value of information services but it is only a good beginning. The Parliament of Finland has started to carry out also knowledge management (KM) projects, which seek to find solutions to the problems like how MPs could best utilize information systems and manage basic information management operations, and what to do with information deluge and the vast spectrum of parliamentary affairs.

In the Finnish Parliament, knowledge management has been considered to include a much wider area than just information technology (Suurla, Markkula & Mustajärvi, 2002). KM consists of systematic development and management of the knowledge, competence and expertise possessed currently by the organization, and that being acquired by it in the future. In order to efficiently manage its knowledge, an organization should be aware of the knowledge it possesses, where this knowledge resides, and how to access it.

In the area of KM, the most interesting trend is to develop personalized and customized IT services to users instead of current standard services. In digital government and especially at the Parliament, those personalized services could be based on MPs' missions. A mission is an MP's personal description of essentials and core interest areas in his or her work (Suurla et al., 2002). A very promising possibility to utilize missions seems to be in creation of personal interfaces for information retrieval and management. These interfaces, also called the trees of information/knowledge, could be in a mind-map form. In the Finnish Parliament the information/knowledge has been organized in the trees according to the missions (Mustajärvi, 2002). Now these information trees have been realized for every parliamentary committee.

How to continue the revolution started by the first steps of the digital government? Possible solutions for improving the current situation lies in more profound utilization of metadata related to the documents created in the governmental activities (Dertouzos, 2001). The semantic web (Berners-Lee, Hendler & Lassila, 2001) extends the current Web technologies by utilizing ontologies and different kinds of vocabularies in assisting information retrieval. With the help of versatile metadata, computers can process more demanding tasks currently processed by humans. In order to accomplish efficient and usable systems based on metadata very deep cooperation between organizations is, however, needed. Metadata standards for e-government information have lately been under development, for example, in the British government (Office of the e-Envoy, 2003) and the Finnish government (JUHTA, 2001).

The Parliament of Finland has started with the Ministry of Finance and the Ministry of Justice a project that aims for more effective utilization of information with the help of metadata in the whole area of legislative information. The project, called RASKE2, continues the work of the RASKE project by extending the standardization to cover also different kinds of metadata needed when dealing with legislative information. The first results in this three-year project are available in 2004. One target is to enable production of personalized, profiled information services for different user groups and even for every citizen.

The Finnish Parliament has also envisioned its information services in the future. At least in principle the Parliament's information services should cover all activities of the society. This could be accomplished by dividing the information services into small components according to predefined missions of the users with the help of metadata. Thus it would be possible to build personalized and profiled services for different user groups like committees and MPs. The solution would benefit both the information producer and the users alike: The producers would be able to offer customized services instead of standard solutions with the same resources than before, and users would have at least a partial relief to the information deluge (Mustajärvi, 2003). A promising and interesting opportunity would be to collaborate with government information services in updating branches and leaves of the information tree. Then the information service of every ministry would update and develop primarily the parts of the tree in its own competence area. The parts could be utilized in other organizations by suitable mechanisms - probably based on metadata and semantic Web. Also ordinary citizens could use the information produced by all the governmental agencies. Everybody could build his/ her own, automatically updated information tree.

# Conclusion

In document-centric governmental agencies effective implementation of electronic document management forms a critical factor in the implementation of digital government. In the Finnish Parliament, electronic document management implementations have been started with document standardization projects that have been going on since 1994. The standardization effort began with document analysis and preliminary DTD design. Document authoring in SGML format started in the Parliament in 1998 with two document types, Committee Reports and Committee Statements. Since then all the structures of the parliamentary documents have been standardized and the documents are now produced with customized authoring software by dozens of people.

The implementation of digital government has so far required a lot of resources, and also taught many important lessons. One of the most central lessons learned during the years is that document standardization is not solely a technical effort, but it also affects people's work tasks. Therefore, cooperation between all involved stakeholders from the very beginning is essential. Also, inter-organizational cooperation was found necessary in order to build a document management chain that could satisfy the needs of all governmental agencies.

From the citizens' and society's point of view the results of the standardization work can be seen in improved Web services: document structures can be utilized in information retrieval, there are links between document parts, and different formats, including HTML, PDF and SGML, are available. Also, the law texts can now be accessed in their consolidated form, which is one benefit of the standardized, structured format of the documents. Better access to parliamentary documents offers the citizens better chances to control and have influence on the decisions concerning them, and thus supports democracy.

# References

Arnold-Moore, T., Clemes, J., & Tadd, M. (2000). Connected to the law: Tasmanian legislation using EnAct. *Journal of Information, Law and Technology, 1.*

Berners-Lee, T., Hendler, J., & Lassila, O. (2001). The semantic Web. *The Scientific American, 284*(5).

Braa, K., & Sandahl, T.I. (1998). Approaches to standardization of documents. In T. Wakayama, S. Kannapan, C.M. Khoong, S. Navanthe & J. Yates (Eds.), *Information and process integration in enterprises: Rethinking documents* (pp. 125-142). Norwell, MA: Kluwer Academic Publishers.

Bray, T., Paoli, J., & Sperberg-McQueen, C.M. (1998). *Extensible Markup Language (XML) 1.0.* Retrieved April 1, 2003, from: *http://www.w3.org/TR/1998/REC-xml-19980210.*

Carmel, J. (2002). Drafting legislation using XML at the U.S. House of Representatives. Retrieved June 30, 2003, from: *http://xml.house.gov/drafting.htm.*

Catteau, T. (1997, December). The European Union's budget: SGML used to its full potential. *Conference Proceedings of SGML'97 US,* 645-653.

Dertouzos, M. (2001). *The unfinished revolution.* New York: HarperCollins.

Fahrenholz-Mann, S. (1999, Spring). SGML for electronic publishing at a technical society - Expectations meets reality. *Markup Languages: Theory and Practice, 1*(2), 1-30.

Goldfarb, C.F. (1990). *The SGML Handbook.* Oxford, UK: Oxford University Press.

Heero, K., Puus, U., & Willemson, J. (2002). XML based document management in Estonian legislative system. In A. Kalja (Ed.), *Proceedings of the Baltic Conference, BalticDB&IS 2002* (vol. 1, pp. 321-330). Tallin: Institute of Cybernetics at Tallin Technical University.

Johanson, B. (1997). *Medieuavhengig publisering i staten (MUP).* Retrieved November 13, 2003, from: *http://www.sgml.no/sgmlinfo/info3_97/mupref.html.*

JUHTA (2001, December 18). *JHS 143, Asiakirjojen kuvailuformaatti.* Retrieved November 17, 2003, from: *http://www.intermin.fi/intermin/hankkeet/juhta/home.nsf/pages/FCCC31E877F89F18C2256BED00291421?Opendocument.*

Kuronen, T. (1998a). *Hajautettu dokumenttien hallinta* (vol. 41). Oulu: Oulun yliopiston kirjaston julkaisu.

Kuronen, T. (1998b). *Tietovarantojen hyödyntäminen ja demokratia* (vol. 174). Helsinki: Sitran julkaisu.

Mustajärvi, O. (2002). Operationalisation of MPs' missions through knowledge management: A Finnish case study. *Proceedings of the 3rd European Conference on Knowledge Management,* 471-480. Trinity College Dublin, Ireland: MCIL.

Mustajärvi, O. (2003, May 26-28). MPs and KM: How strict ICT policy has enabled development of personalized KM services in the Parliament of Finland. In M.A. Wimmer (Ed.), *Knowledge management in electronic government, 4th IFIP International Working Conference, KMGov 2003, Rhodes, Greece, Proceedings* (vol. 2645, pp. 100-105). Springer.

Office of the e-Envoy (2003, May 2). *e-Government Metadata Standard version 2.* Retrieved November 20, 2003, from: *http://www.govtalk.gov.uk/documents/ metadataV2.pdf.*

Poulin, D., Lavoie, A., & Huard, G. (1997, September). Supreme Court of Canada's cases on the Internet via SGML. *E Law - Murdoch University Electronic Journal of Law, 4*(3).

Ronaghan, S.A. (2002). *Benchmarking e-government: A global perspective.* Retrieved July 28, 2003, from: *http://www.unpan.org/egovernment2.asp.*

Salminen, A. (2000). Methodology for document analysis. In A. Kent (Ed.), *Encyclopedia of library and information science* (vol. 67 (Supplement 30), pp. 299-320). New York: Marcel Dekker, Inc.

Salminen, A. (2003). Document analysis methods. In C.L. Bernie (Ed.), *Encyclopedia of library and information science* (2nd ed., pp. 916-927). New York: Marcel Dekker.

Salminen, A., Kauppinen, K., & Lehtovaara, M. (1997). Towards a methodology for document analysis. *Journal of the American Society for Information Science, 48*(7), 644-655.

Salminen, A., Lyytikäinen, V., & Tiitinen, P. (2000). Putting documents into their work context in document analysis. *Information Processing & Management, 36*(4), 623-641.

Salminen, A., Lyytikäinen, V., Tiitinen, P., & Mustajärvi, O. (2001). Experiences of SGML standardization: The case of the Finnish legislative documents. In J.R.H. Sprague (Ed.), *Proceedings of the 34th Hawaii International Conference on System Sciences* (pp. file etegv01.pdf at CD-ROM). Los Alamitos, CA: IEEE Computer Society.

Salminen, A., Tiitinen, P., & Lyytikäinen, V. (1999). Usability evaluation of a structured document archive. *Proceedings of the 32nd Annual Hawaii International Conference on System Sciences.* IEEE Computer Society Press.

Sundholm, E. (1997). *The Odin: The central Web server for official documentation and information from Norway.* Retrieved November 13, 2003, from: *http://www.ifla.org/ IV/ifla63/63hole.htm.*

Suurla, R., Markkula, M., & Mustajärvi, O. (2002). *Developing and implementing knowledge management in the Parliament of Finland.* Retrieved July 28, 2003, from: *http://www.eduskunta.fi/fakta/vk/tuv/KM_Finnish_Parliament.pdf.*

# Endnote

\*   This chapter is based on the paper "Experiences of SGML Standardization: The Case of the Finnish Legislative Documents" by Airi Salminen, Virpi Lyytikäinen, Pasi Tiitinen and Olli Mustajärvi, which appeared in R.H.Sprague, Jr. (Ed.), Proceedings of the Thirty-Fourth Hawaii International Conference on System Sciences. Los Alamitos, CA: IEEE Computer Society. © 2001 IEEE.

## Chapter XI

# Participants' Expectations and the Success of Knowledge Networking in the Public Sector

Jing Zhang, Clark University, USA

Anthony M. Cresswell, University at Albany, SUNY, USA

Fiona Thompson, University at Albany, SUNY, USA

## Abstract

*This chapter reports a study of how participants' expectations of interorganizational knowledge sharing are related to the success of information technology projects that require such sharing. Survey data were collected from 478 participants in six cases based on information technology innovation projects in New York State. Each project was initiated by a single New York State agency, with participants from other state agencies, local government, non-profit organizations, and private sector companies. The data analysis results identified four dimensions of participants' expectations of knowledge sharing:* benefits in providing more effective services, organizational barriers, technological incompatibility, and legal and policy constraints. *Furthermore, building on Theory of Reasoned Action (TRA) and the Theory of Planned Behavior (TPB), we found that the participants' expectations regarding organizational barriers were negatively associated with the success of knowledge networking. The less positive participants' expectations are about the inter-organizational structure and implementation processes, the less likely their efforts are to succeed. This chapter highlights the importance of the behind-the-scenes interorganizational collaboration necessary for public sector agencies to present a coherent public face in electronic government development. The benefits of and barriers to knowledge sharing as they are reflected in participants' expectations provide an opportunity to elucidate the relevant factors that can facilitate or impede the implementation of interorganizational electronic government initiatives.*

# Introduction

In many public policy and social service areas, important decisions are based on information and knowledge beyond the jurisdiction of one agency or one level of government. As public programs grow more complex and interdependent, knowledge and information sharing across the boundaries of government agencies, levels of government, and public, non-profit, and private sector has become an essential element for many applications of electronic government. For example, when the public access geographic information, what may not be noticeable is that behind the electronic interfaces a network of organizations is set into motion to provide such integrated information resources available to both public and private sector contributors and users. Sharing knowledge and information through information technology, therefore, provides strategic advantages for government to improve decision making and enhance the quality of services and programs. Such sharing has the potential to develop integrative applications, to share resources, to adapt to new environments, and to enhance organizational learning (Andersen, Belardo & Dawes, 1994; Bouty, 2000; Kraatz, 1998; Zucker et al., 1995). The expectation of such benefits provides motivation for participants to engage in innovative efforts to share practice-related knowledge. However, achieving these benefits may not be simply based on the technological advancement. Many existing organizational, political, and technical factors may posit serious barriers to the effectiveness of interorganizational knowledge sharing and the success of electronic government initiatives (Dawes, 1996; Landsbergen & Wolken, 1998; McCaffrey, Faerman & Hart, 1995). When participants expect that those barriers are formidable, their commitment to knowledge sharing initiatives and willingness to take risks can be undermined.

This chapter focuses attention on the expectations of participants at the beginning of e-government projects with regard to the benefits of and barriers to interorganizational knowledge sharing by using survey data collected from six cases in New York State (NYS). First, the underlying dimensions of participants' expectations are identified. Second, building on the Theory of Reasoned Action (TRA) and the Theory of Planned Behavior (TPB), we examine the relationship between the participants' expectations and the success of knowledge networking.

The results of this study highlight the importance of interorganizational integration necessary for public sector to present a coherent front of electronic government development. The resulting dimensions of the benefits of and barriers to knowledge sharing as they are reflected in the participants' expectation give rise to an opportunity to expound the relevant factors that could facilitate or impede the implementations of interorganizational electronic government initiatives.

This chapter is arranged in six sections. Following the introduction, we review the literature related to the benefits of and barriers to knowledge sharing as well as the relationship between expectations and knowledge networking successes. In the third section, we discuss the methodology. Next, the analysis results from the surveys are presented, followed by discussion of public sector knowledge networks and their prospects for success. The final section provides the conclusion and recommendations.

# Background

The six cases are based on information technology innovation projects conducted by the Center for Technology in Government (CTG). The approach that CTG uses to help government managers make appropriate IT decisions starts with a specification of the problem and its context, followed by identifying and testing solutions, and completed with evaluating alternatives and "making smart IT choices" (Dawes et al., 2003). Under the facilitation of CTG staff, participants in such innovation projects typically develop a *stakeholder analysis* and a *strategic framework* to identify how an information system

*Table1: Case description*

| Lead Agency, Sample Size, and Success Score | Participants | Purpose of Partnership |
|---|---|---|
| NYS Bureau of Housing Services<br>n=21; SS=86 | Providers of services to the homeless in NYC and region; New York City's Dept. of Homeless Services; contiguous counties' Dept. of Social Services; NYS agencies; private corporations | Develop and implement a Homeless Information Management System |
| NYS Council on Children and Families<br>n=45; SS=37 | NYS agencies related to CCF; Cornell University; local government users of information on children and families; Annie E. Casey Foundation | Develop and implement a Kids' Well-being Indicators Clearinghouse |
| NYS Office of the State Comptroller<br>n=190; SS=71 | NYS agencies | Develop a Central Accounting System |
| NYC's Dept of Information Technology and Telecommunications<br>n=68; SS=31 | NYC Mayoral Agencies | Develop policy for NYC's acquisition and maintenance of IT |
| NYS Office of Real Property Services<br>n=145; SS=30 | Real property assessors across the state; county real property directors; other town and county officials | Develop and implement a program of annual reassessment of properties across the state |
| NYS's Geographical Information System (GIS)<br>n=8; SS=87 | NYS agencies; local governments; private corporations | Develop, implement, and maintain a GIS for NYS |

might affect those connected to potential outcomes, as well as to identify the internal and external factors to be considered in order to achieve the service objectives. To identify solutions and evaluate alternatives, three other important analyses may also be carried out depending on the progress of the project. These are *best practices research, process modeling and analysis,* and *cost-performance modeling.* Some CTG projects go further by building and evaluating a prototype or actually implementing the information systems.

Each project in this study was initiated by a single New York State agency, with participants from other state and local government agencies, non-profit organizations, and private sector companies. The goals and the participating organizations in each of these projects are described in Table 1.

The first project was led by the Bureau of Housing Services (BHS) of the NYS Office of Temporary and Disability Assistance and included the participation of several state agencies, three local governments, and a number of shelter programs operated by nonprofit service organizations, as well as private corporations. The project involved the creation of a prototype of a new system, the Homeless Information Management System, designed to improve ongoing evaluation and refinement of service programs for home-less populations by linking data from shelter programs and government agencies in order to compare information on services to information about outcomes.

The NYS Council on Children and Families (CCF) was the leading agency for the second project. The project was to develop a publicly available, interactive, Web-based reposi-tory of statistical indicator data about the health and well being of the state's children to replace the existing paper publication that presented static information already two-to-three years out of date at the time of publication.

The NYS Office of the State Comptroller (OSC) led the effort in the redesign of the statewide Central Accounting System (CAS) involving all state agencies, all local governments, and many nonprofit service agencies as information providers and system users. The current central accounting system was over 18 years old and provided financial services to all state agencies in budgetary controls, accounting, and reporting. An increasing gap between the capability of the legacy CAS and the accounting and financial management needs of state agencies and other stakeholders led to a project to understand the current and future needs of CAS stakeholders as the basis for building a new system.

The New York City Department of Information Technology and Telecommunications (DOITT) was the leading agency for an interagency effort to implement the city's strategic IT Plan. Working with all mayoral agencies, this project aimed to develop an intranet to support information sharing and services that would enhance IT investment, system development, and information service programs citywide.

The NYS Office Real Property Services (ORPS) initiated a project involving the potential collaboration of over 1,000 appointed and elected real property assessors across the state, as well as county real property directors and other town and county officials, to promote annual reassessment by local assessors employing new procedures and technologies. At the same time, the agency was attempting to shift its relationship and style of working with the assessment community from a supervisory to a collaborative role.

The last project, NYS Geographic Information System (GIS) Coordination Program, involved the development of a Web-based clearinghouse of metadata, data sets, and related information promoting the sharing of spatial data sets statewide. This project represents the state's first successful attempt to create a jurisdiction-wide information resource available to both public and private sector contributors and users. In this initiative, the newly created NYS Office for Technology provided the leadership to a group of participants from a wide range of NYS agencies, local governments, and private corporations.

# Theoretical Framework

Our literature review consists of three sections. The first two sections summarize the incentives of and barriers to knowledge sharing that have been documented by previous studies. The third section primarily builds on the TRA and TPB, and intends to develop the understanding of how these incentives and barriers, as they are reflected in the participants' expectation, are related to the knowledge networking successes.

## Benefits of Knowledge Sharing

Interorganizational knowledge and information sharing offers substantial benefits to the participating organizations on several levels. Sharing has the potential to streamline data management, improve information infrastructure, facilitate the delivery of integrated services, and enhance relationships among participating organizations (Andersen et al., 1994; Dawes, 1996; Dawes, Pardo, Connelly, Green & McInerney, 1997; Landsbergen & Wolken, 1998; McCaffrey et al., 1995).

Information sharing can be a viable way to reduce the duplication of data collection and data handling (Dawes, 1996). For government agencies that essentially use the same or overlapping information about a common group of clients, such as local governments, a data sharing partnership can help them share resources and streamline the collection, organization, maintenance, and distribution of data and information.

Information sharing projects also provide government with opportunities to improve both technology infrastructure and information quality (Dawes, 1996). Agencies can achieve economies of scale by sharing communication networks, standards and common data definitions. As a result, the information about clients and programs will be more consistent from place to place, and each participating organization will have better quality information for its use.

Sharing can also facilitate the design and delivery of integrated services in a more effective, efficient, and responsive fashion (Landsbergen & Wolken, 1998). The goal is to provide clients seamless and integrated access to information and services at a reasonable cost (Linden, 1995). Many social and regulatory problems involve the jurisdiction of multiple agencies. With more consistent and comprehensive information about clients and programs, these agencies can better define and solve joint problems and better coordinate their programs and services.

Information sharing can also enhance trust among participating organizations (Cresswell et al., 2002), and between governments and citizens. Equipped with more complete information, participating organizations can share more equally in decision making about future programs and system designs (McCaffrey et al., 1995). At the same time, positive information sharing experiences can help government professionals build and reinforce professional networks and communities of practice, which can be valuable resources of information about programs, best practices, polities, and environmental changes (Andersen et al., 1994; Bouty, 2000; Kraatz, 1998; Powell, 1998; Zucker et al., 1995). Moreover, when more comprehensive and complete information is accessible by the public, the processes and decisions of government become more transparent, making government more accountable for its choices and performance (Dawes, 1996).

## Barriers to Knowledge Sharing

Despite many benefits, true participative systems have difficulties in sustaining themselves because barriers are deeply embedded in social, economic, and political principles that are usually viewed as having a higher value than the potential gains from such systems (McCaffrey et al., 1995). The ability to adopt an interorganizational information technology strategy or form a coherent joint information solution among heterogeneous organizations is constrained by the technological, organizational, and political reality of each individual organization (Dawes, 1996). Similarly, a number of policy-related barriers to sharing among government agencies have been recently documented by Landsbergen and Wolken (2000). The major barriers include: privacy concerns, ambiguity about statutory authority, openness to public scrutiny, lack of interorganizational trust, lack of experience, lack of awareness of opportunities to share, lack of resources, outmoded procurement methods, incompatible technologies, and lack of data standards.

To enable information exchange and make the exchanged information useful, the participating organizations must have compatible infrastructures as well as consistent data definitions and standards (Dawes, 1996). Although the emergence of open technology standards can help, the continued existence of proprietary hardware and software as well as locally developed conflicting data definitions are major obstacles to success (Landsbergen & Wolken, 1998; Murphy & Daley, 1999). The challenge of mastering the technology is further complicated by the nature and pace of technological change. In the last decade, the nature and use of technology has changed rapidly and radically, challenging the ability of government professionals to maintain adequate levels of knowledge and expertise (Dawes et al., 1997).

The actual process of sharing can be very complicated because of organizational barriers (O'Dell & Grayson, 1998, p.16). In a sense, knowledge sharing initiatives represent a new way of thinking, and require radical process and behavior changes for individuals and collectives. Frequently, organizations and individuals resist change because of structural conflicts, managerial practices, and evaluation and incentive systems that discourage sharing. Failure to address those embedded barriers leads to disappointment and failures.

Adding to such complexity, interorganizational knowledge sharing initiatives may involve large numbers of organizations with diverse missions, goals and priorities.

Organizations are self-interested entities. Achieving agreement on goals can be extremely difficult, and may not even be possible if misaligned missions are involved or a common interest cannot be easily identified (Faerman, McCaffrey & Van Slyke, 2001). Collaboration may not be sustainable simply because the transaction costs of reaching and maintaining consensus with many diverse organizations is too high. Moreover, there can be substantial risks associated with building a knowledge sharing connection. Participants may be concerned that they would lose their autonomy to a powerful party who prefers control-oriented approaches, or that shared information would be misinterpreted against the interests of those provide it (Baba, 1999; Hart & Saunders, 1997).

Even within a single organization, successful adaptation and implementation of information technology requires sharing and the integration of expertise from both program staff and technical staff. However, the traditional emphasis on specialization has created gaps and barriers between the expertise and knowledge of those who specialize in different areas (Wenger, 1998; Wenger & Synder, 2001). In intergovernmental knowledge sharing projects that rely on information technology, the lack of knowledge about technology for policy staff and the lack of knowledge about public service programs for technical staff create difficulties for effective communication and knowledge exchange and negatively impact potential success (Brown & Duguid, 2001; Cohen & Bacdayan, 1994).

Knowledge sharing projects can also be thwarted by financial constraints. Intergovernmental sharing projects often lack dedicated and reliable funding. Public projects are often funded along a vertical line of command or by programs (Dawes & Pardo, 2003). Sharing projects are often initiated on an ad-hoc basis and the continuing growth of the initiatives is not always nurtured by financial and personnel support (Caffrey, 1998), especially at a time of resource constraint. It is difficult for sharing projects to compete with existing programs and other mission-critical and agency-based projects.

Legislative and executive institutions are powerful forces that permit or prohibit sharing. Legislation and policies can influence the process of interorganizational knowledge sharing in complicated ways. On the one hand, the existence of stable and accountable legal or policy guidance about who can access what information can ease the way for risk taking, trust development, and further enhancing interorganizational knowledge sharing (Lane & Bachmann, 1996; Rousseau, Sitkin, Burt & Camerer, 1998). On the other hand, legal factors can harm the development of collaboration, if they create rigidity in resolving conflicts (Sitkin & Roth, 1993; Sitkin & Stickel, 1996). Nonetheless, a lack of legislation does not guarantee a neutral environment for knowledge sharing. Organizations encounter substantial uncertainty created by conflicting political and legal principles, such as public access versus privacy and information sharing versus confidentiality, which constantly threaten to put the restriction of information sharing into legal forms (Caffrey, 1998; Dawes, 1996).

Previous studies not only generate an extensive list of potential gains and losses of knowledge sharing, but also point to the existence of underlying dimensions which can group expectations into conceptual categories. Therefore, the first research question to be answered in this study is:

- **Q1.** What are the underlying factors of participants' expectations about interorganizational knowledge sharing?

# Participants' Expectation, Prior Experience, Work History, and Knowledge Networking Success

Furthermore, participants' expectations of the incentives and barriers may have some bearing on the overall progress of the knowledge sharing projects as well as the knowledge networking efforts. When they contemplate an innovation or collaborative activity, the participants' expectations and perceptions concerning the risks and benefits influence their attitudes and actions, which can lead to different outcomes (Greve, 1998; King, 1974; Levine & McCay, 1987; Uzzi, 1997). The benefits represent the projected utilities that motivate the participants to actively pursue the success of the knowledge sharing projects. The higher the expectations and the more positive the perceptions, the more likely the participants will be to mobilize commitment and resources to bring about the desired results. However, expectations and perceptions of the barriers to sharing have counteractive effects. There can be a "'trade-off' between the probability of an outcome and its utility" (Baron, 1994, p. 313). If an effort is perceived to have a high probability of failure regardless of how beneficial the results might be, participants would be less likely to invest their efforts in it, and moderate their commitment and investment to avoid risks and substantial costs. This reduced commitment in turn can reduce the likelihood of knowledge networking success.

The effect of participants' expectations and perceptions about the success of knowledge networking projects are further supported by the Theory of Reasoned Action (TRA) and the Theory of Planned Behavior (TPB) (Ajzen, 1991; Ajzen & Fishbein, 1980; Fishbein & Ajzen, 1975), which have been widely applied to examine individual technology acceptance and adoption in information system research (Chau & Hu, 2001; Compeau, Higgins & Huff, 1999; Hong, Thong, Wong & Tam, 2002; Karahanna, Straub & Chervany, 1999; Mathieson & Peacock, 2001). According to TRA, attitude and intention are a function of participants' beliefs, and this intention in turn dictates the individual behavior. Therefore, in the context of the projects studied in this research, participants' intentions and behavior are contingent upon their positive or negative evaluation of the benefits and risks of the sharing initiative. Thus, the second research question is:

- **Q2.** How is the success of knowledge networking associated with participants' expectations?

How participants view these benefits and barriers may vary because of their previous experience working on such initiatives, work history with other participating organizations, and their individual characteristics. Dawes (1996) found higher positive expectations were associated with more recent sharing experience, greater amount of experience, and more complexity of sharing experience. The experience public managers have had in other information sharing projects may provide them more realistic and comprehensive expectations about the benefits and barriers. The benefits they achieved in the past, in Dawes's case, especially motivated them to continue efforts toward interorganizational collaboration. It is not clear, however, how the lessons learned from the field would change the view of participants on the existing barriers. They could be more aware of the formidableness of the existing barriers or more confident in overcoming them. Therefore, we are interested to know:

• **Q3.** How are participants' expectations associated with their prior sharing experience?

Beyond such prior sharing experience, McCaffrey, Faerman, and Hart (1995) concluded that difficulties also exist in cooperating with agencies that have an adversarial work history. A contentious relationship in the past affects participants' trust in the partners in the network (Lane & Bachmann, 1996; Zand, 1972), which in turn may lower their expectations about the results or benefits of knowledge networking. Similarly, the degree to which agencies have been cooperative in the past would influence the respondent's expectations about the benefits and barriers. This suggests the fourth research question:

• **Q4.** How are participants' expectations associated with their work history with other participating organizations?

Participants' previous engagement in knowledge sharing and their work history with other participants not only shaped their expectations but are also directly related to the success of knowledge networking projects. Participants with more understanding about the situation and the partners may be able to approach them with modified strategies. So the fifth and sixth questions are:

• **Q5.** How is the success of knowledge networking associated with participants' prior sharing experience?
• **Q6.** How is the success of knowledge networking associated with participants' work history?

*Figure 1: Model relating success of knowledge networking, participants' expectations, and participants' experiences and characteristics*

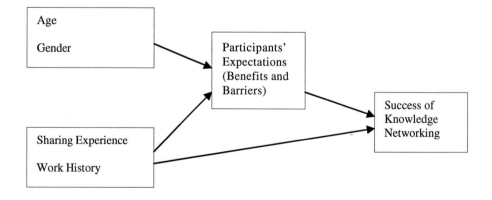

In addition, there is considerable evidence that individual characteristics, particularly age and gender, could have an impact on the users' computer literacy and general attitude toward computing (Chau & Hu, 2001; Hong et al., 2002). Consequently, their general attitude and familiarity with technology could influence their attitude toward such projects that have a strong focus on using new technology. Therefore, in this study, age and gender are controlled variables.

Summarizing the findings from previous studies, a path diagram displays the relationships between the success of knowledge networking, participants' expectations, prior experience, and individual characteristics (see Figure 1). This model provides guidance for the analysis and interpretation of the results and will be further discussed in the next section.

# Method

This study uses survey data collected by the Center for Technology in Government to study individuals' expectations about interorganizational information sharing in the public sector during 1999 and 2000. The survey is part of a longitudinal multi-method study to develop a comprehensive understanding about factors related to success of knowledge networking. This survey is the first of three surveys planned to be administered over the years 1999 through 2002. This initial survey was conducted to measure the original expectations of the participants involved, prior sharing experience, work history, and individual characteristics, in order to better understand the relationship between participants' expectations and the outcomes of knowledge networking.

The survey was administrated to 488 participants in the six projects involved in inter-agency knowledge sharing. Most of the participants work for local government agencies (46.7%) and state government agencies (42.2%), and the rest are from nonprofit organizations (6.6%) or private companies (4.5%). The focus of their jobs range from general administration (49.1%), program management (12.8%), information technology operations or management (18.9%), to direct service delivery (5.3%). The job focus of the remaining 13.9% of participants was not self-identified with any of the four categories. Sixty three percent of the participants have some level of experience in planning or designing programs or projects in which information is formally shared across different organizations, and 37% indicated that participating in the current project is their first such experience. Although a variety of organizations were involved in these seven projects, most of the participants (82.7%) have working relationships with the people who work in the other organizations in their projects, and only 17.3% did not have such relationships prior to the current projects. Since the first survey was mostly administrated on-site, a 96.8% return rate (478 valid responses) was achieved. The unit of analysis for this study is the individual participants, not the projects in which they participated.

Four groups of variables out of five are drawn directly from the survey:

a.   *Participants' Expectations* are measured by Likert-scale responses to 41 items (13 potential benefits and 28 potential barriers). The list of items is generated based on key studies conducted by Dawes (Dawes, 1996; Dawes et al., 1997), Landsbergen and Wolken (1998), McCaffrey et al. (1995), and Hosmer (1995). The respondents were asked to indicate to what extent they personally expected each of the 13 items on potential benefits would be achieved by this project within the next 2-3 years; the expectation range was from "not at all likely to be achieved" (coded as 1) to "very likely to be achieved" (coded as 7). Asked to what extent the respondent personally expected each of the 28 items would be a barrier to success in this project, the choice ranged from "not a barrier" (coded as 1) to "a severe barrier" (coded as 7).

b.  *Prior Experience.* To measure their personal experience of involvement in planning and designing information sharing programs or projects, the respondents were asked to indicate whether this was the first experience, the second experience, or if they worked on at least two other projects.

c.  *Work History.* The survey includes one question asking the respondent to describe the working relationship among the organizations involved in the project by choosing from: usually cooperative, sometimes cooperative and sometimes adversarial, usually adversarial, not working long enough to know the pattern, and don't know.

d.  *Individual Characteristics* including gender and age were also collected as part of the demographic information of participants as individual professionals.

The fifth variable, *Knowledge Networking Success,* is based on the judgment of a panel consisting of researchers and project managers/facilitators at the Center for Technology in Government, all of whom were intimately involved in each of the six cases. The criteria for this judgment focused more on the dynamics of interorganizational collaboration and knowledge sharing than on the achievement of formal programmatic goals. Each case was scored with regard to the degree of knowledge and information sharing, collaboration, service innovation, and improved business opportunity and visibility. The resulting scores are indicated in Table 1: Case Description at the beginning of the chapter. The higher the score, the more successful the project is in achieving this kind of knowledge networking success.

# Results

The means and standard deviations of all the benefit and barrier variables are presented in Table 2. Overall, all the variables have the maximum value of 7 and the minimal value of 1. There are missing data on 276 responses (including the "don't know" response). Since the missing data are not systematic, the factor analysis and regression analysis exclude cases with missing values pair-wise.

The results in Table 2 show that, on average, the respondents have a positive expectation that the listed benefits will be achieved, the average score for all of the benefit items being higher than 4. They are also cautious about the impacts of the barriers. Only the last two items in Table 2, *Lack of respect among organizations* and *Misinterpretation / use of*

*Table 2: Means and standard deviations of individual expectation (N=478)*

| Expected benefits or barriers | Mean | Std. Deviation |
|---|---|---|
| Better quality information | 5.18 | 1.28 |
| Shared information infrastructure | 5.08 | 1.24 |
| More comprehensive information | 4.99 | 1.27 |
| Wider professional networks | 4.99 | 1.31 |
| Improved accountability | 4.88 | 1.34 |
| More effective services | 4.8 | 1.35 |
| Consistent client/program information | 4.65 | 1.44 |
| Better coordinated programs/services | 4.65 | 1.28 |
| More responsive service | 4.55 | 1.41 |
| Reduced duplicate data collection | 4.53 | 1.63 |
| Reduced duplicate data handling | 4.43 | 1.63 |
| More equal program decisions | 4.3 | 1.46 |
| More cost efficiency | 4.23 | 1.54 |
| Too ambitious goals | 5.01 | 1.53 |
| Different organizational priorities | 5 | 1.39 |
| Lack of funding | 4.88 | 1.56 |
| Organizational resistance to change | 4.86 | 1.56 |
| Individual resistance to change | 4.83 | 1.55 |
| Incompatible hardware and software | 4.77 | 1.74 |
| Misallocated funding | 4.57 | 1.72 |
| Control-oriented management | 4.56 | 1.6 |
| Unrealistic time frames | 4.54 | 1.59 |
| Lack of understanding about organizations | 4.52 | 1.55 |
| Misaligned organizational missions | 4.49 | 1.6 |
| No agreement on goals | 4.4 | 1.58 |
| Program staff lack technology knowledge | 4.35 | 1.62 |
| Technology changes too often | 4.31 | 1.57 |
| Restrictive laws and regulations | 4.24 | 1.91 |
| No sharing guidelines or tools | 4.23 | 1.5 |
| Lack technology tools and skills | 4.17 | 1.8 |
| Technical staff lack program knowledge | 4.17 | 1.6 |
| Lack telecommunication network | 4.14 | 1.84 |
| Too much organizational diversity | 4.13 | 1.73 |
| Lack legislative support | 4.11 | 1.89 |
| Lack common data definitions | 4.09 | 1.74 |
| No models to follow | 4.09 | 1.67 |
| Confidentiality | 4.06 | 1.8 |
| Lack executive support | 4.05 | 1.92 |
| Too long for results | 4.01 | 1.63 |
| Lack of respect among organizations | 3.98 | 1.8 |
| Misinterpretation/use of shared information | 3.82 | 1.62 |
| Valid N (listwise) | 202 | |
| Note: for benefit, 7 = very likely to be achieved; 1 = not at all likely to be achieved | | |
| for barrier, 7 = A severe barrier; 1 = not a barrier | | |

*shared information,* achieved a mean score lower than 4. The rest of the items on barriers were viewed on average as a substantial barrier by the respondents. On average, the respondents hold that benefits of *having better quality information for their own use* and *building elements of a shared information infrastructure* are more likely to be achieved than other potential benefits. On the barrier side, on average, *too ambitious goals, different organizational priorities, lack of funding,* and *organizational and individual resistance to change* are viewed as more likely to be severe barriers to success than other potential barriers.

A factor analysis was performed using principal component extraction and varimax rotation techniques to detect common factors among the expectations (Kim & Mueller, 1978). The analysis results strongly indicate the existence of four common factors, as shown in Table 3, the rotated components matrix. The variables with high loadings (over .50) on Factor 1 include all the variables that represent benefit expectations in the survey (reliability coefficient $\alpha = .939$). Variables representing the barriers have high loadings on one or another of the remaining three factors. Examination of the variables with high loadings on the three factors (in almost all cases .50 or above) reveals strong consistency as well (reliability coefficient $\alpha = .891, .837, .763$ respectively). The results suggest that the factors can be conceptualized as follows:

- Factor 1: *benefits* (e.g., more effective and better coordinated services)
- Factor 2: *organizational barriers* (e.g., conflicting organizational priorities and implementation difficulties)
- Factor 3: *technological incompatibility* (e.g., lack of tools and skills, communication networks, and standards)
- Factor 4: *legislative and policy constraints* (e.g., restrictive laws and regulations, and confidentiality regulations)

Two items are loaded relatively high on more than one factor. *Misaligned organizational missions* have a high loading on both the factor of *organizational barriers* and the factor of *legislative and policy constraints*. This indicates that mission misalignment among government organizations is at once related to interorganizational structure and processes as well as the legislative and policy framework. In addition, *no sharing guidelines and tools* are loaded high on both *technological incompatibility* and *organizational barriers*. A viable explanation can be that the tools and guidelines that are needed for sharing information and knowledge is not only just the technical tools, but also the organizational skills, techniques, and guidelines that lead the changes concomitant to the technological innovations. Since we use factor scores in the succeeding analysis, their loading on both factors will be accounted for.

For the subsequent analyses exploring influences on project success, the factor scores from these first four components of the principal components analysis were used to represent the underlying factors shown in Table 3. The correlations among the variables used in this second analysis are shown in Table 4, Correlation Structure. As work history is measured by a categorical variable, it is transformed into three dummy variables (usually cooperative, sometimes cooperative, and don't know, as compared to usually adversarial) to account for the differences in work history and its correlation with other variables.

To test the model in Figure 1, a set of regressions were conducted with the success of knowledge networking as the dependent variable. The results are presented in Table 5. Participants' prior sharing experience, work history, age, and gender account for only 4.6% of the variance in the success variable, and the overall model does not yield a significant result ($p>0.1$). When the set of variables measuring participants' expectations are added in the second equation, the model explains another 6.4% of the variance in success ($p<0.01$). Overall, the group of variables of age, gender, sharing experience, work

*Table 3: Rotated component matrix[a]*

| | Factors | | | |
|---|---|---|---|---|
| | 1 | 2 | 3 | 4 |
| Reduced duplicate data collection | 0.741 | -0.041 | 0.002 | -0.127 |
| Reduced duplicate data handling | 0.735 | -0.098 | 0.016 | -0.153 |
| Consistent client/program information | 0.762 | -0.037 | -0.054 | -0.103 |
| Better quality information | 0.790 | -0.070 | -0.035 | -0.019 |
| More comprehensive information | 0.782 | -0.110 | 0.018 | 0.010 |
| Better coordinated programs/services | 0.787 | -0.104 | 0.021 | -0.016 |
| More equal program decisions | 0.684 | -0.251 | 0.046 | 0.000 |
| Improved accountability | 0.640 | -0.166 | 0.025 | -0.097 |
| Wider professional networks | 0.584 | -0.065 | -0.115 | 0.123 |
| More effective services | 0.801 | -0.107 | -0.008 | 0.059 |
| More cost efficiency | 0.764 | -0.171 | -0.041 | 0.062 |
| More responsive service | 0.798 | -0.117 | -0.055 | 0.072 |
| Shared information infrastructure | 0.701 | -0.128 | 0.005 | -0.092 |
| Misaligned organizational missions | -0.063 | 0.576 | -0.015 | 0.422 |
| Too ambitious goals | -0.228 | 0.523 | 0.125 | -0.013 |
| No agreement on goals | -0.136 | 0.633 | -0.011 | 0.114 |
| Misallocated funding | -0.077 | 0.643 | 0.211 | 0.007 |
| Lack of funding | -0.099 | 0.594 | 0.242 | 0.163 |
| Lack of understanding about organizations | -0.147 | 0.625 | 0.106 | 0.206 |
| Lack of respect among organizations | -0.104 | 0.656 | 0.106 | 0.150 |
| Different organizational priorities | -0.151 | 0.663 | -0.002 | 0.042 |
| Too much organizational diversity | -0.127 | 0.551 | 0.102 | -0.003 |
| Individual resistance to change | 0.109 | 0.501 | 0.145 | 0.008 |
| Organizational resistance to change | -0.024 | 0.493 | 0.119 | 0.214 |
| Misinterpretation/use of shared information | -0.101 | 0.396 | 0.201 | 0.227 |
| Control-oriented management | -0.206 | 0.558 | 0.322 | 0.162 |
| No models to follow | -0.135 | 0.534 | 0.223 | 0.082 |
| Unrealistic time frames | -0.085 | 0.629 | 0.183 | 0.039 |
| Too long for results | -0.223 | 0.391 | 0.192 | 0.175 |
| No sharing guidelines or tools | -0.148 | 0.451 | 0.432 | 0.220 |
| Incompatible hardware and software | 0.027 | 0.134 | 0.651 | 0.033 |
| Lack telecommunication network | 0.075 | 0.166 | 0.723 | 0.152 |
| Lack technology tools and skills | 0.017 | 0.178 | 0.811 | -0.003 |
| Lack common data definitions | -0.020 | 0.165 | 0.527 | 0.381 |
| Program staff lack technology knowledge | 0.006 | 0.191 | 0.716 | 0.127 |
| Technical staff lack program knowledge | 0.026 | 0.209 | 0.642 | 0.245 |
| Technology changes too often | -0.146 | 0.242 | 0.582 | -0.002 |
| Restrictive laws and regulations | 0.005 | 0.266 | 0.164 | 0.629 |
| Lack legislative support | 0.006 | 0.256 | 0.169 | 0.714 |
| Confidentiality | 0.019 | 0.027 | 0.113 | 0.732 |
| Lack executive support | -0.154 | 0.328 | 0.184 | 0.623 |

a. Extraction Method: Principal Component Analysis.
   Rotation Method: Varimax with Kaiser Normalization.
   Rotation converged in 6 iterations.

*Table 4: Correlation structure*

| | Success Score | 1 | 2 | 3 | 4 | 5 | 6 | 7 | 8 | 9 |
|---|---|---|---|---|---|---|---|---|---|---|
| 1. REGR factor score 1 (Benefits) | 0.138* | | | | | | | | | |
| 2. REGR factor score 2 (Organizational Barriers) | -0.251** | -0.068 | | | | | | | | |
| 3. REGR factor score 3 (Technology Incompatibility) | -0.050 | 0.070 | -0.057 | | | | | | | |
| 4. REGR factor score 4 (Legal and Policy Contraints) | 0.051 | 0.021 | 0.033 | -0.001 | | | | | | |
| 5. Prior Sharing Experience | -0.043 | -0.091 | 0.085 | -0.039 | 0.123 | | | | | |
| 6. Usually Cooperative | 0.077 | 0.098 | -0.173* | 0.049 | -0.082 | -0.038 | | | | |
| 7. Sometimes Cooperative | -0.063 | -0.057 | 0.187** | -0.100 | 0.052 | 0.120** | -0.607** | | | |
| 8. Don't Know | -0.001 | 0.005 | -0.051 | 0.056 | -0.033 | -0.126** | -0.474** | -0.363** | | |
| 9. Age | -0.159** | 0.013 | 0.036 | 0.019 | -0.035 | 0.117* | 0.137** | -0.082 | -0.067 | |
| 10. Gender | 0.052 | -0.093 | -0.150* | 0.108 | 0.004 | -0.152** | -0.025 | -0.056 | 0.124** | -0.125** |

* Correlation is significant at the 0.05 level (2-tailed).
** Correlation is significant at the 0.01 level (2-tailed).

*Table 5: Hierarchical regression models with the success of knowledge networking as dependent variable*

| | Models | |
|---|---|---|
| Independent Variables | 1 | 2 |
| (Constant) | 56.124*** | 57.779*** |
| Age | -4.052* | -3.716* |
| Priorn Sharing Experience | 0.111 | 0.362 |
| Gender | 4.445 | 4.000 |
| Usually Cooperative | 5.675 | 2.053 |
| Sometimes Cooperative | 0.472 | -0.987 |
| Don't Know | 4.122 | 0.933 |
| Benefits | | 2.472 |
| Organizational Barriers | | -4.637** |
| Technology Incompetibility | | -1.361 |
| Legal and Policy Constraints | | 1.249 |
| R Square | 0.045 | 0.109 |
| Adjusted R Square | 0.018 | 0.066 |
| **Hierarchical F test** | | |
| R Square Change | | 0.064 |
| F | | 3.704 |
| d.f. | | 4, 207 |
| p | 0.131 | 0.006 |

*p<.05, **p<.01, ***p<.001

history, and participants' expectations accounts for 10.9% of the variance in the success of knowledge networking.

In the second equation, it should be noted that the expectations of technology incompatibility and legal and policy constraints do not have a significant regression coefficient; only the expectation of organizational barriers is significantly related to the success of knowledge networking ($p<0.01$). It appears that the projects are less successful in situations where the participants expect organizational barriers to be more serious constraints to knowledge sharing. In addition, age also appears to be related to the success of knowledge networking ($p<0.05$). The successful cases are associated with a younger population of participants. These results do not, however, indicate whether it is the expectations of the participants that influence the project's success directly or whether the participants are able to identify projects where success is inherently more difficult to obtain.

# Discussion

In general, the respondents hold optimistic expectations of the benefits of knowledge sharing. They tend to expect that those benefits are likely to be achieved. At the same time, they are also very much aware of the potential barriers for achieving those benefits. It is reasonable to expect that these public and nonprofit managers are motivated to achieve the expected benefits and will be approaching these benefits cautiously with knowledge of the policy, organizational, and technological barriers that they have to deal with in initiating a program involving sharing information and knowledge.

Participant expectations in regard to the organizational barriers are negatively associated with the success of knowledge networking. The projects that have higher scores on the severity of these organizational barriers are less successful. This result is consistent with TRA and TPB, which attribute behavior and consequences to individual attitude and belief. Among the six cases studied, projects are more successful when the participants expect less severe organizational barriers will have to be encountered. To further explore how expectations could influence the success of knowledge networking, we provide two explanations. One explanation is related to how the perception of barriers is constructed in relation to organizational realities. Participants' perception may very well reflect the difficulties deeply embedded in organizational structures and processes. As O'Dell and Grayson (1998) pointed out, the actual process of sharing is much more complicated than most people can imagine, as it is "thwarted by a variety of logistical, structural, and cultural hurdles and deterrents present in our organization" (p.16). They noted that these obstacles result from a set of structural conflicts, managerial practices, and evaluation and incentive systems that discourage sharing, and neglecting to address those embedded barriers will only lead to disappointments and failures.

Furthermore, the perceptions may also be a significant factor for success in their own right. The high structural obstacles that participants perceive may define or limit the ways that they themselves engage in the work. They may be less inspired by or committed to the changes and/or be more conservative in taking risks, which in turn can affect the outcomes of knowledge networking. Their expectations may become self–fulfilling prophecies that perpetuate those obstacles. Kanter's (1977) observation about the behavioral and psychological impact of opportunity structure in an organization still holds in the interorganizational context. As she stated,

*Opportunity structures shape behavior in such a way that they confirm their own prophecies. Those people set on high-mobility tracks tend to develop attitudes and values that impel them further along the track: work commitment, high aspirations, and upward orientations. Those set on low-mobility tracks tend to become indifferent, to give up, and thus to "prove" that their initial placement was correct. They develop low-risk, conservative attitudes, or become complaining critics, demonstrating how right the organization was not to let them go further. It is graphically clear how cycles of advantage and cycles of disadvantage are perpetuated in organizations and in society. (p.158)*

Among the public and nonprofit managers in this sample, gender does not account significantly for the differences across expectations and networking success. However, there is a certain level of significant association ($p < .05$) between the age of the participants and the success of knowledge networking.

Surprisingly, the sharing experience that the respondents had in the past does not account for the difference in success. A possible explanation might have to do with the steep learning curve for technology changes. Many systems are still in the stage of trial and error. As Schön (1982) observed, the situation confronting public professionals is characterized by complexity, instability, uncertainty, and uniqueness. The complexity and uniqueness of the technology and process changes involved in projects such as these makes success such a challenging task that even experienced participants have difficulties in grasping.

As the results indicate, work history and participants' expectations of technology incompatibility and legal and policy constraints are not significantly related to the success of knowledge networking. Partly, this result shows that the six cases are situated in similar technological and policy environments. More importantly, it demonstrates the need for studies that include qualitative and dynamic feedback approaches. Quantitative analyses such as this would be stronger supplemented by qualitative data derived from document analysis, observations, and interviews, in order to comprehend the dynamics of the interplay between work history, collaboration, and organizational, technological, and political environments. This line of research is being actively pursued by the Center for Technology in Government. This study points to the limitation of using only a quantitative approach in seeking an in-depth understanding of a dynamic, complex, and multi-faceted phenomenon-the effectiveness of knowledge networking.

Although this study achieved a relatively large sample, the participants were not randomly selected. The available population from six projects was the subject of study. Those projects are self-selected. Each group approached the Center for Technology in Government because of their special interest in innovation projects. This could indicate an exceptionally high preference for information sharing activities or innovation. The attitudes of the participants may not represent those in similar roles in other public agencies in New York state or in other states. However, the results from the survey, especially the factors of potential risks and barriers, offer valuable guidance for those who are planning such projects. This survey of public and non-profit managers' concerns also provides guidance for public policy makers in their attempts to establish a legal and policy environment supportive of information technology innovation and use.

# Conclusion and Recommendations

This study identifies four dimensions of participants' expectations of knowledge sharing: *benefits in providing more effective services, organizational barriers, technological incompatibility,* and *legal and policy constraints.* Furthermore, we find the success of knowledge networking is significantly associated with participants' expectations regarding the organizational barriers to project success. The less positive they are about the inter-organizational structure and implementation processes, the less likely their efforts are to succeed.

These findings have several implications for both the conduct of collaborative innovation projects and further research on this topic. First of all, as the development of electronic government grows more prominent and consumes more resources, it is important to recognize the significance of back-office integration and the many difficulties and risks associated with such interorganizational collaboration. In order to present a coherent electronic government face to the public, it is necessary to develop integrated operations across the jurisdiction of many government agencies, non-profit organizations, and private corporations. Achieving the promises of electronic government thus requires policy makers, managers, and researchers to address those barriers that are deeply embedded in the policy framework, existing interorganizational structures and processes, and technological infrastructure. It should be recognized that innovations geared toward sharing governmental information resources need more than rhetorical support. Success requires executive and legislative actions in adopting fundamental policy principles that "demand that government information be acquired, used, and cared for as jurisdiction-wide resources" on the one hand, and, on the other hand, "give agencies incentives to share data and other information resources... and lay the foundation for organizational and financial mechanisms to support information sharing" (Dawes, 1996, p. 393). Failing to address those discouraging structural conflicts, managerial practices, and evaluation and incentive systems can lead to expensive failures.

Second, to avoid mistakes and control the risks of such undertakings, the strategic planning and implementation processes should be guided with some measures to identify and assess the potential benefits and risks of various innovation initiatives. Understanding the levels of policy constraints, organizational barriers, and technological incompatibility can help public managers, first, choose projects or milestone wisely and, second, manage the interorganizational dynamics and implementation processes more effectively.

In addition, the perception of professionals in the public sector can be guided or influenced in more positive directions by a process called *double-loop learning* described by Argyris and Schön (1978, 1996). According to these authors, learning involves constantly correcting errors by detecting mismatches between expectations and outcomes of a strategy. Single-loop learning occurs when the organization takes actions to adjust strategies to reach the expectations. In this latter case, the underlying value and assumptions governing the establishment of the expectations are untouched; therefore, the learning is limited. Double-loop learning, however, not only connects the error to the strategies but also to the value and assumptions underlying the expectations. Using the double-loop learning process, facilitated discussions of participants' hopes and fears at the beginning of a project can uncover the assumptions underlying these expectations. Consequently, the assumptions can be examined from different angles so that they can recognize that expected difficulties do not necessarily always represent possibilities of failures, but rather can be opportunities for changing long-standing barriers. Thus, the double-loop feedback could be truly instrumental in facilitating such significant changes as the participants in the above innovating projects needed to encounter.

This study also has implications for electronic government initiatives in both developed and developing country alike. This chapter has examined knowledge and information sharing in one state in a country where electronic government has been actively advocated and pursued. Nonetheless, the situation, especially the barriers of interorganizational knowledge sharing, may represent generic difficulties that governments in all countries have to encounter in their information sharing and integration efforts. As such, what has been learnt in this United States study may shed some light on new initiatives in less developed countries. The innovative use of information technology to share information may appear to represent an opportunity for a developing country to carry out social and political reform; the success of such an undertaking, however, largely depends on how well the policy makers and public managers deal with the interactive political, organizational, and technological factors in their entirety.

Lastly, this study points to the need for future studies in two directions. First, it is necessary to combine the strengths of qualitative and quantitative approaches. Case study methods can provide better insights into the dynamics of projects such as these, insights that are not likely to be revealed by cross-sectional survey data. The richness of the connection between different variables, the existence of interactive feedback loops, and the effects of external events can be better understood with the supplementary results from qualitative data analysis and perspectives that draw on concepts from frameworks such as system dynamics. Second, as electronic government grows more mature, it is important to evaluate new initiatives on the grounds of benefits and risks. Through an exploratory factor analysis, this study provides a useful instrument by which the potential benefits and barriers related to technological innovation projects can be identified and assessed, in order to increase the likelihood of success for electronic government development. Future studies can test and refine this instrument and extend its usefulness by conducting confirmative factor analysis in different settings.

# References

Ajzen, I. (1991). The theory of planned behavior. *Organizational Behavior and Human Decision Processes, 50,* 179-211.

Ajzen, I., & Fishbein, M. (1980). *Understanding attitudes and predicting social behavior*. Englewood Cliffs, NJ: Prentice Hall.

Andersen, D.E., Belardo, S., & Dawes, S.S. (1994). Strategic information management: Conceptual frameworks for the public sector. *Public Productivity and Management Review, 17*(4), 335-353.

Argyris, C., & Schön, D.A. (1978). *Organizational learning: A theory of action perspective*. Addison-Wesley Publishing Company.

Argyris, C., & Schön, D.A. (1996). *Organizational learning: Theory, method, and practice*. Addison-Wesley Publishing Company.

Baba, M.L. (1999). Dangerous liaisons: Trust, distrust, and information technology in American work organizations. *Human Organization, 58*(3), 331-346.

Baron, J. (1994). *Thinking and deciding* (2nd ed.). Cambridge University Press.

Bouty, I. (2000). Interpersonal and interaction influences on informal resource exchanges between R&D researchers across organizational boundaries. *Academy of Management Journal, 43*(1), 50-65.

Brown, J.S., & Duguid, P. (2001). Structure and spontaneity: Knowledge and organization. In I. Nonaka & D.J. Teece (Eds.), *Managing industrial knowledge: Creation, transfer, and utilization* (pp. 45-67). Sage Publications.

Caffrey, L. (Ed.). (1998). *Information sharing between & within governments*. Commonwealth Secretariat.

Chau, P.Y.K., & Hu, P.J.-H. (2001). Information technology acceptance by individual professionals: A model comparison approach. *Decision Science, 32*(4), 699-719.

Cohen, M.D., & Bacdayan, P. (1994). Organizational routines are stored as procedural memory: Evidence from a laboratory study. *Organization Science, 5*(4), 554-568.

Compeau, D., Higgins, C.A., & Huff, S. (1999). Social cognitive theory and individual reactions to computing technology: A longitudinal study. *MIS Quarterly, 23*(2), 145-158.

Cresswell, A.M., Pardo, T.A., Thompson, F., & Zhang, J. (2002, August). *Trust and networking: Knowledge sharing in the public sector*. Paper presented at the annual Academy of Management conference, Denver.

Dawes, S. (1996). Interagency information sharing: Expected benefits, Manageable risks. *Journal of Policy Analysis and Management, 15*(3), 377-394.

Dawes, S.S., & Pardo, T.A. (2003). Building collaborative digital government systems: Systemic constraints and effective practices. In W.J. McIver & A.K. Elmagarmid (Eds.), *Advances in digital government: Technology, human factors, and policy*. Boston: Kluwer Academic Publishers.

Dawes, S.S., Pardo, T.A., Connelly, D.R., Green, D.F., & McInerney, C.R. (1997). *Partners in state-local information systems: Lessons from the field*. Albany, NY: Center for Technology in Government.

Dawes, S.S., Pardo, T.A., Simon, S., Cresswell, A.M., LaVigne, M.F., Andersen, D.A., & Bloniarz, P.A. (2003). *Making smart IT choices: Understanding value and risk in government IT investments*. Albany, NY: Center for Technology in Government, University at Albany (also at *www.ctg.albany.edu/publications/guides/smartit2*).

Faerman, S.R., McCaffrey, D.P., & Van Slyke, D.M. (2001). Understanding interorganizational cooperation: Public-private collaboration in regulating financial market innovation. *Organization Science, 12*(3), 372-388.

Fishbein, M., & Ajzen, I. (1975). *Belief, attitude, intention and behavior: An introduction to theory and research.* Reading, MA: Addison-Wesley Publishing Company.

Greve, H.R. (1998). Performance, aspirations, and risky organizational change. *Administrative Science Quarterly, 43*(1), 58-87.

Hart, P., & Saunders, C. (1997). Power and trust: Critical factors in the adoption and use of electronic data interchange. *Organization Science, 8*(1), 23-42.

Hong, W., Thong, J.Y.L., Wong, W.-M., & Tam, K.-Y. (2002). Determinants of user acceptance of digital libraries: An empirical examination of individual differences and system characteristics. *Journal of Management Information Systems, 18*(3), 97-124.

Hosmer, L.T. (1995). Trust: The connecting link between organization theory and philosophical ethics. *Academy of Management Review, 20*(2), 379-403.

Kanter, R.M. (1977). *Men and women of the corporation.* BasicBooks.

Karahanna, E., Straub, D.W., & Chervany, N.L. (1999). Information technology adoption across time: A cross-sectional comparison of pre-adoption and post-adoption beliefs. *MIS Quarterly, 23*(2), 183-213.

Kim, J.-O., & Mueller, C.W. (1978). *Factor analysis: Statistical methods and practical issues.* Newbury Park: Sage Publications.

King, A.S. (1974). Expectation effects in organizational change. *Administrative Science Quarterly, 19*(2), 221-230.

Kraatz, M.S. (1998). Learning by association? Interorganizational networks and adaptation to environmental change. *Academy of Management Journal, 41*(6), 621-643.

Landsbergen, D., & Wolken, G. (1998). *Eliminating legal and policy barriers to interoperable government systems.* Paper presented at the Annual Research Conference of the Association for Public Policy Analysis and Management, New York.

Landsbergen, D., & Wolken, G. (2000). *Realizing the promise: Governmental information systems and the fourth generation of information technology.*

Lane, C., & Bachmann, R. (1996). The social constitution of trust: Supplier relations in Britain and Germany. *Organization Studies, 17*(3), 365-395.

Levine, E.B., & McCay, B.J. (1987). Technology: Adoption among Cape May fishermen. *Human Organization, 46*(3), 243-253.

Linden, R. (1995, May). A guide to reengineering government: Advice from the expert. *Governing,* 63-74.

Mathieson, K., & Peacock, E. (2001). Extending the technology acceptance model: The influence of perceived user resources. *The DATA BASE for Advances in Information Systems, 32*(3), 86-112.

McCaffrey, D.P., Faerman, S.R., & Hart, D.W. (1995). The appeal and difficulties of participative systems. *Organization Science, 6,* 603-627.

Murphy, P.R., & Daley, J.M. (1999). Edi benefits and barriers comparing international freight forwarders and their customers. *International Journal of Physical Distribution & Logistics Management, 29*(3), 207-216.

O'Dell, C., & Grayson, C.J., Jr. (1998). *If only we knew what we know.* New York: The Free Press.

Powell, W.W. (1998). Learning from collaboration: Knowledge and networks in the biotechnology and pharmaceutical industries. *California Management Review, 40*(3), 228-240.

Rousseau, D.M., Sitkin, S.B., Burt, R.S., & Camerer, C. (1998). Not so different after all: A cross discipline view of trust. *Academy of Management Review, 23*(3), 393-404.

Schön, D.A. (1982). *The reflective practitioner: How professionals think in action.* Basic Book, Inc.

Sitkin, S.B., & Roth, N.L. (1993). Explaining the limited effectiveness of legalistic "remedies" for trust/distrust. *Organizational Science, 4,* 367-392.

Sitkin, S.B., & Stickel, D. (1996). The road to hell: The dynamics of distrust in an era of quality. In R.M. Kramer & T.R. Tyler (Eds.), *Trust in organizations: Frontiers of theory and research.* Thousand Oaks: Sage.

Uzzi, B. (1997). Social structure and competition in interfirm networks: The paradox of embeddedness. *Administrative Science Quarterly, 42*(1), 35-68.

Wenger, E. (1998). *Communities of practice: Learning, meaning, and identity.* Cambridge University Press.

Wenger, E.C., & Synder, W.M. (2001). Communities of practice: The organizational frontier. *Harvard Business Review on organizational learning* (pp. 1-20). Harvard Business School Publishing Corporation.

Zand, D.E. (1972). Trust and managerial problem solving. *Administrative Science Quarterly, 17*(2), 229-239.

Zucker, L.G., Darby, M.R., Brewer, M.B., & Peng, Y. (1995). Collaboration structure and information dilemmas in biotechnology: Organizational boundaries as trust production. In R.M. Kramer & T.R. Tyler (Eds.), *Trust in organizations: Frontiers of theory and research.* Thousand Oaks, CA: Sage.

# Endnote

[1]   An earlier version of this chapter was presented at the Eighth Americas Conference on Information Systems. The research is supported by National Science Foundation grant #SES-9979839. The views and conclusions expressed in this chapter are those of the authors alone and do not reflect the views or policies of the National Science Foundation.

Chapter XII

# Shanghai's E-Government: Implementation Strategies and a Case Study

Hongmin Chen, Shanghai Jiao Tong University, China

Qing Zhang, Shanghai Jiao Tong University, China

## Abstract

*This chapter will present and discuss some successful experience of Shanghai's e-government strategies and implementation from the perspective of a developing country. A case study of Social Security Card System (SSCS) in Shanghai will be conducted to further illustrate Shanghai's e-government strategies and implementation experience. Differences of e-government implementation strategies between China and USA are identified and discussed, which may provide some useful insights to the other developing countries, especially to those developing countries that are under the process of transiting to the "market economy" model when implementing e-government in the near future.*

# Introduction

Starting with the "Three-Gold Projects" in the 1980s, China gradually embraced the e-government concept. As the biggest developing country in its transformation from Soviet Union's "plan economy" to the West's "market economy," China has some disadvantages and weaknesses in e-business development, which might be detrimental to its renaissance in the so-called "Information Era". And then, e-government has been considered as an effective driving force for government to promote and enhance e-business development in China.

The coastal provinces and cities in China, due to some historical and geographical advantage reasons, are relatively more prosperous and advanced than the inner provinces and cities. Their economical edge generally results in their leading role in the e-government implementation of China.

Among those coastal provinces and cities, Shanghai, Beijing and the other big cities are rushing to e-government implementation recently. All of them have already set up timetables in their strategic blueprints of "informationization" projects (the term "informationization" is a Chinese word used to describe the diffusion and adoption of modern information technology in industries, public sector and residents' daily life). According to the Mayor of Shanghai (Yan, 2002), Shanghai will try to catch up those central cities of the developed countries in its informationization process in 2005; at that time, the Internet users in Shanghai may reach 50% of its 14 million population, and nearly 90% of traditional government public services will be put on Web sites through e-government implementation.

In order to reap e-government implementation benefits for China in a long run and minimize risks involved in the implementation, it would be a wiser strategy to have a few cities and/or provinces such as Shanghai to lead the way in e-government implementation, so that their successful experience and lessons learned in e-government implementation can provide useful guidance to the rest of the cities and provinces of China in the future.

In the 1990s, Shanghai started its e-government projects. Through detailed analysis of local "5-N" factors (namely, Network Access, Networked Learning, Networked Society, Networked Economy and Network Policy) and the other social and culture factors, Shanghai's e-government strategic goals, Increasing the transparency of government functioning and affairs; Providing the convenience and better services to citizens and enterprises; and improving the efficiency of government administration" (Shanghai Municipal Government, 2003), were worked out and approved by the municipal government. After a few years of implementation of such strategy, some first-stage e-government implementation projects were completed successfully. This book chapter will present and discuss some successful experience of Shanghai's e-government strategies and implementation from the perspective of a developing country. A case study of Social Security Card System (SSCS) in Shanghai will be used to further illustrate Shanghai's e-government strategies and implementation experience. Differences of e-government implementation strategies between China and USA are highlighted and discussed, which may provide some useful insights to other developing countries, especially to those developing countries that are under the process of transiting to the "market economy" model, when implementing e-government in the near future.

# An Overview of Shanghai's E-Government Strategies and Implementation

## History and Current Situation of E-Government in Shanghai

Shanghai, situated at 31.14 degrees north latitude and 121.29 degrees east longitude in the middle of China's east coastline, is a gate to the Yang Zi River valley. It is a municipality under the direct jurisdiction of the central government of China.

Shanghai, with the population of more than 14 million, known as the biggest metropolitan city in China and one of the biggest metropolitan cities in the world, is also the center of China's economy, especially in the industries of finance, manufacturing, trade and shipping. It serves as a bridge linking China to the rest of the world. Shanghai Port is the leading port in China. Its total area is 6,341 sq. km., in which the Pudong New Area occupies 523 sq.km. Shanghai has 55 tertiary universities and colleges with 226.8 thousand college students, 30.6 thousand graduate students, 7.9 thousand PhDs, and more than 2 million residents attending adult education programs each year (*www.shanghai.gov.cn*_(Shanghai eGovernment Web site).

*Figure 1: The home page of Shanghai eGovernment Web site*

*Figure 2: Services provided by Shanghai eGovernment Web site*

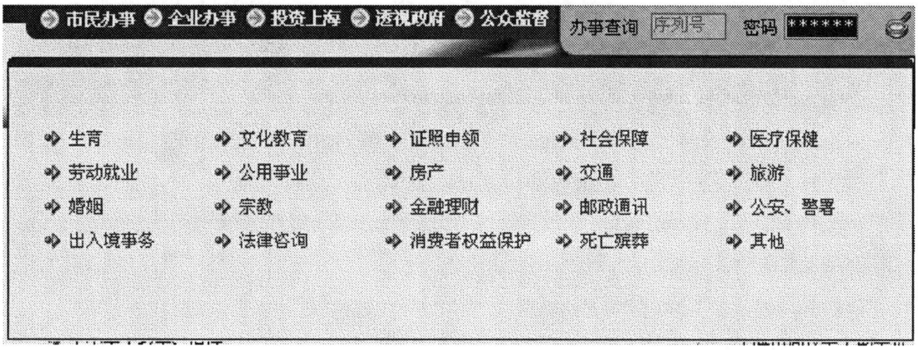

In order to implement Shanghai's e-government strategy and be better prepared for the challenges ahead after China's entry into World Trade Organization (WTO), Shanghai municipal government set up the gateway Web site-"Shanghai eGovernment" (www.shanghai.gov.cn).

This Shanghai eGovernment Web site has been evolving and developing over the years. Today, there are more than 143 governmental agencies' Web sites being connected with this gateway, and among which, there are 51 governmental bureau Web sites, 19 governmental district Web sites, 45 central government's department Web sites and another 28 provinces' government Web sites (Shanghai Municipal Government, 2003).

Besides common governmental services, the Web site also provides local residents and companies with relevant official documents to download, online inquiries, online complaining, and so forth. Every day, more than 100 thousand people visit and make use of this Web site.

Figure 1 is the home page of the Shanghai eGovernment Web site. In order to provide a better online service, the Web site classifies users into five categories: ordinary residents, enterprises, investors, tourists and a special-needs group (senior citizens, women and children). Navigators choose their categories to enter a specific Web site to serve for their specific needs. There is also a personalized page feature, allowing registered users to choose their own page layout and content, and keeping a personal calendar. The center of this page shows the main functions of the Web site. They are Citizen Service, Enterprise Service, Investing in Shanghai, Government Transparency and Monitoring Government. Latest government news is listed in the lower part of the screen.

Figure 2 shows the services provided by Shanghai eGovernment Web site, which include: birth registration service, education service, applying for certificates, social security service, medical care service, employment service, public utility service, real estate service, transportation service, tourism service, registration of marriage, religion service, finance service, postal office, police department, immigration department, legal service, consumer rights protection service, and other services.

So far, Shanghai has implemented dozens of eGovernment projects, including

- *www.smert.gov.cn*   (Shanghai Foreign Economic Relations & Trade),
- *www.sepb.gov.cn*   (Shanghai Environment Protection Bureau),
- *www.shdpc.gov.cn*   (Shanghai Municipal Development & Reform Commission)
- *www.shmec.gov.cn* (Shanghai Education)
- *www.justice.gov.cn* (Shanghai Judicature and Administration)
- *www.123333.gov.cn* (Shanghai Labor Protection Service)
- *www.smhb.gov.cn* (Shanghai Sanitation Information Service),
- *shenji.stc.sh.cn* (Shanghai Audit),
- *stj.sh.gov.cn* (Shanghai Administration Bureau of NGOs),
- *www.shec.gov.cn* (Shanghai Economic Commission),
- *www.stcsm.gov.cn* (Shanghai Technology and Science),
- *jcw.sh.gov.cn* (Shanghai Supervision),
- *www.shucm.sh.cn* (Shanghai Urban Construction),
- www.shanghaiwater.gov.cn (Shanghai Water Service),
- *www.shfao.gov.cn* (Shanghai Foreign Affairs),
- *www.stats-sh.gov.cn* (Shanghai Statistics),
- *tyj.sh.gov.cn* (Shanghai Administration of Sports),
- *www.shfdz.gov.cn* (Shanghai Real Estate Resources),
- *sjr.sh.gov.cn* (Shanghai Finance),
- *fzzx.sh.gov.cn* (Shanghai Municipal Government Development and Research Center),
- *www.commerce.sh.cn* (Shanghai Commerce),
- *www.shac.gov.cn* (Shanghai Agricultures),
- *www.popinfo.gov.cn* (Shanghai Municipal Population and Family Planning Commission),
- *lyw.sh.gov.cn* (Shanghai Tourism),
- *www.ssip.com.cn* (Shanghai Intellectual Property),
- *jtj.sh.gov.cn* (Shanghai Transportation),
- *www.shsz.gov.cn/gov* (Shanghai Municipal Engineering Administration Bureau),
- *nlj.sh.gov.cn* (Shanghai Agriculture & Forestry Bureau), and so forth.

## The E-Government Implementation Strategy of Shanghai

As the powerhouse of China's economy development, Shanghai's e-government implementation can function as a role model for other cities and provinces of China to follow up. Three specific e-government implementation strategies and objectives of Shanghai are specified as follows:

- Increase the transparency of government affairs
- Provide the convenience and better services to residents and enterprises
- Improve the efficiency of government administration

This overall strategy of Shanghai e-government implementation has been worked out by fully analyzing Shanghai's local current conditions and future development. Although different e-government projects of Shanghai might be quite different in terms of functions and services, this strategy guides the design and implementation of all projects. More specifically, the strategy has been based upon the "5-N Factors" analysis (Huang et al., 2003), which is shown in Figure 3.

*Figure 3: The 5-N conceptual research framework*

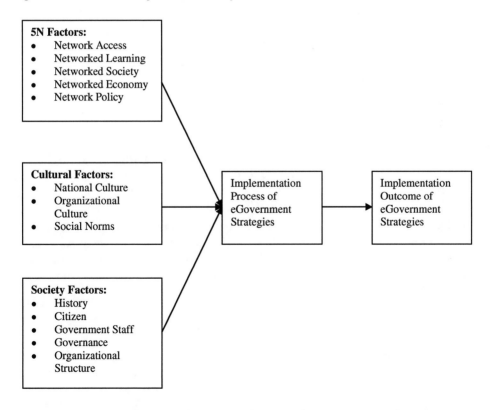

# 5-N Factors Analysis for Shanghai E-Government Strategy[1]

## Network Access

Information infrastructure in Shanghai has achieved big improvements in recent years. Up to the beginning of year 2002, the bandwidth of Shanghai's Internet connection to the outside world was expanded to 2.5GB, and the network cable lines were stretched out for more than 550 kilometers that covered more than 99% of the whole city. The number of broadband Internet users in Shanghai reached 125 thousand that year; the number of fixed phone users exceeded 6 million while mobile phone users exceeded fixed phone users. More than 3.1 million families had access to the Internet, which almost doubled the number of the previous year.

Besides the 99% coverage of broadband in Shanghai, other broadband access services were also adopted and widely used, such as ADSL, HFC+CableModem, FTTB+LAN, Wi-Fi and the other wireless LANs.

## Networked Learning

The development of the network learning is speeding up in Shanghai. The broadband of the main network of Shanghai Science and Education Network (SSEN) was expanded to 1.25GB from 64KB. The fibro-cable connecting the educational institutions in Shanghai was longer than 200 kilometers in 2001. Thus the SSEN was then mainly set up. More than 19 universities in Shanghai made their effects to launch a common-shared database of the book information in the above 19 universities' libraries. In this system, people could also search for the key academic periodicals and borrow through the Remote Borrowing/ Lending Service. Up to the year 2001, the SSEN had a sea-sized collection of materials, including: 12 thousand periodical databases, 200 thousand e-book resources, business sub-databases, science and technology sub-databases, digital periodicals database and so forth. More than 100 multifunctional databases provided a wide range of selections to the students' content. Furthermore, several universities in Shanghai have got the permission from the government to develop their "net-school" projects, which made the e-learning in Shanghai more professional and orderly.

Furthermore, the "remote education" (or to say: the online education) is now provided to the students. More than 23 high education majors such as computer science, transportation management and industrial foreign trade have set up their online education; more than 80 students have already graduated from that.

## Network Society

www.88547.com -Shanghai Community Service Network is a typical example of the "Network Society" in Shanghai. After years of construction, it has become an irreplaceable "virtual society" for the citizen. Besides, the contents and services it provides cover almost all aspects of our daily life. Those hot parts of the Web site are: Housing Service, Senior Citizens' Service, Medical Service, Trading and Procurement Service, Entertainment, Physical Trading Service, Transportation Service, Tourism Service, Financial Service, Education, Decoration Service, Legal Service and so forth.

As for the communities in Shanghai, their informationization paces have never been stopped. More and more social affairs that used to be handled by the upper government department have been passing downwards to the lower levels of communities. Therefore, community management, community services and the education background of community officers become important issues in the adoption and use of advanced information technology.

## Networked Economy

The information industry in Shanghai is keeping a fast developing momentum in recent years. The turnover of the information industry in Shanghai was 130.225 billion Yuan by its growth rate of 24.4%, which maintained its strategic position as Shanghai's first pillar industry. The proportion of the added value in this industry to the GDP amounted to 8.1%, increased from 0.7% more than one year ago. Among the information industry in Shanghai, the turnover of the information product manufactory industry reached 101.3 billion Yuan, so that its growth rate even hit 37.4%. The product sales percentage was also increased by 1.8% and summed up to 97.5%. Meanwhile the information services and software in Shanghai also achieved an output of 28.8 billion Yuan, increased by 52.2% as compared to the previous year. The information technology (IT) industry in Shanghai has maintained the top three positions nationally in terms of its scale and turnover.

The network economy has been greatly enhanced by the economic development strategy Shanghai adopted - "To promote the industrialization by informationization". Among the 1,500 industry companies, 80% of them have set up IT department; 97% of them have popularized the use of computer; 89% of them have become familiar with common software; 12% of them have conducted ERP; and 8% of them have implanted CRM. More than 500 marketplaces have adopted their MIS, Most Convenient chain stores, and supermarkets have launched POS and also had them linked with each other to form a value added network system.

The companies and firms in financial section, trade section, real estate section and the other services sections are also in steady progress in their informationization. And more than 1,500 of them have logged themselves onto the Internet and dealing with their e-business.

## Network Policy

As of 2002, 12 policies, statutes and regulations were taken into consideration by the municipal government. The major ones are listed as follows:

- "Regulations on Shanghai's Informationization Projects Management"
- "Detailed Rules of the Regulations on the IC Industry and Software Promotions in Shanghai"
- "Decision on the Overall Informationization Construction in Shanghai"
- "Suggestions on the Information Security in Shanghai"
- "Management Measures on the Social Insurance Card System"
- "Management Measures on the Public Mobile System,"and so forth

Besides the above-mentioned policies, statutes and regulations, the implementations are also of the same importance. Shanghai's municipal government is dedicated in the administrations, supervisions and mutual discussions of the confusions in order to achieve a better legal environmental situation.

## Cultures and Society Factors of Shanghai E-Government Strategy

As an ideal port, Shanghai is the gateway to the Yangzi River, the longest river in China. But when the British opened their first concession here in 1842, after the first Opium War, it was little more than a small town supported by fishing and weaving. Change was rapid. The French turned up in 1847 and it was not long before an International Settlement was established. By the time the Japanese rocked up in 1895 the city was being parceled up into segments, all autonomous and immune from Chinese law.

The world's greatest houses of finance and commerce descended on Shanghai in the 1930s. The place had the tallest buildings in Asia, and more motor vehicles on its streets than the rest of China at that time.

After the Civil War ended in 1949, Shanghai, as the key city in the new nation, plays an important role as the national industrial and economic center. Especially after the "Opening China to the Outside World" policy adopted by the central government since 1978, Shanghai has been very active and successful to attract foreign capital and investment in this big city.

Since 1992, Shanghai's GDP has increased at a two-digital rate annually. Nowadays, the GDP per capita in Shanghai is reaching US $4000. Meanwhile, the traditional industries in Shanghai have been under reconstruction. With the improving infrastructure and increasing number of talented people in various circles, the investment environment of Shanghai has been greatly improved and huge investment thus has been swarming into Shanghai.

The IT infrastructure construction in the current ninth "Five Year Plan" has set a solid foundation for Shanghai's e-government implementation. During the ninth "Five Year Plan," a series of network infrastructures (for example the "1-5-20" information harbor project) have come into being. This made Shanghai outstanding in China and close to the developed countries. Making full use of advanced ATM technology, Shanghai was the first one to launch the city-range experimental network that was technically ready for the multimedia network practice. Furthermore, the "Broad–Band Information Project" is being completed soon. Shanghai cable-TV has the largest number of city customers and this number is now approaching 2.9 million, and it also has a 98% coverage (the detailed information is referred in the previous 5-N summary.).

The city continues to grow, with a new underground stations highways crisscrossing the city, a modern stock exchange in the world, a US $2-billion airport being built up, and so forth. However, despite the growth and international investment, Shanghai is still a city of contradictions.

The government structure of Shanghai also has undergone great changes. And today, after the reorganizing and restructuring of civil servants in government departments, the structure of a new Shanghai city government is listed in the appendix 5.2.

Almost all the organs and organizations under Shanghai's government structure have launched their e-government projects. Although technical launching of government Web sites may not be very difficult, the change of behavior and attitude of the civil servants who work for the government is by no means easy. Therefore, more transparency in the governmental affairs might be helpful for the conducting of the overall strategy of the e-government in Shanghai.

# E-Government Implementation in Shanghai: A Case Study

## Background of the Case

Social Security Card System (www.962222.net) is connecting with databases of nine governmental departments of Shanghai.

According to the tenth "Five-year Plan" on the informatization and general blueprint of Shanghai's e-government strategy, the Social Security Card System has been identified as a key project of social services. With the development of the Social Security Card System, information will be utilized more efficiently and effectively.

The Social Security Card System in Shanghai has linked the other nine governmental databases. With a small card at hand a citizen can register his/her employment or unemployment status, apply for unemployment benefits, register for job-hunting training, apply for injury benefits, deal with transactions regarding endowment insurance and retirement pension, check bank account, and deal with marriage registration, and so forth.

Figure 4 shows us the front page of Social Security Card System Web site. It has the Online Inquiry function showing social security account information for each card member. The latest news is published in the nether center of this page. In the upper column, there are main categories of this Web site, such as: System Introduction, Forum, News, Services Guidelines, Operations Guidelines, Policy and Laws, Industries Trends, Counties' Section, and Hot-topics Section. On the left column, it presents the hot links, which include: Shanghai-China Web site, Shanghai Informationization Web site, Bank

*Figure 4: The front page of social security card system Web site*

Card System, Transportation Card System, Social Security System, Chinapay, and so forth. On the right column, it shows the main functions that SSCS covers: the civil security service, the labor and social security service, the civil affairs service, the medical care service, the insurance service and the public accumulative fund management.

## Main Functions of SSCS

Main functions of SSCS are in line with the e-Government implementation strategic guidelines. Specific requirements of the whole SSCS system and organization are identified as follows:

*Figure 5: Shanghai social security card system*

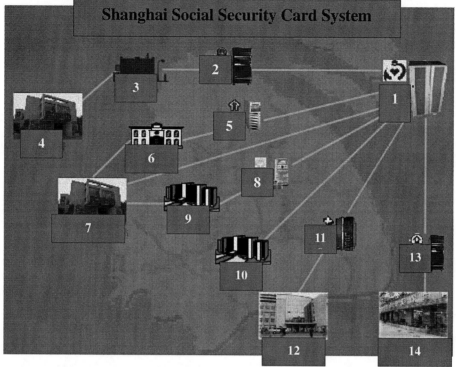

| | | | |
|---|---|---|---|
| 1 | Central information exchange platform | 2 | Public security system |
| 3 | Police bureau | 4 | Street police station |
| 5 | Labor security system | 6 | Labor bureau system |
| 7 | Street SSCS service station | 8 | Civil affairs system |
| 9 | Civil affairs bureau | 10 | Card replacement center |
| 11 | Medical care system | 12 | Medical care institute |
| 13 | Accumulation fund system | 14 | Accumulation management center |

• Responsible for maintaining raw data at the city-level data exchange platform that is used to share common data among different government departments for the purpose of increasing the transparency of government functioning and affairs, as well as improving the efficiency of government administration.

• Responsible for issuing and maintaining Social Security Card, including customized card manufacturing, issuing, and renewing, and so forth.

• Responsible for setting up SSCS service stations in different counties, villages and streets of the city, and also being responsible for organizing and guiding those service stations to develop and provide specific services to the public in their own communities.

- Responsible for the technical support to and maintenance of the system's daily operation.
- Responsible for the training and consultation regarding the usage of SSCS.

Figure 5 shows the structure of SSCS and its functions.

## Main Technical Services Provided by SSCS

1) The IEP (Information Exchanging Platform) and CSD (Common Shared Database)

So far, the IEP and CDS make it possible to share and exchange important data across different government departments. Later on, relevant databases in nearby counties and villages of Shanghai will also be linked to SSCS.

2) The CIC (Card Initialization Center)

The CIC is responsible for issuing Social Security Cards, especially those customized Civil Insurance Cards. At the same time, it also helps the government to promote other application services based on the information of cardholders, such as issuing residential certificate and academic certificate.

3) SSCS Call Center

This call center, as an effective way of oral communication, could help address difficulties and solve problems of the public when using the functions of SSCS.

## Operation and Management of SSCS

1) Internal structure

The internal structure of SSCS organization consists of one office (Shanghai Informationization Office), one company (Tian Min Co.) and four major departments (System Operation Department, Application Development Department, Card Manufacture Department and Call Center Department).

SSCS is planed to create a GMO (General Management Office) which is in charge of expanding services, proposing and planning Research & Development (R&D) projects, establishing rules for maintaining the system, working out production scheme, training technical workers, negotiating on purchasing and/or selling mega-sized equipments, guiding quality management, and carrying out an evaluation annually or periodically.

2) Management Mechanism

a) The following operation management processes are fundamental to SSCS.

- Updating basic operation management platform centralized by MRS (Management Regulation System); setting up practical evaluation system; updating MRS each year

- Further enhancing the management of procurement; making the government purchase strictly according to relevant laws or regulations

- Doing a financial budget and cost management effectively; working out relevant financial supervision regulations and rules

- Maintaining equipments and fixed assets effectively

b) Enhancing training programs and providing a pleasant and effective working environment

- Making the full use of specialists, experts and talents working in SSCS to provide internal training; creating a harmonious working environment and establishing a positive culture;

- Setting up a special fund and mechanism to attract talents to work for SSCS, making full use of those talents and creating a positive atmosphere for them, and finally, improving overall performance of talents and the whole organization

c) Setting up a QAS (Quality Assurance System)

With growing expectations from residents for better-customized services, SSCS has made great efforts to improve its working processes and successfully received the VISA/MSASTER Card Certificate, ISO9002 and ISO14001 certificates. Further, SSCS is continuously upgrading its facilities and equipments, and providing better customized services in order to maintain its leading position nationally.

The general manager of Wan Da Information Company that provides IT services to SSCS, said that "from the cooperation with Shanghai municipal government to implement eGovernment projects, the information technology skills of Wan Da have been enhanced and management expertise upgraded. Wan Da has passed the CMM level 3 assessment in December of 2002, which was the first software company receiving such a certificate in Shanghai. We also received the ISO9001 certificate in 2000. Wan Da's growth is closely related to implementations of SSCS and other eGovernment projects of Shanghai".

The other related governmental departments interviewed by the researchers of this study also expressed that "data sharing across different government departments helps us to make wiser decision and our work is more effectively supported by the other departments".

After three years of construction and two years of initial operation, SSCS has achieved good results. More than 92% of the qualified residents have applied for and received Social Security Cards; up to January, 2003, Social Security Card has been used about 91 million times in 21 different functions. A new method of managing "un-standardized Chinese characters" was one of the five intellectual property rights (IPRs) created for SSCS system and the method is now protected legally by Patent Office of China, which is in the process of commercialization.

296 Chen and Zhang

The Social Security Card System in Shanghai, as one of the key components of Shanghai's big e-government project, also sets up a successful example for other cities and provinces of China in their e-government implementation. More than 19 provincial delegations in China have visited Shanghai for the purpose of learning from Shanghai's successful experience of e-government strategy and implementation, which also helps market SSCS to other cities and provinces.

The municipal government can use this system to be more transparent by sharing relevant information and policies with citizens. With the increasing acceptance and usage of the system from citizens, the Social Security Card System will play a more important role in enhancing social service work for Shanghai government.

SSCS' successful implementation experience can be summarized as follows.

1.  SSCS' system design and development are well in line with the e-government implementation strategy of Shanghai

    The Shanghai e-government implementation strategy is based on a good understanding of Shanghai's local conditions and future development. Therefore, being well in line with the big e-government implementation strategy could result in adequate resources and support from all related government departments, which is key to a successful implementation of SCSS.

2.  A quality feasibility study of SSCS provides a good start for SCSS implementation

    Taking related strengths, weakness and opportunities of SSCS into consideration, the feasibility study of SSCS ensures that SCSS services are designed and provided in an effective sequence in terms of its importance, which in turn helps reduce project implementation risks and increase the chance of success.

3.  Quality system analysis and design for SCSS. Using international standard systems analysis and design methodology and CMM model, clearly defined users' system requirements provide a solid and necessary basis for designing and developing a user satisfactory system with useful functions.

4.  Clear milestones and implementation processes according to the plan and schedule

    The down-to-the-earth practice of implementation process also contributes to the success of SSCS. Compared with the other not-that-successful projects, the milestones of SSCS are achieved according to the plan: from 1998's municipal government's agreement to 1999's introducing of Social Security Card; from the card issued in 2000 to the completion of various functions. All of them are managed effectively according to the scheduled timetable.

5    Online supervision and assessment

In order to further improve and control the quality of SSCS services, an online supervision and feedback function is put in place. Every one could log on SCSS at any time to comment on various issues such as quality of services, response time to their inquiries, and complaining online. This citywide supervision and assessment of services help continuously improve SSCS services.

With the adoption and usage of SCSS, different governmental departments can now join their efforts to cooperate more consistently and efficiently. Also, functions of the government have been gradually changed, and the way and style those civil servants worked before have been altered. The implementation of SCSS can be regarded as a process of social service process reengineer (SSPR). Based on the idea of simplifying processes of social services, social service processes were re-engineered and the related best practices were programmed into SCSS application software. For example, the social insurance service was handled by a simple process of using only one card, instead of former numerous redundant processes.

However, SCSS also has its weaknesses and some problems that need to be addressed in the future. Although system security problem was identified and paid attention initially, it is still a very important issue. Especially after the "9.11" incident in the USA, a more effective and comprehensive security system for the Social Security Card System is urgently needed. Some on-going debate questions about SCSS include: whether or not to set up an integrated database, which may increase system efficiency but also increase systems' vulnerability? How to establish an emergency handling system component and how to maintain it? And so forth....

Historic problems left by the old social insurance system resulted in current data being inaccurate, incomplete and inconsistent. Although efforts have been made to solve this problem, much low-quality data existing in SSCS is still an unresolved problem — about 5 million pieces of data need to be cleaned, which may further influence the overall quality of the system when new data are continuously being fed in. Data cleaning is a challenging issue for the system in the near future.

Completely breaking down boundaries of government's functional departments is an important problem for further development of SCSS. Another challenge faced by SCSS lies in the current legal environment. The incompleteness of the relevant laws and lack of supporting policies directly harm the utilizing and further exploring of existing information resources.

In sum, from the above discussion and analysis, SSCS has generally achieved its main goals, which demonstrated the feasibility and effectiveness of Shanghai's e-government implementation strategy. Shanghai's e-government is generally regarded as a leader in e-government implementation in the whole country. At the same time, SCSS of Shanghai is a successful pioneer project in the city's e-government implementation strategy.

# Future Development of SCSS

The following briefs the future development of SSCS and its related organization issues.

## *Human Resource Plan*

Up to 2005, the human resource plan of SSCS is to adjust human resource structure and allocation to meet demands in the future. A more effective recruiting process and the human resources management policy of "right person for the right position" need to be established.

At that time, the number of the civil servants working for SSCS will be about 150. Except for system operators, all other civil servants should be well educated, with at least university degrees.

A suitable professional composition of SSCS staff should be: management level staff account for about 10% of humanpower (in charge of system center and different departments); technical level staff for about 40% (in charge of software and hardware management, telecommunication, database engineering, system operation, network maintenance and data management); marketing level staff for about 30% (in charge of promotion, procurement, financing, etc.); operation level staff for about 20% (in charge of phone center, card issuing, inventory management, transportation and assistant tasks).

## *Financial Plan*

From 2003 to 2005, SSCS still needs further investment. The financing budget consists of two major parts: fixed assets investment and system maintenance expense.

(1)   Fixed assets investment

The budget on the fixed asset investment for the period from 2003 to 2005 is about USD 36.6 million. The schedule is as follows:

- In year 2003, the third round of upgrading SSCS systems needs about USD18.3 million.

- In year 2004, a comprehensive information service system specifically serving local communities will be under construction, and USD 5.9 million will be invested.

- In year 2005, an operational supervision system will be developed, and about USD 12.2 million will be invested.

(2)    System Maintenance Expense
•    With the expanding scale of SCSS usage, relevant operation and maintenance expense will be increased accordingly (such expenses include devices and equipment maintenance, wages/salaries, resources, etc.).

## System Platform Construction Plan

•    From year 2003 to year 2004, 750 thousand primary school academic certificate cards and 550 thousand middle school academic certificate cards will be issued together with related services being provided.
•    From the end of 2003 to early 2004, SSCS will expand its services to issue endowment insurance and medical care cards to residents of rural areas of Shanghai city.

All the future plans and development of SCSS will be again guided by the three strategic objectives of Shanghai e-government implementation.

# Discussions and Conclusions

From the above analysis and case study, Shanghai, as a major city in the biggest developing country of the world, has chosen the right e-government implementation strategy with the following three specific strategic objectives:

•    Increase the transparency of government functioning and affairs
•    Provide better services to the public and private sectors
•    Improve the efficiency of government administration

Compared with the US's e-government implementation strategy -"Citizen-centered, Results-oriented and Market-based" (www.firstgov.gov, assessed in June 2003), there exist some similarities between US and China. Both strategies recognize that e-government should act to improve the performance and efficiency of government and lead to better cooperation between government and the public, and between government and private sector.

However, the unique feature of the Shanghai e-government strategy lies in the statement "Increase the transparency of government functioning and affairs," as compared to the US "Market-based" strategy. The difference attracts our attention. In order to explain the discrepancy, we need to use the 5-N factors model to do the analysis (see Figure 2).

Generally speaking, the e-government implementation of China is just to keep pace with and further promote the transformation of China's economy from the previous "planning economy" to the current "market economy". Such big change in the country will definitely have profound effects on e-government projects. Furthermore, the restructuring of government in China also influences e-government implementation strategy, for the government nowadays wants to change their role or image from the former "governor" to a real "social servant".

Equipped with existing advanced IT facilities and infrastructures, the e-government implementation in the US has started earlier than many other countries. As a country adopting the capitalism economic model for centuries already, the so-called "market concept" is deeply rooted in its people's minds, and the government's transparent policies are not a major issue there. Therefore, a "market-based" e-government strategy adopted by US government seems a natural and effective choice.

Nevertheless, China is in the developing stage of transforming itself to a more market-based economy. Although the restructuring of government has been underway for years, changes of human mentality and behavior seem always to be slow and lag behind. The government affairs are used to being processed in a so-called "black-box," which starts to become more transparent to the public.

In order to achieve the transparency of government functioning and affairs, a law called "Statute of Publicity of Government Information" has been passed. Guided by this statute, much more information of government will further be released and published to the public.

According to a survey, more than 90% of Web pages of e-government Web sites have been daily updated. Besides the publicity of the latest governmental news in front pages, historical data can also be found in online databases of many e-government Web sites.

In the process of transforming from the old "planning economy" to the new "market economy," Shanghai is playing a leading role in this aspect. Although the "market-based" principle is not clearly stated in Shanghai's e-government strategy, market elements are also reflected in the implementation of e-government projects in Shanghai.

The strategy of e-government implementation of Shanghai is by no means perfect. Some problems still exist that should be addressed in the future, which may also provide useful insights for other developing countries in e-government implementation in the future.

Firstly, process re-engineering of public services is important but difficult, and resistances and barriers for the re-engineering still exist in government departments. Some problems like overlapping functions slow down transactions of public services. These hindrances would be likely to hamper the implementation of e-government strategy. Therefore, reorganization of government functions is necessary. All government departments should be re-organized and re-engineered based on the overall strategy and planning of e-government implementation.

Secondly, the further development and implementation of e-government in Shanghai should be carried out in a coordinated way. E-government development is now faced with difficulties that come from other parts of the society, such as the incompleteness of the legal system and transforming government functions. Therefore, re-organizing other parts of government departments should be coordinated with the development of e-government. Meanwhile, the IT skills and management expertise of civil servants should be further improved to keep pace with the development of the society. Currently, only about 65% of the civil servants have university degrees, which should be increased further.

Finally, the security issue of e-government system appears to become more and more important; otherwise, the public may be "scared" to carry out online public service transactions in the future.

# Appendices

The Main E-government Projects Implemented in Shanghai

- *www.shdpc.gov.cn*: Shanghai Municipal Development & Reform Commission
- *www.shmec.gov.cn*: Shanghai Education
- *www.justice.gov.cn*: Shanghai Judicature and Administration
- *www.123333.gov.cn*: Shanghai Labor Protection Service
- *www.smhb.gov.cn*: Shanghai Sanitation Information Service
- *shenji.stc.sh.cn*: Shanghai Audit
- *www.sepb.gov.cn*: Shanghai Environment
- *stj.sh.gov.cn*: Shanghai Administration Bureau of NGOs
- *www.shec.gov.cn*: Shanghai Economic Commission
- *www.stcsm.gov.cn*: Shanghai Technology and Science
- *jcw.sh.gov.cn*: Shanghai Supervision
- *www.shucm.sh.cn*: Shanghai Urban Construction
- *www.shanghaiwater.gov.cn*: Shanghai Water Service
- *www.shfao.gov.cn*: Shanghai Foreign Affairs
- *www.stats-sh.gov.cn*: Shanghai Statistics
- *tyj.sh.gov.cn*: Shanghai Administration of Sports
- *www.shfdz.gov.cn*: Shanghai Real Estate Resources
- *sjr.sh.gov.cn*: Shanghai Finance
- *fzzx.sh.gov.cn*: Shanghai Municipal Government Development and Research Center
- *www.commerce.sh.cn*: Shanghai Commerce
- *www.shac.gov.cn*: Shanghai Agricultures
- *www.popinfo.gov.cn*: Shanghai Municipal Population and Family Planning Commission
- *lyw.sh.gov.cn*: Shanghai Tourism
- *www.ssip.com.cn*: Shanghai Intellectual Property
- *jtj.sh.gov.cn*: Shanghai Transportation

- *www.shsz.gov.cn/gov*: Shanghai Municipal Engineering Administration Bureau
- *nlj.sh.gov.cn*: Shanghai Agriculture & Forestry Bureau

# The Government Structure of Shanghai

## I. General Office of Shanghai Municipality

Liaison Office of Shanghai Municipality

## II. Government Organizations

Shanghai Development Planning Commission

Shanghai Price Bureau

Shanghai Economic Commission

Shanghai Commercial Commission

Shanghai Education Commission

Shanghai Commission of Science and Technology

Shanghai Commission of Ethnic and Religious Affairs

Shanghai Bureau of Public Security

Shanghai Bureau of State Security

Shanghai Commission of Supervision

Shanghai Bureau of Civil Affairs

Shanghai Municipal Bureau of Justice

Shanghai Finance Bureau

Shanghai Local Taxation Bureau

Shanghai Personnel Bureau

Shanghai Municipal Labor and Social Security Bureau

Shanghai Construction and Management Commission

Shanghai Agriculture Commission

Shanghai Foreign Trade and Economic Cooperation Commission

Shanghai Foreign Investment Commission

Shanghai Administration of Culture, Radio, Film and Television

Shanghai Health Bureau

Shanghai Water Conservation Bureau

Shanghai Population and Family Planning Commission

Shanghai Audit Bureau

Foreign Affairs Office of Shanghai Municipality

Information Office of Shanghai Municipality

## III. Public Agencies Directly Under Shanghai Municipality

Shanghai Municipal Bureau of Environmental Protection

Shanghai Bureau of Statistics

Shanghai Administration of Industry and Commerce

Shanghai Bureau of Quality and Technical Supervision

Shanghai Drug Administration

Shanghai Tourism Administrative Committee

Shanghai Press and Publication Bureau

Shanghai Sports Bureau

Shanghai Intellectual Property Administration

Shanghai Urban Planning Committee

Shanghai Housing and Land Resources Administration

Shanghai Urban Transport Bureau

Government Offices Administration of Shanghai Municipality

Shanghai Informatization Office

Civil Defense Office of Shanghai Municipality

Coordinating Office of Shanghai Municipality

Overseas Chinese Affairs Office of Shanghai Municipality

Legislative Affairs Office of Shanghai Municipality

Restructuring Economic System Office of Shanghai Municipality

Research Office of Shanghai Municipality

State Assets Management Office of Shanghai Municipality

Shanghai Municipal Port Administration Bureau

Research and Development Center of Shanghai Municipality

## IV. Public Agencies Associated with Shanghai Municipality

Shanghai Grain Bureau

Shanghai Bureau of Agriculture and Forestry

Shanghai Urban Infrastructure Engineering Administration

Shanghai Landscaping Administrative Bureau

Shanghai Sanitation Administration

Shanghai Medical Security Bureau

# References

Huang, W., Chen, H.M., Ching, R., & Li, X. (2003, July 4-8). A preliminary study of egovernment strategies and implementation between developed & developing countries: Proposing a conceptual research framework. *Proceeding of Asia Pacific Decision Sciences Institute Annual Meeting, Shanghai.*

Li, T., & Wang, H.C. (2003). Systematic study on electronic governance perspective on developing and research actuality. *Systems Engineering-Theory Methodology Applications, 12*(1).

Mark, F. (2002, February 27). *E-government strategy.* Executive Office of the President Office of Management and Budget.

*The Main Tasks of the Informationization of Shanghai.* (2003). Shanghai Municipal Government, Shanghai, China.

Wang, X.H., & Wang, H.C. (2002). MEI-system economics and e-government. *Journal of Shanghai Jiaotong University (Philosophy and Social Sciences), 10*(28).

*www.shanghai.gov.cn*

*www.962222.net*

*www.88547.com*

Yan, J.Q. (2002). Take full efforts to develop the egovernment in Shanghai. Speech on *"The Third Forum of the Asia-Pacific City Informationization".*

Yearbook of Shanghai Inforationization. (2002). Shanghai Informationization Office, Shanghai, China.

# Endnote

[1]   The data in the following sections are collected from the *Yearbook of Shanghai Inforationization* (2002).

## Chapter XIII

# E-Government:
# Implementation Policies and Best Practices from Singapore

Leo Tan Wee Hin, Singapore National Academy of Science, Singapore

R. Subramaniam, Singapore National Academy of Science, Singapore

## Abstract

*The insertion of an e-government in the public administration infrastructure of Singapore has spawned a bureaucratic renaissance with wide-ranging ramifications in various facets of society. A single entry portal on the Web links citizens to all the government agencies as well as opens a gateway to a plethora of services needed by citizens and businesses. The process of democratic governance has been significantly strengthened with the entrenching of the e-government. This chapter elaborates on some of the important implementation policies and best practices of the Singapore experience with e-government.*

# Introduction

The emergence of the Internet in the mid 1990s has caused structural transformations in various aspects of society and life. Many aspects of society, for example, education, economy and finance have been "virtualized" to a significant extent. The improved work processes and productivity increments achieved in all these sectors are posing challenges for governments to be more responsive to their citizens' needs. More importantly, it is a direct challenge to the way in which democratic processes are evolving.

Citizens in the Internet era are beginning to raise their expectations of what the government can do for them. With the relentless pace at which the economic landscape is being shaped by globalization and competitive pressures, people want their government to be more responsive and to provide the requisite services rapidly and cheaply. The need for the bureaucracy to be in proximity with citizens' everyday life and to be proactive, rather than reactive, has been emphasized in a number of studies (Janssen, Wagener & Beerens, 2003; Tarabanis, Peristeras & Koumpis, 2000).

A direct response to the above challenges has been the e-government movement (Heeks, 2000; Prins, 2001; Ronagan, 2002). The term *e-government* relates to the use of information and communication technologies (ICT) by the bureaucracy to improve their work processes and governance in a manner that simplifies life for the public and businesses when they interact with them online at all times (Norris, Holden & Fletcher, 2001).

The e-government movement started in the USA in 1995, with about 8.7% of local governments having a Web presence where information was dispensed and services delivered (Sprecher, Talcove & Bowen, 1996). By 1997, the number of local governments that had been e-enabled has gone up to 40% (Norris & Demeter, 1999). By late 2000, 83.7% of the governments in the USA had an online presence to some extent (Norris, Holden & Fletcher, 2001).

A number of arguments have been made in support of e-government (Northrop & Thorson, 2003):

- It improves the effectiveness of governments. E-initiatives deployed on the Web have the potential to enhance government productivity whilst achieving cost reductions.

- It makes governments more transparent. When draft policies are posted on the Web, concerned citizens can access these and provide feedback.

- It has the potential to transform government in the way it is structured. For example, the hierarchical clusters in which various agencies are governed presents an inordinate amount of complexity for citizens who want to get in touch with the government or who wish to get involved in some aspect of the decision-making processes of the government.

In the Third Global Forum on Reinventing Government (*http://www.globalforum.org*), delegates from 122 nations espoused on the importance of three key points:

(a)   E-government has the potential to enhance the quality of life for people through diminution of transaction costs and commuting time.

(b)   The civil service is likely to transition to an e-government, where hierarchies are flattened and public sector officials would be more responsive and attuned to the needs of the citizens.

(c)   Developing nations need to give serious thought in transiting their civil service to an e-government. The potential for strengthening capacity building, something that is lacking in the offline version of the e-government, is tremendous. By promoting transparency and openness in government dealings with the public and businesses as well as by improving service delivery, the civil society movement as well as the business community will become more resilient to nation building efforts.

Whereas governments function traditionally through their civil service and public sector, with inter-agency links leaving much to be desired, an e-government allows citizens to be connected to the bureaucracy with a click of the mouse 24/7. This idealized scenario is not yet a reality in most countries owing to a number of factors – basic telecommunications infrastructure has not yet reached ubiquity, the civil service is still a behemoth in many developing countries, infrastructure and standards for e-government are still evolving, best practices that can be emulated in good measure are still being fine-tuned, and so forth.

As a tiny island (682 sq km) with hardly any natural resources, Singapore places great emphasis on the judicious utilization of its available manpower (4 million) as well as the productive use of science and technology to overcome constraints and other problems (Tan & Subramaniam, 1998-2000). When the Internet became a buzz word in the 1990s, the Singapore government realized that it was likely to have more profound ramifications in society than was popularly realized, and took a calculated risk to put in place an advanced telecommunications infrastructure with a view towards riding on the emerging digital economy that is fast taking shape. There was recognition that it was only a matter of time before the government has to be e-enabled if the benefits of information and communication technologies were to be realized for its people.

The sagacity of the foregoing initiatives can be gauged from the fact that Singapore has been consistently ranked high in the world for networked readiness, e-government readiness, and ICT utilization. The e-government in Singapore has matured tremendously over the past few years, benefiting from the fine-tuning of work processes in the public sector on the basis of accumulated experiences and a visionary political leadership that has not shirked from funding investments to make the e-government succeed. With the maturing of the e-government movement in Singapore, its experiences would add to the growing debate on the effectiveness of e-governments in the world.

The objectives of this chapter are four-fold:

(a)   to describe the infrastructure and standards supporting the e-government in Singapore,

(b)   to provide information on some of the key services that have been "virtualized,"

(c)   to place a commentary on the efforts of  putting in place an e-government, and

(d)   to offer pointers, based on the Singapore experience, for other countries contemplating the establishment of an e-government or seeking to improve its effectiveness.

The Singapore e-government Web site is located at http://www.egov.gov.sg

# Infrastructure for E-Government

(a)   Modern telecommunications network

Singapore recognizes that a modern telecommunications network is indispensable for making the transition to e-government. A "virtualized" government by itself has little effectiveness if efforts are not translated into promoting connectivity for its citizenry. A technology-neutral approach was thus taken to roll out a modern telecommunications network in the 1990s. International telecommunication players were incentivised to deploy alternative platforms for access. The spirit of competition was entrenched by the appointment of an independent regulator as well as through the ensuring of a level playing field for all operators.

The following telecommunications platforms are now in place:

* Asymmetric Digital Subscriber Line, for broadband access
* Hybrid Fiber Coaxial (HFC) Cable Modem service, for broadband access
* Asynchronous Transfer Mode, for broadband access as well as for linking ADSL and HFC Cable Modem to the ordinary telecommunications network
* Public Switched Telecommunications Network
* Wireless access

These have been described in detail by Tan and Subramaniam (2000, 2001, 2003).

With the telecommunications network leveraging on a diversity of platforms that are interoperable, a competitive landscape has emerged for cost-effective access.

Tables 1 and 2 provide comparative data on the state of ICT in Singapore with respect to other countries. Table 3 shows the maturation of the telecommunications market in Singapore.

(b)   Public Services Infrastructure

A key feature of the e-government architecture in Singapore is the installation of the Public Services Infrastructure (PSI). It comprises a three-tier framework (http://www.sun.com/br/government/feature_psi.html):

*Table 1: Indicators of Internet infrastructure*

| Country | Internet hosts per 1000 population in 1999 | Internet users per 1000 population in 1999 | Access cost for 40 hours during off-peak in US$ |
|---|---|---|---|
| Australia | 57.58 | 316.84 | 33.85 |
| China | 0.06 | 7.03 | na |
| Hong Kong | 17.09 | 361.57 | na |
| India | 0.02 | 2.81 | na |
| Indonesia | 0.10 | 4.30 | na |
| Japan | 20.84 | 213.90 | 85.65 |
| Korea | 9.84 | 231.76 | 27.13 |
| Malaysia | 2.70 | 68.71 | na |
| New Zealand | 71.12 | 183.69 | 34.80 |
| Philippines | 0.17 | 6.72 | na |
| Singapore | 38.08 | 243.99 | na |
| Taiwan | 27.02 | 205.50 | na |
| Thailand | 0.66 | 13.15 | na |
| USA | 195.00 | 271.74 | 35.40 |

*Source: Wong, 2001*

*Table 2: Networked readiness index for 2002/2003*

| Country | Score | Rank |
|---|---|---|
| Finland | 5.92 | 1 |
| USA | 5.79 | 2 |
| Singapore | 5.74 | 3 |
| Iceland | 5.51 | 5 |
| Canada | 5.44 | 6 |
| United Kingdom | 5.35 | 7 |
| Denmark | 5.33 | 8 |
| Taiwan | 5.31` | 9 |
| Germany | 5.29 | 10 |

*Source: Dutta and Jain, 2002*

*Table 3: Timeline showing growth of fixed line telephony, mobile phone and Internet market in Singapore*

| Sector | 1997 | 1998 | 1999 | 2000 | 2001 | 2002 |
|---|---|---|---|---|---|---|
| Mobile phone | 743 000 | 1 020 000 | 1 471 300 | 2 442 100 | 2 858 800 | 3 244 800 |
| Internet dial-up | 267 400 | 393 600 | 582 600 | 1 940 300 | 1 917 900 | 2 000 700 |
| Fixed line | - | 1 751 500 | 1 850 700 | 1 935 900 | 1 948 900 | 1993 700 |

*Source: http://www.ida.gov.sg*

- a background infrastructural ICT framework,

- a middle layer, which interconnects all government agencies in a manner that allows them to host their data in a central data storage facility as well as integrates all the database software of these agencies, and

- an applications layer, which features security and validation protocols for financial transactions, for example, use of digital signatures.

Prior to the installation of the PSI, it was recognized that if the erstwhile ICT systems of the various agencies were to be integrated, the sheer complexity of the various systems as well as the diversity of the various user interfaces would present enormous technical difficulties in realizing migration of these services onto the e-government platform. The vestiges of these systems would also come in the way of restructuring work processes in a coherent manner that would admit integration with the legacy systems of other agencies. All this would not be conducive for delivering a customer-centric suite of products and services.

The advantage of opting for PSI is that it enables the various agencies to realize operational synergies as well as cost savings by riding on a common platform (http://www.sun.com/br/government/feature_psi.html). For example, by riding on the PSI platform, all government agencies can share the e-payment channels, the electronic data exchange and the security features embedded in the framework. As a result, the cost of introducing new services to the public is drastically reduced, as is also the time taken to roll out these services. The arising economies of scale in the operations also allows for significant overall cost savings to be realized by the government.

There is a services deployment tool called eService Generator, which allows agencies or their appointed vendors to roll out new services and applications rapidly and with a high level of security on the PSI without the need to worry about source codes. For example, when the New Singapore Shares scheme was launched in 2001 by the government to reward citizens for their role in contributing to Singapore's economic growth, the quantum of shares which each citizen gets is determined by factors such as age, income level and type of housing. An e-portal that allows millions of Singaporeans to check on their share allotment was conceptualized and launched in three weeks on the PSI. With any other platform, it would have taken at least six months to launch this service!

In building the PSI, cognizance was taken of the need to embed fundamental technologies such as XML, Java and HTTP into the framework so as to streamline the complexity and reduce cost (http://www.ecquaria.com/clients/pdf/ss.pdf). For example, XML is used for communication and information sharing among the various agencies, as its capacity to e-enable the provision of services to the online public in an expeditious and interoperable manner by a plurality of agencies is well recognized. Where possible, only open standards have been used, for example, LDAP, Java 2 Platform and Enterprise Edition (J2EE Platform) technologies.

For the public who need to engage in financial transactions with the government, the PSI boasts of various payment options such as credit card, cash card, direct debit and online payment.

The modular architecture of the PSI allows scalability of the operations to be boosted when necessary.

# Implementation Policies and Issues

The Singapore experience has been that the transition to an e-government must proceed in a phased manner. As it is, there was little guidance on best practices that it could emulate when it started to "virtualize" its civil service – after all, it was among the pioneers in the e-government movement when it started off in 1995. A phased transition would permit adequate time to iron out bottlenecks and kinks in the network, set the standards, streamline the workflow processes of the various government agencies for automated delivery over the Internet, learn from evolving e-governments elsewhere, and allow for policy issues in the cyber realm to be cognized for proper implementation.

As the public sector initiated its computerization program in the 1980s, it was well positioned to ride on the Internet platform in the mid-1990s. Institutional changes were embarked on internally before up-linking these to the Internet platform. The e-government initiatives started off with the setting up of the government Internet Web site in 1995; this provided the public with an array of information for their needs.

In June 2000, the e-Government Action Plan I was rolled out with an investment of S$1.5 billion, and with the specific emphasis of touching base with three segments of the citizenry through the migration of those government services that can be put online. These are now addressed.

(a)   Government-to-Citizen (G2C) Service

This initiative was configured to facilitate online access for people with the government - the access is on an "anytime and anywhere" basis, unlike the traditional civil service routine of 8:30 am to 5:30 pm on weekdays, and 8:30 am to 1:00 pm on Saturdays.

The G2C portal is a one-stop center for a myriad of information and services that the citizens need. The popularity of this one-stop destination can be gauged from the number of hit counts registered – 240,000 in October 2001 and 8.7 million in May 2003 (http://www.egov.gov.sg/g2c.htm).

In March 2003, the revolutionary SingPass was introduced for citizens aged 15 and above. The scheme offers citizens a single password to transact with any government agency where authentication is required. Previously, each government agency had its own authentication system for such access. This was rather cumbersome for citizens in Singapore who are already saddled with a string of passwords that they have to remember for their various needs– for example, for their e-mail account, for ATM cash withdrawal, and so forth. With SingPass, a high level of security is afforded for all transactions that require verification, and thus the citizen just needs to remember one password when connecting with the government.

(b)   Government-to-Business (G2B) Service

This initiative sought to present the friendly face of the government to local and international businesses (http://www.egov.gov.sg/g2b.htm). It is customary for businesses to deal with governments for various matters, either through the mail

*Table 4: Comparison of some services on civil service and e-government platforms*

| Item | Civil Service | E-government |
|------|--------------|--------------|
| Submitting business plans | Entails separate submission of documents to 12 departments | One-stop submission at G2B portal. Savings of S$450. |
| Incorporating new company | S$1,200 to S$35,000, depending on size of company<br>Approval time of 2 days | Online incorporation at a cost of S$300<br><br>Approval time of 2 hours |
| Opening new entertainment outlet | 2 months for approval | 2 weeks for approval |

*Source: http://www.egov.gov.sg*

or through visits to the various agencies. The availability of the necessary information and services on a 24/7 routine in the e-government means that businesses can realize savings in time, cost and procedures for their various needs.

In Sinapore, there is recognition that a pro-business environment is indispensable for stimulating economic growth and for promoting socio-economic advancement of its people; hence the importance placed on the G2B portal.

An indication of the effectiveness of the G2B portal for businesses can be seen from data displayed in Table 4.

To facilitate ease of navigation on the G2B portal, the information and services are presented in a hierarchical manner, that is, by type of business. The streamlining of services in an integrated manner means that businesses save time, money and effort by capitalizing on the synergies arising from multi-agency cooperation.

As governments are one of the biggest customers of business concerns, an e-government approach allows access to all kinds of works available for tendering. This permits all businesses a fighting chance to land government contracts and build up their portfolios. Such procedures also promote transparency as well as check any lapses on the part of the government. With this in mind, the Government Electronic Business (GeBIZ) portal was established as an online procurement system for the civil service. Whereas, previously, advertisements need to be taken out in newspapers at considerable cost, this new approach allows businesses to be more focused in scanning a one-stop portal for government contracts. It has been estimated that in the year 2002, over S$262 million worth of transactions were done on this portal. The savings in terms of decreased transaction costs, reduced paperwork as well as more competitive quotes for services and goods translate into benefits for the government.

Cohen and Eimecke (2003) have opined that whilst the capacity to purchase on the Web is useful, electronic and streamlined approvals and procedures are as critical, and all of which will aid in decreasing the administrative cost of transactions. These have been effectively addressed in the Singapore e-government.

*Table 5: Timelines for e-commerce development in Singapore*

| Year | Initiative |
|------|-----------|
| Aug 1996 | Introduction of e-commerce Hotbed Programme |
| Jan 1997 | Stock Trading on the Internet<br>Formation of E-commerce Policy Committee |
| Apr 1997 | First Secure VISA Card Payment over the Internet<br>Internet Web site launched for Secure Electronic Commerce Project |
| Jul 1997 | Netrust – South East Asia's first Certification Authority set up |
| Aug 1997 | Singapore IT Dispute Resolution Advisory Committee set up |
| Oct 1997 | Singapore Computer Emergency Response Team set up |
| Nov 1997 | Canada and Singapore sign Information & Communication Technology Agreement<br>S$50 million fund to boost innovation and multimedia content development in Singapore |
| Jun 1998 | Canada and Singapore announce first cross certification of public key infrastructures<br>Electronic Transactions Act introduced in Parliament<br>Singapore, Canada and Pennsylvania sign education technology MOU using digital signatures<br>Electronic Transactions Act passed in Parliament<br>Computer Misuse (Amendment) Bill 1998 passed in Parliament |
| Jul 1998 | E-commerce Co-ordination Committee formed |
| Sep 1998 | Singapore acceded to the Berne Convention for the protection of literary and artistic works<br>Singapore launces e-commerce Masterplan<br>Government Shopfront offers government products and services over the Internet |
| Nov 1998 | S$9 million Local Enterprise Electronic Commerce Programme launched |
| Feb 1999 | Launch of the Regulations to the Electronic Transactions Act<br>Australia and Singapore sign Information and Communication<br>Technology Agreement |
| Apr 1999 | e-Citizen Centre set up |
| Sep 1999 | Berlin and Singapore sign a MOU to cooperate closely in Information and Communication Technology |
| Oct 1999 | Helpdesk for businesses set up for enquiries on e-commerce policies |
| Jan 2000 | IASPs get guidelines on preventive security scanning<br>Lifting of import control on cryptographic products |
| Jul 2000 | First Infocomm Technology Roadmap – charting the future of technology in Singapore |
| Aug 2000 | Singapore paves the way as a trusted e-commerce hub |
| Oct 2000 | IDA and PSB announce S$30 million incentive scheme to spur e-business development and growth in Singapore |

*Source: http://www.ec.gov.sg*

Table 5 shows the evolution of the e-commerce landscape in Singapore. Tables 6 and 7 present some useful data on the growing importance of e-commerce in Singapore. It is important to note that a robust e-commerce ecosystem contributes towards the effectiveness of the e-government.

(c)   Government-to-Employees portal (G2E)

This is a portal for public officers (http://www.egov.gov.sg/gt2.htm). It is recognized that ultimately the service levels of the e-government depend on the quality of the human resources in the public sector. The need for all public sector officers to be ICT-savvy and keep abreast of new developments in technologies and work processes is thus of paramount significance. The G2E publicizes the diversity of ICT training programs available for staff development.

*Table 6: Indicators of e-commerce development in selected countries*

| Country | Secure servers per 1,000,000 population in 1998 | Secure servers with strong encryption per 1,000,000 population in 1998 | Business-to-Business trade in US$M in 2000 | Business-to-Consumer trade in US$M in 2000 | % Internet users who purchased online in past month in 2000 |
|---|---|---|---|---|---|
| Australia | 33.70 | 16.87 | 5,160.55 | 394.09 | 10 |
| China | 0.01 | 0.00 | 954.37 | 72.88 | na |
| Hong Kong | 10.32 | 1.81 | 1,773.28 | 135.42 | 7 |
| India | 0.01 | 0.00 | 675.72 | 51.60 | 5 |
| Indonesia | 0.05 | 0.02 | 110.48 | 8.44 | 3 |
| Japan | 3.39 | 1.13 | 29,618.20 | 2,261.84 | 20 |
| Korea | 0.82 | 0.19 | 5,164.42 | 394.39 | 16 |
| Malaysia | 1.08 | 0.55 | 311.85 | 23.82 | 5 |
| New Zealand | 23.73 | 7.65 | 632.33 | 48.29 | na |
| Philippines | 0.04 | 0.01 | 111.70 | 8.53 | 2 |
| Singapore | 21.18 | 8.02 | 1,097.84 | 83.84 | 5 |
| Taiwan | 1.85 | 0.32 | 3,842.73 | 293.46 | 4 |
| Thailand | 0.10 | 0.05 | 432.15 | 33.00 | 1 |
| USA | 54.29 | 38.39 | 449,900,000 | 38,755.00 | 27 |

*Source: Wong, 2001*

*Table 7: Data on e-commerce activities in Singapore*

| Item | Jan 2001 | Jan 2003 |
|---|---|---|
| Business-to-Business commerce | S$81.5 billion | S$81.5 billion |
| Business-to-Consumer commerce | S$1.9 billion | S$2.1 billion |
| Online banking users (as % of Net users above 15 years old) | 20.1 % | 30.8 % |
| Online shoppers | 21.0 % | NA |

*Source: www.ida.govs.sg*

In Singapore, all civil service officers are encouraged to attend 100 hours of training annually. The availability of these programs is among the reasons why the civil service is a lean but very efficient outfit. Mastering new productivity tools and technologies through the various training programs empowers public officers to be more effective in their work.

(d)  e-Citizen Center

Transcending the weekday 8:30 am to 5:00 pm grind as well as the weekend 8:30 am to 1:00 pm routine, this portal heralds a paradigm shift in the manner in which the public interacts with the government. It was launched in April 1999. All manner of services that the citizen needs are available in this portal (http:// www.ecitizen.gov.sg). It has been estimated that this portal alone contributes to a savings of S$40 million a year (Poon, 2000).

The one-stop Web site now features over 1,600 online services. It is classified into 16 categories, based on the common needs of citizens. The stratification of portal offerings according to key milestones in a person's life has become the de facto standard for logical classification, and this is emulated even by other e-governments (Yeo, 2003). The more important of the services in this portal is outlined below:

- Business - registering a business, applying for a patent, getting a license or permit, and so forth
- Defence - allowing male citizens to register for national service, allowing them to apply for an exit permit when going overseas, allowing reservists to book a date for their annual Individual Physical Proficiency Test, and so forth
- Education - searching for information about the 360+ schools in Singapore, registering for the GCE "O," "N" and "A" level examinations, applying for government scholarships, and so forth
- Housing - checking availability of public housing for sale, applying for ballot for allocation of flats, and so forth
- Employment - searching for jobs in the civil service, filing income tax returns, checking balances in the employee's Central Provident Fund account, and so forth
- Family - registering birth and marriage, finding spouse, applying work permit for foreign maid, applying for birth extract, and so forth
- Parking - online payment of fines for traffic offences, and so forth
- Travel - applying/renewing of international passport, and so forth

These are services that are endemic to the effective functioning of an online government.

The extent to which the e-government movement has impacted on society can be gauged from a consideration of three path-breaking initiatives, all of which are world firsts:

(i)  E-judiciary system

Launched in 2001, it is the world's first paperless civil court system (Wee, 2000). It has virtually eliminated paper transactions in civil litigation cases, as lawyers are now required to file their legal papers online. This allows judicial work processes to be streamlined, thus contributing to more prompt dispensation of justice. The waiting time for litigation has been reduced from two years to a few months. It has been estimated that this system contributes to the realization of about S$4 million in savings a year.

(ii)   TradeNet

This is an electronic trade clearance system (*http://www.tradenet.gov.sg*). With this innovation, the process of obtaining clearances from various agencies such as port authorities and customs department has been migrated to one site. It links freight forwarders and businesses to 35 government agencies. What used to require the completion of 35 forms has now been reduced to just a single form. Processing time has been drastically reduced from 2-7 days to less than a minute. It has been estimated that as a result of these initiatives businesses save between 40-60% on processing fees as well as 30% on their own administrative costs – this translates to about US$1 billion in savings a year.

Currently, there are over 25,000 users of TradeNet.

(iii)   E-stamping System

This service has been a boon to realty agents and lawyers, as all the paperwork required for leasing, renting, mortgaging, and other ancillary services can now be annotated with an online electronic stamp (Wee, 2000). It also has the advantage that the repository of documents uploaded in template format onto the agency's Web site builds up into an electronic archive, thus facilitating easy retrieval of documents. Ownership of stocks and shares can also be transferred electronically, besides being validated by an e-stamp.

It has been estimated that about S$7 million in transaction costs are saved annually through this service. Typically, about 100,000 documents are e-stamped annually.

# Commentary

The pervasiveness of the information economy is posing challenges for governments to remain relevant and responsive. Whilst the private sector has been able to capitalize on the potential of ICT to re-engineer themselves to a significant extent, few governments have demonstrated determination and commitment to dotcom their bureaucracy and re-organize their workings. This is not surprising, as e-bureaucracy calls for a paradigm shift in mindset and governance, which few governments are prepared to embrace.

The literature on e-government has not reached a level where citations have accumulated in sufficient numbers on journal and conference papers for testing the effectiveness of an e-government. This is because the e-government movement is still new and good practices are still evolving. There is thus little consensus on what constitutes an appropriate framework for assessing e-government effectiveness.

It is, however, recognized that establishing an e-government is more than just setting up a Web site. A normative model is available for gauging the scope and breadth of e-government offerings (Layne & Lee, 2001). It assesses the maturity of e-governments on two key aspects – the extent of e-government offerings, as determined by the level of bureaucratic and technological complexity; and the extent to which the offerings, as measured by delivery of data and services, are integrated. Based on an examination of these parameters, a four-phase evolution of an e-government has been proposed by the authors: catalog, transaction, vertical integration and horizontal integration. This model has been used more recently by Holden, Norris and Fletcher (2003).

In the case of Singapore, the e-government movement is of an advanced nature. So far, it has not been the subject of a scholarly study in the international journal literature. We will assess the e-government in Singapore by drawing on the normative model to some extent as well as using other attributes.

To the extent that e-government is more about streamlining the interaction between government and people as well as between government and businesses in a cost-effective manner, the Singapore experience has been a success. The e-government Web site features a catalogue of services and information, and it permits transactions at a secure level. As of now, a significant percentage of the services have been integrated across the various government agencies. It has, however, not reached the desired level, and this would be the thrust of the eGovernment Action Plan 2, which is currently being implemented and is expected to be completed by 2006. Bureaucratic complexity has been drastically streamlined, with new technologies supporting the government Web presence.

*Table 8: Global e-government index for 2001*

| Country | Web presence | PCs /100 | Internet hosts /1000 | % pop online | Tele Lines /100 | Mobile Phones /100 | Human Dev Index | Info access index | Urban % of total pop | E-govt index |
|---|---|---|---|---|---|---|---|---|---|---|
| USA | 4 | 58.52 | 2928.32 | 62.1 | 69.97 | 36.45 | .934 | .999 | 77.0 | 3.11 |
| Australia | 4 | 46.46 | 843.52 | 52.5 | 52.41 | 44.63 | .936 | .999 | 84.7 | 2.60 |
| New Zealand | 4 | 36.02 | 900.87 | 46.1 | 49.57 | 40.25 | .913 | .999 | 85.7 | 2.59 |
| Singapore | 4 | 48.31 | 437.56 | 49.3 | 48.57 | 68.38 | .876 | .333 | 100.0 | 2.58 |
| Norway | 4 | 49.05 | 1009.31 | 54.4 | 72.91 | 70.26 | .939 | .999 | 75.1 | 2.55 |
| Canada | 4 | 39.02 | 768.68 | 46.5 | 67.65 | 28.46 | .936 | .999 | 77.0 | 2.52 |
| United Kingdom | 4 | 33.78 | 280.75 | 55.3 | 56.72 | 66.96 | .923 | .916 | 89.4 | 2.52 |
| Netherlands | 3.5 | 39.48 | 1017.49 | 54.4 | 60.67 | 67.12 | .931 | .999 | 89.3 | 2.51 |
| Denmark | 3.75 | 43.15 | 626.60 | 54.7 | 75.25 | 60.99 | .921 | .999 | 85.3 | 2.47 |
| Germany | 4 | 33.64 | 248.30 | 34.5 | 60.12 | 58.59 | .921 | .916 | 87.3 | 2.46 |

*Source: Ranagan, 2002*

*Table 9: Ranking of Singapore e-government by international agencies*

| Year | Agency and /or Award | Rank |
|------|----------------------|------|
| 2000 | Commonwealth Association for Public Administration and Management International Award | Bronze medal for eCitizen Portal |
| 2001 | Accenture's 2nd Annual Survey on E-government | 2 |
| 2002 | Accenture's 3rd Annual Survey on E-government | 2 |
| 2002 | Economist Intelligence Unit's E-readiness rankings | 11 out of 60 |
| 2002 | Stockholm Challenge Award for Portal Information | 1 for eCitizen Portal |
| 2003 | World Economic Forum's Global Information Technology Report for E-government Category | 1 |
| 2003 | Accenture's E-government Leadership in Engaging the Customer Report | 2 |

*Source: http://www.egov.gov.sg*

The maturity of the e-government in Singapore has attracted international attention from a number of quarters. In an assessment of the progress of member states of the United Nations in moving towards e-government, Singapore was ranked 4th in 2001 (Table 8). The e-government index was calculated by considering three key measures: scope of online presence of government, efficiency of telecommunications infrastructure, and level of human resource capacity.

It can be seen that Singapore is the only Asian country to be among the top ten e-governments in the world for the year 2001. Singapore's 4th rank attests to the high weightage that it has garnered for the three measures used to assess e-government effectiveness. Other rankings from different organizations are reflected in Table 9.

Investments in e-governments have to be made on an ongoing basis. Governments cannot abdicate responsibility after their initial investments. They have to be committed to incremental investments to sustain operations at effective levels. This is because accumulated experiences and cognizance of evolving practices elsewhere necessitate the need for changing or fine-tuning of the format of services delivered online and also for improving service delivery. In the long run, these investments will be more than amortized by the savings in humanpower as well as by the greater generation of economic activity by businesses. Moreover the e-government experiment will succeed only if governments make a conscious effort to be committed. An e-government entails a quantum jump in responsibility for the government. If this objective is not a strategic goal of the government, it is difficult to engage society and business at large. In Singapore, this has been ensured through liberal investments in the ICT infrastructure of the e-government. For example, following the S$1.5 billion invested by the government over the years 2000-2003, another S$1.3 billion has been made available for the years 2003-2006

(Soh, 2003) in order to further streamline the provision of services to the public through the integration of the functions of the various agencies as well as to further bridge the digital divide that exists between them.

A phased development in the setting up of an e-government has advantages. Singapore started off in 1995 with just a portal offering information. With eGovernment Action Plan 1, over 1,600 services have been placed online over the years 2000-2003, this is more a migration of traditional counter services on to the Web platform (Chua, 2003). In a survey carried out in 2002, 75% of people who did transactions with the government did so once through the e-government Web site and, of these, 80% were satisfied with the quality of service (Soh, 2003). With eGovernment Action Plan 2, launched in July 2003, the objective is to integrate the services across the various government agencies over the years 2003-2006 so that the public can get more of the desired services at a one-stop portal (Chua, 2003). The latter is akin to the embedding of a systems solution approach (Dunn & Yamashita, 2003), whereby a total solution is delivered to citizens. It is recognized that this entails creation of a value chain, whereby the various agencies providing point solutions merge seamlessly onto a platform to provide this service. This necessitates a mindset change whereby the agencies do not work separately to justify their effectiveness but instead work to streamline the overall work processes involved in a citizen-centric task. At the same time, the arising synergies can be captured for the common benefit. One concern is the overall accountability, which has to be defined clearly.

Though an e-government is accompanied by the migration of a number of counter services online, citizens will not warm towards these initiatives unless the service is incentivized by lower fees and increased conveniences. The payment regime for such services has thus to be streamlined for the public to make use of it. A raft of changes would thus need to be made for services that entail payment of fees. In putting counter services online in Singapore, the schedule of fees payable has been streamlined downwards so that more people have been encouraged to transact online.

With more than 1,600 government services having been migrated onto the Internet platform, many citizens have realized a slew of conveniences and savings – no more commuting to government agencies to pay for bills and renew licenses, no more waiting in long queues for fulfillment of these services, no more taking of annual leave to attend to mundane tasks, and so forth. With many of the requisite functions Web-enabled, the government chalks up considerable savings in not having to print forms and incur mailing charges for such transactions and services. We reckon that all these must have also contributed to the diminution of congestion levels on the freeways.

A good example of the productivity increments that have been achieved by migrating processes onto the e-platform is afforded by the electronic filing of income tax returns. Set up at a cost of S$2.2 million in 1998, this system has been estimated to contribute to a savings of S$2.70 per e-filing – mainly through reduced paperwork, absence of mailing expenses, and electronic storage of documents (Poon, 2000). The popularity of the system can be gauged from the number of people who have been e-filing their tax returns over the years: 113,000 in 1998, 484,000 in 2000, 690,000 in 2001 and 700,000 in 2003.

In migrating the various processes onto the e-platform, there has been required a drastic dismantling and simplifying of various work processes and protocols. Though these are necessary for the bureaucracy to function, too much red tape can constrain the effectiveness of public administration – in Singapore, an e-platform has been a blessing to do away with unnecessary procedures as well as legacy protocols of earlier times. The enthusiasm of civil servants in warming to this new system has been found to be great.

The hierarchical culture of the civil service in Singapore has been streamlined to a significant extent through the creation of an e-government. The e-mails of all public officers, including ministers and other elected representatives, are available in the public domain, and the public can connect or follow up with the appropriate official for their requisite needs. The fact that the upper echelons of the public administration are within e-mail reach by citizens poses added responsibility on the part of the bureaucracy to remain responsive, effective and answerable – a challenge which has to be realized by prompt service levels and commitment. This has been effective in enhancing governance and promoting transparency in the way the government works. A feedback field is available on the Web sites of all government agencies so that the public can provide feedback as well as comments about the quality of their service. All these have been found to enhance the democratic process of governance. The presence of stakeholders who may pose resistance to changes (Janssen, Wagenaar & Beerens, 2003) has not been found to be a factor in Singapore.

In Singapore, ICT infrastructure is of a very high standard. Internet penetration rates and PC ownership in homes are also high. These have been factors that have helped to pivot the populace to embrace e-government initiatives in good measure as well as allow the dynamics and determinants of the new governance to evolve. One interesting development has been the desire for the online population to have a greater say in government policies and the kind of society that they want to live in. Such facilitation of the decision making process by involving citizens has been found to be a healthy experience. The government has made it mandatory for all its agencies to post their policy consultation papers on the Web in order to get feedback from the public. It is noted that substantial feedback is often provided by the public in this regard.  This has to be taken into consideration by the agencies before fine-tuning the policies for the parliamentary process. Such an accommodative stance in listening to the "ground" has been a development of significance, and it has been harnessed to good effect by the various agencies. The social capital engendered by the visibility of citizen participation has resulted in the evolution of interest groups that are taking a stake in the fine- tuning of polices and enlarging the scope of accountability of public policies and issues – discussion forums on a range of issues abound in the e-government Web site. Northrop and Thorson (2003) have characterized this development as a web of governance in which there are multiple sets of overlapping relationships.

In recent times, global economic conditions have been greatly affected by the forces of globalization and increasing competition. Governments face the challenge of "doing more with less" to an increasingly sophisticated citizenry. The Singapore experience show that e-government initiatives can realize cost savings for people and businesses, and this allows the bureaucracy to remain lean and efficient, all of which have fiscal considerations during budget sessions in parliament.

One aspect of e-government that does not appear to have been adequately addressed in the literature is the use of Intranets by government agencies. In Singapore, all government departments have their own Intranets. Availability of Intranets is an important aspect of streamlining the functioning of public administration – communication is generally by e-mail among officers, circulars are generally sent over this platform, leave form and transport claims are processed electronically, and so forth. All agencies have their own Webmasters and ICT departments, including helpdesks. Availability of Intranets ensures that the necessary citizen-centric tasks are attended to promptly. All these have contributed to decreasing the paper trail as well as allowed workstations of officers to be lean and not crammed with unnecessary filing cabinets.

# Lessons for Other Countries

The Singapore experience with e-government offers several pointers for other countries contemplating the establishment of an online version of the civil service or for improving it further:

- A national ICT plan is important for prioritizing development. Computerization of the civil service followed by reengineering of internal administrative processes is of pressing importance. Availability of Internet access in a cost-effective manner for citizens is imperative for the benefits to be realized by the public.

- A political vision is a pre-requisite to transpose public administration onto an e-government platform in order to realize new age governance. This will provide the necessary momentum for government agencies to reinvent themselves. Public administrators everywhere generally display a certain amount of inertia in embracing new paradigms, especially those which call for mindset changes in the way things are done. A reading of the technological horizon by the political masters helps to pivot public administration on to new horizons, especially when new technologies and policies need to be grappled with and new ways of doing things need to be introduced.

- An e-government that exists merely as a portal with little interactivity or potential for transactions has a lot of drawbacks. Mere provisioning of information on government portals, though serving a useful purpose, makes the e-government a one-way traffic between the civil service and the general public. It is, however, recognized that information provision on the Web is a way to get started on the e-government movement.

- It is essential to identify priority sectors for provisioning the programming of services.

- Multi-agency co-ordination is very important in reducing the paper trail for the public - a one-stop portal is imperative.

- Trained civil service staff who are ICT literate and who are able to configure manual work processes unique to developmental needs into virtual realms are imperative. They need to veer towards a mindset of being citizen-centric rather than process-oriented.

- Setting up an e-government is not cheap. Only a government that places a premium on delivering quality services to its citizenry will sink funds into this, knowing well that the amortization on the investments is far greater in the long term.

- E-government is more about providing citizens and businesses access to the government. Though, in Singapore, home PC ownership stands at 60% and Internet penetration rates exceed 70%, there is recognition that for the realization of the benefits of e-government, it is necessary to also reach out to those who are not connected and to those who are on the wrong side of the digital divide. Access to connecting technologies is not yet a fundamental right for citizens but measures to help veer these people towards the vision of e-government are necessary. To further this aim, a network of e-clubs across Singapore provides free access to the Internet for people who do not have access to such facilities; free training is also provided for them. In developing countries, an e-government approach could perhaps aim to foster the evolution of such e-clubs, as pursuing network connectivity on an ubiquitous basis may not be that easy, given that standards of living and GDP have yet to reach the desired levels. .

- Service provisioning standards need to be set so that work can be cognized for effectiveness.

- The PSI has demonstrated its enabling dimension in the evolution to e-government in an interactive and transactional manner. It is a generic architecture that affords scalability. As it is likely that government agencies have developed their own ICT systems, the challenge of integrating these systems is likely to pose problems with regard to interoperability and presenting a united front to the public. Riding on the PSI also entails the need to review internal administrative processes so that the network synergies help to make these more efficient for e-governance.

- Initiatives such as TradeNet, E-judiciary and E-stamping have proved their effectiveness, and other countries may wish to emulate such practices.

- The necessary metrics of what constitutes good governance needs to be defined. It is necessary to move away from traditional rubrics to a new portfolio of metrics based on customer satisfaction, agency effectiveness and inter-agency integration.

- With advances in technology, cost of PCs and other enabling accoutrements have decreased. The availability of a multi-vendor environment, where competitive pressure is used as an additional instrument to promote cost effective purchases, has been well entrenched in Singapore. This has been a factor in the rise in PC ownership in homes. Civil servants are given interest-free loans to purchase PCs. All libraries, schools and community centres also offer free access to the Internet.

Whilst Singapore's compact city state structure and high ICT infrastructure have permitted the maturation of the e-government movement, it needs to be recognized that such conditions may not exist elsewhere. Accordingly, our recommendations must be qualified with this rider. As one of the top three e-governments in the world, Singapore's experience has, however, useful pointers to offer in terms of best practices and what works. It can also be used as a case study for other countries to replicate such experiments in the context of their own unique circumstances.

# Conclusion

Transition to an e-government is accompanied by increased levels of responsibility for the public sector. This recognition is crucial for sensitizing the civil service to their obligations to the citizenry when a virtual annex is set up. They must also be cognizant of the need to be market responsive and results-oriented when the full transition to e-government become a reality in their country. It is suggested that aspects of the Singapore experience would be useful for other countries.

# References

Achievements of the first e-government action plan in government to citizens (G2C). Retrieved August 19, 2003, from: *http://www.egov.gov.sg/g2c.htm.*

Chua, L. (2003). eGAP II. *Computerworld Singapore, 9*(37), 27-31.

Cohen, S., & Eimicke, W. (2003). The future of e-government: A project of potential trends and issues. *Proceedings of the 36th Hawaii International Conference on Systems Science.* , Los Alamos, CA: IEEE Computer Society.

Dunn, D., & Yamashita, K. (2003). Micro capitalism and the mega corporation. *Harvard Business Review, 81*(8), 47-54.

Dutta, S., & Jain, A. (2002). The networked readiness of nations. In S. Dutta, B. Lonvin & P. Fiona (Eds), *Global Information Technology Report 2002-2003* (pp. 2-25). London: Oxford University Press.

Heeks, R. (2000). *Reinventing government in the information age: Practices in information technology public sector reform.* London: Routledge Publications.

Holden, S.H., Norris, D.F., & Fletcher, P.D. (2003). Electronic government at the grassroots: Contemporary evidence and future trends. *Proceedings of the 36th Hawaii International Conference on Systems Science.* Los Alamos, CA: IEEE Computer Society.

Jakob, G. (2003). Electronic government: Perspectives and pitfalls of online administrative procedures. *Proceedings of the 36th Hawaii International Conference on Systems Science.* Los Alamos, CA: IEEE Computer Society.

Janssen, M., Wagener, R., & Beerens, J. (2003). Towards a flexible ICT architecture for multi-channel e-government service provisioning. *Proceedings of the 36th Hawaii International Conference on Systems Science.* Los Alamos, CA: IEEE Computer Society.

Layne, K., & Lee, J. (2001). Developing fully functional e-government: A four stage model. *Information Quarterly, 18,* 122-134.

Norris, D.F., & Demeter, L.A. (1999). *Computers in American city governments.* 1999 Municipal Yearbook. Washington, DC: ICMA.

Norris, D.F., Fletcher, P.D., & Holden, S.H. (2001). *Is your local government plugged in?* Highlights of the 2000 Electronic Government Survey, Washington, DC.

Norris, D.F., Holden, S.H., & Fletcher, P.D. (2001). *E-government: Web sites and Web access.* Special Data Issue No. 4. Washington, DC: ICMA

Northrop, T.A., & Thorson, S.J. (2003). The web of governance and democratic accountability. *Proceedings of the 36th Hawaii International Conference on Systems Science.* Los Alamos, CA: IEEE Computer Society.

Poon, A. (2000, December 14). E-government site proves popular with Singaporeans. *The Straits Times,* H14.

Prins, J.E.J. (2001). *Designing e-government: On the crossroads for technological innovation and institutional change.* Amsterdam: Kluwer Law International.

Ronaghan, S. (2002). *Benchmarking e-government: A global perspective.* United Nations Division for Public Economics & Public Administration and American Association for Public Administration.

Soh, N. (2003, July 16). Government takes $1.3 billion step to put more services online. *The Straits Times,* 4.

Sprecher, M.H., Talcove, H., & Bowen, D. (1996). *Government Technology, 1,* 47-49.

Tan, F. (Ed.), *Advanced topics in global information management* (pp. 293-311). Hershey, PA: Idea Group Publishing.

Tan, W.H.L., & Subramaniam, R. (1998). Developing countries need to popularizeScience. *New Scientist, 2139,* 52.

Tan, W.H.L., & Subramaniam, R. (1999). Scientific societies build better nations.*Nature, 399,* 633.

Tan, W.H.L., & Subramaniam, R. (2000). Wiring up the island state. *Science, 288,* 621-623.

Tan, W.H.L., & Subramaniam, R. (2001). ADSL, HFC and ATM technologies for a nationwide broadband network. In N. Barr (Ed.), *Global communications* (pp. 97-102). London: Hanson Cooke Publishers.

Tan W.H.L., & Subramaniam, R. (2003). Information and communication technology in Singapore: Lessons for developing nations on the role of government. In Tarabanis, K., Peristeras, V., & Koumpis, A. (2000). *Towards a European information architecture for public administration: The InfoCITIZEN project.* European Conference on Information Systems, London.

Wee, G. (2000). Justice in the high-tech courts. *Computer World, 6*(40), 4-10.

Wee, G. (2001). The e-taxman cometh. *Computer World, 7*(36), 20-26.

Wong, P.K. (2001). Globalization and E commerce: Growth and impacts in Singapore. Report for Centre for Research on Information Technology and Organizations, University of California. Retrieved August 11, 2003, from: *http://www.crito.uci.edu/git/publications/pdf/singaporeGEC.pdf.*

Yeo, G. (2003). On the threshold of a new era, *The Strait Times,* 15 July 2003, p. 6.

**Chapter XIV**

# Towards an
# E-Government
# Solution:

# A South African Perspective

Shawren Singh, University of South Africa, South Africa

Goonasagree Naidoo, University of Cape Town, South Africa

*Cecil Rhodes wanted to build a railroad from Cape Town to Cairo in order to subjugate the continent. Now we want to build an information super-highway from Cape to Cairo which will liberate the continent (Jay Naidoo, X-South African Minister of Communications).*

## Abstract

*With the rapid technological development, electronic governance is a justifiable reality. In this chapter we look at the unique environment under which the South African electronic government is developing. The purpose of this chapter is to report on the first results towards the establishment of an e-government strategy for South African, considering its multicultural and multilingual society.*

# Introduction

While flying into Johannesburg International Airport one looks out of the aircraft's window and sees the South African urban landscape. On the one side is a lush, beautiful first world urban suburb with wide roads, tiled roofs, sparkling swimming pools and double storied houses. To the other side one sees a "human" settlement with dirt roads, shanty living structures and barren looking tree-less wasteland. Yet South Africa can be described as a melting pot of different cultures. These cultures add to the rich South African heritage. South Africa is one of very few countries to boasts 11 official languages. However, this cultural diversity poses quite a unique challenge for designers of software, especially when one has to design Web-based software.

Almost 10 years have passed since South Africa earned its place among the "miracles" of the twentieth century. In an epoch highlighted by the horrors that erupted in the Balkans, the Rwandan genocide and the prolonged violence of the Israeli-Palestinian struggle, a seemingly intractable conflict at the tip of Africa ended in a political settlement that appeared to refute the rhythms of history.

The Global Entrepreneurship Monitor (GEM) (Reynolds, Camp, Bygrave, Autio & Hay, 2001) report describes South Africa as follows. *Entrepreneurial Activity* – in terms of the proportion of adults engaged in entrepreneurship, South Africa ranks in the middle (9.4%) among GEM 2001 countries. A relatively high proportion of entrepreneurship (31%) is motivated by necessity. More than 1 person in 25 has invested in a start-up business in South Africa. This is a relatively high proportion and ranks third among the GEM 2001 countries. *Unique National Features* – South Africa's economy has been dramatically liberalized following several decades of isolation and protection. Although the economy is stable, economic growth remains weak. Historically, the economy has been highly concentrated, dominated by a handful of large state-owned enterprises and corporations, and relying heavily on commodities in mining and agriculture. Until the 1990s, policy makers largely neglected smaller entrepreneurial enterprises. South Africa is a country of stark contrasts, socially, economically and geographically. In urban areas, sophisticated industrial centers contrast with informal settlements. In rural areas, commercial agriculture contrasts with communities lacking the most basic services and relying on remittances from migrant workers. A highly educated, globally mobile minority contrasts with the majority who face poverty and high unemployment. *Key Issues* – The previous apartheid policies prevented black people from owing and running business, and many Black South Africans have little business experience. Despite a recent explosion of entrepreneurial activity, successful entrepreneurs do not receive wide recognition. Professional or corporate careers are held in greater esteem than business ownership. In the past, the education system and an authoritarian society actively discouraged creativity and independence, leading many South Africans to have a negative view of their ability to succeed on their own. The new school curriculum has a strong focus on entrepreneurship and management skills. However, the lack of basic literacy and numeracy, as well as more technical skills, continues to exert a serious constraint. Access to micro-enterprise finance is limited. Poverty, a lack of resources and a lack of business skills and experience make it difficult for many potential entrepreneurs to access financial resources. The administrative burden placed on small firms by the requirements of legislation is substantial and discourages many entrepreneurs from formalizing their business.

Designing the electronic frontier in this environment is therefore a major challenge. This is further complicated by the language and cultural diversity of the people of South Africa. The purpose of this chapter is to report on the first results towards the establishment of an e-government (EG) strategy for South African multicultural and multilingual society.

# The State of the Internet in South Africa

Internet access in South Africa continues to grow year-on-year, but the rate of growth is slower than ever before. South Africa has little more that 3 million Internet users; however South Africa lags behind the rest of the world, and will continue to do so until the local telecommunication climate is more favourable.

The Goldstuck Report: Internet Access in South Africa (2002) reveals that only 1 in 15 South Africans had access to the Internet at the end of last year. By the end of 2002, Internet access will have improved only marginally, to 1 in 14 South Africans. According to the report, the slow growth is largely a factor of delays in licensing a second network operator, Telkom's own uncompromising attitude towards Internet service providers, and market ignorance about the continued value of the Internet in the wake of the technology market crash of 2000 and 2001 (Goldstuck, 2002).

The key findings of the report are:

- One out of every 15 South Africans had access to the Internet at the end of 2001. This compares with at least one out of every two people in countries like the USA, Canada, South Korea, Singapore and Hong Kong. China, at one out of 18, is catching up fast despite its huge population and underdeveloped infrastructure. At current growth rates, there will still be only 1 in 10 South Africans with Internet access by 2006.

- The total number of South Africans with access to the Internet at the end of 2001 was 2.89 million.

- This grew by less than 10% to 3.1 million by the end of 2002. This is the lowest growth rate since the public was first given access to the Internet in 1994.

- Sluggish dial-up growth stands in dramatic contrast to the growth in the total number of leased lines - permanent high-speed connections to the Internet - installed in South African businesses. The number reached just under 7,000 at the end of 2001, reflecting an insatiable demand for bandwidth among corporate users of the Internet. This year the number of leased lines will see a growth rate of around 20% in total market size.

- Only a small handful of ISPs are profitable, but there is no specific business model that guarantees profitability. Neither size small or large, nor target market (corporate or consumer) is an indicator of success. In the corporate market, Internet Solution is the most profitable ISP, while in the dial-up space World Online is the only major ISP operating profitably. An increasing number of ISPs are profitable on an EBITDA basis (earnings before interest, tax, depreciation and amortisation). In short, it is no longer uncommon for ISPs to be operating profitably, but they still have a legacy of debt.

- The number of ISPs has grown dramatically in the past year, largely due to the rollout of a Virtual ISP service by Internet Solution and the continued heavy use of the equivalent service from SAIX.

- Business strategies in the ISP industry are maturing to the extent that it has become possible to create a model that explains not only how ISPs evolve, but also how they meet their clients' needs as those needs evolve.

- While the industry faces seemingly insurmountable challenges, it remains a stable industry. Only a tiny proportion of ISPs in South Africa have gone out of business through bankruptcy.

- Mobile access to the Internet has been a non-starter, with only a tiny proportion of those people who have appropriate devices actually using the devices to connect to the Internet.

- The arrival of GPRS, the so-called 2.5 generation of mobile network technology, may alter the mobile access picture during 2003, but only if appropriate handsets become available.

- Community centres, resource centres and digital villages in townships will continue to underachieve in their goals of bringing Internet access to a sizeable proportion of residents in disadvantaged areas.

"There are positive signs amid the access gloom," Goldstuck points out. "The educational environment in particular is poised for a boom in access, with numerous projects under way to connect schools up to the Internet. That will not only be a positive intervention in the short term, but will provide a healthy underpinning for long-term growth of Internet access in South Africa."

## What is Electronic Government?

An e-delivery strategy in public management is not only about the automation of the current way of doing business. It is about re-engineering the current way of doing business, by using collaborative transactions and processes required by the government departments to function effectively and economically, thus improving the quality of life for citizens and promoting competition and innovation. To put it simply, EG is about empowering a country's citizens. The vision is ultimately about inclusion, that is, the ability of all people to take part in the economy. The Internet makes it possible for the government to streamline its interaction with business people, private citizens and government agencies, while ensuring:

- improved public access to government information and services;
- improved quality and cost-effectiveness of government services;
- effective information sharing and communication with its citizens;
- improved opportunities for participation in democratic institutions; and
- better relationships with business people and private citizens.

At the heart of the e-delivery strategy is the recognition that e-business or EG is not about technology; rather it is about changing the way in which organisations operate. Business processes need to be changed and re-aligned to be able to take advantage of electronic technology. Furthermore, if customer satisfaction is not ensured, the systems will fall into disrepute. Thus, metrics must be clearly defined and continuous and accurate measurement implemented. The three critical metrics to measure the effectiveness of EG are application and service relevance; citizen and business satisfaction; and preservation of trust.

The business drivers of EG are somewhat different from the standard e-business drivers and cognisance of this must be taken. There are a number of key business drivers which are both internally and externally focused in relation to the government departments, namely:

- e-enabling citizens;
- information management;
- channel expansion;
- social inclusion;
- universal access;
- accessibility; and
- economic service delivery.

The key is to find technology platforms and applications that can drive the transition towards a new model for doing business in government. These must satisfy such basic requirements as the empowerment of citizens, ease of access to services, the enhancement of government image, the inclusion of citizens and leverage of emerging technologies. EG initiatives will help transform many industries, but organisations must understand the factors that will inhibit and those that will stimulate this change.

In South Africa, the small medium and micro enterprise (SMME) sector is vital to the economic success of the country. This is because the contribution of the SMMEs to stimulating economic growth and job creation is unparalleled in terms of speed-to-market, financial flow, informal channels, sources of innovation and countrywide reach.

It is not enough to assume that the SMME entrepreneurs will take advantage of available technologies. There needs to be a clear definition of this environment in terms of EG initiatives, which require that the respective government departments are knowledgeable about EG, and that the required functionality is available with minimum requirements for financial or technological input from the SMMEs. It is therefore important that suitable EG structures are in place to assist the SMME marketplace.

Closely linked to EG is the overall concept of e-governance, which deals with the transformation of the business of government and the transformation of governance itself. Citizens are becoming accustomed to going online, ordering exactly what they want and then receiving the item within a few days. They will inevitably expect the same kind of fulfillment from their government officials. It is not enough to simply put in new systems; the government has to find ways to respond to people timeously as well. As users begin to interact with the government online and experience the increased benefits, a greater degree of trust will be created. This is the arena in which it will ultimately be decided whether EG succeeds or fails.

Electronic technology can be used in all facets of the public service. It should be seen as the necessary infrastructure for government into the 21st century. The medium-term goal should be to implement an EG which allows citizens instant access to information and services through an efficient process and which will fundamentally change the relationship between the government and the people in South Africa.

The information revolution is affecting how governments respond to the needs of their clients in the public sector. It has opened up new possibilities for the delivery of programs and services in government ministries. A defining characteristic of the South African public sector has been the existence of infrastructure to deliver programs through a network of points of service to certain communities. The South African government is now experimenting with new organisational models, such as the electronic model, to deliver services to all communities; namely, those that were denied basic services, as in the case of disadvantaged rural communities. The information revolution lessens the need for a large physical infrastructure to deliver programs and services to the public. Efficiencies can be achieved through the sharing of data among departments, and the provision of a "single-window" of service delivery. With the use of networks and information sharing, organisational boundaries do not serve as impediments to service delivery, as is the case with traditional organisational models. New information technologies allow for integrated databases and common program delivery. Clients will be able to face a "seamless" government in their daily interactions for programs and services. Hence, the legitimacy and relevance of government can actually be enhanced by improved service delivery. New information technologies thus offer the possibility of close and ongoing interaction between government and citizens. More importantly, online information would result in the affirmation of previously disadvantaged groups. Online forms of governance are non-discriminatory, faceless and consistent. Furthermore, online forms of governance are replicable and empowering.

# Impact of Electronic Technology on South Africa

According to Shilubane (2001) electronic technology "is the continuous optimization of government service delivery, constituency participation and governance by transforming internal and external relationships through technology, the Internet and new media". This implies the transformation of how citizens, be they legal or natural persons, perceive and experience government.

It is evident that globalisation and information technology are impacting on how South Africa (SA) conducts business and how government implements its day-to-day activities. Globalisation suggests that South Africa should be linked to the international community and to the degree to which companies can interact productively with the global community. Hence, the electronic model of service delivery will open up new opportunities for South Africa; for example, global markets and small business will be able to compete on an equal footing with big business. The electronic model is also an opportunity to promote economic growth through the creation of SMMEs and the expansion of South African businesses into new markets. The electronic model will also level the playing field for small and large entities in South Africa, as these entities can extend into local and international markets and increase revenue potential. Hence, South African companies need to become globally profitable and to measure up to international benchmarks. The electronic model thus presents new opportunities to achieve a more level playing field vis-à-vis larger, more developed economies. The Internet can thus be a great force for economic development, the spread of democracy and for the promotion of communication and understanding. Furthermore, it diminishes existing advantages of cost, communication, and information and can create huge markets for indigenous products and services. The electronic model is, therefore, the indispensable prerequisite for sustainable economic development, for job creation, promoting social equality, improving service delivery and overcoming poverty in South Africa (Singh, 2002).

Another important feature of the electronic model is that it expands the size of any organizational entity from its immediate geographic area to a potentially worldwide area. This expansion into other markets and opportunities for existing and new businesses has created a potential for accelerating economic growth in South Africa, including relatively poor and rural areas. There will be a huge need for business development support programs and for training in the electronic model applications such as the Web design, interactive media, different languages and other training. There is also a need for sharing of information and experience among Web-based businesses, as market opportunities, strategic advantages, and unique approaches could be of value to all counterparts in South Africa (Department of Communications, 1999).

One of the most important benefits of the electronic model for South Africa is the opportunity to "leapfrog" into the knowledge paradigm. In this respect, the electronic model will have an impact on all aspects of society, not just the commercial or public sector. Nevertheless, progress with respect to the electronic model has been mainly evident in the private sector. The government can play an important role in examining the economic and social impact of the electronic model and promote an understanding of the model as well as create an enabling environment so that the model can succeed also in government (Liebenberg, 2000).

However, while many companies and communities in South Africa are beginning to take advantage of the potential of electronic technology, critical challenges remain to be overcome before its potential can be fully realised for the benefit all South Africans. The government, therefore, has an important role to play, in that it must establish policy for improving the quality of life of all citizens through equitable development, and thereby set new precedents for the role of the electronic model in the country. It must, however, adhere closely to international principles, while nevertheless maintaining the broad focus on fostering widespread economic growth, opportunity, and global integration (Department of Communications, 1999).

In this regard, South Africa is committed to promoting economic growth and development in the region, since Southern African Development Community (SADC) constitutes an important market for South African goods and services. The government, together with business, can therefore play a vital role in promoting the growth of the electronic model by instituting appropriate policies with respect to education, industry, technology, the economy, technical assistance and human resource development programs, to enable the country to move from a traditional to an information society. Thus, government must become familiar with rules, frameworks, vague pointers, to assist in understanding and dealing with the electronic model (Liebenberg, 2000). The government's influence must take on new dimensions.

The electronic model can also be an important strategy in building the country's comparative or competitive advantage (Evans, 2001). The electronic model presents unique opportunities for South Africa to greatly expand its markets, both internally and externally. Externally, the Internet and other technologies may allow for low-cost international trade, even for small local businesses. Internally, marginalised communities may gain affordable access to, amongst others, government services and financial services, and may participate in all aspects of the economy. Companies and the public can conduct their business from any location. Hence, rural areas may become the focus for investment and market expansion and also for relocating corporate offices (Department of Communications, 1999).

With respect to job opportunities, if the electronic model generates significant economic growth, this should lead to increased employment opportunities both in the private and public sector. However, initially workers could be displaced as a direct result of transformation as the skills and experience required for the electronic model could be significantly different from traditional employment skills. There could be a short-term risk to workers whose current jobs and skills may become obsolete. The counterpoint to this argument is that there should be considerable long-term opportunities. Nevertheless, the Internet can provide direct employment opportunities in software, data processing and many other information-intensive jobs for those skilled in ICTs (Department of Communications, 1999).

However, an efficient and versatile infrastructure, finances and a skilled labour force are required for the electronic model of service delivery in South Africa. Such an environment can facilitate electronic service delivery, domestic trade and also enable rapid growth in international markets, which is an area of critical growth, since export markets will be the largest single source of gross domestic product expansion for South Africa (Evans, 2001).

# Implications of the Electronic Model for Public Sector Delivery in South Africa

Governments globally are demonstrating the advantages of electronic government, namely by conducting transactions electronically as well as electronic service delivery. Business imperatives entail improving customer service, focusing resources on core areas, and increasing competitiveness both nationally and internationally. By changing to the electronic model of service delivery, government will be based on business-like practices and principles, cost savings and an enhanced environment (Department of Communications, 2000). The electronic model is vital for the public sector as it can open up new opportunities, namely a reduction in the number of paper transactions involved in government operations, public participation in decision making, government purchasing of goods and services, electronic payments and improvements in service delivery. In this regard, Keen and McDonald (2000) argue that the electronic model of service delivery is an opportunity not to be missed. The electronic model is important as it can rapidly improve service delivery and productivity.

In order to obtain real benefits of the electronic model for better service delivery, better procurement, efficient working and better communication with citizens and businesses, government is preparing a comprehensive system for implementation in the public sector. The electronic model entails a shift to the customer, where citizens must be able to access more public services online at their convenience at any time and at any place. Thus, services must be integrated and "customer centric," aligned to the "Batho-Pele" service delivery framework of the South African government. Hence, the electronic model presents both opportunities and challenges for government. As a catalyst for economic growth, the government simultaneously faces demands to make services more accessible, responsive and affordable to the public. The South African government sees the value of the electronic model as efficient means to deliver public services, such as education and health care, to the broader population (Evans, 2001). In this regard, the fact that many services can now be delivered electronically has implications for the government's service commitments, since many of these commitments were made without considering electronic service delivery (Department of Communications, 2000).

The advances in technology hold great potential for helping government respond to its challenges, namely, better service delivery, better procurement, efficient working and better communication with citizens and businesses. The public sector should be responsive to the needs of citizens and service delivery should be of high quality (Evans, 2001). By linking government at all levels within and across department lines, and by improving citizen access, convenient and efficient methods of conducting government business are enabled. Hence, the organisational and operational changes will take place on many fronts and in many ways. However, at their core, all are driven by an architecture and an infrastructure that allow for information to be seamlessly moved across government, between its various programs and ultimately, to citizens and businesses. By providing online access to information and services through phones, faxes, self-service kiosks and World Wide Web, government can provide higher quality, faster service to the public. Such initiatives hold great benefits, but the lack of strategy and synergy among various ministries may continue to be a significant barrier (Department of Communications, 2000).

Through the application of advanced network technology and the deployment of multiple service delivery points, government can overcome barriers of time and distance and become better positioned (Liebenberg, 2000). Continued progress in areas such as competitiveness, quality and effectiveness of traditional government services will enable government to address a number of criticisms, namely, that government is not customer-focused, it is not delivering, and it fails to stimulate economic growth. As a result, the South African government is striving not only to improve the efficiency and quality of services, but also to ensure that services are delivered at the most convenient times and locations via electronic media. The adoption of the electronic model will, however, involve a fundamental shift in government because the changes implied by the electronic model will affect the core operational and managerial aspects of government. The scope of the electronic model in government will extend to what it can do, to a network of stakeholders (such as the public/customer, a network of suppliers, intermediaries and others). However, government must integrate vertical operations with virtual integration (Liebenberg, 2000).

The benefits of EG for South Africa must be tangible and should include at least the following (Babcock, 2000; Czerniawska & Potter, 1998):

- It should make it easier for businesses and individuals to deal with government;
- It should enable government to offer services and information through new media such as the Internet or interactive TV;
- Improve government efficiency and effectiveness through automating processes and streamlining processes;
- Communication between different government departments and functions should be improved so that people do not have to be asked repeatedly for the same information by different service providers;
- EG should improve access to information – either via call centres or the Internet – so that government departments can deal with members of the public more efficiently and more helpfully;
- Different parts of government should be more easily able to work in partnership: central government with local authorities or the voluntary sector, or government with third party delivery channels such as SAPO or the private sector; and
- EG will help government to become a learning entity by improving access to, and organisation of, information.

Some of the ultimate benefits of the electronic model are better-informed citizens, increased productivity, improvement in service delivery and more efficient government.

By using the model applications, for example, in procurement, the impact on operation and service delivery will be tremendous. The South African government is the largest purchaser of products and services, amounting to approximately R65 billion a year. Internet based e-procurement will therefore present tremendous opportunities for the government, namely (Department of Communications, 2000) "reduced prices of materials, shortened acquisition and fulfilment cycles, decreased administration burdens and cost and improved inventory practices; and increased control over purchases".

# Challenges Facing the South African Government

The challenges facing the South African government in transforming conventional government into electronic government are tremendous. In the USA, the huge Internet user base is 100 million, which has given rise to a thriving Business-to-Consumer (B2C) marketplace. It is different in South Africa, where the Internet users number only three million. Although it is agreed that the Internet is a great way to do research and establish customer contact, government departments as well as businesses are generally afraid of the technology (Evans, 2001). Moreover, many organisations are not willing to spend a lot of money on the Internet approach. They are also reluctant as the human element is lacking with this approach. Many government departments, businesses and consumers are still wary of conducting extensive business over the Internet because of the lack of a predictable legal environment governing transactions. Furthermore, most sites on government are no more than electronic brochures. There is a dire lack of understanding of the powerful role the Web can fulfil. For example, government Web sites look electronically enabled but generally are not. Hence, from an on-line strategy point of view, there is no consideration of the customer. Furthermore, there is no effort to market these sites online. Thus, very few government departments are employing the electronic model, despite claims that it is the online element of the Web that is the key to entrepreneurial government based on business like principles and cost savings.

Other challenges that the South African government will face with respect to the electronic model are (Liebenberg, 2000):

- ensuring effective methods of protecting privacy over the Internet;
- identifying possible legal barriers to the development of the electronic model;
- providing education and training on the usage of the electronic model;
- addressing the lack of preparedness by government institutions, consumers, companies and SMMEs; and
- managing the negative socio-economic impacts, for example, job losses and other associated risks.

Concerns centering on issues such as enforcement of contracts, liability, intellectual property protection, privacy, security and other matters have caused government departments, businesses and consumers to be cautious. There are major drawbacks that the South African government must address (Johnson, 2000). The South African government will need to consider the development of a national policy to support and expand the electronic model in South Africa both in government and industry. This should also serve as the underlying philosophy for the establishment of the electronic model for South Africa. Another area on which the electronic model will have an impact is the area of international and national global trading legislation, which will have to be aligned in the context of global trading on the Internet.

Consequently, initiatives over a horizon of 10 years will force the South African government to contend with the ensuing issues (Shilubane, 2001):

- ICT infrastructure is weak in geographical areas in which the majority of citizens live because of the apartheid separate development legacy;

- ICT related goods and services are made available on suppliers' terms, most of which are foreign companies, and the low per capita purchasing power does not allow markets to mature;

- the general education level is lower and ICT degrees are difficult to obtain; hence there is over-dependence on imported ICT goods and services, rather than the development of local solutions;

- organisations have less and shorter experience in using ICT; consequently it takes some time to offer a comprehensive range of services leveraging ICT capabilities;

- information sharing is not common among organisations, and sometimes within an organisation itself, given the old silo/command structures; hence the provision of seamless services is usually hampered by fragmented information systems, and fragmented systems will take a while to inter-operate;

- EG readiness varies significantly between government departments, provinces and local authorities;

- there are pressing demands in the public service, which make ICT development a lower priority in budget terms. The gap between the ICT development scenario and the reality is big, and needs financial priority;

- governments the world over find it difficult to recruit and retain competent ICT professionals. EG endeavours require some in-house champions to undertake planning and oversee developments.

From the above, it is evident that the South African government is confronted with innumerable challenges, similar to other developing economies that need to be addressed.

# Role of the South African Government in Creating an Enabling Environment for the Electronic Model of Service Delivery

The information society will undoubtedly have an impact on ways of communicating, receiving and sending information and new ways of working in South Africa. It offers South Africa an opportunity for development and progress, and also presents new and demanding challenges. Electronic technology has created a new marketplace in which government is required to operate. Hence, we have an arena without conventional rules, which challenges existing practices and notions. This new phenomenon may also defy regulation. This requires careful consideration by the South African government in terms of its implications for the public sector, society and business. Those that are affected by the electronic model will have to play a vital role to help government to move ahead on some of the crucial issues that the model presents (Department of Communications, 1999).

In government use, e-business is about Internet applications that enable the public to access information and interact with government departments on the Web. It is not about reinventing the organisation. It is about providing citizens with better information and new knowledge to make faster, more informed decisions possible. As with any other successful project, it is necessary to formalise the processes in order to realise the benefits. The processes may then be driven by means of standard project management methodologies and, typically, using a program office scenario (Babcock, 2000).

Successful EG takes a strategic approach, leveraging their knowledge and information over time. They capitalise on the information. Government departments need to re-design themselves and the way they provide services to take advantage of the technologies enabling the new digital economy. This means that there must be a definite focus on the way a department connects to its external environment. However, being effective in the external environment requires introspection. Issues that should be considered should include (Roodt, 2001):

- how a government department wants to be relevant in the new economy; and
- how the government organises itself internally and how it allies itself to partners to achieve this.

For EG to provide benefits and value to government and citizens, it will be essential for the functional steps be followed and implemented. The success of EG depends on insight, planning and total commitment. Nevertheless, the main point of contention for government is on how to formulate a coherent policy strategy on the electronic model.

The main concerns for the government on the electronic model in South Africa are identified as (Department of Communications, 1999):

- Deciding on the governing philosophy that guides nation-wide decisions on priorities and options concerning the electronic model of service delivery;

- How and under what organisational structure will the electronic model be co-ordinated;

- Formulation of polices to overcome real and perceived risks to businesses and consumers that can arise in electronic transactions;

- Formulating policies that establish the ground rules applicable to electronically based businesses, on a national and international level;

- Formulating polices for enhancing the information, telecommunication and financial services technologies and facilities that are essential for participation in global e-commerce; and

- Formulation of policies that focus on promoting new business opportunities and on easing the transformation of the economy.


The effective development of the electronic model will require a well co-ordinated and participatory process that involves a wide range of stakeholders in both the public and private sectors. The adoption of the electronic model will involve the integration of many elements of technology, infrastructure, business operation and public policy. The technologies must be fully operational to the operational needs to implement innovative approaches that will promote market development. These requirements will be applicable to all sectors of society, including the public and private sectors. An effective national policy on the electronic model can be established only if disparate operational, legal, regulatory, and enforcement actions within the government, along with technical, marketing, financial, and management strategies in the business sector, are closely aligned. The key concern is whether the government has the capacity to co-ordinate and understand the various issues and initiatives, especially in the area of infrastructure, which must underlie all electronic service delivery. The other areas of concern are briefly outlined below (Department of Communications, 2000):

*Consumer Protection, Privacy and Security:* The South African government will need to secure networks, access points and business-critical applications against theft, fraud, electronic abuse and misuse. Therefore, a number of countermeasures are to be undertaken to ensure that the electronic model is as secure as traditional forms of transaction (Department of Communications, 2000). The South African government must develop policies that build trust in electronic transactions, as there has been an increase in fraud and abuse with transactions online. There must be confidence that electronically based purchases, fund transfers and business deals are valid as traditional practices. Hence, personal information and finances must be secure so that consumers can be well protected against fraud and mistreatment. There must be accountability for the quality, reliability and legality of products and services. This also raises issues, mainly for the South African government, such as national security and facilitating law enforcement, protection of citizens' privacy, encouraging economic well being, and maintaining public safety. Furthermore, as the use of encryption spreads, the result can be access to cryptographic codes or decryption keys by government agencies such as law enforcement and national security (Department of Communications, 1999). The use of the

Internet has also raised new issues concerning confidentiality of records in terms of access to personal details, jurisdiction over storage and use of data, and protection of financial information disclosed in electronic transactions. With respect to enhancing users' sense of privacy protection in the online environment, government regulation could play an important role through specific legislation, to require Web site operators and database owners to conform to certain standards regarding the use of data (Department of Communications, 2000).

*Taxation:* One of the major difficulties that the South African government must face as the electronic model grows is the question of taxation with respect to electronic transactions, and of import duties when they cross international boundaries. Specific new taxes called "bit taxes" may have to be applied to digital transmissions, separate from ordinary taxes, for products and services purchased electronically. With respect to tax collection under the electronic model, there are complications around issues of jurisdiction and institutional roles. Operating on the Internet implies that the physical location of a business is almost irrelevant, and possibly undetectable, as data files and related hardware can be easily moved from one location to another. Hence, tax laws based upon the seller's place of business can become increasingly difficult to enforce (Department of Communications, 1999). In South Africa, there are no specific provisions that cover electronically transmitted goods and services. The tax and tariff policies in South Africa have not yet been updated to encompass the realities of electronic technology.

*Intellectual Property Rights and Domain Names:* Other issues of concern are intellectual property rights and domain names. The future development of the electronic model is dependent on the protection of copyrights and related rights and the protection and equitable allocation of trademarks and domain names. South African laws must conform to treaties with respect to intellectual property rights, including software, recordings and technical designs against illegal pirating and from unfair use of South Africa trademarks. Furthermore, there is no other established legal precedent to ensure protection of companies' trademarks in the virtual environment in South Africa (Department of Communications, 2000).

*Enhancing Infrastructure:* The lack of infrastructure in South Africa has impeded the progress of the electronic model both in the public and private sectors. For the vast section of the population in rural areas, infrastructure is often limited or non-existent, and is unaffordable. Hence, one of the major concerns for the South African government is the need to enhance the national infrastructure to support the electronic model. However, the possibility of participating in the global electronic marketplace and/or electronic model of service delivery is remote for the majority of the population, as there is a low level of basic telephone services in rural areas, and access to computers and data services are even lower (Liebenberg, 2000). Furthermore, the Internet is restricted to particular geographic locations and segments of the population, due to historical inequities in society, and the lack of access to basic telephone service and computers particularly to rural areas (Department of Communications, 1999, 2000).

*Telecommunications Market and Pricing Policy:* Regulation of the telecommunication industry is an important public responsibility to support fair competition and to oversee appropriate pricing and service responsibilities. The prices charged by telecommunications operators for access to crucial services can be an important factor in determining the effectiveness and affordability of the electronic model opportunities on the whole. It is extremely difficult for smaller entrepreneurs, ISPs, and public operators such as telecentres to afford to connect themselves. This will inevitably form a barrier to the electronic model of development. This could create economic barriers, especially for the most disadvantaged users (Evans, 2001).

Although 2.8 million telephone lines will be made available in the next five years throughout South Africa, it is not sufficient to achieve the entire infrastructure needs of the electronic model (Department of Communications, 1999). Many questions will need to be addressed in the context of the market opening policy. These will, amongst others, include the interconnection regulation, treatment of Universal Service Fund contributions, tariff regulation, cross ownership with other industries and the role of ICT in government (Department of Communications, 1999; Evans, 2001).

The South African government must deal with these critical challenges to ensure the successful entrance of the electronic model of governance. In line with its Constitutional mandate, the Department of Public Service and Administration is developing an EG strategy as part of its overall service delivery improvement program. In preparation for a more convenient, efficient, effective and integrated government service delivery system, the Department of Public Services and Administration (DPSA) has commissioned a scooping study. The objective of the scooping is to describe the optimal process by which government can deliver services to citizens, according to critical life cycle events, rather than as defined by government structures and systems. The study will capture the entire interface that takes place in the Government-to-Citizen (G2C) and Government-to-Business (G2B) relationship, from the point of view of providing a single gateway through which citizens can interact with government. The study will focus on mapping both technology enabled information flows, as well as the institutional mechanisms through which they are delivered. The desired outcome of the study is to develop a vision of optimal service delivery, which will reflect those government departments which are better positioned to collect, process, store and disseminate various types of information, as well as suggest the most appropriate mechanisms through which services should be made available to the public (Shilubane, 2001; Singh, 2002).

# Current Initiatives Undertaken by South African Government

The South African government's commitment towards improving service delivery across the population was illustrated in 1995, when Mr. Thabo Mbeki (the then Deputy President of South Africa) stated at the G8 meeting of the information society in Brussels, "we must strive to ensure that each individual whatever his or her station in life, play a meaningful role in decision making and in governance. One of the ways this can be done is to ensure that citizens have access to information." This was reiterated by the South African Minister of Communication in 2001, whereby it was stated that "the South African government believes that every region, province, community and citizen whether urban or rural has to benefit from access to the information economy" (Van Jaarsveld, 2003).

In the budget vote speech for 2002, the South African Minister of the Department of Public Service and Administration announced that "South Africa on-line" is a single electronic gateway that will facilitate access to all information about and services provided by the South African government (Van Jaarsveld, 2003). This initiative implies an end to the tedious process of visiting a multitude of South African government departments to conduct business. Citizens will be able to access all the government services from a single point, for example multipurpose walk-in community centres or kiosks that will be established across South Africa.

The key areas in which the South African government departments and other bodies are currently involved in to effect a national e-governance strategy are (Central Government, 2002):

- Department of Education: Education policies on information technologies and distance learning;
- Department of Labour: Programmes on skills training, technology job placement, policies on industry evolution;
- Department of Health: Tele-medicine programmes, health information database and education initiatives;
- Department of Trade and Industry: World Trade Organisation (WTO) negotiations, imports and customs issues, harmonisation of South African policy with global treaties, and local industrial strategies;
- South African Bureau of Standards (SABS): The establishment and management of standards;
- Department of Finance and the South African Revenue Service: Policies on tax treatment, revenue collection for electronic transactions and imports and customs issues;
- South African Communications Security Agency (SACSA): Looking into policies on cryptography including digital signatures, certification authorities, public key infrastructures;
- Department of Arts, Culture, Science and Technology (DACST): Policies relating to development of technology, particularly the information and communications technology (ICT) sector of the national research and technology foresight project, also cultural expression via new technologies;
- Department of Justice, National Intelligence Agency: Investigation into cyber fraud, illegal transmissions and other security threats, establishment of information technology security policies for government;
- Department of Public Service and Administration (DPSA): Establishment of information technology and information management policies for government;
- Department of Public Works: Electronic archiving of policies and strategies;
- Department of Home Affairs: Development of a national identity card with a smart chip catering for various users; and

- South African Reserve Bank: Initiatives on electronic payments, funds exchange, inter-bank technologies and electronic money.

The South African government's application of ICT in a variety of settings would undoubtedly improve the quality and cost-effectiveness of service delivery, and establish the foundation for the development of ICT applications in the South African private sector. However, there are various perceptions of information and communication technology that would undoubtedly have a major impact on policy and implementation in South Africa. A case study was therefore undertaken to examine these perceptions.

# Case Study on Perceptions of Technology in South Africa

The South Africa population can be described as a fragmented portion of a whole. Each race group (Indigenous Africans [IA], South Africans of mixed decent [SAM], Afro-Asians [AA] and Afro-Europeans [AE]) is uniquely different. For example, the South African democratic government inherited a divided and unequal system of education. Under apartheid, South Africa had 19 different education departments separated by race, geography and ideology; that is, before 1994, IAs, SAMs, AAs and AEs grew up in very different social-political, educational and cultural environments. This education system prepared children in different ways for the positions they were expected to occupy in

*Table 1: Contrast between monochronic and polychronic people (Hall, 1989, 1990)*

| Monochronic People | Polychronic People |
|---|---|
| Do one thing at a time | Do many things at once |
| Concentrate on the job at hand | Are highly distractible and subject to interruptions |
| View time commitments as critical | View time commitments as objectives |
| Are low context and need information on specific task | Are high context and already have general information |
| Are committed to the job at hand | Are committed to people and human relationships |
| Adhere religiously to plans | Change plans often and easily |
| Emphasize promptness in all situations | Base promptness on the importance of and significance of the relationship |
| Are accustomed to short-term relationships | Have a strong tendency to build lifetime relationships |

social, economic and political life under apartheid. In each, the curriculum played a powerful role in reinforcing inequality (Singh & Kotze, 2003).

When designing Web applications such as EG software the design team has to be aware of cultural diversity (Preece, Rogers & Sharp, 2002). There are many views to the issue of cultural diversity and many angles from which it can be approached (see for example Evers & Day, 1997; Hofstede, 1997). One aspect of this diversity is related to whether the intended users are monochronic or polychronic. Table 1 summarises the main characteristics of monochronic and polychronic people.

American society, as well as those of northern Europe, is predominantly monochronic (Hall, 1989, 1990). Some cultures such as Arab, Latino, or Black (African) cultures are polychronic (Hall, 1989, 1990). Not all nations are predominantly of only one culture. South Africa's sizable AE population is recognised as monochronic and the majority IA as polychronic (Morrison, Conway & Douress, 1999; Prime, 1999). Members of polychronic cultures find delay significantly more tolerable than do members of monochronic cultures. Members of monochronic cultures find delay to be a source of great anxiety. In fact, members of polychronic cultures have been noted as having little anxiety at delay levels 50 times greater or more than those found very troubling to monochronic individuals (Hall, 1989, 1990). Research conducted by Walton, Vukovic & Marsden (2002) confirm that IA are polychronic in general.

Therefore, it would seem sensible to assume that AE and IA would respond differently to excessive delay in system response time and other issues relating to monochronicity and polychronicity. One of the aspects researched and presented in this chapter links up with this.

# Experiment

The South African environment as well as the cultural differences influences users' perception of technology. As part of a wider research project we have conducted an experiment to test if the chosen samples was monochronic, polychronic, both monochronic and polychronic, or predominantly one of the two. The following features, amongst others, were identified for investigation by the researchers: instructions, speed of Web site, communication (e-mail, fax, phone), appearance and navigation. Communication as a feature of investigation was chosen because in the social-political context, not all South Africans have access to basic communication.

The investigation was done through an experiment involving the design of two Web sites (site A: experiment 1 (E1) and Site B: experiment 2 (E2)) and a questionnaire to assess these sites. The sample of subjects for the experiment was selected using judgment sampling (Groebner & Shannon, 1990). This study was aimed at the net-generation [N-Gen] (Tapscott, 2000). N-Gen refers to the generation of people who are between the ages 2 and 22, not just those who are active on the Internet. The total number of respondents was 219.

The experiment was designed in the following way: the two sites addressed the same content but E2 adhered to general usability and design principles, while E1 broke some of these principles. The main principles on which these two sites can be distinguished and which have relevance on the work being reported here are: (1) *Consistency:* this refers to designing interfaces to have similar operations and use similar elements for achieving similar tasks (Preece et al., 2002). E1 was illogically designed with the use of poor spelling and grammar. (2) *Navigation:* this refers to avoiding orphan pages, long pages with excessive white space that force scrolling, narrow, deep, hierarchical menus that force users to burrow deep into the menu structure, and non-standard link colours; providing navigation support, such as a strong site map that is always present; as well as providing a consistent look and feel for navigation and information design (Preece et al., 2002). Navigation for site E1 was unstructured and totally linear, while E2 was designed with all the above in mind. (3) *Structured information:* E1 did not follow a structured approach for the specific content, leading the user to access the information in a particular way, and provided random bits of trivial information mixed up with the remainder of the content. The information for E2 was designed to lead the user through the content of the Web site. E1 appealed to the unstructured nature of the polychronic culture and E2 appealed to the organised nature of the monochronic culture.

The questionnaire consisted of the following main sections: demographic information about the respondents; a section to assess past computer experience; a set of instructions for assessing the first Web site (either Site A or B), and 32 statements, each on a 5-point Likert-scale, relating to the first Web site; respondents' open comments on the first Web site; a further set of instructions for assessing the second Web site (either site B or A), and 32 statements, each on a 5-point Likert-scale, and respondents' comments relating to the second Web site; and respondents' open comments on the second Web site.

The respondents from each institution would look at E1 and then E2, or vice versa. To avoid sample set bias subjects from culturally diverse institutions from different regions were selected for the experiment.

An intrinsic part of the questionnaire is its ability to collect quantitative and qualitative data, giving the respondents the opportunity to comment on or justify answers.

For this chapter we limit our discussion to the subsections of the questionnaire relating to: speed of Web site, communication (e-mail, fax, phone), and navigation. The outcomes of the following questions are specifically addressed. *Speed of Web site:* "It is important that the website process my request quickly" (specific to our Web sites) and "A fast response time is important to my activities on the web" (the Web in general). *Communication:* "Help features via phone, fax or e-mail are important aspects of a website" (Web in general). *Navigation:* "On-line help features such as navigation tutorials are unimportant to my activities on the web" (Web in general).

# Findings

The results give the E1 and E2 results of respondents looking at each site respectively for the above questions. Figures 1 to 4 contain the attitudes of the respondents

*Figure 1: It is important that the Website process my request quickly.*

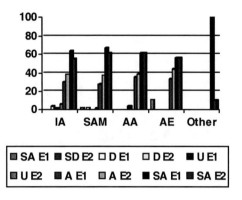

*Figure 2: A fast response time is important to my activities on the Web.*

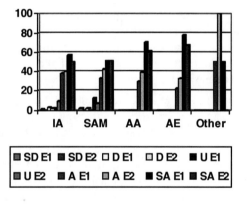

*Figure 3: Help features via phone, fax or e-mail are important aspects of a Website.*

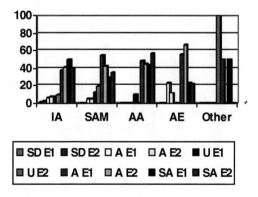

*Figure 4: On-line help features such as navigation tutorials are unimportant to my activities on the Web.*

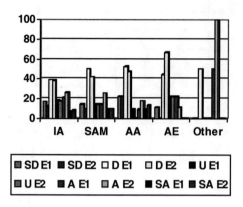

represented as a percentage where SD, D, U, A, SA respectably stand for strongly disagree, disagree, undecided, agree and strongly agree. We can summarise the findings as follows: (1) Among all the population groups the respondents became more critical of the site they where seeing/assessing second. Their pre-knowledge of the site/questions caused the respondents to be extremely critical of the second Web site. (2) A significant difference between the population

groups is expected. These results paint a different picture. Our results are supported by the work de Wet, Blignaut, and Burger (2001), indicating that there is a shift in literate IA to become more monochronic. Our results suggest that the entire population is monochronic. This could be explained because the sample group was from the N-Gen, all possessing basic computer literacy skills, and all having been through similar education systems during the last few years at least. Their cultural background did not seem to influence their requirements and performance on the Web. If the target population was the wider South African community, we expect that the results might have been more mixed. (3) A closer look at Figure 1 indicates that there are significant differences in the E2 for IA users. In Figures 2, 3 and 4 the same pattern again emerges for IA users. This indicates that IA users are monochronic. The results in Figure 4 reflect a type of status quo in the E1 and E2, with the majority of all respondents, independent of population group, seeing support material as important (again leaning to the monochronic side).

The chosen usability principles that were applied to site A and site B affected the respondents' attitude to the sites in question, illustrated by some of the open-ended comments by the respondents:

*Site A:* "...navigation was not well organized, i.e. I did not know where I was going next"; "the pictures and text were congested, there should be a space in between"; "the website frustrated me and put me in a bad mood"; "navigation was totally linear and highly frustrating". *Site B:* "the right amount of picture = the right speed"; "the screens were very well organised in a logical order, i.e. menu on left of screen => worked its way down the menu". Here again, comments from the IA group led the researchers to believe that the entire group is monochronic.

The respondents could see the difference that design according to human-computer interaction and usability principles made, and therefore "demanded" more. The aphorism that "ignorance is bliss" is therefore true; given the differently designed Web sites the respondents aggressively commented on what they considered as poor design, even when given a better design the second time around.

The results above strongly suggest that designers should look very carefully at the audience for which they are designing. Every market has a wide spectrum of people from skilled computer literate people to unskilled farm labourers, the ones who came through very different educational systems as opposed to those who had equal opportunities. It would be unrealistic for designers to think that they could design for the whole market. A realistic approach could be for design teams to know who the target audience is; this could possibly be achieved by conducting a marketing survey (by a group of experts) and giving these data to the design team.

The research indicates that cultural differences for the N-Gen target audience do not affect their activities on the Web. If it is accepted that there is a N-Gen or computer/ technology subculture, then efforts should be directed towards developing this culture with a sensitivity to beliefs, customs, and the intrinsic meaning of words and symbols in the context in which it is to be used. The results further suggest that as long as users have achieved a certain level of computer literacy and exposure to EG and other Web applications, they would accept similar designs without customisation of the user interface. The results are supported by the research of Norton (2002) on corporate culture in South Africa. There are, however, little to no longitudinal studies that have been conducted in usability and cultural differences. Further research is therefore needed to make long-term and validated claims on the issue of culture in designing for the Web.

# Lessons for Developing Countries

The success of the electronic model in developing countries requires strong and high-ranking political and bureaucratic leadership. Equally important is vast amounts of time, as well as capital. Government and business must debate and address issues and initiatives required to create an enabling framework for the electronic model both in the private and public sectors in these countries. Moreover, efforts must be speedily made to ensure that policies and processes are put in place that addresses the needs of society.

Governments in developing countries can thus refocus their attention to customers and value network relationships. Governments should also take the necessary steps to ensure that their public managers understand the electronic model, for ensuring its effective implementation. Managers must understand approaches for implementing the electronic model that will span multiple network players and channels. Governments should look at what it means to establish the electronic model, which involves embedded rules and regulations, application program interfaces and the accelerating move to component-based technologies and approaches. It means designing and operating the business from the public perspective (the customer) and recognising that all aspects of governmental operation will affect the public. The new fit will entail understanding the fit between government rules, capabilities and technology. The implications of integrating technology into public sector departments in developing countries will be far reaching. The initiatives or steps that can be undertaken by developing countries to ensure the successful entrance of e-government are summarised in Table 2.

Broadly speaking, *a suitable four-step program for e-government for developing countries* should entail the transformation of the core business processes, organisations

*Table 2: Initiatives/steps to be undertaken to ensure the successful entrance of e-government (adapted from discussion)*

| Initiatives/steps | Remarks |
|---|---|
| Strong and high-ranking leadership | Competent leadership is required to drive the whole e-government initiative. Bureaucratic leadership should be well trained to implement the whole e-government initiative. |
| Strategic and operational Issues | There should be a strategic fit between government rules, capabilities and technology. There is a need for the transformation of core business processes. |
| Development of Partnership | Collaboration with the business sector and civic organization is essential. |
| Regulation of Telecommunication Industry | It is necessary to support fair competition and to oversee appropriate pricing and service responsibilities. |
| Institute appropriate policy | Institutions should become familiar with rules, regulations, frameworks and vague pointers. |
| Sufficient Resources should be made available | Financial, human resources and time should be made available. |
| Education and Training | Education and training is crucial for recipients of the services. Education and training is crucial for implementers of the e-strategy. Ongoing education and training of ICT specialists is essential. |
| Provision of Infrastructure | The provision of basic infrastructure is essential for the success of e-government, for example electricity, telephones, computer hardware and software. |

changing their work processes and having a vision of how such a transformation will improve their operations, and the building of a new generation of e-business applications, which will allow governments to build the required functionality, without reinventing the wheel. Such an approach will allow the systems and applications that they already have in place to become more functional, with the appropriate emphasis on application that are non-existent or that require integration. The adoption of such an "electronic architecture" that is scalable, open and secure is essential, and finally, it is also suggested that governments should establish a hardware infrastructure that can grow easily, as requirements and demand increases. Hardware and software alternatives should also be made available, in such a manner that they can provide for high levels of security. Such a mammoth task requires a well-strategised, thoroughly planned and carefully coordinated approach to ICT and electronic government.

The implementation of an e-government approach in developing countries will require a sustained effort, as well as collaboration with the business sector and civic organisations. The success of the electronic model in developing countries will require an effective partnership between the private and public sectors. Partnerships between governments and industries will be required, not only to develop the actual strategies, but also to become involved in the integration of the existing, future and newly created digital world entities.

Regulation of the telecommunication industry is an important public responsibility, to support fair competition and to oversee appropriate pricing and service responsibilities (Electronic model of service delivery, e-gov examples shine abroad, 2000). The prices charged by telecommunications operators for access to crucial services can be an important factor in determining the effectiveness and affordability of the electronic model opportunities on the whole in developing countries. It is extremely difficult for smaller entrepreneurs, ISPs, and public operators such as tele-centres to afford to connect themselves.

Governments in developing countries, together with businesses, can therefore play a vital role in promoting the growth of the electronic model, by instituting appropriate policies with respect to education, industry, technology, the economy, technical assistance and human resource development programs, to enable their countries to move from traditional to information societies. Thus, governments must become familiar with rules, frameworks, and vague pointers, to assist in understanding and dealing with the electronic model (Liebenburg, 2000). The critical challenge for governments will center on how they sources their capabilities, how to ensure implementation of rules, and how to manage their networks, both within and outside the public sector. Other important issues include the fact that sufficient resources must be made available to ensure successful policy implementation in developing countries. Accordingly, governments in developing countries must encourage and promote the electronic model by creating the necessary conditions in this regard, namely consumer protection and privacy and establishing and enhancing the necessary infrastructure.

Finally, with the new tools of a networked society, governments in developing countries must completely rethink and re-engineer themselves as new and innovative issues of government, and become central players in the new global economy. Developing countries should set the climate for wealth creation, which is vitally important in these economies. It can act as a deadening hand on change or be a catalyst for creativity. They can cause economic stagnation through runaway deficits, or they can set a climate for growth. The ultimate goal for innovation is not fear but the ability to reform and transform in the electronic era. There is a major quest in developing countries to attempt to address the electronic divide in the information age.

The electronic model will have far reaching implications and impact in developing countries. In an era where the communication of information has become so vital for generation of knowledge, it is most apparent that developing countries utilise the expediency of faster and reliable means of the transportation of these databases and deliver services. Governments in developing countries should thus see their role as an enabler, facilitator, educator and law enforcer to prevent cyber crimes, as well as a model user of the electronic model of service delivery. The government influence must take on new dimensions. Governments' participation in developing countries must be coherent and cautious, avoiding the contradictions and confusion that can sometimes arise when different organisations assert their authority too vigorously and operate without co-ordination. There is undoubtedly a great opportunity on the Internet and other ICT media for developing countries. If private sector and government in developing countries act appropriately, this opportunity can be realised for the benefit of all countries. However, without a cohesive outlook and attitude to such a challenge, the anticipated benefits may not accrue.

# Conclusions and Recommendations

The electronic model will have far reaching implications and impact on South Africa. There is undoubtedly a great opportunity for commercial and government activity on the Internet. If private sector and government act appropriately, this opportunity can be realised for the benefit of all South Africans. EG is thus about competing in an electronically enabled world, which creates fundamental shifts in existing markets and creates new industry opportunities. The maxim of having to be "worldly-wise" in a global village has now become a reality for South Africa. South African government departments thus need to have this global village wisdom. As the South African government progresses on its journey towards EG, it must select specific applications, promote them to the citizens and define auditable security and privacy policies. In this way, the Information Communication Technology (ICT) return on investment will be more rapid for government while the value creation for citizens will be maximised and visible. In the digital world, value creation will no longer be cordoned off within the boundaries of a single corporation. The extended enterprise will become the essential element and way of transacting business. It is necessary to take cognisance of this fact when designing the elements of EG.

The authors suggest the following approach to designing effective EG sites for South African institutions. The letters ABCD symbolise the grass roots approach: start at the beginning, do not assume anything about your audience, as illustrated (by an example that will be added to the chapter based on our research). *A stands for atmosphere;* the organisation should understand the atmosphere in the particular environment that it is operating in, such as socio-political, law, local customs, and amongst the local languages spoken. *B stands for build-up;* you may be an electronic entity, but you have to build up a culture of trust between yourself and the citizens. *C stands for communication;* build up good communication lines between citizens, intermediaries and government. *D stands for discipline;* work with in the rules and regulations of the community. The ABCD approach is a simple approach that assists the government to assess the social environment that it exists in. Such a mammoth task requires a well-strategised, thoroughly planned and carefully coordinated approach to ICT and EG in South Africa.

There are a number of areas for further study that need to be explored in South Africa that are considered vital to the success of the electronic model, namely:

- how the digital medium for export and trade can be exploited;

- which government departments in South Africa should provide training and education initiatives and what funding mechanisms can be employed to support these;

- what the impact of the electronic model will be on the workforce, in terms of both job losses and job creation;

- what resources should be devoted to retraining and compensation for workers who may be at risk due to the electronic model, namely, automation, shifting of jobs offshore, or elimination of the need for certain intermediary activities; and

- how the South African government and the private sector should share the responsibility and cost for easing the transformation of the workforce through these changes?

E-government forms a very important part of future governance in South Africa. It is necessary that public servants and citizens acquire the applicable skills and knowledge. Without proper training, it will be impossible to optimise the use and usage of e-government and its associated benefits. By availing programmes online to public servants and equipping them with information technology commodities, the required skills and knowledge that will be needed for future e-government applications could be inculcated. Professionals must be in a constant learning situation to keep abreast with the developments in their areas of specialisation. Skills in using computers, the Internet, telecommunication and related technologies also need to be part of the core curriculum for schools, beginning at the primary level, through universities and graduate programmes. The provision of locally relevant content should be added to the South African government's e-strategy. Government agencies should work together with the private sector partners and other institutions to help maximise the benefits of e-government through coordinated policies and programmes. Extensive research, both normative and empirical, is needed to cement the fusion between the realities associated with South Africa's capacities and the possibilities presented by advances in information technologies.

# References

Babcock, C. (2000, October 2). *Africa's Internet Newspaper - Inter@ctive week,* 13.

Central Government. (2002). White paper on electronic commerce. Available: *http://www.polity.org.za/govdocs/*.

Czerniawska, F., & Potter, G. (1998). *Business in a virtual world.* Great Britain: Macmillan Press Ltd.

Department of Communications. (1999). *Discussion paper on electronic commerce.* South Africa: Department of Communications.

Department of Communications. (2000). *Green paper on e-commerce. "Making it your business".* South Africa: Department of Communications.

de Wet, L., Blignaut, P., & Burger, A. (2001). *Comprehension and usability variances among multicultural Web users in South Africa.* Paper presented at the CHI-SA 2001.

Evans, U. (2001). Director: Department of Public Service and Administration. Pretoria.

Evers, V., & Day, D. (1997). *Role of culture in user interface acceptance.* Paper presented at the of Interact 97, 6th IFIP TC 13 International Conference on Human Computer Interaction.

Goldstuck, A. (2002). *The Goldstuck report: Internet access in South Africa, 2002.* World Wide Worx.

Groebner, F.D., & Shannon, W.P. (1990). *Business statistics: A decision-making approach* (3rd ed.). New York: Macmillan Publishing.

Hall, E.T. (1989). *Beyond culture.* New York: Anchor Books.

Hall, E.T. (1990). *The silent language.* New York: Anchor Books.

Hofstede, G. (1997). *Cultures and organizations: Software of the mind, intercultural cooperation and its importance for survival.* New York: McGraw-Hill.

Johnson, R. (2000, September 18). The same trends, another decade. *Africa's Internet Newspaper. Interactive week.*

Keen, P., & McDonald, M. (2000). *The eProcess edge.* USA: McGraw-Hill.

Liebenberg, K. (2000). e-Government. Dawn of thee-state (137). Have you Heard. Available: *http://kid/kid/hyh.nsf/48bb38f07.*

Morrison, T., Conway, W.A., & Douress, J.J. (1999). *Dun & Bradstreet's guide to doing business around the world.* Prentice-Hall.

Norton, D. (2002). *Implementation of an electronic report viewing application for multicultural users.* Paper presented at the CHI2002: Changing the world, changing ourselves, Minneapolis, Minnesota, USA.

Preece, J., Rogers, Y., & Sharp, H. (2002). *Interaction design: Beyond human-computer interaction.* New York: John Wiley & Sons.

Prime, N. (1999). *Cross-cultural management in South Africa: Problems, obstacles, and agenda for companies.* Paper presented at the Seventh Cross Cultural Research Conference, Cancun.

Reynolds, D.P., Camp, S.M., Bygrave, D.W., Autio, E., & Hay, M. (2001). *Global entrepreneurship monitor: 2001 executive report.*

Roodt, J. (2001). *Government news: SARS to go e-commerce* (vol. 20). IT Web.

Shilubane, J. (2001). e-Government: An overview. *Service Delivery Review. A Learning Journal for Public Service Managers.*

Singh, S. (2002). Deputy Director: Department of Trade and Industry. Pretoria.

Singh, S., & Kotze, P. (2003). *The socio-political culture of users.* Paper presented at the INTERACT 2003 - Bringing the bits together, Zurich, Switzerland.

Tapscott, D. (2000, May). Minds over matter: The new economy is based on brains, not brawn. The only thing that counts is smart. *Intelligence,* 20-24.

Van Jaarsveld, L. (2003). *Implementing EG in South Africa: A critical development perspective.* Unpublished paper.

Walton, M., Vukovic', V., & Marsden, G. (2002). *'Visual literacy' as challenge to the internationalisation of interfaces: A study of South African student Web users.* Paper presented at the CHI-2002: Changing the world, changing ourselves, Minneapolis, Minnesota, USA.

Chapter XV

# Building the Network State

Dieter Spahni, University of Applied Sciences Berne, Switzerland

## Abstract

*The administration portal for Switzerland,* www.ch.ch, *is based on a powerful meta-database of available resources and services of the public administration and allocates a unique name, the Uniform Resource Name (URN), to every resource. The URN:Technology, adapted to the requirements of* www.ch.ch, *has become an open standard and a building block of the Swiss e-government platform. This chapter shows why portals in widespread, long-established federal structures with decentralized responsibility for the resources and interlinking can benefit from the URN:Technology, enabling the implementation of the vision of a network state. In this chapter, a blueprint of the network state in Switzerland based on URN:Technology will be presented.*

## Introduction

After several years of concept design and development work, Switzerland's administration portal, the Virtual Desk Switzerland *www.ch.ch*, was opened to the public in January 2003. Figure 1 shows the home page in German. The information presented, structured by subject (typically life events such as birth, school, work, etc.), leads the visitor step by step to the relevant information source in the public administration sector, be this in the Federal Confederation, in a canton or commune[1]. The portal is to be understood primarily as a guide. The number of links that must be maintained in this portal is enormous. Thus, for instance, each of the 2,880 communes responsible has to maintain links at the local level to all relevant subjects.

The URN:Technology outlined later in this chapter solves the maintenance problem with the aid of a central meta-database in which all portal partners (the Federal Confederation, cantons and communes) independently maintain the description of the resources they offer on the relevant subjects, in particular, providing the current valid address of the resources.

Resources vary from providing simple information and forms that can be downloaded to Web applications and Web services. Resources keep a unique name, the URN, which serves to identify them. The URN:Technology is particularly suited for cross-linking in complex and federally structured portals with decentralized responsibility for the resources and interlinking but is in no way limited to e-government in its application.

Similar to users locating appropriate services using the meta-database, developers will find Web services[2], respectively their interface descriptions, to integrate them into their own applications. In order to foster the coupling of distributed applications irrespective of available interfaces or data formats, a central transaction hub reduces system complexity, for example by converting data formats and providing store-and-forward capabilities to merge different media and channels.

*Figure 1:The Virtual Desk Switzerland, www.ch.ch, provides explanatory texts in all four national languages (German, French, Italian and Romansch), leading the user step by step to the information source in the public administration sector in Switzerland.*

Drucken

**www.ch.ch**

Privatleben
Gesellschaft
Arbeit
Gesundheit, soziale Sicherheit
Mobilitat
Sicherheit
Staat und Politik
Wirtschaft

www.ch.ch ist ein Wegweiser, welcher die Benutzerinnen und Benutzer zu den Verwaltungsstellen aller Staatsebenen fuhrt: Bund, Kantone, Gemeinden. www.ch.ch gibt Kurzinformationen zu den ublichen Behordengangen.

**Testphase**
Das Portal befindet sich in der Testphase und hat deshalb noch Lucken. Weil nicht jede Gemeinde uber ein ausgebautes Web-Angebot verfugt und auch noch nicht alle Themen erfasst sind, finden Sie die gewunschte Information nicht in jedem Fall. Wir bitten um Verstandnis. Mit Ihrer Meinung helfen Sie uns, www.ch.ch weiterzuentwickeln. Vielen Dank!

**Privatleben**
Ausweise / Leben im Ausland
vorgesehen: Zivilstand / Kinder / Familie / Seniorinnen und Senioren / Wohnen / Auslanderinnen und Auslander in der Schweiz

**Gesellschaft**
Bildung / Medien / Tiere / Konsum
vorgesehen: Kultur / Internet / Kirche und Religion / Gleichstellung

E-Quest
Info
Ubersicht
de fr it rm

[          ]
Suchen

Erweiterte Suche

**Gesundheit, soziale Sicherheit**
Gesundheit / Soziale Sicherheit

**Mobilitat**
Auto, Motorrad
vorgesehen: offentlicher Verkehr / Umwelt

**Staat und Politik**
Steuern

**Arbeit**
vorgesehen: Arbeit

**Sicherheit**
Militardienst
vorgesehen: Justiz

**Wirtschaft**
Handel und Gewerbe
vorgesehen: Telekommunikation / Versicherungen

**Support**
Brauchen Sie Unterstutzung? Zogern Sie nicht, uns telefonisch oder per E-Mail zu kontaktieren.

**Info**
Wie funktioniert www.ch.ch?
Wer betreibt www.ch.ch?
Was kommt noch?

Thus, services and business processes not previously connected, or even not yet aware of each other, successively build a network of services. Consequently, the administration, enabled by the technology of Web services, arranges its tasks more efficiently and effectively, focusing on its core competences. The network state becomes attainable.

This chapter presents the vision of a network state in general and a blueprint of the network state in Switzerland based on URN:Technology. In case study format, it describes the first steps in this direction made by the Swiss government when implementing the URN:Technology as a core building block of the national e-government platform[3].

# Vision of the Network State

## Technology Enabling the Network State

The task of administration consists to a large extent of the processing of data and this can be supported by technology. Often data or information from external suppliers are required to provide this service. Today, with contemporary information and communication technologies, access can be gained to external resources without transferring them to other media. Great attention is therefore given to the building and maintenance of virtual production networks for the provision of public services in the context of e-government. The key to success with these lies in the integration of suppliers' and partners' systems into one's own service supply chain. For this reason, there is a requirement for enterprising decision-making in e-government in the so-called "supply network" (Meir, 2002). In general, supply network management can be understood as an approach, characterized by organizational and information technology, to the creation and coordination of logistical networks. Classic hierarchically arranged organization models are facing barriers in the context of supply network management.

The network organization as a new organization concept could contribute to a reduction in complexity. In connection with increased orientation in administration towards efficiency and service that is supported by more flexible organization structures and based on the idea of contract management, networks become a promising form of cooperation for state institutions: "Networks attempt to combine the different strengths of the cooperating partners in order to achieve common goals or for problem solving" (Thom & Ritz, 2000). As a customer, the administration is in a contractual relationship with service providers (which can, in turn, be other administrative offices) and is connected with these in a vertical and horizontal network.

The vision of the network state and the strategy of electronic service provision assume the prior integration of heterogeneous systems across organizational boundaries into a common system. Looking closely at the multiplicity of decentralized administrative solutions arising from federal systems, one recognizes the need for integration of processes across organizational boundaries, regardless of platforms or programming languages used.

Here, the potential of Web services and their future role in the network state become visible. Web services allow the state to provide services and functions to other authorities via new, standardized protocols (e.g., UDDI (OASIS UDDI Specifications, 2002), WSDL (Chinnici, Gudgin, Moreau, Schlimmer & Weerawarana, 2003), SOAP (Mitra, 2003)) and they are, at the same time, independent of platform and programming language.

Web services, therefore, influence the form of the processes of state service provision, which, in turn, can lead to the discovery of new strategic potential for combining administration functions by innovative process design. Web services support the implementation of the vision of the network state taking into account federal structures and heterogeneous systems. In this, they support the more efficient formation of supply networks for state service provision as process networks.

# Three-Level Model of the Network State

The introductory reflections make it clear that the elements of the system to be created in connection with Web services are to be found at three different levels: at the strategic level with the idea of the network state, at the process level with the idea of process networks and at the level of information systems and telecommunication networks (Meir, 2002).

- The strategic level contains the vision of the network state as a normative superstructure and is based on the cooperation of business units. Central to the cooperative relationship is willing collaboration based on mutual advantage. The network state consists, on the one hand, of formal elements, for example general agreements between authorities and partners and, on the other hand, of informal elements such as mutual trust and shared norms and values.

- The process level relates to the form of the process network, which can be understood as a connection of business processes extending beyond the business world. The cooperative strategy is implemented on the operational level and services are made available to clients of the process. In the context of the process network, the coordination between the partners' processes is a central theme.

- The information system level concentrates on the form taken by the IT systems, which consist of procedures, data and technology. IT systems support process networks by the electronic exchange of services at the process level. Thanks to open standards, Web services make possible an exchange of services, independent of platform and programming language and spanning different systems.

The next section focuses on the information system level as the enabling technology to implement the sketched strategic issues with their profound impact on the process level.

# Blueprint of the Network State in Switzerland

This section outlines the author's personal view for proposed enhancements of the Virtual Desk Switzerland currently being evaluated by the Swiss Federal Chancellery.

## E-Government Platform: The Basic Building Blocks

As the central service provider, the federal government sensibly makes available Web services frequently requested countrywide by cantons, communes and third parties, and operates a corresponding service registry. While the cantons concentrate on specific requirements within their area of jurisdiction, the federal government provides services requested at a more general level, in so far as technical and legal constraints and security requirements permit this. This is no more an empty vision but already a present reality thanks to the Virtual Desk. So, for example, links can lead to resources irrespective of their current address (URL) by means of a unique name (URN). The link to the cantonal passport office in Berne can be written, for instance, as shown in Figure 2 and the same applies for all other cantons.

The advantages of this linking are obvious, since adjustments for changes of URN-based links are then unnecessary and this name is simple and memorable.

Available Web services must be placed in the central resource registry so that they can be located by potential users and application developers. In Switzerland, the Virtual Desk is admirably suited to this, being already the central registry with metadata on available resources. If these registries contain not only detailed listings but also the interfaces to the service processes of the individual administration units, such a registry can be further developed into a hub for business processes and transactions extending beyond single authorities.

The vision resulting from this approach consequently places the Virtual Desk in the middle of the business processes extending beyond the authority which, apart from directing clients to information sources of all administration units, also actively supports the location, access, handling, combination, synchronization and running of the business processes for all involved.

The Virtual Desk as a core building block of the e-government platform of the Federal Confederation (see Figure 3) is the prerequisite for secure and seamless cooperation within the federal administration as well as between it and the cantonal and communal administrations. With its central registry and hub of processes extending beyond single authorities, it increases their efficiency. It also integrates the varied systems of decen-

*Figure 2: URL with the URN of the cantonal passport office in Berne*

```
http://urn.ch.ch/urn:Passbüro,Bern
```

*Figure 3: E-government platform in Switzerland as a fundament of the e-government project portfolio*

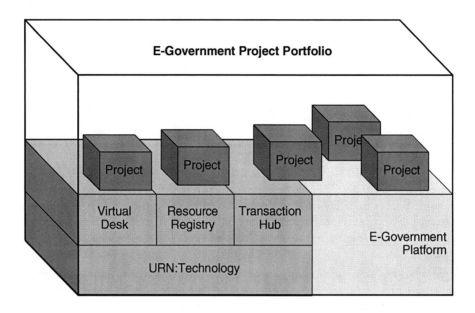

tralized authorities, irrespective of the transmission medium used with open, standardized interfaces and thereby actively promotes cooperation between the state and its clients. This platform-supported integration of the tasks of the government and administration units improves the information flows significantly and creates the desired transparency.

## Virtual Desk: The Administration Portal for Switzerland

To the user, the Virtual Desk *www.ch.ch* presents itself as a common portal with its information structured by subject. This portal is one of the many government portals worldwide - a comprehensive list of governmental portals is presented in "Guichets virtuels weltweit" (2002). The goal of these portals is to provide an intuitive integrated view of available resources. Together with the links to internal and external resources, a search engine offering more exact and specific requests and a classification schema of information categories for easy retrieval are common portal features. One of the key challenges of government portals is the provision of classification schemas not based on governmental hierarchical structures (Detlor & Finn, 2002) but on life events (Vintar & Leben, 2002).

Because the Swiss cantons have remained, to a large extent, sovereign entities, administrative procedures, responsibilities, mandatory regulations and even the wording of legal texts vary to a large extent from canton to canton, even from commune to commune.

Therefore, the Virtual Desk authority has to delegate the responsibility of interlinking local resources with the subjects given, since citizens need government portals providing information that is relevant, reliable and timely, as a recent study (Golder & Longchamp, 2003) pointed out. Thus, the Virtual Desk is to be understood primarily as a guide and leads the visitor finally to the appropriate information source in the public administration sector determined by the resource registry. The section "URN:Technology" explains the details with the core technology used in the Virtual Desk.

## Resource Registry: Locating, Accessing and Integrating Processes

With the Virtual Desk, Switzerland is the first country to have not only a comprehensive guide but also a standardized national resource registry. This registry is, together with the improved functions for location and access of business processes, the place to turn for both users and application developers. Via the portal both client groups find the desired information for the approach to a process or for building Web services into their own applications.

All partners can publish the description of their client processing in the resource registry, irrespective of the interface technology used, so that automatic access to processes and, in connection with that, transmission of electronic data between linked processes across the boundaries of authorities is made possible irrespective of the communication medium used.

*Figure 4: UDDI like registry of the Virtual Desk*

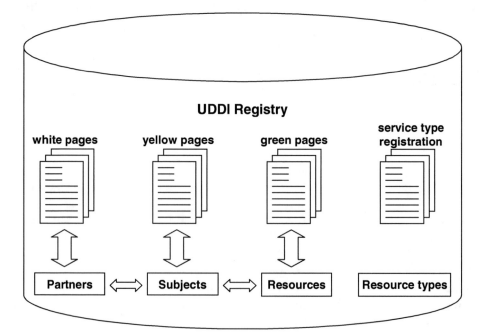

Support for carrying out processes requires the publishing of process descriptions and examples. The resource registry, as a knowledge and transaction database, must be conceived in such a way that this can be developed in corresponding stages.

The portal guides the user, right through from navigation structures with the support of explanatory text, not only to the information but also to the entry points of the relevant processes. Then, depending on each particular service provided by the administration units, one is referred by the URN to the related Web site or online form, whose content is approved and transmitted, securely and with regard to appropriate data protection regulations, via the most suitable communication channel.

By the same route, applications developers find the descriptions of the technical interfaces (per WSDL (Chinnici et al., 2003)) for the integration of available Web services.

Interestingly, in its structure the Virtual Desk is already seen as a registry conforming to UDDI in its approach, as depicted in Figure 4. All the partners are listed in it (white pages) and their resources described (green pages) if they fall within the subject structure of the portal (yellow pages). The list of resource types corresponds to the list of supported data formats (see section "Identification of Resources" for details).

# Transaction Hub: Processing, Combination, Synchronization and Running of Processes

The individual transactions of processes that cross administrative boundaries are combined by the transaction hub. The exchange of information inside the administration as well as between it and the parties from society and economy is thus noticeably simplified. This approach allows a large number of those involved to build their own solutions as required and, at the same time, to interconnect with each other across authority boundaries. The data to be passed between the transaction partners can be automatically converted on demand into a suitable format used by the transaction hub - preferably based on XML (see Figure 5). The portal provides various and secure communication channels transparently to the partners. The synchronization tools needed for batching individual transactions into higher-level transactions are also part of the transaction hub.

With the transaction hub, the Virtual Desk becomes the central backbone of business processes extending beyond the authority. The transaction hub is seamlessly integrated into the pre-existing navigation system of the Virtual Desk, whilst alongside the information resources of the partner, the location, access, handling, combination, synchronization and running of its business processes are also actively supported by the portal for all those involved.

The next section presents the first steps made by the Swiss government toward the implementation of the vision of the network state. It will describe the backbone of the transaction hub, the resource registry as a core building block of the national e-government platform implementing the URN:Technology, in more detail. This has been in operation since January 2003.

*Figure 5: Transaction hub enabling application-to-application interaction*

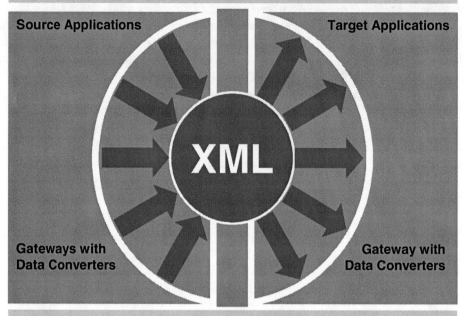

**The transaction hub handles process- and meta-data between source and target applications applying data conversions where required**

Source Applications

Target Applications

**XML**

Gateways with
Data Converters

Gateway with
Data Converters

**The core component of the transaction hub handles at least the data needed to monitor and control concurrent transactions.**

# URN:Technology

The URN:Technology has been developed in order to manage access to distributed resources by naming them. As this next section outlines, a uniform resource name (URN) is a persistent resource identifier. Thus, a portal like the Virtual Desk Switzerland designs its own namespace to access resources.

## Access to Resources

For access to resources available via the Internet, various partly overlapping approaches exist under the title Uniform Resource Identifier (URI (Berners-Lee, Fielding & Masinter, 1998; Connolly, 2002) as shown in Figure 6. A distinction is made between Uniform Resource Locator (URL) and Uniform Resource Name (URN (Moats, 1997)). URL designates an addressing scheme for finding resources on the Internet. URLs represent the most familiar approach because of their use in the World Wide Web.

*Figure 6: Uniform Resource Identifier URI with the commonly used Uniform Resource Locator URL and the Uniform Resource Name URN*

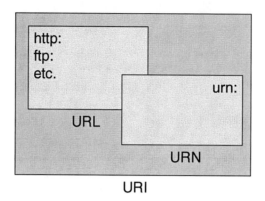

URL

URN

URI

URN:Technology is based, in contrast, on the concept of the URN, whose aim is the allocation of a globally unique and permanent name to resources. The referencing of such resources thus becomes independent of the place of storage. In addition, opportunities arise for the preparation of different data formats (e.g., HTML, PDF, RTF) and language versions of a resource.

## Identification of Resources

Resources can be described by numerous attributes, some of which are particularly suited to referencing resources. The URN:Technology of the Virtual Desk Switzerland uses the four following attributes for referencing:

| | | | |
|---|---|---|---|
| Language | e.g. | de | "German" |
| Partner | e.g. | ch.be.6509 | "communal administration of Urtenen/BE" |
| Subject | e.g. | ch.01.01.02.01 | "Passport" |
| Data format | e.g. | 01 | "HTML" |

In combination, these four attributes are sufficient for the identification of resources by a URN and thus build the namespace. For the Virtual Desk, all valid values of the identifying attributes were coded (Spahni & Gygax, 2002). Open standards were used in this as far as possible.

Figure 7 shows the URN for the above example. The prefixed "urn:ch" indicates the URN's namespace name "ch," the country code for Switzerland according to ISO (ISO Country Codes 3166-1:1997, 2003). Following RFC 2611 (Daigle, van Gulik, Ianella & Faltstrom, 1999), the Internet Assigned Numbers Authority (IANA, 2003) maintains the list of

*Figure 7: Example of a URN for the Virtual Desk Switzerland*

```
urn:ch:de:ch.be.6509:ch.01.01.02.01:01
```

globally reserved namespace names. The language is determined by "de" (German). Then follow the hierarchical codes "ch.be.6509" to indicate the commune of Urtenen (which is in the canton of Berne: BE) and the subject "passport," (accessible via the subjects "private life," "proof of identity" and "identity cards and passports"). The final "01" stands for the data format HTML. The individual attributes are separated by colons (":").

## URN:Resolver

In order to access resources via URNs on the World Wide Web, the portal partners must put each URL into the description of the resources stored in the central meta-database. This is so that portal users can access resources via the URN with the widespread technology of the World Wide Web; hence with almost any browser just by embedding the URN into an URL, the URN:Technology brings the URN:Resolver to bear. The URN:Resolver has the task of turning a URN into a URL (see Figure 8). A unique assignment can then only take place if the correct URL was assigned to the URN in the central meta-database by a portal partner.

## Primary Task of the URN:Resolver

The user puts the URN into a URL and thus sends a request to the URN:Resolver. In the case of the Virtual Desk Switzerland for the example in Figure 7, only the address of the URN:Resolver is prefixed to the URN in Figure 9.

It is important to note that this kind of URL is primarily intended for machine usage. Users prefer simple and memorable notations behind smart interfaces hiding the details of the syntax.

*Figure 8: The URN:Resolver turns a URN into a URL based on a complex procedure.*

*Figure 9: URN embedded within a URL for resolving*

```
http://www.ch.ch/urn:ch:de:ch.be.6509:ch.01.01.02.01:01
```

*Figure 10: URN:Resolver in operation mode HTTP Redirect*

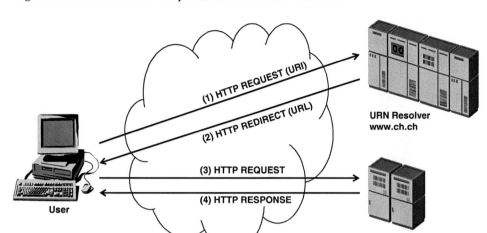

Two possible modes of operation of the URN:Resolver can be visualized. Either the URN:Resolver can redirect the client's request to the desired URL or it loads the resource filed under the URL itself on behalf of the client calling it up and delivers it to that client. In this function the URN:Resolver acts as a proxy server. For the time being, the implementation for the Virtual Desk Switzerland envisages only the first mode of operation: the client with the enquiry passes a URN embedded in a URL (hence as a URI) to the URN:Resolver in the form of an HTTP request. It extracts the URN from the URI and searches for the URL that corresponds to a URN in its database. It sends an HTTP response (content: HTTP Redirect) back to the client's browser. The client then directs a request to the URL supplied and so accesses the desired resource. This procedure is illustrated in Figure 10.

## Further Tasks of the URN:Resolver

The URN:Technology tries to ensure that the most appropriate resource is actually transmitted to the user even if:

1.  no resource at all was recorded by the relevant portal partner for the URN sought,

2.  the supplied URN proves to be not unique or

3.  instead of a URN, natural language search terms are used.

In the first case, that is, when absolutely no resource was recorded by the desired portal partner for the URN sought, the URN:Resolver searches with a complex procedure for the most suitable resources on the basis of the descriptions recorded in the central meta-

*Figure 11: URNs embedded in URLs are used throughout the Virtual Desk Switzerland in the explanatory texts. The providing partner is omitted in the URN when the residential canton or commune of the user must be identified. Thus the URN:Resolver will ask the user and guide him or her correctly.*

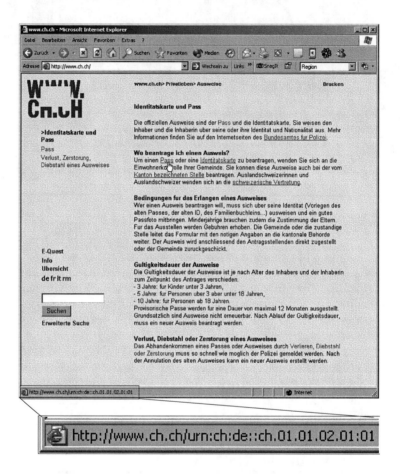

database. Thus, for instance, it checks whether resources are available in other languages or on lower or higher level subjects instead of on the subject sought. In this, the URN:Resolver follows the hierarchical structures of both the subjects and the partners and thus leads the user to an appropriate target. This complex procedure has been carefully designed for the special requirements of the Virtual Desk Switzerland.

In the second case, the use of URNs that are not unique is only permissible and logical if the expression for an attribute, for example the language or the portal partner, is omitted. This function is particularly important for the direction to resources, for instance, for which the partner providing them can only be identified after determination of the residential commune or canton of the user. The omission of the partner in the URN (e.g., when being directed to check the resident's commune in urn:ch:de::ch.01.01.02.01:01) allows the URN:Resolver to ask users for their residential canton or commune - based on

*Figure 12: URN resolving - from free-form query to unique URN: Three levels of abstractions for valid and resolvable URN: A free-form enquiry (URN Level 2) is transformed by the URN resolver into a descriptive form (URN Level 1) and then translated into a URN Level 0 before assigning the appropriate URL.*

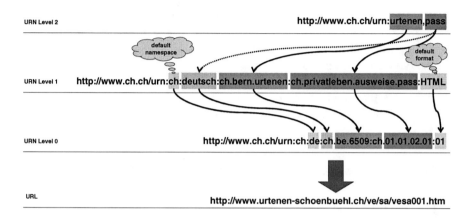

the assignment of responsibility to each subject in the meta-database - and then to guide them correctly. This interlinking feature is used throughout the Virtual Desk when the residential canton or commune of the user must be identified, as illustrated in Figure 11.

Alongside the omission of individual attributes, the use of wild cards is also permitted. Searching, for example, for the same subject as with the URN in Figure 7, but replacing the language and only a part of the partner id with wild card "*", for example urn:ch:*:ch.be.*:ch.01.01.02.01:01, the URN:Resolver will compile a list of all available resources from communes in the canton of Berne written in any language.

In the last case, even natural language terms instead of coded expressions for attributes are permissible and they allow a free-form query (URN Level 2). It is not, in this instance, a typical full text search but an intelligent-as-possible algorithmic transformation of a URN based on the list of all valid values of all attributes. The example in Figure 12 shows the transformation for the very short URN "urn:urtenen,pass". The URN:Resolver derives the desired language "de" from the language of the chosen subject "pass" (passport). The code of the appropriate commune is determined from the commune identifier, which proves to be unique in this example. Further assumptions relate to the domain "ch" and the data format HTML, which are provided as default by the Virtual Desk Switzerland. In the conversion to a URN, the order of the attributes is not important, as the URN:Resolver automatically recognizes the individual attributes. As shown in Figure 12, multiple levels of URNs are handled by the URN:Resolver. Given a complete vocabulary, in other words the list of all valid values of all attributes in all languages[4] used within the namespace, the URN:Resolver is able to transform even free-form natural language terms (URN level 2) or URNs in valid syntax but with natural language values (URN level 1) into a single URN or – if natural language terms prove to be not unique – into a set of valid and unique URNs (URN level 0), which are then presented to the user.

# Resource Description

For the description of resources, the URN:Technology applies an open standard, the Resource Description Framework, RDF (Lassila & Swick, 1999). RDF is based on XML and offers a syntax that contains consistent rules for the generation of metadata. RDF gives Web site authors the opportunity to describe resources with the help of metadata (Hjelm, 2001). Future search engines that support RDF will be capable of answering enquiries by this means and guiding the user much more accurately to the targeted resource. Hence the resource descriptions are not only recorded in the central database but also made available to the portal partners in RDF format; the partners can publish the descriptions on their own Web sites in a manner accessible to the search engines. Variants of this with different advantages and disadvantages are currently available as follows:

- The descriptions of all resources of a Web site are published as a single RDF document as part of the Web site.

- For each individual resource of a Web site the description is published as an RDF document. Within the resources, for instance within HTML documents, there is a reference to the descriptive RDF document.

- In HTML documents the description is embedded as an RDF sequence.

*Figure 13: Portal partners register their resources with a simple online form in their extranet.*

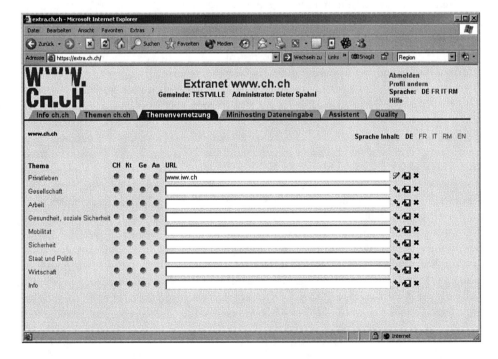

The attributes used by the Virtual Desk Switzerland to describe the resources have been selected with several recommendations in mind, especially with the Dublin Core Metadata Element Set (Dublin Core Metadata Initiative, 2003) (title, author, subject, contributor, language, format, date, rights) and include further domain specific attributes (e.g., validity date, codes identifying the separation of powers), as shown in Figure 13.

# Conclusion

Switzerland is the first country to have not only a comprehensive guide and portal but also a standardized national resource registry, visited by more than 3,000 users per day. The success of such a portal is heavily dependent on the support of all partners, because they maintain all the links to the resources available. Today, the Federal Confederation, all 26 cantons and even all 2,880 communes are online with at least some standardized pages and nearly all of them have interlinked the relevant subjects with their own Web sites. In November 2003, more than 167,800 URNs were recorded in the central meta-database. This number will increase until the end of the test phase in winter 2004 as administrative tools supporting the URN management improve and new subjects are added to the portal by the Swiss Federal Chancellery.

Organizational aspects proved to be of great importance for a project spanning institutions in federal structures not previously working together alike. In order to build and run the Virtual Desk Switzerland, the Federal Chancellery established a cooperation between the Federal Confederation, the 26 cantons and communal administrations (Poupa, 2002). The federal project team is supported by the consultation group, with more than 50 representatives from the Federal Confederation, all cantons and selected communes. This group is responsible for the roll-out within the administration and acts as a sounding board to the project team. Strategic decisions are made by a small management committee with about 10 members from the federal administration, the cantons and a representative from the association of cities as well as another from the association of communes. This cooperation proved to be crucial with respect to the information flow and motivation, since with this approach a central meta-database had to be maintained locally by all the portal partners.

To achieve a balance between effort and benefit for portal partners working for the Virtual Desk, organizational and technical support is provided centrally. A hotline offers technical support for Webmasters in most national languages and relevant documents are available in an extranet. Moreover, a quality-assurance team audits the links in the meta-database manually and verifies that they point to proper resources. Of course, all links are repeatedly checked for availability by a spider. In any event of fault, notifications are sent to the persons in charge. Furthermore, a set of reports shows how relevant subjects are actually interlinked with the resources provided by the portal partners.

For portal partners with no information online as yet, the Virtual Desk offers a small Website hosting application based on restricted templates. Thus, even very small communal administrations, typically with a population of fewer than 1,000 people, were able to participate actively from the beginning.

The central meta-database provoked requests from the private sector for detailed information about the system and especially for interfaces connecting local content management systems directly to the central database. A basic interface is now available and will be improved when shifting to a new, Web services enabled platform.

The URN:Technology has generally become accepted by all portal partners, because of its decentralized responsibility for resources and interlinking, matching the political structures of Switzerland. All partners – including all Webmasters linking to public resources - benefit today from the URN:Technology, due to the fact that the responsibility for accurate links using URNs has shifted onto the providers.

Several portal partners now intend to use the URN:Technology for their own purposes independently too, but interlinked with the subject structures provided by the Virtual Desk Switzerland.

Other non-governmental portals (Ruf Gruppe, 2003b) have started using the same meta-database to provide access to selected resources with their own navigational structures meeting special requirements of their users. New search engines, such as the eFinder (Ruf Gruppe, 2003a), dynamically integrate the meta-database to sort the results by governmental structures or other attributes. As the central meta-database of the Virtual Desk improves in terms of quality and quantity, more applications using this database will become available.

The realization of a transaction hub is characterized by technical as well as organizational complexity. It is precisely because of the ongoing technological development in the area of business-to-business integration (in this case also government-to-government integration) that an ongoing review of the technology used is necessary.

The resource registry is the central UDDI-like registry of public administration in Switzerland. Interestingly, the Virtual Desk has already shown itself in its structure to be a registry conforming to UDDI in its approach. However, further research and development is necessary in order to make a complete UDDI registry out of the URN:Technology currently applied by the Virtual Desk.

With the present operational infrastructure, the further development in the UDDI registry with the help of Web services will succeed in fulfilling the special requirements for comprehensive public registries in the public sector.

To conclude, with the enabling technology available, it will become a major political issue to implement a network state with its profound impact on the integration of business processes spanning multiple government agencies. New forms of cooperation and coordination emerge and even public-private partnerships are fostered by the central meta-database approach.

# References

Berners-Lee, T., Fielding, R., & Masinter L. (1998, August). *Uniform Resource Identifiers (URI): Generic Syntax*. Retrieved December 20, 2003, from The Internet Engineering Task Force IETF: *http://www.ietf.org/rfc/rfc2396.txt*.

Chinnici, R., Gudgin, M., Moreau, J.-J., Schlimmer, J., & Weerawarana, S. (2003). *Web Services Description Language (WSDL) Version 2.0*. Retrieved December 20, 2003, from World Wide Web Consortium W3C: *http://www.w3.org/TR/wsdl20/*.

Connolly, D. (2002, October 23). *Naming and addressing: URIs, URLs*. Retrieved December 20, 2003, from World Wide Web Consortium W3C: *http://www.w3.org/Addressing/*.

Country Codes. (2003). Retrieved December 20, 2003, from International Organization for Standardization ISO: *http://www.iso.org/iso/en/prods-services/iso3166ma/02iso-3166-code-lists/index.html*.

Daigle, L., van Gulik, D., Ianella, R., & Faltstrom, P. (1999, June). *URN Namespace Definition Mechanisms*. Retrieved December 20, 2003, from Internet Engineering Task Force IETF: *http://www.ietf.org/rfc/rfc2611.txt*.

Detlor, B., & Finn, K. (2002). Towards a framework for government portal design: The government, citizen and portal perspectives. In A. Grönlund (Ed.), *Electronic government: Design, applications & management* (pp. 99-119). Hershey, PA: Idea Group Publishing.

Dublin Core Metadata Initiative. (2003, June 2) (Dublin Core Metadata Element Set, Version 1.1: Reference Description). Retrieved December 20, 2003, from Dublin Core Metadata Initiative: *http://www.dublincore.org/documents/dces/*.

Golder, L., & Longchamp, C. (2003, June 24). *Einfach, informativ und sicher*. Retrieved December 20, 2003, from GfS Research Institute: *http://www.admin.ch/ch/d/egov/gv/aktuell/gfs-d-gesamt.pdf*.

*Guichet Virtuel > Spezifische Themen > URN*. (2002). Retrieved December 20, 2003, from Swiss Federal Chancellery: *http://www.admin.ch/ch/d/egov/gv/themen/urn/urn.html*.

*Guichets virtuels weltweit*. (2002). Retrieved December 20, 2003, from Swiss Federal Chancellery: *http://www.admin.ch/ch/d/egov/gv/links/links.html*.

Hjelm, J. (2001). *Creating the semantic Web with RDF*. New York: Wiley.

*IANA*. (2003). Retrieved December 20, 2003, from Internet Assigned Numbers Authority IANA: *http://www.iana.org*.

Lassila, O., & Swick, R.R. (1999, February 22). *Resource Description Framework (RDF) Model and Syntax Specification* (W3C Recommendation). Retrieved December 20, 2003, from World Wide Web Consortium W3C: *http://www.w3.org/TR/REC-rdf-syntax/*.

Meir, J. (University of Applied Sciences). (2002). Center of Competence in eGovernment, Institute for Business and Administration IWV. *Working Paper (Bern) No. 5.5*.

Mitra, N. (2003). *SOAP Version 1.2 Part 0: Primer* (W3C Recommendation 24 June 2003). Retrieved December 20, 2003, from World Wide Web Consortium W3C: *http://www.w3.org/TR/soap12-part0/*.

Moats, R. (1997). *URN syntax*. Retrieved December 20, 2003, from Internet Engineering Task Force IETF: *http://www.ietf.org/rfc/rfc2141.txt*.

*OASIS*. Retrieved December 20, 2003, from Organization for the Advancement of Structured Information Standards OASIS: *http://www.oasis-open.org/*.

*OASIS UDDI Specifications.* (2002). Retrieved December 20, 2003, from Organization for the Advancement of Structured Information Standards OASIS: *http://www.oasis-open.org/committees/uddi-spec/doc/tcspecs.htm.*

*The political structure of Switzerland.* Retrieved December 20, 2003, from Swiss Federal Chancellery: *http://www.admin.ch/ch/e/bk/buku/buku2003/01.pdf.*

Poupa, C. (2002). Electronic government in Switzerland: Priorities for 2001-2005. In A. Grönlund (Ed.), *Electronic government: Design, applications & management.* Hershey, PA: Idea Group Publishing.

Ruf Gruppe. (2003a). *EFinder Version 2.* Retrieved December 20, 2003, from Ruf Gruppe: *http://www.ruf.ch/produkte/egov/images/efinder_v2.pdf.*

Ruf Gruppe. (2003b). *Guichet Schweiz.* Retrieved December 20, 2003, from Ruf Gruppe: *http://www.guichet-schweiz.ch.*

Spahni, D., & Gygax, U. (2002, June 26). *Normenkatalog Guichet Virtuel.* Retrieved December 20, 2003, from Swiss Federal Chancellery: *http://www.admin.ch/ch/d/egov/gv/kurzportraet/normenkatalog.pdf.*

Thom, N., & Ritz, A. (2000). *Public management.* Wiesbaden: Gabler.

Vintar, M., & Leben, A. (2002). The concept of an active life-event public portal. In R. Traunmüller & K. Lenk (Eds.), *Electronic government - Proceedings of the First International Conference, EGOV 2002* (pp. 383-390). Berlin: Springer-Verlag.

*Web Services Activity.* (2003). Retrieved December 20, 2003, from World Wide Web Consortium W3C: *http://www.w3.org/2002/ws/.*

# Endnotes

[1]    Switzerland has a federal structure with three different political levels: the Federal Confederation, the 26 cantons and 2,880 communes (The political structure of Switzerland).

[2]    Web services are an emerging technology enabling application-to-application interaction removing human intervention. A complex set of open standards for this technology is being developed, for example by the World Wide Web Consortium (Web Services Activity, 2003), the OASIS consortium (OASIS ), private vendors and others.

[3]    The Swiss Federal Chancellery maintains a Web site dedicated to this implementation; see (Guichet Virtuel > Spezifische Themen > URN, 2002).

[4]    Switzerland has four national languages: German, French, Italian and Romansch.

# Chapter XVI

# Semiotic Analysis of E-Policing Strategies in the United Kingdom

Kecheng Liu, The University of Reading, UK

Michael Hu, The Police IT Organisation, UK

## Abstract

*Technological infrastructure must satisfy business requirements, and more importantly, it must be able to evolve to meet the new requirements. This requires not only a good understanding of business strategies, visions and functions, but also the evolvability built into the architecture. This chapter first presents a semiotic approach to the business and information technology (hereafter IT) systems. This approach treats the IT system as an integral part of the business organisation. The chapter then discusses the applicability of a semiotic framework in the e-government in the UK, particularly in an evolvable architecture for e-policing. The semiotic framework is applied in the assessment of the e-government strategies and systems requirements, and in the analysis of these requirements to the e-architecture. A case study demonstrating the applicability of the framework is conducted to evaluate the implementation of the national Information Systems Strategy for the Police Service (ISS4PS) and the Crime Justice Information Technology community (CJIT) in the UK.*

# Introduction

Three categories of e-government applications can be identified (Marchionini et al., 2003): access to information, transaction services and citizen participation, each of which represents a stage of the development history of e-government.

In the United Kingdom, the e-government initiative is underpinned by the UK government appointing in 2001 its e-envoy, who reports directly to the Prime Minister. The e-envoy's office has three core objectives: 1) to make all government services available electronically by 2005, with key services achieving high levels of use; 2) to ensure that everyone who wants Internet access has it by 2005; and 3) to develop the UK as a world leader for business. As the first step, the most popular government services will be made available online as soon as possible, to allow more efficient access through the Internet to the information available in different statuary bodies and ministries, as well as different government agencies/organisations. This will be followed by transaction services and citizen participation including services to business, benefits and personal taxation, transport information and booking, education, health, citizen interactions with the justice system, land and property, agriculture, and e-democracy (BCS, 2003).

Drawing experience from e-commerce and e-business from industry, the advocates of e-government agree that the aims of e-government should not be cost saving, but other more profound benefits. PCIP (2002) has suggested a list of possible reasons and goals for e-government:

- Improving services to citizens;
- Improving the productivity (and efficiency) of government agencies;
- Strengthening the legal system and law enforcement;
- Promoting priority economic sectors;
- Improving the quality of life for disadvantaged communities; and
- Strengthening good governance and broadening public participation.

This list represents the vision of most governments and organisations in most countries. In a study by SOCITM (2003a) conducted in the 441 local authorities in England, Wales and Scotland (over 230 councils took part and responded to the survey), it shows that is an optimism within councils about e-government to deliver better services to citizens, with service improvements forecast at 100% in some areas and an average of 20% across all services. Local authority spending on information and communication technology is forecast to rise by 25% to almost £2.5 billion this fiscal year. However, the success of e-government will reply on multiple factors: appropriate telecommunication infrastructure, business process re-engineering, integration of IT and business processes, citizen participation, readiness of government staff, officials' readiness for change, and many more. Amongst all these, human and organisational factors are more crucial than technological aspects. Successful examples of e-government, experience and best practice, particularly in small councils, are disseminated by SOCITM (2003b) for others to share.

As an important part of the e-government initiative in the UK, the e-policing programme is introduced to revolutionise the Police Service and improve the effectiveness of crime prevention and detection, by providing the following (PITO, 2002).

- ready access for the public to the police information and services through a variety of easy to use, safe and secure channels, including the use of intermediaries;

- provision of information and services of relevance to the citizen, particularly victims of crime, in a timely and efficient manner;

- support for joined-up working across police forces and with other criminal justice agencies and local authorities;

- better use of information across all forces and with other criminal justice agencies to support the implementation of the National Intelligence Model and to make policing more effective in combating criminality;

- the collection, exchange and storage of information in a secure and trusted environment;

- flexibility to accommodate new business requirements and to take advantage of changes in technology.

Implementing and rolling out the e-policing programme demands an extension of the traditional police service with the more efficient, more transparent, and more citizen-centred business process and underlying technical infrastructure. This requires the change of culture and business processes that have been in place for crime reporting, intelligence gathering, crime analysis, command and control, and many other parts of the business; it also requires an integrated and modernised police IT systems deployed in the business in parallel to the national systems re-engineering and modernisation programmes to the police IT systems throughout the country. In this chapter, an approach for co-design for business and IT systems will be presented. The theoretical framework derived will be used in the assessment of business and IT strategies for e-policing, one of key e-government initiatives the UK.

# Background

Historically, more than 50 police forces in UK independently developed their own IT systems to support their work, which, although guided by principles defined by the Home Office, has resulted in separate systems with different structures and functions. These IT systems, usually initially developed in 1980s, are based on dated technologies; some are still running on the terminal-mainframe platform. The Police National Computer (PNC), launched in 1977, provides the police forces with key information needed for crime investigation, usually via direct terminal access. Now an important question is how to deal with these legacy systems to meet the new business requirements in police and criminal justice systems.

PITO, the Police Information Technology Organisation, as a non-departmental public body was established in 1997, and acquired its statutory status in 1998, with the UK British Home Office as its sponsor department. The organisation's remit includes England, Wales and Scotland. PITO provides information technology and communications systems and services to the police and other criminal justice organisations within the United Kingdom. Recognising that "information and communication technology (ICT) capabilities play a key role in meeting the Government's objectives and the Home Secretary's priorities for policing" (PITO, 2003), PITO has been leading the strategic planning and implementation of organisational and technological infrastructure for e-policing. One of the important items on PITO's agenda is re-engineering and migration of the legacy police information systems to a web-enabled platform which supports the online police information exchange and processing, and enables the revolutionary concept of e-policing.

# An Organisational Semiotic Approach

The co-design of business and IT systems is an approach towards the development of the two systems in a flexible and adaptable manner (Liu et al., 2002). Within an organisation, the deployment of information technology does not change the business nature, but only the way the business is conducted. This lends to a holistic view of two parts (business and IT systems) being interrelated. Following the Organisational Semiotics (Stamper et al., 1988; Liu, 2000; Liu et al., 2001), a business organisation is by and large a system of information and communication. This is because in the organisations, information is created, stored, and processed for communication and coordination and for achieving the organisational objectives. In some organisations, information processing may be the core business, such as in service industry, for example, banking, insurance and consultancy. In this type of industry, information and services are their products. In other organisations, information processing and communication is to support the production of physical goods and other substantive activities. To a large extent, e-government involves a great deal of the first type of activities, which produce information. An IT system should be viewed as an integral part of the business organisation; the design of both the IT and business systems must be conducted simultaneously. The organic integration of IT into the business processes will allow both systems to evolve naturally.

An organisation, as an integrated business and IT system, can be seen as an architecture having multiple layers, three of which constitute the technical infrastructure:

- *physical* devices and their interconnections - the computer hardware, the network, the optical fibres, the satellites, and so forth, which generate and carry a cause-and-effect chain of events quickly and cheaply, across the globe if necessary;

- *signalling* protocols, the validation, authentication and encryption routines that exploit the basic physical phenomena, so that a varied stream of patterns originating in one place can be reproduced, ideally without error, at another place, or corrected in case of error;

- *structures* that enable signals to be combined into messages, to be analysed into parts (parsed), stored in files, retrieved, used in calculations, and recombined into new messages.

The design, implementation and maintenance of these three layers are the tasks of the IT department, whose responsibilities are to make sure these technical components are functional and adequate to support business operations.

Other three layers in the system architecture are perhaps more important in conducting the business:

- meanings of the numbers, words and expressions that form a message, and the ways that meanings combine to create the meaning of the message as a whole;

- communicating the intentions of the message, through interaction and negotiation between appropriate actors;

- social consequence in the form of established commitment, obligation and responsibly between the people involved.

All these are close to the core business issues that are related to the business objectives of police operations.

Adopting Stamper's Semiotic Framework (Stamper, 1996), we can summarise the above key issues of an IT embedded system at the six semiotic levels (Figure 1). On the left of the diagram suitable names for the levels are given; the key issues are mentioned in the middle; and, on the right are listed the solutions available or approaches to be attempted.

We shall develop the organisational system with IT component at all these levels, but at the technical levels, our solutions are distinguished by being formal and precise. The physical level solutions are implemented in the form of interconnecting networks of standardised telecommunication devices and computers. We can be almost certain when these are correctly established and when they break down; thus the quality of the physical systems can be assured. At the empiric level we use various standard communication protocols (such as PC/TIP) to exploit the physical devices. These take care of encoding, switching, error detection and correction, the confirmation of transmission and so forth. They, like the physical standards, are established globally. The syntactic level is also formal and precise but here it is more difficult to establish global standards. Great efforts in industry have been made to bring in standard forms of communications in computer and information technology, for example SOAP and UDDI in Web services. Some standards have been established but it is difficult to agree on global solutions and the standards tend to be modified at the local level according to the business norms of the industry.

The problems at the upper three layers are less studied and difficult to find "standard" solutions, though organisational semiotics places a great emphasis on them. The problems at the semantic level can be explained by the need to encapsulate meanings of

*Figure 1: Key issues of Internet based systems analysed using the Semiotic Framework*

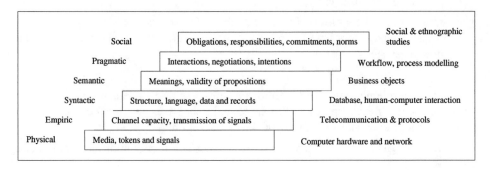

communication within the message syntax solutions, which is commonly acknowledged as the most difficult task. The representation of intentions and social obligations by any IT system is more of a challenge that many systems development methods would not consider, although the semiotic approach (Liu, 2000) has offered mechanisms and techniques whose benefits have been increasingly recognised. Semiotic methods have been applied in examining how information is used in virtual and distributed organisations to enhance the competitiveness (De Moor, 2002; Gazendam, 2001, 2002). Industrial applications have also been carried out in requirements engineering and process modelling for e-policing (e.g., Xie et al., 2003).

# Systems Requirements and Architecture for E-Policing

PITO, as a national organisation responsible for IT policies and strategies for the UK police forces, has set up many task forces to look into different issues, including the IT infrastructure and functionality of the e-policing systems. As a result of the investigation, it has emerged that the environment for the future e-policing should include:

- Information from all police and criminal justice (CJ) organisations that is up-to-date, of known provenance and readily available for use at the point of decision-making
- Enhancement on data and information sharing among the police forces and national agencies, and between the police and other CJ partners
- The capacity for a co-ordinated response across force boundaries using the intelligence generated from multiple information sources
- Greater capability to tackle serious and major crime
- More direct, efficient, and interactive interfaces between the police and public
- Common standardised business processes to harness "best of breed" police systems that support those ACPO (Association of Chief Police Officers) endorsed business processes

- A business information framework that points the way to reuse such systems (as software components) at minimum cost within other forces and/or complex processes
- A common minimum standard for the technical infrastructure, with advancements planned and co-ordinated
- Solutions to address local, regional and national business problems as appropriate.

Many current initiatives have been driven by immediate business needs. For example, the online vehicle number plate enquiry enables the cruising police officer to check the vehicle details on the road. On top of all these, we believe a more thorough understanding of the police work will lead to significant changes in the manner and quality of services. Understanding of the police business processes will be the basis for embedding the Web enabled technologies into the daily workflow of the police forces, which will provide a solid foundation for the e-policing strategies and implementations.

PITO has been tasked to lead the national programme of implementing and rolling-out the e-policing in UK. The principal strategic/business driver for such a programme is to make all government services (with exclusions for policy or operational reasons) available electronically by 2005 as set by the UK government (e-envoy's office paper at www.e-envoy.gov.uk).

It is important for the police service to plan the provision of electronic facilities for the range of communications expected from citizens as an alternative to the traditional face-to-face contact. In addition to the improved accessibility to police services, other factors in the modernising government agenda are of importance for e-policing:

- building services around citizen choices;
- providing for social inclusion; and
- making better use of information.

Thus, any new facilities brought in as part of e-policing, wherever possible, should be focused on the citizen rather than being designed around the sole needs of the police. E-policing must help the police to make better use within and between forces of the information in their possession to combat criminality.

Whilst the operational aspects of the police response to these strategic drivers will be through local forces, because of the federated nature of the police service, a common and joined-up approach in the way that central government envisages is likely to be achieved only by a corporate response and co-ordinated strategy.

## Current Infrastructure

There exists a well-established and fairly efficient business process in the police service in UK that has been in application in the 53 police services throughout the country. This

380 Liu and Hu

is supported by an underlying technical infrastructure that is developed in the last three decades, including

- A portfolio of core IT systems used in the police forces;
- A substantial data repository in the Police National Computer (PNC);
- A backbone of secure communication network.

A wide range of IT systems have been developed in the last several decades in the 43 police forces in England and Wales (not counting in Scotland), serving thousands of on-duty police officers throughout the UK as well as the Criminal Justice System (CJS) community. Many of these systems are currently being upgraded with added functionality, while new systems are continuously being developed and rolled out. The backbone of IT systems to support policing nationwide is the Police National Computer (PNC), which has been in service for 30 years. Over the years, the system has grown to embrace many technological advances, incorporating advice from the government and policing bodies, as well as from in-house and industry technical experts. It has developed from a record keeping service to a sophisticated intelligence tool. It holds extensive data on criminals, vehicles and property, which is accessible in a matter of seconds, through more than 10,000 terminals in police forces across the country (PITO, 2003).

The police IT systems and PNC are connected via the Police National Network Communications that link all police forces, the Home Office and other criminal justice organisations.

Whilst the police/public interface had improved through the introduction of the Police Portal and in some areas "one stop shops," there is no formally agreed upon strategy to ensure the development and delivery of a coherent programme. Common facilities across the service will only succeed if supported by the introduction of standard business processes. There is a slow adoption of best practice in individual forces, and little central promulgation of best practice and little overall programme management function to drive the business process improvements forward. More generally, there is only limited interoperability and integration between systems within forces and a low level of data sharing between forces and with other criminal justice agencies. This impacts on the forces' abilities to make best use of the valuable data held throughout the service. While interfacing and business process improvement may be seen as part of the overall information systems strategy or contained within other programmes of work, the Police/Public Interface programme set the goals to improve these interfaces to deliver all the benefits of e-policing.

There is also little coordination of approach to common services such as security and presentation of information. A wide range of interfaces to core systems exist, as there are no service-wide standards to follow and a plethora of local applications operating in individual forces. As there is no mandate for forces to adopt common systems and standards, there is an inconsistent approach and the potential for duplication of effort is enormous. Data quality is variable between forces. These factors impact on the service's ability to present a "joined-up" appearance and cannot be regarded as cost-effective nor provide best value.

*Figure 2: Information shared amongst the key members of the CJS*

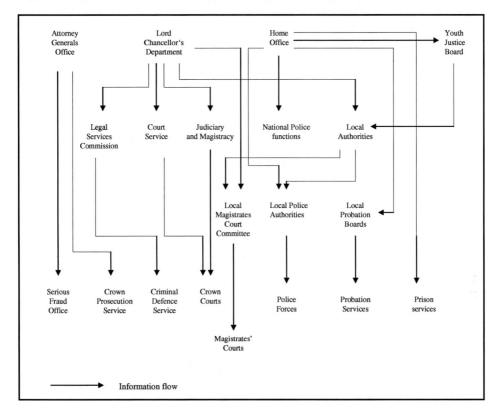

Many of the initiatives in PITO are in the form of studies or pilot projects. There is a danger that the strong messages to come out of these may not be disseminated to forces or embraced by the wider police service partly because of the absence of an overall strategy and programme management function. Moreover, with the police service as one of the key members of the criminal justice system (CJS), it is within PITO's remit to enable a full integration between the police IT systems and other parts of the CJS, so that a seamless collaboration is achieved. Figure 2 shows the key member organisations within the CJS and how information is shared between them (Parsons-Hann, 2003).

## Business and Systems Requirements

Business targets in several business areas have been identified for the next few years (*ww.pito.org.uk/what_we_do*):

•     Communications: This target is to achieve clear and secure voice and data communication, as it is vital to any successful police operation. This area is important because officers rely on it for their safety and that of their colleagues.

- Criminal Justice: All police information systems must be able to share information with other CJS systems. Access to the police systems will be provided to CJS agencies. Information and communications technology holds the key to joining together criminal justice organisations and improving the way they work together.

- Identification: The ability to identify "one person from many" is a fundamental concept in policing. Technology now enables the police to do this more quickly and accurately than ever.

- Intelligence and Investigation: Successful police operations need to be founded on reliable intelligence and sound investigative practice. Collating that intelligence, sharing it with police colleagues and giving them the tools to unlock its potential are key aims in this area.

- Police National Computer: The PNC is an unparalleled source of police intelligence available to all forces nationwide. Steady infrastructure upgrade and the addition of new databases have been implemented to make sure the PNC continues meeting the police needs.

- Police Support Services: Improving police efficiency and effectiveness is not all about front line policing. Forces need IT applications that help them to report and analyse performance and get the most out of the resources they have available.

*Figure 3: The police services information systems architecture*

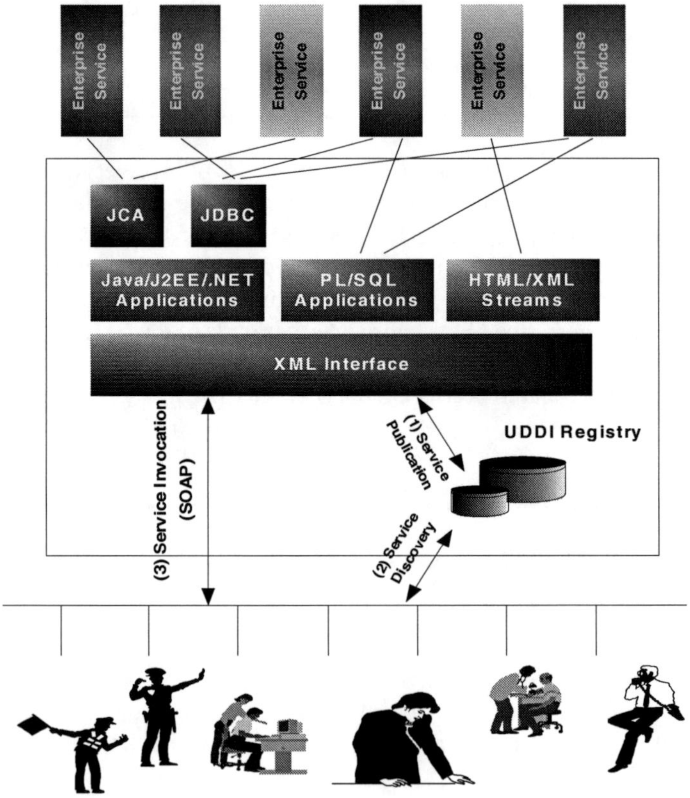

Whilst the definition of e-policing at first glance could include the whole spectrum of policing, it is appropriate to focus the initial e-policing programme on the police/public interface as that must be delivered electronically by 2005 to meet the government's targets. This will build on the current Police/Public Interface programme and is consistent with the agreed scope of the police service information systems strategy (code name Valiant) as shown diagrammatically in Figure 3. A number of core systems are listed for illustrative purposes only and not all potential channels for public access are depicted.

For the police/public interface (PPI) to be effective, there is a requirement for the scope of e-policing programme to include interconnection to those back-office or legacy systems necessary to achieve the vision. The scope will also extend to include areas of data warehousing to make effective use of the information held in core systems. Apart from the necessary links to back-office systems, all other police core business systems and systems serving staff are considered to be outside the current scope of e-policing. Also, whilst e-policing depends on the Criminal Justice Extranet (CJX) for its delivery, the provision and operation of this network is to be considered outside the scope of the initial e-policing programme

In the long run, police information systems in the UK will go through the modernisation and transformation process, as specified by the national Information System Strategy (as seen in Valiant document 2002). The modernised systems will provide ubiquitous access for the police forces and officers. The capability of knowledge-based processing is also required to support effective policing and collaboration between the police and the CJS organisations.

# Case Study: Analysis of the E-Policing Strategies

In this section, the Semiotic Framework (see Figure 1) will be used to evaluate the design and implementation of IT infrastructure for e-policing.

To meet the requirements for e-policing, PITO has developed a strategic framework (PITO, 2002) to address the challenges of organisational and technological issues, and the management of expectations and the implementation of infrastructure. The strategic framework for e-policing illustrated in Figure 4 comprises five component strategic areas:

- Governance and Management Strategy
- Applications Strategy
- Enabling Services and Infrastructure Strategy
- Procurement and Implementation Strategy; and
- Information and Content Management Strategy.

*Figure 4: The e-policing strategic framework*

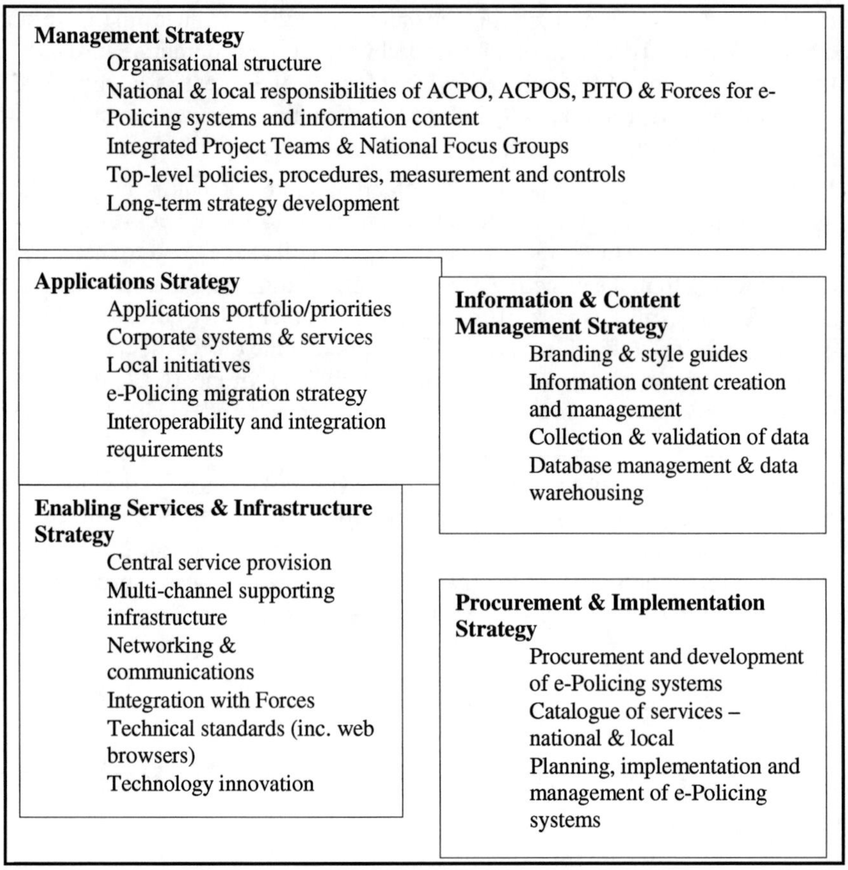

**Management Strategy**
    Organisational structure
    National & local responsibilities of ACPO, ACPOS, PITO & Forces for e-Policing systems and information content
    Integrated Project Teams & National Focus Groups
    Top-level policies, procedures, measurement and controls
    Long-term strategy development

**Applications Strategy**
    Applications portfolio/priorities
    Corporate systems & services
    Local initiatives
    e-Policing migration strategy
    Interoperability and integration requirements

**Information & Content Management Strategy**
    Branding & style guides
    Information content creation and management
    Collection & validation of data
    Database management & data warehousing

**Enabling Services & Infrastructure Strategy**
    Central service provision
    Multi-channel supporting infrastructure
    Networking & communications
    Integration with Forces
    Technical standards (inc. web browsers)
    Technology innovation

**Procurement & Implementation Strategy**
    Procurement and development of e-Policing systems
    Catalogue of services – national & local
    Planning, implementation and management of e-Policing systems

This framework summarises all the important aspects of the current practice of design and implementation of organisational and technological infrastructure for e-policing. An analysis based on organisational semiotics will enable us to evaluate the e-policing framework by examining the methodological underpinnings.

## Governance and Management Strategy – The Social Aspect

In the planning and implementation of IT infrastructure, governmental requirements and police organisations' commitments to the UK society have been seen as the fundamentals. The Governance and Management Strategy covers the following:

- organisational structure to support e-policing
- top-level policies, procedures and controls

- development of the long-term strategies for e-policing; and
- responsibilities of different government agencies and each individual force in e-policing.

## A Semiotic Analysis

As suggested by the semiotic framework, the design of any information systems infrastructure must start from definition of responsibilities, obligations and commitments. The e-policing strategic framework is consistent with this theory by putting the governance and management strategy as the fundamentals. E-policing requires full collaboration between police forces and other criminal justice services. Technologies deployed are only part of the infrastructure, but coordination and collaboration between all organisations involved is more essential in a functional e-policing infrastructure. Guided by the top-level policies and definition of responsibilities, collaborative work processes between agencies, institutions and forces will build an organisational foundation, while modern technologies can enhance the collaborative e-policing.

# Applications Strategy – The Pragmatic Aspect

To meet the vision for e-policing, the single biggest challenge is to move from a police-based system development environment to a citizen-centric business model. In the traditional model, the office of Central Customer acts on behalf of police forces by establishing the service requirements and priorities for development. The focus of e-policing on the police/public interface necessitates an extension of this role to capture also the expectations of the citizen.

In the first instance, the developments will be prioritised based on the recent consultation exercise with all forces and ratified by the Central Customer and the EPMG team. PITO will continue to manage the central programme portfolio including systems, services, infrastructure and common practices. Some systems and services within the central e-policing programme portfolio will be provided locally by forces.

The applications strategy will be developed to include:

- strategy for e-policing corporate systems and services, and local initiatives;
- e-policing migration strategy; and
- specification of interoperability and integration requirements to meet the long-term e-policing strategy.

A key issue is the determination of what should be provided centrally and what may be considered at the local level. The proposed strategy for systems and services to be provided centrally will be based on the premise that these provide:

- corporate single points of contact for the public to engage electronically with the police service; or

- e-policing systems and services that are generic to the police service as a whole and may be replicated across force boundaries.

The e-policing business process model is shown in Figure 5. The citizen expectations, as seen in the model, are the fundamentals to determine the criteria for technical and service performance. These criteria are then applied to the measurement of current services, systems, practices and infrastructure.

## A Semiotic Analysis

The applications strategy covers the issues identified in the pragmatic aspect. It takes into account the different perspectives of the various stakeholders and aims at achieving effectiveness of the integrated systems. The strategy considers how the systems and services interact with the citizens as well as other users (i.e., police officers and CJS staff). Measuring the systems and services will lead to identification of possible gaps between what is expected and what is available with the current infrastructure, which may lead to identification of further improvements and solutions to reduce the gaps.

*Figure 5: An e-policing business process model*

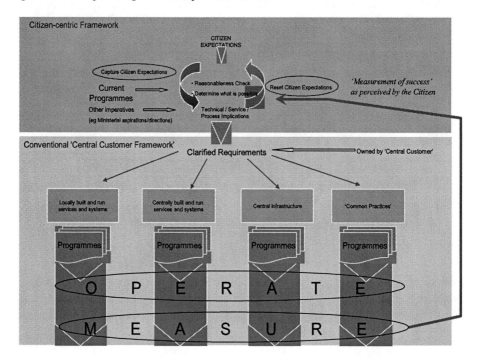

# Information and Content Management Strategy – The Semantic Aspect

An overall strategy for the management of data submitted by citizens, and the provision and updating of published information will be developed. This strategy will be provided to the forces as a "toolkit" to ensure a generic framework is used in information and content management throughout the forces. For the majority of the projects within the PPI programme, the information and content management will be the responsibility of forces following policies and procedures issued by the Association of Chief Police Officers and Association of Chief Police Officers of Scotland (ACPO/ACPOS) and the EPMG team within PITO. Part of the planning, design and training for each project will focus on this important area.

The strategy will focus on the branding of police service Web sites and other electronic display facilities so that the public can gain assurance of the ownership of the information and the security of the communication channels used. Other aspects of content and information management will also be covered in this strategy, including responsibility for the collection and validation of data through e-policing channels, database management and data warehousing as it affects e-policing, and the creation and management of the content published electronically by the police service.

## A Semiotic Analysis

The information and content management strategy addresses the issues at the semantic level. Information content, meaning and validity are essence for all systems that provide information and services, as described in the semiotic framework. Information should be provided timely and shared by relevant stakeholders. The quality of information provision impacts directly on the quality of police services through e-policing. As shown by experience in many information systems development projects, the semantics of information presents the most challenges, as it is difficult to capture in information models and to represent in information systems. Effective methods for dealing with information semantics have to be identified and deployed in the implementation of e-policing infrastructure.

# Enabling Services and Infrastructure Strategy – The Syntactic and Empiric Aspects

In order that the public may be encouraged to use the police portal and other channels in providing often sensitive information to the police and for the police service to make better use of information in its possession in combating criminality, a suitable resilient multi-channel supporting infrastructure is to be provided

The strategy to be developed for enabling services and infrastructure is a key component in the delivery of trusted, secure and joined-up e-policing services. It will include strategies for:

- provision of central services (e.g., Web hosting, common directories);
- communications infrastructure to support multiple channels (e.g., channel strategy);
- integration with local force infrastructures (e.g., browser interface standards).

A backbone communications infrastructure, CJX, is in place linking all forces and the police portal will be connected to it. This will ensure secure routing of data traffic and the ability for forces to share information. Forces will be responsible for compliance with data protection legislation, conformance to system security policies and the observance of the Government Protective Marking Scheme. The accreditation of other criminal justice agencies to use CJX will continue to be the responsibility of ACPO. The requirement for and viability of adopting the replacement government-wide secure communications network being delivered under GSISP, as the principal communication network for the police service or connecting CJX to it, will be assessed centrally at the appropriate time.

Whilst the strategy is being developed, additional features will be provided through the police portal and the forces will become more dependent on it. As it is supporting operational policing, rigorous testing of new features will be necessary prior to their introduction in a live environment and resiliency will be introduced to ensure its continuous availability.

PITO is well placed to provide information and guidance to forces wishing to link their systems into the e-policing infrastructure. There are a series of national focus groups already in existence, which will be used to review elements of this framework to accommodate e-policing as a priority covering policy/role issues across a range of topics. For example, guidance notes will be provided to cover:

- security elements to be considered across all channels;
- technical and architectural standards to be adopted;
- infrastructure  installed to provide the recommended functionality to be used;
- standards for interfaces to back office legacy systems (e.g., Web browsers);
- performance measures and targets for the fulfilment of citizen enquiries and commitments made;
- business process standards (e.g., call centre procedures and practices, data quality, data validation, data cleansing);
- presentation standards for police Web sites (e.g., branding, image, style guides);
- protection of information and codes of practice.

In the longer term, the whole premise, in line with modernising government, will be to provide choices. There is no desire to limit public use of any channel to access e-policing services. A national channel strategy will be developed and it is the intention to provide choices for the public in being able to access police services through a range of channels, including:

- the police portal;
- Internet Web sites;
- one stop shops;
- kiosks;
- call centres;
- digital telephony including text messaging;
- intermediaries (e.g., local authority staff); and
- face-to-face contact (e.g., at police stations).

It is important to develop and maintain coherence between the channels so that an individual may choose to use different channels (e.g., Internet to report a minor crime, telephone to report additional information and SMS text messaging to enquire about progress) while the police officer responding is made fully aware of all the information received to date through all channels. This is a central feature of commercial call centre and client relationship models and has important reference value for the integration with back-office systems.

E-policing services delivered through the police portal will continue to be provided centrally but the content for specific features will be requested to be provided and maintained locally. The use of Internet Web sites by forces is to be encouraged to provide information and discrete services better handled at local level. Consideration will be given to the provision of a national Web hosting service, and to standardising the appearance and the function of force Web sites. It is our intention to recommend a form of branding to enhance the appreciation of the police service as a whole and to provide guidance on the overall appearance and functional content of the Web sites. Links through to force Web sites will be provided on the police portal and vice versa.

It may be appropriate for one-stop shops, kiosks and call centres to be operated on a joint agency basis and the use of intermediaries will be encouraged where it is to the advantage of both parties (e.g., abandoned vehicles, noise nuisance), does not compromise security and is likely to provide a higher level of service to the public (e.g., rural areas). Forces will determine locally with partners the most effective and efficient method of providing these facilities.

The provision of conventional face-to-face contact and telephone services locally will be supplemented by a shared non-emergency telephone number, if proven by the concept demonstrator. Calls will be routed to the local force for response. Additionally, the provision of a single number for text messaging is being considered and is at an early stage of investigation. In the long-term, to ensure that e-policing is citizen-centric, all channels will be supplemented by strong links with back-office systems. Due to the disparate nature of these legacy systems, local forces have to provide interfaces with systems that have been developed in-house.

The key decisions required concern the extent to which e-policing in the long-term moves towards a fully functional customer relationship management (CRM) environment. This will determine the extent of the citizen focus provided, the integration required with back-office systems and the data warehousing facilities needed. CRM implies potential intelligence gathering opportunities and we need to be aware of the implications of this, particularly with regard to the customer relationship. Assuming that full citizen-centric capability is required, the integration strategy will provide a road map for the two-stage migration from the current CJX-connected forces to:

a.    limited interoperability with back-office systems in forces as required for the first phase of e-policing; and

b.    full integration of core systems, data warehousing and e-policing applications as envisaged in the Police Service Information Systems Strategy (Valiant).

It is recognised that for many years forces will be at different stages on the migration towards the fully integrated solution. The integration strategy will be developed as part of ACPO Information Systems Strategy and the need to cater for the diversity of local infrastructures and systems, together with the expectation that different elements of the police community will migrate at different speeds to the centrally provided infrastructure.

### A Semiotic Analysis

The enabling services and infrastructure strategy covers the issues of the syntactic and empiric aspects. It defines standards for data structure, information exchange, communication between systems, and interfacing between application layers and back office or legacy systems. Channels for accessing police services and information sources are also defined; for example, the police portal, Internet Web sites, call centres and digital message exchanges. The appropriate syntactic and empiric setting provides the necessary basis for the correct representation of semantics.

## Procurement and Implementation Strategy – The Physical Aspect

PITO will take responsibility for the implementation of centrally provided and managed projects within the overall e-policing PPI programme. Forces will be expected to provide project management for local implementations and initiatives. During implementation, business continuity will be a priority and the migration to new systems will be achieved in a manner commensurate with maintaining operational capability at all times. PITO will assist the forces in training for new systems and will provide support to local initiatives taking consideration of the fact that forces will be at different stages in their adoption of e-policing techniques.

### A Semiotic Analysis

The procurement and implementation strategy is concerned with the physical aspect of the e-policing infrastructure. PITO has deliberately allowed freedom for the individual forces to choose their own hardware platforms, as long as the syntactical and empiric standards are reinforced, which enables the correct representation and interpretation of information semantics. This separation between the physical platforms from the rest of the aspects in the semiotic framework maximises the flexibility for systems changes. As witnessed in many cases, the need for systems changes arises from both the changes in business requirements and technologies available. The separation between the hardware platforms and other aspects of the e-policing infrastructure will enable the whole set of integrated systems evolve with minimal unnecessary interruption to the rest.

# Summary and Future Work

One important initiative similar to e-policing in the USA is COPLINK (Chen et al., 2003). COPLINK recognises the problems that most local police have database systems used by their own personnel, and lack an efficient mechanism for sharing with other forces and agencies. To enhance the national and local police forces' ability to handle massive amounts of information and improve the efficiency of policing, COPLINK sets the target of developing an integrated information and knowledge management environment for capturing, accessing, analysing, visualising and sharing low enforcement related information. Researchers at Virginia Tech and Purdue University, teamed up with Indiana's Family and Social Services Administration (FSSA), have been developing a WebDG infrastructure for e-government (Medjahed et al., 2003).

In our work, input has been drawn from research work of other going e-government and e-policing projects such as US CJIT and Intelligence Service, Dutch Police and Belgium Police, which we shall continue to benefit from.

This chapter presents only a part of the work currently undertaken in PITO of which the second author is responsible for the architectural design. In this chapter, we introduced an organisational semiotic approach to information systems design and implementation. A business organisation is comprised of people and technology. People are teamed up in a certain structure, with defined responsibilities and governed by the norms (rules and regulations). From the perspective of organisational semiotics, these organisations produce and consume information, and therefore are information systems. The organisational as well as technological components of such information systems have to be co-designed together, so that technologies are best fit into the workflows and business processes. The semiotic framework offers an effective guideline in analysing and designing information systems by carefully examining the issues at the six semiotic levels.

PITO, as an organisation responsible for UK's IT strategies, policies and advice on IT systems implementation, has been playing an important role in organisational and technological infrastructure for e-policing in the UK. The e-policing infrastructure will be built on the existing work by all police forces and CJS agencies. Coordination and collaboration between police forces and CJS agencies are required more than before, which is the prerequisite for a successful implementation of e-policing. The research of the current state of the work shows a firm foundation is available in the UK amongst the police forces and CJS services but much more work is needed before an integrated infrastructure is brought into place. The PITO e-policing strategic framework presents the direction for all the working parties involved in the implementation of the e-policing infrastructure.

A semiotic analysis has been performed on the e-policing strategic framework with a view to assess the e-policing strategies. It shows that the e-policing strategic framework covers well the entire range of the semiotic framework. Careful considerations have been given in the e-policing framework to the social, pragmatic, semantic, syntactic, empiric and physical aspects, as suggested in the theory of organisational semiotics. This has given us much confidence about the current work. Our analysis also suggests that semantics of information is, though its importance is recognised, difficult to capture in the information models and systems. The work we have presented here is an analysis of the current practice in the planning and implementation of e-policing infrastructure after the majority of the work has been completed by PITO. It could be more beneficial if organisational semiotics could have been applied earlier. In further work, semiotic methods, such as semantic analysis and other methods for analysing organisational and technical infrastructure, will be considered for detailed planning and implementation of e-policing infrastructure.

E-government involves a large group of stakeholders: government and non-government, service providers and users from all sectors of the society. The key "product" and "commodity" is information, which will be produced and consumed by the government and citizens (note that both will be providers and consumers, as the interactions can be bidirectional). To understand the nature and characteristics of information is crucial for the design and implementation of e-government systems; and is necessary for effective use of information both in provision of the service and response to it. These services are different from in the traditional form of governance, but supposedly should be equivalent socially and legally. To deliver and enjoy the information-based service through e-government will require an integrated social, legal and technical system that encompasses the technical infrastructure, government and citizens. This system should be built on a sound technical and non-technical basis, covering all semiotic aspects.

# References

BCS. (2003, March). Bulletin interview with Andrew Pinder. *The Computer Bulletin,* 16-17.

Chen, H., Zeng, D., Atabakhsh, H., Wyzga, W. & Schroeder, J. (2003). COPLINK: Managing law enforcement data and knowledge. *Comm. of the ACM, 46*(1), 28-34.

De Moor, A. (2002). Language/action meets organisational semiotics. *J. Information Systems Frontier, 4*(3), 257-272.

Gazendam, H.W.M. (2001). Semiotics, virtual organisations, and information systems. In K. Liu, R.J. Clarke, P.B. Andersen & R.K. Stamper (Eds.), *Information, organisation and technology: Studies in organisational semiotics* (pp. 1-48). Boston: Kluwer Academic Publishers.

Gazendam, H.W.M. (2002). Information system metaphors. *Open semiotics resource center: The semiotic frontline, www.semioticon.com.*

Hu, M. (2003) *Systems integration and re-engineering using XML/Web Services.* WWW2003, Budapest.

Liu, K. (2000). Semiotics in information systems engineering. *Cambridge University Press.*

Liu, K., Clarke, R., Stamper, R., & Anderson, P. (Eds.). (2001). *Information, organisation and technology: Studies in organisational semiotics.* Boston: Kluwer Academic Publishers.

Liu, K., Sun, L. & Bennett, K. (2002). Co-design of business and IT systems. *J. of Information Systems Frontiers, 4*(3), 251-256.

Marchionini, G., Samet, H., & Brandt, L. (2003). Digital government. *Comm. of the ACM, 46*(1), 25-27.

Medjahed, B., Rezgui, A., Bouguettaya, A., & Ouzzani, M. (2003, January/February). Infrastructure for e-government Web services. *IEEE Internet Computing,* 58-65.

Parsons-Hann, H. (2003). *Information infrastructure for e-policing.* BSc thesis, Computer Science Department, The University of Reading, Reading.

PCIP. (2002). Roadmap for e-government in the developing world. The Work Group on E-Government in the Developing World, Pacific Council on International Policy. Retrieved January 10, 2003, from: *http://www.pacificcouncil.org/pdfs/e-gov.paper.f.pdf.*

PITO. (2002). *e-Policing strategic framework.* Police Information Technology Organisation, London.

PITO. (2003). *Forward Plan 2003 to 2008.* Police Information Technology Organisation, London.

SOCITM. (2003a). ICT spending up by 25% as councils make progress on e-government. Socitm's IT trends. December 17, 2003, from: *http://www.socitm.gov.uk.*

SOCITM. (2003b). Small councils' e-government achievements celebrated. Socitm Insight. Retrieved November 16, 2003, from: *http://www.socitm.gov.uk.*

Stamper, R.K. (1996). Signs, information, norms and systems. In P. Holmqvist, P.B. Andersen, H. Klein & R. Posner (Eds.), *Signs of work: Semiotics and information processing in organisations.* Walter de Gruyter.

Stamper, R.K., Althaus, K., & Backhouse, J. (1988) MEASUR: Method for Eliciting, Analyzing and Specifying User Requirements. In T.W. Olle, A.A. Verrijn-Stuart & L. Bhabuts (Eds.), *Computerized assistance during the information systems life cycle.* North-Holland: Elsevier Science.

Xie, Z., Liu, K., & Emmitt, D. (2003). Improving business modelling with organisational semiotics. In H. Gazendam, R. Jorna & R. Cijsouw (Eds.), *Dynamics and changes in organisations – Studies in organisational semiotics* (pp. 89-102). Dordrecht: Kluwer Academic Publishers.

Chapter XVII

# Digital Government Development Strategies:
## Lessons for Policy Makers from a Comparative Perspective

Yu-Che Chen, Iowa State University, USA

Richard Knepper, Indiana University, USA

## Abstract

*This chapter provides policy makers with a comprehensive framework for developing national digital government strategies. This framework raises the importance of technical and economic situations, cross-country comparison of laws and institutions, and the necessity of considering political contexts. More importantly, it outlines the general developmental strategies and critical success factors for improving the practice of national digital government efforts. To illuminate the utility and application of the framework through an examination of Poland and Taiwan's experience, this chapter also yields insights into specific considerations for designing and improving digital government.*

# Introduction

Digital government has a better chance of success if it follows a well-articulated and sound strategy. Failures of digital government projects in terms of cost overrun, delay in delivery, and problems in implementation are the rule rather than the exception (Heeks, 1999). Having a sound strategy is considered as the first and most important step in securing the success of information technology projects (Fletcher, 1999). More importantly, a strategic master plan helps align information and communication technology investment and resource allocation with the objectives of organizations. If done properly, a strategic plan can help public organizations realize the full potential of an information technology investment.

The key question that guides this study is: How can a national digital government strategy be better designed and developed? As reflected in the research question, this chapter takes a normative perspective of policy and institutional design with emphasis on policy makers. A large number of countries around the world have recognized the importance of information and communication technology for staying competitive in the information age. Moreover, it is recognized that a national strategy is the critical first step in building an information and communication infrastructure and allocating the necessary critical resources to build digital government. Some European countries, Asian economies, and North and South American nations, have some form of a national digital government plan, such as UK Online, e-Japan, and e-Korea.

However, there is a shortage of research-based frameworks for guiding the development of a national strategy. This chapter fills this gap by offering policy makers a comprehensive framework for developing national digital government strategies. Moreover, the authors further examine the experiences of Poland and Taiwan to illuminate the proposed framework and to provide insights into specific considerations for designing and improving digital government through strategic planning.

# Background

Digital government refers to the use of information and communication technology to better the relations between government and its employees, citizens, businesses, nonprofit partners, and other agencies by enhancing the access to and delivery of government information and services.1 The terms of digital government and e-government are used interchangeably in this chapter because, in the authors' view, they cover the same set of activities as outlined in the definition of digital government. Digital government strategic plans are national plans to guide the development of a country's efforts to deliver information and service via digital means.

An overarching national digital government plan is less studied than individual digital government projects. Most of the critical success factors come out of studies of individual IT projects at state and local levels (Dawes et al., 1997; Heeks, 1999). Since national strategic plans provide the framework in which most digital government projects are prioritized, designed, and implemented, it is important to study those. There is lack of a research-based guidance on strategic planning for digital government at the national level and this study aims to fill the gap by drawing from three streams of literature to develop a framework for developing a national digital government strategic plan: digital government, institutionalism, and strategic information system planning. Each body of literature, as reviewed below, points out some key factors for the development of a conceptual framework. By choosing Taiwan and Poland, which are at markedly different points in their implementation of digital government plans, the authors believe that they can more rigorously test the validity and salience of the framework.

# Digital Government

The broad literature on digital government points out the importance of political forces, institutions, and the all-encompassing notion of digital government to include citizen participation and electronic production of public services. In addition to these broad environmental factors, this body of literature offers a set of critical success factors that should be an integral part of national digital government strategies, including building management/rational decision-making capacity, establishing national information and technology infrastructure, developing IT-related human resources, protecting privacy and security, and managing government information resource management.

In addition, political forces and institutional settings play a significant role in national digital government efforts. Digital government plans and projects, unlike other private sector information technology projects, need to be attentive to political considerations and governmental processes at all levels of government (Bozeman & Bretschneider, 1986; Rocheleau, 2003). In the international arena, countries need to harmonize their digital government plans with regional associations that they aspire to be associated with. For example, current and future European Union members look for EU e-governments' plan for guidance on what components need to be included in their digital government plan to take advantage of the resources available at the regional level. A number of unique political challenges face development of digital government at the domestic level. These include the election cycle, budget requirements, politics of intergovernmental information sharing, competing policy objectives, and existing civil service systems.

Moreover, legal and institutional incentives and constraints shape the design and use of information technology in the public sector (Fountain, 2001; Landsbergen & Wolken, 2001). For example, privacy laws may govern how information is collected and shared among public agencies. Institutional incentives are critical for soliciting cooperation from individual public employees and agencies as a whole to share information and resources. Moreover, security law allows governments to win the trust of citizens and business to conduct transactions with government without the fear of information fraud or identity theft.

Citizens and their participation also constitute an important environmental element of digital government (Marchionini, 2003; Schedler & Scharf, 2001; UN/ASPA, 2002). When an active civil society and well-established information and communication infrastructure is in place, an e-government strategy that is more responsive to citizen needs is more likely to be implemented.

Keeping these environmental conditions in mind, the broad digital government literature has pointed out some critical elements needed in a sound national plan. First, rational/ administrative capacity is one critical factor for digital government, as various studies of e-government projects around the world have suggested (Heeks, 1999). This is a precondition for any successful implementation of national digital government strategy. Second, national governments need to facilitate citizen participation in establishing an information and communication (hereafter referred to as ICT) infrastructure. As highlighted in the United Nations' report on an e-government survey, accessibility to e-government services depends on the information and communication infrastructure of a country (UN/ASPA, 2002). Since building ICT infrastructure usually has an economy of scale, national government is best suited for conducting its design and development.

Third, the training of IT related personnel should also be included in a national plan. The building of human infrastructure for the use of information technology is as critical as building the physical one. This is a particularly severe challenge at the local level in the United States and probably for most countries a challenge at all levels of government. The International City/County Management Association has conducted two e-government surveys of local government and has consistently ranked the lack of IT personnel as the number two barrier to e-government (ICMA 2000, ICMA 2002).

Fourth, the importance of launching a national campaign for the protection of privacy and security has been increasingly recognized by countries around the world. Cyber-crime, such as identity theft and child pornography, has greatly affected many people's lives. The protection of privacy and security is also critical for winning citizens' trust in government and for them to conduct transactions online (Edmiston, 2003). Lastly, the management of government information resources has been discussed as a critical component for a national digital government plan (Fletcher, 2003). Government information is the underlying content base on which information and transaction services are created. National government is in a good position to set a common standard for data format and information sharing protocols.

# Institutionalism

Institutionalism has contributed to the study of national digital government strategies in a number of ways.2 First, it points out the importance of national administrative and legal institutions. Therefore, a sound national digital government plan should have a component on building an administrative and legal institution. Second, it explains the ways in which institutions may shape the design and implementation of digital government projects. Specific programs can be developed when there is a good understanding of how incentive structure works in various national and sub-national context. Third, institutionalism stresses the link between institutional arrangements and performance. A comprehensive national strategy should have a mechanism to track performance. Lastly, for a design of an institution or policy, it is important to address the physical environment (Farris & Tang, 1993; Ostrom, 1990).

National institutions are critical for the success or failure of national digital government efforts. The comparison between various nations' economic performance has articulated the importance of developing national institutions (North, 1990). Countries with similar resources may perform quite differently if one has efficient and rational national institutions and another is plagued with corruption and mismanagement. Institutions are broadly defined as rules that govern relationships in the specific domain of human interchange, such as the rule of law and democratic governance. In the digital government domain, privacy and security laws are fundamental for developing trust for citizens, businesses, and other governmental agencies to conduct transactions with one another. The health of national digital government institutions is in part judged by the effectiveness of national government in making rational decisions and implementing policies. The lack of rationality in government decision-making has undermined digital government projects in many developing countries (Heeks, 1999). A comprehensive digital government strategy should include the effort to build rational decision-making if so lacking. Institutions shape not only the selection of digital government projects but also their design and implementation (Fountain, 2001). For example, a national identity card is permissible in Singapore but raises heated debates in the United States, which are due to the difference in legal protection requirements for privacy. The role of institutions is particularly pronounced when a cross-country comparison is concerned. As a result, a national strategic framework needs to factor in the role of institutions.

The link between institutions as an incentive structure and performance is another important insight (Ostrom, 1990; Ostrom et al., 1993). For example, an IT training program can only be successful when the perceived expected benefit of participation outweighs the costs involved. A national digital government plan needs to think through the costs and benefits. Performance is critical for linking incentives and outcomes (North, 1990; Ostrom et al., 1993). A national digital government strategy needs to have performance measures specified for the evaluation and modification of strategies.

The last important insight that institutionalism has for digital government is that it is critical to match policy and institutions to address the conditions of the physical information and communication infrastructure. Any strategy and policy developed needs to be sensitive to the unique challenge of each individual country's ICT infrastructure.

## Strategic Information System Planning

Strategic information system planning is another key body of literature that provides insights into the development of a national digital government strategy. A national strategic plan, if implemented properly, can anticipate and address the political, institutional, economic, and technical context in which a national digital government strategy is formulated. The strategic information system planning literature states the important components of strategic planning, the role of context, and specific issues for public sector strategic information system planning.

Strategic planning literature offers guidelines on the essential components of an effective strategy. An effective strategy has a statement of strategic goals, an articulation of policies that affect the achievement of strategic goals, and more detailed programs to carry out the strategy (Mintzberg & Quinn, 1991). Similarly, an effective digital government strategy should at least include explicitly stated strategic goals. For example, the state of Minnesota has articulated its goals as to create a technologically literate public and to both create and maintain an efficient and effective state government. Moreover, that strategy should list relevant policies that limit or facilitate the deployment of such strategies as well as specific programs to achieve these strategic goals. Information system (IS) planning adds a technical component to strategic planning in general. In particular, strategic IS planning looks at the inventory of information technology resources both inside an organization and in the marketplace.

Strategic IS planning literature has pointed out the importance of scanning societal, organizational, and managerial issues before formulating a strategy. These organizational and managerial issues are usually more difficult than the technical ones. Taking organizational issues into account before drafting strategy increases the fit between strategy and organization.

Public sector strategic information system planning needs to consider several unique characteristics of government. First, government usually has multiple and usually competing objectives (Bozeman & Bretschneider, 1986). A public sector strategic IS plan needs to take that into account. Second, the planning horizon needs to correspond with election cycles, so that the planning horizon is usually shorter than the one advocated by the private sector (Caudle, Gorr & Newcomer, 1991; Guy, 2000). Lastly, stakeholders' involvement is regarded as critical for the successful implementation of an IS strategic plan (Bryson & Alston, 1996). However, a balance needs to be made between timeliness and extent of stakeholder involvement.

# An Analytical Framework

The framework developed below draws from the insights offered by the three streams of literature as identified by their respective opening paragraphs presented in the previous section. As shown in Figure 1, these insights are organized into digital government strategies (center), environmental conditions (left), and performance results (right). Each group of factors is grounded either in these bodies of literature or some empirical evidence.

Four principles govern the development of the framework. First, a good strategic plan needs to address the unique challenges posed by the environmental circumstances facing a national digital government effort. What matters is the extent to which a strategy addresses its environmental conditions rather than setting ambitious goals. Second, there exists a set of principles and success factors, which, if done correctly, will increase the likelihood of success. Third, the framework acknowledges the evolutionary nature of digital government efforts. A strategy also needs to adapt to and possibly shape the environment that a national government is in. Lastly, performance of digital government is an important element of the framework to trace the effect of strategies on outcomes.

*Figure 1: A conceptual framework for the development of a national digital government strategy*

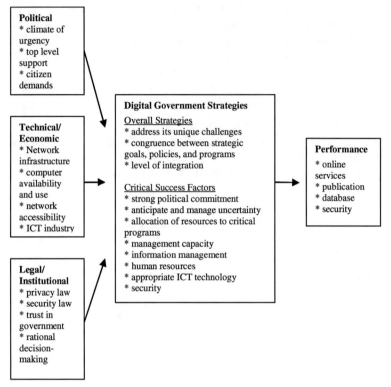

## Environmental Factors

### Political Considerations

Three political drivers, as shown in the top left box of Figure 1, set the stage for the development of a national digital government strategy. International political pressure may have an impact on a strategic plan. For example, a national digital government plan can be used as a precondition for a membership in an international organization, or for external help.

Another driver for a national digital government plan is the policy agenda of administration. A country's leaders may recognize the need for digital government as being part of a coherent strategy to stay competitive in the information era. They may view digital government as a means to revitalize public services (Snellen, 2000). The digital government plan could be supported by national legislature and the executive branch.

Citizen demand is another driver for digital government (Kamarck & Nye, 2002). Citizens, after becoming accustomed to the convenience and efficiency accompanied by e-commerce, will probably demand that government do the same. Grass-roots demand involves both electronic voting and civic participation in the government decision-making process. This is an important area of development for a digital government plan to pay attention to (Marchionini et al., 2003). From a management perspective, electronic democracy should be integrated into the core mission of digital government. It should be noted that the extent to which civic participation may shape a national digital government plan depends on the power of democratic institutions in shaping public policy.

## Technical/Economic Conditions

Several technical/economic conditions, as shown in Figure 1, are relevant for the design and formulation of a national digital government strategy. A good strategy needs to first assess the current condition as the first step to developing a path to the desired results. The national information and communication technology infrastructure is the first critical element for assessment. In particular, the UN/ASPA report has pointed out the importance of network availability (UN/ASPA, 2002). The availability of a high-speed network for both government and private use is an important indicator of the maturity of an infrastructure.

Second, computer availability and use determines whether the information and communication infrastructure is utilized. Citizens and businesses need to have computers and Internet service providers for them to get access to government information and services online. This is usually measured by the number of computers per capita. Wide disparity is seen among countries around the world. For example, in the United States, more than half of population has a computer, whereas in Brazil less than 5% of the population has one (UN/ASPA, 2002).

Third, the distribution of use and accessibility among various groups also shapes national digital government strategies. *Digital divide* is usually the term used to capture this issue. Different socio/economic groups and demographics have unique needs and uses for digital government.

Lastly, the existence of a viable domestic IT industry is beneficial to the design and implementation of a national digital government strategy. This factor has a positive spill-over effect on the affordability of computers, the establishment of an information and communication network, and the viability of building e-commerce applications for government use.

## Legal and Institutional Issues

Two prominent legal and institutional issues pertaining to digital government are privacy and security (see Figure 1). These two issues have been identified by various levels of US government as important (GAO, 2001; ICMA, 2000, 2002). Privacy laws govern the use and distribution of information by government and businesses. For example, US Privacy Act dictates the protection of sensitive individual information from improper distribution. An exception can only be made when there is strong public interest such as public safety or national security. The EU has also developed directives to specify policies for the protection of individual data. The protection of privacy aims to foster consumer confidence and encourage e-commerce.

Security is a major concern when government information systems store vital information about individuals and government units. Unauthorized access to critical information could have devastating consequences. Social security information may be stolen as a result of identity theft. Individuals' lives are shattered as a result. Countries around the world started to experience security problems associated with increasingly computerized government information systems. The US instituted the Computer Security Act of 1987 to spell out principles for computer security.

A national digital government strategy needs to address both privacy and security to win the trust and willingness of citizens and businesses to submit personal information and conduct transactions online. If privacy is not adequately protected to facilitate private and business transactions with government online, a national digital government strategy needs to include efforts to pass relevant laws and regulations. A national digital government strategy should also address gaps in the area of security. Some countries have launched the Public Key Infrastructure Initiative and other security measures to address this issue.

As institutionalist literature suggests, administrative capacity is one of the key elements for enhancing performance. As a governmental effort, digital government also relies on the institutional capacity of government to be efficient and rational. If such capacity does not exist, a national digital government strategy needs to make this a high priority and incorporate it into its plan.

# Digital Government Strategies

A successful national digital government strategy should be able to appropriately address the political, institutional, social, and technical challenges outlined above as environmental factors. As suggested by the review of relevant literature, digital government strategies have two components (see Figure 1). The first component is overall strategies that a country should follow to address its environmental challenges. Since each country faces unique challenges, an assessment of the overall strategy should focus on the extent to which these challenges are addressed. Having a congruent strategic plan and striving for a higher level of integration of electronic services are two additional indicators of a sound strategic plan.

The second component includes critical factors for the success of a national digital government strategy. These factors include strong political support, management of uncertainties, allocation of resources, development of management capacity, the use and quality of managed information, the development of human resources, an appropriate level of technology, and the protection of privacy and security. Each factor will be detailed in the following section.

## Overall Strategies

A successful digital government strategy needs to have the following three character-istics. First, the strategy needs to address its unique environmental conditions as articulated in institutionalism and strategic planning. For instance, if a country is still behind in setting up the network infrastructure, then this should receive the highest priority. This is consistent with the strategic planning literature. The UN/ASPA survey of digital government around the world also supports the need for addressing its social, political, and economic composition.

Second, strategic goals, policies, and programs should be congruent with one another. The internal consistency between goals, policies, and program as three integral components of a strategic plan are the preconditions for successful implementation. For instance, a national objective of bringing access to all citizens should have policy and programs that address digital divide issues. The congruence can be seen when policies and programs support the outlined strategic goals.

Another common characteristic is the integration of various digital government infrastructure components and services. The integration of government networks and infrastructure is the foundation for seamless e-government services. Such integration usually involves a common platform for all government services and protocol for information and resource sharing. This is also a sign of maturity in the development of digital government (Layne & Kim, 2001).

## Critical Success Factors

A good strategic plan addresses the constraints of political authority. A good plan mobilizes the support for digital government, particularly high-level support. In addition, it will reflect citizen demands and other political considerations. Another critical success factor of a national strategic plan is the anticipation and management of political and technological uncertainties.

Government is subject to the turnover of political appointees and elected officials. Changes in the course of policies are commonplace. A strategic plan needs to identify and anticipate those political uncertainties. Another source of uncertainty is technology. A leading technology today may be obsolete tomorrow. As a result, the cost projection for information technology may be incorrect.

Moreover, a strategic plan needs to allocate necessary resources to critical programs. One main challenge of digital government initiatives is finding the resources. A plan without committed resources is very likely to fail. One main resource that most countries are short of is skilled IT personnel. A strategic plan needs to address the recruiting and training of IT staff for critical programs.

Quality and security control of government information resources is at the center of any successful national digital government strategic plan. Ensuring the quality and security of information is the necessary groundwork for disseminating government information and providing government services online.

Rational decision-making and implementation capacity is central to a national strategic plan. This institutional capacity affects both the design and implementation of a digital government plan. This is the foundation for much successful decision-making at national and local levels. With this capacity, a national government is able to identify what is lacking in its political, economic/technical, and institutional conditions and develop a plan to address those.

## Performance

The performance of digital government usually has multiple dimensions (see Figure 1). The main indicators include the availability of online services, the number of government publications online, the access to government databases for information retrieval, the level of security control, and the extent to which a national information and communication infrastructure is developed.

Online government services range from the simple provision of information to client-centered transaction environments. Most developing countries are capable of delivering static information and forms for a number of standard services over the Internet. Many governments are beginning to offer a limited range of services via the Internet. The most advanced online government portals provide services, such as filing for benefits and renewing identification cards, which are organized by clients' needs, rather than by organizational structures. This client-centered model for a transactional portal requires a high degree of both horizontal and vertical cooperation between agencies and levels of government, or an intermediary agent that aggregates disparate functions into a single interface. Public service portals and government information systems require a database containing information relevant to public services and functions, and these systems must ensure security and privacy for their users. These include such data as records of vehicles and insurance, social security, medical, and demographic information. One of the most difficult pieces in any information system is to ensure that it provides privacy and security to its users. Secure information systems require thorough investigation and testing at implementation and long-term maintenance.

In order for public information systems to be used by clients, and not just public administrators, a healthy telecommunications infrastructure must be in place to convey information to clients. In order to provide access to as many citizens as possible, many government plans emphasize the development of high-speed networks and public access points, as well as the stimulation of Internet service provider markets. These development plans include links to the global network infrastructure, fast connections between metropolitan area networks and research institutions, and the provision of network infrastructure to public places such as post offices and public transportations stations.

# Illustrative Cases: A Comparison Between Taiwan and Poland

The utility of the proposed framework (see Figure 1) is illustrated with the analysis of Taiwan's and Poland's digital government strategies. When guided by the framework, policy makers are able to identify the strengths and weaknesses of digital government strategies. The results of analysis are presented below with summary tables.

Poland and Taiwan were selected because each country is at a different point along the developmental curve. Selecting cases with significant differences in context and outcomes provide theoretical insights (Miles & Huberman, 1994; Yin, 1994). Moreover, it assists with the assessment of applicability of the framework in a wide variety of situations. By investigating two cases with different characteristics, this chapter identifies success factors that are common to both situations, investigates which factors seem to be isolated to specific developmental processes, and provides policy recommendations.

# Performance of National Digital Government Strategies

The result of implementing existing digital government plans varies between Taiwan and Poland. According to a 2003 report comparing countries around the world (West, 2003), Taiwan was ranked number 5 among 169 countries surveyed in terms of its digital government performance. In contrast, Poland ranked 44 among them. Taiwan outperformed Poland in all five main areas examined in the report: online services, online publications, use of databases, privacy policy, and security policy. Taiwan was particularly advanced in making publications online and employment of integrating databases for services.

Poland's progress in implementing its plan has been slow, although some areas are showing success. The number of ministry, regional, and local government Web sites continues to grow. Many online services, such as tax services and an online system for entering complaints and requests for information, are still in pilot stages. However, databases and internal systems for bureaucratic functions are being introduced, and some programs to ensure the safe transmission of data are in place. A large part of Poland's plan focuses on the reengineering and replacement of old civil service information systems. Poland appears to be focusing on developing a strong internal structure before opening that structure to its citizens.

# Analysis of Environmental Factors

Taiwan's overall political environment is in favor of a digital government strategy. Taiwan's political authority has recognized the importance of becoming a "green silicon island." The government's commitment to a digital island is seen in the emphasis it places in e-government as an important piece of its overarching national development strategic plan – the sixth national economic developmental plan (Lin, 2002). Top-level government officials have touted the current achievement in the area of information technology and hope to sustain growth in this area. Citizens are used to the convenience provided by e-commerce. As a result, they tend to demand similar services from their government.

The information and communication infrastructure in Taiwan is relatively more mature than most of the emerging economies. In September 2000, Internet users have grown to 5.94 million, about 25% of the total population. The communication infrastructure has both domestic and international components. In December 2000, the connection between major cities in Taiwan has reached 45 Gbps, a 29000-fold increase over the 1.544 Mbps in April 1995. A direct international connection has been established between Taiwan's major trading partners such as United States, Japan, Hong Kong, and Singapore. In terms of broadband service coverage, ADSL services covered 97% of Taiwan in 2000.

Moreover, Taiwan has a vibrant IT manufacturing industry and aspires to further develop network related industries. In 2000, Taiwan was the fourth IT hardware manufacturing country in the world with the total value of approximately 23 billion dollars. Taiwan has over 60% of the global market share in products such as keyboards, hubs, and motherboards. The National Science Council, a Taiwanese counterpart to the National Science Foundation in the United States, has aimed to promote collaboration among industry, academia, and government to promote wireless communications and next generation Internet technologies (Yo et al., 2001).

For the past few years, Taiwan has made efforts toward formulating laws and policies in the areas of digital transactions and security. The legal framework governing electronic signature to facilitate electronic commerce and electronic transactions with government was in place before the year 2002. The revision of existing laws on digital property rights, regulations on fair trade in electronic commerce, protection of online consumer transactions, and online banking practices was planned to be underway in 2002 (Executive Yuan, 2001). Digital security efforts center on the establishment of new offices inside policy departments to handle computer crime and creation of a new reporting system. Specific attention is paid to the prevention of computer crime and problems with pornography (Yo et al., 2001). Privacy has not been specifically discussed as part of the e-Taiwan initiative.

Poland has only recently started to embark upon market and ICT infrastructure development, and requires extensive infrastructure development and education of public administrators and citizens in order to ensure the success of its initiatives. Poland is on the way to joining the European Union and needs to rapidly adopt EU practices and standards in order to become a member state. The political motivation for the implementation of a strategic development plan is strong. The ePolska plan also emphasizes the benefit of ICT for business and government effectiveness. At the same time Polish citizens are increasingly frustrated with government inefficiency and irrational processes, which can benefit (or possibly suffer) from the use of ICT and reengineering. In contrast to Taiwan, however, citizens are used to doing business personally and have little experience with government on the Internet. Some statistics find that only 4% of Polish Internet users access public administration Web sites (Taylor Nelson Sofres & Center for Public Opinion Research, 2002). Providing Polish citizens with channels to access government services must precede the adoption of those services.

Information technology infrastructure in Poland is still maturing, and many citizens are still without some means of Internet access. Currently about 2 million of Poland's 38 million citizens are listed as Internet subscribers (SourceOECD, 2001). Poland has one major telecommunications company, Telekomunikacja Polska S.A. (TPSA), which is undergoing a lengthy privatization and market rationalization process, and this company provides a subscription-free dial-up Internet service to every telephone client, as well as subscription-based ISDN and broadband services. Broadband subscriptions are much less frequent, around 1000 subscribers (SourceOECD, 2001). Poland's metropolitan area networks are connected by a single (originally academic) network, and there are three connections to the European backbone. Poland's information and communications technology industry is small; there are few Polish companies producing new technology. The relatively high price of computers has kept computer ownership low: 23% of households have computers, and computer ownership is concentrated in the 25% of households with the highest income (Main Statistical Office, 2002).

The Polish government is struggling to improve its practices and make administrative procedures more rational, as well as to maintain citizens' privacy and security. Laws against unauthorized access and computer and telecommunications fraud are part of the criminal code, although police forces may not be well equipped to deal with computer crime. Ensuring identity and reliability of documents on the Internet in order to regulate e-commerce has been a concern for some time, generating a project to create an electronic signature that has been working for several years. The Ministry of Internal Affairs and Administration is working to rationalize Poland's personal identification system. Implementation of policy initiatives has been difficult so far; Poland's scarce resources have limited the introduction of new programs, although a number of plans have been drafted. Engendering trust in these new programs may be difficult, even if Poland succeeds in providing access for all citizens. Public trust in the government is low, and government services are often seen as inefficient and operating without rationality, and new initiatives may not be better. As an example, a program to allow business owners to report income tax with their computer met with difficulties that severely limited the program's efficacy. Digital government offers Poland the chance to rationalize administrative decision-making and make government services easier to deal with by eliminating problems such as multiple collections of data and paper-based archives.

## Assessing Digital Government Strategies

Both countries address three overall strategy areas well. Both the ePolska and e-Taiwan plans fit well with external concerns, fitting their e-government development plan well into an overall strategy. Both plans also clearly delineate relationships between goals and policy measures, and initiatives clearly move towards overarching goals. Taiwan and Poland are also able to integrate those measures effectively. Multiple initiatives are dependent upon each other for eventual success.

Poland and Taiwan both seem to be facing the challenges effectively, but both development plans have weaknesses that require attention. The two countries focus on network infrastructure and have a strong commitment to address universal access issues, as well as high-level support and standardization. However, both plans require extensive interagency cooperation, which is often difficult to secure. Poland and Taiwan also score low in data quality and training areas, as well as in the area of security. In many of the areas Taiwan performs better, owing to a strong existing infrastructure and support for the measures in the plan.

Following the proposed framework, the analysis of digital government strategies includes two phases. The first phase involves the overall fitness of a digital government strategy to address external challenges, the congruence between strategic goals, policy, and programs, as well as the level of integration among different components of the strategy. Table 1 illustrates the main findings. The second phase discusses the strengths and weaknesses of specific areas of the digital government strategies by comparing Taiwan with Poland. A summary table for this section is Table 2.

*Table 1: Strengths and weaknesses of the overall digital government strategies of e-Polska (2003) and e-Taiwan (2001)*

| | Poland | | Taiwan | |
|---|---|---|---|---|
| **Criteria** | **Strengths** | **Weaknesses** | **Strengths** | **Weaknesses** |
| **Meeting external challenges** | *catch up to EU standards<br>* addressing digital divide | * goals are set too high, timelines too short | * efficiency<br>* addresses legal and institutional issues<br>* G2G, G2B, G2C<br>* use of multiple channels<br>* strong ICT infrastructure and IT industry<br>* addressing digital divide | * unable to scan external changes |
| **Congruence between goals, policy, and programs** | *Three long range goals<br>* aligned with eEurope initiatives<br>* creating standards | * large infrastructure investment<br>* lack of reengineering | * clear overall strategies<br>* clear measurable goals<br>* clear role of common platform<br>* process reengineering | * lack of training |
| **Level of integration** | *Portal (Wrota Polski)<br>* Central Administrative Database<br>* unification of identification schemes | * Agency cooperation difficult<br>* Inertia | * portal<br>* common service platform<br>* one-stop services | * lack of organizational strategy<br>* lack of resource commitment |

## Assessing the Overall Digital Government Strategy

In addressing external concerns, Poland ranks slightly behind Taiwan. Each country stresses competition as a driving force behind improvement, as well as digital divide issues, and both focus on relationships between government, business, and citizens (G2G, G2B, and G2C). Each country's plan recognizes the gains in efficiency and efficacy that e-government offers.

The Polish strategy notes several gaps in ownership access equipment between Poland and its neighbors (ePolska, 2003) and accordingly sets goals for increasing citizens' access. Measures for success in the ePolska plan include the number of stationary and mobile phones, computers, and the number of homes with broadband access. Access-related goals also include the construction of public Internet kiosks and provisioning schools with computers and high-speed Internet access, as well as the creation of a tax credit or other economic incentive for computer owners. Another part of the plan calls for improving Poland's telecommunications market. By stimulating price-and service-based competition, the plan aims to improve Internet access prices and service. Poland's initiatives also include a number of public-private partnerships with foreign firms, especially in education.

Impending EU accession is a driving factor in Poland's development plans and serves to tie together a number of initiatives, in order to bring Poland into compliance with EU requirements, as well as to prepare for participation in the Schengen Information System. Poland's portal will include a "Polish Gateway to Europe," which will increase the efficiency of requests for EU financial aid both before and after accession. The structure of Poland's plan follows the foundation laid out in the eEurope plan, dividing digital government development into providing access for all, training and education of citizens and public administrators, and the creation of resources and applications.

However, Poland's strategy has a two-fold weakness, which gives rise to its relatively poor fit between government strategy and external environment. First, the goal set for building communication infrastructure and improving network access is overly aggressive since most of the goals are modeled after eEurope without giving consideration to feasibility. Second, Poland seems to rely heavily on technological solutions when human capital should receive more attention. For example, there is an emphasis on telework and telemedicine while the fundamental issue of training of personnel is not properly addressed.

In contrast, Taiwan scores relatively high in addressing its environmental conditions. Its assessment of the feasibility of its digital government plan seems to be reasonable. This is evident in the achievement of key objectives ahead of schedule in the first three years of e-government efforts from 1997-2000. Moreover, the e-government strategy included partnership with Taiwan's vibrant IT manufacturing industry to quickly establish and upgrade the ICT infrastructure. In its e-government plan, Taiwan understands the need for multiple channels of service delivery to address the problem of the digital divide. For instance, in the area of health care service, electronic service is integrated into a broader strategy of service delivery rather than being the only service delivery channel. The e-Taiwan plan also covers some aspects of the legal and institutional framework such as electronic transactions and digital signatures necessary for e-government to function.

Nonetheless, Taiwan's digital government strategy also has its weaknesses. The common problem that Taiwan shares with Poland is the lack of a proactive mechanism for environmental scanning. Due to fast-changing technology and political conditions, a good strategic plan must constantly scan changes in environment and make adjustments accordingly. However, no section of the digital government plan has been devoted to that.

With regard to each country's plans in terms of long-term strategic goals, the two countries score close to each other. Each country defines clear strategic goals in its plan, and Poland's plan identifies clear goals and their relation to wider targets. The ePolska plan also calls for the development of overarching standards, such as common file formats, applications, protocols, and a system for document exchange. The primary goal of Taiwan's e-government plan is to provide seamless online service to citizens, businesses, and government employees. Specific policies are formulated to achieve a secure and reliable information exchange environment, reduction in paperwork, and online access for all government units. This is supported by programs for establishing a government-wide service network with a common platform supporting various public service applications, setting Web sites for all national agencies, putting application forms online, and e-routing for government (Research Development and Evaluation Commission, 2001).

Both countries still have some flaws in the area of strategic goals that prevent them from receiving high marks. As part of its preparation for EU membership, Poland is reforming a number of other areas as well, from agriculture to public health to transportation.

Financial and administrative support for IT reforms may be overshadowed by demands in other areas. In order to marshal the funds necessary to implement the ePolska plan, leaders will have to ensure that there is enough impetus year-by-year to make sure that continuous funding supports plan initiatives, rather than leaving them without financial support in the middle of implementation.

Other areas in the framework are also lacking. Process reengineering is not mentioned in the Polish plan, and this could be fatal to the execution of the plan as a whole if public administrators hold to the old way of conducting business, rather than adopting new practices. Taiwan's challenges include the deficit problem that limits the resources available for e-government projects. Another related documented deficiency is the lack of training for government employees to establish Web sites and move services online.

Turning to the integration of different components of a national digital government strategy, both countries have a modest plan. The key element of their plan is a unified portal for their services. The ePolska plan calls for the creation of a "Gateway to Poland," which will include services and content for Polish citizens as well as the goal of promoting Poland to other countries. Poland will create a unified data model, which will ensure that databases for personal identification, vehicle registration, and taxes are interoperable and rational. Poland also proposes the unification of its various identification schemes. These schemes are strongly ingrained at the organizational level and replacing multiple systems will prove to be a challenge.

Taiwan has identified one-stop shopping in the form of a portal as an objective in its strategy. This portal is supported by a common service platform that integrates all government services. In the year 2000, 61% of government offices had local area networks to connect computers at the office. Seventy-four percent of government offices had Internet connections, while 47% of total government offices had a Web site. These numbers are expected to reach 100% by the end of 2002, according to Taiwan's e-government plan (Research Development and Evaluation Commission, 2001).

Both countries are likely to meet problems with interagency cooperation. Interagency cooperation has been identified as one main barrier to seamless e-government. In Taiwan's digital government strategy, there is a lack of specific reference to any systematic way of addressing potential barriers to interagency sharing of resources and information. A council at the cabinet level is required to facilitate interagency coopera-tion. However, no acknowledgement of the need for a high-level coordinating agency is in the plan and a description of such a coordinating body is not yet available. The ePolska plan also lacks a high-level coordinating agency to oversee collaboration among various agencies to deliver seamless e-government services.

## Individual Critical Success Factors

Concerning the success factors that we have identified in the framework, Taiwan seems to be ahead in several areas, but both strategies have some common weak points. These critical success factors and their assessment for Taiwan and Poland are summarized in Table 2. Each factor will be discussed separately.

*Table 2: Strengths and weaknesses of the specific areas of digital government strategies of e-Polska (2003) and e-Taiwan (2001)*

| Specific Areas | Poland | | Taiwan | |
|---|---|---|---|---|
| | Strengths | Weaknesses | Strengths | Weaknesses |
| Political commitment | * Strong support<br>* Reorganization | * Low funding,<br>* Lack of follow-through | * Strong support | |
| Uncertainty management | * Leaves technology choices open<br>* Does not dictate broad solutions | * Vulnerable to uncertainty | | * Vulnerable to change |
| Resource allocation | | * Funds not allocated | * Large allocation of funds | |
| Management capacity | *Periodic evaluation | *No oversight | * Tied to NICI<br>* Periodic evaluation | |
| Information management (use & quality) | *Creating information resources<br>* Standards and common systems | *No use of existing information | * Creating information resources<br>* Use of existing information | * Lack of quality assurance |
| Human resources | *Training for disadvantaged groups | * lack of trained professionals<br>* Lack of training programs | * Training emphasized in all areas | * Lack of training of government officials |
| ICT Technology | *Focus on disadvantaged groups<br>* efforts to broadband access | * Market rationalization far off | * maturity of network technology<br>* broadband access | |
| Security | * Some training<br>* Emergency response | * Lack of standards<br>* still under development | * PKI<br>* Vulnerability scanning<br>* Emergency response<br>* Training | * Still developing |

Both strategies have a fair amount of political commitment behind them. Taiwan's e-government strategy is part of digital Taiwan, a major component of the national development plan, the blueprint for Taiwan, which is evidence of major political recognition of the importance of having a digital Taiwan. Implementation of the plan will come directly from Taiwan's Executive Yuan, the primary executive branch of government. Another sign of support is numerous statements on the important role that information and communication will play in securing Taiwan's competitiveness in the global market.

Poland's plan comes from the State Committee for Scientific Research, although it has some high-level backing and input from important ministries. Unfortunately, initiatives in the Polish strategy may not be not followed through, and a lack of resources has severely reduced the number of initiatives implemented on time. The ePolska plan outlines agencies responsible for the execution of plan initiatives as well as target completion dates, but it does not define sources for funding of individual initiatives and it appears that government branches are responsible for securing their own funding for initiatives.

Neither plan seems to adequately prepare for unexpected developments. Digital government needs to be particularly sensitive to technological changes and possible social changes. In a strategic plan, these changes should be considered as risks and a plan to manage risks should subsequently be in place. Poland makes no mention of any ways to adapt to possible technological change or change in political regime. In its e-government plan Taiwan also makes no reference to possible risks and the management of those risks. As a result, both countries score low in risk management.

Taiwan performs better in resource allocation. Strong resource commitment can be seen in the NT $36.6 billions (approximately one billion US dollars) allocated for e-Taiwan over 2003-2008 under the framework of the six-year development plan. Institutional resources are also available. For instance, the National Information and Communication Initiative (NICI) was formed to outline the blueprint for e-Taiwan with e-government as a major component. In contrast, Poland's economy is going through a recession and government resources are scarce. Implementation of individual measures requires the presence of a strong leader to gather and protect funds in an environment where resources are often contested. Funding sources are not identified for individual initiatives in the Polish plan, nor does there appear to be a funding source for the plan overall.

In terms of management capacity, Taiwan's strategy seems to be well grounded. The e-Taiwan plan undergoes periodic evaluation, and planning for the strategy was executed under the oversight of the National Information and Communication Initiative (NICI). The existence of technocrats who serve a rational decision-making capacity has been documented. Further evidence of management capacity is the comprehensive and specific nature of Taiwan's e-government plan. Specific measures are used to gauge the progress of e-government. For instance, according to the plan, the use of e-mail by government employees needs to reach 100% by 2003, compared to 33% use in 1999. Poland's plan also has a periodic evaluation that sets multiple milestones for completion and also outlines the responsible agency or office for each initiative in the plan. The measures for success are open-ended, and there are no set levels to be reached for each measure. For example, success is measured by the number of homes with broadband connections, but there is no number or percentage that represents success or failure of initiatives related to providing access to citizens. In addition, there is no facility for oversight by either government or citizens, or for assessment by external bodies such as the European Union.

With regard to information resource management, the two countries have different problems and goals. Taiwan concentrates on the need for more information resources in its own language as well as the use of existing informational resources. As stipulated in the e-government plan (Research Development and Evaluation Commission, 2001), content needs to be further developed to meet the needs of citizens and businesses. Another area of information resource management emphasized in Taiwan is the use of geographic information systems and health information systems. This is accomplished by information sharing between governments. However, one weakness of the current information resource management effort is the lack of a concerted effort in ensuring information quality. Since information quality is the most fundamental issue for information resources, missing it has serious consequences.

In contrast, the Polish strategy focuses on the creation of content and new resources, as well moving the flow of information from paper to computer for initiatives such as a

Polish Internet Library, medical databases, or encouraging electronic trade. The ePolska plan also mandates the creation of standards for data quality and a national data model with majority of public bodies adopting the data model as one of the measures for success. Poland makes no mention of converting existing older records to an electronic format, but initiatives to create an electronic document exchange service for government bodies are included in the plan.

Both Taiwanese and Polish plans mention a lack of trained professionals and the difficulty of training citizens to ensure that they are able to use new services. The ePolska plan mandates a minimum level of computer and Internet skills for K-12 students, certifiable by examination. The Polish plan also encourages cooperative partnerships between schools and firms such as Cisco and Intel, and emphasizes the educational use of IT in all subject areas, rather than just in computer science classes. The Polish plan addresses issues of access by creating training programs for adults and those outside the school system, including special programs for the unemployed, disabled and those in rural areas.

Taiwan's e-government plan has recognized that the lack of training for government employees was one main drawback of the first phase of the e-government effort from 1998-2000. To address such a deficiency, the second phase of e-government effort from 2001-2004 has proposed to include the use of online e-government transactions as part of performance measures for government employees. Training and e-learning are also part of the overall strategy. The overall e-Taiwan plan has proposed a "Knowledge and Learning Logistic Center" that helps improve both quality and access to knowledge. This begins by addressing the need of various industries and then extends to the general public for a range of educational opportunities.

Taiwan is much further ahead in the use and application of ICT, and demonstrates an excellent understanding of implementing and managing networks. Taiwan has emphasized having a broadband connection to 6 million households in an island of 22 million people. To increase its capacity for managing domains on the Internet, Taiwan has also proposed to establish an IPv6 framework. In government, a common communication platform has been developed called the government service network and this lays the foundation for information exchange and seamless service delivery. The Polish plan identifies a number of essential factors for reaching a similar level of development. The Polish telecommunications market requires strong intervention in order to ensure that businesses and citizens get the level of access they require at fair prices, and the ePolska plan details a number of milestones on the way to providing broadband access to schools and citizens. ePolska also focuses on ways to provide Internet access to the disadvantaged. There is also an initiative to create PIONIER, a high-speed optical academic network linking research universities, which will increase linkages across the country.

Security is an area that both Taiwan and Poland emphasize. Currently, Taiwan has done a better job than Poland in addressing security issues for its digital government. Taiwan has set out to protect its critical information infrastructure. For example, a center has been set up to track computer crimes. Another main initiative is the use of a Public Key Infrastructure. Government has planned to have security policy and measures in place for at least 50% of main government offices by 2007. Training for computer security should reach more than 5% of government employees during the same period. However, the goals do not seem to be aggressive enough to address the potential threats properly.

The ePolska plan focuses on the propagation of best practices, assuming that users will implement measures on their own. The ePolska plan also places emphasis on the protection of intellectual property. The Polish government intends to implement multiple security levels for communication, such as authentication and digital signatures, as well as an advanced authentication method for every citizen to use: the Integrated Packet of Personal Documents. Finally, ePolska calls for the proper qualification of judges and legal staff in order to prosecute electronic crime effectively.

Between the two countries, Taiwan appears to be in a stronger position, with good political and financial support for the plan as well as sound initiatives. Poland's plan is well in line with the objectives outlined by eEurope, but lacks the financial support of Taiwan's plan. Both ePolska and eTaiwan have well-reasoned initiatives that span a number of developmental dimensions, and concentrate on areas that are central to continuing long-term development. Viewing each country through the framework outlined in this chapter allows comparison of two development strategies that at first glance may seem wildly disparate. With Taiwan's existing advanced infrastructure and strong political and financial commitment to the plan, it might seem that Taiwan's plan is far ahead of where Poland could hope to be. By examining the two plans through the analytical framework, however, areas where the two plans diverge and correspond can be seen. Both plans could use more risk management, as well as increased training and security measures, and both plans have strengths in the area of information management, management capacity, security and use of technology. Each country can benefit from the other's strengths by incorporating initiatives that the other plan contains, and other national digital government strategies can also act on the differences seen here to ensure success.

# Development and Trends

Examining these development strategies yields a number of implications for public administrators in other countries. In order for a country to see the benefits offered by digital government, development must be coordinated strategically with broad goals outlined in a plan. Both Poland and Taiwan's development plans make use of initiatives that cut across agencies and depend upon successive stages. A strategic plan allows a government to pick out large-scale goals and outline the steps required to reach those goals, which may take a number of years. Without such a plan, implementation of individual measures will occur haphazardly, without coordination of efforts. Resource allocation will be carried out on a case-by-case basis, resulting in gaps in implementation. Common data models and application models are impossible to implement without some top-level planning.

As these plans and others like them are implemented, a number of concerns still remain. Security and privacy will continue to be important for any government activity, and needs for secure systems and private means of communication will only increase. A system designed to be secure today will undoubtedly have some vulnerabilities months or years down the road. Secure systems and privacy safeguards are a matter of constant maintenance and testing, as no program, tool, or protocol is perfect, and often only time brings security holes to light. In order for digital government systems to be secure, these systems will not only need to be built with security in mind to protect against the exploits used today, but also constantly updated and audited to defend against future attacks.

Another concern unlikely to disappear is the issue of the "digital divide". Despite countries' best efforts to provide as many access channels as possible for citizens, some citizens will remain out of reach, either because they are somehow denied access by disability or situation, or because they choose traditional means of interacting with government. Governments have a responsibility to constantly improve accessibility for the disadvantaged, provide training for citizens to allow them to effectively use access channels, and create systems that are both effective and easy to use. One way of addressing the digital divide is to make services easy, effective, and appealing enough to encourage citizens to seek out the means to use them.

In order for services to become and remain effective, government institutions will need to be constructed and maintained to reflect the current environment. Governments need up-to-date privacy and security laws, as well as legal professionals capable of making informed decisions. By creating a body of policy and law that is conversant with technological issues, governments need to increase their ability to adapt to changes and be more prepared for future digital government initiatives. Having strong and current institutions allows a government to support continuous reform. Governments that do not have institutions that take technological change into account will be forced to reengineer these institutions in order to move forward.

In keeping with the idea of maintenance, both of security and government institutions, government entities need to maintain flexibility with regard to their environment and act correspondingly. Constant assessment of changing capacity, such as resources, expertise, and time, which dictate the courses of action open to public administrators, is necessary to be prepared for changes. While implementing digital government initiatives is an exercise in closing the gaps between the current and desired situations, it is possible for these gaps to change. In order to be sure that initiatives are successfully implemented, public administrators must therefore constantly scan the environment as well as internal capabilities in order to see what changes may be necessary. It is critical for a strategy to be flexible in order to adapt initiatives to best fit changing gaps.

Further research can improve this analytical framework in a number of ways. This examination of two countries is rather limited, and a multi-country study would undoubtedly refine the elements of the framework, and highlight some areas that have been left unexplored. The choice of Poland and Taiwan uses subjects that are quite distant, in terms of culture, development, and geography, and a regional study of Asian states or Central European states may serve to better ground the framework with a range of subjects that are closer together, and improve the rating system for each of the framework's elements. Increasing the number of subjects for study will also bring greater variety to the elements of the framework, and can serve as a cross-pollination of initiatives, as similar situations and success factors for more cases are compared.

A future study might follow digital government strategies in a longitudinal study of plans from drafting to implementation to completion and maintenance. Such a view of strategies put into action can expose factors that the plans themselves do not contain, such as social networks that cause governments to behave differently than expected, or non-rational behavior that obstructs implementation, or problems related to the public-private partnership aspects that are part of many strategies. Long-term studies will also serve to better identify which factors are most important for success. Furthermore, the contrast between issues in building initial capacity for putting strategy into place versus flexibility in adapting to environmental changes may be highlighted, showing if governments with more capacity or more flexibility are more successful in implementing strategy.

# Conclusions and Recommendations

The framework of national digital government strategy is useful in incorporating various building blocks for the success of digital government. This framework addresses the environmental conditions necessary for various advances in digital government, including political, institutional, technical, and economic ones. A less inclusive approach is likely to cause problems. Moreover, this proposed framework provides a list of key factors for a successful digital government endeavor. As the above comparison has demonstrated, if these factors are not attended to at the national level, implementation and performance are likely to be problematic.

Moreover, the proposed framework offers several general guidelines for developing national digital government strategies. First, the broad political, technical, economic, and institutional conditions are of critical importance for the development of a digital government strategy. Second, it is the role of a national digital government strategy to address its unique setting and give priority to its areas of critical need. Third, various components of a national digital government strategy should complement each other. One productive way of looking at the integration and interoperability is the portal concept and the network infrastructure that supports it.

However, it should be acknowledged that this framework does have some limitations. The framework could be complex and the interactions between its various elements may not be fully understood. Moreover, the policy recommendations that it provides are largely normative in nature. This framework, although aiming to be comprehensive, may not be able to account for all possible initiatives embodied in existing digital government plans.

The analysis of Taiwan's and Poland's digital government strategies has yielded specific recommendations for both countries. For Poland, more emphasis needs to be placed on the development of information and communication infrastructure. More reasonable goals need to be set to take into account its resource issues. Poland also needs stronger political support for the implementation of its ePolska plan. This political support may come in the form of establishing a higher central office to oversee the ePolska plan or in the form of more resource allocation. Management of information and risk is another area for potential improvement for Poland. The conversion of existing information resources to an electronic format would be useful. A risk management plan that anticipates changes in technology and political and social conditions is also critical. Training and security are another two areas for Poland to improve upon. Currently, training is one of the main barriers to establishing and utilizing e-government services. Training should be conducted for users in the rural areas as well as government employees. Security is in its infancy for Poland. Specific measures need to be taken to further develop this area of capacity.

Taiwan is lacking in the mechanism to conduct a scan of environmental factors as outlined in the proposed framework. This is critical for the government's ability to align its overall strategy to its environment. A specific section on building this mechanism should be included in the next version of the plan. The other area that needs further emphasis is interagency cooperation. This is at least one factor that needs to be explicitly dealt with. The current e-government plan is limited in its ways of addressing interagency cooperation when turf fighting is likely to become a barrier to information exchange and resource sharing. Risk management capacity also needs to be further developed for Taiwan. In the Taiwanese e-government plan, there seems to be no explicit mentioning of any particular risk. The discussion has only focused on lessons learned from the first phase of e-government. The training of both government employees and the general public needs to be strengthened. Some progress has been made, but the real implementation may be challenging. The last area for improvement is security. In particular, security training seems to be the weakest link of the comprehensive security policy. Until 2007, only less than 5% of government employees are expected to get computer security training.

This chapter is the first significant step to formulate a comprehensive framework for the development and implementation of national digital government strategic plans. The knowledge of such a comprehensive framework can be further advanced in two ways. First, the proposed framework can be applied to more countries to test its comprehensiveness and utility. Second, more research can be done to link a national strategy to e-government performance. As a result, a more comprehensive framework will provide even more detailed guidance for the development and implementation of national digital government strategies.

# References

Bozeman, B., & Bretschneider, S. (1986). Public management information systems: Theory and prescription. *Public Administration Review, 46* (Special Issue), 475-487.

Bryson, J.M., & Alston, F.K. (1996). *Creating and implementing your strategic plan: A workbook for public and nonprofit organizations.* San Francisco, CA: Jossey-Bass Publishers.

Caudle, S.L., Gorr, W.L., & Newcomer, K.E. (1991). Key information systems management issues for the public sector. *MIS Quarterly, 15*(2), 171-188.

Dawes, S., Pardo, T., Green, D., McInemey, C., Connelly, D., & DiCatireno, A. (1997). *Tying a sensible knot: A practical guide to state-local information systems.* Albany, New York: Center for Technology in Government.

Edmiston, K. (2003). State and local e-government: Prospects and challenges. *American Review of Public Administration, 33*(1), 20-45.

Executive Yuan. (2001, December 26). *National information and communication infrastructure development plan.* Taipei, Taiwan: Executive Yuan.

Ferris, J.M., & Tang, S.-Y. (1993). The new institutionalism and public administration: An overview. *Journal of Public Administration Research and Theory, 3*(1), 4-10.

Fletcher, P.D. (1999). Strategic planning for information technology Management in state government. In G.D. Garson (Ed.), *Information technology and computer applications in public administration: Issues and trends* (pp. 81-98). Hershey, PA: Idea Group Publishing.

Fletcher, P.D. (2003). The realities of the Paperwork Reduction Act of 1995: A government-wide strategy for information resources management. In D. Garson (Ed.), *Public information technology: Policy and management issues* (pp. 74-93). Hershey, PA: Idea Group Publishing.

Fountain, J. (2001). *Building the virtual state: Information technology and institutional change.* Washington, D.C.: Brookings Institution Press.

General Accounting Office. (2001, July 11). *Electronic government: Challenges must be addressed with effective leadership and management.* Washington, D.C.: General Accounting Office.

Guy, M.E. (2000). Public management. In J.M. Shafritz (Ed.), *Defining public administration* (pp. 166-168). Boulder, CO: Westview Press.

Heeks, R. (1999). *Reinventing government in the information age: International practice in IT-enabled public sector reform.* London: Routledge.

International City/County Management Association. (2001). *2000 electronic government survey dataset* [Data file]. Washington, D.C.: International City/County Management Association.

International City/County Management Association. (2002, August). *2002 electronic government survey dataset.* Washington, D.C.: International City/County Management Association.

Kamarch, E.C., & Nye, J.S. (2002). *Governance.com: Democracy in the information age.* Cambridge, MA: Visions of Governance in the 21st Century Brookings Institution Press.

Landsbergen, D., Jr., & Wolken, G. (2001). Realizing the promise: Government information systems and the fourth generation of information technology. *Public Administration Review, 61*(2), 206-220.

Layne, K., & Lee, J. (2001). Developing fully functional e-government: A four stage model. *Government Information Quarterly, 18*(2), 122-136.

Lin, K.H. (2002, June 5). Cabinet to pour NT$36 billion into 'e-Taiwan' Project. *Taiwan News.*

Main Statistical Office. (2002). *Household situation in 2002 from the results of the household budget survey.* Retrieved July 15, 2003, from: *http://www.stat.gov.pl/serwis/nieregularne/gosp_dom2002.htm.*

Marchionini, G., Samet, H., & Brandt, L. (2003). Digital government. *Communications of the ACM, 46*(1), 25-27.

Miles, M., &. Huberman, M. (1994). *Qualitative data analysis.* Thousand Oaks, CA: SAGE Publications.

Mintzberg, H., & Quinn, J.B. (1991). *The strategy process.* Englewood Cliffs, NJ: Prentice-Hall, Inc.

North, D.C. (1990). *Institutions, institutional change, and economic performance.* Cambridge, MA: Cambridge University Press.

Ostrom, E. (1990). *Governing the commons: The evolution of institutions for collective action.* Cambridge: Cambridge University Press.

Ostrom, E., Schroeder, L., & Wynne, S. (1993). Analyzing the performance of alternative institutional arrangements for sustaining rural infrastructure in developing countries. *Journal of Public Administration Research and Theory, 3*(1), 11-45.

Research Development and Evaluation Commission (RDEC). (2001). *E-government implementation plan.* Taipei, Taiwan: Research Development and Evaluation Commission, Executive Yuan.

Rocheleau, B. (2003). Politics, accountability, and governmental information systems. In D. Garson (Ed.), *Public information technology: Policy and management issues* (pp. 20-52). Hershey, PA: Idea Group Publishing.

Schedler, K., & Maria Christina Scharf. (2002). *Exploring the interrelations between electronic government and the new public management: A managerial framework for electronic government.* Paper presented at APPAM 2002 Conference.

Snellen, I. (2000). Public service in an information society. In G. Peters & D.J. Savoie (Eds.), *Governance in the twenty-first century: Revitalizing the public service.* Montreal & Kingston: Canadian Centre for Management Development.

SourceOECD Telecommunications Database. (n.d). Retrieved July 15, 2003, from: *http://www.sourceoecd.org/content/templates/el/el_location_ivt.htm?comm=telecomm.*

State Committee for Scientific Research. (2003). *Strategy for information technology cevelopment of the Republic of Poland – ePolska.*

Taylor Nelson Sofres & Center for Public Opinion Research. (2002). *Government online: A national perspective. Annual Country Report: Poland.*

United Nations — DPEPA & ASPA. (2002). *Benchmarking e-government: A global perspective: Assessing the progress of the UN member states.* New York: United Nations American Society for Public Administration.

West, D. (2003). *Global e-government.* Providence, RI: report published by author.

Yin, R. (2003). *Case study research: Design and methods* (3rd ed.). Thousand Oak, CA: SAGE Publications, Inc.

Yo, C.-D., Tsai, W.-C., & Tien, D. (2001). National information infrastructure development in R.O.C. *Industrial Forum.*

# Endnotes

[1]    This definition is adopted from the General Accounting Office's (2001) report on e-government.

[2]    Institutions are sets of rules that constrain and guide behaviors (North, 1990; Ostrom, 1990). These rules manifest themselves in laws, regulations, governing structures, patterns of behavior, and so forth.

**Chapter XVIII**

# E-Government Applications and User Acceptance in Taiwan

Shin-Yuan Hung, National Chung Cheng University, Taiwan, R.O.C.

Cheng-Yuan Ku, National Chung Cheng University, Taiwan, R.O.C.

Chia-Ming Chang, National Chung Cheng University, Taiwan, R.O.C.

## Abstract

*E-government has become one of the most important issues in the transformation of the public sector in many countries. However, it is not easy to implement. According to a report by the Center for Public Policy at Brown University, Taiwan's e-government was ranked the first among the 198 countries in 2002. Therefore, the developing experience of Taiwan may be a useful lesson for other countries. In this chapter, we briefly introduce the history, current status and the architecture of Taiwan's e-government. To further help, this chapter also identifies the critical factors of e-government adoption in Taiwan, using the Online Tax Filing and Payment System.*

# Introduction

The emergence of the Internet has made tremendous changes in people's lives and has connected people in unprecedented ways. Thus, the Internet has not only revolutionized the way people interact but has also reshaped lifestyles. With usage of Internet, routine transactions in many fields can be automatically processed and completed online quickly without human intervention. Since the mid-1990s governments around the world have been executing major initiatives in order to tap the vast potential of the Internet to improve the governing process (Ronaghan, 2002). Accordingly, electronic government (e-government) has become one of the most important issues in the transformation of the public sector in many countries, and many global areas have been used as subjects of e-government research. Chen (2002) discussed the e-government outsourcing projects in the context of U.S. local government. Huang et al. (2002) explored the adoption factors of e-government in the Australian public sector. For Asia, Hu and Li (2003) provided an overview of the e-government developments in Mainland China. Poon (2002) explored the "ESDLife," an e-government application in Hong Kong. Hence, e-government studies and implementations in many global areas have attracted many researchers' attentions.

What exactly is e-government? According to Gefen and Straub (2000), e-government has the potential to fundamentally change how public services are provided by increasing the responsiveness, immediacy and quality of service, while reducing costs compared with traditional alternatives. Defined broadly, e-government is the use of information and communication technology to promote more efficient and effective government, facilitate more accessible government services, allow greater public access to information, and make government more accountable to citizens (Working Group on e-Government in the Developing World, 2002). The primary goals of e-government are to make it easier for citizens to obtain services and interact with the government, improve government efficiency and effectiveness, and improve government's responsiveness to citizens (Forman, 2002). However, e-government is not easy to implement, and most governments experience problems when implementing large IT projects. Budgets are exceeded, deadlines are over-run and often the quality of new systems is far below the standards determined when the project was undertaken (OECD, 2001). Before spending time and resources in successfully implementing an e-government initiative, it is necessary to understand the basic reasons for pursuing (or not pursuing) e-government (Working Group on e-Government in the Developing World, 2002).

Many governmental units across the world have recognized the digital trend in the future and placed a wide range of materials online for public services. Although global e-government is still in its infancy, it has improved over the past two years. Some of these significant improvements are (West, 2002):

1.    Twelve percent of offered services in governmental Web sites are fully executable online, up from 8% in 2001.
2.    Seventy-seven percent of Web sites provide access to publications and 83% have links to databases, up from 41% in 2001.

3.   Fourteen percent (up from 6% in 2001) show privacy policies, while 9% (up from 3% in 2001) have security policies.

4.   Thirty-three percent of government Web sites have some form of disability access, which is a dramatic improvement over the level of 2%in the previous year.

5.   Seventy-eight percent of national government Web sites have an English version, which is up from 72% in 2001.

# Research Incentive

As can be seen, global e-government is improving rapidly. The United States offers the most organized portal Web site in all investigated 198 countries (West, 2002). Singapore's "eCitizen" site provides the largest amount of e-services. The Canadian e-government Web portal focuses on functionality and ease of use. The Australian e-government portal excels aesthetically in its successful incorporation of color, without diminishing its disability access compliance. According to a report by the Center for Public Policy at Brown University, Taiwan's e-government was ranked the first among the 198 countries in 2002 (West, 2002). Moreover, the distinct feature of e-government implementation in Taiwan is that 100% of offered services for the evaluated sites can be fully executable online. Therefore, the developing experience and architecture of Taiwan's e-government may be a useful lesson for other countries which would like to make their public services available on the Web. In the following section, we briefly describe the development of e-government in the U.S. and then introduce the history, current status, architecture, and future work of Taiwan's e-government. To further the knowledge of the Taiwan e-government success, this study identifies the critical factors of e-government adoption in Taiwan, using the Online Tax Filing and Payment System. Within all the e-government services provided by Taiwan, the Online Tax Filing and Payment System in its e-taxation plan is one of salient successful implementations (http://www.rdec.gov.tw/eng). From the perspective of users' adoption, there has been little empirical study on this key aspect of successful e-government implementation. The major objective of the e-taxation plan is to reduce operating costs, and raise quality of service and administrative efficiency at tax offices. In addition, this plan aims to ensure that all citizens could use high-speed communication links in any time or at any place to obtain comprehensive tax information from taxation agencies, in order to lower the tax compliance costs of businesses and individuals, and enhance corporate and national competitiveness. It is clear that the Online Tax Filing and Payment System has become the best practice in e-government plan in Taiwan. However, as is well known, the technological success of a system does not guarantee the adoption by users. Therefore, in the second half of this chapter, we will focus on investigating users' adoption of the Online Tax Filing and Payment System in Taiwan. Hopefully, the results from this empirical study will be a valuable reference for other countries.

# Development of E-Government in the United States

Facing the impact of information technology, developed countries, like the United States, the United Kingdom, Japan, and so on, have adopted various information policies to improve their public service, industrial competitiveness, and citizen welfare. According to the statistics compiled by the United Nations in May 2002, among the global e-government online service, United States was ranked first (Ronaghan, 2002). Hence, the development of e-government policies in the United States is described below (Ronaghan, 2002):

1.  From 1993 to 1996

    Although United States government began to incorporate an e-government plan into its principal policies in 1999, an e-government initiative was developed early by the Clinton administration's "Reinventing Government Program" in March 1993. The Clinton administration, to spread the benefits of the technological revolution, had appointed Vice President Gore to establish the National Performance Review (NPR) with the intent of establishing the National Information Infrastructure (NII) and promoting the adoption of e-business applications. The NII served as a foundation for e-government development. Thus, it was the Clinton administration's initiatives in 1993 that enabled the United States to remain on the leading edge of information industries and e-commerce applications in the next 10 years.

2.  From 1997 to 1999

    After the first stage (1993-1996), the network infrastructure and the environment of application reached maturity. The Clinton administration took the lead and proposed a global e-commerce infrastructure in 1997. Subsequently, the deployment of e-government took off in the second stage (1997-1999), integrating the results of government reinvesting engineering and NII with the global e-commerce infrastructure in order to develop the e-government environment.

3.  From 2000 to the present

    As the infrastructure of information integration between the federal government, state government and citizens was completed in the second stage, the subsequent goal was to implement a software infrastructure. Thus, the focus shifted from hardware infrastructure to network security and information services. Accordingly, issues such as articles of digital signature and information security were proposed. Afterwards, as the Bush administration took over in August 2001, a special team was appointed to improve the e-government services, which has had a positive effect in the long-term development of e-government in the United States.

# The History and Current Status of Taiwan E-Government

Taiwan is undergoing a social transformation and aims to integrate information technology into every facet of society. The developing progress of e-government can be categorized into the following three stages. In November 1997, the Research, Development, and Evaluation Commission (RDEC) in Taiwan started the four-year e-government Implementation Plan (RDEC, 2002a). This plan implemented the full-scale deployment of a governmental network and the development of online services and administrative applications. It also accelerated information exchange between all levels of the government and established an infrastructure for electronic certification and network security. To further broaden the applications of e-government, in the second stage, the RDEC launched the e-Government Program in April 2001, which is scheduled to be completed in 2004. This program aims to link all governmental agencies through the Internet and to provide versatile Web-based services. The scheduled goals are listed as follow (RDEC, 2002a):

1.   All levels of governments should have electronic official documents exchanged by the end of 2001.

2.   All levels of governments should build their own Web sites by the end of 2002.

3.   All government employees should be equipped with computers and know how to use them by the end of 2003.

4.   All government services should be provided on the Internet by the end of 2004.

As wireless technology matures, the available bit rate increases, and the price of mobile usage continues to fall, wireless e-government services will be brought to citizens in the near future. To meet this demand, in the third stage, the Taiwan government is planning to implement a mobile government to efficiently deliver wireless information and services (RDEC, 2002b).

As mentioned above, Taiwan's e-government was ranked first among the 198 countries in the 2002 report. This report noted that the site for the Executive Yuan of the Republic of China contains information varying from national statistics, history of Taiwanese art and culture policy papers and timely news updates (West, 2002). It seems that the Taiwan authorities' plan was used well for meeting those goals of future governments. As stated in the official Taiwan government documents published in March 2003, the current status of Taiwan e-government can be summarized as follows (RDEC, 2003a, 2003b):

1.   The Government Service Network (GSN) has been developed to link all government organizations/agencies. By the end of 2002, 97% of government organizations were connected to the Internet.

2.   4,863 government agency Web sites had been established by the end of 2002.

3. To alleviate the digital gap between urban and rural areas, Taiwan government has established many Internet access points in remote areas. Furthermore, it also helped more than 6,500 villages and boroughs to establish their own Web pages (*http://village.gov.tw*).

4. The government has developed an interdepartmental e-mail delivery infrastructure and a Certification Authority. All levels of government agencies/organizations deliver official messages via electronic delivery system.

5. Administrative applications of the Internet:

   (1) The electronic interchange of official documents began a test run in July 2000, and today all levels of governments and major agencies have implemented electronic interchange of official documents.

   (2) The completion of the online procurement, tender, and bid information systems has made this governmental process much more transparent and efficient (*http://gpic.pcc.gov.tw*).

   (3) The government has provided online access to laws and official regulations (*http://law.moj.gov.tw*).

   (4) The government has also created an online access point for personnel administration (*http://www.cpa.gov.tw*) and government publication services (http://gpnet.nat.gov.tw).

6. Development of online public services:

   (1) The Taiwan government has developed an online tax-filing system and tax-tracking system to provide better tax services (*http://www.itax.com.tw*).

   (2) A driver's license and vehicle certificate system already provides many online services (http://www.mvdis.gov.tw).

   (3) A database for job openings and applicants has been implemented to provide online employment services.

7. The government has established a portal site (*http://www.gov.tw*) to integrate all the online information and government services. More than 1,300 application forms were available to download and 183 online services were offered by the end of 2002.

8. The government has established a certificate mechanism to provide network authentication services. A Government Certification Authority (GCA) (*http://www.pki.gov.tw*) was established in February 1998. In October 2002, a Government Root Certification Authority (GRCA) (http://grca.nat.gov.tw/) was established as well to prevent identification theft and misuse. The GCA has issued 430,000 certificates for services such as online tax filing, driver's licenses and vehicle certificate services, online procurement, and electronic document interchange.

9. The government has developed a Gateway System and defined an e-government Common Platform Guideline to integrate interdepartmental information in order to reduce the need for redundant copies of official documents.

   (1) Query, inspection, and transmission of corporate information and registration data across cities and counties were provided by the end of 2001 (implemented on trial between five cities and counties). This enables government agencies to efficiently share information.

(2) The Inter-city Land Title Transcript Application and Checking System came into use in May 2001 in Taipei City, Taipei County, Taichung City, and Kaohsiung City.

(3) Other trial gateway systems provide online data query services across cities and counties for police, taxation, law affairs, immigration entry and exit, road management, fiscal administration, and health care information.

# Architecture of Taiwan E-Government

Based on the related documents of the US government, their 24 initiatives of e-government implementation will be managed using a portfolio management process. The four portfolios are (Forman, 2002):

1.   The Government-to-Citizen (G2C) initiatives will provide online benefits and services.

2.   The Government-to-Business (G2B) initiatives are intended to reduce the burden on businesses.

3.   The Government-to-Government (G2G) initiatives will enable sharing and integration of data of federal, state and local governments.

4.   The Internal Efficiency and Effectiveness (IEE) initiatives bring commercial best practices to key government operations.

*Figure 1: An overview of implementation of e-government in Taiwan (RDEC, 2002a)*

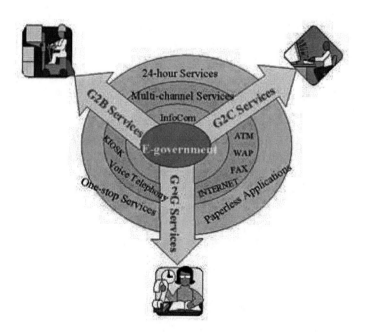

*Figure 2: Government Service Network (RDEC, 2003a)*

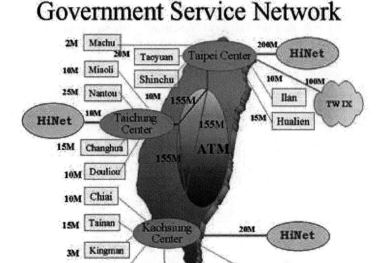

In Taiwan, the government proposed an e-government concept based on the above-mentioned portfolios except the IEE initiatives, which will be implemented in other innovative plans. The strategy of implementation is illustrated in Figure 1.

The e-government services can be categorized in the following three groups: G2C, G2B or G2G. These services in each group are planned and implemented by each specific committee, although the common implementation platform and infrastructure is the Government Service Network (GSN). GSN's island-wide broadband backbone network was deployed in accordance with RDEC's 1997 Mid-term e-Government Implementation Plan and the 2001 e-Government Action Plan (RDEC, 2002a). The GSN backbone, which currently consists of 18 network nodes, is linked directly to three major domestic networks, as shown in Figure 2. The GSN SDH (Synchronous Digital Hierarchy) backbone, which was established at the end of 2001, provides total bandwidth in excess of 1,000Mbps. All government units were linked to the GSN by using about 1,000 fixed lines, roughly 3,000 ADSL lines, and nearly 10,000 dial-up connections as of the end of 2001 (RDEC, 2002a).

The Government Service Network (GSN) backbone system, the fundamental infrastructure, was developed to integrate government agencies at different levels. Through it, information is automatically updated between agency Web sites and the e-government portal (*http://www.gov.tw/*). The e-government entry point, a so-called portal, acts as an integrated service station where all government agencies are required to make their primary services available online. The deployment and management of this Taiwan e-government entry point has been entirely outsourced to private contractors, including the development of application service systems, data updating, education and training, as well as advertising and promotion. The current project contractors are Digital United

Inc. (SEEDNET), Taiwan's second-largest ISP, and its main strategic partner, Yam Digital Technology Inc. Yam's Web site is one of Taiwan's major e-commerce portals.

This entry point Web site also integrates the electronic procurement, electronic publishing, taxation, motor vehicle oversight, electronic payment, household administration, and land administration strategic e-government application systems. Oversight and management functions include adjustment of system performance, data backup management, database management, Web hosting system management, e-mail system management, discussion area and user group management, as well as catalog and account management. All of these aspects are monitored 24 hours a day by official specialists. To strengthen the network security, GSN has also organized a network security team and established a related Web site. This Web site provides security-related information and collects incident reports. It also is responsible for new technology acquisition and development, maintains the contents, accepts any requests for various security-incident handling, and provides network security training for all levels of governments (RDEC, 2002b). GSN online security services include two parts: backbone security and user security services. The responsibilities of backbone security are (RDEC, 2002b):

1.   Backbone network equipment and Web site security compromise detection.
2.   Establishment of equipment and Web site defense mechanisms.
3.   Attack investigation functions to keep watch over common interagency areas and public service areas.
4.   Online scanning service.
5.   IP filtering.

For user security services, their responsibilities are (RDEC, 2002b):

1.   Security compromise detection services.
2.   Network attack investigation services.
3.   Network and Web site defense mechanisms.
4.   Web site mail-relay scanning.
5.   Consulting services.

# Taiwan E-Government in Comparison with Other Countries

Since the initialization of e-government plan, the Taiwanese government, supported by its strength in hardware manufacturing, has dedicated great efforts to build online services and transactions. Currently, notable results are clear, and as mentioned above, Taiwan's e-government was ranked first among the 198 countries in 2002 based on a survey conducted by the Center for Public Policy at Brown University (West, 2002). In addition, Taiwan was already ranked second, just behind the U.S., in the first annual survey in 2001 (West, 2001). The second annual update (West, 2002), used a 0-100 point e-government index and applied it to each nation's Web site based on the availability of contact information, publications, databases, portals, and number of online services. Taiwan's overall point was 72.5, which is much higher than the 64.0 of South Korea, which took second place. From the detailed information in the appendix of this report, it can be found that the Taiwan government is doing very well in providing online services (74%), publications (100%), databases (100%), and privacy policy (96%). However, it needs to improve the security policy (35%) and disability accessibility (0%). In Taiwan, the privilege of disabled citizen has long since been neglected in public infrastructure, and this report may stimulate to improve these two items. In addition, 96% and 100% of the official Web sites in Taiwan have provided features of foreign language translation and search engines, respectively. None of these sites showed commercial advertisement on requested users to pay fees. Notably, the Taiwanese government portal and Ireland Revenue Department were the only two sites in the September 2001 report that used digital signatures (West, 2001).

# The Future Work of Taiwan E-Government

Even though the implementation of Taiwan e-government was already ranked top worldwide, the governmental officials are still working hard to promote various applications of e-government. Future areas they are going to focus on are listed below (RDEC, 2002a):

1.  Online services

    (1) Enhance the contents and usability of the e-government portal and implement evaluation processes for government Web pages.

    (2) Promote the online law database and governmental regulations, so citizens can conveniently access and download online information.

2.  Information dissemination, integration and sharing

    (1) Information on government agencies at all levels is integrated to provide online service through a single portal Web site, www.egov.gov.tw.

    (2) The government will implement e-procurement, online quotation, catalog and information sharing service to interact with enterprises more effectively.

3.  Widespread computerization and raising the level of government information application

    (1) Promote widespread governmental computerization and information sharing among agencies. All government agencies should work using an automatic office with advanced information systems.

(2) Improve the infrastructure of information technology for suburban and rural areas. Local agencies should be equipped with computer equipment to reduce the digital divide between urban and suburban areas.

(3) Promote e-learning for governmental officials to enhance their understanding of information technology and to ensure their capability to serve citizens online.

(4) Further implement the infrastructure of information technology in Taiwan, promoting the usage of broadband service, teleconference, wireless network, and so forth.

# Critical Factors Towards User Acceptance of the Online Tax Filing and Payment System

From above-mentioned description of the e-government applications in Taiwan, we can see that the Online Tax Filing and Payment System is one of the most successful examples. Subsequently, we will explore the critical factors affecting users' adoption of e-government in the second half of this chapter, using the Online Tax Filing and Payment System as an example.

To understand critical factors towards user acceptance of an e-government application, the study aims to (1) identify the critical factors of Online Tax Filing and Payment System service adoption; (2) explore the relative importance of each factor for users who adopt Online Tax Filing and Payment System and those who do not.

## Research Hypotheses

Based on empirically well-tested theory for investigating the level of acceptance of IT services among users, we include the theory of planned behavior (TPB), innovation diffusion theory (IDT), technology acceptance model (TAM), and other importance predictors in e-government literature.

The 10 identified predictors in this study include perceived usefulness, perceived ease of use, trust, perceived risk, compatibility, personal innovativeness, interpersonal influence, external influence, self-efficacy, and facilitating condition. The hypotheses of this study are listed as follows:

- $H_1$: Perceived usefulness significantly influences Online Tax Filing and Payment System service adoption.

- $H_2$: Perceived ease of use significantly influences Online Tax Filing and Payment System service adoption.

- $H_3$: Perceived risk significantly influences Online Tax Filing and Payment System service adoption.

- **H$_4$:** Online Tax Filing and Payment System service adoption increases with individual trust towards the service.

- **H$_5$:** Online Tax Filing and Payment System service adoption increases with individual innovativeness towards the service.

- **H$_6$:** Compatibility significantly influences Online Tax Filing and Payment System service adoption.

- **H$_7$:** Peer influence significantly affects Online Tax Filing and Payment System service adoption.

- **H$_8$:** External influence significantly affects Online Tax Filing and Payment System service adoption.

- **H$_9$:** Self-efficacy significantly influences Online Tax Filing and Payment System service adoption.

- **H$_{10}$:** Facilitating conditions significantly influence Online Tax Filing and Payment System service adoption.

# Research Method

The research method in this study is illustrated as follows. Firstly, the data were collected from the field using a questionnaire survey. The sampling frame created in this study was assisted by authorized governmental units in the National Tax Administration in Taiwanese Ministry of Finance. In this sampling frame, the subjects were classified as adopters and non-adopters. Second, this study gathered data using a systematic sampling method and analyzed the data using logistic regression and structural equation modeling. Regarding the construction of the research model and measurement instruments, several taxpayers and experts were also interviewed to modify the research model and the construction of the questionnaire.

# Instrument Development and Pretest

To construct the instrument, items used to manipulate the constructs of each investigated variables were mostly adopted from relevant previous studies, as shown in Table 1, with necessary validation and wording changes. Specifically, the items, which measure perceived usefulness and ease of use, were adapted from Davis (1989), whereas items for measuring subjective norms, perceived behavioral control, and attitudes were taken from Taylor and Todd (1995). In addition, measurements of behavioral intention were derived from both of the above-mentioned articles. The items measuring trust and perceived risk were adapted from Gefen et al. (2002). Additionally, constructs shared by different investigated models were measured using the same items. All items were measured using a seven-point Likert scale with anchors ranging from "strongly agree" to "strongly disagree". The items used to measure each variable are listed in the appendix. To ensure the desired balance and randomness in the questionnaire, half of the items were worded with proper negation and all items in the questionnaire were randomly sequenced to

*Table 1: Research variables and measurements*

| Construct | Source |
|---|---|
| Perceived usefulness | Davis (1989) |
| Perceived ease of use | Davis (1989) |
| Perceived risk | Gefen et al. (2002) |
| Trust | Gefen et al. (2002) |
| Personal innovativeness | Agarwal and Prasad (1998) |
| Compatibility | Taylor and Todd (1995) |
| External influence | Taylor and Todd (1995) |
| Peer influence | Taylor and Todd (1995) |
| Self-efficacy | Taylor and Todd (1995) |
| Facilitating condition | Taylor and Todd (1995) |

reduce the potential ceiling (or floor) effect, which induces monotonous responses to the items for measuring a particular construct. Moreover, the final version of the question-naire was validated by two professional translators to ensure that no syntax errors or semantic biases had occurred in the process of translation.

Furthermore, to ensure data validity and reliability, this study first pre-tested the questionnaire by having several consumers and telecommunication professionals re-view it. Once the final survey was taken, analysis of the responses of 28 random respondents revealed no problems in the research design. Regarding reliability, the Cronbach's alpha values of all items exceeded 0.78, all exceeding the recommended value of 0.7 for social science research. Moreover, the average variances extracted (AVE) value for each construct was between 0.5 and 0.82, exceeding the minimum value of 0.5 (Fornell & Larcker, 1981).

As for the validity of the measurements, Fornell and Larcker (1981) suggest the criteria determined by whether or not the AVE value exceeds the squared correlation between the constructs. In this case, it demonstrated good discriminant validity. In addition, Anderson and Gerbing (1988) suggest that the assessment of convergent validity requires assessing the loading of each observed indicator on its latent construct. The results of the confirmatory factor analysis found that all loadings were significant. Thus, strong evidence demonstrates satisfactory convergent validity.

# Data Collection and Sample Representativeness

Using a systematic sampling method, 8,500 questionnaires were e-mailed to individuals and a 14-day period was allowed for responses, after which the same questionnaire was resent to non-respondents.

*Table 2: Profile of the respondents*

| Variable | Level | Count | Percentage |
|---|---|---|---|
| Gender | Female | 214 | 18.14% |
| | Male | 966 | 81.86% |
| Age | < 20 years old | 4 | 0.34% |
| | 21-30 years old | 144 | 12.20% |
| | 31-40 years old | 523 | 44.32% |
| | 41-50 years old | 350 | 29.66% |
| | > 50 years old | 159 | 13.47% |
| Education | Junior high school | 7 | 0.59% |
| | High school | 93 | 7.88% |
| | Undergraduate degree | 715 | 60.59% |
| | Graduate school | 365 | 30.93% |
| Marital status | Single | 310 | 26.27% |
| | Married | 870 | 73.73% |
| Hours using computer per week | < 7 hours | 88 | 7.46% |
| | 7-14 hours | 206 | 17.46% |
| | 14-21 hours | 137 | 11.61% |
| | 21-28 hours | 106 | 8.98% |
| | > 28 hours | 643 | 54.49% |
| The Online Tax Filing and Payment System use | Have not used | 106 | 8.98% |
| | Used | 1074 | 91.02% |

Of the 1,201 returned questionnaires, 21 were excluded because of incomplete answers, leaving 1,180 usable responses, a response rate of 13.88%, which compares favorably with similar e-mail surveys. The profile of the respondents is shown in Table 2. The $\chi^2$ goodness-of-fit test was used to test whether the sample data ratio, including Online Tax Filing and Payment System's users and non-users, matches the structure of population with a specific distribution. The results indicated that this sample is representative of the population in Taiwan. Moreover, this study also tested for response bias between the responses and non-responses using the independent samples t test. The results revealed no significant differences in terms of gender, age, education level, annual income, and marriage status. Thus, no response bias existed in this study.

# Results and Discussions

We used the logistic regression to identify important factors affecting Online Tax Filing and Payment System's adoption. As shown in Table 2, 106 (8.98%) of the respondents

*Table 3: Results of the logistic regression analysis*

| | β | Standard deviation | Wald | Significance | Exp(β) |
|---|---|---|---|---|---|
| Perceived Usefulness | -0.052 | 0.133 | 0.15 | 0.699 | 0.95 |
| Perceived Ease of Use | -0.422 | 0.158 | 7.08 | 0.008** | 0.66 |
| Personal Innovativeness | 0.064 | 0.121 | 0.28 | 0.596 | 1.07 |
| Compatibility | 0.479 | 0.159 | 9.08 | 0.003** | 1.62 |
| Trust | 0.142 | 0.138 | 1.05 | 0.305 | 1.15 |
| Perceived Risk | -0.214 | 0.109 | 3.88 | 0.049* | 0.81 |
| Interpersonal Influence | 0.067 | 0.136 | 0.25 | 0.621 | 1.07 |
| External Influence | -0.234 | 0.137 | 2.91 | 0.088 | 0.79 |
| Self-efficacy | 0.329 | 0.153 | 4.61 | 0.032* | 1.39 |
| Facilitating Conditions | 0.356 | 0.119 | 8.94 | 0.003** | 1.43 |

* denotes significance at the p < 0.05 level.
** denotes significance at the p < 0.01 level.

had never used the Online Tax Filing and Payment System in Taiwan and 1074 (91.02%) of respondents had used the Online Tax Filing and Payment System. The results also indicated that the respondents included more males (81.86%) than females (18.14%), and the age of 31-50 years was the largest group of respondents in the survey (73.98%). Almost all (91.52%) of the respondents had at least graduated from college.

Furthermore, a logistic regression analysis was conducted to identify those factors affecting Online Tax Filing and Payment System adoption, with results as shown in Table 3. Judging by the Wald statistic for each regressor in each model, together with a corresponding significance level, the results revealed that significant differences exist in perceived ease of use, perceived risk, compatibility, self-efficacy, and facilitating condition. Hence, we know that respondents who have used the Online Tax Filing and Payment System and those who have not have given significant different weights on these five critical factors.

To focus on the five significant factors affecting use of the Online Tax Filing and Payment System, we further analyzed the mean value difference between users and non-users, as indicated in Table 4, which shows that Online Tax Filing and Payment System users have a higher perceived ease of use for this system than non-users. As for compatibility, the results indicate that those who perceived a higher level of system compatibility with their experience of usage will be more likely to use it. Although Gefen et al. (2002) have suggested that trust and perceived risk are two of the most important predictors toward use of e-government applications, this study in the context of Taiwan only confirmed that perceived risk is an effective predictor for use of the Online Tax Filing and Payment System. This may indicate that the relative importance of trust perceived between Online

*Table 4: Mean differences between users and non-users*

|  |  | Number | Mean | Standard Deviation |
|---|---|---|---|---|
| Perceived Ease of Use | Non-user | 106 | -0.48 | 1.23 |
|  | user | 1074 | 0.05 | 0.96 |
| Compatibility | Non-user | 106 | -0.81 | 1.42 |
|  | user | 1074 | 0.08 | 0.91 |
| Perceived Risk | Non-user | 106 | 0.48 | 1.24 |
|  | user | 1074 | -0.05 | 0.96 |
| Self-efficacy | Non-user | 106 | -0.72 | 1.27 |
|  | user | 1074 | 0.07 | 0.94 |
| Facilitating Conditions | Non-user | 106 | -0.72 | 1.27 |
|  | user | 1074 | 0.07 | 0.94 |

Tax Filing and Payment System's users and non-users reveals almost no difference. But the system users did perceive less risk in this system usage than non-users. Considering the perceived risk level on the system, individuals in Taiwan themselves determine whether or not to use the Online Tax Filing and Payment System. As for individual self-efficacy, this system's users generally have higher level of self-efficacy than non-users, which indicates that individuals with higher confidence with the system's use are more likely to use the Online Tax Filing and Payment System. In addition, users consider that the facilitating condition is sufficient to offer necessary external resources for system use, whereas non-users perceived that it was not sufficient.

# Conclusions

These research findings from Taiwan have important implications to e-government implementation for other developing and developed countries. Although e-government has the potential to fundamentally change how public services are provided by increasing quality of service and reducing costs, there still exists a large gap from concept to implementation. In this study, we have contributed two useful points to e-government implementations. First, this study has captured a "snapshot" of successful e-government development strategies and activities in Taiwan. It will be a helpful qualitative example illustration for future research or practical use concerning e-government implementation. Second, some studies have emphasized the issue of adoption by users of a new system. Gefen et al. (2002) suggested that users' adoption is a very important factor for successful online public services in the e-government. This empirical study of users' adoption toward a completed and effective e-government subsystem, Taiwan's "Online Tax Filing and Payment System," provides helpful quantitative data for other e-government implementation strategies' formulation. Some marketing strategies to increase the use of e-government services are as follows.

To successfully promote e-government services, perceived ease of use, compatibility, perceived risk, and facilitating conditions must be acceptable to users. That is, perceived ease of use, compatibility, and perceived risk should be emphasized to increase positive attitudes towards e-government services. In addition, resources such as hardware, software, and other facilities, which are required to use e-government services, are clearly perceived by users as being sufficient in Taiwan, and e-government services are perceived as being effective. Finally, a market segment focusing on the low self-efficacy users will clearly be the most efficient means of achieving a reduction in perceived behavioral control. Low self-efficacy users have lower perceived behavioral control than other users, and their perceived behavioral control has a relatively weak suppressive effect on the use of e-government services. Thus, actions should be taken to increase users' self-efficacy.

Of course, the cultural dimension is an important consideration in judging research findings replicable in other varied contexts. For understanding the development in each area of global e-government applications (Hu & Li, 2003; Huang et al., 2002; Poon, 2002; Pupp, 2002; Strejcek & Theil, 2003), the e-government implementation of Mainland China, Taiwan, Singapore, and Hong Kong could be considered. Taiwan is one of the top-ranked e-government implementation examples and has distinct features in its Online Tax Filing and Payment System. To explore this successful e-government case in Taiwan, we could provide more in-depth understanding of e-government applications in other Chinese-speaking areas. This would make this study's empirical results more helpful for academic researchers or practitioners focusing on the e-government development in these areas.

# References

Agarwal, R., & Prasad, J. (1998). A conceptual and operational definition of personal innovativeness in the domain of information technology. *Information Systems Research, 9*(2), 204-215.

Aldrich, D., Bertot, J.C., & McClure, C.R. (2002). E-government: Initiatives, developments, and issues. *Government Information Quarterly, 19*(4), 349-355.

Anderson, J.C., & Gerbing, D.W. (1988). Structural equation modeling in practice: A review and recommended two-step approach. *Psychological Bulletin, 103*(3), 411-423.

Boonthanom, R. (2003). Strategic information systems planning: A case from public organization. *Proceedings of the Ninth Americas Conference on Information Systems,* pp. 778-782.

Chan, C.M.L., Pan, S.L., & Tan, C.W. (2003). Managing stakeholder relationships in an e-government project. *Proceedings of the Ninth Americas Conference on Information Systems,* pp. 783-791.

Chen, H. (2003). Digital government: Technologies and practices. *Decision Support Systems, 34*(3), 223-227.

Chen, Y.C. (2002). Managing e-government outsourcing projects: Lessons from U.S. local government. *Proceedings of the Eighth Americas Conference on Information Systems,* pp. 558-563.

Chen, Y.C., & Gant, J. (2001). Transforming local e-government services: The use of application service providers. *Government Information Quarterly, 18*(4), 343-355.

Chircu, A.M., & Lee, D.H.D. (2003). Understanding IT investments in the public sector: The case of e-government. *Proceedings of the Ninth Americas Conference on Information Systems,* pp. 792-800.

Davis, F.D. (1989). Perceived usefulness, perceived ease of use, and user acceptance of information technology. *MIS Quarterly, 13*(3),. 319-340.

Devadoss, P.R., Pan, S.L., & Huang, J.C. (2003). Structurational analysis of e-government initiatives: A case study of SCO. *Decision Support Systems, 34*(3), 253-269.

Elgarah, W., & Courtney, J.F. (2002). Enhancing the G2C relationship through new channels of communication: Web-based citizen input. *Proceedings of the Eighth Americas Conference on Information Systems,* pp. 564-568.

Forman, M. (2002). *E-government strategy.* Executive Office of the President Office of Management and Budget.

Forman, M. (2002). E-government strategy: Simplified delivery of services to citizens. *http://www.whitehouse.gov/omb/inforeg/egovstrategy.pdf.*

Fornell, C., & Larcker, D.F. (1981). Evaluating structural equation model with unobservable variables and measurement error. *Journal of Marketing Research, 18*(1), 39-50.

Gefen, D., Pavlou, P.A., Warkentin, M., & Rose, G. M. (2002). E-government adoption. *Proceedings of the Eighth Americas Conference on Information Systems,* pp. 569-576.

Gefen, D., & Straub, D. (2000). The relative importance of perceived ease of use in IS adoption: A study of e-commerce adoption. *Journal of the Association for Information Systems, 1*(8).

Golden, W., Hughes, M., & Scott, M. (2003). The role of process evolution in achieving citizen centered e-government. *Proceedings of the Ninth Americas Conference on Information Systems,* pp. 801-810.

Hu, H., Li, Q., & Lin, Z. (2003). From concept towards implementation: E-government in China. *Proceedings of the Ninth Americas Conference on Information Systems,* pp. 1104-1108.

Huang, W., D'Ambra, J., & Bhalla, V. (2002). Key factors influencing the adoption of e-government in Australian public sectors. *Proceedings of the Eighth Americas Conference on Information Systems,* pp. 577-579.

Jaeger, P.T. (2002). Constitutional principles and e-government: An opinion about possible effects of federalism and the separation of powers on e-government policies. *Government Information Quarterly, 19*(4), 357-368.

Jain, A., & Patnayakuni, R. (2003). Public expectations and public scrutiny: An agenda for research in the context of e-government. *Proceedings of the Ninth Americas Conference on Information Systems,* pp. 811-820.

Kaylor, C., Deshazo, R., & Van Eck, D. (2001). Gauging e-government: A report on implementing services among American cities. *Government Information Quarterly, 18*(4), 293-307.

Lagroue, H. J., III. (2002). The impact of e-government initiatives: Louisiana's "Express Lane" license and vehicle registration system. *Proceedings of the Eighth Americas Conference on Information Systems,* pp. 580-584.

Lee, J.K., & Rao, H.R. (2003). A study of customers' trusting beliefs in government-to-customer online services. *Proceedings of the Ninth Americas Conference on Information Systems,* pp. 821-826.

Lowry, P.B., Albrecht, C.C., Nunamaker, J.F., Jr., & Lee, J.D. (2003). Evolutionary development and research on Internet-based collaborative writing tools and processes to enhance e-writing in an e-government setting. *Decision Support Systems, 34*(3), 229-252.

Navarra, D.D., & Cornford, T. (2003). A policy making view of e-government innovations in public governance. *Proceedings of the Ninth Americas Conference on Information Systems,* pp. 827-834.

Organisation for Economic Co-operation and Development (OECD). (2001). The hidden threat to e-government. *www1.oecd.org/puma/Risk/ITfailuresE.pdf.*

Poon, S. (2002). ESDLife of Hong Kong e-government application with an e-business spirit. *Proceedings of the Eighth Americas Conference on Information Systems,* pp. 585-591.

Research, Development, and Evaluation Commission (RDEC). (2002a). Innovating and transforming government through information technology — Taiwan's experience. *http://www.rdec.gov.tw/eng.*

Research, Development, and Evaluation Commission (RDEC). (2002b). The government service network. *http://www.rdec.gov.tw/eng.*

Research, Development, and Evaluation Commission (RDEC). (2003a). E-government development in Taiwan. *http://www.rdec.gov.tw/eng.*

Research, Development, and Evaluation Commission (RDEC). (2003b). E-government in Taiwan—Policy, strategy, and status. *http://www.rdec.gov.tw/eng.*

Ronaghan, S.A. (2002). *Benchmarking e-government: A global perspective.* United Nations and American Society for Public Administration.

Rupp, C. (2002). Best practice in EAustria: The Austrian electronic economic chamber project. *Proceedings of the Eighth Americas Conference on Information Systems,* pp. 592-596.

Sanchez, A.D., Koh, C.E., Kappelman, L.A., & Prybutok, V.R. (2003). The relationship between IT for communication and e-government barriers. *Proceedings of the Ninth Americas Conference on Information Systems,* pp. 835-844.

Strejcek, G., & Theil, M. (2003). Technology push, legislation pull? E-government in the European Union. *Decision Support Systems, 34*(3), 305-313.

Taylor, S., & Todd, P.A. (1995). Understanding information technology usage: A test of competing models. *Information Systems Research, 6*(2), 144-176.

Vassilakis, C., Laskaridis, G., Lepouras, G., Rouvas, S., & Georgiadis, P. (2003). A framework for managing the lifecycle of transactional e-government services. *Telematics and Informatics, 20*(4), 315-329.

Wagner, C. (2003). Knowledge management in e-government. *Proceedings of the Ninth Americas Conference on Information Systems,* pp. 845-850.

West, D.M. (2002). *Global e-government survey.* World Markets Research Centre, Brown University.

West, D.M. (2003). *Global e-Ggovernment, 2003.* Center for Public Policy, Brown University.

Working Group on e-Government in the Developing World. (2002). *Roadmap for e-government in the developing world.* Pacific Council on International Policy.

Zhang, J., Cresswell, A.M., & Thompson, F. (2002). Participants' expectations and the success of knowledge networking in the public sector. *Proceedings of the Eighth Americas Conference on Information Systems,* pp. 597-604.

# About the Authors

**Wayne Huang** is an associate professor in the Department of Management Information Systems, College of Business, Ohio University (USA). Professor Huang has more than 12 years' teaching and research experience at research universities worldwide including USA, Australia, Singapore and Hong Kong. He worked as a system analyst in the IT industry before joining the academic field. His research areas include e-commerce, mobile commerce, groupware, computer-mediated communication, and e-education. Dr. Huang has published more than 70 academic and professional papers including *JMIS, DSS, I&M, IEEE Transactions, European Journal of Information Systems,* and *JGIM*. He has been invited to present his research work in the USA, UK, Australia, Austria, Denmark, and Japan. His research paper has been awarded with the Highest Quality Rating certificate by ANBAR Electronic Intelligence, UK, 1999.

**Keng Siau** is an associate professor of Management Information Systems (MIS) at the University of Nebraska, Lincoln (UNL). He is currently serving as the Editor-in-Chief of the *Journal of Database Management* and as the Book Series Editor for *Advanced Topics in Database Research*. He received his PhD degree from the University of British Columbia (UBC), where he majored in Management Information Systems and minored in Cognitive Psychology. His master and bachelor degrees are in Computer and Information Sciences from the National University of Singapore. Dr. Siau has over 150 academic publications. He has published more than 60 refereed journal articles, and these articles have appeared in journals such as *Management Information Systems Quarterly, Communications of the ACM, IEEE Computer, Information Systems, ACM SIGMIS's Data Base, IEEE Transactions on Systems, Man, and Cybernetics, IEEE Transactions on Information Technology in Biomedicine, IEICE Transactions on Information and Systems,* the *Journal of Database Management,* the *Journal of Information Technology,* the *International Journal of Human-Computer Studies,* the *International Journal of*

*Human-Computer Interaction, Behaviour and Information Technology,* the *Quarterly Journal of Electronic Commerce,* and others. In addition, he has published more than 70 refereed conference papers, edited/co-edited nine books, edited/co-edited nine proceedings, and written more than 15 book chapters. He served as the Organizing and Program Chairs of the International Workshop on Evaluation of Modeling Methods in Systems Analysis and Design (EMMSAD) (1996–2004). He also co-chaired a number of minitracks at AMCIS and HICSS. For more information, please visit his Web site at URL: *http://www.ait.unl.edu/siau/.*

**Kwok Kee Wei** is a professor (chair) and department head at City University of Hong Kong in Information Systems. He has published widely in the information systems field, with more than 150 publications including articles in *MIS Quarterly, Management Science, and Information Systems Research.* He was the Senior Editor of *MIS Quarterly* (2000-2003). Professor Wei is currently the President of the Association of Information Systems (2003-2004).

********************

**Michael Bates** is Director of Consultancy and Research at Oxford Analytica. He has previously worked 12 years in the UK financial services industry. He was elected in 1992 to the UK Parliament, serving for five years as a member and three years as a minister. Mr. Bates is a graduate of Wadham College (Oxford), where he also obtained his MBA.

**Chia-Ming Chang** is a doctoral student in the MIS program at the National Chung Cheng University (Taiwan, ROC). He received his Master in MIS from the same University and his Bachelors degree in Foreign Languages and Literature from the National Taiwan University (Taiwan, ROC). In addition to electronic government implementation, his current research interests include decision support systems and e-commerce.

**Hongmin M. Chen** is a professor and associate dean of the Management School, Shanghai Jiaotong University (SJTU), Shanghai, China. He received his PhD from the School, Shanghai Jiaotong University (1991). He was a visiting scholar at Sloan School, Massachusetts Institute of Technology, USA (1999-2000). His main research interests are in industrial organization (mergers and acquisition), negotiation and bargaining theory, transportation management (air transportation), and technology innovation. Professor Chen published dozens of papers in academic journals and conference proceedings.

**Yining Chen** is an associate professor at the School of Accountancy, Ohio University. Professor Chen's current teaching and research interests are in accounting information systems, auditing, and accounting education. Professor Chen earned her doctorate from the College of Business Administration, University of South Carolina. She was Assistant Professor of Accounting at Concordia University in Canada for two years. She has also held instructional positions at the University of South Carolina. Professor Chen has authored articles in *Auditing: A Journal of Practice & Theory,* the *Journal of Management Information Systems, Issues in Accounting Education, Review of Quantitative Finance & Accounting, Internal Auditing,* the *Journal of End User Computing,* the *Journal of Computer Information Systems,* and the *Journal of Global Information Management.*

**Yu-Che Chen** is an assistant professor of e-Government and Public Management at Iowa State University. He is the lead faculty member of the Public Policy and Administration Program's e-Government concentration. He received his PhD in Public Policy in 2000 from Indiana University, where he also earned his MPA. Dr. Chen's current research focuses on management of IT outsourcing and partnerships as well as on the role of management networks in the production and delivery of e-government services. He has published in the *Public Performance and Management Review, Government Information Quarterly,* and *Public Administration Quarterly.* In 2003, he also published a management report on IT outsourcing with the IBM Endowment for the Business of Government.

**Anthony M. Cresswell** is the Deputy Director of the Center for Technology in Government, University at Albany-SUNY (USA). His responsibilities include directing and participating in the Center's current research and innovation projects, developing new research proposals, and working as a member of the Center's leadership team. A longtime University at Albany professor, Cresswell began working with CTG in 1994 as a senior research fellow. His current faculty appointments are as an associate professor of Information Science and of Educational Administration and Policy Studies. An expert in management and organizational behavior, he has applied this knowledge in a number of international development projects as well. Prior to his appointment at the University at Albany he served on the faculties of Northwestern University and Carnegie-Mellon University, and as an advisor in the US Office of Management of Budget. Cresswell holds a doctorate in educational administration from Columbia University.

**Khalil El-Khatib** received his BS in computer science from the American University of Beirut (AUB) (1992). From 1992 to 1994, he worked as a research assistant in the Computer Science Department at AUB. In 1996, he received his MSc in computer science from McGill University. His research topic was dynamic load balancing for parallel discrete event simulation. In 1996, he joined the High Capacity Division at Nortel Networks as a software designer. After two years, he joined the Distributed System Research Group at the University of Ottawa as a PhD candidate under the supervision of Prof. G.V. Bochmann. His research work includes QoS for multimedia applications, personal mobility, IP telephony, feature interaction for VoIP, and ubiquitous computing. He joined the National Research Council of Canada in February 2002, as a member of the Network Computing group, researching into security and privacy issues for the Internet and ubiquitous computing environments.

**Roberto Evaristo** is an assistant professor in the Information and Decision Sciences Department at the University of Illinois, Chicago (USA). He is currently involved in several projects related to the management of distributed projects, with work done in Japan, USA and Europe. He has published in outlets such as *Communications of the ACM,* the *International Journal of Project Management, Database,* the *Journal of Global Information Management, Competitive Intelligence Review, European Management Journal, Human Systems Management,* the *Journal of Organizational Computing and Electronic Commerce, International Information Systems,* and elsewhere. He also serves on the editorial board of the *Journal of Global Information Management* and the *Journal of Global Information Technology Management.*

**Xuetao Guo** is a PhD candidate in the Faculty of Information Technology at the University of Technology Sydney, Australia. His current research interests include e-government, recommender system, Web mining, and Web intelligence. He earned a Master of Science in Computing Science from the University of Technology Sydney. To contact: *xguo@it.uts.edu.au.*

**Michael Hu** is the lead solutions architect in Police Information Technology Organization (PITO), UK, responsible for the information and technical architecture of the Police National Computer (PNC) Modernization Programme and Information System Strategy for the Police Service (ISS4PS) Programme in UK. Dr. Hu has a PhD on global information systems from University College London, and has been working in both the public and private sectors on telecommunication, electronic publishing and digital library initiatives, electronic document and information indexing, as well as IS/database management systems.

**Shin-Yuan Hung** is an associate professor of Information Systems at National Chung Cheng University. He holds a PhD in Information Systems from the National Sun Yat-sen University. His current research interests include executive information systems, financial support systems, group decision support systems, electronic commerce, and knowledge management. Dr. Hung has published a number of papers in *Decision Support Systems, Information and Management, Information Technology and People, Electronic Commerce Research and Applications,* among other journals.

**Beomsoo Kim** is an assistant professor in the Graduate School of Information at Yonsei University, Seoul, Korea. After receiving his PhD from the University of Texas at Austin in 1999, he joined the University of Illinois at Chicago as an assistant professor in the Department of Information and Decision Sciences. His research interests include information systems economics, virtual field experiments, market mechanisms in a digital economy, knowledge management, and electronic government.

**Lori Klamo** is currently doing her research work on information systems as a student at College of Business, Ohio University, USA.

**Richard Knepper** finished his undergraduate studies at New College of Florida in 1997. He started graduate studies at Indiana University in 1999, and completed his Masters in Public Administration and Masters of Arts in Polish Studies in 2002, with a Masters thesis evaluating the effectiveness of Poland's ePolska plan for information and communications technology development. He currently works for the Digital Media Network Services group in Indiana University's IT services division as a lead digital media analyst, administrating videoconferencing infrastructure, streaming media, and collaboration technology services for the university.

**Larry Korba** is the group leader of the Network Computing Group of the National Research Council of Canada in the Institute for Information Technology. He is currently involved in several projects related to security and privacy. His research interests include privacy protection, network security, and computer supported collaborative work.

**Cheng-Yuan Ku** is an associate professor of Department of Information Management at National Chung Cheng University, Taiwan, ROC. Dr. Ku received his PhD in 1995 from Northwestern University. His current research interests include e-commerce, mobile commerce, supply chain management, network management, and wireless network. His publications may be found in *Decision Support Systems, Performance Evaluation, European Journal of Operational Research,* and *IEEE Transactions on Automatic Control,* among other journals.

**D. Li** is a professor of information systems and chair of MIS department at Guanghua School of Business, Peking University, China. He received his PhD from Tokyo Institute of Technology, Japan and was a visiting scholar at Kellogg School of Management, Northwestern University, USA. His research interests include theories of management information systems, decision support systems, e-commerce, and artificial intelligence. He published numerous research papers and books on information systems in academic journals internationally.

**Kecheng Liu,** Fellow of the British Computer Society, holds a chair of Applied Informatics and E-business at The University of Reading. He has published more than 100 papers in the fields of computing, spanning from information systems methodology, requirements studies, software engineering, e-business, to normative modelling of software agents. His research monograph of *Semiotics in Information Systems Engineering* (Cambridge University Press, 2000) is the first treating the topic in a systematic manner, followed by four edited books on organisational semiotics. He chaired the programme committees of the International Workshops of Organisational Semiotics (1999, 2000, 2003), and of the IFIP WG8.1 Working Conference (in Montreal 2001) on "Organisational Semiotics: Evolving a science of information". His Applied Informatics with Semiotics Laboratory has been a key base station and received many international visitors in recent years. Dr. Liu is a visiting professor at Fudan University, Beijing Institute of Technology, and Southeast University in China.

**Jie Lu** is a senior lecturer of Software Engineering at the Faculty of Information Technology and Director of the E-service Research Group at the Institute of Information and Communication Technology, University of Technology Sydney (Australia). She received a BS and MS from Hebei University in China, and her PhD in Information Systems from Curtin University of Technology in Australia. Her research interests include e-business modeling, e-service evaluation, decision support systems, group decision support technologies and fuzzy optimization. Dr. Lu has published more than 90 research papers in journals and conferences.

**Virpi Lyytikäinen** is a PhD student at the University of Jyväskylä, Department of Computer Science and Information Systems, in Finland. For eight years she has been active in research and development projects in public administration and industry, where methods for electronic document management have been developed. Her research interests include structured documents, contextual metadata, and methods for electronic document management.

**Bryane Michael** is currently at Oxford University, where he reaches organizational performance and teaches economics and management. He also advised a number of international organizations, businesses and educational institutions. While at the World Bank and OECD, he was involved in a number of collaborative projects in Nicaragua, Bolivia, Russia and Turkey and has been involved in the training of more than 200 senior policymakers and business leaders at both organizations. He publishes extensively in international development, business and economics, and presents at a wide range of international conferences.

**Olli Mustajärvi** received his master's degree in computer science at the Helsinki University of Technology. Currently he works as head of Information Technology in the Finnish Parliament, and is preparing his PhD thesis on the knowledge management of Parliament members. Mustajärvi is also one of the authors of the book *Developing and Implementing Knowledge Management in the Parliament of Finland* (2002).

**Goonasagree Naidoo** pursued a B.Bibl at the University of Durban-Westville. She worked for the Department of Education as an educator while pursuing her Honors (1991). On completion of her MA in public administration (1992), she joined the South African Public Service, where she was involved in transformation and reform of provincial and national departments. She has published widely both nationally and internationally on policy issues, namely, ICT, human resources management and development, affirmative action, gender equity, diversity and transformation in the workplace. She was nominated to various committees, bodies and councils to chair various projects viz.; Human Sciences Research Council (HSRC); Department of Water Affairs and Forestry; Department of Public Service and Administration (DPSA); the Ford Foundation-US; and the Institute of Personnel Management (IPM) (1994-1997). In 2002, whereby she passed her PhD coursework with distinctions. She is currently employed by the University of Pretoria as a lecturer. She is currently actively involved in various projects towards the uplifting of disadvantaged communities in South Africa.

**Andrew S. Patrick** is a senior scientist at the National Research Council of Canada. He is currently conducting research on the human factors of privacy protection, computer interface issues for trustable software agents, the human factors of security systems, and advanced collaboration environments. Dr. Patrick holds a PhD in Cognitive Psychology from the University of Western Ontario. For more information, visit www.andrewpatrick.ca

**Airi Salminen** is a professor at the University of Jyväskylä, Department of Computer Science and Information Systems, Finland. She has worked as a visiting professor at the University of Waterloo, Canada, and headed several projects where research has been tied to document management development efforts in major Finnish companies and public sector organizations. Her current research interests include digital government, document management, structured documents, user interfaces, software maintenance environments, and semantic Web.

**Hans J. (Jochen) Scholl** is an assistant professor at the University of Washington. He earned a PhD in Information Science from the University at Albany and an MBA from the GSBA Zurich, Switzerland. His research interests focus on modeling complex systems using system dynamics. He also engages in qualitative research. Study areas include information systems success, e-government, and firm survival. Previously, Jochen was a researcher at the Center for Technology in Government at Albany, New York.

**H.Z. Shen** is a professor of information systems at School of Management, Shanghai Jiaotong University, China. He received a PhD in System Engineering from Tianjin University. His research interests include group decision-making, group decision support system and e-commerce. He published numerous research papers internationally.

**Shawren Singh** is a lecturer at the University of South Africa in the School of Computing. Shawren is actively involved in research relating to e-economy, human computer interaction (HCI), Internet security, Web-based courseware tools, Internet applications, Web-based education and accounting information systems. He is a member of SAICSIT (South African Institute for Computer Scientists and Information Technologists, SAICSIT Council member) and SACLA (South African Computer Lecturers Association). His research has been recognized internationally.

**Ronggong Song** received his BSc in Mathematics (1992), M.Eng in Computer Science (1996), and a PhD in Network Security from Beijing University of Posts and Telecommunications (1999). He was employed as Network Planning Engineer at Telecommunication Planning Research Institute of MII, P.R.China. He is currently working as a research officer at National Research Council of Canada. His research interests are network security and privacy protection, e-commerce, and multi-agent applications.

**Dieter Spahni** is a professor at the University of Applied Sciences Berne, Switzerland, and Director of the Institute for Business and Administration IWV (*www.iwv.ch*) since 1997. He is Vice President of the Ecademy, The National Network of the Swiss Universities of Applied Sciences for E-Business and eGovernment and member of the Federal Consultation Group for the Swiss Virtual Desk. Professor Spahni is actively involved with governmental, business and non-profit organizations concerned with the research and development of e-government strategies and applications. He has published several books and articles about e-government. His research focuses on emerging uses of ICT in the public sector, information systems architectures and design of complex systems. To contact: *dieter@spahni.com*.

**Bernd Carsten Stahl** (Dr. rer. pol., Dipl.-Wi.-Ing., MA, DEA) studied mechanical engineering, business, economics, and philosophy in Hamburg, Hagen, Bordeaux, and Witten. From 1987 to 1997 he was an officer of the German Armed Forces. From 2000 to 2003 he lectured in the Department of MIS and the German Department of University College Dublin, Ireland. Since 2003 he has been working as a senior lecturer in the Faculty of Computer Sciences and Engineering and as a Research Associate at the Centre for Computing and Social Responsibility of De Montfort University, Leicester, UK. His area of research consists of philosophical, more specifically of normative, questions arising from the use of information and communication technology. The emphasis in this area is on the notion of responsibility. He researches the application of such normative questions in economic organisations, but also educational and governmental institutions. His second area of interest consists of epistemological questions in information systems research.

**R. Subramaniam** has a PhD in Physical Chemistry. He is Honorary Secretary of the Singapore National Academy of Science. He is also Assistant Professor at the National Institute of Education at Nanyang Technology University. Prior to this, he was acting Head of Physical Sciences at the Singapore Science Center. His research interests are in the fields of physical chemistry, science education, theoretical cosmophysics, museum science, telecommunications, and transportation. He has published several research papers in international refereed journals.

**Matthew Ka Wing Tam** obtained his MPhil from the Chinese University of Hong Kong in 2003 and his research area is the application of component technologies in e-government. He obtained his BS of Computer Science in the same university. Matthew has more than 15 years of working IT experience with extensive experience in system development and support both in the local and international environment. He is also a member of the British Computer Society (BCS), a chartered holder of the Engineering Council (EC) and an affiliate holder of the Association of Chartered Certified Accountants (ACCA).

**Efthimios Tambouris** is Founder and Manager of the e-Government Unit at Archetypon S.A. (*http://egov.archetypon.gr*). He holds a Diploma in Electrical and Computer Engineering from NTUA, Greece and an MSc and PhD from Brunel University, UK. Dr. Tambouris was initiator, project manager and scientific coordinator of the IST projects EURO-CITI and eGOV. He is co-initiator and senior consultant of the IST project SmartGov and leads CEN's project on e-government metadata standardization. Dr. Tambouris leads and/or participates in a number of national and international e-government initiatives and projects. His research interests are in the areas of e-democracy and e-government, where he has published several papers. To contact: tambouris@archetypon.gr, Archetypon, S.A., Athens, Greece.

**Leo Tan Wee Hin** has a PhD in Marine Biology. He is President of the Singapore National Academy of Science. He also holds the concurrent appointments of Director of the National Institute of Education and Professor of Biological Sciences at Nanyang Technological University. Prior to this, he was Director of the Singapore Science Centre. His research interests are in the fields of marine biology, science education, museum science, telecommunications, and transportation. He has published numerous research papers in international refereed journals.

**Fiona Thompson** is a sociologist specializing in qualitative research methods. She has been a researcher for the Center for Technology in Government at the University at Albany since 1999 and has over 15 years of research experience in academic and government settings. She is co-principal investigator on projects funded by the National Science Foundation. In her current work as project manager, she is responsible for the design and execution of the research components of CTG partnership projects. Her research interests include why and how people and organizations work together.

**Pasi Tiitinen** is a PhD student at the University of Jyväskylä, Department of Computer Science and Information Systems, in Finland. Since 1996 he has participated in research and development projects in both industry and public administration, where methods for electronic document management have been developed. His research interests include user needs analysis and usability engineering in document management projects, and structured documents.

After her two years of postgraduate work in Italy within the domain of safety critical systems and after one year of completing her PhD at the University of Linz, **Maria Wimmer** put her focus on e-government developments. She is a lecturer and senior researcher at the Institute of Applied Computer Science and she leads the e-Government research team there. She is a member of IFIP (International Federation of Information Processing) and acting as vice-chair of working group 8.5. Furthermore, she is vice-chair of the Austrian forum e-Government heading the workgroup "Organization". Assoc.-Prof. Wimmer organizes annual international and local conferences and workshops in the field. For more information, visit http://falcon.ifs.uni-linz.ac.at/. To contact: wimmer@ifs.uni-linz.ac.at

**Kam Fai Wong** obtained his PhD from Edinburgh University, Scotland (1987). After his Ph.D., he has performed research in Heriot-Watt University (Scotland), UniSys (Scotland) and ECRC (Germany). At present, he is a professor in the Department of Systems Engineering and Engineering Management, the Chinese University of Hong Kong (CUHK) and in parallel serves as the Director of the Centre for Innovation and Technology (CINTEC), CUHK. His research interest centers on Internet programming and applications, Chinese computing and parallel database and information retrieval. He has published more than 100 technical papers in these areas in various international journals and conferences and books. He is a member of the ACM, CLCS, IEEE-CS AND IEE (UK). He is the founding Editor-in-Chief of *ACM Transactions on Asian Language Processing (TALIP)* and a member of the editorial board of the *Journal on Distributed and Parallel Databases, International Journal on Computer Processing of Oriental Languages, International Journal on Computational Linguistics* and *Chinese Language Processing*. He is the general co-chair of the 1st Asia Information Retrieval Symposium (AIRS04), Beijing, Oct 2004, panel chair of VLDB2002, PC co-chair of IRAL03, ICCPOL01 and ICCPOL99 and general chair of IRAL00 and also PC embers of many international conferences. For example, some recent ones are: WISE02, ICWL02 and COLING02. He is the Vice Chairman of the Hong Kong I.T. Joint Council (2002-03) and ex-chairman of ACM, Hong Kong Chapter (94/95).

**Yuefei Xu** is a research officer in the Network Computing Group, Institute for Information Technology, National Research Council of Canada. Before this, Dr. Xu was a postdoctoral fellow in the University of Calgary (Canada) focused on agent-based reconfigurable distributed control system. He received his BSc, MSc, and PhD from the Northwestern Polytechnical University, China. His research interests include distributed information system, e-business, information security and privacy. His current activities are on the research of privacy protection and trust management for e-learning applications.

**George Yee** is a senior researcher in the Network Computing Group, Institute for Information Technology, National Research Council Canada (NRC). Prior to joining the NRC in late 2001, he spent over 20 years at Bell-Northern Research and Nortel Networks. George received his PhD (Electrical Engineering), MSc (Systems and Information Science), and BSc (Mathematics) from Carleton University, where he is now an aadjunct professor. He is a senior member of IEEE, and member of ACM and Professional Engineers Ontario. He has also been the chair of the Ottawa IEEE Computer Society for many years and is an active volunteer for conferences. His research interests include security and privacy for e-services, system reliability, and system performance. For more information, visit www.georgeyee.ca.

**Jing Zhang** is an assistant professor of the Graduate School of Management of Clark University. Her research focuses on interorganizational knowledge sharing and knowledge networking, and on the organizational impact of technology and innovation in e-government initiatives. Her work has been presented in some major conferences such as Academy of Management Conference and Hawaii Conference on System Sciences. Prior to her graduate study in the U.S., she worked as a project manager for educational projects sponsored by the World Bank in the Ministry of Education. She received her PhD in Information Science from the University at Albany, State University of New York.

**P.Z. Zhang** is a professor of information systems at School of Management, Shanghai Jiaotong University, China. He has more than 10 years of research experience in information systems and published numerous papers internationally.

**Qing Zhang** is a master's degree student at the Management School, Shanghai Jiaotong University (SJTU), in Shanghai, China.

# Index

## W

## X

## Y